W9-AZU-467

Mathematics Methods
for Elementary and
Middle School Teachers

Sixth Edition

Mary M. Hatfield

Professor Emeritus, Arizona State University

Nancy Tanner Edwards

Missouri Western State University

Gary G. Bitter

Arizona State University

Jean Morrow

Emporia State University

BICENTENNIAL
1807
WILEY
2007
BICENTENNIAL

John Wiley & Sons, Inc.

Vice President & Publisher: Jay O'Callaghan
Acquisitions Editor: Robert Johnston
Marketing Manager: Jeff Rucker
Production Manager: Dorothy Sinclair
Senior Designer: Kevin Murphy
Media Editor: Lynn Pearlman
Editorial Assistant: Carrie Tupa
Production Management Services: Thomson Digital
Cover Photo: © Emanuele Taroni/Photodisc/Getty Images, Inc.
Cover Design: David Levy
PRAXIS II™ is a trademark of Educational Testing Service (ETS).

This publication is not endorsed or approved by ETS. This book was set in New Aster by Thomson Digital and printed and bound by Courier Westford. The cover was printed by Courier Westford.

This book is printed on acid-free paper. ⊗

To order books or for customer service please, call 1-800-CALL WILEY (225-5945).

ISBN 978-0470-136294 pbk.

Printed in the United States of America

10 9 8 7 6 5 4 3 2 1

We dedicate this edition and the companion Web site to our students,
our colleagues, our families, and our friends
who offered their support and encouragement
throughout our writing.
Jean offers a special dedication and a word of thanks
to the Servants of Mary for their unwavering support.

To the Instructor and the Student

ABOUT THE BOOK

Welcome to the sixth edition of *Mathematics Methods for Elementary and Middle School Teachers*. This book will provide preservice prekindergarten through grade eight teachers with ideas, techniques, and approaches to teaching mathematics appropriate for the twenty-first century. You will find that the book emphasizes problem solving, mathematical connections, estimation, mental math, portfolio and journal assessment, cultural diversity, and technology. You will find TIMSS lessons that use the scientific approach known as COMIC-E. COMIC-E is a mnemonic device to help you remember the steps in the scientific process—classify, observe, measure, infer and predict, communicate, and experiment. The lesson plans accompanying these lessons are designed to include the major ideas of active learning and assessment along with the five strands to promote mathematical proficiency. You will learn more about this beginning in Chapter 3.

Much of the technology—WebQuests, spreadsheet activities, Internet scavenger hunts, and a variety of online activities—can be accessed by going to the companion Web site developed for this book at www.wiley.com/college/hatfield. Video vignettes of experienced elementary and middle school teachers teaching mathematics lessons in their classrooms are found on the accompanying Web site. You will be invited to view the videos from multiple perspectives as you look at how teachers handle different aspects of a mathematics lesson. Most importantly, you will be reminded often to ask "Where's the mathematics?" as you view these vignettes. It's easy to get caught up in the student behavior or the "fun activity." What is essential is that you can describe where and how the mathematics is being taught and learned as well as what mathematics is being taught.

The book models the approach of concrete-to-abstract developmental learning. A variety of manipulatives are emphasized throughout the book. In addition, paper models of many of the manipulatives are found in full size on the companion web site for readers' personal use.

SPECIAL FEATURES

Praxis-II™-Style Questions are provided at the end of each chapter. This feature readies the teacher candidate for the high-stakes testing required for teacher certification in 80 percent of the states. Other national exit tests also use similar test questions.

Most chapters feature a **WebQuest** to be used by P-8 students and are available at the companion web site. These WebQuests have been written by practicing teachers and preservice candidates. The WebQuests have been used in actual classroom settings with P-8 students.

Each chapter begins with a **graphic organizer** and **Self-Help Questions** to guide the reader to identifying important topics throughout the chapter. Beginning with Chapter 6, "At the Start—Know What Children will Be Doing . . . " provides a partial listing from the National Council of Teachers of Mathematics (NCTM, 2006) *Curriculum Focal Points*. The *Focal Points* are intended to help curriculum developers, school districts mathematics planning teams, and classroom teachers by providing a focus on the significant concepts at each grade level that will provide a foundation for understanding and lasting learning. These *Focal Points* include related ideas, concepts, skills, and procedures that should be taught in the context of the processes—communication, reasoning, representation, connections, and, particularly, problem solving—found in the *Principles and Standards* (NCTM, 2000).

Most chapters provide a bibliography of children's literature. Children's literature used in mathematics teaching and learning emphasizes the interconnectedness of mathematics with the thoughts and experiences of language in the child's world.

Journal and portfolio assessment techniques are included in each chapter where appropriate. Actual children's work is provided for preservice and inservice teachers to review and evaluate. Included in each discussion are the needs of different types of special learners and methods of correcting common student errors. Teachers who work with students with special needs will find these materials helpful, with direct application for classroom use.

Activities are provided throughout the book and on the student companion Web site (the Extended Activities) for the following categories:

Problem Solving—emphasizes strategies and higher-order thinking.

Manipulatives—uses concrete experiences for developing concepts.

Calculators—emphasizes problem solving and de-emphasizes tedious computations.

Mental Math—builds methods of doing computation mentally.

Cultural Relevance—emphasizes activities to illustrate historical cultural contributions to mathematics along with activities promoting equity in mathematics.

Computers, *spreadsheets, databases, and graphing*—uses exploration in problem solving.

Estimation—emphasizes techniques to determine reasonable answers.

Mathematical Connections—encourages interdisciplinary approaches to learning mathematics.

Computers, *Internet and WebQuests*—emphasizes the power of technology to enhance the learning of mathematics with real-world applications.

Portfolio and Journal Assessment—uses actual children's work and explanations to help teachers analyze the development of children's mathematical thinking and explore rubric scoring guides for classroom use.

Video Vignettes—emphasizes the power of modeling good teaching practices for quality mathematical understanding.

The following icons will be used to alert the reader to the emphasis of each category when it appears throughout the text

CALCULATORS   **COMPUTERS**   **ESTIMATION**   **MANIPULATIVES**

PROBLEM SOLVING   **MATHEMATICAL CONNECTIONS**   **MENTAL MATH**   **CULTURAL RELEVANCE**

PORTFOLIO   **INTERNET SEARCHES**   **VIDEO VIGNETTE**   **CHILDREN'S LITERATURE**

WEBQUESTS

ORGANIZATION

- The book has 15 chapters. Chapter 1 presents an overview of our teaching philosophy, a review of the current standards movement in mathematics education and of the current state of the field, and a brief discussion of its future. The history of mathematics is described on the Web site.

- Chapter 2 discusses culturally relevant mathematics with the acknowledgement that all cultures of our world have contributed to the discoveries of mathematics. The book attempts to bring students' cultural heritage to various teaching situations. Culture-relevant assessment materials are included throughout the book. Equity for all students to learn quality mathematics in modeled.

- Chapter 3 discusses the assessment of children's mathematical understandings. The use of rubrics or scoring guides for assessing children's work is introduced here and will be put into practice throughout the book. To understand appropriate assessment means to also understand how children learn mathematics. Learning theories are briefly reviewed in relation to effective teaching and assessment models and lesson plan development, including brain research studies as applied to the learning of mathematics. The chapter emphasizes the importance of good lesson planning in effective teaching.

- Chapter 4 reviews some of the characteristics of middle school students, examines the type of mathematics program appropriate for the preparation of middle school teachers of mathematics, and introduces some of the current standards-based mathematics curricula for middle school. Whether or not the reader is planning on teaching middle school mathematics, this chapter provides information on students with special needs and the mathematics in the middle school curriculum.

- Chapter 5 offers problem-solving strategies and activities. Characteristics of good problem solvers are outlined and related to lesson planning. The NCTM *Standards* form the underpinnings of this chapter.

- Chapter 6 discusses number readiness and the beginning of the numerical aspects of mathematics. Number readiness is the initial introduction of numbers, including one-to-one correspondence, counting, and the general concept of number.

- Chapter 7 discusses operation sense of the whole number system in relation to the basic facts of addition, subtraction, multiplication, and division. Concrete materials and mental arithmetic are emphasized in the development process.

- Chapter 8 covers numeration and the development of counting systems. The base 10 numeration system is discussed in the context of the more general idea of numeration as it applies to any base system. Base 10 blocks and chip trading activities are developed as examples of proportional and nonproportional materials to use with children.

- Chapter 9 discusses the algorithms for addition, subtraction, multiplication, and division using base 10 blocks followed by chip trading activities. The calculator and computer are an integral part of the development. Alternative algorithms are discussed and illustrated by example.

- Chapter 10 covers rational numbers and decimals, specifically common fractions, using concrete materials. The operations are explored with several models. The approach emphasizes understanding the algorithm rather than memorizing procedures.

- Chapter 11 discusses ratio, proportion, percent, and rate. Pattern blocks and other manipulatives are used to develop an understanding of percent. The calculator, estimation, and mental math are stressed in relation to ratio, proportion, percent, and rate.

- Chapter 12 discusses geometry. Concrete experiences are the key to developing informal, plane, and solid geometry. Hands-on exploration is the theme of this chapter.

- Chapter 13, on measurement, follows geometry and emphasizes the metric and customary systems. The topics of linearity, area, volume, capacity, temperature, mass, money, and time are carefully developed, including their related units of measurement. Activities are provided for each topic. Many of the activities encourage exploration to develop frames of reference for various units of measurement.

- Chapter 14 develops patterns, functions, and number theory in the light of algebraic thinking and algebra. The middle school teacher will find the topics useful in developing number "sense."

- Chapter 15 explores data analysis, statistics, and probability. Types of graphs and their interpretation are discussed and illustrated with examples, including graphing calculators. Statistics and probability theory are highlighted. Real-world examples are provided, and activities to motivate students are presented. Mathematical connections are emphasized throughout the chapter.

The companion Web site at www.wiley.com/college/hatfield consists of

- An online study guide that can be accessed either by category (WebQuests, sample exercises and solutions, annotated Web sites, test questions) or by chapter (1–15). Each chapter will offer the same four category selections mentioned previously, with links to the appropriate category.

- Sample exercises with an emphasis on creating student activities, additional samples of student work with a rating scale (rubric), and technology-related activities.

- Annotated Web sites—two or three Web sites that relate specifically to the chapter at hand with either lesson plans and activities or sites that expand the students' knowledge of the particular concept.

ACKNOWLEDGEMENTS

Our special gratitude goes to the professors and students at Arizona State University, Missouri Western State College, and Emporia State University (KS) who have given valuable suggestions for improvement as we have updated the sixth edition to meet the challenges of the twenty-first century. We also thank those who have reviewed this edition for their thoughtful comments and suggestions:

Joyce Hoellein, *Westminister*
Kathleen Anderson, *Piedmont College*
Martha Tapia, *Berry College*
Nell Cobb, *DePaul University*

Haywood Mayton, *University of West Alabama*
Kevin J Reins, *University of South Dakota*
Beth Vinson, *Athens St. University*
Cathy Castellan, *Loyola*
Terry Lashley, *Tennessee Tech University*

We wish to thank the following people for their help in the production of the sixth edition of the book: Janice Rey, Saint Joseph's College, and her students for their questions and list of errors and misspellings; Robert Johnston, our acquisitions editor at John Wiley & Sons for his unfailing support, encouragement, and good humor.

Last, but certainly not least, thanks go to the participating teachers who allowed us windows into their classrooms, sharing their mathematics teaching with others to improve the teaching and learning of mathematics.

To the Instructor

HOW TO USE THIS BOOK

This book is a resource for teaching mathematics in the elementary and middle school. Problem solving, cooperative learning, and manipulatives are emphasized at all levels. Different learning styles are emphasized, and concrete-to-abstract materials are a prerequisite for each concept development.

Throughout the book, preservice and inservice teachers will be referred to as *the teacher*. The book has been class tested in college courses, and teachers have successfully used the activities with children. Using the computer as a tool offers many learning experiences for teachers as well as elementary and middle school children. We hope this careful, realistic presentation makes mathematics meaningful to elementary and middle school teachers and their students.

This book and the companion Web sites are to be used with classes that emphasize the teaching of elementary and middle school mathematics. Field experiences in relation to learning from the book are encouraged. Generally, the book is organized into seven sections per chapter—introduction, teaching strategies, assessment, summary, Praxis II^{TM}-style questions, integrating technology, and children's literature bibliography. The bibliography for citations within each chapter is found at the end of the text.

Each chapter begins with a brief preview of the contents of the chapter to prepare the reader. If additional review of the mathematics that may have been covered in prerequisite college content courses is desired, you may refer to *Check Your Mathematics Knowledge* on the companion Web site. This is especially true in the content chapters where teachers need to see the mathematical understandings to which children will be exposed from an "adult" viewpoint. The mathematical content there is presented in a more symbolic, formal structure.

The *teaching strategies* present developmental activities that can be used with elementary and middle school students. These emphasize a variety of techniques in concrete/pictorial experiences, problems solving, cooperative learning, and computer/calculator technologies. Additional activities are available on the companion Web site, many of which may be printed and copied as activity pages to use with your students. In order to get a feel for the mathematics classroom in which manipulatives are used, the companion Web site contains eighteen video vignettes that exemplify the mathematics teaching advocated by the National Council of Teachers of Mathematics *Principles and Standards*.

The *assessment* sections present techniques for evaluating what the student actually knows and for correcting common error patterns and other frequently occurring difficulties of elementary and middle school students. Sample student work is included and analyzed for error patterns, a practice that we encourage in all teachers. Portfolio assessments are included in the book as well as on the companion Web site to assist the teacher in developing a professional portfolio.

Integrating technology contains WebQuests, Web sites, and a variety of computer activities. The computer activities are to be integrated into the curriculum as tools to understand and teach mathematics. Please note that a spreadsheet and a database program are needed to do the spreadsheets and databases. The computer activities can be done as explorations in an individual setting or in cooperative learning groups where work is shared among students to draw conclusions.

The *Praxis II^{TM}-style questions* in the text prepare the teacher candidate for the high-stakes testing required for teacher certification in 80 percent of the states. Over a hundred additional *Praxis II^{TM}-style questions* are available on the instructor's companion Web site in the *Test Bank*. You will need to register, a simple process, to get a password to access the companion Web site. Additionally, there are *exercises* on the written on three levels of difficulty. There are many exercises so that you can choose assignments that student companion Web site are most appropriate for your course objectives. It is not our intent that everyone complete every exercise. The exercises are to encourage understanding of the content covered in the text as well as prepare a preservice teacher

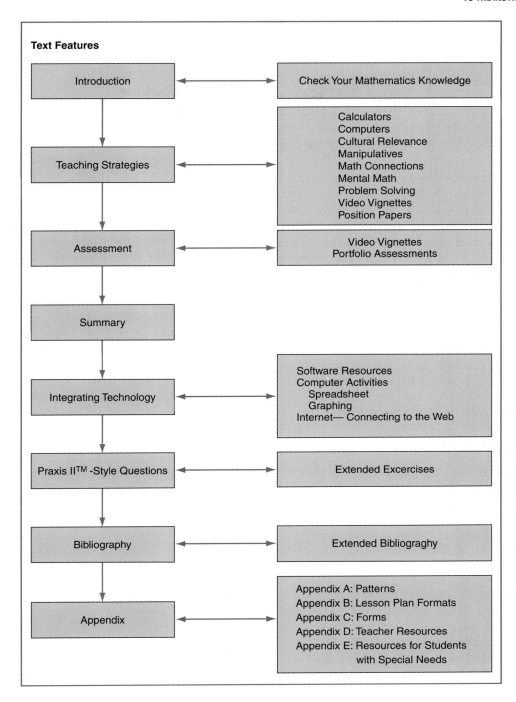

Text Features

Introduction	⟷	Check Your Mathematics Knowledge

| Teaching Strategies | ⟷ | Calculators
Computers
Cultural Relevance
Manipulatives
Math Connections
Mental Math
Problem Solving
Video Vignettes
Position Papers |

| Assessment | ⟷ | Video Vignettes
Portfolio Assessments |

| Summary |

| Integrating Technology | ⟷ | Software Resources
Computer Activities
Spreadsheet
Graphing
Internet— Connecting to the Web |

| Praxis II™ -Style Questions | ⟷ | Extended Excercises |

| Bibliography | ⟷ | Extended Bibliograghy |

| Appendix | ⟷ | Appendix A: Patterns
Appendix B: Lesson Plan Formats
Appendix C: Forms
Appendix D: Teacher Resources
Appendix E: Resources for Students
with Special Needs |

for classroom instruction and to strengthen the inservice teacher's mathematics presentations. Many of the exercises can be used in future teaching, so teachers are encouraged to save them.

SUPPLEMENTS

The *Instructor's Manual* consists of additional worksheets for further evaluation of common errors, suggestions to the professor for using the text for early childhood and middle school preservice methods, quarter versus semester courses, and graduate versus undergraduate courses; suggestions at the beginning of each chapter for activities, that can be used as introductory, developmental, or assessment purposes; an updated testbank; solutions to *Praxis II™-style questions* in the text and exercises on the student companion web site; additional spreadsheet activities for various chapters.

The companion website at **www.wiley.com/college/hatfield** consists of:

- An online study guide that can be accessed either by category (WebQuests, sample exercises and solutions, annotated websites, test questions) or by chapter (1-15). Each chapter will offer the same four category selections mention previously, with links to the appropriate category.

- Sample exercises with an emphasis on creating student activities, additional samples of student work with a rating scale (rubric), and technology-related activities.

- Annotated - two or three websites that relate specifically to the chapter at hand with either lesson plans and activities or sites that expand the students' knowledge of the particular concept.

- Additional test questions, with answers, to be used for practice, for feedback, or as an online quiz option, with the student submitting answers by e-mail.

The student companion Web Site also includes patterns for several of the manipulatives, observation forms, lesson formats, and teacher resources that may be printed and copied. We suggest using and integrating the book, and student companion Web site as shown in the diagram on the following page.

The bibliography is a listing of references cited in the book. Extended bibliographies are on the student companion Web site for teachers interested in further information on a topic. Readers who are asked to search professional journals for assignments will find the bibliography a good starting point.

Contents

CHAPTER 3
The Development of Mathematical Proficiency: Using Learning Research, Assessment, and Effective Instruction   41

CHAPTER 4
Middle School Mathematics   78

CHAPTER 7
Operations and Number Sense **147**

CHAPTER 8
Numeration and Number Sense   187

CHAPTER 9
Operations with Whole Numbers   218

Mathematics Education Today and into the Future

A few years ago, one of the television ads for a fast food chain featured a senior citizen asking, "Where's the beef?" At various times in the history of mathematics education, much the same question has been asked: "Where's the mathematics?" This question was asked by those who championed the "back to the basics" movement in the 1980s, for instance. It has also been asked by those who support the standards movement of this millennium. To gain a better perspective on the cyclical history of mathematics education, read "History of Mathematics Education" on the companion Web site that accompanies this text (Chapter 1, Extended Activities). There you will find a more comprehensive description of the movements in the history of mathematics education. You will see that the world of mathematics education is a world with a rich heritage in the past, an exciting and sometimes overwhelming present, and a challenging future in this, the twenty-first century. What is the most appropriate way of teaching mathematics to children living their lives in the twenty-first century? Perhaps it is different from the way you were taught mathematics. As mathematics educators, you must help prepare children for this ever-changing world by being aware of the expanding field of knowledge in mathematics and mathematics education.

This text has three main goals: to build on the strengths of past mathematics education, to model the successful techniques of the present, and to prepare for changes in the future. Mathematics education has always been and will continue to be an expanding field of knowledge. As human beings grow in understanding and in awareness of new possibilities, mathematics education changes. It is not the stagnant body of knowledge that many people assume. Basic mathematical principles, such as the commutative and associative properties, will continue to be taught, but new methods of teaching, such as the use of fact strategies, are constantly emerging as new insights. Ways to teach mathematics will continue to change as more effective methods develop along with new technologies that support them. This book will show you how the International Society of Technology Education (ISTE) standards for technology use in the classroom will help integrate technology in your lesson planning. You will use the World Wide Web to find information for your class, examples of lesson plans, and interactive Web sites appropriate for the students you will teach. The Web is today's way of keeping up with the growth of knowledge in mathematics education.

What are the newer techniques of mathematics education that research indicates are the best for teaching all students mathematics? What are the techniques from the past that we can continue to use? What must be changed if we are to teach successfully in our dramatically changing world? How should we prepare elementary school children and middle schoolers for mathematical experiences we have never had ourselves?

This chapter presents an overview of our teaching philosophy, a review of the current standards movement in mathematics education and of the current state of the field, and a brief discussion of its future. The ideas presented here will be

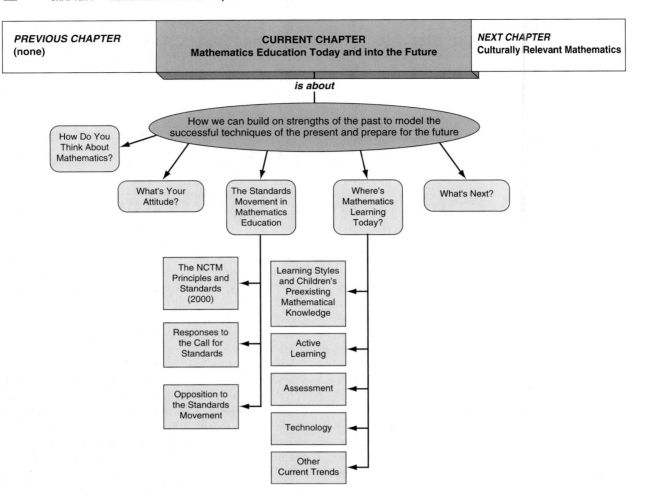

| PREVIOUS CHAPTER
(none) | CURRENT CHAPTER
Mathematics Education Today and into the Future | NEXT CHAPTER
Culturally Relevant Mathematics |

is about

How we can build on strengths of the past to model the successful techniques of the present and prepare for the future

- How Do You Think About Mathematics?
- What's Your Attitude?
- The Standards Movement in Mathematics Education
  - The NCTM Principles and Standards (2000)
  - Responses to the Call for Standards
  - Opposition to the Standards Movement
- Where's Mathematics Learning Today?
  - Learning Styles and Children's Preexisting Mathematical Knowledge
  - Active Learning
  - Assessment
  - Technology
  - Other Current Trends
- What's Next?

SELF-HELP QUESTIONS

1. Why is it better to understand mathematical concepts as "packages of knowledge" rather than as sequences of steps for solving problems?

2. Why is it important to understand both the "how" and the "why" of mathematical procedures?

3. What are the six guiding principles of the NCTM's *Principles and Standards for School Mathematics* (2000)?

4. What are the six process standards that comprise the *learning principle?*

5. What is the significance of NCATE's teacher accreditation standards?

6. What is TIMSS?

7. What does "active learning" mean?

8. Which types of assessment are emphasized within the NCTM's standards? How would traditional teaching and assessment methods have to change to meet those standards?

9. What are the Praxis™ exams and why are they important?

10. Which technologies currently play important roles in mathematics education?

11. How will technology impact education in the coming years?

studied in greater detail as relevant in subsequent chapters.

HOW DO YOU THINK ABOUT MATHEMATICS?

Mathematics is nothing to be afraid of; it is our human heritage from all cultures. This is a powerful message for children—and for many of their parents. But you are not alone if you question your own mathematical background and your ability to teach mathematics. One approach to teaching mathematics is to ask "Where's the mathematics?" in each concept you are preparing to teach. This leads to a further question: "What do my students and I need to know to master this concept?" Mathematics educator Liping Ma (1999) reminds us that there are two ways of thinking about how to teach a mathematical topic. Some see teaching a mathematical topic as teaching a sequence of steps leading to a concept. For example, you might think that to teach two-digit addition you first teach the basic addition facts, then how to add a one-digit number and a two-digit number, and finally how to add two two-digit numbers. Others see mathematics teaching as teaching a "package of knowledge" whose elements contribute in different ways and at different points to the knowing. You will be given the opportunity to develop knowledge packages for various mathematical concepts as you proceed through the text. In Chapter 7, you will examine a specific package of knowledge in depth. For now, spend a few minutes familiarizing yourself with the basic idea. Briefly, a knowledge package is a "network of conceptual and procedural topics that support and are supported by its learning" (Ma and Kessel, 2001). Ma (1999) delineates a "knowledge package for subtraction" that every teacher of elementary mathematics needs to have. In Figure 1.1, the shapes represent different elements of this knowledge package. Ovals are the topics in the curriculum. Rectangles with rounded corners are the basic principles. Key pieces have thick borders. The rectangle is the topic under discussion. If you look at the diagram, you can identify conceptual topics such as "addition and subtraction as inverse operations" and procedural topics such as "Subtraction without regrouping." The topic under discussion is "Subtraction with regrouping between 20 and 100." The learning of that topic is supported by those topics with arrows leading toward the rectangle. The learning of that topic supports "Subtraction with regrouping of large numbers."

As you study this diagram, ask yourself what is meant by "composing and decomposing a higher value unit" and "the rate of composing a higher value unit"? What importance do these ideas have for children's knowing and doing mathematics? Consider the subtraction problem 17 − 9. The solution to this problem is one of the "basic facts." But elementary students, before

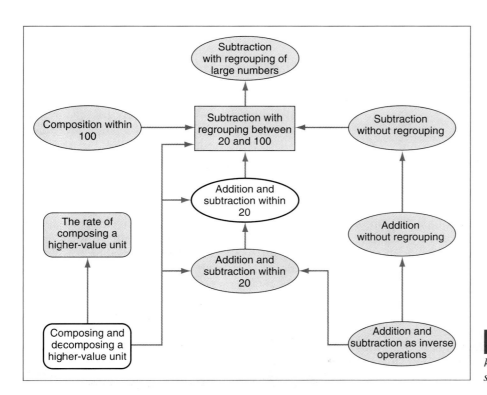

FIGURE 1.1 *Ma's (1999) knowledge package for subtraction.*

they are ready to memorize that fact, may already have discovered that they can decompose the 17 to $10 + 7$, then decompose the 10 to $8 + 2$, then recompose the 17 as $8 + 2 + 7$ or, with parentheses, as $8 + (2 + 7,$ or $9)$, and finally subtract the 9 (i.e., $8 + 9 - 9$) and have a final answer of 8. Many adults find this a tedious, if not confusing, means of subtracting. For children who are learning to do mathematics, it is a meaningful approach to the problem. Elementary mathematics teachers must understand the concepts and procedures that support children's learning and doing of mathematics. From the direction of the arrows in the diagram, you can see that "Composing and decomposing a higher-value unit" supports the learning of "the rate of composing a higher-value unit." Take a moment now and write down your definition or an example of "rate of composing a higher-value unit." Compare your definition or example with that of a classmate. For more information, see Chapter 7, page 152.

If these ideas seem overwhelming, consider how a knowledge package is like the maps you get when you use MapQuest.com. When you request driving directions, you are given two maps—one that shows the broad outline of the trip and one that gives detailed directions with distances and road names. As a prospective teacher of elementary or middle school mathematics, you have to know both the broad outlines of the mathematical concepts you are teaching and the many connections among them, and among your students' past, present, and future understanding of mathematics. Liping Ma (1999) refers to this kind of knowledge as a "profound understanding of fundamental mathematics."

WHAT'S YOUR ATTITUDE?

As a teacher of mathematics, you should both "know how" and "know why" and assign high value to both—that is, you should take the attitude that it is important not only to know mathematical procedures, but also to know the rationale for those procedures. It is important for you to have that attitude, and it is important for you to instill that same attitude in your students. A teacher who does not have this attitude may *know how* and *know why* but think the latter is unimportant and not teach for it. Or the teacher may *know how* but not *know why* and thus be unable to answer students' questions. In either case, students hear an-all-too-familiar refrain—"Trust me, it works," or "Just do it this way and you'll learn why when you get

to. . . . " These attitudes—both the right one and the wrong ones—go back a long way.

Mathematics education began as a discipline in the mid-1800s. In those days, the textbook for children and the manual for teachers were one and the same. Teacher training in mathematics typically consisted of a one-page introduction to the student book (Ray, 1850). It is of interest that the big ideas found on such pages sound very much like the big issues of today. A detailed look at a book from the 1850s is available on the Companion Web site (Chapter 1, Extended Activities, "Mathematics Book from 1850"), but the main ideas can be summarized as follows:

- Teachers should keep oral recitation (now called oral discourse) short and lively.
- Students have a range of abilities; different accomplishments need to be recognized for different students. (Compare this idea to Gardner's ideas of multiple intelligences, discussed in Chapter 3.)
- The primary focus should be on how well a child can analyze and give reasons for answers, rather than on memorization of facts. (Compare this to similar emphases in the standards movement, discussed next in this chapter.)
- Students should be able not only to describe the methods they chose to arrive at an answer but also to explain why they used those methods (a *must* according to current research, as explained later in this chapter).

These constants of mathematics education show that no matter what new mathematics and technologies we may have now or in the future, we will still have to teach children to reason out answers and analyze the relationships presented in models. The models will change, but the processes of good mathematical thinking will remain. A mathematics teacher in the 1800s would have been astonished to see today's students learning mathematics with a computer—creating their own mathematical equations and checking to see if their answers are correct, all within a few seconds. The cognitive process, however, by which children can do this, would have been understood in schools 150 years ago.

Despite this general agreement on the best way to teach mathematics, there has always been a shortage of teachers with the right attitude. After all, teachers are human, and they tend to teach the way they themselves were taught—putting more emphasis on teaching procedures, especially computation procedures, and less on teaching how to develop concepts. During the 1900s, there were many attempts to reform mathematics teaching and promote the growth of that "right attitude." Until quite recently, however, those attempts bore little fruit.

The Third International Mathematics and Science Study (TIMSS, discussed later in this chapter) and the National Assessment of Educational Progress (NAEP), conducted at intervals since 1973, showed U.S. students scoring low, with little ability to solve challenging problems requiring conceptual understandings, compared with students from higher-scoring countries. In this text, we use the NAEP as our basis for assessing how well students do in meeting standards. The NAEP is the only test given nationally to representative samples of students over a period of years, so scores can be compared and contrasted. The test itself has evolved as standards have changed. The NAEP information is analyzed in many different ways, using the latest statistical methods available at each testing period. Beginning in the 1990s, U.S. students' NAEP scores in mathematics became more promising, showing that when instruction is aligned more with the recent mathematics standard movement stressing conceptual development, students have better scores (NAEP, 2006). This encouraging trend continues with all social groups individually and with the nation's scores collectively gaining higher scores with each NAEP. It shows the standards movement of the 1990s had positive effects on mathematics instruction and holds promise for more improvement in the twenty-first century.

THE STANDARDS MOVEMENT IN MATHEMATICS EDUCATION

Remember the question asked near the beginning of this chapter: How should we prepare elementary school children and middle schoolers for mathematical experiences we have never had ourselves? The answer lies in recognizing the "big picture" that people need to know about, because the little facts, figures, and other specifics change too quickly for teachers and students to keep up with them. Learning the *process of thinking* and how to approach solving problems is more important than memorizing one way of getting an answer. The method and the answer may change before one has a chance to use them. How could educators develop a curriculum that would support change itself? That was the challenge for educators during the final decade of the twentieth century, and they responded by going on record about what really mattered in mathematics learning. Thus, the standards movement was born.

Mathematics educators were the first to take on the challenge of creating new academic standards to prepare people for a rapidly changing world. Under the auspices of the National Council of Teachers of Mathematics (NCTM), three sets of standards were written—*Curriculum and Evaluation Standards* (1989), *Professional Standards for Teaching Mathematics* (1991), and *Assessment Standards* (1995). In 2006, NCTM added the *Curriculum Focal Points*. Together, they cover all the bases of *who, what, when, where, why, how,* and *how much* in mathematics teaching.

The overall vision of these mathematics standards deals with the "big picture" of mathematics, how to solve problems, reason out answers, and communicate mathematically. Each set of standards is and will remain classic because of its impact on public and teacher awareness. If you want to read a summary of the original standards, you can do so on the student companion Web site (Chapter 1, Extended Activities, "The Original Standards"). Throughout this book, specific standards are described whenever relevant to the concepts being studied. Activities in the text and on the companion Web site often show which parts of the NCTM standards are being emphasized. In the interest of brevity, not all activities are so marked, but all do support the standards.

The NCTM *Principles and Standards* (2000)

The *Principles and Standards for School Mathematics* (NCTM, 2000) combines the original three documents into one, with certain changes as described below. If you do not have your own copy of this document, you can view it in its entirety on the NCTM Web site, **http://standards.nctm.org/index.htm**. We encourage you to do so.

The following summary of the *Principles and Standards* reflects the four main changes from the original documents:

- The professional teaching standards and the assessment standards have been condensed and renamed "guiding principles."
- A new curriculum process standard called "representation" has been added.
- The curriculum standards have been condensed from thirteen to ten.
- Grade levels have been divided into smaller clusters in the early years of child development.

The Guiding Principles The original standards (1989, 1991, 1995) and the *Principles and Standards* (2000) were never meant to prescribe specific mathematics objectives and/or performances, but rather to broadly guide people about what needs to be valued as we work with students in the twenty-first century. The word *principles* was chosen to convey the idea of broad tenets that guide quality mathematics instruction. Think about the set of classroom teaching hints from the 1850s as you review these six guiding principles. How do they differ and how are they similar across the years?

Equity Principle Mathematics instructional programs should promote the learning of mathematics by all students. To achieve this goal, teachers must believe in their students and actively work to help students have high expectations of themselves. Teachers must provide strong support to all students if inequities are to be successfully overcome.

Mathematics Curriculum Principle Mathematics instructional programs should emphasize important and meaningful mathematics through curricula that are coherent and comprehensive. This implies teaching fewer topics and promoting deeper understanding of mathematical ideas through a well-chosen curriculum, organized and integrated in a meaningful manner. Studies should emphasize the interconnectedness among mathematics topics and among mathematics and other disciplines. What students know and are able to do should become progressively deeper, reflecting an ever-broadening system of mathematical understanding.

Teaching Principle Mathematics instructional programs depend on competent and caring teachers who teach all students to understand and use mathematics. This implies that teachers plan the use of worthwhile mathematics tasks that involve analysis and that reflect student learning. The learning environment should promote positive attitudes toward mathematics and should encourage oral and written discourse among students and with the teacher, in both small group and large class settings. Students need experience in reading, writing, and orally communicating their mathematical ideas so that discussing mathematics with others feels natural.

Learning Principle Mathematics instructional programs should enable all students to understand and use mathematics. This implies that students need to build on prior experiences by using the processes of problem solving, reasoning and proof, communicating, and making connections, as well as the new process called *representation* (see page 7). Students need to grapple with complex and interesting problems that take time to solve; as they begin to enjoy using their minds, they become confident in their own abilities. They will have the sense of possessing the mathematical power needed to solve new sets of problems.

The use of many problem forms is advocated so that students become widely competent mathematical problem solvers. Some problems should be open ended, with no one right answer, whereas others should have models to follow, with predictable formulas. The time allotted for solving problems should approximate the real world, in which some problems can take days or months to solve and others occur on a daily basis and can be solved more quickly. People need to value mathematics. Students should have a variety of experiences involving the cultural, historical, and scientific evolution of mathematics so that they can anticipate the importance of mathematics in their lives and in the lives of their children.

Assessment Principle Mathematics instructional programs should include assessment to monitor, enhance, and evaluate the mathematics learning of all students and to inform teaching. Assessment is a cyclic process of (1) setting clear goals in the planning stage, (2) gathering evidence using various methods, (3) interpreting evidence through valid inferences enabled by teacher expertise, (4) using the inferences to make decisions and take action, and (5) repeating the process. One never really finishes assessment; it is ongoing. Even when teachers use summative assessment at the end of a semester, it is added to the ongoing evaluation of students as they progress through the education system, as evidenced by the all-too-familiar piece of paper called a school transcript.

Technology Principle Mathematics instructional programs should use technology to help all students understand mathematics and should prepare them to use mathematics in an increasingly technological world. Technology is a tool that can be used to enhance mathematical thought. It should free students to concentrate on the big ideas of mathematics by making it easier for students to perform the complex calculations that can otherwise hinder mathematical development. When calculations are few and easy, however, technology is not an appropriate tool—mental math and quick paper calculations are more appropriate in these situations. If students understand the purposes, strengths, and limitations of technology, it can help them prepare for the increasing demands of a competitive society. As always, students will need guidance from knowledgeable teachers to determine when the use of technology is appropriate.

The Curriculum Standards   Representation was added to the original process standards of problem solving, reasoning and proof, communication, and connections as one of the five processes that permeate all mathematical thinking. Representation is the process of modeling and interpreting physical, social, and mathematical phenomena in meaningful ways that enhance mathematical understanding. Numerous learning theories stress that children learn mathematics first by concrete representations, then by moving to pictorial representations, and finally through symbolic representations. Numerous research studies have shown that good mathematics teaching involves the continual use of representations.

Curriculum Standards   Five standards describe the mathematical content that students should learn:

- Number and operation
- Patterns, functions, and algebra
- Geometry and spatial sense
- Measurement
- Data analysis, statistics, and probability

The other five standards describe the mathematical processes through which students should acquire and use their mathematical knowledge:

- Problem solving
- Reasoning and proof
- Communication
- Connections
- Representation

The content standard of number and operation now takes in the three 1989 curriculum standards of estimation, number sense, and numeration; concepts of whole number operations; and whole number computations. Each of these is a natural subset of number and operation. This text divides the number and operation content into chapters on number readiness; numeration; operation sense; operation with whole numbers, common fractions, and decimals; and percent, ratio, proportion, and rate. The chapters mirror the way this content is usually divided in school mathematics curricula.

Figure 1.2 shows the curriculum standards and gives a brief description of each one (NCTM, PSSM, 2000, pp. 48–50).

Grade Levels Divided into Smaller Clusters   Grade levels have been divided into pre-K–2, grades 3–5, grades 6–8, and grades 9–12. The division of pre-K to grade 5 into two clusters reflects current research in early childhood development, which indicates that preschool and primary school children have thought structures different from those of third, fourth, and fifth graders. The next division, grades 6–8, reflects the fact that more middle schools start at grade 6 than grade 5. Sixth graders can hold their own much better with eighth graders than can fifth graders. The new grade level divisions allow for more developmentally appropriate materials to be created for each group.

More on the NCTM Standards

Support for Teaching the NCTM Standards   Programs as well as students must be evaluated with respect to the standards. Concerns include providing appropriate resources for support of mathematics goals, such as concrete manipulatives (physical objects to be handled) used to help children actively construct their world mathematically. (On the companion Web site, suggestions for using hands-on materials are in Chapter 1, Extended Activities, "Tips for Using Manipulatives in the Classroom.")

Equity for *all* students is also a program goal. If all students are to experience the exhilaration that mathematical power brings to people, then procedures must be in place to make everyone part of the program.

More and more excellent resources are being produced to help teachers plan activities that teach concepts in line with the NCTM standards. The NCTM *Addenda Series* can help a novice teacher see what some of those concepts are and how to structure classroom activities to get the job done. The *Addenda Series* will be referenced in this book where appropriate. The *Navigation Series*, a series of books to accompany the *Principles and Standards* is in process. *Navigating through Algebra* was released in 2001; *Navigating through Geometry* was released in 2002, and more *Navigating through . . .* books for each of the content standards are under development. A Web site, Illuminations **(http://illuminations.nctm.org/index.html)**, contains a wide variety of Web-based resources to help improve the teaching and learning of mathematics. NCTM journals, as well as other leading journals in elementary and

NUMBER AND OPERATIONS

Instructional programs from prekindergarten through grade 12 should enable all students to

Understand numbers, ways of representing numbers, relationship among numbers, and number systems.

Understand meanings of operations and how they relate to one another.

Compute fluently and make reasonable estimates.

ALGEBRA

Instructional programs from prekindergarten through grade 12 should enable all students to

Understand patterns, relations, and functions.

Represent and analyze mathematical situations and structures using algebraic symbols.

Use mathematical models to represent and understand quantitative relationships.

Analyze change in various contexts.

GEOMETRY

Instructional programs from prekindergarten through grade 12 should enable all students to

Analyze characteristics and properties of two- and three-dimensional geometric shapes and develop mathematical arguments about geometric relationships.

Specify locations and describe spatial relationships using coordinate geometry and other representational systems.

Apply transformations and use symmetry to analyze mathematical situations.

Use visualization, spatial reasoning, and geometric modeling to solve problems.

MEASUREMENT

Instructional programs from prekindergarten through grade 12 should enable all students to

Understand measurable attributes of objects and the units, systems, and processes of measurement.

Apply appropriate techniques, tools, and formulas to determine measurements.

DATA ANALYSIS AND PROBABILITY

Instructional programs from prekindergarten through grade 12 should enable all students to

Formulate questions that can be addressed with data and collect, organize, and display relevant data to answer them.

Select and use appropriate statistical methods to analyze data.

Develop and evaluate inferences and predictions that are based on data.

Understand and apply basic concepts of probability.

PROBLEM SOLVING

Instructional programs from prekindergarten through grade 12 should enable all students to

Build new mathematical knowledge through problem solving.

Solve problems that arise in mathematics and in other contexts.

Apply and adapt a variety of appropriate strategies to solve problems.

Monitor and reflect on the process of mathematical problem solving.

REASONING AND PROOF

Instructional programs from prekindergarten through grade 12 should enable all students to

Recognize reasoning and proof as fundamental aspects of mathematics.

Make and investigate mathematical conjectures.

Develop and evaluate mathematical arguments and proofs.

Select and use various types of reasoning and methods of proof.

COMMUNICATION

Instructional programs from prekindergarten through grade 12 should enable all students to

Organize and consolidate their mathematical thinking through communication.

Communicate their mathematical thinking coherently and clearly to peers, teachers, and others.

Analyze and evaluate the mathematical thinking and strategies of others.

Use the language of mathematics to express mathematic ideas precisely.

FIGURE 1.2 *Mathematics Curriculum Standards: Pre-K–12.*

CONNECTIONS

Instructional programs from prekindergarten through grade 12 should enable all students to

Recognize and use connections among mathematical ideas.

Understand how mathematical ideas interconnect and build on one another to produce a coherent whole.

Recognize and apply mathematics in contexts outside of mathematics.

REPRESENTATION

Instructional programs from prekindergarten through grade 12 should enable all students to

Create and use representations to organize, record, and communicate mathematical ideas.

Select, apply, and translate among mathematical representations to solve problems.

Use representations to model and interpret physical, social, and mathematical phenomena.

FIGURE 1.2 *Mathematics Curriculum Standards: Pre-K–12 (Continued).*

middle school curricula, have featured ideas for teaching the NCTM standards.

Curricula Projects The National Science Foundation (NSF) is funding eight ongoing programs to develop curricula in line with the NCTM standards. To date, there are three elementary programs and five middle school programs scattered around the nation. The National Centers for Implementation of Standards-Based Mathematics Curricula (1999) have the charge of disseminating the curricula to interested people working with elementary and middle school students. The centers maintain Web sites where teachers can explore activities and engage in dialogue with other teachers as they try the activities with students. Visit the elementary Web site, **www.arccenter.comap.com**, and the middle school Web site, **www.showmecenter.missouri.edu**, to get ideas for activities to use with your students.

Learning about the problems, concerns, and successes of practicing teachers can be enlightening. Become part of this new network that is helping teachers at all levels use the Internet to talk with and learn from colleagues across the country.

Responses to the Call for Standards

There have been a large number of studies, recommendations, proclamations, and other responses to the call for higher standards in mathematics education. These include the Third International Math and Science Study (TIMSS) and the teacher accreditation standards of the National Council for the Accreditation of Teacher Education (NCATE), both of which are discussed below and described in detail on the student companion Web site, along with a variety of other standards-related documents and activities (see Extended Activities).

National Council for the Accreditation of Teacher Education The National Council for the Accreditation of Teacher Education is an organization

that accredits colleges of education that meet certain standards in their preparation of teachers, including specific mathematics guidelines for the preparation of elementary and middle school teachers (NCATE, 2005, 2007). These standards were written in conjunction with the NCTM to ensure that teachers can instruct the way the new student standards require. (The CD presents these standards and discusses what they mean for elementary education candidates; see Chapter 1, Extended Activities, "NCATE Program Standards for Elementary Teacher Preparation" and "NCATE Program Standards for Grades 5–8 Mathematics Teachers.")

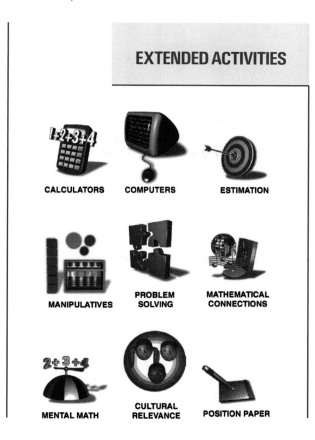

EXTENDED ACTIVITIES

CALCULATORS   COMPUTERS   ESTIMATION

MANIPULATIVES   PROBLEM SOLVING   MATHEMATICAL CONNECTIONS

MENTAL MATH   CULTURAL RELEVANCE   POSITION PAPER

On the Web Site (Chapter 1, Extended Activities 1.1) read/do the following activities:

- History of Mathematics Education
- Mathematics Book from 1850
- Mathematics Contributions by the Decades
- The Original NCTM Standards (1989, 1991, 1995)

    Curriculum and Evaluation Standards
        Curriculum
            K–4
            5–8
            9–12
        Evaluation Standards
    Professional Standards for Teaching Mathematics
    Assessment Standards

- Standards for the Professional Development of Teachers of Mathematics
- NCATE Program Standards for Elementary Teacher Preparation
- NCATE Program Standards for Grades 5–8 Mathematics Teachers
- Project 2061
- Introduction to TIMSS
- Measuring What Counts (MSEB)
- Current Trends and Issues in Mathematics Education

    Issue: Journal Writing
    The "Every Child" Statement
    Early Childhood Mathematics Education
    Teaching Mathematics in the Middle Grades
    Calculators and the Education of Youth
    The Use of Technology in the Learning and Teaching of Mathematics
    Mathematics Anxiety
    Issue: Links to Literature
    Issue: Cooperative [Collaborative] Learning

- Tips for Using Manipulatives in the Classroom

Included in the general elementary sections of the NCATE standards is the requirement that teachers know about the contributions of many cultures in each academic area and can teach that material to students. Chapter 2 of this text prepares you to teach children about the contributions of different cultures in the field of mathematics. A second requirement is that teachers acknowledge that all students can learn each subject area. Chapter 3 of this text and subsequent content chapters describe ways you can teach mathematics to all students, including special needs students. The NCATE middle school standards and the standards for elementary mathematics specialists follow along the same lines.

Research from the National Commission on Teaching and America's Future found that the number of institutions that were NCATE accredited in a state is the strongest predictor of well-qualified teachers. All three states that required NCATE accreditation for their colleges in the 1980s experienced higher-than-average gains on national student testing scores in the 1990s. That may be one reason why knowing both the teacher and the student standards has become important when interviewing for a teaching position. For example, interviews with school administrators from the East Coast to the Midwest verify that those hired first for teaching positions in many districts are those who know and can use the current student and teacher mathematics standards in actual classroom experiences.

NO CHILD LEFT BEHIND

On January 8, 2002, President Bush signed into law the *No Child Left Behind Act of 2001*. The Act was the most sweeping reform of the Elementary and Secondary Education Act (ESEA) since ESEA was enacted in 1965. It redefined the federal role in K-12 education with the goal of helping to close the achievement gap between disadvantaged and minority students and their peers. It is based on four basic principles: stronger accountability for results, increased flexibility and local control, expanded options for parents, and an emphasis on teaching methods that have been proven to work. "Stronger accountability for results," in particular, has resulted in an emphasis on high-stakes assessments in mathematics and reading from grades 3–8.

In his State of the Union Address in January 2007, President Bush discussed his plans for the law's reauthorization. **Building On Results: A Blueprint for Strengthening the *No Child Left Behind Act*** proposes providing additional tools to schools and educators to help America's students read and do mathematics at grade level by 2014. The President proposed among other things extending the provisions of NCLB to high schools. At the time this book is going to press, the reauthorization of NCLB is still being discussed in Congress.

WHERE'S MATHEMATICS LEARNING TODAY?

Learning Styles and Children's Preexisting Mathematical Knowledge

New brain research (see Chapter 3) and the standards movement have influenced mathematics educators to look at new alternatives for teaching mathematics. These alternatives include different curricula for different groups of students with different ways of studying (i.e., with different learning styles). Teachers who can target students' learning styles are better able to expand students' future prospects. Brain research has also shown that educators need to get past the assumption that their students have no mathematical knowledge before they enter the classroom, and they have to help students bring what they already know about mathematics into the classroom. That is, educators must identify and reinforce students' out-of-school mathematical experiences and knowledge. Young children typically engage in all kinds of mathematical activities. For example, looking at pictures of buildings acquaints students with two-dimensional representations of three-dimensional objects, and there are of course many other ways in which mathematics appears in everyday life.

Active Learning

Given the new standards, the new brain research, and the new recognition of students' out-of-class mathematics activity, the challenge is still to teach students to reason mathematically. To do that, the classroom teacher must know how to actively engage students by posing tasks that

- Children with a variety of levels of knowledge and skill will find challenging but not impossible.
- Involve serious mathematics.
- Provide an opportunity to develop mathematical reasoning.

Research (Sullo, 2007) shows that students learn best when they are actively engaged in the experience, with new learning connected to things they already know. This also applies to students with special needs (Meyer, 2002). Connections can grow increasingly more complex by the middle school years, when students begin to decide what their real-world occupations may be. If you are planning to work with middle school students, read the NCTM focus issue on middle school connections (NCTM, 2006).

Children's literature can be a good connection for active learning. Many stories have mathematics-related themes or can be used to teach special mathematics concepts. Thiessen (2004), and Whitin and Whitin (2004) list many works of children's literature with notes on how each can be used in teaching mathematics; their book is an excellent resource for any teacher. In addition, a selected set of children's literature that can be used with various mathematics content is listed at the end of each of this text's content chapters.

Recognizing that students need to reflect on and record their mathematical knowledge and behaviors through oral and written discourse, educators are emphasizing communication, especially journal writing and oral reporting. This text also presents ideas for mathematics communication in the content chapters.

Assessment

Assessment issues accompany today's curriculum reform efforts. Many teachers claim they would like to change their teaching practices, but they need to cover material that is "on the test." Teachers are well aware of the importance of standardized achievement tests—results are published in local newspapers and used for district-to-district, school-to-school comparisons, and even classroom-to-classroom comparisons. As educators begin to recognize the importance of providing a different mathematics education for American youth, improved means of measuring student learning and attitudes are needed. The following statement is as true today as it was more than a decade ago, particularly in this era dominated by high-stakes testing at all levels of education: "We must ensure that tests measure what is of value, not just what is easy to test. What is tested is what gets taught. Tests must measure what is most important" (National Research Council, 1989, p. 8).

Assessment activities and ideas are included in the NCTM's original *Assessment Standards* (1995). You can adapt them to suit your needs, but in doing so you should keep in mind the underlying assessment principles and practices. Figure 1.3 presents a performance task from the *Assessment Standards* that illustrates several of the standards. Which standards do you think relate to the task?

Take an acute triangle with an interior point P. Consider the perpendiculars from point P to the sides and the triangle formed by the three feet of these perpendiculars on the three sides. This is the pedal triangle of pedal point P.

1. Measure

    a. The sum of the perpendicular distances to the three sides of the original triangle from P.

    b. The sum of the distances from P to the three vertices of the original triangle.

    c. The area of the pedal triangle.

    d. The perimeter of the pedal triangle.

2. Explore how these measures change for different locations of P inside the triangle.

3. What conjectures can you make about the sums, areas, and perimeters found in your explorations? Do you think your conjecture will apply to any triangle?

    • Make a convincing argument for your answer. Your argument can be written or oral.
    • Support your argument with the data you collected.
    • Use tables or graphs to present your data.
    • Explain a situation where someone would want to know this information.

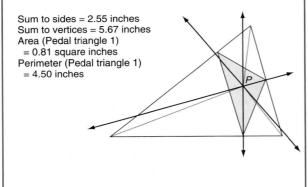

Sum to sides = 2.55 inches
Sum to vertices = 5.67 inches
Area (Pedal triangle 1)
= 0.81 square inches
Perimeter (Pedal triangle 1)
= 4.50 inches

FIGURE 1.3 *Performance task. Source: National Council of Teachers of Mathematics, 1995, p. 37. Reprinted with permission from Assessment Standards for School Mathematics, copyright 1995 by the National Council of Teachers of Mathematics. All rights reserved.*

See Chapter 3 for a detailed discussion of the nature, purposes, and techniques of assessment.

Assessment of Teachers: Praxis™ Exams Even as educators develop a better understanding of assessment and how to assess in ways that are meaningful to students and allow them to demonstrate what they know and understand about mathematics, so are schools of education and state departments of education developing more rigorous types of assessments that allow you to demonstrate what you know and understand about teaching. The test most commonly used by universities and states is one or more of the Praxis™ exams. In fact, Praxis™ is required by 35 of the 43 states that use tests for licensure. Many colleges and universities also use one or more of the Praxis™ series as part of their entrance and/or exit requirements for teacher education. To help you prepare for this type of test, the authors have provided Praxis™-style questions at the end of each chapter, and there are additional questions available to your instructor at the Web site developed for this text.

Technology

Technology has the power to motivate students and teachers alike. We strongly advocate the use of technology to enhance mathematics learning. Throughout this text, we will describe ways of using technology in mathematics education, including technologies such as interactive multimedia, the Internet and World Wide Web, and mathematics-related programming with Logo with Turtle Math and LEGO MINDSTORMS (LEGO Group, 2002). Consult the ASCD yearbook, *Learning with Technology* (ASCD, 2006), for discussions of how and why technology works as an educational tool.

The Internet and the World Wide Web The World Wide Web was created in 1993, with the goal of making parts of the Internet more quickly and easily accessible. Today, you can create, access, and download an enormous variety of information, games, and interactive activities on the Web. The Web is very fluid, constantly changing, so you will surely find more Web sites related to mathematics education than the authors were aware of when this text was written. The Web sites listed in Activity 1.1 demonstrate the range of material on the Web.

At the end of each chapter in this text, you'll find a list of one or more Web sites related to the content of that chapter. There is a Web site developed for this text to keep you updated on new and emerging topics and issues in mathematics teaching. Our Web address is **www.wiley.com/college/hatfield**.

Activity 1.1

EXPLORING WEB SITES

DIRECTIONS

Visit these Web sites for interactive activities. From this list which three did you enjoy the most? Why?
http://neptune.galaxy.gmu.edu/~drsuper/
http://discoveryschool.com/schrockguide/math.html

- Educators Reference Desk
  http://eduref.org/Virtual/Lessons/
- Swarthmore forum
  http://mathforum.org/library
  http://forum.swarthmore.edu/~steve/
- New Hampshire Public Television
  http://www.nhptv.org/kn/vs/mathgames.htm
- Columbia Education Center
  http://www.col-ed.org/cur/#math3/
- Busy Teachers
  http://www.ceismc.gatech.edu/busyt/
- Girls Tech
  http://www.teachertech.rice.edu
- GoENC (subscription)
  http://www.goenc.com
- Teachers for Teachers
  http://www.pacificnet.net/~mandel
- Teachers
  http://www.teachers.net/curriculum/mathematics.html

Supporting the NCTM *Principles and Standards* (2000):

- Mathematics as Problem Solving: Communication
- Worthwhile Mathematical Tasks—The Learning Principle
- The Technology Principle

Calculators Technology also includes calculators of all types. Middle school students are using sophisticated calculators that plot and display graphs in seconds, eliminating the need to perform long, tedious computations. Some first grade students are using motion sensors and graphing calculators to learn about graphing. Students get a quick sense of how changes in an equation's variables affect the equation's graph, and this type of knowledge can be useful in solving new problems. Research supports the idea that calculator use has a positive impact on the development of problem-solving strategies (Heid et al., 1998). The NCTM's *technology principle* (see page 7) calls for all students to have access to calculators. All students should be able to determine when and where calculator use is appropriate.

Other Current Trends

Figure 1.4 lists the current trends and issues in mathematics education receiving the most attention as reflected in mathematics research and professional journal articles. Scan the list in Figure 1.4 and then do the activity in the Video Vignette on p. 15.

Professional organizations such as the National Council of Teachers of Mathematics issue position statements on many current trends and issues. Visit the NCTM Web site (www.nctm.org)

CURRENT TRENDS IN MATHEMATICAL LEARNING

No Child Left Behind Requirements
Trends in Problem Solving
Trends in Estimation and Mental Math
Trends in Communication
    Issue: Cooperative Learning
    Issue: Journal Writing
Trends in Mathematical Connections
    Issue: Links to Literature
Trends in Mathematical Reasoning
Trends in Early Childhood Mathematics
Trends in Equity: Mathematics for ALL Students
    Issue: Culturally Relevant Mathematics
    Issue: Math Anxiety
    Issue: Women in Mathematics
Trends in the Use of Manipulatives
Trends in Technology
    Calculators
    Microcomputers
    Computer-Assisted Instruction
        Drill and Practice Programs
        Problem-Solving Programs
        Application Programs
            Databases
            Spreadsheets
            Graphics
Computer-Managed Instruction

FIGURE 1.4 *Current trends and issues on the student companion Web site.*

and follow the links **About NCTM/Position Statements** to read the council's position statements, including "Calculators and the Education of Youth," "Early Childhood Mathematics: Promoting Good Beginnings," "Teaching Mathematics in the Middle Grades," and "The Use of Technology in the Learning and Teaching of Mathematics."

 Video Vignette

Teacher's Reflection on Mathematics Teaching

On the CD, view the Video Vignette "Teacher's Reflection on Mathematics Teaching" (Chapter 1, Video Vignettes). The teacher, Mrs. Torres, discusses her vision of how a mathematics classroom should look. As you view the video, think about these questions and be ready to discuss them with your colleagues:

- How are the trends and issues in Figure 1.4 reflected in the video?
- What points does Mrs. Torres stress about the mathematics classroom? How does her vision of a classroom relate to what you have read in this chapter about the standards?
- What beliefs about children's learning are evidenced in the video? How are they similar to or different from your beliefs about mathematics instruction?

WHAT'S NEXT?

It is exhilarating to project into the future. In the field of mathematics education, many projections are now on the drawing boards, or should we say, on computer drives. They indicate that the profession of teaching may undergo a change

in focus, but there will still be plenty for teachers to do.

The school will still have a physical plant, and there will still be a mathematics curriculum, but not all mathematics lessons will need to be taught in the school building. Students will use the Internet to call up lessons or last-minute assignments at home. Still, human beings are social creatures who will need to come together to discuss what they have learned. There will still be a need for a gathering place—the school.

But just think . . . no more heavy book bags! "Books" will be thin, round CDs, or portable flash drives. Students will carry one lightweight laptop or an iPod instead of many weighty books. Streaming video will bring mathematics studies into the "real world," with students being able to see mathematics at work. Students will problem solve along with teachers and other professionals via the Internet at home and at school.

Increasingly, technology will enhance students' ability to come up with new and different solutions to mathematics problems. Teachers must understand the mathematics deeply enough to know how to respond when students give solutions that aren't in the teacher's manual (Fennell, 2006). The activities in this text and on the Web are geared to get you thinking on your own about mathematics. Some problems have one correct answer, but many ways to get to it. Other problems have many answers. Whether there's one answer or many, teachers must change the question from "What is the answer?" to "Why is the answer correct?" A teacher must know when and how to switch from one approach to another when helping students solve a problem. These are some of the essentials if we are to be ready for twenty-first-century students.

Burrill (1998) state the challenges that will face all mathematics teachers in the future:

Connect the mathematics that you teach with the curriculum that you are supposed to teach. Find out what mathematics is taught in your grade cluster. Think hard about technology and how it can be used. Design your lessons carefully, and choose tasks that matter. Bring closure to the lessons that you teach. Help your students see the mathematics in what they do. Keep families informed about the mathematics as you are teaching and why. (p. 593)

Remember, we are all in this together—parents, teachers, administrators, and students. No one must be left out of the loop when planning for mathematics education in the future.

SUMMARY

- Mathematics education is an ever-changing, ever-expanding field of knowledge. Mathematics education is more than "learning the steps" for working problems; rather, it means understanding mathematical concepts as "packages of knowledge" that support the ways children naturally approach learning and doing mathematics.

- Teachers of mathematics should have the attitude that it is important to both "know how" and "know why." This attitude is being actively promoted for the first time as a result of the current standards movement.

- Under the auspices of the NCTM, three sets of standards deal with the "big picture" of mathematics. The six "guiding principles" of these standards broadly state the foundations of high-quality mathematics education: the *equity principle*, the *mathematics curriculum principle*, the *teaching principle*, the *learning principle*, the *assessment principle*, and the *technology principle*.

- Many different resources are available to help mathematics education programs support the NCTM standards, including a number of curricula projects.

- The accreditation standards developed by NCATE are designed to ensure that teachers can teach the way the NCTM standards require.

- Mathematics educators today recognize that students learn best when they are actively engaged in the experience. To promote active learning, curricula and teachers should respond to children's different learning styles and their preexisting mathematical knowledge. Children's literature can be a good connection for active learning.

- Evaluation of student learning must include classroom assessment as well as standardized tests. Standardized tests must test what is important, not just what is easy to test. The NCTM's assessment standards envision a classroom environment very different from that of most present classrooms.

- Schools of education and state departments of education are developing teacher assessments that allow teachers to demonstrate what they know and understand about teaching. Universities and states most commonly use the Praxis™ exams.

- Technology should be used to enhance mathematics learning, including technologies such as interactive multimedia, the Internet and World Wide Web, and mathematics-related programming, as well as calculators of all types.

- In the not-too-distant future, much learning will take place over the Web rather than at school. Flash drives and iPods will replace heavy books and CDs. Teachers will face new challenges related to the new modes of learning.

PRAXIS II™-STYLE QUESTIONS

As noted in this chapter, high-stakes testing will be part of your life as a teacher, just as it will be for your students. All U.S. states and all the provinces of Canada require that you pass a test in your teaching area before you can be granted certification to teach. Whether you are seeking teacher certification in a Praxis II™-state or elsewhere, you will have to take a test with questions like the Praxis II™-style questions found at the end of each chapter in this text. We want to help you get ready to pass the test in the mathematics area. For elementary teachers, the mathematics section has the second-largest number of questions, exceeded only by reading. We will present Praxis II™-style questions in the two common formats for the tests—multiple choice and constructed response.

Prospective teachers have also found it helpful to adopt the role of a test writer by writing their own test questions for others to answer, and we have designed an activity like this on the Web (Chapter 1, Extended Activities, "Write Your Own Praxis II™-Style Questions"). You can download a form for writing text questions from the Web. Share your work on this activity with a colleague. See if he or she can answer your questions and say why the wrong answers are wrong. The student companion Web site also contains test questions written by teacher candidates in the past (Chapter 1, Extended Activities, "Praxis II™-Style Questions by Teacher Candidates"). Once you have learned to structure your thoughts like a test writer, you will find yourself working on the higher cognitive levels required to pass the test.

EXERCISES

Answers to this chapter's Praxis II™-style questions are in the instructor's manual.

Multiple-Choice Format

1. You are observing a mathematics teacher who believes in the ideas and concepts promoted in the NCTM's *Principles and Standards for School Mathematics* (2000). You can expect the students to be

   a. Communicating the results of their mathematical investigations to other students.

   b. Using the computer to verify mathematical computations done with a slide rule.

   c. Using problem solving and higher-order thinking skills to memorize the 100 basic facts.

   d. Doing math drills at the blackboard.

2. Which of the classroom scenes below supports the use of calculators in effective instruction, as advocated by the NCTM?

   a. Students are using calculators only to check their paper and pencil work.

   b. Students are using calculators to complete mathematical reasoning tasks.

   c. Students are using calculators to quickly come up with the basic 100 number facts.

   d. Students are using calculators instead of performing tedious computations.

Constructed-Response Format

3. A parent comes to your classroom and says, "I don't like it that you make my child reason out an answer in different ways. Just tell him the one right way to get the answer and then move on to other math concepts." In three sentences or less, state what you would say to the parent.

4. State three things you would do as you taught mathematics if you were a teacher who believed in NCTM's equity principle.

Integrating Technology

Video Vignettes

Observations of Good Teaching with the Standards
On the CD, view the video vignettes listed below. Read the questions accompanying each vignette before viewing it. Be prepared to discuss your answers with your colleagues after you have watched the five video vignettes.

- Chapter 7: "Pizza Perimeters"
- Chapter 9: "Whale Math"
- Chapter 9: "Numeration Games" (note the brief clip of a college mathematics methods class at the beginning)
- Chapter 10: "Dinosaur Legs"
- Chapter 15: "Graphing Probability"

Internet Activities

WebQuest

Design Your Own Virtual School
On the Web site for this text www.wiley.com/college/hatfield, open the activity "Design Your Own Virtual School." Follow the directions there to complete this Web-based activity. Apply what you have read in this chapter as you do the WebQuest.

Web sites

The LEGO MINDSTORMS system permits children to link their Lego programs to the Lego Systems home page. Games, tutorials, and more can also be found at this Web site: **http://mindstorms.lego.com/**. To access the games and tutorials, click on the **MIND-STORMS Community** link. You will need a set of LEGO-Logo materials to actually do the activity entitled "Missions."

National Library of Virtual Manipulatives http://nlvm.usu.edu/en/nav/vlibrary.html (also in Spanish) Virtual manipulatives, with suggestions for teachers and parents, useful for teaching the content standards in NCTM's Principles and Standards.

Culturally Relevant Mathematics

No student should leave elementary school without a sense of the importance of mathematics in human history. Our rich mathematical understanding has evolved from the contributions of diverse cultures of the past and the present. All students deserve the right to know about, appreciate, and benefit from these contributions. *Culturally relevant mathematics* is a term that shows awareness on the part of educators that mathematics exists within a cultural environment, which must not be ignored.

The term *culturally relevant mathematics* comprises two main ideas:

1. *Multiculturalism.* Mathematics has been present in every culture in recorded history. The giftedness of many cultures in mathematics is well documented.
2. *Equity.* Mathematics is important to all cultures and their people. Everyone has the right to acquire the mathematical power needed for success in today's world.

Both aspects of cultural relevance will be discussed in this chapter. Equity is the overriding challenge for mathematics teachers—to help *all* students pursue mathematical success (Nelson, Joseph, and Williams, 1993; Campbell and Rowan, 1997; Michael-Bandele, 1998). An important part of that is multiculturalism—helping students see that all cultures have giftedness in mathematics and that all people can be successful in mathematics.

This challenge raises two key questions for mathematics teachers: How can we give students from culturally diverse backgrounds the mathematical understanding needed to be full partici-

pants in society? How much of a part do diverse cultural backgrounds and beliefs play in the acquisition of mathematical understanding? This chapter explores some of the research being done to help answer these questions. We also examine some of the exemplary teaching practices that show the most promise in helping all students acquire mathematical power.

MULTICULTURALISM: THE GIFTEDNESS OF MANY CULTURES IN MATHEMATICS

Respect for one's own culture and for the cultures of others is essential as we strive for quality in our lives. Knowledge about the contributions of diverse cultures to mathematics and about the different ways those cultures use mathematics can foster that respect. Zaslavsky (2002) states that the discipline of mathematics can no longer be viewed as culture free. *Ethnomathematics* is one term used to describe the awareness that different cultures, societies, and ethnic groups bring their unique approaches to the performance of mathematics. The International Study Group on Ethnomathematics was organized in 1985 as an affiliate group of the National Council of Teachers of Mathematics (NCTM). Information on the group is available at the NCTM Web site (**http://www.nctm.org**). Membership is open to all interested persons, and many countries are represented in its list of members.

The Chicago public school system has led the way in emphasizing the contributions of diverse cultures in each strand of the mathematics curriculum. When this approach is followed

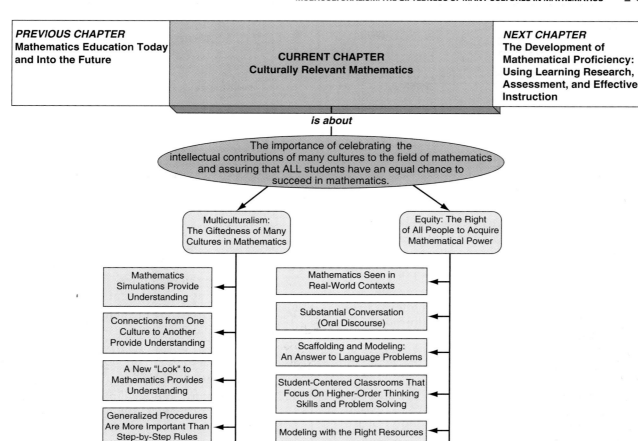

consistently from year to year, children truly begin to accept the fact that all cultures, including their own, really have made contributions to the areas they are studying. In mathematics, pride and a sense of hope replace learned helplessness, and students who previously would never have considered mathematics as a possible area for success can begin to achieve at high levels. The authors of this text thank Dorothy Strong and the mathematics administration of the Chicago public schools for sharing their work with us; their multicultural goals for mathematics learning appear in Figure 2.1.

The cultural contributions summarized in Figure 2.1 are presented to acquaint you with some basic information that you can share with students in the future. Subsequent chapters discuss these contributions in greater detail as relevant to the mathematics concepts. Subsequent chapters also feature mathematics activities celebrating different cultures where appropriate for elementary and middle school students. The range of possible mathematics activities is great, so the authors have picked culturally relevant activities they think are especially appropriate for students

at strategic skill levels. These activities are denoted with the cultural relevance icon:

**CULTURAL
RELEVANCE**

Starting in the mid-1980s, many multicultural resources in mathematics began to appear in print (Closs, 1986; Kunjufu, 1987a, 1987b, 1987c; Caduto and Bruchac, 1989; 1991; Akoto, 1990; Voolich, 1993; Secada, Fennema, and Adajian, 1995; Mingo, 1997; Taylor, 1997; Edwards, 1999; Ortiz-Franco, Hernandez, and De La Cruz, 1999; Secada, 2000; Strutchens, Johnson, and Tate, 2000; Hankes and Fast, 2002, to name only a few). You should start making your own list of resources. With more and more mathematics resources in print, classroom teachers have the opportunity to provide a wide variety of exciting culturally relevant mathematics lessons for elementary and middle school students (Wiest,

SELF-HELP QUESTIONS

1. What is culturally relevant mathematics?

2. How can I use mathematical ideas from other cultures to give students a greater understanding of the accomplishments of others?

3. What can I do to help students from underrepresented populations realize how important their cultures have been to the development of mathematical ideas?

4. What can I do to help bilingual students and those from underrepresented populations succeed in mathematics?

5. How do mathematical simulations help children understand multiculturalism in mathematics?

6. How does making connections between cultures help children understand multiculturalism in mathematics?

7. How can I use different cultures' different thought patterns to help all children learn mathematics?

8. Why are generalized procedures more important than step-by-step rules in teaching mathematics?

9. How can I use the power of storytelling to teach mathematics concepts?

10. How can I be sure to teach mathematics using real-world contexts for all students? How does poverty impact these contexts?

11. How can I be sure that oral discourse in my mathematics classes meets the needs of all students?

12. How can I use scaffolding and modeling to help all students understand mathematics?

13. How do student-centered classrooms promote learning in mathematics?

14. What resources are available to highlight the unique contributions and characteristics of different cultures? What resources are available to highlight women's contributions to mathematics?

15. How can an awareness of different learning styles help me teach mathematics to all children?

2002; Morris, 2000). You should also take a look at the lists of children's multicultural literature in mathematics at the end of this chapter.

Mathematics Simulations Provide Understanding

Students learn to appreciate the unique mathematical contributions of other cultures when they perform tasks similar to ones performed in those cultures. If the tasks are challenging and require mathematical reasoning and perseverance, the message is clear—the people in those cultures are smart and determined!

People in Other Cultures Today   Where and how people live often explains why they have discovered things that other cultures haven't. Two excellent examples come from African cultures. To highlight cultural contributions, Zaslavsky (1993) prepared lessons for sixth and ninth graders on the mathematics used by African societies. Zaslavsky reports that students were fascinated to see how Tanzanians built round houses with the greatest floor area for a given amount of building material. The students discovered this principle for themselves after a difficult hands-on experience involving surface areas of circles and squares. The scarcity of building materials provided the impetus for the people of Tanzania to apply mathematical formulas to solve problems involving surface area.

The students were equally fascinated to learn that the Bakuha children of Zaire can do graphing based on network theory that adult Belgian ethnographers could not do. The students were also given lessons on graphing based on network theory that showed the intelligence of the Chokwe elders of Angola. Zaslavsky reported that many students looked for traceable networks in other designs after the lessons. Several African American students expressed delight to learn that the Bakuha children could perform mathematics that adult whites could not. Davidson and Kramer (1997) described the same effect from similar units of study.

People in Ancient Times   Many students think modern technology shows that people today must be more intelligent than people in ancient times. As one student expressed it, "If they were really smart, they would have had cars, TV, and computer

Multiculturalism is summarized in a statement following each of the seven strands related to the State Goals for Learning in Mathematics. A multicultural statement precedes the list of objectives for each strand at each grade level K–12.

Arithmetic: Many peoples contributed to the development of the modern system of numerals. (Africans were the first to use numerals. Ancient Egyptians in Africa invented a symbol for ten that replaced 10 tally marks and a symbol for one hundred that replaced 100 tally marks. The Chinese invented negative numbers. Native Americans were the first to use a symbol for zero. Ancient Egyptians invented unit fractions.)

Quantitative Relationships: Students should know that the ancient Egyptians invented proportional scale drawing. They enlarged figures proportionally by transferring drawings from grids of small squares to grids of large squares.

Measurement: Students should be able to relate the origin of geometry to real-life situations. (Examples: The annual flooding of the Nile River in Africa created a need to measure the area of triangles, rectangles, and circles. The building of the pyramids created a need to develop formulas for the volume of pyramids. The unit of measurement was the cubit, the length of the pharaoh's forearm. The 24-hour day—12 hours of day and 12 hours of night—originated in Egypt.)

Algebraic Concepts: Students should know that Africans invented rectangular coordinates by 2650 B.C. and used them to make scale drawings and starclocks. The students should examine the Egyptian use of the distributive property in multiplication. (Example: Ancient Egyptians multiplied 21 ′ 34 by selecting (1 + 4 + 16) ′ 34 from successive doublings of 1 ′ 34.) They should explore patterns to find the next term in the sequence *1, 7, 49, 343*, which was taken from an ancient Egyptian papyrus. Students should know that the word *algebra* is Arabic in origin and that Europe received algebra as a gift from Asia and Africa.

Geometric Concepts: Students should know that the first concepts of congruence were developed in Africa and Asia and that cotangents and similar triangle principles were used in the building of the African pyramids. The students should examine the contributions to geometry made by people all over the world. (Examples: Eskimos built igloos in the shape of a catenary. Mozambicans built rectangular houses by using equal-length ropes as the diagonals. The Babylonians used the right triangle theorem 1500 years before Pythagoras was born. The term *Pythagorean theorem* is a misnomer.)

Data Analysis: Students should know that many peoples used and contributed to statistics and probability. (Examples: The Mayan people learned to predict eclipses by analyzing astronomical tables that they had made over the centuries. The peoples of Egypt and Mesopotamia developed geometric formulas through experimentation and data analysis.) Students should explore methods for collecting statistics and predicting outcomes related to real-life problems. (Examples: In Africa, ancient Egyptian governments prepared budgets and levied taxes based on data analysis. Measurements of the annual flood, made with a Nilometer, were used to predict the size of the harvest.)

Applications: Students should explore methods for collecting statistics and predicting outcomes related to real-life problems. (Examples: In Africa, ancient Egyptian governments prepared budgets and levied taxes based on data analysis. Measurements of the annual flood, made with a Nilometer, were used to predict the size of the harvest. The modern method of using the so-called pascal's triangle was actually invented in Asia by the Chinese and the Persians 500 years before Pascal was born.)

FIGURE 2.1 *Chicago public schools mathematics objectives that reflect multiculturalism.* Source: *Strong, 1991c, p. 38.*

games." Activities 2.1 and 2.2, presented here for you to do with your classes, are simulations that dispel the idea that ancient peoples could not solve hard mathematical problems.

A Numeration System from Ancient Africa Activity 2.1 is based on a numeration system used in ancient Africa. Bohan and Bohan (1993) started elementary lessons by having children find the similarities between the ancient system and our current system. Children were asked to write large numbers in the ancient system. They found that the string of numerals seemed very long and tedious to write. Bohan and Bohan then encouraged students to problem solve ways they could make the ancient system less cumbersome. The journal article shows the work of several students.

After reading the journal article, a student teacher decided to motivate her class by telling them that other children across the country had done the activity too. She said she would let her

Activity 2.1

CULTURAL
RELEVANCE

PROBLEM
SOLVING

PORTFOLIO

CREATING YOUR OWN NUMERATION SYSTEM BASED ON A SYSTEM FROM ANCIENT AFRICA

MATERIALS
- Pictures shown to children from the Bohan and Bohan (1993) article
- Pencil and paper to make their own systems

DIRECTIONS
1. Show how to write a large number in the Egyptian system from Africa as presented in the article.
2. Use these words to start the activity: "The ancestors of our African Americans invented a great numeral system in a country called Egypt. The African numerals in the activity are much too long to write every time. What way could you invent to make the number shorter to write? Write out how you would explain your system to a first grader."
3. Figure 2.2 shows Teisha's work and explanation.
4. Teisha took a ruler and measured her numeral to the one in the journal each time. This was her own idea; no one had told her to do this.

FIGURE 2.3   *Teisha compares her work to Mary's.*

5. Then Mary's King Tut system from the journal article was shown to Teisha. Figure 2.3 shows Teisha's response. Teisha meticulously measured her numeral and Mary's numeral with the ruler. She demonstrated that her numeral took up less space. She was quite proud of this discovery.
6. Then Teisha was shown that Mary's numeral for 9642 would be shorter than hers. Mary's 9642 was not shown in the book, so the student teacher drew it like this (Figure 2.4)

FIGURE 2.4   *Student teacher's drawing of 9642 as Mary's system would show it.*

FIGURE 2.2   *Teisha's numeration system.*

Activity 2.2

CULTURAL RELEVANCE   MATHEMATICAL CONNECTIONS

FINDING THE MISSING MAYAN NUMBERS

MATERIALS

- Each child copies a Mayan numeral chart (Figures 2.5 and 2.6)

DIRECTIONS

Elementary Students (use Figure 2.5)

1. Use these words to start the activity:

   "This lesson shows the smart thinking of the Mayan people. They are the ancestors of the Hispanic Americans today. Study the numerals of the Mayan system. Fill in the blanks for the missing numbers."

2. Explain how you figured it out by writing in your journal. Then tell a friend.

Middle School Students (use Figure 2.6):

1. Use these words to start the activity:

   "This lesson shows the smart thinking of the Mayan people. They are the ancestors of the Hispanic Americans today. Study the numerals of the Mayan system. Fill in the blanks for the missing numbers. Think what is happening with the oval eye. How many times larger are things becoming?"

2. Explain how you figured it out by writing in your journal. Then tell a friend.

3. Think of several new numerals you could write following the system. Show your choices to a friend. Decide together if each numeral follows the Mayan pattern.

Supporting the NCTM *Principles and Standards* (2000):

- Mathematics as Reasoning and Logic; Mathematics as Communication
- Worthwhile Mathematical Tasks; Mathematics as Oral and Written Discourse—The Teaching Principle
- Monitoring Students' Progress and Achievement—The Assessment Principle

---

Our Numeral	1	2	3	4	5	6	7	8	9	10
Mayan Numeral	•	••	•••	••••	—	•—		••• —		=

Our Numeral	11	12	13	14	15	16	17	18	19
Mayan Numeral	•=	••=			≡		••=		•••• ≡

FIGURE 2.5 *Mayan numeral chart for early grades.*

Our Numeral	1	2	3	4	5	6	7	8	9	10
Mayan Numeral	•	••	•••	••••	—	•—		••• —		=

Our Numeral	11	12	13	14	15	16	17	18	19
Mayan Numeral	•=	••=			≡		••=		•••• ≡

Our Numeral	20	40	60	80	100	120	140	160	180	200
Mayan Numeral	⊙	⊙•			— ⊙	•— ⊙		••• ⊙		= ⊙

FIGURE 2.6 *Mayan numeral chart for middle school.*

students compare their number systems with those she had found in the Bohan and Bohan article, after her class had finished the work. The following reflection became part of the student teacher's professional portfolio: *Important—Notice that the students are always told which cultural group is being celebrated in the mathematics activity.* This is essential in helping students understand the mathematical giftedness of all cultures. The student teacher's words are modeled in Activity 2.1.

In this example, the student teacher found a clever way of using professional journals in teaching. There are many new assessments in which children's actual work is shown in journal articles. It often works to motivate a class with the promise that they can see the work of others doing the same activity. Students like the idea that other children are doing the same things they are. If the students' answers are not as good as those of the journal group at first, encourage them by saying that the journal group has probably been doing it a lot longer than they have. That is almost certainly true, because authors generally practice a strategy or skill with a class before publishing.

A Numeration System from Ancient Mayan Culture The Mayan society of Central America provides a prime example of the power of the mind to create efficient mathematics. They invented the most remarkable number system of all the ancient civilizations. They needed only three symbols to write any number they wished—a dot, a line, and an oval eye. Just as a 0 is a place holder in our system that makes things ten times larger, the oval eye meant that things were twenty times larger. Activity 2.2 can be used with young children or expanded to teach middle school students. It is adapted from a similar exercises presented in classrooms. The activities stress the reasoning and patterning skills first used by the Mayans.

Other creative lessons using the mathematics of the Mayan culture (Lara-Alecio, Irby, and Morales-Aldana, 1998; Overbay and Brod, 2007) stress the relationship between numeral and number, geometry, and mathematical calculations in astronomy. Other teaching ideas appear on the Web site (Chapter 2, Extended Activities). All prove that simulations are an effective way of doing mathematics and appreciating cultural contributions at the same time.

Connections from One Culture to Another Provide Understanding

My First Kwanzaa Book (Chocolate, 1992), which shows the connections teachers can make from one culture to another, can be used with beginning counting activities (see Chapter 6 for a variety of counting activities suitable for children of all cultures). Kwanzaa is a nonreligious holiday celebrating seven principles of African life—unity (helping each other), self-determination (deciding things for ourselves), collaboration and responsibility (working together to make life better), cooperative economics (supporting our own businesses), purpose (having a reason for living), creativity (using our minds and hands to create things), and faith (believing in self, ancestors, and the future). Each day from December 26 to January 1 a candle is lit in commemoration of one of the seven principles. A teacher can feature the number 7 in honor of Kwanzaa. Certainly, the seven principles are desirable ones for all peoples. Jacobs and Becker (1997) describe the mathematical pattern used in the lighting of the Kwanzaa candles:

There is one black candle, three red candles, and three green candles. On the first night the black candle is lit in the middle position. The second night the black candle and a red candle are lit. The third night the black, the red, and a green candle are lit. This pattern continues with each night having an additional candle lit, alternating red and green as the additional candle. On the seventh night, all candles are lit, with three red, then a black candle, and then three green. If each night's candles are burned completely in a single night, what is the total number of candles used and how many of each color are used over the seven days? (p. 109)

Jacobs and Becker (1997) also point out that the similarity of Kwanzaa candle lighting and Chanukah candle lighting can be shown to students, with similar math problems created to figure out how many candles would be needed for the eight-night celebration of Chanukah. Students from one culture are often surprised to see that students from another culture have similar rituals for commemorating different things. Activities like those described here make for a rich environment in which to explore mathematics. Other children's books that add cultural interest to mathematics lessons are listed at the end of this chapter.

The activities listed in the Extended Activities have been used with middle school students. The first, "Black History Connections," is actually a unit of activities. The second, "Pyramid Measurements," lets students experience the tremendous size of the Great Pyramid of Giza, in Egypt, by using ratio and proportion measurements on the athletic field and in the classroom.

The third, "Babylonian Logo Activity," shows the work of African American eighth graders from Kansas City, Missouri, who had been studying the early Babylonian numeration system. In that system, the physical size of the numeral is significant. The bigger the numeral, the larger the number it represents. The students invented their own Babylonian-type system on a computer, using the Logo computer language, which they had been working with since early elementary school. The program is presented in the activity on the student companion Web site so you can see how students can integrate mathematics, computer technology, and cultural awareness in one mathematics project. Working in cooperative groups, the students programmed the keystrokes to make each numeral.

A New "Look" to Mathematics Provides Understanding

Many cultures view the world quite differently from the way white Europeans do, but it is the white European view that dominates in most schools in the United States and Canada today. People from other cultures may pattern their thoughts differently, and this can give a new "look" to mathematics. Students exposed to new thought patterns in mathematics may find that a different way of thinking can make difficult concepts easier to understand rather than memorizing a set of rules. For example, many teachers have seen students with special needs flourish when presented with other ways to solve mathematics problems.

EXTENDED ACTIVITIES

| MATHEMATICAL CONNECTIONS | CALCULATORS | CULTURAL RELEVANCE | PROBLEM SOLVING |

On the Student Companion Web Site (Chapter 2, Extended Activities), read/do the following:

- Black History Connections—A Middle School Unit
- Pyramid Measurements
- Babylonian Logo Activity Created by African American Middle School Students

Generalized Procedures are More Important Than Step-by-Step Rules

Too many teachers teach concepts using a step-by-step approach that overemphasizes a rule-governed way of looking for a solution (NCTM, 2000). This approach may work for one type of problem, but not for multiple types in multiple contexts. The approach also has the fault of prompting students to think of mathematics as rule based rather than concept based.

The western European worldview tends to separate knowledge into categories. Writing on Native American cultural contributions to scientific thought, DeLoria and Wildcat (2001) note the limitations of the western European approach by pointing to "chaos theory, nonlinear models of development and change in physics, and complexity, emergent properties, and bio- and phytoremediation in biology as evidence that cutting-edge science now recognizes the holistic worldview as necessary to solve today's problems" (p. 16). Native American tribal cultures recognize the interrelatedness of things and the necessity of integrating knowledge to deal with complex problems. In mathematics, this holistic way of thinking leads to an emphasis on generalized procedures over step-by-step rules, because generalized procedures are readily applicable across a range of problems.

The idea of a holistic view can be seen in African and Latino cultures as well. African American and Latino American students who were taught general procedures for approaching word problems, rather than step-by-step techniques scored higher on standardized achievement tests (Carey et al., 1995) (see Chapter 5 of this text for similar types of problems). Using the program, Cognitively Guided Instruction, teachers eliminated keyword approaches to problem solving in favor of general processing strategies. They stressed asking students three questions: What do you think? How did you get that? Did anyone solve the problem another way? These are the questions associated with mathematical flexibility in the NCTM *Principles and Standards* (2000).

The Power of Storytelling

Mathematics teachers traditionally use either the rule method of teaching procedures or the discovery approach in which students are given a problem and encouraged to manipulate variables to see what they can "discover." Noting that African American, Latino American, and Native American cultures all value the power of storytelling, Payne (2005) suggests that storytelling be used to teach mathematical and scientific ideas. Payne also reports a structure to such storytelling:

1. The end of the story is told first.
2. The part with the greatest intensity (importance) is told next.
3. The narrator stops at intervals for audience participation.
4. The story ends with a comment about the characters and their values.

Activity 2.3 contrasts the discovery approach and the storytelling approach. Notice that both approaches culminate with students understanding the same things. It's the means to the end that are important. For example, to a person from a noncompetitive culture, *how many* ways one can discover to do something is not important. Finding the message or theory behind the activity is the important thing. The discovery approach implies that everyone is alone in discovering what they can, but the storytelling approach involves the teacher and students together, walking through the problem. Other storytelling approaches can be seen on the Web site (Chapter 2, Extended Activities, "Problem Solving by Chicago Inner City Students"), where minority students from the Chicago public schools problem solve in authentic ways in programs for "at risk" students. The topics, experiences, names, and written examples were created solely by students for students.

Activity 2.3

CULTURAL RELEVANCE   **PROBLEM SOLVING**

THE DISCOVERY APPROACH AND THE STORYTELLING APPROACH

MATERIALS

Use the activity for symmetry on the Student Companion Web Site (Chapter 2, Extended Activities, "Finding Native American Designs with Mirror Puzzles"). You will need:

- A pocket mirror.
- The "Mirror Puzzle with Native American Symbol" from the activity on the student companion web site. (You can print this out from the Student Companion web site.)

DIRECTIONS

1. As you follow along with both approaches, think of other questions students could ask or comments they could make on the story.
2. Discuss your impressions, comparing yours with those of your colleagues.

CONTRAST THE DIFFERENCE IN APPROACHES

(In both approaches, the students have mirrors and the mirror puzzle from the Student Companion Web Site, so they can work along with the teacher.)

The Discovery Approach

Find ways of moving the mirror around the symbol of the sun in the upper left-hand corner of the puzzle so the image in the mirror matches each of the 10 drawings. How many ways of moving the mirror did you find? Did you find all of them? Which ones were difficult to find? How could you do the activity again to find more matches next time? Can you discover another way to do the activity? Come up with another way. See how many ways of doing the activity you can find.

The Storytelling Approach

(**Bold type is the teacher-narrator.** Plain type is the student; Several can talk at once.)

You know that these ten Native American images can be made by putting the mirror on different parts of the sun drawing in the square. Yea, okay! **Well, there once was a person with a very little brain; we'll call him PeaBrain. He couldn't figure out what to do with the mirror in the square.** Poor slob, how dumb can he be! **He first tried to tilt the mirror, but the image looked too far away.** He should know better. He should try putting the mirror straight up. **Ah yes, at right angles with the image. How smart of you.** Yea, dumb PeaBrain should sit next to Dion. He could have showed him. **I wonder how to move the mirror around that little square to make sure I could find all of the 10 matches for PeaBrain.** Yea, that's hard. Put it down in different places. I know; move the mirror around in a circle until you find them all. **Ah, move the mirror around a center point. Smart!** Yes, I see all those matches being made as you do it. Yea, dude! We're a smart class. **PeaBrain could have done well if he had been in this smart class with you, thinking about right angles and center points and all. You saw the things mathematicians see!** Yea, nobody's got stuff any better than us.

Supporting the NCTM *Principles and Standards* (2000):
- Mathematics as Problem Solving; Mathematics as Communication
- Worthwhile Mathematical Tasks; Mathematics as Oral and Written Discourse—The Teaching Principle
- Monitoring Students' Progress—The Equity Principle

There are times when students just do not seem to understand a mathematics concept no matter what the teacher does. That is a time to try the storytelling approach. If the story is successful, write it down and share it with others. What is successful with one set of students is worth trying with another. The Extended Activities lists a variety of activities for both the discovery approach and the storytelling approach.

EXTENDED ACTIVITIES

CULTURAL RELEVANCE

PROBLEM SOLVING

CALCULATORS

COMPUTERS

MANIPULATIVES

On the Student Companion Web Site (Chapter 2, Extended Activities), read/do the following:

- Native American Story Starters with Mathematics Concepts
- Wild Animal Math: A Native American Lesson
- Graphing Calculator with Anasazi Math
- Greg's Halloween Counting Book
- Algebra Coordinates Add-On Book
- Abacus Fun
- Creating a New Counting Book Like Anno Did
- Problem Solving by Chicago Inner City Students
- Finding Native American Designs with Mirror Puzzles
- Accomplishments of African Americans: Voices of Triumph and Leadership

This section has discussed a variety of ways in which mathematics lessons can incorporate a multicultural perspective. The following testimony of a beginning teacher of Latino heritage best explains why an emphasis on multiculturalism in mathematics is of the utmost importance (Figure 2.7).

"Coming from a bi-cultural family, I feel that multi-cultural education is very important. Whenever we talked about Hispanics or other cultures in school, I felt a sense of pride. I think it

FIGURE 2.7 *Monique Mesa. (Photo taken by Anne Adams.)*

is important for all children to experience that feeling of pride in their cultural background. It does wonders for their self-esteem."

EQUITY: THE RIGHT OF ALL PEOPLE TO ACQUIRE MATHEMATICAL POWER

Every student has the right to acquire the mathematical power needed for success in today's world. However, equity in mathematics education has not always been the rule. Research studies (NCES, 2000; Sutton and Krueger, 2002) report that mathematics learning is facilitated by three critical factors:

- Mathematics seen in real-world contexts
- Substantial conversation (oral discourse)
- Student-centered classrooms that focus on higher-order thinking skills and problem solving

To the extent that any of these three factors is lacking for some groups over others, mathematical equity is diminished. Cultural differences in thinking patterns, gender differences, language acquisition problems, and lower socioeconomic status have been seen as barriers to mathematical success in classrooms (NCMST, 2000). However, research and best practices have shown that these apparently insurmountable problems can be overcome by good teaching.

Mathematics Seen in Real-World Contexts

The challenge is to know enough about other cultures to be able to place mathematics in real-world contexts for students whose backgrounds are different from our own. Well-meaning but uninformed teachers often give mathematics assignments without being aware of the deep cultural implications of word problems. For example, a teacher cut several food coupons from a local paper and asked the children to find the best buy for their money if they had only $7 to spend. The teacher evaluated one child's responses to the assignment as unsatisfactory when the student chose only lettuce and green beans, leaving out obvious bargains on beef. The teacher did not realize that the child's Hindu culture did not permit eating beef. The student, who received a failing grade, was left thinking that something was wrong mathematically (Mestre and Grace, 1986). Teachers must exert themselves to learn about important aspects of their students' cultures.

Poverty and Its Implication for Mathematics

Unfortunately for a growing number of our nation's children, part of their real-world context is a low socioeconomic status. Ruby Payne (2005) refers to the poor in our society as the *poverty class* rather than the lower class. She rightly points out that the class is not lower; it is different because of *the lack of resources available to individuals,* which is the definition of poverty. A disproportionate number of people from nonwhite cultures in the United States find themselves in the poverty class. In 1996, one out of every four students under the age of 18 in the United States was living in poverty (Center for the Study of Poverty, Columbia University, 2002). Unfortunately, this inequity in availability of resources is often accompanied by a corresponding inequity in the opportunity to acquire mathematical power. That this truly is an inequity in opportunity, and not a reflection of some lack of ability, is shown by the fact that nonwhite children from affluent families (whether African American, Latino American, Asian American, or Native American) achieve at the same levels as their affluent white peers. Payne, quoting Oscar Lewis, points out that poverty classes around the world are remarkably similar. The poverty class in Harlem has the same characteristics and hidden class rules for survival as those in London, Glasgow, Paris, and Mexico City (Payne, 2005, p. 62).

The lack of resources affects mathematics learning in many ways. Ladson-Billings (1995) cites one example involving African American students working with a problem in a different social context from that of their white, middle-class counterparts. Here is the problem:

It costs $1.50 to travel each way on the city bus. A transit system "fast pass" costs $65 a month. Which is the more economical way to get to work, the daily fare or the fast pass?

The white, middle-class students from suburbia figured on the basis of five days of work at a fare of $3 a day for four weeks in a month, a total of $60, making the daily fare more economical. The inner-city African American students said the problem could not be solved without more information, such as, "How many jobs are we talking about?" They knew that people often held several low-paying part-time jobs in order to make a living. Thus, it was conceivable that a worker would need to ride the bus several times a day (and pay several fares) to get to different jobs. In addition, some students pointed out that most people they knew rode the bus because they did not own a car and thus would be using the bus for more than just going to work.

This example stands as a warning signal to teachers, just like the example of the Hindu child who couldn't choose beef. Not only do we all need to constantly evaluate the kinds of problems we give students to solve but we also have to use oral and written discourse in authentic assessment (see Chapter 3). When teachers give students the opportunity to tell why they chose their answers to real-life problems, test scores improve and teachers realize how bright their students really are. Morgan and Watson (2002) caution that teachers have to be trained to watch for their own prejudices when scoring. The educational community in the United States and Canada can be proud of its choice to use authentic assessment in testing programs; the challenge is to make sure that these alternative types of assessment receive as much weight as the multiple-choice standardized testing assessments, especially when evaluating students from the poverty class. Teachers must be on the forefront in insisting that the contexts in mathematics be real for all students.

Poverty and Its Impact on Technology

The farther away students are from the mainstream culture of white America the less opportunity they have to actively use the new interactive technologies. The only way to rectify this situation is to provide these technologies in *all* schools. Moreover, the National Assessment of Educational Progress (NCES, 2001; NAEP, 2006); Lott and

Souhrada (2000); Silver, Smith, and Nelson (1995); Leder (1995); and Tate (1995) all report that teachers in poverty schools where computers are available tended to assign computer time to do more drill and practice of minimal mathematics skills rather than taking advantage of the computer's potential to help students apply logical and critical reasoning skills in programming. The NCTM's technology principle takes a stand against such practices (NCTM, 2000), as does the International Society for Technology in Education–National Educational Technology Standards (ISTE-NETS, 2002). Programs, such as the Logo programming language for children, LEGO Group's MINDSTORMS Robotics (2002), and interactive programs on the Internet and on CDs with mathematics textbooks, all help children unlock for themselves the power of mathematical reasoning through the use of applied computer technology. Computer activities for prekindergarten to grade two show what young students can do to explore possibilities based on the Logo programming ideas of slides, flips, and rotations (Clements, 2003). We have seen students of varying socioeconomic levels, in white and nonwhite populations, create such Logo procedures in the early grades, confirming that all students can achieve mathematical power with computers if given the chance.

The calculator may very well be the "technology of choice" in mathematics education because its cost is minimal compared to the purchase price of classroom computers. Virtually all students participating in the National Assessment of Educational Progress in 1996 reported that they or their family owned a calculator. Access to school-owned calculators was greater at each level than access to school-owned computers (Reese et al., 1997). Scores on the 2000 National Assessment of Educational Progress (NCES, 2001) also showed that there was a clear relationship between calculator use and performance on the assessment, with more problems answered correctly when the calculator was used. This result presents further evidence that time spent on the appropriate use of calculators in mathematics classrooms will pay off with higher scores in mathematics assessments. Calculator activities for elementary and middle school students that promote mathematical reasoning are featured throughout this text. Such technologies *are* the real-world context of the twenty-first century.

Substantial Conversation (Oral Discourse)

Research cited in Chapter 1 shows the importance of oral discourse in mathematics. Numerous studies reported by Einhorn (2002), Abrams, Ferguson, and Laud (2001), Bucko (2001), Garrison and Mora (1999), Khisty (1995), and Warren and Rosebery (1995) document the important role that language plays in problem solving when one goes beyond rudimentary skills in basic mathematics. It becomes even more important when non-native speakers of English, called *English language learners* (ELLs), are placed in mathematics classrooms. By the year 2010, it is predicted, one in every ten children in the United States will be foreign born and therefore classified as an ELL (Lindeman, 2002). Frequently, these students are mainstreamed into mathematics classrooms because it is thought that mathematics involves minimal language skills; yet that assumption is not true with respect to problem solving, logic, and real-world applications. This practice often leads to student failure and a sense of hopelessness when dealing with mathematics. In this regard, two important elements of mathematical discourse have received attention by researchers—"if–then" statements and variable reversal errors.

"If–Then" Statements Consider this typical "if–then" math problem:

If a man takes 3 minutes to run 500 meters, how long will it take him to run a kilometer?

Now see it reconstructed:

A man took 3 minutes to run 500 meters. He kept running at the same speed. How much time did it take him to run a kilometer?

Thomas (1997) points out that the implied logical connectives of "if–then" statements are difficult for young people to understand, even if their native language is English. Speakers of some other languages would not use an "if" statement unless they were looking for an exception. For example, in the problem above, they might think the speed varies, which would make the problem impossible to solve. Thomas also points out that the word *long* in this problem means time duration rather than distance, but this may not be apparent to many non-native speakers of English. The reconstructed version would be understood by all learners and still enable teachers and test writers to judge the students' mathematical ability.

Variable Reversal Errors Mestre and Gerace (1986) report on the difficulties people have in constructing equations that represent word problems with simple algebraic statements. The most common mistake is what has come to be called the "variable reversal error," which occurs with problems such as the following:

Write an equation using the variables S and P to represent the following statement: "There are six times as many students as professors at a certain university." Use S for the number of students and P for the number of professors. (Mestre and Gerace, 1986, p. 143)

The incorrect "variable reversal" answer, $6S = P$, was given by approximately 35 percent of white American students and 54 percent of Latino American students. Student interviews revealed that the most common misconception involved using the *S* and *P* as labels standing for "students" and "professors" instead of mathematical variables standing for the *number* of students and the *number* of professors. Students apparently then constructed their equation by mindlessly reading left-to-right:

six times as many students as professors

$$6 \quad \times \quad S \quad = \quad P$$

or $6S = P$

If they had recognized that the problem was really asking about the *number* of people in one group compared to the *number* of people in the other group, they would have been led to the correct answer, $S = 6P$. When this problems was reworded as "6 times the number of professors is equal to the number of students," all the Latino American students in the Mestre and Gerace study answered the equation correctly.

It should be noted that rewording this problem to help students avoid making a "variable reversal" error does not, in itself, lead students into good mathematical thinking. In this case, for example, students could still use the sequential left-to-right literal translation of the problem, but this time to get the right answer instead of the wrong one! Thus, in addition to rewording, teachers have a responsibility to teach in a way that encourages students to think about the mathematical principles involved in solving mathematical problems.

Scaffolding and Modeling: An Answer to Language Problems

Khisty (1995, 1997) and Hernandez (1999) talk of the need to develop teachers who use modeling and scaffolding in oral discourse, especially for the benefit of English language learners (ELL). *Modeling* is the process of performing the kinds of actions or using the kinds of discourse needed to be successful in a learning task while others watch, listen, and observe the results. For an example of a teacher modeling mathematical understandings for ELL, see the Video Vignette "Math in the Bilingual Classroom" on the Web site (Chapter 2, Video Vignettes), where Mrs. Torres talks about what she is doing as she draws the answers to fraction problems on the chalkboard. She carefully models the questions she needs to ask herself to achieve the correct answers (the results). These questions also involve the ELL, so they become models for each other in the classroom discourse.

Scaffolding is the process of providing support for students' answers by asking progressively more probing questions and giving cues as the students construct their responses. It is similar to the elaborating technique discussed in Chapter 3. The difference is scaffolding's emphasis on the support structure; the scaffold does not come down until the answers are secure and firmly grounded. An example of scaffolding is seen in Figure 3.14 (page 59).

The ideal situation for ELL is to have a mathematics teacher who is proficient in both English and the student's primary language. In the Video Vignette "Math in the Bilingual Classroom" on the Web site (Chapter 2, Video Vignettes), Mrs. Torres provides an excellent example. She switches from one language to another so quickly and easily that you may need to watch the video more than once to notice every instance. She also encourages students to talk with one another and to write journal entries about their mathematics discoveries. Of course, not all teachers are capable of dealing with language issues so adroitly, but all teachers can do other things that research shows culturally diverse students need to be successful learners. The innovative mathematics program called Project IMPACT (Campbell and Rowan, 1997, p. 65) sets guidelines in accord with the TIMSS recommendations discussed in detail in Chapter 3. The Video Vignette asks you to analyze how Mrs. Torres uses the Project IMPACT guidelines.

The Extended Activities lists four statements of educational goals for different groups.

Student-Centered Classrooms That Focus on Higher-Order Thinking Skills and Problem Solving

Student-centered classrooms are classrooms where teachers take the time to "mentor" students,

Video Vignette

Math in the Bilingual Classroom

View the Video Vignette with Mrs. Torres (Chapter 2, Video Vignettes, "Math in the Bilingual Classroom"). Then:

- Consider the approaches of Project IMPACT for helping culturally diverse learners (Figure 2.8).
- Describe how Mrs. Torres uses these approaches in her bilingual classroom.

- Use mixed-ability groups as often as possible to promote the language growth of students who are less facile.
- Have students write in journals about the mathematics they are learning.
- Have students share their ideas in small groups or pairs before sharing with the entire class.
- Have students write their own story problems using personal experiences, and then expect students to share their problems with the rest of the class.
- Have students explain the information in a word problem or restate the problem in their own words using whole-class sharing before expecting students to work on the problems individually, in pairs, or in groups.
- During class discussions, first call on students with language difficulties or with fewer experiences. Doing so allows these children to share the ideas that are more apparent and challenges those with more experience or language to stretch for ideas.
- Allow students to adjust the numbers in, or the circumstances of, a problem if they are having difficulty understanding the problem or using the numbers given. Always ask the students to explain why they made the adjustments.
- When students with no English fluency come to the classroom, assign them a buddy who can help with translation. If that is not possible, use concrete materials or diagrams and connect them to words so that the students can understand the problem as much as possible without necessarily understanding all the language.

FIGURE 2.8 *Project Impact:Approaches to support the effective use of language.*

EXTENDED ACTIVITIES

CULTURAL RELEVANCE   **POSITION PAPER**

- Mathematics for Second Language Learners
- Mathematics Education of Underrepresented Groups
- Goals for Native American Education
- Women and Mathematics Education Aims

taking a personal interest in their achievements and stressing high expectations (Stiff, 2002). Teachers in student-centered classrooms also make sure to reword mathematics problems so they reflect students' interests and experiences (Kersaint and Chappell, 2001), and they help students see how these problems are like those in the textbooks and on tests (Slavin, 2002).

NAEP results (2000) showed that all ethnic groups made statistically significant gains in mathematics scores over the last decade and that nonwhite groups who took more mathematics courses showed greater gains in test scores than their white counterparts who took the same kind and number of math courses. Reports also showed that early intervention, before the high school years, was important in motivating nonwhite students to take more mathematics courses. By providing the right kind of intervention, student-centered classrooms foster the critical thinking and problem-solving skills that help students from all cultural groups succeed in mathematics.

The same is true for girls (Levi, 2000). For example, Karp and Niemi (2000) report standing room only when girls were given a chance to join the Math Club for Girls and Other Problem Solvers in a middle school. Girls thrive in student-centered classrooms geared toward noncompetitive, non-speed-related mathematics activities.

It is also important to recognize that speed of performance is not viewed as an important quality in many nonwhite cultures. Mathematics programs and tests that stress speed put nonwhite students and females at risk for failure. Moreover, as discussed in Chapter 5, good problem solving may actually require a slow pace, where time must be taken to consider all options before the best solution can be obtained.

Modeling with the Right Resources

Choosing resources that are relevant to students' cultures is of the utmost importance. It sends the message that the teacher cares enough about students to find resources that show people from their cultures being smart and doing mat ematics. Such resources also show students that people from all cultures make valuable contributions, even cultures quite different from their own.

Resources for Contributions of African Americans Jawanza Kunjufu has written several books to help teachers and students learn more about the contributions of African Americans. The books are in both elementary and junior-senior high editions, and each comes with a teacher's guide (Kunjufu, 1987a, 1987b, 1987c). Students can use the bibliographies in these books to find additional information about African American scientists and inventors who used mathematics in their work (Gazin, 2000). This information includes the fact that African Americans were responsible for many "firsts": first traffic light, first book on electricity, first parallel circuitry, first machine to mass produce shoes, first tires on moon buggy, first surgeon to operate on human heart in United States, first to develop blood plasma, first drafted plans of telephone for Alexander Graham Bell, and first railroad car coupler, and the list could go on and on. A WebQuest celebrates the accomplishments of African Americans and their use of mathematics (Chapter 2, WebQuests, "Accomplishments of African Americans—Using Mathematics in Many Fields").

The first African American mathematician, Benjamin Banneker (1731–1806), deserves special mention. His accomplishments included:

- Made the first clock in America.
- Surveyed and designed the layout of Washington, DC (with five others) and reconstructed the whole plan from memory after the original was stolen.
- Wrote an almanac in 1792 that received international acclaim.
- Wrote the first science book by an African American.

Teachers interested in the work of African American mathematicians and the education of African American children in mathematics are welcome to join the Benjamin Banneker Mathematics Association, an affiliated group of the NCTM (for information, contact NCTM). Eighteen additional resources for learning mathematics from the African American perspective can be reviewed in Strutchens, Johnson, and Tate (2000).

Teachers need to be aware of the following major elements in the African American heritage:

- The importance of extended family (the "kinship code").
- The importance of living in the present, as opposed to emphasizing duration or time elements.
- The importance of speaking in proverbs, because proverbs reflect holistic thought patterns that let you see the whole picture or system of events.

Waters (1993, 2001), whose extensive listings of ancient African and African American accomplishments is shown on the Web site (Chapter 2, Extended Activities, "Accomplishments of African Americans: Voices of Triumph and Leadership"), state that these qualities had much to do with the creative spark seen through the generations of great African American scientists and mathematicians.

Resources for Contributions of Native Americans Each year, the U.S. Bureau of Indian Affairs sponsors a week-long workshop at Haskell All Nations Indian University in Lawrence, Kansas, where Native American elementary and secondary teachers come together to write culturally relevant mathematics and science lessons. The lessons are bound into books and are available through the Bureau of Indian Affairs; some are featured in this text and on the Web site (e.g., Chapter 15, Extended Activities, "Pictographs with Sandpaintings").

In addition, mathematics teachers can use Native American stories as starters for activities.

Three beautiful books of Native American stories that can be put to such use have received high praise: *Keepers of the Earth, Keepers of the Animals,* and *Keepers of Life* (Caduto and Bruchac, 1989, 1991, 1994; teacher's guides are also available). In these books, each story comes from a different tribal nation. When using such stories, teachers must remember the importance of telling the name of the tribal nation during the telling of the story, as a way of acknowledging the tribe for its contribution to Native American culture. Each tribal nation has its own language, customs, and stories; so it is just as much a mistake to put all Native Americans in one "basket" as it would be to lump together the European Americans who are proud to be of French, Italian, British, or other extraction. Every group strives to preserve its identity and have its contributions recognized.

Other Native American story starters are incorporated in activities throughout the text and on the CD, along with teaching ideas for mathematics lessons on such topics as symmetry, tessellations, and probability and statistics (e.g., the activity on mirror puzzles [see pages 316–317] and the activity "Creating Proportions with Native American Stories," in Chapter 11). The Web site includes several middle school activities created by Clo Mingo (1997) involving the TI-82 graphing calculator, using stories from the Anasazi tribe (Chapter 2, Extended Activities, "Graphing Calculator with Anasazi Math").

Although each Native American tribe has a distinct culture and has made its own unique contributions, Native American culture as a whole also expresses some common values, including the value of cooperation and the deep value of the extended family. Nature speaks and teaches the worth of cooperation and deep care for others. Students from other cultures may see Native American stories as always ending with a moral, but teachers should point out that these "morals" do not preach morality; rather, they affirm the worth of the soul from which the story was born. Twenty-five additional resources for learning mathematics from the Native American perspective may be reviewed in Hankes and Fast (2002).

Resources for Contributions of Latino Americans
Did you ever wonder when the first mathematics book was written in the Americas and who wrote it? The honor goes to an early Latino American, Juan Diez. His book was published in 1556 in Mexico City. Its topic was business mathematics, the most needed mathematics of the time. With Europeans coming to Central America in large numbers, the Old World people and the New World people needed to communicate with each other about business transactions and use money to trade with one another fairly.

We have made a conscious decision to use the term "Latino American" (or simply "Latino") rather than "Hispanic American" because, as Ortiz-Franco, Hernandez, and De La Cruz (1999, p. 1) state:

Although the people of Latin America are aware that their language (Spanish), their names, and their dominant religion (Catholicism) are cultural elements transplanted from Spain to the New World, they prefer to call themselves Latinos rather than Hispanics. The term Latinos can be viewed as a statement of cultural self-determination, and it should be respected as such by society at large, including the mathematics education community.

Aspects of the Latino American heritage that teachers should know about include:

- A strong emphasis is placed on the work ethic.
- Family is highly valued, and extended family is very important. The father is revered as the head of the family, family activities are valued, and a sense of celebration prevails when the extended family is together. Celebrations of feast days, marriages, and special holidays may last several days.
- Children are the responsibility of the whole extended family, not just the mother and father (Morales-Jones, 1998). That is why family math projects have been successful in many communities of Latino Americans: if the father or mother isn't available, a member of the extended family will be there for the child.
- As in the African American community, living in the present is more important than excessive concern about the future.

Resources showing how to teach mathematics to Latino students focus on the approaches discussed in Chapter 3 of this text, emphasizing the constructivist perspective, performance-based analytic thinking, and the five strands for mathematical proficiency (Bustamante and Travis, 1999; Garrison, 1999; Ivory, Chaparro, and Ball, 1999; Moschkovich, 1999). These approaches have yielded higher scores on achievement tests for Latino students (Khisty and Viego, 1999). Resources showing the importance of parental involvement in their children's mathematical development are found in Ortiz-Franco (1999) and in Lo Cicero, Fuson, and Allexsaht-Snider (1999). Various models for successfully tutoring Latino students in mathematics emphasize problem solving strategies, oral discourse in Spanish and English simultaneously, and the use of manipulatives (De La Cruz, 1999; Garrison, 1999; Ramirez and Bernard, 1999; Seda and Seda, 1999).

A group of Latino educators met at the annual NCTM meeting in April 2003 to organize a group interested in the work of Latino American mathematicians and the education of Latino children in mathematics, similar to the Banneker Association (for information, contact the NCTM).

Resources for Contributions of Asian Americans

Elementary and secondary mathematics education includes many mathematical discoveries that have their roots in Asian culture. Some of the most interesting ideas in number theory have come from people of Chinese heritage (see Chapter 14). Origami, the art of Asian paper folding, can be the focus of fascinating geometric investigations. A legend about tangrams is featured in Chapter 12. This delightful story can be used to introduce many activities involving tangrams, and it points to the ingenuity of Asian people. You should consult the chapter bibliography for other resources to include in your lessons. On the student Companion Web site, the extended activities for Chapters 5–15 include a variety of activities with elementary and middle school teaching ideas. Four of the extended activities in Chapter 2 are inspired by Asian American ideas: "Greg's Halloween Counting Book," "Algebra Coordinates Add-on Book," "Creating a New Book Like Anno Did," and "Abacus Fun" (the first three are based on *Anno's Counting Book*).

You can find ancient problem-solving activities and children's games in Krause (1993), Vogt (1994), and Zaslavsky (1996, 2000). Some student game activities seen in these resources are particularly well suited for the middle school. Activity 2.4 presents a problem-solving activity suitable for both elementary and middle school students.

An abacus can be the focus of various activities. For example, if one or more Asian American students in your class know how to use an abacus (or have a family member who knows how), arrange for a demonstration. If the person uses an abacus regularly, set up a race between the abacus and an electronic calculator. Let the class choose the most proficient class member on the calculator; then have the class predict who will win. Almost always, the abacus user will win easily, to the great surprise of most students, who will be

Activity 2.4

CULTURAL RELEVANCE   PROBLEM SOLVING   MATHEMATICAL CONNECTIONS

HINDU PROBLEM SOLVING FROM INDIA

MATERIALS
- Paper with copies of the figures in Figure 2.9

DIRECTIONS

Elementary Students:

1. Use these words with Figure 2.9 to start the activity:

   "This lesson shows the smart thinking a man named Bhaskara from India did long ago. He is one of the ancestors of the Asian Americans today. He used a number system invented by his people. It looks like this":

FIGURE 2.9   *Hindu numerals from ancient times.*

2. "Does it look familiar? From where do you think we got our numbers?"

3. "Bhaskara wrote a math book to make his daughter happy when she was very sad. He told number stories about bees and animals using big numbers in the tens and hundreds. Write some stories about bees using the numbers the way Bhaskara would have written them."

4. Do other examples you think up yourself. Tell a classmate your stories and show your Hindu numerals. Decide together if the numeral fits the correct pattern.

Middle School Students:

1. Use these words to start the activity:

   "This lesson shows the smart thinking a man named Bhaskara from India did long ago. He is one of the

	First Hand	Second Hand	Third Hand	Fourth Hand
1st way	Hammer	Shell	Flower	Discus
2nd way	Hammer	Shell	Discus	Flower
3rd way	Hammer	Flower	Shell	Discus

ancestors of the Asian Americans today. He told many math stories about Hindu gods. Here is one of them" (from Mitchell, 1978, p. 39):

Bhaskara had a problem about Hari, a god who had four hands. He wanted to pick up a hammer, a shell, a flower, and a discus . . . . Hari wonders in how many ways he can pick up these four things. Can you figure it out? (Hint: Make a chart like this and finish it. The total number of ways may surprise you.)

2. Do other examples to finish the chart. Show your problem-solving chart to a classmate. Decide together if the answers fit the correct pattern.

filled with admiration for the person's speed and skill. Finish the lesson by asking, "Why do you suppose Asian Americans still use the abacus today?" The class will know that answer for sure!

Many Asians and Asian Americans have distinguished themselves in the fields of science and mathematics. The best known of modern times may be the Indian mathematician Srinivasa Ramanujan, who is often cited in middle school mathematics books and in journal articles (Perl and Manning, 1982; Voolich, 1993). Perl and Manning's book also features Native American, Latino American, and African American mathematicians. Voolich points out that there are very few individual Chinese mathematicians who can be cited by name because historical writings generally did not include names of the individuals responsible for mathematical discoveries.

Asian cultures vary widely of course, but teachers should be aware of some basic values and beliefs that most Asian cultures hold in common:

- The ideas of elders are revered, because wisdom comes with living a long, honorable life and overcoming many trials and hardships.

- Respect for others is fundamental, permeating how people communicate with one another. Other people's ideas are considered before one's own. An Asian person who finds that his or her ideas on a subject differ from another person's would not say, "I disagree with you. Let's look at this again." Instead, the person would avoid an "I" statement in favor of a third-person statement and say something like, "There are those who may have thought of

another answer. They may have expressed it this way."

It is of interest that teachers who encourage their students to use this approach when working in cooperative settings have found that conflicts are less likely to erupt into violent disruptions, as reported by the Kansas City, Missouri Public Schools Police Division (1993). If we are to use student-to-student discourse as advised in the NCTM *Principles and Standards* (2000), we need to apply this valuable lesson from Asian culture and encourage students to try rewording "I" statements into third-person statements, and watch the positive effect it has on others. Eight additional resources for learning mathematics from the Asian American perspective are reviewed in Edwards (1999).

Resources for Contributions of Women in Mathematics Students need to know that there are women who have succeeded in mathematics— *women of all cultures.* Women and Mathematics Education (WME) has been an affiliated group of the National Council of Teacher of Mathematics since 1983. Its purpose is to promote the mathematics education of girls and women (on the Web site, see "Women and Mathematics Education Aims," in Chapter 2, Extended Activities). Since 1990, the WME has published a bibliography of pertinent articles and research findings, which currently has over 1000 listings (Mark, 1998). As with all NCTM-affiliated groups, the WME is open to all interested persons. Updated information on the group may be found on the NCTM Web site (**http://www.nctm.org**).

Women mathematicians are not new. An early example was Hypatia (circa 415 B.C. to 370 B.C.). Born to Greek parents living in Alexandria, Egypt, she joined her father as a teacher of mathematics at the university (Cooney, 1996; Nichols, 1996). Hypatia explored conic sections and diophantine equations, which are now part of the high school curriculum in mathematics. An activity honoring Hypatia, involving cuts in conic sections to produce hyperbolas, was published for student use over 25 years ago (Perl, 1978). New resources containing similar activities (Morrow, 1996; Morrow and Perl, 1997) are available for middle school teachers who want to show young women that a career in mathematics is a realistic possibility.

Middle school is the time when girls decide what math courses they will pursue in high school. It may be the last time a teacher has the opportunity to effectively influence math choices by showing them how other women have used mathematics in successful careers. Young girls who may have no idea how mathematics is used in the real world need exposure to such examples. A series of videotapes (Riley, 1999) showing successful women using math at work has won several prestigious awards, including the Gold Medal of the International Film and Video Festival in New York and the Young Adults Award from the American Library Association. In these videos, women tell in their own words what mathematics has done for them in the world of work. Each video is no longer than 15 minutes, allowing teachers time to show and discuss the video during a class period. Resource guides are available to aid middle school teachers in planning the postvideo discussions. The video *Math at Work: Women in Nontraditional Careers* may be shown separately if teachers feel they cannot allot class time for all eight videotapes.

Students should study famous women mathematicians and find examples of their mathematical work (*Celebrating Women in Mathematics and Science* [Cooney, 1996] is an excellent resource). Fifteen additional resources on multiculturalism and gender equity may be reviewed in Secada (2000). Activity 2.5 is designed to motivate students to learn the role, importance, and national heritage of various woman mathematicians.

In Celebration of All Mathematicians   Mathematicians of many nationalities and both genders are included in Voolich's (1993) wonderful list of mathematicians' birthdays, along with clever ideas for writing biographies. An innovative teacher can use the list in several ways; for example, have students look at the list to see whether they share a birthday with a famous mathematician (with 121 names, students can always find a mathematician born on or close to their birthday). The students can learn more about the person and about his or her mathematical contributions. Assignments like this are especially important in the middle school years, when students are making decisions that affect not only their choice of high school courses in mathematics and science but also the career choices that may be available to them.

Learning Styles

Malloy (1997), Wilson (1992), Cheek (1984), and Hale-Benson (1986), among others, believe that Native Americans, African Americans, and Latino Americans tend to be field-dependent learners as opposed to field-independent learners. A field-dependent learner sees a learning task as a whole. Learning facts is seen as an integrated part of the

Activity 2.5

CULTURAL RELEVANCE   MATHEMATICAL CONNECTIONS

WOMEN IN MATHEMATICS

MATERIALS

- Names are given on a sheet.

DIRECTIONS

1. Use these words with Figure 2.10 to start the activity:

    "This lesson shows the smart thinking of women from many cultures, starting long ago. Some examples are shown here. Find out more about these women. Come ready to tell others what you discovered."

FIND OUT WHAT THEY DID

Maria Angeal (Italian)	Grace Hopper (American)
Emmy Noether (Jewish from Germany)	Evelyn Boyd Granville (African American)
Mary Fairfax Somerville (Scottish)	Edna Paisano (Native American)
Sophie Germain (French)	Marjorie Lee Brown (African American)

FIND OUT WHICH ONE OF THE ABOVE

Shared ideas with Einstein

Was called a witch—and why

Made patterns of sand on a drum (inventing many unique number patterns)

Invented COBOL computer language

FIGURE 2.10   *Famous women mathematicians.*

2. Students follow the names on the sheet, going to the library to look up more information to make a correct match.

3. Find other examples. Explain how you found out the contribution of each woman mathematician by writing in your journal. Show your choices to a friend.

Supporting the NCTM *Principles and Standards* **(2000):**

- Mathematics as Connections; Mathematics as Communication
- Mathematics as Oral and Written Discourse— The Teaching Principle
- Monitoring Students' Progress—The Equity Principle

whole task (a detailed analysis of mathematics tasks for field-dependent learners is presented in Chapter 3). Some of the researchers cited above believe that people in the white population tend to be field-independent learners, who focus on facts and other features of a learning task without any initial need to see the task as an integrated whole. From an information-processing perspective, the term *simultaneous synthesis* is associated with field-dependent learners, whereas *successive synthesis* is associated with field-independent learners. Brain research (Jensen, 2005) indicates that people in general, even field-independent learners, may prefer a whole-to-part, simultaneous view of material when it is seen for the first time. Mathematics textbooks, however, have tended to introduce concepts using the part-to-whole, successive view. As discussed more fully in Chapter 3, mathematics educators generally have been slow to change their teaching practices based on learning style research, but if children could profit from it, teachers would be remiss not to try introducing concepts with both simultaneous and successive approaches. This text uses both approaches in the assessment parts of Chapters 6 through 15.

SUMMARY

- The term *culturally relevant mathematics* comprises two main ideas—*multiculturalism* (mathematics has always been part of every culture) and *equity* (everyone has the right to acquire mathematical power). *Ethnomathematics* denotes the awareness that different cultures, societies, and ethnic groups bring their unique approaches to mathematics. By consistently emphasizing the contributions of diverse cultures in mathematics, we can help all children develop pride and a sense of hope that make it possible for them to begin achieving at high levels.

- When children perform mathematical tasks like those performed by other cultures (mathematics simulations), they learn to appreciate the unique contributions of those cultures. When we show children how mathematical tasks performed by one culture are similar to those performed by another culture, they see how each culture brings its own unique approach to mathematics.

- People from different cultures have different thought patterns, different ways of looking at things. Looking at things in a new way can make difficult mathematical concepts easier to grasp.

- In teaching mathematics, generalized procedures are more important than step-by-step rules. Teachers can learn to appreciate this idea by relating it to the holistic worldview of many non-Western cultures.

- Storytelling is a powerful means for teaching mathematical concepts.

- Equity means making sure that mathematics is placed in real-world contexts for all students. To do this, teachers must be sensitive to the impact of poverty, both on the way children use mathematics in their lives and on children's access to technology.

- Oral discourse is highly important in teaching mathematics, but teachers must make sure that oral discourse is appropriate for all students, including English language learners. Two elements of mathematical discourse are particularly important in this regard—word problems stated using "if–then" statements and word problems stated in ways that lead to "variable reversal errors."

- For English language learners, it is especially important that teachers use scaffolding and modeling to promote understanding.

- In student-centered classrooms, teachers take the time to "mentor" students. They also reword mathematics problems to reflect students' interests and experiences. All ethnic groups benefit from student-centered classrooms, as shown by higher mathematics scores on standardized tests, and the same is true for girls.

- It is important to choose the right resources when modeling mathematics, resources that are relevant to students' cultures. Many available resources highlight the unique and valuable characteristics and contributions of the four main U.S. minority cultures—African American, Native American, Latino American, and Asian American. Other resources highlight women's contributions, whereas still others focus on mathematicians of many nationalities and both genders.

- By recognizing students' different learning styles—particularly, the difference between field-dependent learners and field-independent learners—teachers can significantly promote children's learning.

- Each child's culture can and should be a strength, not a detriment. We cannot hope to make an equitable world unless we help build a sense of pride in all its people. As teachers, we must let students know that they can be anything they want to be. If we can be mentors who care, we will find ways to get through to every student. As we move forward in the twenty-first century, the Swahili admonition *Harambee!* ("Let's all pull together!") will be increasingly relevant. Mathematics is an important stepping stone to success in many careers. Students don't have to leave their dreams behind in fear of mathematics. We offer this thought in the spirit of our Native American sisters and brothers:

You, Too, Can Feel the Wind

Do not be afraid to walk in the footprints of time.
The wind will hold you uplifted in your flight to the eagle's eye.
See the earth below; all is clear as you fly to the circle of life.
The eagle goes before you keeping the promise . . . . you, too, can feel the wind.

Nancy Tanner Edwards
Descendant of One Who Lost His Tribal Identity
In Pennsylvania, Carlisle Indian School (circa 1882)

PRAXIS II™-STYLE QUESTIONS

Answers to this chapter's Praxis II™-style questions are in the instructor's manual.

Multiple-Choice Format

1. When working with English language learners, which of the following statements should a teacher use when asking students to set up equations using letters to represent mathematical variables?

   a. There are six times as many dogs as there are cats.

   b. Six times the length of a stick is 24 feet.

   c. Both a and b.

   d. Neither a nor b.

2. The _____ were the first people to use negative numbers. They are the ancestors of the

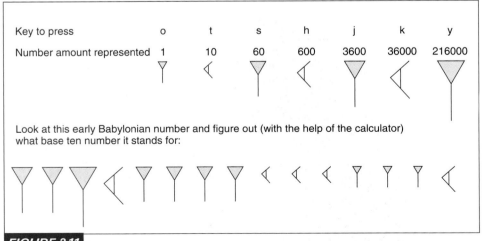

Key to press	o	t	s	h	j	k	y
Number amount represented	1	10	60	600	3600	36000	216000

Look at this early Babylonian number and figure out (with the help of the calculator) what base ten number it stands for:

FIGURE 2.11 *Early Babylonian numerals made by African American middle school students in Kansas City, Missour by using the Logo computer language.*

_____ children in our classrooms. (Hint: Remember Figure 2.1)

a. Chinese; Asian American.

b. Mayans; Latino American.

c. Egyptians; African American.

d. Native Americans; Native American.

3. The _____ were the first people to use numerals. They are the ancestors of the _____ children in our classrooms. (Hint: Remember Figure 2.1)

a. Chinese; Asian American.

b. Mayans; Latino American.

c. Egyptians; African American.

d. Native Americans; Native American.

4. African American and Latino American students are likely to score higher on standardized achievement tests in mathematics if they are taught _____ procedure(s) to approach word problems.

a. a 3-step.

b. a 2-step.

c. general.

d. both a and b.

5. For students from noncompetitive cultures, which approach to mathematics learning is considered BEST?

a. Discovery.

b. Storytelling.

c. Drill and practice.

d. Rote memory.

Constructed-Response Format

6. Figure 2.11 shows early Babylonian numerals made by African American middle school students in Kansas City, Missouri (on the student companion web site, see Chapter 2, Extended Activities, "Babylonian Logo Activity") using the Logo computer language:

   Write the equivalent base ten number here:

   _____

7. Write an equation using mathematical variables to represent the statement: There are six times as many dogs as there are cats.

   _____

   Would you expect an English language learner to answer this correctly? Why or why not? If not, reword the problem to make it easier for an ELL to solve.

8. Who were the first people to use a symbol for zero? _____.
   They are the ancestors of _____ in our classrooms today. (Hint: Remember Figure 2.1.)

9. Rewrite this typical textbook problem so students from a nonwhite culture have a greater chance for success. Blend three ways covered in the chapter.

   Janice expects 32 friends to come to her party. If each friend will get an 8-ounce serving of soda, then how many 12-ounce bottles of soda does Janice need for the party?

Integrating Technology

Internet Activities

WebQuests

Accomplishments of African Americans—Using Mathematics in Many Fields

ESTIMATION   MATHEMATICAL CONNECTIONS   CULTURAL RELEVANCE   INTERNET SEARCHES

1. On the text Web site, open the WebQuest "Accomplishments of African Americans—Using Mathematics in Many Fields" (**www.wiley.com/college/hatfield**).

2. You will be asked to pick an occupation in which famous African Americans used their talents in mathematics to become noted leaders.

3. Follow the directions in the WebQuest to see what it was like to become famous and have a successful career using mathematics.

Animal Tracks (a Native American Approach)

COMPUTERS   PROBLEM SOLVING   CULTURAL RELEVANCE   INTERNET SEARCHES

1. On the text Web site, open the WebQuest "Animal Tracks—a Native American Approach" (Chapter 2, WebQuests).

2. Follow the directions in the WebQuest to solve the mystery of which animals are in the forest by identifying and measuring their tracks (shape recognition and linear measurement techniques).

Web sites

Go to the NCTM Web site (**http://www.nctm.org/affiliates**) and review the information available there on Benjamin Banneker, on ethnomathematics, and on women and mathematics education.

Go to Douglas Clements's Web site (**http://www.gse.buffalo.edu/org/buildingblocks/index_2.htm**) to see examples of young children working with computer activities. Dr. Clements' work is being pilot tested in various socioeconomic areas throughout the United States as part of an NSF grant project.

The Development of Mathematical Proficiency: Using Learning Research, Assessment, and Effective Instruction

Prior knowledge

Picture yourself in the "perfect" classroom. You are due to teach a complex mathematics concept to your students. You are not worried because all the students always learn all of their mathematics concepts at the highest level the first time the concepts are presented, and this learning lasts for the duration of their lives. In such a classroom, there would be no need to assess how well students were learning or what level or rate of learning was attained. Everyone would be at the same level, at the same rate, learned in the same way, all of the time. Teachers would pick a concept to teach, and students would learn it perfectly . . . and on to the next concept they would go.

But ours is NOT a world of "sameness!" Our classrooms abound in variety—different personalities, different learning rates, different ways of learning, different preferences for learning, different achievement levels, and so forth. When variations exist, human beings find ways to note the differences and to compare and contrast them. Even parents of identical twins spend the first hours after their birth looking for the presence of minute differences so they can know one twin from the other. It is in the differences that we become interesting, unique human beings.

This chapter discusses the three essential parts needed to develop mathematical proficiency of all students in a world of differences: (1) the understanding of how students learn mathematics, (2) the application of assessment techniques to analyze student learning, and (3) the planning and execution of quality mathematical experiences to ensure continued growth based on what was learned during the assessments. This introductory chapter sets the stage for learning and assessment in the content chapters. Each content chapter features specific ways to assess student learning on the important mathematics concepts unique to that chapter. Students with special needs are assessed in this chapter as well as throughout the content chapters.

HOW STUDENTS LEARN MATHEMATICS—THE BRAIN RESEARCH CONNECTION

Understanding the developmental nature of how students learn and construct their own mathematical knowledge will help you plan more effective instruction for those students entrusted to your care. This must be done in light of new research and best practices coming from brain research. It is possible to analyze students' ability to do quality

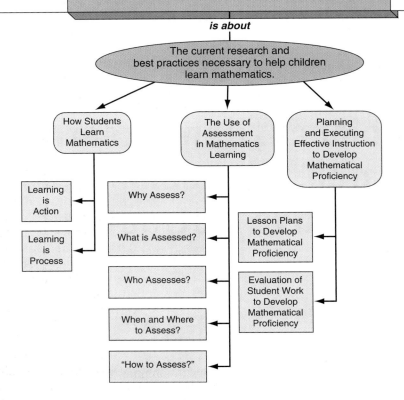

PREVIOUS CHAPTER	CURRENT CHAPTER	NEXT CHAPTER
Culturally Relevant Mathematics	The Development of Mathematical Proficiency: Using Learning Research, Assessment, and Effective Instruction	Middle School Mathematics

is about

The current research and best practices necessary to help children learn mathematics.

How Students Learn Mathematics
- Learning is Action
- Learning is Process

The Use of Assessment in Mathematics Learning
- Why Assess?
- What is Assessed?
- Who Assesses?
- When and Where to Assess?
- "How to Assess?"

Planning and Executing Effective Instruction to Develop Mathematical Proficiency
- Lesson Plans to Develop Mathematical Proficiency
- Evaluation of Student Work to Develop Mathematical Proficiency

SELF-HELP QUESTIONS

1. How can I use the knowledge of brain research and subsequent learning theories to prepare better lessons that will help my students understand mathematics at a deeper and more lasting level?

2. How can I create quality assessments to help my students achieve greater mathematics understanding?

3. What ways are more successful in helping children with special needs to learn mathematics?

4. How can the variety of learning theories help me understand and use the many processing and learning styles of children?

5. How can I apply the teacher study lesson approach to my own teaching?

6. Which assessment techniques are the best ones for me to use when working with students?

7. How can I construct my lesson plans to promote mathematical proficiency of my students?

8. How does the Praxis II™ exit exam assess my ability to perform as a mathematics teacher who knows how to apply the things explained in this chapter?

mathematical thinking when presented tasks that correspond to their individual unique ways of learning.

The knowledge of how human beings learn is expanding daily. Research studies of the brain continue to add growing insights across many disciplines. The research both challenges our previous knowledge of how things are supposed to work, and in many cases, seems to reaffirm widely held theories on which we have based formal mathematics instruction in the past. The study of the brain is still in its infancy, so we can expect to see many changes in our understanding over the next decade. Although there are many theories of learning, only those with the most impact on mathematics education have been included for study in this text. Many of the new insights fit very well with the developmental learning theories that stress active learning with growing complexity of mental structures. The insights have led educators to coin the phrase, "Learning is Action." Still other insights fit well with the theories of information processing and their diversified ways of storing and retrieving information in the brain, leading to the phrase, "Learning is Process." Table 3.1 shows how the two main areas are divided with the principal ideas that come from each respective category listed by the leaders or major terminology used in the field of learning.

Learning is Action—The Brain as Resilient, Growing More Complex: The Cognitive/ Constructivists Theories

Research studies of the brain (Sylwester, 2000; D'Arcangelo, 2001; Wolfe, 2001; Jensen, 2005) are proving the brain to be marvelously resilient and flexible, a quality known as *plasticity*. One part of the brain is capable of taking over the actions normally done by another part if the need arises as a result of some unforeseen malfunction or impairment. It appears that the brain is "wired" with trillions of *neurons*, nerve cells so small that 30,000 can fit on a pinhead. These neurons make connections with other neurons through *synapses*, the point at which electric impulses pass from one neuron to another. It is a very active process; one neural connection spurs the connections of other neurons.

The more stimulation children receive in their environment, the more they can interact with the things around them. The more interaction a person has with the environment, the more diversified neural connections are made. These connections form *networks*. These growing networks of more and more complex neural connections are how we learn and remember. Neural networks virtually control everything that keeps us going. These networks can be seen in two pictures of brain activity—the magnetic resonance imaging (MRI) and the positron-emission tomography (PET) scan. The MRI and the PET allow researchers to observe brain activity as a person performs a learning task. The image of the brain's activity shows on a computer monitor. The more mentally active the learning task, the greater the brain activity appears to be on the monitor, confirming the phrase—Learning is Action!

The description of brain activity fits very well with the Constructivist learning theory. Constructivists believe that children must be allowed to experiment physically with the things around them if they are to learn. They believe active learning builds mental structures. The works of Jean Piaget, Lev Vygotsky, and most recently, Constance Kamii (Kamii, Kirkland, and Lewis, 2001) have had a great impact on the study of how children learn mathematics. These theories coincide well with the developments of brain research as active, continually changing neural connections growing more and more complex.

TABLE 3.1	Learning Theories with Implications for Mathematics Instruction

LEARNING IS ACTION		LEARNING IS PROCESS
Cognitive/Constructivist Theories *Piaget*		**Information Processing Theories** *Sensory Pathways* • Concrete → Pictorial → Symbolic
Stages of Development 1. Sensorimotor 2. Preoperations 3. Concrete operations 4. Formal operations (13 years and older)	*Action Needed* • Actions on objects • Actions on reality • Actions on operations • Operations on operations	***Thought Processing*** • Field dependent • Field independent
Vygotsky • Zone of proximal development • Mapping • Covert actions with same-named objects		***Learning Styles*** *Perceptual Factors* • Visual • Auditory • Tactile
		Gardner Multiple intelligences

Jean Piaget Jean Piaget, a Swiss philosopher-epistemologist, conducted extensive research for over sixty years (1920s–1980) on the development of children's cognitive abilities. Piaget and his co-workers devised ingenious learning tasks, some of which tested children's understanding of mathematics. These tasks and their results are presented throughout the book where appropriate. Some tasks have become benchmarks in measuring students' mathematical capabilities at varying intervals and are used by teachers to assess how much might be reasonable to expect children to do, given their mental structures at particular points in their school experience. Several tasks are presented as number readiness benchmarks in Chapter 6.

The focus in this chapter is Piaget's theory as it applies to the general learning of mathematics. Piaget believed that people go through definite developmental stages in their lives. Each stage must be completed before a person can attain the next stage. It is of interest that Piaget found that the historical development of mathematics proceeds through the same stages in a collective sense (taking many generations) that each person goes through individually in a relatively short amount of time. People must act on their environment at each stage until bits of knowledge form schemes that interlock the bits of knowledge together to perform meaningful actions. These schemes then form changed mental structures. These changed mental structures thrust a person into the next developmental stage. In a literal sense, the person no longer sees the world the same way. Notice in Table 3.1 the Piagetian stages through the approximate age of twelve require action on the environment. In mathematics, this means that elementary-age children must learn the operations of addition, subtraction, multiplication, and division through the use of hands-on, concrete materials that allow them to physically examine what is happening when an arithmetic operation is performed.

When students enter the formal operational stage, Piagetians believe that mental transformations can take place without the need of concrete materials. Students are then capable of understanding abstract concepts that cannot be easily proved in the physical world. An example would be the existence of irrational numbers having no repeating decimal pattern that can be keyed back to a basic building unit in our numeration system, explained in greater detail in Chapters 8 and 10. Some studies have shown that not all people may attain formal operational thought, and still others may attain it far beyond the age of twelve. For this reason, some eighth graders have trouble understanding irrational numbers.

Piaget himself did not adhere to a strict age theory in the last ten years of his research. He continued to stress the progression from one set of mental structures to another as seen in Activity 3.1. The Piagetian approach of asking questions and building on the answers of children aligns well with the need for oral discourse as seen in the NCTM *Principles and Standards of School Mathematics* (2000) and works well with the elaborating technique to be explained in the assessment section of this chapter. Piagetian theory has helped teachers have a more realistic view of what children can be expected to do at the appropriate developmental times.

Activity 3.1

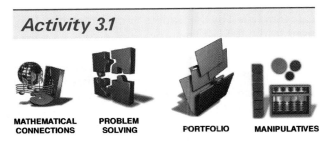

MATHEMATICAL CONNECTIONS · PROBLEM SOLVING · PORTFOLIO · MANIPULATIVES

ASSESSMENT OF PIAGET'S DEVELOPMENTAL STAGES WITH CHILDREN

MATERIALS
1. Pan of sand, salt, or paper filler.
2. Several containers in various shapes, to include those pictured in Figure 3.1. Each should be hollow.

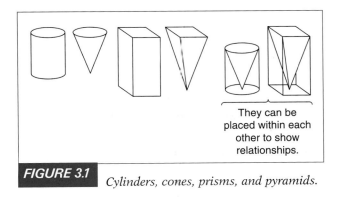

They can be placed within each other to show relationships.

FIGURE 3.1 *Cylinders, cones, prisms, and pyramids.*

DIRECTIONS
1. Select a child in each of the following age groups:
   - Toddler to two years old
   - Two to six years old
   - Six to twelve years old
   - Over twelve years old

2. Try the activities listed below and allow each person to explore with the containers.

3. Record what each child does. This becomes a good *professional portfolio item*, documenting your ability as a keen observer of student actions.

4. Check with the responses Piaget found in each of these age groups as seen below. Reflect on the responses of your child. See how well they match Piaget's explanations.

5. WHAT PIAGET FOUND:

SENSORIMOTOR STAGE (TODDLER TO TWO YEARS OLD)

Do not use filler with young child. This is the "oral" time; children will eat the filler! They truly "act" on everything.

Teacher says: "Here are some objects just for you."

Actions on Objects

Children will touch, taste, squeeze, pinch, drop, and bang (to hear noise), roll, throw, stack, pretend to drink from can, and so on.

Children see the objects as extensions of themselves. Out of sight, out of mind describes this time of action.

Toward the end of this stage, children will use two-word oral language to describe what they are doing.

Expect language such as: "can go" "me drink" "see box," and so on.

PREOPERATIONAL STAGE (TWO TO SIX YEARS OLD)

Teacher says: "Here are some objects and some filler. Show me what you can do with them."

Actions on Reality

Children know that objects exist outside of themselves (have their own reality), recognize that objects have properties, will use words to tell you so.

Children will scoop up filler in containers and dump it all over surfaces; may fill one container from another; may hide containers in filler, and so on.

Children say that objects are "pointed, square, flat, pointed, round," and so on.

CONCRETE OPERATIONAL STAGE
(SIX TO TWELVE YEARS OLD)

Teacher says: "Here are some objects and some filler. Explore and find out what you can do with them. Tell me what you have discovered."

Actions on Operations

Children will "operate" on objects by systematically filling containers back and forth; will make state-ments that acknowledge the interrelatedness of the objects; will show that they understand how to reverse actions by filling and unfilling containers.

Children will figure out which containers hold the most, the least, equivalent amounts, and so on. They will predict before they do the actions.

If they do not think about predicting things on their own, teacher says: "Can you predict what will happen before you pour the filler in the containers?"

Children's oral discourse will include such descriptions as the following: "the rounded and square cans hold three times as much filler as the 'pointed' cans." They can also express it as "the pointed cans hold one-third as much as the ones with all sides flat."

FORMAL OPERATIONAL STAGE (OVER 12 YEARS)

Teacher says: "Tell me what you know about these objects from using other objects like these in the past. Explore to check out any predictions you make."

Operations on Operations

Children no longer need the objects to work on the relationships; can generalize a simple volume formula for the operations on pyramids and cylinders, not just the ones shown to them. They can symbolize the formula as well.

For cylinders

$$V = \pi r^2 h$$

For pyramids

$$V = \frac{1}{3}(l \times w \times h)$$

Supporting the NCTM *Principles and Standards* (2000):

- Mathematics as Reasoning, Communication, Problem Solving, and Representation

- Student Representation; Teacher's Role in Developing Representation; Analysis of Teaching and Learning—The Teaching Principle

- Monitoring Student Progress; Judging Progress Toward Mathematical Power—The Learning Principle

---

Piagetian Theory in Practice Nothing helps a person understand a complex, intricate theory like Piaget's better than conducting one's own assessments with children in the various stages of cognitive development. Activity 3.1 on Piagetian developmental stages is presented to help you begin to place yourself in the role of an assessor. It is hoped that the basic outline in Table 3.1 has more meaning after reading Activity 3.1 in its entirety. You are encouraged to find children of each developmental age group and try the activity with them. Review the interview techniques in the assessment section before you start your work with the children. Use the Krulik and Rudnick (2001) holistic scoring guide (see Figure 3.20) to score the degree to which each child is firmly entrenched in a developmental stage. When you do the tasks with elementary and middle school students, you will notice that some students do the task completely for their expected developmental stage, rating a "3" on the Krulik and Rudnick rubric. Others do partial work at any stage, rating a "2." Students who have a great amount of difficulty even starting the task at any stage would rate a "1." A score of "1" is your notice to move your interview questions back to the stage immediately preceding the level where you started. Figure 3.1 shows the physical materials (manipulatives) you will need for the activity. They may be made from models available on the Web site in Appendix A.

We explore more of Piaget's theory in later chapters. Piaget's ideas concerning conservation of quantity, liquid, weight, and volume are noted in the measurement Chapter 13.

Lev Vygotsky Lev Vygotsky's theory stresses continually constructing and restructuring knowledge. His work also delineates stages of development. At first, names of things, including beginning mathematical concepts, are not arbitrary; instead, names are assigned to objects and used intentionally. Children from the age of eighteen months experience an urgency to assign each object a unique name. The name fuses together with the covert action on the object, and children will not decenter from it until they reach five to six years of age (Vygotsky, 1962). Covert actions and the disposition to perform the same action with the same-named object are called mapping. Eventually, children come to accept that a name may represent a variety of meanings, enlarging that which is included in the mapping. When people can produce and analyze a complex skill on their own, Vygotsky says the skill is internalized in the *zone of proximal development* (Vygotsky, 1978).

Vygotsky's work has appeal to today's Constructivists because his research gives credence to the idea that children can be guided to better mathematical understandings as they progressively analyze complex skills on their own (Snowman and Biehler, 2006). Vygotsky's research showed that children could internalize actions involving complex knowledge more quickly with

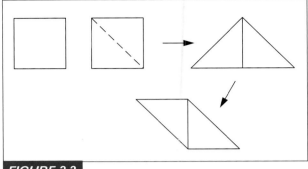

FIGURE 3.2 *Square with first cut and two of the earliest transformations.*

the guidance of good analyzing questions from a teacher. This is where the use of the questioning techniques discussed in the assessment section comes into play with Vgotsky's theory. Concepts approximate real understanding, action by action, construct by construct. Therefore, no two people will have the same understanding of the concepts. Each builds (constructs) his or her own reality depending on the kinds of discourse and experience each has. Teacher intervention and quality instruction become very important in Vygotsky's view of learning.

Vygotsky's Theory in Practice Activity 3.2 explores the differences in two children's construction of concepts in geometry. Figures 3.2–3.5 show the children's work with geometric transformations. The activity uses Vygotsky's ideas to help each internalize the experience. Both children were in the same class and both were exposed to the same initial instruction. Use this as a starting point to do your own observation and assessment of children's work for your professional portfolio. On the Krulik and Rudnick scoring guide, a student with a "3" is one who has internalized his or her understanding

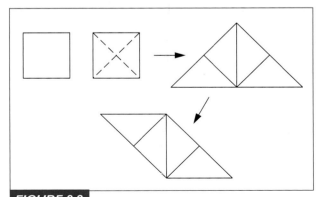

FIGURE 3.3 *Square with two cuts and same transformations.*

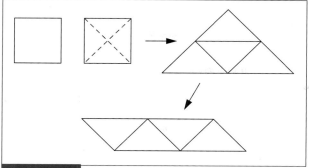

FIGURE 3.4 *Square with two cuts and resulting new transformations.*

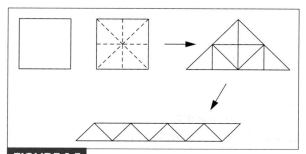

FIGURE 3.5 *Square with four cuts and resulting eight triangles in new forms.*

of the concept in the zone of proximal development. A score of "2" shows the need for the teacher to continue good questioning strategies to help the student internalize the actions needed to understand the concept at a greater depth.

Activity 3.2

PORTFOLIO   PROBLEM SOLVING   MATHEMATICAL CONNECTIONS   MANIPULATIVES

ASSESSMENT OF VYGOTSKY'S CONSTRUCTIVISM

MATERIALS

1. Three 10-cm squares cut from paper
2. Scissors, pencil, and a straight edge

DIRECTIONS

1. Read the experience of the two fourth graders described here.

2. Then pick a student from an elementary grade of your choice and follow the same activity, checking to see at which point your student may approximate the same understandings of these children.

3. *Teacher:* "Here are three squares. Do they cover the same amount of area? How do you know?"

Both children place all three squares on top of each other, proving congruency.

Teacher: "Place a straight edge diagonally from one-corner to its opposite corner on one of the squares. Mark the line with a pencil and cut the square into two pieces." (Teacher models the placement of the straight edge.)

Both children follow the directions.

Teacher: "Find other ways to put the two pieces together."

Both children perform the following actions:

Teacher: "Now take the next square and mark it with two diagonals and cut it apart. Can you arrange the pieces to match the triangle and the parallelogram you made first?"

Child 1: "Yes, I can do it if I can use the first two I made to put these pieces on." (Teacher nods and child makes the figures seen below on top of the first two pieces.)

Child 2: Makes no verbal commitment but moves quickly to make the following arrangement *without* using the first two pieces to match. Then child 2 says: "The parallelogram is getting longer and thinner."

Teacher asks: "Does the longer parallelogram cover the same area as the wider parallelogram you made before?"

Child 2: "Yes it does. See." (Child places longer, thinner parallelogram on the other one.)

Child 1: Watches what is going on but when asked, he states that "it is different because it changes to be longer and thinner. It's the same when it's like the first one but it is different when it is here like the long and thin one."

Teacher to Child 1: "Did you take anything away or add anything to change the area?"

Child 1: "No, nothing's gone but it is still different. Its area can't be the same because it is different. Its area is the same only when I match it up."

The teacher then gives a third square to both children and asks them to cut it into eight pieces like the one shown in Figure 3.5.

Child 1: Cuts the eight triangles but says, "They are too little to do anything with them, to make the big triangle or anything else. There are just too many pieces."

Child 2: "I know I can make an even longer parallelogram. See." (Child places pieces as seen at the bottom of Figure 3.5.)

Teacher to Child 2: "What do you think will happen if I kept giving you more and more squares to cut?"

Child 2: "I would keep making longer and thinner parallelograms with the same area."

Teacher: "How do you know that?"

Child 2: "I know because you started me out matching them all up from the same square so I know it all has the same area."

TEACHER REFLECTION

1. What do you know about each child as a learner from this experience?

2. Which child pushes his or her zone of proximal development further during the lesson?

3. Was the teacher wise in not asking Child 1 the last question? Why or why not?

4. What do you expect would have happened if the teacher had asked Child 1 the last question?

5. Could the teacher have worked any questions differently to help children arrive at an understanding without telling the answer?

6. What activity(s) should be planned next for Child 1? for Child 2?

Supporting the NCTM *Principles and Standards* (2000):

- Mathematics as Reasoning, Communication, Problem Solving, and Representation

- Student Representation; Teacher's Role in Developing Representation; Analysis of Teaching and Learning—The Teaching and Learning Principles

- Monitoring Student Progress; Judging Progress Toward Mathematical Power—The Assessment Principle

---

Vygotsky's theory would state that the teacher took each child to his or her own zone of proximal development based on the variety of meanings that each child was able to use in mapping the activity at that point in time. Each constructed his or her own reality of the events. A teacher believing in Constructivism would continue to work with both children, providing activities to stimulate the mapping of their own events within their own mental structures. The teacher would use each child's reasoning ability and suppositions as a starting place to help the child grow to more complex understandings. As you can see from the teacher reflection questions in the Vygotsky activity, it takes an alert teacher to use the Constructivist teaching technique.

The Current Constructivists There are many theorists who are advocating the Constructivist viewpoint today. Many education articles have been written for the classroom teacher, showing ways to structure the classroom environment to enhance cognitive development in mathematics (Kamii, 2001). All advocate an environment where young students are constructing their own knowledge through careful, competent guidance of a teacher, asking questions to clarify thoughts while not telling the answers. The section on assessment supports student construction of mathematics knowledge through the use of elaborating techniques in questioning and diagnostic interview techniques in interviewing students. The Cognitive/Constructivists' view the minds of young people as resilient, vibrantly alive, constantly growing in neural connections to handle more and more complex thoughts. It is an exciting picture of today's classrooms, supporting the belief that LEARNING IS ACTION!

Learning is Process—The Brain as Highly Diversified, Must Use It or Lose It: The Information-Processing Theories

We know that if a person decides not to use a perfectly good arm, over time he or she loses the ability to use the arm altogether. It appears that this is true for the brain as well. If the neural connections are not continually activated, knowledge governed by that network connection will be lost. Researchers point to the ability that infants have to vocalize all sorts of sounds. Children in any culture can trill an *r* sound or place a click in between their babbling. If the children come from a culture where they do not use the trilled *r* sound, as used in Spanish, or the fast click between syllables of words, as used in several African tribal languages, the ability to produce those sounds will be lost. Linguists point to the fact that adults who learn another language later in life will never become native speakers of the language as if they had learned it in infancy. They can learn to make the sounds, but they are never as natural sounding as a native speaker. Brain research supports the idea that neural connections must be used if they are to remain vital in the life of human beings. There must be a constant encoding, storing, and retrieving of learned information if it is to remain vital—hence, the phrase, "use it or lose it."

In pyschology, the study of how humans encode, store, and retrieve information is known as Information-Processing Theory; it compares well with the current brain research. Table 3.1 shows parts of the information-processing theory that have direct relationships to mathematics learning and teaching.

Sensory Pathways If you are on a boat that capsizes, swimming becomes essential to your survival. Would you rather have had the concrete experience of swimming in the past, or would you feel fine having only read a book on how to swim or seen slides of someone else swimming? Human beings have been genetically programmed for survival; hence, the concrete experiences make the strong, long-lasting neural connections. Wolfe (2001) points out that the concrete experiences engage more senses and use multiple pathways to store information in the brain. The more ways students can hook abstract, symbolic learning to concrete experiences, the greater and more lasting the learning will be. Mathematics researchers have long held the same belief (Baratta-Lorton, 1976; Heddens, 1986; Ball, 1992; Kilpatrick, Swafford, and Findell, 2001; Kilpatrick and Swafford, 2002). Figure 3.6 shows the multiple representations a child might use to discover the conceptual meaning of $2 + 1 = 3$. The multiple representations go from the concrete experiences to the symbolic abstract understandings through various intermediate connections to help store the abstract mathematical knowledge in meaningful ways. The intermediate connections are often seen as iconic or pictorial representations.

Researchers caution that physical manipulatives in and of themselves are not necessarily concrete to students. If the manipulatives have no meaning to the students or their connections to the mathematical concept are not readily apparent, the manipulatives might actually hinder rather than help mathematics learning.

Concrete experiences to pictorial representations to the symbolic abstractions are routinely a part of lesson plans and teaching techniques as seen in the mathematics literature, and they appear throughout the *Principles and Standards in School Mathematics* (NCTM, 2000). The gradual progression from concrete to abstract is modeled many times in this text as we talk about how students can learn various concepts throughout the book.

Students with Special Needs The model in Figure 3.6 is important when working with students with special needs who may require more gradual changes during the middle transition period from the concrete to the abstract. These models presuppose that the student is *ACTIVELY MANIPULATING* the materials. When new or additional knowledge is being learned, people must progress through one mode to the next for strong connections to take place. However, gifted students and students with Asperger's syndrome or other sensory issues are examples of students who do not follow a predictable path of learning. Gifted students may appear to jump to the abstract (symbolic) mode without the need for the concrete or transitional (pictorial/iconic) mode. They are capable of seeing relations quickly and do not need the repetition of the same concept in more than one mode. Those with Asperger's syndrome and other sensory issues may have a low tolerance for activities that involve movement, called *vestibular hypersensitivity;* whereas others may have difficulty exerting the right amount of pressure when handling objects, called *proprioceptive sensitivity.* These students may need to watch as others handle the materials or move immediately to the iconic modes so the concrete objects do not hamper the learning that needs to take place. A strategy that works one day may not work the next.

CONCRETE EXPERIENCES ◄─────►	CONNECTING TRANSITIONAL MODES		◄─────► ABSTRACT/SYMBOLIC
Logical relations among objects; free to explore by manipulation; hence, objects called manipulatives.	Familiar activities now done with math symbols; may be connected to iconic (visual/pictorial) representations; higher level of abstraction is seen.		May still use concrete objects or iconic representations of the concrete, but emphasis is on symbols and what can be learned from them
Actual objects are used. 	*Semiconcrete* Pictures of actual objects. 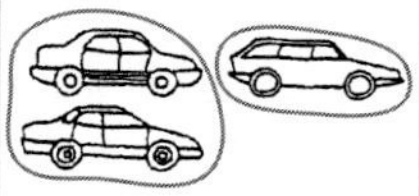	*Semiabstract* Tally marks or stylized symbol.  /|| |	Numerals seem as preferred way to solve problems. $2 + 1 = 3$

FIGURE 3.6 *Multiple representations used to discover conceptual meaning.*

Myles et al. (2000) recommend that classroom teachers work with occupational therapists and other personnel trained in sensory integration issues to select the appropriate strategy to use. The Myles et al. book contains many checklists and accompanying strategies to help classroom teachers, parents, and other caregivers make the appropriate links that enable learning to occur. In some cases, special manipulatives can be purchased that minimize the problems. Suppliers of special education materials and their respective Web sites are listed on the Web site in Appendix E. Further ways to handle complex issues for children with special needs are mentioned in the content chapters where appropriate to a particular mathematics concept.

Thought-Processing Styles   Neurons can create more and more intricate network connections, always changing with no two people having the same exact connections. This gives rise to the individuality component in learning (Wolfe, 2001). The general public as well as educators have been intrigued with the notion that people have different processing styles and various learning style preferences that may be completely different from one person to another.

Thought processing is defined as the strategies used to organize and classify new information or skills to obtain order out of a confusing series of stimulus events (Snowman and Biehler, 2006). Two of these strategies have a direct relationship to how children perceive mathematics. *Simultaneous thought processing* requires stimulus material to be presented all at once (simultaneously), seeing the whole before its parts. A person begins to look for patterns and relationships to break down the whole into its respective parts to arrive at appropriate solutions. Persons using this thought processing are said to be ***field-dependent learners.*** *Successive thought processing* requires stimulus material to be presented from one component part to the next (successively), leading from detail to detail until the whole is seen. A person begins to look for patterns and relationships between details, building the respective parts into the whole to arrive at correct solutions. Persons using this thought processing are said to be ***field-independent learners.***

At the beginning of this chapter, a graphic organizer showed how the chapter would be divided into manageable parts so the concepts could have meaning to persons who may not be schooled in brain research or learning theories. Table 3.1 and Figure 3.6 also presented material in a graphic or clustered form. Readers who are field-dependent learners may find themselves referring to the chapter organizer, the table, and figures as they read these paragraphs to see how all of the material fits together. Other readers may have profited little from them and skipped immediately to the paragraphs that outlined details of each theory. Such readers would be using successive thought processing as field-independent learners. Material has been presented by using both thought-processing modes in this text. Perhaps you will be able to analyze your own processing preferences as you work in the text.

Some people may adopt processing styles depending on their perception of how difficult the material is from task to task. Figures 3.7 through 3.9 show typical mathematical problems seen in elementary and middle school books and worksheets. In each set, both problems are teaching the same concept. The problems on the top of each set require students to process the information by (1) counting the objects one by one until the entire set is calculated or (2) constructing the information one part at a time to get the answers. This is successive synthesis—the part-to-whole processing strategy used by field-independent learners.

The problems on the bottom of each set require students to process the information by (1) receiving the entire set of answers all at once, deciding which sets do not belong, and partitioning them away from the whole or (2) seeing the

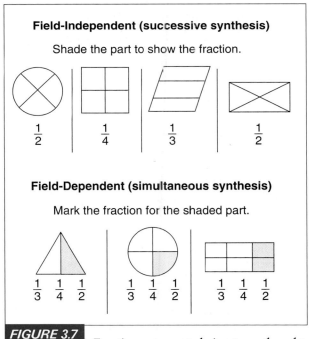

FIGURE 3.7   *Fractions presented in two thought-processing styles.*

CRAZY

Field-Independent (successive synthesis)

1			4				8
			12				16
							64

Write the numerals from 1 to 64
in the blocks going across.
What patterns do you see with
eights and fours?

Field-Dependent (simultaneous synthesis)

1	2	3	4	5	6	7	8
9	10	11	12	13	14	15	16
17	18	19	20	21	22	23	24
25	26	27	28	29	30	31	32
33	34	35	36	37	38	39	40
41	42	43	44	45	46	47	48
49	50	51	52	53	54	55	56
57	58	59	60	61	62	63	64

Look at the filled-in chart above.
What patterns do you see with
fours? With eights?
What addition combinations can
you see easily?

FIGURE 3.8 *Fact strategy chart presented in two
thought-processing styles.*

Field-Independent (successive synthesis)

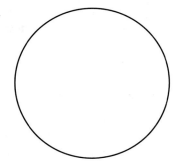

Create your own:
   Draw a tangent. Label it *CD*.
   Draw a radius. Label it *AS*.
   Draw a diameter. Label it *RS*.
   Draw a chord. Label it *XY*.
   Draw a ray. Label it *AZ*.

Field-Dependent (simultaneous synthesis)

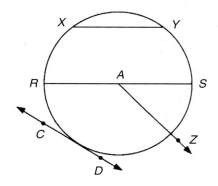

Find and label:
   The tangent is _____.
   The radius is _____.
   The diameter is _____.
   The chord is _____.
   The ray is _____.

entire relationship pattern that o
another.
   This is simultaneous synthesis
part processing strategy used by
learners.
   Some students are very confus
material seen at once as shown on
Figures 3.7 to 3.9. They may know
the problems, but they may not b
what they really know because
information in this format is so dif
Other students are equally confused
asked to determine an answer with

1) Field In/Dependent

2) Use it or loose it - kids need
    experience →

3) must use physically happen
    → conceptual meaning
    concrete → transitional - abstract
                                symbols

4 prior knowledge

Perceptual Learning Styles　*Perceptual learning style* refers to a person's preference for material presented through one or more of the five senses. The visual, auditory, and tactile modalities are the ones most appropriate for the study of mathematical concepts. The visual and tactile modalities are seen most clearly in the use of the physical manipulatives (so named because of the tactile manipulation that is possible). They are shown in every chapter and even have their own icon to represent their presence in the mathematical activities throughout the book. The auditory modality is the one most associated with school—listening to the teacher and other classmates; however, research shows that the visual modality has consistently gained favor as the modality of choice with children in recent years (Jenson, 2005). The iconic connecting level may be gaining more importance for visual learners.

Gardner's Multiple Intelligences　Howard Gardner has received much recognition in the 1990s for his theory of multiple intelligences. Gardner (1993) believes that there are at least eight different basic intelligences that human beings use to process information about the world around them. The eight intelligences as they might be applied to a mathematics lesson are represented in Figure 3.10.

The theory has appeal because all teachers know that they can reach some children better through one medium than another (Prescott, 2001). Gardner believes that people of all ages learn better if the material is presented through the areas of intelligence in which they are most gifted. It may be wise for elementary and middle school teachers of mathematics to present new mathematics concepts through the eight areas of intelligence. This means planning eight different approaches to the same content. Proponents of multiple intelligences say that students' sense of well-being and willingness to grapple with hard concepts far outweigh the expanded time a teacher needs to plan multiple activities. When students learn the material more easily, a teacher's job becomes easier as well. As you plan for effective instruction in the pages to follow, look for ways to integrate all eight intelligences in your teaching.

Many Differing Views　Many researchers differ on their beliefs about learning styles, processing strategies, and multiple intelligences. Different studies are cited in support of processing styles and learning styles. The proponents point to general classroom situations of success, more so than empirical research studies (Strong, Silver, and Perini 2001; Dunn, 2001). Generally mathematics educators have been slow to adopt the idea of field-dependent and field-independent processing styles and multiple intelligences (Bruer, 2001; Ormrod, 2002). They point to research that shows children solve most mathematical concepts with similar strategies rather than different ones. They feel each person must know how to reason mathematically whichever way a concept occurs in the real world.

The authors are in agreement with the real-world approach. However, it does make sense to start the learning of any new concept using the strengths of each student, whatever the processing strategy or modality may be. Then students can be switched to other strategies that simulate the real world more closely once they have found success and initial understanding of a new concept. Therefore, a variety of visual, auditory, and tactile techniques and processing strategies are shared throughout the text in the hope that teachers will use a variety of learning aids to reach as many students as possible when teaching difficult mathematical concepts.

Learning modalities and processing styles show an individual's unique neural connections to encode, store, and retrieve more and more complex information. It paints an exciting picture of today's classrooms, supporting the belief that LEARNING IS PROCESS!

THE USE OF ASSESSMENT IN MATHEMATICS LEARNING

Assessment is a systematic way to mark the differences that exist in learning rate, level, duration, and type. In and of itself, assessment does not imply judgment of one element better than the other, nor does it imply a hierarchy of desirable traits. The judgment factor applied to assessment is called evaluation. In school settings, assessment is done so that teachers can evaluate the quality and quantity of learning as a necessary factor to plan for more effective learning in the future. Through a variety of assessments, teachers and researchers study how people learn mathematics (the rates, levels, durations, and ways) so that the information can be used to plan for more efficient and effective learning for students.

Assessment in student learning is here to stay! Local, state, and national legislation mandates the use of assessment in the schools. In many instances, funding for schools depends on evidence that assessment of student learning has taken place. The whole gamut of assessment—the why, what, who, when, where, and how—has

FIGURE 3.10 *Gardner's eight multiple intelligences in a math lesson.*

become essential knowledge for teachers because they are held accountable for the use of assessment in effective classroom teaching and learning.

Why Assess?

The purpose of assessment is to provide useful information regarding students' understanding and skills. Appropriate assessment contributes to the teacher's ability to understand students' needs to provide opportunities to develop students' mathematical abilities. Quality assessment provides multiple measures of information about stu-

dents' learning strategies, knowledge, and abilities as they are allowed to show what they are able to do. Assessment should provide information to

- Students to get information about themselves as learners of mathematics
- Teachers to make informed decisions about instruction
- Parents to obtain information about their children's mathematical competencies and abilities
- Administrators to become informed about the effectiveness of mathematics programs

- Interested public to learn about the effectiveness of a school's educational system

What is Assessed?

As Chapter 1 has emphasized, the needs of the twenty-first century are very different from what was expected in the majority of the twentieth century before the advent of computers and calculators. Tedious computations had to be done "by hand," so accuracy of manual computation was a major factor. Today there are calculators inside wristwatches and others are tiny enough to fit into a pocket or purse. Convenience stores sell them for as little as two dollars. The message is clear; calculators are affordable and portable for everyone to use. The calculator will not tell students how to think; it only does what the humans tell it to do. Therefore, today's challenge is to ensure one's ability to reason and problem solve in authentic, real-world situations. When to use the correct formula, equation, or algorithm to match the appropriate situation is crucial for success in the working world of the twenty-first century. Students are being required to show they can perform the thinking required to survive in the years ahead as productive workers in the new age. As a result, teachers have made a major shift in their thinking. McDonald (2002) makes this important observation:

Teachers often say that they want their students to **know** *certain things, but they mean something subtly different . . . they want their students to* **perform** *the reasoning or the application of the algorithm. (p. 121)*

That calls for a way to measure the quality of the performance when reasoning or applying what is learned. The key is performance-based assessment.

What is Meant by "Performance-Based Assessment"?
Concerned educators who want to change the scope and focus of assessment have coined a number of words to describe the change from the simple close-ended, multiple choice tests to new assessment methods. Some of the new terms are authentic assessment, performance-based assessment, and alternative assessment. Multiple choice tests may be used if they are accompanied by a form of constructed response that requires the students to explain their answers. Whichever terminology applies, basically the same concept of assessment is envisioned:

- Students perform, create, and produce solutions to tasks.

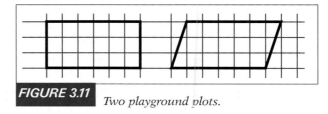

FIGURE 3.11   *Two playground plots.*

- Tasks require problem solving or higher-order thinking.
- Problems are contextualized—are not produced in isolation; they have meaning in real-world applications.
- Tasks are often time-consuming; some may even need days to complete.
- Scoring rubrics or scoring guides are required.

Activity 3.3 shows an example of a performance-based task that has all of the characteristics stated above with the exception of the scoring guide. The task includes two iconic representations of playground plots in Figure 3.11. The scoring guide is presented as Figure 3.12, known as the performance-based ladder.

Teachers who ask students **what** they know are finding that students do NOT produce a quality answer. Instead, students produce a laundry list of items with no connection or relationship from one thing to another. Performance-based assessments call for students to explain **how** they reason to achieve a solution and **how it relates** to other ways to solve problems. This is a keystone of the NCTM *Principles and Standards* (2000). When teachers focus on student refinement of explanations and integration of solutions, students achieve higher scores on state and national assessments (Hall, 2000). The "higher-level performance-based" ladder (Figure 3.12) shows how students can move up to quality assessment answers by checking their own thought processes as they work.

The authors of this text have seen that the ladder works equally well with college students as it does with younger students. All students need to check how they are performing mathematics tasks. Often one discovers it is easy to move up to a higher level on the ladder if one were to take the time to read the performance-based phrases as one works. Try it with Activity 3.3. On which level would you place yourself after doing the task? Do you see some things to change to move to a higher step? Later in the chapter you will see how these phrases can be used to write quality mathematics journals. The ladder becomes a scoring guide or rubric for student self-assessment and for teacher assessment of student work.

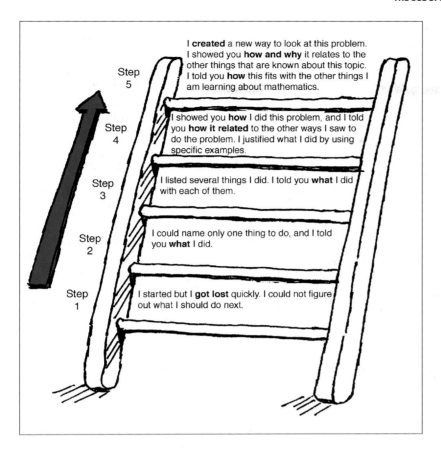

I **created** a new way to look at this problem. I showed you **how and why** it relates to the other things that are known about this topic. I told you **how** this fits with the other things I am learning about mathematics.

I showed you **how** I did this problem, and I told you **how it related** to the other ways I saw to do the problem. I justified what I did by using specific examples.

I listed several things I did. I told you **what** I did with each of them.

I could name only one thing to do, and I told you **what** I did.

I started but I **got lost** quickly. I could not figure out what I should do next.

Step 5

Step 4

Step 3

Step 2

Step 1

FIGURE 3.12 *Higher-level performance-based ladder.*

Activity 3.3

PROBLEM SOLVING

MATHEMATICAL CONNECTIONS

PORTFOLIO

PERFORMANCE-BASED TASK: PREPARING FOR NATIONAL ASSESSMENT TESTS[1]

DIRECTIONS
Think carefully about the following question. Write a complete answer. You may use drawings, words, and numbers to explain your answer. Be sure to show all of your work.[1]

PROBLEM
You want to make a playground for you and your friends. You have been given two plots of ground from which to choose. You want to make it on the biggest area possible. Which playground area would you choose? Justify your answer.

1. In what ways are the figures above alike? List as many ways as you can.
2. In what ways are the figures above different? List as many ways as you can.
3. How did you go about solving the problem?
4. How do you know your decision is the correct one?

> **Supporting the NCTM *Principles and Standards* (2000):**
> - Mathematics as Problem Solving, Reasoning, Representations, Measurement
> - Written Discourse by Students, Tools for Enhancing Discourse—The Teaching Principle
> - The Assessment Principle

[1]Task adapted from National Center for Educational Statistics, NAEP, 4th Grade Released Test Items, Web site **http://www.nesc.ed.gov./nationalsreportcard/itmrls/qtab.asp** (November 2002).

In summary, in today's mathematics classrooms, performance-based tasks are the focus of assessment.

Performance-based assessment should be consistent with curriculum goals, embedded in real-world situations, require problem solving or higher-order thinking, and encompass a number of procedures for observing, collecting, and evaluating student learning. These procedures are discussed in the section, "How to Assess?"

Who Assesses?

Ask teachers the question, "Who assesses mathematics learning?" and the answer will be, "Just about everyone!" It appears that many groups want to be a part of the action in today's educational climate. Local administrators and teachers, state or provincial legislators, national and international government officials—all have claimed mathematics assessment as their turf. The United States seems to be a nation obsessed with assessment, constant evaluation, and achievement. However, the Western world has largely followed the same path. Canada, Wales, and England, to name a few, are dealing with the same issues. The history of evaluating and testing human knowledge and capabilities dates back to the beginning of historical record. Early measurements were primarily oral examinations such as those used by Socrates in 400–300 B.C. to measure the understanding of the young men in his care.

International Studies Profile tests have been administered to study mathematical performance across cultures. The International Association for the Evaluation of Educational Achievement has conducted a cycle of international comparative studies since 1960. This nongovernmental organization represents thirty-five countries interested in assessment of outputs of national education systems. Data from the First International Mathematical Study, the Second International Mathematical Study, the Assessment Performance Unit in England, and the Third International Mathematics and Science Study (TIMSS) provide information for setting standards for international survey research, as well as valuable insights into aspects of the teaching and learning process (Forgione, 1997).

A major focus of TIMSS is an analysis of the curriculum for cross-national comparisons. Another component of the TIMSS relates to the incorporation of alternative assessment methods. Participation in international studies such as TIMSS can provide information about national educational systems that become critical for policy decisions made by educational leaders. The disappointing results of American students' scores have prompted some of the push for national assessments in the United States. The TIMSS report has recently spawned the Lesson Study Approach to help teachers work together to improve their own teaching as seen in several articles featured in the *Kappan* (Phi Delta Kappa, 2002) and outlined later in this chapter. The detailed report of TIMSS is found on the student companion Web site.

National Studies: National Assessment of Educational Progress Since the 1960s, student mathematics achievement in the United States has been measured by the National Assessment of Educational Progress (NAEP), a program of the United States Department of Education. Based on a sample size of 25,000 students at three grade levels, NAEP data are collected on trends in eleven academic areas. In recent years, data on student achievement has been reported as "The Nation's Report Card" giving group comparisons by race and ethnicity, gender, type of community, and region. Interest in state-comparative information resulted in the data providing state-by-state or state-to-nation comparisons of student achievement. Results may be seen at the Internet address found at the end of the chapter.

A significant number of educators are concerned that federal, state, and local policymakers may misuse such data to make inappropriate comparisons and inaccurate conclusions. External assessment expectations play a powerful role in determining what curriculum is taught, particularly when student performances are compared and reported. With new emphasis on the NAEP data for state-by-state comparisons, teachers place increased importance on preparing students for the test and, thus, may narrow the curriculum to cover NAEP topics.

To counter this concern, the 1990 NAEP assessment established mathematical objectives based on expectations from the NCTM *Standards* documents (1989, 2000). The items reflected a balance from five content domains (Numbers and Operations; Measurement; Geometry; Data Analysis, Statistics, and Probability; and Algebra and Functions). Items included multiple choice, constructed-response, and use of a calculator. Since 1996, the assessments of fourth, eighth, and twelfth graders have included performance tasks on the mathematics tests with constructed response items included. Specific results from the NAEP are included in the content chapters when appropriate.

State Assessment Programs The push to measure educational progress continued to increase.

By 1989, every state in the United States had a mandated testing program. Statewide testing is generally conducted at three grade levels, such as grades 4, 8, and 12. Teachers found themselves spending more instructional time on topics included on the state tests. The tests now include higher-order thinking skills, and for the most part, deal with complex problems that take time to solve. The assessment systems in many states are closely aligned with the outcomes for change in mathematics supported by what is called state systemic initiative programs. These are state-initiated, systemwide, reform efforts that reflect broad consensus building with an infrastructure to sustain and expand the reform efforts in a whole state. The variety of state objectives in mathematics and the diversity of state assessment programs limit state-to-state comparisons. States continue to seek ways of obtaining reliable data for comparing performances among schools. Educators are faced with many questions regarding the multiple purposes and uses associated with statewide assessments.

Students with Special Needs   Some states include students with special needs in the testing and the related statistical information; others may report the scores as if all students were functioning without special services. Still others do not require students with special needs to be tested. The detailed testing regulations in the test examiner guide are the only way to know how students will be scored. This further complicates state comparisons of data.

Local School Districts   The public in many local school districts has given great attention to published standardized test scores. Local districts will often supply their own tests or purchase ones that go along with the texts to show local constituents that their tax money is being spent for quality education of its students. This assumes that the tests really do measure quality performance, an assumption that is sometimes questioned by test experts. Indeed, many teachers teach to the test and learning goals become determined by the content of the tests. Researchers have evidence that testing shapes instruction. The more performance-based testing is done, the more teachers will create performance-based tasks for classroom use. Such tasks are shown through the content chapters of this text to help teachers begin to plan classroom math activities like the one shown in the section, "What to Assess?"

There are Web sites maintained by each of the national and international groups listing the results of their assessments. Many states also have assessment center Web sites usually listed on a state's department of education Web site. The Web site addresses are named in the technology section at the end of the chapter. Some of the sites include released test items that can be used to help current elementary and middle school students prepare for the assessments, such as the NAEP test item seen in Activity 3.1. You are encouraged to look at the items. You will see that they meet the criterion of being performance based, requiring students to show their ability to reason and problem solve in areas written with the standards in mind.

Benchmaking to Reach Standards   Local, state, and national groups have spent a large part of the last decade deciding which levels of attainment should be expected of students at each grade level. This process is called benchmarking. If students are to reach the top expectations of the standards by the end of their formal education, they must meet reasonable subgoals along the way. It has largely been the work of teacher committees throughout local school districts meeting after long days of teaching who have made these decisions. It seems fitting that the people who will guide students to competency in mathematics should be the ones with this responsibility. National benchmarking is beginning to take place. Chapter 6 shows the work of early childhood mathematics educators who have just finished national benchmarking in pre-kindergarten to grade 2.

When and Where to Assess?

Traditionally, international testing is every four to five years, whereas NAEP national testing in mathematics and reading is every two years. The other subjects areas in NAEP are spread out at longer intervals. The message is clear: mathematics and reading are the two important skill areas that everyone is watching. The No Child Left Behind Act (2001) has moved reading and mathematics to the forefront as well. State testing is done yearly. Even during the recent financial downturn in states when some subject area tests were placed "on hold," mathematics and reading tests continued as annual assessments. All of these are summative assessments, marking a critical moment in time when achievement is given a final grade or score.

In reality, assessment never stops. In classrooms, assessment should be an ongoing process. Figure 3.13 shows the continual aspect of assessment. Once it is started, it follows a four-point cycle.

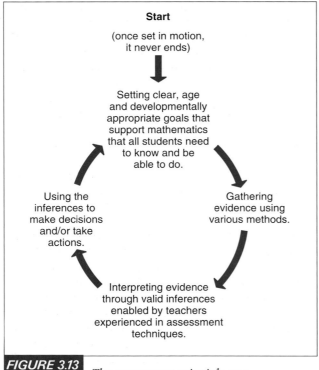

Start

(once set in motion,
it never ends)

Setting clear, age
and developmentally
appropriate goals that
support mathematics
that all students need
to know and be
able to do.

Gathering
evidence using
various methods.

Interpreting evidence
through valid inferences
enabled by teachers
experienced in assessment
techniques.

Using the
inferences to
make decisions
and/or take
actions.

FIGURE 3.13 *The assessment principle as a coherent, ongoing process.*

The onus for quality assessment is on the shoulders of classroom teachers. The daily ongoing practice is known as formative assessment to monitor progress and plan further instruction. Critical thinking skills must become a way of life—a natural response. That does not happen without continual effort on the part of classroom teachers. They are the unsung heroes of the assessment movement!

"How to Assess?"

The performance-based assessment requires careful scrutiny of student work. Not all students will understand a task well enough to achieve success without well-placed guidance on a teacher's part. How a teacher gets students to think critically is the key to quality assessment. The teacher must become an expert at all kinds of techniques to elicit quality student performance—questioning, observing, interviewing, creating, and scoring student journal and portfolio pieces and encouraging student self-assessment.

Questioning The issue of questioning is embodied in the *Teaching Principle* (NCTM, 2000). This principle calls for teachers to limit the number of questions that can be responded to with a yes/no answer or with a short, one-word response. Teachers need to develop more open-response questioning techniques and to ask students to explain their answers. Students should be asked to defend their answers, to think of other ways to solve the problem, and to share their thinking with a partner. When teachers develop this kind of questioning environment, students begin asking good questions of one another. Teachers need to consciously practice allowing children a longer time to respond. Right and wrong answers should be given the same degree of respectful listening followed by probes for explaining the answer.

Elaborating Techniques Effective classrooms must include time for students to think aloud. Students who have trouble expressing their thoughts should be taught elaborating techniques (ways to guide their thought structures) to reach appropriate mathematical conclusions. An example of an elaborating technique may be helpful at this point. Some readers may have had no previous experience with the Logo computer language. A procedure could be frightening the first time it is tried. This is a good simulation of how students feel when a task is strange to them. Figure 3.14 shows an elaborating technique to help students understand some of the things Logo can do with numbers. The student's words and the teacher's words should be read alternating back and forth as a dialogue.

The teacher never told the answer but guided the responses to (1) promote transfer of learning from that which was familiar to that which was unknown, (2) direct problem solving on the student's own, and (3) guide the encoding process so that the student would associate the term, PR, with producing that which is seen on the screen. These three points are essential steps in developing the elaborating technique with students.

Student-to-Student Discourse To facilitate student-to-student discourse, students should talk to each other and verify their solutions. Teachers should direct questions like, "Amy, do you agree with Shalonda?" "Explain your thinking about her answer." Many teachers serve as megaphones repeating answers given by students rather than requiring students to speak more clearly and to interact directly. Teachers should pose interesting questions and then become the facilitators for orchestrating good discourse. Rowan and Robles (1998, pp. 505–506) present a list of possible questions to be used to open avenues of thinking for students. The list can be downloaded from the Web site. It can "save" the teacher who is just starting to develop questioning skills.

Observations Teachers observe students working individually and in groups every school day,

STUDENTS ELABORATING TECHNIQUES	WITH TEACHER'S GUIDANCE
I can't tell what this program will do.	Key words are sometimes helpful in solving any mystery. What do you see?
I see the word MAKE used more than any other word, but I don't know what the A and mean. I MAKE a picture with red paint.	Create a sentence with the word MAKE in it . . . just like you do in everyday language. What were the important words after MAKE in your sentence?
Picture and red paint.	So red paint told you what you would do to the picture. Now what do you think A and 1 are doing in the Logo program? Use the same wording.
tells what to do to. So 2 must tell what to do to B, and A + B must be 1 + 2 which is 3. But I still don't know what PR means.	You could run the program and see if it helps you find out.
The program just answered 3. So PR must mean I get some kind of answer.	Yes, anytime you see PR, it means something is going to be done that you can see or it will be PRINTED so you can see the answer.
I was right.	You were right.

FIGURE 3.14 *Alternating dialogue between student and teacher.*

and they acquire a great deal of information about what students know and understand. The difficult task becomes knowing how to document students' learning from informal observations. In the past, objective data collection was preferred over subjective information. To make observing and recording a reasonable task, teachers use a variety of checklists. Some focus on very specific objectives as in Figure 3.15; others assess general processes like the problem-solving checklist in Figure 3.16. Checklists can be put on the computer and quickly scored by the touch of the screen or by any handheld palm device. Total class records can be updated and printed in a few minutes.

Information can be recorded in an orderly, focused fashion without interfering with instruction. Some teachers elect to focus on one group of students at a particular time with a specific list of skills; other teachers prefer a total listing of the class with broad objectives. Observations can also be made about individuals. An effective plan is to record the comments of students on small index cards. These dated cards can be placed directly into the student's assessment folder. Another efficient approach is to write comments on Post-It Notes, which can be easily transferred to the student's assessment folder.

Interviews Interviews provide a source of rich information concerning what a child is thinking or feeling about mathematics. Information about students' conceptual knowledge of mathematics may reveal the shallow understandings even the talented students may have about some concepts. Questions should be prepared in advance and include probing questions to gather additional information. The lesson plan form to promote mathematical proficiency has a place to write such questions. It is presented in the next section on effective instruction. Encourage

WEEK OF_____ TASKS	ANDY	CLARA	FERNANDO	MARIA	NICK
Uses counting-on to find sums					
Counts by twos					
Touches objects for counting					
Uses models to show sets					
Ready for connecting level					
Uses counting-on to find sums					

FIGURE 3.15 *Checklist for observations.*

PROBLEM-SOLVING STRATEGIES USED	JUAN	TUSHAN
1. Estimation and Check	√	
2. Drawing Pictures, Graphs, and Tables		
3. Elimination of Extraneous Data		√
4. Simplifying the Problem		
5. Developing Formulas and Writing Equations		
6. Looking for Patterns		√
7. Modeling		
8. Flowcharting		
9. Working Backwards	√	
10. Acting Out the Problem		
11. Insufficient Information		

FIGURE 3.16   *Problem-solving checklist.*

students to use drawings, illustrations, manipulatives, or models in addition to oral discourse to explain their thinking.

Diagnostic Interview Technique   Mathematical achievement improves as teachers understand students' misconceptions about mathematics and move to remediate the problems before they become too ingrained in a student's thought. The diagnostic interview technique has proven helpful in assessing problem areas. The teacher observes a student's thought process through questioning to learn the degrees of understanding or misconception of a mathematical concept or principle. Interviews may occur individually or in a group. It is recommended that teachers tape the interviews to improve their questioning techniques over time. Audiotapes or videotapes work well as long as they do not distract students from sharing their thoughts. The wait time between teacher question and student responses may require adjustment to meet the individual or group needs. There is no one ideal wait time, but it is widely known that most teachers wait only a second or two between responses. That is definitely not long enough. Teachers must remember that they are not correcting student misconceptions at this point; they are learning what the misconceptions are.

Discouraging the "Parroting" Responses of Students
Students frequently give an explanation back to the teacher just as the teacher has worded it in a teaching session. Many teachers use phrases to get students to verify their answers such as:

"How do you know that?" "Is there another way to get the answer?"

"How would you explain that answer to *a third grader?*" (supply the grade level just below the student's grade level). The authors have found that this phrasing has helped many students who are not precise enough in their explanations without this wording.

Asking Students to Justify Their Answers   Students may answer an example correctly but have no idea what the reasoning is behind it, and some students can reason correctly but still come up with erroneous answers. Sometimes they have trouble with both. Students should be asked to prove that their reason or their answer is the correct one.

Keeping a Student Elaborating on a Procedure or Reason   Teachers must remain noncommittal and nonjudgmental if they are to learn what students really think. Enough encouragement should be provided without implying that the student explanation is correct or incorrect.

Use phrases like: "Keep going"   "I'm listening"
Rather than: "Okay"   "Good"
                 "Tell me more"
                 "All right"

Words like okay, good, and all right imply that the answers are correct. These responses should be avoided because a teacher does not want to imply that a wrong answer is correct when it will need to be retaught later, possibly confusing the student even more. Teachers should not interrupt the child nor begin to teach the correct way of doing the problem no matter how tempting it may be.

When a teacher moves from the role of assessor to the role of teacher, it is helpful to use the pupil-teacher elaborating technique demonstrated under the preceding "questioning" section. It guides the student to correct responses without negating the work a student has done in the interview session. A list of Interview Do's and Don'ts is found on the Web site under Chapter 3.

Student Self-Assessment   Although self-assessment is a common activity in which we all frequently engage, many students would not list it as an aspect of mathematics assessment. However, the new focus on assessment encourages students to learn about themselves as a mathematics student. When selecting pieces for a student portfolio, many teachers ask students to include a piece of work that illustrates their best work and select one that represents the work needing the most improvement. Encouraging students to write about what they know about mathematics is another aspect of self-assessment.

Self-evaluation places the responsibility of learning on the student. It also involves turning a critical eye on one's own mathematical knowledge, feelings of confidence, and attitudes toward mathematics. Some teachers ask students to predict the mathematics grade they should get from an assignment or on a project. According to research, self-assessment is associated with less math anxiety and an increase in understanding mathematics content (Heuser, 2000). Both self-assessment and self-evaluation occur simultaneously. An example of a self-assessment sheet for elementary and middle school students is shown as a part of the following section on math journals.

Math Journals and Diaries   The NCTM *Principles and Standards for School Mathematics* (2000) advocate the use of "written discourse" by asking students to explain in writing the rationale for the choices they make, thereby gaining insight into how students are thinking about mathematics (Pugalee, 2001). When states or provinces use student written explanations of mathematics in their high-stakes testing, written discourse becomes a routine part of grade level lessons. Math journals need to be constructed carefully to elicit quality responses. Two journal forms are presented side by side to show the work of the same teacher candidate. The first journal form (Figure 3.17) does NOT challenge the way the writer is thinking. It shows only categories for self-evaluation. The second journal form (Figure 3.18) adds the wording of the higher-level performance-based ladder (seen in Figure 3.12). It serves two purposes: (1) a guide for self-reflection leading to (2) a self-evaluation score. The teacher candidate was given no instruction in circumference between settings. The only difference was the change in journal format. The candidate moves from blaming the instructor for creating an insufficient task to a quality answer by following the higher-ordered performance cues.

Student with Special Needs   Figure 3.19 shows a sixth grade student doing the same task. The student has been diagnosed with a developmental delay in small muscle development affecting his handwriting ability. Notice it does not stop the child's ability to think clearly and remember an earlier mathematics lesson based on *pi*. The student even remembers how to spell *pi* which cannot be said for the teacher candidate! Teachers must be careful when working with students with special needs not to let the visual appearance of the paper distract from the quality of thought. A copy of the journal form is included for download on the Web site in Appendix B for your use with students in your teaching experiences.

The quality of writing may also be graded as a part of writing across the curriculum (Whitin and Whitin, 2004). Mathematics "quick writes" are one way to start students on the math writing process with performance-based tasks. The tasks are short and explanations do not need to be long or involved. A list of possible activities for quick writes can be seen in Activity 3.4.

Some classroom groups keep mathematics diaries. A diary is defined as a running record of how a student solves mathematics problems. Diaries may be written by the student or stated orally, called oral discourse (NCTM, 2000). Oral responses are recorded for the record by an aide or teacher. Progress is evaluated by comparing reasoning from project to project over an extended period of time. The two math journals (Figures 3.17 and 3.18) could have functioned as math diaries for the purpose of comparing reasoning ability over time.

Student Portfolios   Portfolios are common in art or writing to show a record of one's work, but now portfolios are being used in many mathematics classes to show student progress. In the past, teachers have kept folders of students' work, but a portfolio represents a large collection of materials, papers, projects, pictures, copies of group reports, reports of student investigations, and math journal writings. The collection often is a year-long reflection of one's work. Student portfolios can provide evidence of performance tasks that illustrate conceptual understanding. They also can represent a record of student reflections, feelings, and self-assessments.

Portfolios offer a powerful tool for communicating to students and parents what is valued as important information about students' mathematical endeavors. Teachers should develop a purpose for their use that considers the function served, intended audience, and demonstrated competencies. Some guidelines to consider for developing portfolios are found on the Web site under Chapter 3. The portfolio should signify a vision of mathematics that goes beyond the right answer and should emphasize worthwhile mathematical tasks in a supportive learning environment.

Multimedia technology provides an effective way to collect information for portfolio assessments. Large amounts of information can be added to or retrieved easily and managed efficiently. Students can type their reflections using

General Criteria: Circle where you think you are after solving the problem.

4+	Advanced	•I did this perfectly. I was AWESOME!
4	Proficiency	•I was almost perfect.
③	Nearing Proficiency	•I knew what I was doing ~~but I forgot a few things.~~ *I was not given correct information to solve problem*
2	Progressing	•I thought I knew what I was doing, but I forgot a lot of things.
1	Starting	•I started but I got lost quickly.

Kind of Problem: ☐ Open-ended ☒ Discovery ☐ Guided Discovery
I made up a new problem   I found a way to solve   I followed the clues

I used the following problem solving strategies:

_____ 1. Estimation and Check   _____ 5. Modeling   _____ 9. Simplifying the Problem
_____ 2. Developing Formulas and Writing Equations _____ 6. Flowcharting   _____10. Acting out the Problem
_____ 3. Drawing Pictures, Graphs, and Tables   _____ 7. Working Backwards   _____11. Looking for Patterns
_____ 4. Elimination of Extraneous Data   ☒ 8. Insuf cient Information

Work the problem (showing all your work)

Today's Problem:

In the length of the larger half-circle longer (along the circumference), shorter, or equal to the sum of the lengths of the three other half-circles? Tell how you answered the question. What was the reasoning you used?

Draw or visualize how to work the problem:

If given some string or a radius or diameter, you could work this problem but there is lack of information needed to do this problem.

It appears to be the same but it could be different.

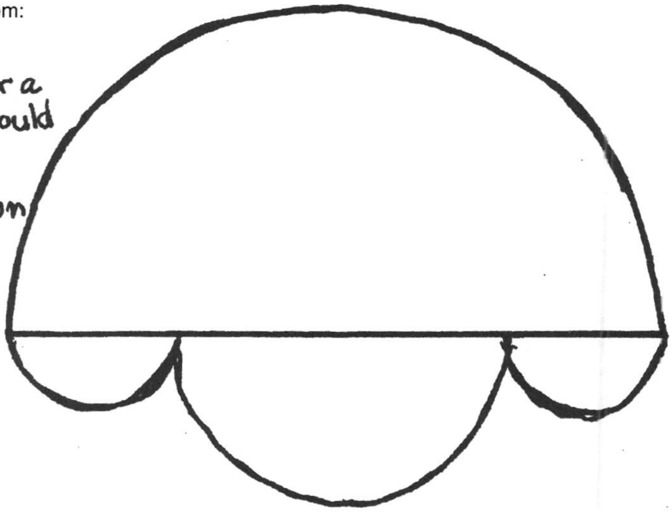

Journal Entry:
Defend your answer. How did you know it is correct? How would you explain this to a sixth grader?

I just knew there was not enough information.

FIGURE 3.17 *Student scoring guide, first response of teacher candidate.*

hypertext electronic notebooks, and teachers can review the work to determine interests, understandings, and skills. The reduced paperwork and easy retrieval are important benefits. Students' work can be scanned directly into the portfolio and digitized photos and video can be included. Portfolios have gained popularity to the point of becoming part of some school districts' school improvement plans in statewide assessment programs. As it becomes easier to press one's own

General Criteria: Circle where you think you are after solving the problem

4+	Advanced	•I **created** a new way to look at this problem. I showed you **how and why** it relates to the other things that are known about this topic. I told you **how** this ts with the other things I am learning about mathematics.
(4)	Proficiency	•I showed you **how** I did this problem, and I told you **how it related** to the other ways I saw to do the problem. I justi ed what I did by using speci c examples.
3	Nearing Proficiency	•I listed several things I did. I told you **what** I did with each of them.
2	Progressing	•I could name only one thing to do, and I told you **what** I did.
1	Starting	•I started but I **got lost** quickly. I could not gure out what I should do next.

Kind of Problem: ☐ Open-ended   ☒ Discovery   ☐ Guided Discovery
         I made up a new problem   I found a way to solve   I followed the clues

I used the following problem solving strategies:

_____ 1. Estimation and Check	_____ 5. Modeling
_X_ 2. Developing Formulas and Writing Equations	_____ 6. Flowcharting
_X_ 3. Drawing Pictures, Graphs, and Tables	_____ 7. Working Backwards
_X_ 4. Elimination of Extraneous Data	_____ 8. Insuf cient Information

         _____ 9. Simplifying the Problem
         _____ 10. Acting out the Problem
         _X_ 11. Looking for Patterns

===

Work the problem (showing all your work)

Today's Problem:

In the length of the larger half-circle longer (along the circumference), shorter, or equal to the sum of the lengths of the three other half-circles? Tell how you answered the question. What was the reasoning you used?

Draw or visualize how to work the problem:

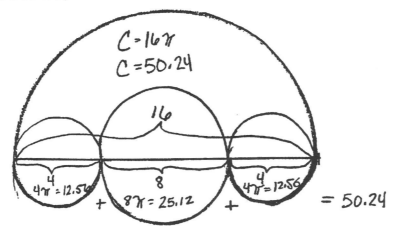

Journal Entry:

Defend your answer. How did you know it is correct? How would you explain this to a sixth grader?

I first made up a diameter for the larger circle. I gave it a value of 16. I then noticed that the three circles lined up and took up the same amount of space at the diameter of the larger circle. I made the diameter of the smaller circles equal 16 when added together I then took the individual diameter of each circle and multiplied it times pic. I added the 3 products of the 3 smaller circles together and compared them to the product of the large circle.

FIGURE 3.18 *Student scoring guide, second response of teacher candidate.*

General Criteria: Circle where you think you are after solving the problem

4+	Advanced	•I **created** a new way to look at this problem. I showed you **how and why** it relates to the other things that are known about this topic. I told you **how** this ts with the other things I am learning about mathematics.
4	Proficiency	•I showed you **how** I did this problem, and I told you **how it related** to the other ways I saw to do the problem. I justi ed what I did by using speci c examples.
3	Nearing Proficiency	•I listed several things I did. I told you **what** I did with each of them.
2	Progressing	•I could name only one thing to do, and I told you **what** I did.
1	Starting	•I started but I **got lost** quickly. I could not gure out what I should do next.

Kind of Problem: ☒ Open-ended (I made up a new problem) ☐ Discovery (I found a way to solve) ☐ Guided Discovery (I followed the clues)

I used the following problem solving strategies:

____ 1. Estimation and Check
____ 2. Developing Formulas and Writing Equations
____ 3. Drawing Pictures, Graphs, and Tables
____ 4. Elimination of Extraneous Data
____ 5. Modeling
____ 6. Flowcharting
____ 7. Working Backwards
____ 8. Insuf cient Information
_X_ 9. Simplifying the Problem (I gave numbers)
____10. Acting out the Problem
_X_ 11. Looking for Patterns

Work the problem (showing all your work)

Today's Problem:

In the length of the larger half-circle longer (along the circumference), shorter, or equal to the sum of the lengths of the three other half-circles? Tell how you answered the question. What was the reasoning you used?

Answer

Draw or visualize how to work the problem:

I learned about pi at pi day last year so I showed you how it fits

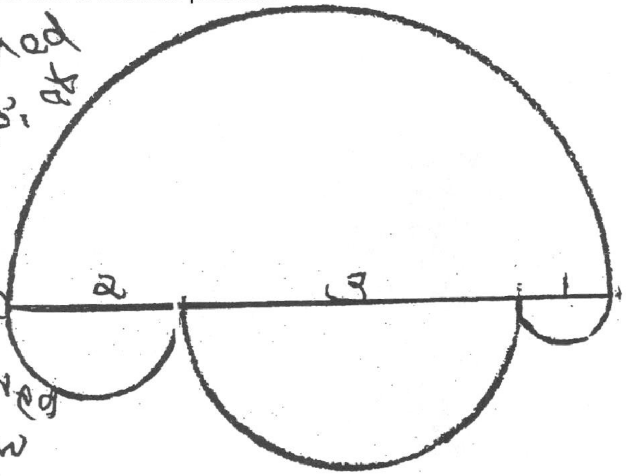

as the others added together

Journal Entry:

Defend your answer. How did you know it is correct? How would you explain this to a sixth grader?

I know 3.14 is always the same & the only thing that changes is the diameter number, since the 3 small diameters add up to the big diameter, the larger circumference is the same.

FIGURE 3.19 *Student scoring guide, response of student with special needs.*

Activity 3.4

MANIPULATIVES **PROBLEM SOLVING** **SHOW YOU KNOW HOW**

In a newspaper or magazine, find pictures that have examples of similarity and congruence (or rectangular solids, and so on).

Draw a picture to show how you can make regions that are partitioned equally.

Make a spinner to show that the probability of getting red is twice that of getting blue and the probability of getting yellow is half of that of getting blue.

Make a paper triangle that shows the different lines of symmetry—the medians.

With the blocks, show me the difference between addition and subtraction.

With a paper circle, show how it can be folded into a square, an octagon, and a triangle.

student companion Web site in the classroom, portfolios may be used by more school districts in the future.

Creating and Scoring Performance-Based Assessments

Alternative ways to grade students' work become necessary when using performance-based assessment systems. Some assessments will need to be created by the teacher although more assessment tasks are being published every year. Performance assessment and open-ended tasks must be relevant to the child's world to take on the claim of being "authentic assessments." For example, to ask children in inner-city schools to imagine going on a vacation to Disney World and calculating cost, mileage, meals and tips, amusement ride costs, and so on, may not be appropriate, meaningful tasks for these children. When constructing performance tasks, ask the question, "Is this task using a contrived context?" Issues of diversity, gender, socioeconomic levels, appropriate language and context, and interest level should be given attention. Getting students to communicate and explain their thinking requires a great deal of sensitivity on the teacher's part. Teachers must remain vigilant to choose the tasks most relevant to students' past experiences as possible.

Creating One's Own Assessment Tasks

Teachers report that it is not easy to write quality assessment tasks. It is helpful to have a model of successful ones from experienced teachers. The Web site contains over 30 portfolio assessments for your use; they appear at the end of each content chapter. Each assessment has been used successfully with students from low to high socioeconomic levels. The assessments range from kindergarten to grade eight and contain samples of actual student responses. They are labeled "Portfolio Assessments" because they make excellent teaching activities for teacher portfolios. Try several of the assessments with your own classes and include them in your professional portfolio. For more practice, Moskal (2000) and Stylianou et al. (2000) show the work of multiple students doing the same task at varying levels of understanding. This will give you practice in analyzing student thought. Once you have seen the format and tried several assessments with real students, you will be more ready to write your own assessment pieces. School officials want to hire teachers who have had experience teaching, creating, and scoring student performance assessments.

Using Scoring Guides (Rubrics)

The term associated with scoring of assessment tasks is "rubric" or "scoring guide." Rubrics must come from the qualities desired in the task. Teachers find themselves creating the scoring guides for the assessments they have written. Two methods that are commonly used are analytic and holistic. In analytic scoring, specific points are identified in detail. Points are given if the student's response includes that particular point. The Taxman Game shows how a three-point rubric can be used with specific criteria to score the assessment.

Activity 3.5

PROBLEM SOLVING **TAXMAN GAME**

The game of Taxman is a number game played with you and the Taxman. Every time it is your turn, you can take any number in the list, as long as at least some factors of that number are also in the list. You get your number, and the Taxman gets all of the factors of that number.

Play several games of Taxman with these ten numbers.

1   2   3   4   5   6   7   8   9   10

Make a record of your best game. Be sure to show which numbers you took and the order in which you took them, not just the final score.

Then answer the following questions:

Did you beat the Taxman?_____

What number did you choose first?_____Why?

Do you think anyone could ever play a better game than your best game?_____. Explain why or why not.

Suppose you were going to play Taxman with whole numbers from 1 to 95.

What number would you choose first?_____Why?

Source: Mathematical Sciences Education Board, 1993, p. 107.

PROTORUBRIC FOR SCORING TAXMAN

Characteristics of the High Response:
- The high-level response is one that demonstrates an optional game, communicates it effectively, and generally shows an understanding of choosing the largest available prime as the best first move.

Characteristics of the Medium Response:
- A winning game is described, although it need not be an optimal one.
- The first number chosen is justified simply on the basis that it works out to be a winning first move.
- A correct answer, with some justification. (Of course, this response will have to depend on the best game that the students can find. If a less-than-optimal game is described, then an answer of yes is correct here.)

Characteristics of the Low Response:
- Some game is described, but sketchily and perhaps ambiguously (that is, it may not be possible to tell in what order the numbers were selected.)
- No justification is provided for the first number chosen, or the justification does not take into account the factors of the number.

Source: Mathematical Sciences Education Board, 1993, p. 107, 113–114.

Holistic scoring means that the entire response is considered and assigned a point. This scoring method allows the teacher to make more subjective decisions about the student's thinking. An example of a holistic scoring guide is shown in Figure 3.20 (Krulik and Rudnick, 2001). The advantage of holistic scoring is that it is quicker. This technique is used in large-scale assessments when an overall

3	The student accomplishes the purpose of the question or task. Understanding of the mathematics in the task is demonstrated and the student is able to communicate his reasoning.
2	The student partially accomplishes the purpose of the question or task. Understanding of the mathematics may not be complete *or* the student may not be able to communicate his reasoning adequately.
1	The student is not able to accomplish the purpose of the question or task. Understanding of the mathematics is fragmented and the communication is vague or incomplete.

FIGURE 3.20 *Holistic scoring guide.*
Source: Krulik and Rudnick (2001).

judgment of performance is needed, and it is easier to get consistency among assessors with holistic scoring. The Piagetian and Vygotsky assessments seen earlier in the chapter will give you a chance to score students on the holistic scoring guide.

Some teachers may want the benefit of one instrument to do both analytic and holistic scoring. Such a rubric is shown in Figure 3.21. It allows the teacher to write specific criteria (analytic) for any performance-based task on the same form while being used as a holistic guide for quick assessment.

EXTENDED ACTIVITIES

CALCULATORS   MANIPULATIVES   PROBLEM SOLVING   MATHEMATICAL CONNECTIONS

On the student companion Web site (Chapter 3, Extended Activities), read/do the following:

- Interview Dos and Don'ts
- Create a Graph
- Hidden Digits
- Use Questioning Skills with Student Assessments
- Student Portfolio Guidelines

LEVEL	GENERAL CRITERIA	SPECIFIC CRITERIA (CHOSEN BY THE TEACHER)
4 + Advanced	• Shows understanding of concepts • Reasoning pattern is consistent and well structured • Gives clear explanations • Allows for more than one approach or solution • Performs the task with accuracy • Goes beyond the requirements of the task	
4 Proficient	• Shows understanding of concepts • Reasoning pattern is consistent and well structured • Gives clear explanations • Allows for more than one approach or solution	
3 Near Proficiency	• Shows understanding of concepts • Reasoning pattern is consistent and well structured • Gives clear explanations	
2 Progressing	• Shows understanding of concepts • Reasoning pattern is consistent	
1 Starting	• Shows some understanding of concepts • Little if any reasoning pattern	

Comments on Student Growth: _____

FIGURE 3.21 *Generic scoring guide for performance-based assessments.*

You can practice using this rubric with the student work in the Web site portfolio assessments found throughout the chapters. At the end of each assessment you will be able to compare your scores with the teacher who used the task in her classroom.

This section has attempted to show the many facets of the assessment—the why, what, who, when, where, and how assessment is accomplished in today's schools. The work of teachers has expanded to respond to the demand for developing quality student mathematical thought. At the same time, researchers are continuing to understand more about how children learn. A teacher needs to use both assessment and learning research tools together.

PLANNING AND EXECUTING EFFECTIVE INSTRUCTION TO DEVELOP MATHEMATICAL PROFICIENCY

Classroom instruction can be structured so that students attain a greater understanding of mathematics, using the ideas and concepts featured in the previous sections of this chapter. However, one key factor is still missing! If one does not understand the mathematical concepts to be taught, all the knowledge of brain research, learning theories, and assessment techniques will not be sufficient to enable students to develop mathematical proficiency. *Mathematical proficiency* is defined as the mathematical knowledge, skills, and confidence needed to succeed in the twenty-first century world. Recent research from the National Research Council (Kilpatrick and Swafford, 2002) and other research reports (Ma and Kessel 2001; Ma, 1999) point to the fact that U.S. teachers in elementary schools do not always have a depth of understanding about the mathematics they are teaching. The definitive work of the National Research Council, *Adding It Up* (Kilpatrick, Swafford, and Findell, 2001), suggests that all students can achieve success in mathematics if teachers learn to interweave five strands of mathematical proficiency in their lessons. The five strands will also help teachers gain mathematical proficiency themselves, thereby strengthening their own depth of mathematical understanding. The five strands, their technical

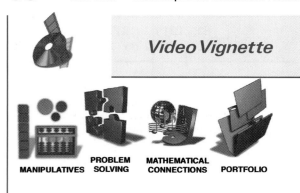

MANIPULATIVES PROBLEM SOLVING MATHEMATICAL CONNECTIONS PORTFOLIO

How Do I Know What My Students Understand?

DIRECTIONS

After viewing the video, answer these questions:

- In what ways did Mrs. Castenda say she assesses students?

- What ways were shown in the actual classroom with students?

- Which scoring guides in this chapter could be adapted for use in scoring the kinds of work shown by the students in Mrs. Castenda's class? Justify your choices by telling why each guide would be good to use.

terms, and definitions appear in Table 3.2 and are adapted from *Helping Children Learn Mathematics* (Kilpatrick and Swafford, 2002, p. 9).

Not every lesson lends itself to use all five strands, but lessons should not be planned without a conscious effort to interweave several strands together within a lesson.

Lesson Plans to Develop Mathematical Proficiency

The lesson plan forms used in this text have been created to include the major ideas of active learn-ing and assessment along with the five strands to promote mathematical proficiency. When novices first create lessons, it is recommended that the form be followed, including all segments of the plan. It is recognized that not all areas will be suited for every lesson, but even experienced tea-chers should review lessons at the end of each week to see if all areas have been covered over the week of instruction. Without a self-check, tea-chers may find they are leaving out important seg-ments over time, denying students the change to grow in their full understanding of mathematics. Figure 3.22 shows the lesson plan form.

There is a blank form like the one in Figure 3.22 that can be printed from Appendix B on the student companion Web site to help you plan your own classroom instruction. The major points of this chapter can be seen in the lesson plan. There is a completed lesson plan on the Web site for this chapter, called "Sample Lesson Plan for Mathe-tical Proficiency." There are other sample lesson plans throughout the content chapters so you can see how teachers have planned with use of this format in real classrooms.

A Research Base for Quality Lesson Plan-ning The lesson plan format is adapted from the extensive research that followed the results of TIMSS (Ma and Kessel, 2001, 1999; Kilpatrick and Swafford, 2002). TIMSS researchers studied Japa-nese classrooms because Japan was a high scoring country on the international tests. The researchers found that Japanese classrooms are structured to emphasize reasoning, problem solving, using representations meaningfully and on communi-cating mathematically first by the student alone, then in a small group, and then in the total class. When performance tasks follow this format, they are sometime referred to as TIMSS performance-based tasks in the research literature.

The same points have been advocated by the NCTM *Principles and Standards for School Mathe-matics* (2000) and complement the work being done with the five strands of mathematical profi-ciency. Many of the state assessment tests require more constructed responses and journal explana-tions. The mathematical proficiency format devel-ops the same things being tested in many of the state examinations. At the end of this chapter, on the student companion Web site, and where appropriate throughout the text, you will be shown lesson activities and portfolio assessments of actual students' work so you can sharpen your skills at trying to write and teach mathematics lessons using the five strands of mathematical proficiency. An example of student work is seen

TABLE 3.2	The Five Strands of Mathematical Proficiency	
NAME OF STRAND	**TECHNICAL TERM**	**DEFINITION**
Understanding	Conceptual Understanding	Comprehending mathematical concepts, operations, and relations—knowing what mathematical symbols, diagrams, and procedures mean.
Computing	Procedural Fluency	Carrying out mathematical procedures, such as adding, subtracting, multiplying, and dividing numbers flexibly, accurately, efficiently, and appropriately.
Applying	Strategic Competence	Being able to formulate problems mathematically and to devise strategies for solving them using concepts and procedures appropriately.
Reasoning	Adaptive Reasoning	Using logic to explain and justify a solution to a problem or to extend from something known to something not yet known.
Engaging	Productive Disposition	Seeing mathematics as sensible, useful, and doable—if you work at it—and being willing to do the work.

in the performance-based task, "Laura's Dinner," on the Web site. It shows a connection to children's literature and was written by a classroom teacher in response to the low scores of U.S. students seen in the international test (TIMSS). The task allows for depth of thought and open-ended discussion in small groups before a presentation of each group's chosen recipe to the whole class. The scoring guide and the work of three students are included, The book is one from Laura Ingalls Wilder's *Little House* series.

Teachers constructing alternative performance assessments have reported a rise in the state assessment scores dealing with math problem solving after using the approach for only half a year (Sharp and Ingram, 1998). The TIMSS research showed that the U.S. curriculum spent more time on overpracticing procedures and focusing on little topics before students understood how and why they related to the big picture of mathematics. What little topics should be eliminated in the elementary/middle school curriculum? What would you give up if you had to? Look for journal articles and research studies that deal with this issue. There will be many opinions. No one knows for sure what topics will remain in the curriculum by the end of this decade, but one would predict there will be a greater focus on the big picture of mathematics.

Lesson Study Using the Video Vignettes: Actual Teachers in Classrooms *Lesson Study* is a new term involving quality teacher reflection to be done with colleagues after one teaches a mathe-

matics lesson (Yoshida, 2002). This approach is common practice in Japan; unfortunately in the United States, teachers are not given the planning time to visit daily with their colleagues for structured, high-level thinking about their teaching. School districts are beginning to see academic benefits to the lesson study reflection approach (Freiberg, 2002; Glickman, 2002), and many districts are beginning to find time for such discussions at least some time during the week, if not daily. College courses make excellent lesson study arenas because preservice and graduate teachers learn from this new approach. If the course does not have an in-school component from which to judge one's own teaching, it is possible to watch videos of quality mathematics teachers provided on the Web site that accompanies this text. A structured lesson study guide was developed for the Video Vignettes and is shown in Table 3.3. It is possible to use the guide on your own if class time is not available for the lesson study approach. The guide's detailed questions will lead you through the analysis of quality mathematics learning seen in the videos. The same format is used for all the video vignettes on the Web site.

Use the Lesson Study Guide for Video Vignettes as you do A Lesson Study on "Candy Sales." Which of the five strands of mathematical proficiency to you see in the lesson?

Homework in Light of the New Approaches to Instruction If classroom instruction is changing, it stands to reason that homework assignments are changing also. The general rule is never to send

Lesson Topic: _____ Grade Level: _____ Date: _____

Multicultural Emphasis (if applicable; what culture(s) first introduced the concepts?): _____

Ancestors of the _____ group(s) in our world today.

Conceptual Understanding Outcomes (Objectives) (tell what concepts, operations, and relations need to be stressed; tell what symbols, diagrams, and procedures mean just as you will explain them to students).

Standards Emphasized (what do you want students to learn?):

State standards: _____

Local standards: _____

National NCTM standards: _____

Assessment (how will you and they know they are learning? what are your standards for success?)

Scoring Guide

Teacher States Criteria (how flexible, accurate, efficient, and appropriate)

4+ Advanced: _____

4 Proficient: _____

3 Nearing proficiency: _____

2 Progressing: _____

1 Starting: _____

Planning the Active-Learning, Performance-Based Task:

List what concrete manipulatives are needed: _____

_____

_____

How does this task apply to concrete experiences in the real world? _____

_____

_____

Procedural fluency—tell which kinds of addition, subtraction, multiplication, and/or division are needed: _____

_____

Strategic competence—check which of the following problem-solving strategies can be used to solve the performance-based task:

_____ 1. Estimation and check

_____ 2. Developing formulas and writing equations

_____ 3. Drawing pictures, graphs, and tables

_____ 4. Elimination of extraneous data

_____ 5. Modeling

_____ 6. Flowcharting

_____ 7. Working backwards

_____ 8. Insufficient information

_____ 9. Simplifying the problem

_____ 10. Acting out the problem

_____ 11. Looking for patterns

Learning processes—tell how the task can be completed using:

Field-dependent by _____

_____

Field-independent by _____

_____

Gardener's multiple intelligences—state which ones and how they should be applied to the task (not all eight intelligences have to be used):

_____ 1. Logical-mathematical by _____

_____ 2. Linguistic by _____

_____ 3. Bodily-kinesthetic by _____

_____ 4. Spatial by _____

_____ 5. Musical by _____

_____ 6. Naturalist by _____

_____ 7. Intrapersonal by _____

_____ 8. Interpersonal by _____

FIGURE 3.22 *Lesson plan form to develop mathematical proficiency.*

Executing the Lesson Procedure:

- **Anticipatory set by teacher** (what will you say or do to capture students' interest?)

- **Teacher gives performance-based task and directions to students** (read task to younger children; write task and directions for older students): (ATTACH TASK TO LESSON PLAN)

- **Students work alone and/or in small groups** (what are the student responses you expect to see? note **how** they are actually solving the problem as you walk around observing):   Estimated time needed: _____

- **Adaptive reasoning:**   Estimated time needed: _____

   1. Students decide which solution(s) they will present to the class and **how** they will explain the solution(s).

   2. Students decide who is responsible for which part of presentation to the whole class. (If in groups, everyone has a part.)

- **Productive disposition:**

   Students report to the whole class (list teacher questions and elaborating techniques (be ready to use techniques if students do not see concepts):   Estimated time needed: _____

- **Closure** — class decisions on the *best* answers.

Appropriate Technology for This Lesson: _____

Lesson Evaluation — **After the Lesson Has Been Presented:**

- **Report of assessment results** (How do you know you had a positive effect on student learning? What did you see and hear?):

   _____
   _____
   _____

- **Scoring guide results** (How many?):   4+ _____   4 _____   3 _____   2 _____   1 _____

- **Students with special needs** (if needed; How did you adapt the lesson for students with special needs?):

   _____
   _____
   _____
   _____

- **Student reactions:**

   _____
   _____
   _____
   _____

- **The best parts of this lesson:**

   _____
   _____
   _____
   _____

- **Steps I would change should I teach this lesson again:**

   _____
   _____
   _____

FIGURE 3.22 *Lesson plan form to develop mathematical proficiency (Continued).*

TABLE 3.3	Lesson Study Guide for Video Vignettes

This is an example of a lesson plan to use for analyzing the vignettes based on the NCTM *Principles and Standards for School Mathematics* (2000).

Tasks

Tasks are the projects, problems, questions, applications, and exercises in which students are engaged. Worthwhile mathematical tasks are those that encourage students to develop their understandings, skills, and conceptual development. Such tasks have alternative solutions strategies, fuel students' curiosity, facilitate classroom discourse, and help make sense of the mathematics course. Think about the task in the vignette:

- How does the teacher encourage students to analyze important mathematical ideas?
- Do the tasks nurture mathematical thinking and make connections with past experiences?
- Do they provide for a diverse range of student learning and encourage all students to participate?
- Do the tasks fit into a coherent curriculum?

Discourse

Discourse refers to the ways of representing, thinking, talking, agreeing, or disagreeing about mathematics. The nature of discourse is to provide insight into mathematics thinking that teachers can use to make decisions about curriculum and purposeful teaching.

Think about the discourse in the vignette:

- How does the teacher use discourse to engage students in mathematical ideas?
- How does the teacher use discourse as a tool to generate legitimate mathematical reasoning?
- Does the discourse build mathematical confidence and allow for an exchange of ideas?
- In what ways does the teacher orchestrate discussions and balance knowing when to ask, tell, and redirect the discourse?

Learning Environment

The learning environment is the context in which the tasks and discourse are embedded. It represents the setting for learning and shapes the ways of knowing what is expected in the mathematics classroom. Think about the learning environment in the vignette:

- How does the learning environment engage students to build new understanding, refine their thinking, and develop confidence in their abilities?
- How does the environment provide for alternative ways of approaching tasks?
- How does the environment promote mathematical reasoning, communicating, and representations?
- How does the teacher use tasks and tools such as technology and engagement with concrete materials to support mathematics learning?

material home that has not been taught at school. Teachers cannot expect parents or guardians to do the teaching. If mathematical procedures are to be practiced, it should be for short amounts of time (20 minutes or so) without the need for parental instruction. Parents ARE encouraged to take an active interest in their children's work in the thought development and explorations that are possible as children study mathematics. Increased parental involvement is one of the goals for the twenty-first century. Family math has become a major theme in some school districts. Children, along with their parents or guardians, can work on math projects started at school and finished with the family at home. Some districts even have Saturday family math days where parents and children come to school to work on math projects together. One district has combined the reading of children's literature and the reinforcement of mathematics concepts by creating learning pack-

ets that parents or guardians can do in 20 to 30 minutes at night with their children. A series of these family math packets are available on the Student Companion Web Site where appropriate in the content chapters. The packets were created by preservice teachers in association with a local school district. The school is in an area of low socioeconomic resources so the books and games are appreciated as many letters from parents/guardians attest (Honeycutt, Edwards, and Hunt, 2001). Sixth graders manage the program, replenishing the packets upon their return to school.

The new innovations in mathematics homework activities require thinking skills that go far beyond the basic-fact drill and practice associated with the homework of yesteryear (Cooper, 2001). As you will see in chapter 7, basic facts are taught more as thinking strategies rather than speed drills. So even when basic facts are sent home for practice, they do not appear in drill form. Morrow

Video Vignette

PROBLEM SOLVING   **MATHEMATICAL CONNECTIONS**

Activity 3.6: A Lesson Study on "Candy Sales"

DIRECTIONS

1. View the video vignette, "Candy Sales," on the Web Site in Chapter 3.

2. After viewing the video, use the Lesson Study Guide for Video Vignettes in Table 3.3 in the text to stimulate a thoughtful discussion on the ideas presented in Chapter 3.

3. How many ideas from this chapter are being used in the video?

4. What evidence is there to talk about the student's productive disposition—a sense of enablement about mathematics?

5. Analyze the classroom environment in terms of the Learning Principle (NCTM, 2000).

Morrow and Harbin-Miles also include a form for a letter home to parents and a report on the activity to be filled out by the parent (1996, pp. 21–23). The form is available in the activity for you to download and use with the students in your own classroom.

Appropriate Use of Technology As noted in the lesson-planning model, technology questions should be a part of each lesson-planning situation. One may decide not to use technology in a lesson, but the question remains on the lesson plan form so teachers have to ask themselves if the lesson could be enhanced through technology—either WebQuests, computer interactive software, calculators, sketch pad, and so forth. If there has been no connection to technology for over a week's worth of lessons, it may be time to rethink one's approach to lessons. The ISTE Standards (2002) found at http://cnets.iste.org can help in planning quality use of technology in the classroom. The student companion Web site also includes many WebQuests for children to do in mathematics. They are highlighted throughout the text where appropriate in the content chapters.

EXTENDED ACTIVITIES

CALCULATORS   **COMPUTERS**   **MANIPULATIVES**

PROBLEM SOLVING   **MATHEMATICAL CONNECTIONS**   **PORTFOLIO**

On the Student Companion Web Site (Chapter 3, Extended Activities), read/do the following:

- The Black Hole of 3 and 6

- Performance Assessment Task—Laura's Dinner

- Sample Lesson Plan for Mathematical Proficiency

- Teacher Candidate's Assessment of Student Mathematical Proficiency

and Harbin-Miles (1996) have designed mathematics activities that give a challenge to children and permit communication between parent and child at the same time. The classroom activities are engaging and definitely model many worthwhile mathematical tasks. One example is included on the Companion Web Site, called "the Black Hole of 3 and 6." It shows how an activity started at school can become an assignment for enjoyment at home. At the end of the activity, the children's homework assignment is to share what they discovered with their parents or guardians.

A. Analyzed conceptual understanding in light of the problem difficulty:

POINTS	CRITERIA
_____ 1	Saw the basic problem through error pattern analysis.
_____ varies	Analyzed intricate component parts of what was known and unknown to the child.
_____ 1	Score given and justified using five-point scoring guide criteria (see Figure 3.21).

B. Adapted method of instruction:

POINTS	CRITERIA
_____ 2	Child's learning style identified and analyzed.
_____ 2	Approach changed to correct child's misconception; developmentally appropriate by age and individual.
_____ 2	Sample elementary textbook page shown (or sketched) and adapted to child's math needs.

C. Adapted manipulative materials:

POINTS	CRITERIA
_____ 2	Set up actual problem correctly with drawn manipulatives (level of difficulty like one example from child's worksheet).
_____ 3	Answered problem with correct moves of materials (shown in actual drawings).

D. Appropriateness of technology and procedural fluency:

POINTS	CRITERIA
_____ 4	Could justify which was appropriate to use, which was **not** appropriate, and why:

computer: _____ calculator: _____

mental math: _____ computational flexibility/fluency _____

E. Constructed a new learning plan:

POINTS	CRITERIA
_____ 2	Realistic beginning point for strategic competence (ability to form, represent, and solve problems).
_____ varies	Each component part handled from second criterion in **A** above. (Analyzed intricate component parts of what was known and unknown to the child.)
_____ 2	New task created with adaptive reasoning (student reflection, explanation, justification) included.
_____ 3	Steps in correct sequence (concrete experiences to iconic transitions to symbolic abstract).

Total Average Points _____

FIGURE 3.23 *Scoring guide for analysis of student work to develop mathematical proficiency.*

Evaluation of Student Work to Develop Mathematical Proficiency

Creating and teaching quality lessons do not ensure that every student will comprehend every concept at the desired depth of understanding. Student misconceptions can still emerge even with the best lessons. Therefore, effective instruction also involves the evaluation of student work when misconceptions have occurred for individual students. This involves the need to reteach concepts differently from the student's previous experience. The five-step thought procedure outlined in Figure 3.23 is one that stresses the five strands of mathematical proficiency as they relate to teacher analysis and reconstruction of learning for individual students.

The procedure has been used with more than one thousand preservice teachers as they have begun to analyze student work. Research has shown that doing this type of analysis and reconstruction of the mathematical learning three times with separate student work has a high correlation ($r = 0.91$) with teacher candidates' abilities to score well on the Praxis II™ elementary tests (Edwards, 2003). A sample of a teacher candidate's analysis of student work is on the companion Web site in Chapter 3, called "Teacher Candidate's Assessment of Student Mathematical Proficiency."

SUMMARY

This chapter has explored how teachers can use the knowledge of brain research and its matching learning theories to create mathematics lessons involving active learning opportunities for students, moving experiences from the concrete

through transitional modes to the symbolic/abstract knowledge of mathematics. The individual learning preferences of students make the teachers' lessons more diversified and challenging to create, but they also hold more promise to help all students understand mathematics at higher levels than students have in the past. When curriculum has been written with all those factors in mind, the students have achieved at higher levels than did the students in classrooms taught in a more traditional way (UCSMP, 2001, 2006). An effective teacher uses all theories wisely, coordinating the difficulty of the task with stages of cognitive development. We have seen why teachers need a better understanding of mathematical concepts themselves if they are to teach the bigger picture of mathematics to their students with the five strands of mathematical proficiency in mind.

Teachers have become diagnosticians to assess the thought development level of students as scored on a variety of rubrics through open-ended questioning, keen observations, and well-documented interviews. Because these assessments are ongoing and embedded in the mathematics curriculum, the teacher will use all of this information to continue creating more relevant, effective instruction. This is no small order! It calls for teachers who are intellectually aware and excited about learning themselves.

PRAXIS II™-STYLE QUESTIONS

Answers to this chapter's Praxis II™-style questions are in the instructor's manual.

Multiple-Choice Format

1. Which phrase(s) should be used to encourage quality student explanations?
   a. "How would you explain this to a first grader who doesn't understand it?"
   b. "Prove your answer is the correct one by doing the work again."
   c. "Reread the problem aloud to justify your answer."
   d. Both b and c

2. Here is a dialogue between a teacher (T) and a student (S) in the class:
   T: Mr. Smith delivers 840 pounds of office supplies to stores in the immediate area every month. How many pounds of office supplies does he deliver in a week?
   S: Gee, that's a big number to handle. There's 840 pounds added 4 times.
   T: Let's see . . . we only need to know about one week's office supplies.
   S: Oh, four weeks is too much. I only need to know about one week's worth.
   T: I wonder if a person in one week would need more or less supplies than 840 pounds.
   S: Okay . . . I would need less away for four times.

   T: So how could you figure out what to take away evenly for four times?
   S: I could divide 840 by 4 to get 210 for each week.

   THE TEACHER IS USING:
   a. the "parroting" technique
   b. the Baratta-Lorton "connecting level" technique
   c. the elaborating technique
   b. Both a and b

3. Using the work of the student in problem #2, what score would you give the student on the scoring rubric in Figure 3.21?
   The student should receive a score of_____

   a. 1 because she shows no ability to reason and is just guessing at the answer.
   b. 2 because she has a justified reason for her answer, but she is misled by looking only at one side of the parallelogram.
   c. 3 because she is partially correct; she just did not look at all the sides before answering.
   d. 4 because her answer is correct, showing understanding of area even though she did not refer to the figure by its more precise name of a parallelogram.

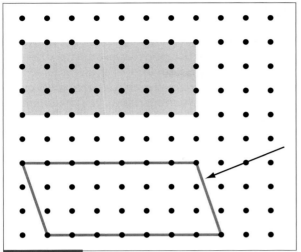

FIGURE 3.24 *Paper used with student response.*

4. A student was asked to tell what she observed about each figure on the sheet of paper seen in Figure 3.24.

   The student traced around both figures and then said, "The bottom figure has more area. You can tell because the side sticks out more right here (pointing to the side shown by the arrow in the picture below)." This student is in the _____ stage of Piagetian theory because the student is doing _____ .

   a. preoperations; actions on reality
   b. concrete operations; actions on operations
   c. formal operations; operations on operations
   c. sensorimotor; actions on objects

Constructed Response Format

5. Figure 3.25 shows is a student's work after studying the multiplication strategies for factors from 0 to 9. What numerical score would you give the student using the Krulik and Rudnick rubric (Figure 3.20)? Justify your answer.

6. What thought processing style might the student in #5 have? How could you redo the activity to more closely match the student's processing style?

7. Using the form (Figure 3.23), analyze the student work in #5 to develop greater math proficiency. List what is known by the student and what math concepts are still unknown to this student.

X	0	1	2	3	4	5	6	7	8	9
0	0	0	0	0	0	0	0	0	0	0
1	1	1	2	3	4	5	6	7	1	9
2	2	2	4	6	8	10	12	14	16	18
3	3	3	6	9	12	15	18	21	24	27
4	4	4	8	12	15	18	21	24	27	30
5	5	5	10	13	20	25	30	35	40	45
6	6	6	12	18	21	24	27	30	33	36
7	7	7	14	21	24	27	30	33	36	39
8	8	8	16	24	27	30	33	36	39	41
9	9	9	18	26	29	31	34	37	41	43

FIGURE 3.25 *Student's multiplication tables.*

Integrating Technology

Internet Activities

Scavenger Hunt
On the student companion Web site you will find several internet based scavenger hunts. "Measuring Up" was created by an elementary math methods students as an exploratory activity for her class.

Web sites

TIMSS Site
Go to the TIMMS site (**http://timss.bc.edu/TIMSS1/Items.html**) and review the information available there on assessment in other countries compared to the United States.

NAEP Sites
http://www.ed.gov/pubs/ncesprograms/assessment/surveys/naep.html
http://www.nces.ed.gov/nationsreportcard/itmrls/search.asp
Compare test questions and results from various grade levels and various states as you browse the sites.

Sample of State Site
Go to this example of a state site to help teachers prepare students for state assessment tests (**http://services.dese.state.mo.us/divimprove/assess/**). Analyze the types of questions on the performance-based tests.
Search for your own state or province to see if Web sites contain assessment information.

Interactive: Home Page
http://www.shodor.org/interactivate
Developed for middle school mathematics explorations but several are adaptable to elementary mathematics.

Middle School Mathematics

Middle school adolescents are extremely complex. In fact, the reasons why they act the way they do are often a mystery. I never thought that I'd enjoy teaching middle school because I thought the curriculum wouldn't be intellectually challenging. Wow, was I wrong. After three weeks in middle school, I realized that it wasn't the content that was challenging, but the methodology involved in teaching middle school learners that was complicated. And I quickly discovered that I enjoyed this aspect of middle school.

(Fantauzzo, 2002)

Perhaps, like Michael Fantauzzo—a secondary education major student teaching in a middle school—you question whether you would like to teach mathematics to middle school students. To help you answer that question, this chapter reviews some of the characteristics of middle school students, examines the type of mathematics program appropriate for the preparation of middle school teachers of mathematics, and introduces some of the current standards-based mathematics curricula for middle school. It is not the authors' intention to review the material presented in an adolescent psychology class but to highlight some of those psychological characteristics impacting middle school learners of mathematics.

MIDDLE SCHOOL STUDENTS

Middle school students are enthusiastic, energetic, curious, and idealistic. The physiological, emotional, and cognitive changes that occur as students enter adolescence make middle school an important transition period. Cognitively, middle school students' thinking ranges from concrete operational to formal operational, as defined in the work of Jean Piaget. Some mature early; others later. Peer influence is strong. This age group strives for independence and seeks opportunities to have more control over their lives as they find their identity within a social context. It is to their peers that they look for validation of their feelings about themselves. Their peers are also a source, although not the only source, of support as they develop their concept of self.

Middle school students want and need work—assignments, projects, tasks, and performances—that give them the opportunity to demonstrate and increase their sense of themselves as competent and successful students. For this to occur in the classroom, three conditions must exist (Strong et al., 1995):

- Students must know the criteria for success or the rubric for assessment, and they must receive clear, prompt, and constructive feedback.
- Students must know that they have the skills, or can acquire the skills, to successfully complete the work.
- Students must know that success is a valuable asset to their personalities.

Motivation

The type of stimulation provided by today's highly visual, fast-paced video games, combined with the fact that television is often used as a baby sitter, often results in students feeling lethargic or apathetic during school lessons. One of the most important skills for a teacher is the ability to motivate

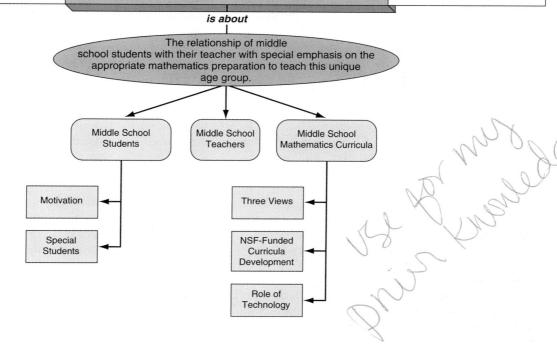

PREVIOUS CHAPTER	CURRENT CHAPTER	NEXT CHAPTER
The Development of Mathematical Proficiency: Using Learning Research, Assessment, Effective Instruction	Middle School Mathematics	Problem Solving

is about

The relationship of middle school students with their teacher with special emphasis on the appropriate mathematics preparation to teach this unique age group.

- Middle School Students
  - Motivation
  - Special Students
- Middle School Teachers
- Middle School Mathematics Curricula
  - Three Views
  - NSF-Funded Curricula Development
  - Role of Technology

SELF-HELP QUESTIONS

1. Can I describe the different theories about what motivates students to learn?
2. How can I use what is known about motivation of middle school students to help me plan interesting activities that increase the chances of mathematical success for all my students?
3. Can I describe the characteristics of the diferent types of special students in schools today?
4. What are some strategies I can use in teaching students with learning disabilities?
5. Which mathematics curriculum materials hold the most promise for teaching the deep ideas of mathematics within a context that will keep the attention of middle schoolers?
6. What mathematics preparation do I need to be a successful middle school teacher of mathematics?
7. What technology applications in mathematics are available that will "grab" the interest of middle school students?
8. How could I explain to parents the role of technology in middle school mathematics classes?

students to learn, to study, and to practice skills. You may already have learned in other classes that there are a number of different theories about motivation and the characteristics of motivation. You probably realize from your own experiences in classrooms that motivated students tend to spend more time on task, accomplish the work assigned, and enjoy learning, whereas unmotivated students tend to be off task, rarely do the work assigned or do it poorly, and do not enjoy learning, at least in the particular classroom setting. In this section, we review some motivation theories and some of the steps teachers can take to increase student motivation for learning mathematics.

Attribution Theory Experienced teachers often note that as students enter middle school, there seems to be a decline in motivation and performance for many students. Research indicates that students may persist in studying in an area such as mathematics if they believe they are unsuccessful because of factors they can control (e.g., a lack of necessary skills or poor study habits). Students who believe that their lack of success is due to factors beyond their control tend to see no hope for improvement and, thus, are unmotivated to study. If you have studied adolescent psychology, you will most likely recognize that this reflects a tenet of attribution theory. Simply put, in attribution theory of motivation, students will be motivated to continue studying mathematics, for instance, if they believe that they can improve through their own efforts. Students who believe that their lack of success is due to factors such as poor teaching or the mathematics being too hard or that "the teacher doesn't like me" will lose the motivation to study.

Goal Theory Another theory offered to explain students' motivation, or lack thereof, is known as goal theory. In goal theory, there are two primary goal orientations: task goals and ability goals. Students who establish task goals believe that personal achievement and progress in mastering skills and knowledge are the criteria for judging success. A task goal might be passing algebra or learning to create box-and-whisker graphs. On the contrary, students who rely on ability goals believe that success lies in appearing competent, usually in comparison to others. An example of an ability goal might be getting an "A" in algebra. Students who rely on a task goal orientation are better able to use effective learning strategies, are more willing to seek assistance, are more likely to undertake challenging work, and have more positive feelings about themselves as learners and about school (snowman and Biebler, 2006). Conversely, students who rely on an ability goal orientation are less likely to use effective learning strategies, are less likely to seek assistance, are less likely to take challenging courses, and have more negative feelings about themselves as learners and about school.

Self-Determination Theory The theory of self-determination as an explanation for students' motivation states that students have three types of needs: a need for a sense of competence, a need for a sense of relatedness to others, and a need for a sense of autonomy. Competence refers to knowing how to reach a certain goal or outcome and believing in one's ability to do so. Relatedness refers to developing satisfactory connections, or relationships, with others, particularly one's peers. Autonomy refers to the ability to initiate and regulate one's own actions. Most research in self-determination theory, particularly within the classroom, focuses on the need for a sense of autonomy (Armstrong, 2006). Factors that support a middle school student's growing need for autonomy include the ability to choose the type of task to engage in and to gauge the time needed for the task. Giving students the option of choosing one of several projects or assignments for demonstrating mastery of a skill or concept, or the option of working with a partner on a team of three or four classmates, or individually are ways the middle school teacher can support student autonomy without creating havoc in the classroom. Allowing such options in your mathematics classroom does not guarantee immediate and continuous success for students. It takes time and practice to develop good time-management skills and decision-making skills. Here your classroom management practices can support learning by limiting the number of options, providing guidelines or a timeline for completion of the steps in a project, and teaching students how to break a large task into a series of smaller tasks.

Intrinsic and Extrinsic Motivation Two other terms used to describe student motivation are intrinsic and extrinsic motivation. Briefly, intrinsic motivation describes those students who engage in learning out of curiosity, interest, or enjoyment, or to accomplish their own personal goals. These students do not need balloons or candy or other rewards. They will complete a task simply because it is challenging. In contrast, students who are extrinsically motivated will complete a task to receive a reward or to avoid a punishment. Such students rarely do more than the minimum amount of work or expend more than the minimum effort necessary to meet the goal or finish the work. They are more likely to be discouraged and to give up when they feel unsuccessful in comparison to their classmates (Brewster and Fager, 2000).

It should be noted that some researchers object to this categorization of student motivation as being too simplistic to adequately describe the many complex and interrelated factors that influence students' motivation to succeed in school. Most of us can probably identify times in our lives when we were extrinsically motivated and other times when we were intrinsically motivated.

Teacher's Role in Motivating Middle School Students Teachers' actions and attitudes can have a great influence on students' motivation to learn mathematics. Teachers who are knowledgeable about mathematics and are committed to the belief that all students can learn (see discussion of the equity principle in Chapter 1) are more successful in motivating students. Teachers can also help students develop increased motivation to learn by praising them for their substantial efforts *and the progress that results* from those efforts. Praise and/or rewards for completing work requiring little effort or for being "smart," or just arbitrarily praising students, do little, if anything, to motivate middle school students to learn.

Teachers must remember that although middle school students are moving toward formal operational thinking, they are still in the process of developing their thinking skills. One way to support middle school students in their development is to provide concrete examples before moving into abstract concepts such as those found in algebra. Here manipulatives—or models, as some prefer to call them at this level—can be helpful, and the students themselves can be part of the modeling. For instance, when studying linear equations and the role of the intercept, you can create an x–y axis outside on the school parking lot or on a grassy field and then have the students form the line $y = x + 2$. Then ask them to move one step to form the line $y = x + 3$. What changed? By how much? Repeat this with other equations such as $y = x$ or $y = x - 2$.

Teachers are essential in creating the classroom environment and tasks that assist middle school students in demonstrating that they are competent and successful. When assigning a project or assignment, clearly articulate the criteria for success—give students a copy of the rubric along with the assignment—or engage the students in helping to define the criteria. To help students with the skills they need for the particular task, teachers must model the skills. If the assignment is solving a nonroutine problem, such as the one in Activity 4.1, use a technique called "think-alouds." Talk with the class as you think about what the problem is asking you to do, what strategy you are going to use, why you chose that particular strategy, difficulties that you may encounter, other strategies that could be used, and finally, why your solution is reasonable. Have your students do the same type of think-aloud during small group discussions of the problem or as they share their solutions with the class. The problem in Activity 4.1 is called nonroutine because it is not solved using a standard algorithm such as addition or division. A model think-aloud can be found on the student companion Web site (Chapter 4, Think-Aloud).

Other Considerations If students in middle school are, in fact, enthusiastic, energetic, curious, and idealistic, then middle school is a great time to take advantage of alternative learning.

Activity 4.1

PROBLEM SOLVING

CHANGING A DOLLAR

PROBLEM

Determine how many different ways you can make change for a one dollar bill using coins in circulation today: pennies, nickels, dimes, quarters, half dollars, and dollars.

DIRECTIONS

1. Determine a strategy to use.
2. Spend the next five to ten minutes identifying and listing solutions.
3. Move to your assigned group and spend the next ten to fifteen minutes sharing your strategy and the solutions you have found to this point.
4. As a group, decide which strategy the group wants to use and continue working on solutions for another five to ten minutes.
5. Each group will present its reasoning and solution to the problem to the class.

Supporting the NCTM Standards (2000)
- Mathematics as Problem Solving, Communicating, Reasoning and Proof
- Worthwhile Mathematical Tasks for Teachers—The Teaching Principle

---

Where's the Mathematics?

1. What "knowledge packet" would middle school students need before they could solve this problem? To answer this question, consider the following questions:
   a. What is the topic, the primary mathematical concept, needed for this problem? This goes in the rectangle (see the sample knowledge packet in Figure 1.1).
   b. What are the key concepts, skills, and procedures students need to work with the topic identified in a? These go in the thick-bordered ovals.
   c. What are the basic principles related to this topic? These go in the rectangles with rounded corners.
   d. What topics in the curriculum studied thus far relate to the current topic? These go in the ovals.

e. What are the relationships among these elements? Draw arrows to indicate the relationships.

2. Are there any terms students would have to know the definition of before they could solve this problem?

3. What choice(s) of strategy would be more appropriate for this problem (at the middle school level)?

4. How would you expect students to show their reasoning?

5. If students need help "getting started," what hints or suggestions would you offer?

6. How will students know when they have found the correct solution (i.e., all the ways that change can be made for a dollar)?

7. What adaptations would you make for students with special needs?

Note: The directions for this activity are adapted from the Lesson Plan Form to Develop Mathematical Proficiency (see Chapter 3, Figure 3.23). The solution to the problem is in the instructor's manual.

If classes are designed so that all students are being taught the same things, in more or less the same way—working at a set pace, listening to the teacher, and discussing topics chosen only by the teacher, that is a surefire method for squelching natural curiosity and a love for learning. Ask yourself—are you confident enough in your own mathematics knowledge that you can present mathematics as an interesting and accessible intellectual game and not just as a set of practical rules and processes? If your answer is yes, your attitude will have a positive influence on students' motivation. If your answer is no, you may want to consider ways to improve your mathematics knowledge and your confidence in your ability to know and do mathematics.

When middle school students ask, "Why do we have to learn this?" take the question seriously. Students are asking for a reason why they should be engaged. They want to know if what they're studying will prepare them for what they want to do with their lives, even if they're not certain what that will be. The task of the middle school teacher is to help students stretch and test their limits. Each new task must have the potential to bring the learner one step closer to his or her dreams (Sullo, 2007; Greene, 2001).

Perlin (2002) recommends a program he calls "rewrites" to motivate middle school students to master mathematical concepts. Rather than give extra-credit assignments, he offers students the opportunity to regain some of the points lost on an assessment. Students demonstrate that they have reflected upon and mastered concepts by completing a rewrite form in which they describe in detail what they did wrong in the original assessment, give a detailed explanation of the correct solution (including an explanation of the mathematical reasoning and the underlying concepts), and give the correct solution, with all work shown. A successful rewrite earns half of the lost points back.

Finally, nothing succeeds like success. One way to enhance comprehension and memory is to stimulate learners to relate relevant memories and schemata to the information they are about to learn. Middle school students are entering the formal operational period of cognitive development. They can think logically not only about objects and events in the environment but also about abstractions. In effect, they are capable of thinking and acting like scientists. One way to capitalize on this is to present information organized in one way and have the students reorganize the information in another way. For instance, if in a geometry lesson, you have reviewed properties of polygons by sides, organized as shown in Figure 4.1, what different organizational format might you assign for homework?

If you are uncertain of an appropriate organizational format, check the "Geometry Terminology Review" on the student companion Web site (Chapter 12, "Check Your Mathematics Knowledge"). As you study the chart in Figure 4.1, do you

POLYGON	NUMBER/TYPE OF SIDES
Triangle	**3 Sides**
• Equilateral	All same length
• Isosceles	Two same length
• Scalene	None same length
Quadrilateral	**4 Sides**
• Parallelogram	Opposite sides parallel and congruent
• Rectangle	Parallelogram with right angle
• Square	Rectangle with all sides congruent
• Rhombus	Parallelogram with all sides congruent
• Trapezoid	Exactly one pair parallel sides
Pentagon	**5 Sides**
Hexagon	**6 Sides**
Etc.	

FIGURE 4.1 *Properties of polygons.*

have any questions? Why do you think the teacher who prepared this chart defined a rectangle the way you see here? Is this definition mathematically accurate?

Children's Literature as a Motivational Tool Most teachers, when they hear "children's literature" and "mathematics class" in the same sentence, automatically think that a primary mathematics lesson is being planned. However, children's literature can be just as effective in setting a context for problem solving or skill development in middle school. Stories that in primary grades are used to teach measurement can be used for teaching ratio or proportional reasoning in the middle grades. Throughout this text you will find suggestions for using children's literature.

Special Students

In the early 1990s, Congress passed legislation requiring that students be educated in the least restrictive environment appropriate to their needs. Many students who had once been assigned to special classrooms with special teachers were mainstreamed into regular classrooms. At the same time, the increasing immigration of people from Asia, Eastern Europe, Africa, and Central and South America means more English Language Learners (ELL) are attending our schools and being placed in regular classrooms. In addition, the improvement of diagnostic tools means that students with learning disabilities are more readily identified; thus, today's classroom teachers are more aware of their many students with special needs. Clearly, one of the major challenges facing today's teachers is helping *all* these students learn. This section reviews some of the characteristics of these special students and some of the ways that teachers can help them learn mathematics.

Students At-Risk For students who are considered "at-risk," the middle school years are critical in terms of whether they will stay in school or drop out. Over 13 million youth in America have been identified as at-risk. The majority of students who drop out of school do so during the tenth grade year (Womble et al., 1997). The most commonly recognized characteristics of students at-risk are that they generally read below grade level, are older than their classmates, have excessive absenteeism, and are seldom involved in extracurricular activities.

You can greatly help students who are at-risk by teaching them the importance of setting goals and that preparation is the key to achieving those goals. The classroom environment also should encourage the idea that asking for help is not admitting failure; rather, asking for help shows the desire and the will to learn. Finally, success in the classroom depends on students' willingness and ability to make good choices: the choice to work hard, to care about what happens in the classroom, to attend class, and to pay attention and participate in class.

Students with Special Needs The latest statistics indicate that students with special needs make up 10 to 15 percent of the school-age population. They include students with learning disabilities, with physical challenges, and with special interests or exceptional talent in mathematics. For these students, like students at-risk, the middle school years are critical. Will they be supported in a way that accommodates their needs and gives them access to a challenging and coherent mathematics program? "The vision of equity in mathematics education challenges a pervasive societal belief in North America that only some students are capable of learning mathematics" (NCTM, 2000).

Students with Learning Disabilities Students with learning disabilities make up more than 50 percent of students with special needs. The federal definition of learning disabilities includes disabilities in one or more of the following ways:

- Listening
- Speaking
- Basic reading
- Reading comprehension
- Arithmetic calculation
- Mathematics reasoning
- Written expression

As this list indicates, students with learning disabilities are those whose problems are the result of deficits in essential learning processes involving perception, integration, and verbal and nonverbal expression. These deficits may or may not have a neurological basis.

There are a variety of approaches that can be used with students who have learning disabilities to increase their chances of success. Steele (2002, page 141) provides the following summary of strategies that can be used in the classroom:

- Present advance organizers.
- Review prerequisite skills or concepts no matter how long ago they were taught.

- Model procedures enough times for clarity.
- Use step-by-step procedures.
- Provide sufficient guided and independent practice.
- Teach the skill of generalization specifically and directly.
- Use real-life and meaningful examples.
- Focus on essential ideas for connections and foundations.
- Use mnemonic strategies.
- Teach self-questioning and self-monitoring.
- Teach and practice the use of visual aids.
- Teach gradually from the concrete to the abstract.
- Use cooperative learning groups.

Good teaching for students with learning disabilities is good teaching for all students. The use of these strategies for your entire class will be well worth the time and effort it takes to integrate them in your teaching. As you read through this list, you should recognize some that you have already encountered in this text—not because we assume that your students will have learning disabilities but because they are effective teaching and learning strategies for everyone.

Another way to look at teaching students with learning disabilities is to consider that all students differ in the way they best learn and express themselves. Students make up a continuum of learner differences, with no special category for those with disabilities. Thus, as a teacher, you must make adjustments for learner differences for all students, not just for those with the "disability" label. (To learn more about students with learning disabilities, read Choute's *Successful Inclusive Teaching: Proven Whys to Detect and Correct Special Needs* (4th ed., 2003).

Gifted and Talented Students   Is talent innate or is it the result of experience, hard work, and education? Psychologists and others have debated that question for over a hundred years. The Russian psychologist Krutetskii (1976) devoted much of his research to identifying the characteristics of mathematical talent. Among the characteristics he described are resourcefulness and flexibility, economy of thought, the use of visual thinking, mathematical memory, and the ability to abstract. Krutetskii identified these characteristics based on surveys of teachers and case studies of students. It should be noted that practically all methods for identifying the gifted and talented depend almost exclusively on an examination of students' oral or written products—performance on a test, solutions to problems, or demonstrations of proof.

Lev Vygotsky, another Russian psychologist, suggests that teachers must be observant to identify those students whose mathematical talents are in the process of development. Vygotsky's insights suggest that teachers can create classroom environments that encourage students to display their developing talents and that teachers can model a "mathematical cast of mind" (Krutetskii, 1976)—a tendency to analyze the world around them from a mathematical point of view.

Unfortunately, in all too many school districts, if there are programs available for those with special interests or exceptional talent in mathematics, they are generally limited to one of the following types:

- *Enrichment.* Many schools claim to offer enrichment for the gifted students within the regular classroom; however, this is an extraordinary burden to put on already overly busy teachers, especially because there are rarely more than one or two gifted students in a classroom. A true enrichment program requires a great deal of planning, preparation, and experimentation, not just haphazardly providing an extra worksheet or puzzle.

- *Acceleration.* This refers to the practice of double promoting or teaching courses a year or two early. Questions about social readiness are often raised if the practice is double promoting, especially if the student might end up attending high school as a nine-year-old and college at the age of twelve or thirteen.

- *Ability grouping or "tracking."* Many teachers and parents find ability grouping attractive, but unless teachers are willing and able to adjust the curriculum and methodology to the students in the classroom—whether they are gifted, "average," or students with special needs—this approach is difficult to justify. In "tracked" classes, teachers must avoid the temptation to teach the regular school curriculum either too slowly and repetitiously, because low-ability students "don't get math anyway," or too quickly, because gifted students "can get it on their own."

As a teacher of mathematics in a middle school, you need to be alert and receptive to students' unexpected, even "off-the-wall," mathematical observations. For instance, if Student A in your class incorrectly adds two fractions by adding the numerators and adding the denominators (i.e., $7/10 + 3/4 = 10/14$), and Student B says that

that's wrong because then 3 + 5 would equal 4 rather than 8, would you recognize the mathematical talent of Student B? Student B, who has just demonstrated that the addition of fractions must preserve the results of whole number addition, may or may not be able to recite the "rule" for adding fractions, but how sad it would be to dismiss this student's insight for that reason. Just as sad would be to focus praise on a student just because he or she can recite the rule. (If you are not sure of what Student B meant, see Chapter 10, page 261 for a more detailed discussion of this example.)

Students Who Are Underserved It's the rare middle school classroom that does not have students who are traditionally considered "underserved." They include those who are not native speakers of English, those who live in poverty, those who are female, and many of those who are nonwhite. These students, as you read in Chapter 2, are often victims of their teachers' low expectations, particularly with regard to their need or aptitude for learning mathematics. However, it should go without saying that the equity principle (NCTM, 2000) applies to them as well.

Research by Lubienski (2000) indicates that students who are underserved can be motivated by mathematics activities that involve games or individual interests such as sports or dream homes, where the mathematics itself is not the focus of the activity or the motivating force behind their engagement in it. These students are often very sophisticated in their ability to consider multiple real-world variables when solving problems; however, they tend to miss the mathematical learning at the heart of the problem, as indicated by difficulty in articulating their reasoning. These students also tend to focus on individual problems and not see the mathematical ideas connecting different problems. It is important to support these students by helping them see "where the mathematics is" as they engage in problem solving.

All students in the middle grades can be drawn toward mathematics if they have a context or anchor for their learning, find the mathematics challenging, and know that they have the support they need in the mathematics classroom (NCTM, 2000). Throughout this text, you will study ways that will assist you in teaching middle school students in the mathematics classroom. The video vignette shows how one middle school teacher uses music to reinforce the order of operations (the activities for you to do after viewing the video vignette will help you begin to build a file of resources for when you start teaching).

Video Vignette

The "Order of Operations" Song

On the view the video vignette "Order of Operations Song" (Chapter 4, Video Vignettes). As you watch Ms. Valerie Jones and her eighth grade class sing the song, notice the number of students who seem to be enjoying themselves while they learn mathematics material that might otherwise be considered "boring"—or, as the students would say, "BORE-ing!"

DIRECTIONS
- Before viewing this vignette, you might want to review what you read about perceptual learning styles and Gardner's theory of multiple intelligences in Chapter 3.
- Develop at least three other ways that involve different senses (perceptual learning style) or intelligences that would help students learn and remember the order of operations. Share these with your colleagues to expand one another's repertoire of activities.
- Take a familiar melody and write lyrics to help middle school students remember a procedure, definition, or process in mathematics. Choose either the spatial or bodily-kinesthetic intelligence and develop an activity to complement or reinforce the lyrics you just wrote. Again, share these with your colleagues.

MIDDLE SCHOOL TEACHERS

Programs for preparing middle school teachers are relatively new in many colleges and schools of education. State departments of education often gave certificates only for "K–9" or "7–12" teaching, but with the introduction of algebra classes in seventh or eighth grade and geometry (i.e., the traditional high school geometry course) in eighth or ninth grade, principals and parents began demanding that teachers at the middle school level have a strong background in these content areas.

It is generally recognized that what has been the typical mathematics preparation expected of elementary teachers is not sufficient for today's middle school teachers. Certainly, middle school teachers need to know the mathematics learned by those preparing to be elementary teachers, but those who teach middle school mathematics must also understand the more sophisticated and complex reasoning that reflects the growing maturity of middle school students' thinking.

Activity 4.2 shows a problem from the NCTM's *PSSM* (2000) that middle school students can solve during their study of number theory. (If you need a hint to get started on this problem, go to Chapter 4 on the student companion Web site and click on "Hints" for Activity 4.2.)

In 2001, The Mathematics Association of America (MAA) published its recommendations for the mathematical education of teachers. Chapter 8 of this report discusses in some detail the mathematical content needed by prospective middle grades teachers in the four major areas:

- Number and operations
- Algebra and functions
- Measurement and geometry
- Data analysis, statistics, and probability

The important types of mathematical reasoning applied in these four major content areas include proportional reasoning, reasoning about quantitative relationships, spatial reasoning, and statistical and probabilistic reasoning. Each of these content areas and types of mathematical reasoning will be addressed in greater depth in later chapters of this text.

Activity 4.2

NUMBER THEORY PROBLEM SOLVING

PROBLEM SOLVING

PROBLEM

A number of the form *abcabc* always has several prime-number factors. Which prime numbers are always factors of a number of this form? Why?

PSSM (2000), p. 217

DIRECTIONS

1. Determine a strategy to use.
2. Spend the next five to ten minutes applying your strategy.
3. Move to your assigned group and spend the next ten to fifteen minutes sharing your strategy and the progress you have made to this point.
4. As a group, decide which strategy seems to be most promising.
5. Each group will present its reasoning and solution to the problem to the class.
6. Each person will turn in a report on his or her problem-solving process—the strategy chosen first, the results from that strategy, reasons for choosing a different strategy (if you did), and an explanation of why you believe your solution is correct.

> **Supporting the NCTM *Principles and Standards* (2000)**
>
> - Mathematics as Problem Solving, Communicating, Reasoning and Proof
> - Worthwhile Mathematical Tasks for Teachers— The Teaching Principle

Where's the Mathematics?

1. What "knowledge packet" would middle school students need before they could solve this problem? (Review the questions in Activity 4.1, page 85, if you need help getting started.)
2. Are there any terms students would have to know the definition of before they could solve this problem?
3. What choice(s) of strategy would be more appropriate for this problem (at the middle school level)?
4. How would you expect students to show their reasoning?
5. If students need help "getting started," what hints or suggestions would you offer?
6. How will students know when they have found the correct solution (i.e., *all* the prime-number factors for numbers of the form *abcabc*)?
7. What adaptations would you make for students with special needs?
8. Are there other NCTM standards that you believe are supported by this activity, in addition to those listed above? If so, which would you include in this list? (You can view the standards on the NCTM Web site: **http://nctm.org/standards**.)

At a conference on using classroom teaching for professional development, Ball (2002) offered a somewhat different list of what teachers need to learn to teach mathematics. The list is short, but the task is not easy.

- First, teachers must learn to pay attention to and teach every student in the classroom.

- Second, teachers need to know how to know mathematics and to use that knowledge to help their students learn. In other words, more than knowing the mathematics to do the mathematics, you must know how to organize the content, create activities, and adjust the activities so that the lesson addresses both the goals of the curriculum and the interests of the students.

- Finally, teachers must learn how to work with other teachers in developing knowledge for teaching. Too often, a teacher's classroom is his or her kingdom . . . it's the "I'll close the door and do my own thing" syndrome.

Throughout this text, with its emphasis on knowledge packets and questions relating to the activities, we are trying to help you learn to meet the challenges posed by this list.

MIDDLE SCHOOL MATHEMATICS CURRICULA

There is considerable evidence to show that the textbooks adopted by schools in the United States have a great influence on the mathematics that is taught in the schools (Grouws and Smith, 2000; Weiss, 2001). Whether measured by the percent of teachers who report using a textbook on a daily basis or by the number who report "covering" three-fourths or more of the textbook, the reliance of teachers on commercial textbooks is high. By implication, the content and instructional strategies provided in those textbooks strongly influence middle school students' learning.

Three Views
School districts, in general, take one of three views when considering mathematics programs (text-books, materials, etc.). The first is best described as favoring a continuation of the series adopted for grades K–5. Such continuation series may well be focused on reviewing the mathematics taught in the previous grades, with a little algebra at the end of the text for the seventh and eighth graders (this is most often the case in a K–8 school). The second view is that the "best" mathematics students will take prealgebra as seventh graders and algebra as eighth graders, with the remaining students in "regular" classes. The third view is that middle school students need a challenging alternative to the first two views in the form of a mathematics program that focuses on, and integrates, the major concepts of number, algebra, geometry, and data analysis. The materials associated with this third

view have come to be known as *middle grade standards-based mathematics curriculum materials.*

NSF-Funded Curricula Development
Standards-based mathematics curriculum materials are comprehensive materials developed primarily through funding from the National Science Foundation (NSF). There are basically four such programs: Connected Mathematics Project, Mathematics in Context, MathScape, and Math Thematics. Two other NSF-funded curriculum development projects are Integrated Mathematics, Science, and Technology and Pathways to Algebra and Geometry.

Connected Mathematics Project (CMP)   CMP is a complete middle school mathematics curriculum that helps students develop understanding of important concepts, skills, procedures, and ways of thinking and reasoning in the areas of number, geometry, measurement, algebra, probability, and statistics. It is problem centered but does not neglect skill development.

Mathematics in Context (MiC)   The MiC curriculum features a total of 40 units developed for grades 5 through 8. Units stress the interrelationships among mathematical areas such as number, algebra, geometry, and statistics. The initial drafts of the units were prepared by Dutch researchers with more than 20 years of experience in the development of materials oriented to the real world. University of Wisconsin personnel revised the units to make them appropriate for U.S. students and teachers.

MathScape   The MathScape curriculum has as its central theme "mathematics in the human experience." The curriculum was developed to help students experience mathematics as it is used in fundamental human activities: planning, predicting, designing, exploring, explaining, coordinating, comparing, and deciding.

Math Thematics   Originally known as Six Through Eighth Mathematics (STEM), *Math Thematics* consists of curricular materials that provide students with connections to science and other mathematical fields and that integrate the appropriate use of technology.

Pathways to Algebra and Geometry   Originally called Middle-school Mathematics through Applications Project (MMAP), this series is a comprehensive middle grades mathematics curriculum integrating computer technology and interdisciplinary connections. The program is intended to be completed in the two years prior to beginning algebra. Projects integrate mathematical software developed for use with the program; about half of the students' work in these units requires the use of computers.

Integrated Mathematics, Science, and Technology (IMaST)

IMaST promotes active learning for students and teamwork among teachers. A key instructional approach is problem solving. A common problem-solving terminology was developed for all disciplines involved in teaching with the IMaST curriculum: DAPIC (define, assess, plan, implement, and communicate).

Criteria for Standards-Based Mathematics Curricula

The Show-Me Center (**http://showmecenter .missouri.edu**) designates these criteria, among others, for standards-based mathematics curricula:

- Designed to reach *all* students.
- Focused on investigations that interest, challenge, and motivate students.
- Identify and explore "significant" mathematical concepts that will prepare students for continuing to learn mathematics in high school.
- Engage students as active learners of mathematics.
- Require teachers and students to assume different roles, including coach and co-investigator.
- Illustrate the use of alternative forms of assessment, such as portfolios.

Study the NCTM Standards for grades 6 to 8 in Figure 4.2 before beginning Activity 4.3.

NUMBER AND OPERATIONS

Instructional programs from prekindergarten through grade 12 should enable all students to

1. Understand numbers, ways of representing numbers, relationships among numbers, and number systems.

   In grades 6 to 8 all students should

   Work flexibly with fractions, decimals, and percents to solve problems.

   Compare and order fractions, decimals, and percents efficiently and find their approximate locations on a number line.

   Develop meaning for percents greater than 100 and less than 1.

   Understand and use ratios and proportions to represent quantitative relationships.

   Develop an understanding of large numbers and recognize and appropriately use exponential, scientific, and calculator notation.

   Use factors, multiples, prime factorization, and relatively prime numbers to solve problems.

   Develop meaning for integers and represent and compare quantities with them.

2. Understand meanings of operations and how they relate to one another.

   In grades 6 to 8 all students should

   Understand the meaning and effects of arithmetic operations with fractions, decimals, and integers.

   Use the associative and commutative properties of addition and multiplication and the distributive property of multiplication over

addition to simplify computations with integers, fractions, and decimals.

Understand and use the inverse relationships of addition and subtraction, multiplication and division, and squaring and finding square roots to simplify computations and solve problems.

3. Compute fluently and make reasonable estimates.

   In grades 6 to 8 all students should

   Select appropriate methods and tools for computing with fractions and decimals from among mental computation, estimation, calculators or computers, and paper and pencil, depending on the situation, and apply the selected methods.

   Develop and analyze algorithms for computing with fractions, decimals, and integers and develop fluency in their use.

   Develop and use strategies to estimate the results of rational-number computations and judge the reasonableness of the results.

   Develop, analyze, and explain methods for solving problems involving proportions, such as scaling and finding equivalent ratios.

ALGEBRA

Instructional programs from prekindergarten through grade 12 should enable all students to

1. Understand patterns, relations, and functions.

   In grades 6 to 8 all students should

   Represent, analyze, and generalize a variety of patterns with tables, graphs, words, and, when possible, symbolic rules.

   Relate and compare different forms of representation for a relationship.

FIGURE 4.2 *NCTM standards overview for grades 6 to 8.*

Identify functions as linear or nonlinear and contrast their properties from tables, graphs, or equations.

2. Represent and analyze mathematical situations and structures using algebraic symbols.

In grades 6 to 8 all students should

Develop an initial conceptual understanding of different uses of variables.

Explore relationships between symbolic expressions and graphs of lines, paying particular attention to the meaning of intercept and slope.

Use symbolic algebra to represent situations and to solve problems, especially those that involve linear relationships.

Recognize and generate equivalent forms for simple algebraic expressions and solve linear equations.

3. Use mathematical models to represent and understand quantitative relationships.

In grades 6 to 8 all students should

Model and solve contextualized problems using various representations, such as graphs, tables, and equations.

4. Analyze change in various contexts.

In grades 6 to 8 all students should

Use graphs to analyze the nature of changes in quantities in linear relationships.

GEOMETRY

Instructional programs from prekindergarten through grade 12 should enable all students to

1. Analyze characteristics and properties of two- and three-dimensional geometric shapes and develop mathematical arguments about geometric relationships.

In grades 6 to 8 all students should

Precisely describe, classify, and understand relationships among types of two- and three-dimensional objects using their defining properties.

Understand relationships among the angles, side lengths, perimeters, areas, and volumes of similar objects.

Create and critique inductive and deductive arguments concerning geometric ideas and relationships, such as congruence, similarity, and the pythagorean relationship.

2. Specify locations and describe spatial relationships using coordinate geometry and other representational systems.

In grades 6 to 8 all students should:

Use coordinate geometry to represent and examine the properties of geometric shapes.

Use coordinate geometry to examine special geometric shapes, such as regular polygons or those with pairs of parallel or perpendicular sides.

3. Apply transformations and use symmetry to analyze mathematical situations.

In grades 6 to 8 all students should

Describe sizes, positions, and orientations of shapes under informal transformations such as flips, turns, slides, and scaling.

Examine the congruence, similarity, and line or rotational symmetry of objects using transformations.

4. Use visualization, spatial reasoning, and geometric modeling to solve problems.

In grades 6 to 8 all students should

Draw geometric objects with specified properties, such as side lengths or angle measures.

Use two-dimensional representations of three-dimensional objects to visualize and solve problems such as those involving surface area and volume.

Use visual tools such as networks to represent and solve problems.

Use geometric models to represent and explain numerical and algebraic relationships.

Recognize and apply geometric ideas and relationships in areas outside the mathematics classroom, such as art, science, and everyday life.

MEASUREMENT

Instructional programs from prekindergarten through grade 12 should enable all students to

1. Understand measurable attributes of objects and the units, systems, and processes of measurement.

In grades 6 to 8 all students should

Understand both metric and customary systems of measurement.

Understand relationships among units and convert from one unit to another within the same system.

Understand, select, and use units of appropriate size and type to measure angles, perimeter, area, surface area, and volume.

2. Apply appropriate techniques, tools, and formulas to determine measurements.

In grades 6 to 8 all students should

Use common benchmarks to select appropriate methods for estimating measurements.

FIGURE 4.2 *NCTM standards overview for grades 6 to 8 (Continued).*

Select and apply techniques and tools to accurately find length, area, volume, and angle measures to appropriate levels of precision.

Develop and use formulas to determine the circumference of circles and the area of triangles, parallelograms, trapezoids, and circles and develop strategies to find the area of more complex shapes.

Develop strategies to determine the surface area and volume of selected prisms, pyramids, and cylinders.

Solve problems involving scale factors, using ratio and proportion.

Solve simple problems involving rates and derived measurements for such attributes as velocity and density.

DATA ANALYSIS AND PROBABILITY

Instructional programs from prekindergarten through grade 12 should enable all students to

1. Formulate questions that can be addressed with data and collect, organize, and display relevant data to answer them.

In grades 6 to 8 all students should

Formulate questions, design studies, and collect data about a characteristic shared by two populations or different characteristics within one population.

Select, create, and use appropriate graphical representations of data, including histograms, box plots, and scatterplots.

2. Select and use appropriate statistical methods to analyze data.

In grades 6 to 8 all students should

Find, use, and interpret measures of center and spread, including mean and interquartile range.

Discuss and understand the correspondence between data sets and their graphical representations, especially histograms, stem-and-leaf plots, box plots, and scatterplots.

3. Develop and evaluate inferences and predictions that are based on data.

In grades 6 to 8 all students should

Use observations about differences between two or more samples to make conjectures about the populations from which the samples were taken.

Make conjectures about possible relationships between two characteristics of a sample on the basis of scatterplots of the data and approximate lines of fit.

Use conjectures to formulate new questions and plan new studies to answer them.

4. Understand and apply basic concepts of probability.

In grades 6 to 8 all students should

Understand and use appropriate terminology to describe complementary and mutually exclusive events.

Use proportionality and a basic understanding of probability to make and test conjectures about the results of experiments and simulations.

Compute probabilities for simple compound events, using such methods as organized lists, tree diagrams, and area models.

FIGURE 4.2 *NCTM standards overview for grades 6 to 8 (Continued).*

Role of Technology

In every generation, a new tool is invented, which when first introduced in the schools, provokes a cry that this new tool will be the death of students' ability to write or think or learn some necessary skill. The ballpoint pen, the typewriter, the adding machine, television, the computer, and the calculator are all cases in point. Nevertheless, according to a 2001 report by the National Research Council (NRC) a "large number of empirical studies of calculator use, including long term studies, have generally shown that the use of calculators and technology does not threaten the development of basic skills and that it can enhance conceptual understanding, strategic competence, and disposition toward mathematics."

Activity 4.3

INTERNET SEARCHES

INVESTIGATING MIDDLE SCHOOL MATHEMATICS CURRICULA

DIRECTIONS

1. Review the criteria that standards-based mathematics curricula must meet, as outlined by the Show-Me Center.

2. Examine the description of each standards-based mathematics program described in this chapter

and then explore the sample modules/units available on the Web sites listed on page 95. Then answer these questions for each module/unit:

a. In what ways was this module/unit designed to reach *all* students? What modifications or adaptations were suggested for students with special needs?

b. What was challenging, interesting, and/or motivating to middle school students in the choice of the central investigation/topic/problem in this module/unit?

c. What significant mathematical concepts did you see in this module/unit?

d. What alternative forms of assessment were recommended?

e. What do you think middle school students would find engaging about this module/unit?

f. In what ways do you see yourself as a coach or a co-investigator if you were to teach this module/unit?

g. What uses of technology were integrated in this module/unit?

WEB SITES

- IMaST
  http://www.cemast.ilstu.edu/programs/imast/index.shmtl
- Pathways
  http://mmap.wested.org
- MathScape
  http://www.glencoe.com/sec/math/mathscape/index.php
- Mathematics in Context
  http://www.hrw.com/math/
- Math Thematics
  http://classzone.com/books/math_thematics1
- Connected Mathematics Project
  http://connectedmath.msu.edu

Supporting the NCTM *Principles and Standards* (2000)
- Mathematics Curriculum Principle
- Equity Principle
- Technology Principle
- Assessment Principle

Supporting the ISTE NETS-T Standards (2000)
- Planning and Designing Learning Environments and Experiences

---

In grade school or high school, you rarely hear a student call out to the teacher, "Look what I learned on this page of my math book!" In contrast, students are often eager to show the teacher what they discovered by pushing a button on the calculator or working on the computer. The real issue with technology is not what equipment you have in your classroom, but how you use the technology in your classroom. Properly used, technology in the classroom helps students visualize mathematical ideas, organize and analyze data, and compute efficiently and accurately. The key to success in using technology in the classroom is identifying the right times for integrating the technology into the mathematics class so that it supports students' learning.

Graphing Calculators   A study of the results of the 1996 NAEP mathematics scores for the fourth and eighth graders showed that technology had a greater impact on middle schools than it did in elementary schools (Valdez et al., 1999). Graphing calculators, computer programs such as Geometer's Sketchpad, and application software such as spreadsheets are three examples of technology that can play a valuable role in encouraging students to be active learners who truly *study math*. If you ask your parents or grandparents about their experiences in algebra, they will probably tell you that a major challenge was learning to graph accurately. Today, inexpensive graphing calculators do the tedious graphing and allow students to truly study the mathematics—what is the impact of changing the slope or moving the intercept? The graphing calculator also allows students to move easily among numeric, graphical, and symbolic representations to solve problems using multiple representations.

GPS/Geocaching   **GPS** is the use of a network of 24 satellites in geosynchronous orbit around the earth to determine nearly exact longitude and latitude coordinates through the use of hand held device. The satellites circle the earth twice a day in a very precise orbit and transmit information to earth. GPS receivers take this information and use triangulation to calculate user's exact location. The position can then be displayed on the GPS unit's moving electronic map, which may include nearby landmarks, streets, and other geographical detail. GPS is funded can controlled by the United States Department of Defense. **GeoCaching** is a hide-and–seek type activity where you hide something, upload the longitude and latitude coordinates to a Web site so that other users can seek out the hidden "something" based on those coordinates.

GPS receivers are used for many purposes by many people–hikers, drivers, fishermen, balloonists, surveyors to name a few. The curricular integration in mathematics, science, geography, and language arts that is possible using GPS technology makes this one of the newer technology tools for the middle school mathematics classroom. A few of the Web sites containing lessons plans for using GPS are included in the "Integrating Technology" sections at the end of this chapter.

Computer Software Perhaps you have had experience with Geometer's Sketchpad. If not, visit the Key Curriculum Press Web site (**http://www.keypress.com/x5521.ml**) and download a functioning version of Geometer's Sketchpad for evaluation purposes. (The demonstration package is good for 60 days from the first day of use. The downside of the demonstration version is that there is no saving or printing, no copying and pasting to other programs, and no exporting of work as a dynamic Java Sketchpad Web page.)

Simply put, students use Geometer's Sketchpad to construct a figure (called an object) and then explore its mathematical properties by dragging it with the mouse. Because students can examine an entire set of similar cases in a matter of seconds, they can make generalizations, visualize and analyze problems, and make conjectures before ever attempting a proof. Many third-party vendors and Web sites support teachers' use of Sketchpad. See Figures 4.3 and 4.4 for examples of figures constructed using Sketchpad. Activity 4.4 presents a problem found in a Chinese fifth grade mathematics text and a Japanese elementary school text, which you can try solving with Sketchpad.

Most school computer labs today, as well as most home computers, have an integrated "suite" of application programs installed, such as Microsoft Office or Microsoft Works, or ClarisWorks. The ready availability of spreadsheets enables mathematics teachers to bring an investigative environment to their classrooms that encourages active learning on the part of students. Examples of interactive spreadsheets appropriate for different concept areas in mathematics are referred to in this text and are available both on the student companion Web site accompanying this text and on the Web site.

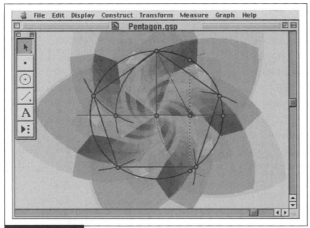

FIGURE 4.3 *A pentagon constructed using Geometer's Sketchpad.*

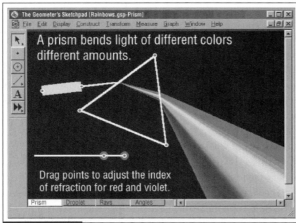

FIGURE 4.4 *A prism constructed using Geometer's Sketchpad.*

Activity 4.4

COMPUTERS   **PROBLEM SOLVING**   **CIRCUMFERENCE MATHEMATICS TASK**

PROBLEM

A. Is the length of the larger half-circle (along the circumference) shorter than, longer than, or equal to the sum of the lengths of the three other half circles?

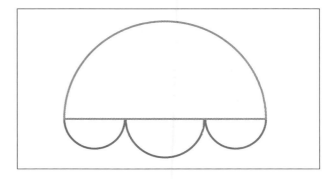

B. How does the problem change, or does it, if the figure is drawn in the manner shown below? Is the length of the larger half-circle (along the circumference) shorter than, longer than, or equal to the sum of the lengths of the three other half circles?

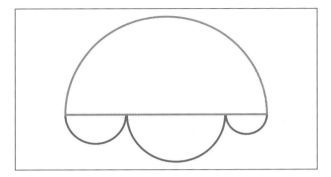

DIRECTIONS

1. Work the problem (both part **A** and **B**) for yourself using paper and pencil first.

2. Tell how you answered the question. What was the reasoning you used?

3. If you have access to Geometer's Sketchpad, or have downloaded the trial version, try solving the problem with it. Did the results from Sketchpad support your first solution?

4. Look at the solutions below that were offered by three different students and answer the questions.

SOLUTIONS OFFERED BY STUDENTS

Here are solutions offered by three different students to parts **A** and **B** of the problem.

1. Solutions to part **A**:

- *Student 1.* It is. Because I used a problem to figure out the problem. It is hard to explain. I know it is.
- *Student 2.* The sum of the three half circles is equal to the length of the larger half circle. When you line up the three half circles next to the larger half circle—they are the same length.
- *Student 3.* I first made up a diameter for the larger circle. I gave it a value of 16. I then noticed that the three circles lined up and took up the same amount of space as the diameter of the larger circle. I made the diameters of the smaller circles equal 16 when added together. I then took the individual diameter of each circle and multiplied it times pi. *[Authors' question: Why multiply by pi?]* I added the three products of the three smaller circles together and compared them to the product of the larger circle.

2. Solutions to part **B**:

- *Student 4.* I think there was insufficient information.

- *Student 5.* Shorter. Since I know that circumference equals pi times the radius squared, I could assign numbers.
- *Student 6.* The length of the larger half circle is equal to the sum of the lengths of the smaller circles. The sum of diameters of the smaller circles is the same as the diameter of the larger circle. If the circles are true, they should have an equal circumference.

Do any of these match your solution? If not, where do you differ? Who is correct? Why?

Supporting the NCTM *Principles and Standards* (2000)

- Mathematics as Reasoning; Communication; Representation; Geometry and Spatial Visualization
- Worthwhile Mathematical Tasks—The Teaching Principle
- Mathematics Curriculum Principle

Supporting the ISTE NETS-T Standards (2000)

- Technology Operations and Concepts
- Planning and Designing Learning Environments and Experiences

---

Where's the Mathematics?

1. What "knowledge packet" would middle school students need before they could solve this problem (both parts **A** and **B**)? Review the questions in Activity 4.1, page 85 if you need help getting started.

2. What terms would students have to know the definition of before they could solve this problem?

3. What type of proof would be acceptable for this problem?

4. How would you expect students to show their reasoning?

5. If students need help getting started, what hints or suggestions would you offer?

6. How will students know when they have found the correct solution?

7. What adaptations would you make for students with special needs?

8. Did any of your responses to these questions change between parts **A** and **B**?

9. How do you know your solution is correct? How would you explain the solution to a sixth grader?

10. What did you learn about this problem by using Sketchpad?

11. Are there other NCTM standards that you believe are supported by this activity, in addition to those listed above? If so, which would you include in this list? (You can view the standards on the NCTM Web site: **http://standards.nctm.org/index.htm**.)

12. Are there other ISTE standards from NETS that you believe are supported by this activity, in addition to those listed above? If so, which would you include in this list? (You can view the standards on the ISTE Web site: **http://cnets.iste.org/students/index .shtml** for the student NETS or **http://cnets.iste .org/teachers/** for the teacher NETS.)

Note: See Chapter 12 for more about this problem, common misunderstandings revealed in students' work, and the correct solution.

SUMMARY

- Middle school is an important transition period in early adolescents' cognitive development.
- Theories that attempt to explain students' motivation include attribution theory, goal theory, and self-determination theory.
- Another characterization of students' motivation to learn is as intrinsic and extrinsic motivation.

- Teachers have an important role in increasing students' motivation.
- More than 13 million youth in America have been identified as students at- risk.
- Students with special needs comprise 10 to 15 percent of the school-age population.
- More than half the students with special needs have learning disabilities.
- Students with special needs include those who are gifted and talented.
- Middle school teachers of mathematics are expected to have in-depth preparation in the four areas of number and operations, algebra and functions, measurement and geometry, and data analysis, statistics, and probability.
- Several standards-based mathematics curricula have been developed for middle school programs.
- Appropriate use of technology will help students visualize mathematical ideas, organize and analyze data, and compute efficiently and accurately.

PRAXIS II™-STYLE QUESTIONS

Answers to this chapter's Praxis II™-style questions are in the instructor's manual.

Multiple Choice Format

1. An eighth grade student rarely turns in math assignments, stares into space thinking about dropping out of school as soon as possible, and struggles to read the math problems when asked to do so in class. This student is displaying the characteristics of _____.
   a. Students with special needs.
   b. Students at- risk.
   c. Students who are underserved.
   d. There is not enough information to tell.

2. Mathematics teachers who want to provide the best help to a student like the one described above should respond by
   a. Praising any small accomplishment, even when the student knows that it required little effort.

   b. Emphasizing ability goals for the students.
   c. Emphasizing task goals for the students.
   d. Supporting attribution theory in the classroom.

3. Teachers who want middle school students to understand how humans use mathematics to predict, design, explore, coordinate, compare, and make quality decisions would most likely choose which of the following curriculum materials?
   a. Math Thematics
   b. MathScape
   c. Mathematics in Context
   d. Integrated Mathematics, Science, and Technology

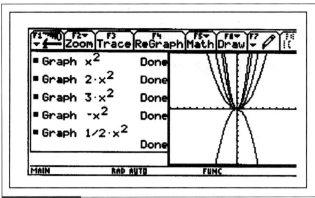

| FIGURE 4.5 | *Graphs using graphing calculator.* |

Constructed Response Format

4. Figure 4.5 shows work done with a graphing calculator. Which of the multiple representations is (are) NOT being used here?
   a. Numeric
   b. Graphical
   c. Symbolic
   d. All are being used

5. Using the work displayed on the graphing calculator in Question 4, what would be a likely response of a middle schooler asked to follow with another graph building on the sequence of graphs shown on the calculator? Tell how the middle schooler is likely to explain his/her thinking.

6. Using the work displayed on the graphing calculator in Question 4, sketch on the drawing where the graph $-2x^2$ would be. Middle school students should be able to do the same work *without* using the graphing calculator. This reinforces the NCTM Processing Standard of _____. Tell why.

7. If you are teaching in a middle school where graphing calculators are not part of the curriculum materials, but spreadsheets in a "suite" of applications are readily available, how could you teach lessons about the effects of changing variables on an equation?

Integrating Technology

Internet Activities

WebQuest

Prove the Pythagorean Theorem!

On the Web site for this text, open the WebQuest "Prove the Pythagorean Theorem!" (**www.wiley.com/hatfield**). Follow the directions there to complete this Web-based activity. You studied the Pythagorean theorem in your high school geometry class. Today, as a middle school teacher of mathematics, you may find yourself teaching geometry with its axioms, postulates, theorems, constructions, and proofs.

Web sites

Geometer's Sketchpad (Key Curriculum Press Web Site)

Download a functioning version of Geometer's Sketchpad for evaluation purposes from **http://www.keypress.com/x5521.xml**.

Jack Finn Project

http://www.in.gov/igic/project/huckfinn/classmaterials.html. Lessons plans by grade level for using GPS technology also include science and mathematics connections (spatial reasoning, map reading, the environment).

Lesson Plan Links

http://www.computercooks.com/andy/lessonplanlinks.htm. Provides links to a variety of lesson plans based on GPS/Geocaching technology.

GPS Lesson Plans

http://www.uen.org/utahlink/activities/view_activity.cgi?activity_id= 15969. Lesson plans using GPS technology in a variety of content areas.

Graphing Calculator Activities

Check calculator companies' Web sites for sample activities: Texas Instruments, Casio, Sharp, and Hewlett-Packard would be among those to investigate. Here are two to get you started:

- Texas Instruments (TI)
  http://education.ti.com/sites/us/homepage/index.html
- Casio
  http://www.casioeducation.com/activities
  Interactivate: Home Page
  http://shodor.org/interactivate
  Java-based coursewave for middle school mathematics explorations

Spreadsheet

Planetary Adjustments
Open the file "Planetary Adjustments" (Chapter 4, Spreadsheet Activity) on the student companion Web site. Follow the directions to create your own interactive spreadsheet for students.

CHILDREN'S LITERATURE

Myller, Rolf. *How big is a foot?* New York: Bantam Doubleday Dell Publishing Group, 1962.

Schwartz, David. *If you hopped like a frog.* New York, Scholastic Press, 1999.

Scieszka, Jon, and LaneSmith. *Math curse.* Viking Penguin Publishing Group, 1995.

Problem Solving

Problem solving is the oldest intellectual skill known to humanity. The ability to understand a problem, relate it to a similar problem or to past experiences, speculate about the possible solution, and carry through until the problem is solved is basic to human survival. Without the ability to solve problems, human beings would have become extinct.

STANDARDS IN PROBLEM SOLVING

The vision of the Principles and Standards (NCTM, 2000) is that problem solving permeates all topics of mathematics. It serves as the foundation for developing mathematical knowledge and reasoning. Problems are formulated by children from everyday situations and may extend over several days. Figure 5.1 shows the standards for problem solving. You may also find it helpful to review the entire problem-solving strand in the Principles and Standards (2000) from the NCTM Web site (**http://standards.nctm.org/index.htm**). There are many facets of problem solving to be considered in this chapter. Contemplate a teacher's role in weaving methods, procedures, and strategies of problem solving with the principles espoused in the NCTM Standards for elementary and a middle school mathematics curricula to benefit all children. We have a huge and exciting task to do!

COMPLEXITY OF PROBLEM SOLVING

As writers and researchers started to work with the concept of problem solving, it became apparent that problem solving is a complex topic that can be viewed in different ways: (1) as an educational method, (2) as a broad definition, and (3) as an environment in and of itself.

As an Educational Method

Problem solving as an educational method has received a good deal of attention. Some people may remember solving mathematical problems dealing with how many hours two painters would require to paint a room if one worked twice as fast as the other. For many people, this is an unpleasant memory because they felt as though they were stumbling blindly through problems without much guidance from the teacher or the textbook. Sometimes teachers resist teaching problem-solving skills because of their own frustrating experiences with problem solving. Yet, Jerome Bruner, the constructivist, believed that constructivist teaching and learning was best accomplished through problem solving. Eric Jensen (2005), in his book *Teaching with the Brain in Mind*, says, "The single best way to grow a better brain is to engage in challenging problem solving. Surprisingly, it doesn't matter to our brains whether we come up with the right answer or not: neural growth happens because of the process, not because we have found the correct answer." This is not to say that finding the correct answer is not important, or that the process is more important than the correct answer. Rather, we must help students to understand that finding the answer is part of the process and we can learn as much, if not more, from our mistakes. Mistakes are a natural and even necessary part of learning.

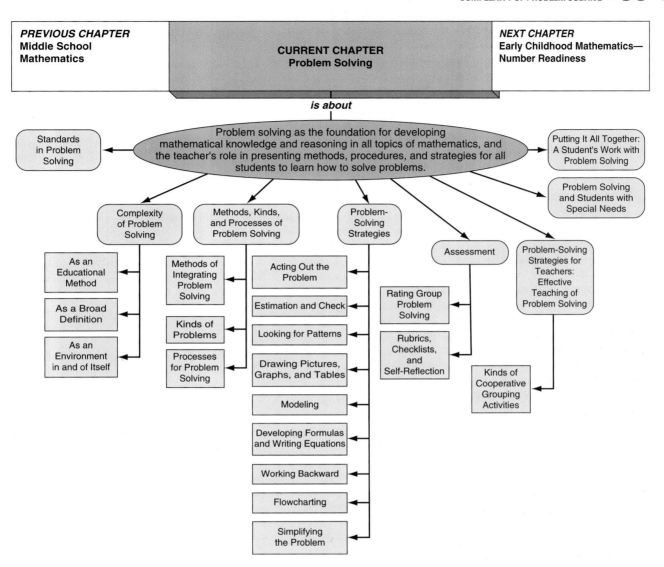

| PREVIOUS CHAPTER
Middle School
Mathematics | CURRENT CHAPTER
Problem Solving | NEXT CHAPTER
Early Childhood Mathematics—
Number Readiness |

is about

Problem solving as the foundation for developing mathematical knowledge and reasoning in all topics of mathematics, and the teacher's role in presenting methods, procedures, and strategies for all students to learn how to solve problems.

Standards in Problem Solving

Putting It All Together: A Student's Work with Problem Solving

Problem Solving and Students with Special Needs

Complexity of Problem Solving
- As an Educational Method
- As a Broad Definition
- As an Environment in and of Itself

Methods, Kinds, and Processes of Problem Solving
- Methods of Integrating Problem Solving
- Kinds of Problems
- Processes for Problem Solving

Problem-Solving Strategies
- Acting Out the Problem
- Estimation and Check
- Looking for Patterns
- Drawing Pictures, Graphs, and Tables
- Modeling
- Developing Formulas and Writing Equations
- Working Backward
- Flowcharting
- Simplifying the Problem

Assessment
- Rating Group Problem Solving
- Rubrics, Checklists, and Self-Reflection

Problem-Solving Strategies for Teachers: Effective Teaching of Problem Solving
- Kinds of Cooperative Grouping Activities

SELF-HELP QUESTIONS

1. What does research say about the role of problem solving in the mathematics curriculum?

2. What are some strategies that my students and I can use in solving problems?

3. Can students engage in problem solving without knowing all of the strategies?

4. What are some strategies that I can use to be a more effective teacher of problem solving?

5. What are some of the different types of problems used in problem solving?

6. What are some of the adaptations I can use to help my students with special needs develop their problem-solving abilities?

As a Broad Definition

The term *problem solving* is broad and refers to a complex of cognitive activities and skills. George Polya, a noted scholar in the area of problem-solving theory, held that solving a problem is finding the unknown means to a distinctly conceived end

STANDARD

Instructional programs from PreK through grade 12 should enable all students to:

Build new mathematical knowledge through problem solving.

Solve problems that arise in mathematics and in other contexts.

Apply and adapt a variety of appropriate strategies to solve problems.

Monitor and reflect on the process of mathematical problem solving.

GRADES PREK TO 2

In PreK through grade 2 all students should:

Involve a variety of contexts from problems related to daily routines to mathematical situations arising from stories.

Use and extend their knowledge from the content standards as needed to solve specific problems—especially as they relate to classification, shape, and space.

Generate new questions in mathematical contexts with persistence.

See a variety of strategies to solve a problem through shared experiences with other children in cooperative learning.

GRADES 3 TO 5

In grades 3 to 5 all students should:

Engage in problem solving involve important mathematical concepts where answers are not immediately obvious.

Generate and organize information; evaluate and explain results.

Begin understanding of predicting likelihood of an event.

Formulate new questions to extend the problem to new situations and see new strategies for solving the problem.

Apply mathematical skills learned in class to help solve the problems.

GRADES 6 TO 8

In grades 6 to 8 all students should:

Work through carefully selected problems to allow mathematical applications in other contexts.

Share their methods of solving with others to see the strengths and limitations of alternative approaches to solving the same problem.

Probe more deeply into relationships within problems.

Formulate their own problems based on a wide variety of situations with frequent opportunities to explain their problem strategies and solutions; explaining and generalizing and reflecting on their own work while monitoring solutions by themselves and others.

Use technology to handle "messy" problems too complex to solve in other ways.

FIGURE 5.1 *NCTM expectations of problem solving. Source: A partial listing as it pertains to Problem Solving from NCTM Principles and Standards for School Mathematics (2000, pages 116–117; 182–183; 256–257).*

(Polya, 1957). To solve a problem is to find a way where no way is known, to find a way out of a difficulty, to find a way around an obstacle, and to attain a desired end that is not immediately attainable, by appropriate means.

As an Environment in and of Itself

The environment of problem solving involves a problem with no immediately obvious solution and a problem solver who is capable of trying to find the solution by applying previously learned knowledge. Problem solving involves problem posing (Manouchehri, 2001), offering and testing conjectures, puzzles, word problems, "real-world"

problems, and nonroutine problems. A problem-solving session might be initiated by the teacher saying to the class, "What are some good questions to ask about decimals? You have five minutes to write down as many questions as you can about decimals in your math journal." Students are engaged in the process of problem posing that will lead to problems to be solved by the class.

Furthermore, it is helpful to remember that one essential aspect of problem solving is basic logic. Consider that most story problems contain words like *and, not,* and *or,* and basic logic can present a problem in the elementary classroom where it is not usually taught. Yet, to solve problems, students must master logical means for finding a solution. Means for solving such problems are presented later in this chapter.

METHODS, KINDS, AND PROCESSES OF PROBLEM SOLVING

As with any complex issue, problem solving has been broken down into several parts in an attempt to understand this broad topic more fully. We have constructed Figure 5.2 for those who are field-dependent learners and like to see the whole field and how everything fits into the big picture. However, each of these facets of problem solving will be considered separately in this section of the text for those field-independent learners who want to concentrate on one thing at a time.

Methods of Integrating Problem Solving

There are three common methods of interpreting problem solving:

1. As a goal
2. As a process
3. As a skill

As a Goal When problem solving is interpreted as a goal, it does not rely on particular procedures and methods, specific problems, or even mathematical content. Instead, it becomes an end in itself. Problem solving opens up the mind to see new possibilities performed in unique ways. If we apply the ideas of constructivism presented in Chapter 3, we would ask ourselves, "What would an effective classroom look like if the teacher were to follow the constructivist/standards approach?" The teacher would have the student actively engaged in constructing the subject matter, first concretely, then pictorially, and finally symbolically. This includes a heavy emphasis on appropriate manipulatives in mathematics. The primary concepts, the "big ideas" of all subjects (mathematics included), would be presented rather than looking at separate, isolated skills (Sutton and Krueger, 2002). The curriculum material would be presented as questions to be posed and problems to be solved rather than facts to be learned. How to structure effective problem-solving experiences is so important that we have reserved this entire chapter to problem solving and how to help students learn from it. We encourage you to read this chapter carefully as a beginning to the structure of good mathematics lessons.

METHODS OF INTERPRETING	KINDS OF PROBLEM SOLVING	HOW TO STRUCTURE YOUR MIND— THE PROCEDURES[a]	WHAT TO DO— STRATEGIES TO USE[b]	WHEN TO APPLY— NCTM *PRINCIPLES* ON PROBLEM SOLVING
1. As a goal	1. Open-ended	1. Understand the problem.	1. Estimate and check.	*K–8 Grades*
2. As a process	2. Discovery	2. Devise a plan using strategies.	2. Look for patterns.	1. Use approaches to investigate content.
3. As a skill	3. Guided discovery	3. Carry out the plan.	3. Insufficient information.	2. Formulate problems from everyday and math situations.
		Look back to check solution to see whether correct; if not, try again.	4. Draw pictures, graphs, or tables.	3. Develop and apply strategies to a wide variety of problems.
			5. Eliminate extraneous data.	
			6. Develop formula and write equation.	4. Verify and interpret results.
			7. Model.	5. Generalize solutions and strategies to new problem.
			8. Work backward.	
			9. Flowchart.	6. Acquire confidence.
			10. Simplify problem.	
			11. Act out the problem.	

[a]*Source:* Polya, 1957.
[b]This is not a definitive list; more can be added.

FIGURE 5.2 *The facets of problem solving.*

As we learned in Chapter 2, the celebration of people's cultural heritage gives all children in the classroom a sense of pride. There are various collections of stories coming from different cultures that show how people have been clever problem solvers through the ages. One such collection tells fifteen folktales from around the world in which the heroes and heroines have been clever problem solvers (Shannon, 1994). Each story is presented and then children are asked to explain how the problem was solved. The children then turn the page to see the solution as the folktale ends. This book and others are excellent resources if you are teaching problem solving as a goal to be enjoyed for the power it brings to the mind.

As a teacher you can take any folktale or story and give it the same suspense that Shannon gives in his delightful book. Just stop the story before the ending is told and ask children to think of ways to solve the problem. After reading the following story coming from Africa and told around campfires over the years (Edwards and Judd, 1976), you are given directions for creating your own problem-solving story in Activity 5.1.

An airplane had taken off from the Nairobi airport loaded with medical supplies for several remote villages far away from the African city. Approaching the landing field on a plateau above one of the villages, the pilot was alarmed to see no landing lights on the field. In the dense darkness of the night he could see neither forms nor outlines to help guide him to a safe landing. It was too far to fly to the next village on the limited gas supply he had. HE HAD TO LAND! He circled several times with his mind running helplessly from one idea to another—none of which looked workable.

Activity 5.1

CULTURAL RELEVANCE **PROBLEM SOLVING**

CREATING YOUR OWN PROBLEM-SOLVING STORY FROM CULTURAL FOLKTALES

MATERIALS

Stories you find in the library or have heard told over the years.

DIRECTIONS

1. Read over the story and decide where you want to stop and let the student problem solve a successful ending. This may be oral discourse or written discourse.

2. Then finish the story, making sure the students see the cultural group in the story as heroes and heroines for their ability to problem solve in a tough situation.

Supporting the NCTM *Principles and Standards* (2000):

- Mathematics as Connections . . . with Cultures; Mathematics as Problem Solving and as Communication
- Worthwhile Mathematical Tasks for Teachers— The Teaching Principle

---

Stop and let the students suggest possible ways to solve the problem. Then continue on:

How the Problem Was Solved in the African Village

Then he saw a very faint flicker—a little dot of yellow. It was still no help. One dot in the thick darkness gave no guidance at all. It was impossible to tell what in the world it was. Then a startling thing began to take place. As if out of nowhere the pilot began to see another flickering dot, and another, and another until there must have been over a hundred of them! Very methodically, in a well-organized, unified fashion, the dots became two rows of landing lights showing the outline of the landing strip. As the pilot gradually descended onto the field, he could see the people standing on either side of the field holding their burning torches high above their heads.

One torch just could not do the mammoth job needed. It took a well-organized, purposeful, committed people who knew that the sound of an approaching plane at dark meant action on their part as a whole village. (pp. 28–29)

As a Process As a process, problem solving is seen as an opportunity to exercise certain methods, strategies, and heuristics. *Heuristics* involves the discovery of the solution to the present problem on one's own. New assessment tasks are being developed in many states and provinces with questions that require the students to come up with a heuristic to solve a problem. The students can draw from any of life's experiences or what they have learned in school to help them. An example of such a task asks fourth grade students to think of more than one way to solve a problem (Kansas State Board of Education, 1993):

If two of your classmates each have three dimes and four nickels, demonstrate and explain two different ways to determine the total amount of money the students have. (p. 27)

When students demonstrate and explain, teachers can see how well students are developing mathematical power in the process of problem solving.

As a Skill   Problem solving as a skill demands more attention to specific types of problems and methods of solution. The interpretation that the teacher brings to problem solving will determine the approach taken in the classroom.

Here is a typical task that may help children see the relationship of addition and multiplication with the number 9 in our number system:

How many different patterns can you find?

9

18

27

36

45

54

63

72

81

Teachers who want to stress the problem-solving strategy of looking for patterns would choose a task like this one. It focuses on that particular skill in problem solving. There are many books and journal articles that feature skill development in problem solving.

Kinds of Problem Solving

The approaches to teaching problem solving can be classified generally into three types: open-ended, discovery, and guided discovery. Figures 5.3, 5.4, and 5.5 are examples of three teachers asking higher-order thought questions in which children were asked to respond in three different ways. These are examples of the three approaches to teaching problem solving. Let's look at the activities and classify each type of problem.

FIGURE 5.3   *The open-ended question in problem solving.*

FIGURE 5.4   *The discovery question in problem solving.*

Open-Ended Questions   The open-ended question has a number of possible solutions, so the process of solving the problem becomes more important than the answer itself. Notice in Figure 5.3 that the teacher's interest is not in having students solve any of the problems they write. The purpose is to see whether they understand when such a procedure would be appropriate to apply in problem solving.

Discovery Questions   Discovery questions usually require a justification of the solution, and there are a variety of methods the student can

FIGURE 5.5 *The guided discovery question in problem solving.*

use to reach the solution. Figure 5.4 shows an example of a discovery situation.

There are a limited number of solutions to this problem, but the students can arrive at the answers from their understanding about numbers. As in this illustration, some students will approach the answer from an understanding of odd and even numbers; others from a knowledge of products in multiplication; and still others from a visual awareness of the difference in "look" between single- and double-digit numbers.

Guided Discovery Questions Guided discovery questions, by far the most common type, include clues and even directions for solving the problem so that the student does not become overly frustrated and give up. Figure 5.5 shows a typical teacher question with guided discovery. The teacher channels the students' thinking by giving clues that narrow the focus of possible solutions.

Kinds of Problems

Problems can be broadly categorized as either "word" problems or "process" problems. You may remember doing a lot of word problems during your elementary and high school years. Generally, those problems were found at the end of the section and were mostly the drill problems at the top of the page wrapped in words. In first-year algebra,

those problems were often subdivided as age problems, coin problems, mixture problems, distance problems, one-step, two-step, and multistep problems. When the standards were published, instructors began to realize that such artificial distinctions in the surface characteristics of problems were at least a nuisance and often a hindrance to students developing their problem-solving skills. A better approach seems to be that of using a few problems in any given lesson and discussing their similarities and differences to foster the students' metacognition (i.e., their ability to think about their own thinking). Such an approach encourages students to look at the mathematical structure of the problems rather than focusing on less helpful details such as the characters in the problem or the "key words." An example of three problems that could be used in this way is shown here:

1. Jose is collecting pretty stones during his vacation in the Rockies for his classmates. If he wants 4 stones for each student and there are 18 students in his class, how many stones must he collect?

2. Carla is moving 18 small blocks across the front step using a toy truck. She can only put 4 blocks on the truck at a time. How many trips will it take to move all 18 blocks?

3. Renee is bringing brownies for her Brownie troop meeting. If there are 16 brownies in the box and she gives 2 brownies to each person, how many are at the Brownie troop meeting?

Questions to be asked include the following: In what ways are problems 1 and 2 alike? In what ways are they different? In what ways are problems 2 and 3 alike? In what ways are they different?

Process problems are generally written in word form, but they are significantly different from the common word problem, which is usually solved through an application of known facts or algorithms. Process problems do not often yield to the simple application of basic facts and/or algorithms. Generally, process problems call for logical reasoning and the use of problem-solving strategies. An example of a process problem is the "Handshake Problem," which is described in the discussion of the "Act It Out" strategy later in this chapter (Morrow and Harbin-Miles, 1996).

Whether using word problems or process problems, it is important to include from time to time problems that have either too much information or not enough information. These two types of problems create difficulties for students who have reading problems and students who have trouble focusing on the task at hand.

An example of a word problem with insufficient information is: How much will it cost to buy a 5-pound bag of dog food today if it cost $.20 less last week? For a solution, students should identify the missing information as what the actual cost of the dog food was last week. Without knowing this, $.20 cannot be added to the base price to find out this week's price.

Many problems are designed with information that is necessary to solve the problem as well as information that is not needed. The students' first task is to sort through the information given to determine what is necessary and what is extraneous. If students fail to do this, they may waste time trying to produce irrelevant and insignificant data. Operating on clues about relevant and extraneous data, students can narrow the range of possible solutions instead of trying to use meaningless information.

An example of a word problem with unnecessary information is as follows: Rambo is a 35-pound dog. He eats a 5-pound bag of dog food that costs $3.14 every week. How much does it cost to feed him for 4 weeks? Before reporting an answer for the problem, students should identify the weight of the dog and the weight of the bag of food as extraneous to this problem.

Processes for Problem Solving

Polya's Process Whatever approach in using problem solving in the classroom is taken, it is important to understand the process of solving problems. Polya (1957) identified four phases of the process:

1. The student understands the question and is motivated to answer it.
2. The student has learned facts and strategies that are useful in solving problems.
3. The student applies various strategies until the problem is solved.
4. The student checks the solution to see if it is correct. If not, another strategy must be tried.

Accepting Polya's phases as a working model, the teacher is presented with step-by-step instructions in teaching. The problem must be designed and posed in such a way that (1) the student is capable of deciphering clues and determining what information is being requested and (2) the student becomes involved in the problem and is interested in solving it. Many books and teaching aids on the market present more or less effective problem-solving exercises. A number of computer-assisted instruction programs rely on problem solving as a way of teaching organizational and decision-making skills. Other teachers can be an excellent source of advice about what types of problems are effective.

Cognitively Guided Instruction Another model for teaching problem solving is based on the research in Cognitively Guided Instruction (Carpenter et al., 1999). The teacher poses a rich (worthwhile) mathematical task for students. After students have had an opportunity to work on the problem, the teacher asks students to begin explaining their work. Students share the process they used in solving the problem. The focus of the classroom discourse is the process. Students are encouraged to listen to and question one another. The role of the teacher in planning instruction and assessment in this approach to problem solving is critical and depends in great part on his or her ability to analyze children's thinking and on his or her knowledge of what is developmentally appropriate for these learners. A well-worded problem or task that leads to good discourse in the classroom can be more productive, mathematically speaking, than fifty isolated "drill and kill" exercises (van Zoest and Enyart, 1998).

Share and Compare A third model for teaching problem solving is "Share and Compare" (Buschman, 2003). Share and Compare is an instructional approach to teaching mathematics that encourages children to solve open-ended problems in ways that make sense to them. Buschman (2003, page 5) describes his approach as "a culture of discourse that children create to learn mathematics with confidence and understanding . . . (and) a learning model that places problem solving at the center of mathematics activities in the classroom." Buschman advocates direct instruction of problem-solving strategies only after children have developed or created their own strategies. You will recognize this as a constructivist approach. There are four elements to the typical share and compare lesson:

1. The warm-up, usually consisting of mental math exercises, is designed to help students acquire knowledge and practice skills.
2. The problem of the day is solved by the students in ways that make sense to them. They may work individually, in pairs, or in small groups and use any of the problem-solving tools available in the classroom: manipulatives, calculators, even the Internet.

3. Mathematician's chair is the time that children share their solutions to the problem of the day.

4. Compare, the final activity of the lesson, is the time for the children to compare solutions and look for similarities and differences in the solutions and the methods of arriving at the solution.

All three of the processes described above include the element of discourse, either written or oral. Students are expected to be able to describe the method used for solving the problem and justify or verify the reasonableness of the solution. We can see that problem solving involves several aspects of learning and teaching, including how to decode the problem (a reading skill) and how to translate the answer to a meaningful end (a writing skill). Many educators support the technique of having students write the numerical answer in a full sentence. This approach forces the students to reflect on their answer as they translate it. It may also provide an opportunity to consider the reasonableness of the answer. Asking students to verify and justify their answers in a written form often helps them clarify their thinking.

PROBLEM-SOLVING STRATEGIES

Strategies are methods by which a problem can be solved. The strategies used to solve problems are determined by two factors: (1) the skill and sophistication level of the student and (2) the range of mathematical tools that the student has previously mastered. The degree to which the student is able to compare a problem to a familiar situation, problem, or experience tends to dictate which strategy he or she uses. The more complex the problem to be solved, the more strategies that are often required to solve the problem. Therefore, some researchers argue, that students need to learn as many strategies as possible to become effective problem solvers. Research (Gravemeijer and Galen, 2003) shows that students may become more proficient problem solvers by using various strategies. Other researchers (Clements and Samara, 2007; Carpenter et al., 1999) have concluded that children become better problem solvers if they first develop their own natural problem-solving abilities. Strategies and teaching ideas are shared in the NCTM series *Navigating through Problem Solving* (House and Greens, [Eds.], 2004) Several strategies are described here. Teachers must be knowledgeable about a variety of strategies if they are going to teach problem solving. Sample problems are given for each strategy described.

Acting Out the Problem

Acting out a problem is similar to the modeling strategy, although it differs in that it does not depend on physical objects or visual aids that students can manipulate. Students who are in the concrete stage of learning will frequently call on the acting out strategy for solving problems. Students are more likely to view the problems as real-life situations if acting is encouraged and it will be easier for them to see the steps involved.

Example 1

If a salesperson sells 20 cents worth of gum to one customer, 15 cents worth of candy to another, and 30 cents worth of balloons to a third customer, how much has the salesperson sold altogether? What is the total dollar value if that same amount is sold every day for 4 days?

Solution: Students take the roles of the salesperson and the customers in the store. They may actually exchange play money to simulate earnings and expenditures, but for some students the visual aids are not necessary. They can see just by acting that the process is one of addition. If play money is used, then students may also see that subtraction is involved and they will have some practice in making change.

Example 2

The sixth grade girls' basketball team at Washington School won the district championship. All 12 members of the team congratulate each other with a handshake. How many handshakes would that be?

Solution: Have 12 students in the class represent the team members. Have the other students keep a written record of the number of handshakes. The first person shakes hands with the other 11 team members. The second person shakes hands with the remaining 10 team members. The third person shakes hands with the remaining 9 team members, and so on until the next to last person shakes hands with the 1 remaining team member. That is a total of $11 + 10 + 9 + 8 + 7 + 6 + 5 + 4 + 3 + 2 + 1$, or 66 handshakes.

Example 3

Many of today's mathematics textbooks provide lessons on problem-solving strategies. Our advice to you is to read the problems carefully or you may find one like the following. The strategy to be used is "Act It Out."

Maria can run 5 laps around the school track in the time it takes Susan to run 3 times around the track. How many laps will Maria have run when Susan has run 12 laps?

Solution: The "Act It Out" strategy would be difficult to employ here—not many students can pace their running so exactly. A table or chart, or writing an equation using proportional reasoning would be far more effective strategies.

Estimation and Check

Estimation is the strategy of proposing an approximate answer to determine a range within which the solution might fall. The assumed answer is checked in relation to the solution. Estimation can be done on a daily basis in the classroom. Such a strategy is effective in two types of problem solving:

1. In problems where there are too few data to allow for elimination of unlikely answers
2. In problems that deal with very large unknown quantities

Example 1

Your school principal has enough ribbons for 350 science fair participants. If the following number of students from each grade level had entries in the science fair, does the principal have enough ribbons? Use front-end truncation and compensation to estimate the number of ribbons the principal needs.

Grade 3	102	Grade 5	165
Grade 4	127	Grade 6	139

If you are not familiar with the terms "front-end truncation" and "compensation" as a method for estimation, review Check Your Mathematical Knowledge, "Estimation Strategies," on the Web site, chapter 5.

Solution: Adding the leading digits (front-end truncation) gives an initial estimate of 4 (hundred). This information is sufficient to determine that the principal does not have enough ribbons for the science fair participants. To estimate how many ribbons the principal needs, students use compensation. In using compensation, students look at the remaining digits in each number—65 and 35 is another 100; the remaining digits come to about 35. Therefore, the principal needs to order another 135 ribbons to have enough for this year's science fair participants.

Example 2

Jho-Ju held a yard sale and charged a dime for everything but would accept a nickel if the buyer were a good bargainer. At the end of the day, she realized that she had sold all 20 items and taken in the grand total of $1.90. She had only dimes and nickels at the end of the day. How many of each did she have?

Solution: To make our estimation and check useful, it would be helpful to build a chart or table to help us organize our guesses. For instance, a student might begin by guessing 5 dimes. Then, because there are 20 coins, that means there would be 15 nickels. But the total must also come to $1.90. So the student decides to create a column for the value of the dimes, the value of the nickels, and the total value. Finally, the guess is rated as "high" or "low" in relation to the answer of $1.90. Several guesses are illustrated below.

Dimes	Nickels	Value of Dimes	Value of Nickels	Total Value	Rating
5	15	$0.50	$0.75	$1.25	Low
15	5	1.50	0.25	1.75	Low
20	0	2.00	0.00	2.00	High
18	2	1.80	0.10	1.90	This is it!

Source: Herr and Johnson (1994).
This problem will be revisited in Chapter 14.

Estimation can also be the content of a problem-solving situation. Consider this problem from the TIMSS middle school problem set. Internationally, about 50 percent of the students answered this item correctly (43 percent of seventh graders; 53 percent of eighth graders). Of the U.S. students participating, 32 percent of the seventh graders and 34 percent of the eighth graders responded correctly (Beaton et al., 1996).

Example 3

Rounded to the nearest 10 kg the weight of a dolphin was reported to be 170 kg. Write down a weight that might have been the actual weight of the dolphin.

Solution: Any number in the range from 165 to 174 kg.

Looking for Patterns

Some problems are designed in such a way that the only way to solve them is to identify patterns in the data given to predict the data not given. Students need to practice examining given data to see whether it reveals a predictable pattern. Once the pattern is established, the student can calculate the unknown data to solve the problem. Putting data into table format often will help show the pattern.

Example 1

The peg puzzle can be used to create patterns to make a generalization. In the activity, the object is to exchange the black and white pegs shown in Figure 5.6 by moving in a prescribed order.

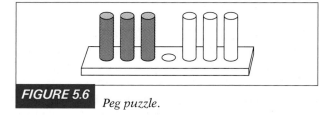

FIGURE 5.6 *Peg puzzle.*

Directions:

1. Move a peg forward one space into an empty hole, jump one peg if it is a different color. Pegs can only move forward.

2. Play with a partner—one player moves the whole time while the other partner counts the moves. Then switch positions.

3. First start with one pair (a peg of each color), find the minimum number of moves to exchange pegs from one side to the other. Record in the following table. Try again with two pairs and find the minimum number of moves. Look for a pattern in the table:

Number of Pairs (x)	Number of Moves (y)
1	3
2	8
3	15
4	?
5	?

Example 2

Students must be made aware that patterns are not always as projected from a few samplings. Figure 5.7 is an example of a time when the beginning pattern does not hold.

What is the maximum number of regions formed by connecting all the points in a circle?

Find out what the next one would be.

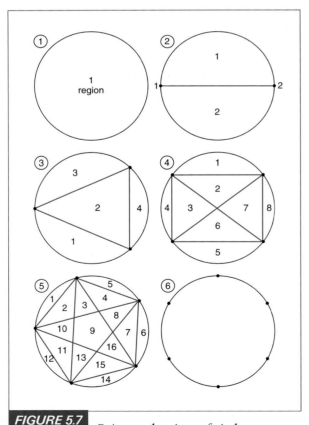

FIGURE 5.7 *Points and regions of circles.*

Number of Points	Number of Regions
1	1
2	2
3	4
4	8
5	?
6	?

Drawing Pictures, Graphs, and Tables

If students have difficulty grasping a problem that seems too complex or abstract, they might find it helpful to create a visual image to assist them. Aids such as drawing pictures, graphs, and tables provide a graphic means of displaying numerical data in a way that students can see. Graphs can help to demonstrate relationships among data that may not be apparent immediately. A visual image can also help students keep track of intermediate steps required to solve the problem.

Example 1

A farmer planted 8 rows of beans and put 12 beans in each row. How many beans did the farmer plant?

Solution: Drawing a sketch such as this one will quickly indicate the repeated addition or multiplication needed for solving the problem.

```
XXXXXXXXXXXX
X
X
X
X
X
X
X
```

Example 2

If four friends go bowling every week, how can they keep track of their weekly average?

Solution: One solution is to create a bowling average computer database (a computerized method of organizing and storing information that can be easily retrieved) to keep continuous, up-to-date records of bowling results each week. The information can be ordered by using the database, and the table is convenient for displaying the data to solve problems. A sample database follows:

Name	Week	Bowling Game 1	Average Game 2	Game 3	Average
Bitter	1	155	185	175	172
Hatfield	1	182	175	180	179
Edwards	1	158	192	188	179
Morrow	1	177	182	188	182
Bitter	2	182	189	188	186
Hatfield	2	182	178	168	176
Edwards	2	155	187	177	173
Morrow	2	177	166	197	180

Modeling

Constructing a physical representation or model of the problem is another way of helping students to conceptualize the operations necessary to solve a problem. Students may even be more interested in a problem that they can manipulate manually, as evidenced by the popularity of puzzles in teaching arithmetic and geometry. Teachers who have access to computers and graphics software can make good use of the modeling strategy. Students can be given problems that ask them to construct a variety of shapes. Computer graphics can be used to motivate students to take an active interest in the problem-solving process. Moone, Grace and Cornelis de Groot. "Fraction Action." *Teaching Children Mathematics 13* (December 2006/January 2007): 266–271.

Example

Have students arrange six markers in the following triangular pattern.

Move just two markers and turn the triangle "upside down."

Solution: Students can try different moves. The solution is to move the outside markers in the bottom row to the top row.

Activity 5.2 shows the modeling approach applied to a typical algebra problem. The models developed by the students are then compared to an algebraic approach.

Developing Formulas and Writing Equations

It is often useful to invent a formula into which one can plug numbers to arrive at an answer. Students learn that routine formulas often have real-world applications and that numbers stand for objects and concepts in a mathematical formula. It is helpful to give students exercises that

Activity 5.2

CULTURAL RELEVANCE **PROBLEM SOLVING**	**MODELING STRATEGY**

Students in Ms. M's class were given the following directions and problem.

DIRECTIONS

1. Read the following problem.
2. Create a model for the problem.
3. Solve the problem.
4. Pair off with someone who solved the problem differently.
5. Compare your models and solutions.

PROBLEM

Bill and Ivan are neighbors. Each has a fence running the length of his backyard. Together the fences are long. If Bill's fence is 5′ shorter than Ivan's fence, how long is each fence?

When the students had completed step 5 in the directions, Ms. M asked volunteers to share their models and solution with the entire class. Anita was the first volunteer.

Anita's Model

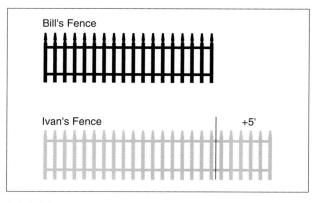

Anita's Solution

If the two fences are 87′ feet long, then I can add 5′ to Bill's fence to make them the same length. Then the fences together will be 92′ long. I can divide the in half to get the length of each of the fences. Half of 92 is 46. So, Ivan's fence is 46′ long. I subtract 5′ from that (because I originally added on 5′) and get 41′ for the length of Bill's fence.

Tamika's Model

Tamika's model was nearly the same as Anita's, but her approach to the solution was different.

Tamika's Solution

If the two fences are 87′ feet long, then I can subtract 5′ from Ivan's fence to make them the same length. Then

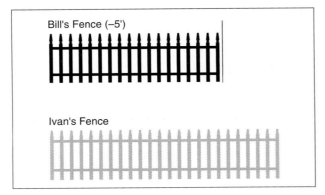

Bill's Fence (−5')

Ivan's Fence

the sum of the lengths of the two fences is 82'. I can divide the 82' in half to get the length of each of the fences. Half of 82 is 41. So, Bill's fence is 41' long. I add 5' to that (because I originally subtracted 5') and get 46' for the length of Ivan's fence.

When most of the students in class identified with either Anita's or Tamika's approach to the solution, Ms. M asked the students if they would like to compare their model and approaches to how it might be done in algebra. Ms. M pointed out that the length of the two fences could be identified with a single variable and then the expressions for the fences could be written in an equation.

$$\text{Bill's fence in feet}: x$$
$$\text{Ivan's fence in feet}: x + 5$$
$$\text{Total fence length}: x + x + 5 = 87$$
$$2x + 5 = 87$$
$$2x + 5 - 5 = 87 - 5$$
$$2x = 82$$
$$x = 41$$

Bill's fence is 41' in length; Ivan's fence is 46' in length.

Supporting the NCTM *Principles and Standards* (2000):

- Mathematics as Problem Solving, Communication
- Worthwhile Mathematical Tasks for Teachers— The Teaching Principle
- The Assessment Principle

---

require the translation of ideas into words and numbers.

Example

Micha must take an aspirin a day every day for the next six weeks. How many aspirin will Micha take in six weeks?

Solution: First, translate "every day for six weeks" into numbers. Then the student can write an equation and solve it: $a = 6 \times 7$. $a = 42$. Micha will take 42 aspirin in six weeks.

Working Backward

Geometric proofs call for the strategy of working backward. More common everyday problem solving calls for this skill as well.

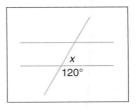

Example 1

Prove that angle x is 60 degrees.

Note: The answer, that $x = 60$ degrees, is given. Now the student needs to work backward to find out how to get the answer.

Solution: The student might reason this way: The angle adjacent to the 120 degree angle is its supplement so it must be 60 degrees. When two parallel lines are cut by a transversal, the alternate interior angles are congruent. So, angle x must be 60 degrees.

Example 2

The lumber truck left enough lumber to build three recreation rooms, but only one-half of that is needed for even the biggest recreation room. This room will be only 2/3 as large as the biggest recreation room. Will I have enough if I offer to give 5/8 of it back?

Solution: The student might reason this way: If this room is only 2/3 as large as the biggest recreation room, then I only need 2/3 of one-half of the lumber for this room. Two-thirds of one-half is one-third. One-third is 8/24. Five-eighths is 15/24. If I give back 15/24 of the lumber for this room, I will still have 9/24 of the lumber which is more than the 8/24 that I need. So, yes, I will have enough to build this room if I give back 5/8 of the lumber originally left for this room.

Flowcharting

Borrowing the concept of flowcharting from the field of computers, teachers can assist students in visualizing the process of solving a problem by using a flowchart. *A flowchart* is a detail-by-detail outline of steps that must be taken and conditions that must be met before the solution is reached. It is not necessary to use the various symbols that programmers use in flowcharting. If presented like the example in Figure 5.8, the shape of the boxes can help young children decide where to place each decision. Children can be shown the process of problem solving by a chart with directional arrows, showing the way one step leads to another or requires testing for a certain condition.

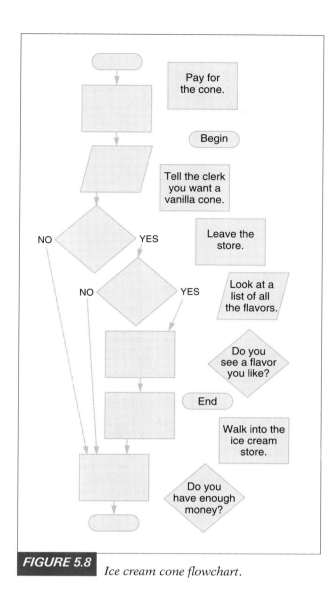

FIGURE 5.8 *Ice cream cone flowchart.*

Simplifying the Problem

Substitute smaller numbers that can be handled with quick estimation skills so students can test the reasonableness of their answers before doing the problem with the original numbers. Have students substitute basic facts or easy number combinations so they can get a sense of the appropriateness of the operation chosen.

Example 1

A person bought a car for 25 percent less than the original price of $3495. How much was paid?

Solution:

Think: 25 percent off $100 would be $25 off or $75 for the sale price.

Think: 25 percent off $1,000 would be $250 off or $750 for the sale price.

Think: 25 percent off $3,000 would be 3 × 250 = $750 for a sale price of $2250.

Each answer fits into the general pattern,

$$0.25 \times \text{old price} = x \text{ and old price} - x = \text{sale price}$$

Then the original numbers can be supplied.

Another way to approach this problem would be to substitute 10 percent of $3,000. Think about how that answer is obtained, then work up to 25 percent of $3,000, and finally to the actual numbers.

Example 2

A new school is set to open. There are 1,000 lockers in the school, all with closed doors. On the first day of school, the students decide they must do something special to start the year in their new school. So they decide to enter the building one at a time. The first student to enter opens the doors of every locker. The second person closes the doors of the even-numbered lockers. The third person changes the door (from open to closed or closed to open) of every third locker. Likewise, the fourth, fifth, sixth, and on to the one-thousandth student. After all the students have changed the locker doors, which locker doors are closed?

Solution: Suppose instead of 1,000 lockers, there were only 25 lockers. Now, students can either act it out using their school lockers, or they can create a chart similar to the one in Figure 5.9:

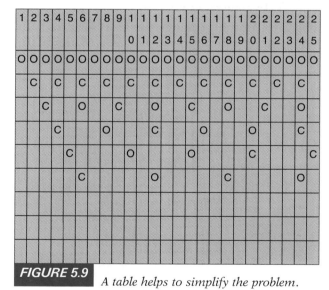

FIGURE 5.9 *A table helps to simplify the problem.*

Fill in as much more of the chart as you need to. Take time to look for a pattern as well. At this point (only 6 students completed) it may be difficult to see what the pattern might be. When you have completed the chart for 10 students, you will see that lockers 1, 4, and 9 are open; all the others are closed. You may recognize these as the first three perfect squares. A pattern seems to be emerging. Continue to see if you are right. Other problems can be found on the Web site (Chapter 5, Extended Activities, "More Process Problems").

EXTENDED ACTIVITIES

| PROBLEM SOLVING | MATHEMATICAL CONNECTIONS | PORTFOLIO | CHILDREN'S LITERATURE |

- More Process Problems
- Checklist Assessment of You as a Good Problem Solver
- Family Math Packet [using Children's Literature] Problem-Solving Game

PROBLEM-SOLVING STRATEGIES FOR TEACHERS: EFFECTIVE TEACHING OF PROBLEM SOLVING

Yes, our job as teachers of problem solving does seem monumental. We must remember that " . . . in real life, few mathematical situations can be clearly classified as belonging to one content strand or another, and few situations require only one facet of mathematics thinking". Figure 5.10, an illustration from the NAEP 1996 Mathematics Report Card for the Nation and the States, helps us to visualize this reality.

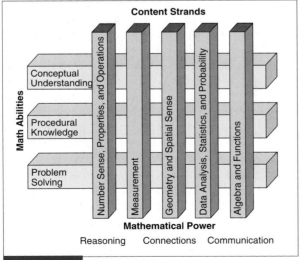

FIGURE 5.10 *The interrelatedness of mathematical content, processes and skills. Source: National Assessment Governing Board, Mathematics Framework for the 1996 National Assessment of Educational Progress.*

There are techniques to use and assessments with rubrics to evaluate ourselves and our students when we start to slip back into old, nonproductive habits. A rubric is a standard by which to assess one's level of ability in a topic or concept in a structured, objective manner. We explore some techniques and rubric assessments in this section. Effective teaching of problem solving involves techniques, other than the strategies discussed, to make students feel more comfortable with the problem-solving experience (Buschman, 2003). Some techniques are emphasized in the following paragraphs and may be used as a checklist for teachers:

- *Model a positive attitude for your students.* If you convey the excitement, satisfaction, and sense of accomplishment that successfully solving a problem can provide, your students will catch the spirit and be more willing to tackle problems themselves.

- *Choose problems carefully, paying special attention to interest and difficulty level.* Students are not motivated to solve problems that they find boring, irrelevant, too easy, or too difficult. Other teachers can be excellent advisors on appropriate problems to present. Collect students' work when they are asked to generate word problems, and use these settings as examples.

- *Let students choose the problems.* Problem posing, such as that described previously, engages students in solving problems they have generated and are interested in. Problem posing, like problem solving, takes practice.

- *Put students in small groups and allow them to work together on problem-solving exercises.* Some teachers have found that students are more successful at problem solving when they work in pairs or teams (Manouchehri, 2001). Cooperative learning enables the exchange of ideas about which strategies to use and provides assistance in estimating and testing results. Each student needs to experience several ways of conceptualizing the problem and selecting strategies. Cooperative learning establishes an environment that supports problem solving. "A small group structure has the potential to maximize the active participation of each student and reduce individual isolation. Small groups increase the opportunity for individual participation and immediate feedback. Both are valued as needed social interaction for children (Burns, 2007). In addition, combine collaborative problem solving with individual accountability. Provide a five- to ten-minute individual "think time" before the cooperative group work begins, or have each student respond individually in a journal, perhaps justifying the process/solution the group used, or solving a similar type of problem.

- *Identify wanted, given, and needed information.* Before students can solve a problem, they must understand the three types of information that are involved in the problem itself:

  a. Wanted information—the solution.

  b. Given information—presented in the problem.

  c. Needed information—information not presented in the problem but required to solve it.

It may be useful for students to create a list or table showing what data apply to the three categories above. Include the likely source of the needed information because students cannot solve a problem if they do not have access to the information required.

- *Pose the problem in such a way that students clearly understand what is expected of them.* No matter how motivated students are, they will not be able to solve problems unless the problem and accompanying instructions are stated clearly and simply. Ask students to repeat directions to check for understanding. Foster an environment in which they feel comfortable asking questions when they do not understand. If necessary, introduce them to vocabulary words that are used in the problems. This point also supports English as a subject for mathematical connections.

- *Present a wide range of problems.* Students may become bored if they are expected to work similar problems repeatedly. They should practice a strategy or problem type only until it is mastered. At that point, it is time to introduce a new type of problem so that students continue to feel challenged.

- *Present problems often.* Make problem solving a frequent part of class instruction so that students do not see it as an isolated skill but as an ongoing, familiar, and necessary process.

- *Give students the opportunity to solve problems in a way that makes sense to them.* Careful scaffolding of students' strategies will increase students' exposure to different and more efficient strategies.

- *Provide opportunities for students to structure and analyze problems.* Discuss the makeup of a problem as well as its components. Students will develop a language for discussing strategies and patterns for analyzing problems that would not be possible otherwise.

- *Provide opportunities for students to solve different problems with the same strategy.* Such opportunities provide the practice necessary for students to master a given strategy. Students also develop an important sense that strategies are flexible and can be applied to a wide range of situations. Also encourage students to solve the same problem with different strategies. This approach makes them aware that they have choices about how to approach a problem.

- *Help students consider appropriate strategies for a particular problem.* Model problem-solving strategies for students each day. Use the "think-aloud" method to share your approach to a problem rather than just springing the strategy or answer on them. At first, students have little experience on which to base judgments about which strategies are most effective with specific types of problems. Trial and error are frustrating ways to choose a strategy. If students are assisted in selecting the best strategy and in defining the qualities that make it effective, they gain experience that will aid them later when making judgments on their own. Ask three questions of your students during any problem-solving situation. "What are you doing?" "Why are you doing that?" "How is it helping you?" These questions are not meant to be sarcastic or demeaning, nor to be asked only of those who are having difficulty with the problem at hand. Rather, these questions are intended to help students learn to be reflective about their problem-solving processes and strategies—to think about their thinking. Another question to ask is "What strategy should we **not** use for this problem?" This encourages students to think about the practicality or efficiency of creating a chart for 1,000 lockers or acting out a solution that involves 1,000 students. Students can then focus on making the problem simpler, for instance, and/or looking for patterns.

- *Help students recognize problems that are related.* Students need to be trained to see structural relatedness of problems. Teachers need to create related problems by varying the data and condition of a single problem. Ask students to list key words and features of the problems to identify their similarities.

- *Allow students plenty of time to solve problems, discuss results, and reflect on the problem-solving process.* Students need to be able to discuss their methods and rationales as a way of organizing and processing their experience. As mentioned earlier in this book, research shows that elaborating techniques are rewarded by higher achievement in mathematics. In addition, have students communicate in written and oral form daily. One school in Massachusetts credits their high performance on the state assessment to their use of this learning strategy (Gallagher and Kaufman, 2005).

- *Demonstrate to students how they can estimate and test their answers.* This process can save students the frustration of wasted time and effort in problems in which the range of results is not immediately obvious. Students also need to be shown how they can work a problem backward or use other methods of testing their answers.

- *Discuss how the problem might have been solved differently.* With many problems, a variety of strategies will result in correct solutions. Ask students what other methods they could have used after a problem is solved successfully. Help students see that various approaches to the problem are acceptable. The selection of strategies depends, in part, on learner style and preference. Various strategies that can be used with different learning styles are mentioned where appropriate throughout this text.

Kinds of Cooperative Grouping Activities

Reflection on the above techniques reveals the possibilities for cooperative group activities in problem solving. Problem solving is one type of assignment that can work well in cooperative groups. Students who have learned to listen to one another's ideas, pose problems, and probe for understanding are better able to monitor their own thoughts, the thoughts of their teammates, and the problem-solving process, during group problem-solving sessions (Lampert and Cobb, 2003).

1. **Think-Pair-Share** (adapted from Kagan, 1989). In this cooperative group activity, students first work individually on the problem. Then, when each has prepared some initial work (a statement of what the student understands the problem is asking, a possible strategy or two to use), students pair off and discuss what each has brought to the table for the problem under consideration.

The pair then continues working together on the problem. Later, the pairs are invited to share their understanding, the strategies used, the solution found, and why the solution is a reasonable one, with the entire class.

2. **A grid approach.** Using a grid to structure beginning thought processes has proved helpful to some groups. A problem-solving grid from Learning 91 (Trahanovsky-Orletsky, 1991) in Figure 5.11 could be adapted to a cooperative learning lesson. The basic parts of the grid are as follows:

   a. Finding: What are you looking for? What is the answer you want to find?

   b. Given: What does the problem tell us? What information is given?

   c. Conditions: Does the problem set any limits, or requirements?

   d. Noise: Is there information included in the problem that you do not need?

   e. Key words: Are there important words that tell you what operation to use—addition, subtraction, and so forth?

   f. Hidden numbers: Are there numbers that do not look like numbers—two for 2, first for one, quarter for 0.25, and so forth?

   g. Planning the solution: What are you looking for? What is given?

   h. Finding the solution: Solve the equation. What does x represent?

   i. Looking backward: Does the number make sense?

Finding?	Given?	Conditions?
Noise?	Key words?	Hidden numbers?
Planning the solution	Finding the solution	Looking backward

FIGURE 5.11 *Problem-solving grid.*

Each cooperative group of four students may be given a problem to solve and asked to go through the problem-solving steps in order. To ensure that each member of the group has a definite role, two of the sections of the grid could be the assigned responsibility of each student, with the entire group responsible for the last step.

semester long

3. **A weekly problem approach.** Another possible way of organizing problem-solving activities (Artzt and Newman, 1990a) would be assigning problems on Monday with each group asked to solve the problem by the end of the week. Some problems require more time to solve than one math session may provide. Groups can find time to meet before recess, or at the end of the day, to continue to explore solutions. Teachers report hearing children giving each other assignments to do before they meet again. The groups present their solutions and how they went about solving the problem for the whole class to hear. The teacher asks the students to keep track of how many different solutions and strategies were used to solve the problem. Over time this becomes a powerful message that there is more than one way and often multiple solutions to math problems. Weekly problems and extended projects can come from many sources. Note that we are suggesting this as a strategy with cooperative group problem solving. We are **not** recommending that problem solving is a once-a-week activity.

PROBLEM SOLVING AND STUDENTS WITH SPECIAL NEEDS

"Once we say that some children are not capable thinkers or problem solvers, we have all but guaranteed that they will not be so" (Robert, 2002). Too often, students with special needs are denied the opportunities to become problem solvers because "they need to learn the basics first." Or "these students are too easily frustrated and just look for someone else to do the work for them." Yet, it is important to remember that " . . . there is abundant research evidence that proficient calculation skills and basic facts mastery need not precede conceptual understanding and problem solving" (Sutton and Krueger, 2002).

Researchers and curriculum developers at the Education Development Center, based in Boston, Massachusetts, have developed a profession devel-opment series called Addressing Accessibility in Mathematics. Some strategies for making mathematics more accessible for students with learning disabilities are shown in Figure 5.12. A more complete list of strategies can be found at their Web site, **www2.edc.org/accessmath.**

ASSESSMENT

Chapter 3 described a variety of assessment strategies, tools, and rubrics. Many of those strategies, tools, and rubrics can be applied to assessment of students' work in problem solving. Here are a few additional ideas related to assessment and problem solving.

Rating Group Problem Solving

There will be times when you will decide to assess the class during a collaborative problem-solving activity. With this approach, students may be asked to solve a problem as a collaborative group and to submit one group solution. An analytic scoring rubric based on Polya's plan for problem solving (Figure 5.13) may be used at this time. In this situation, all the members of the group received the same score or rating. Many teachers recommend including some form of individual accountability at the same time. Thus, students might be asked to submit individual papers describing the solution process, or justifying the solution, or applying the process to a similar problem.

Rubrics, Checklists, and Self-Reflection

Teachers can use the assessment rubrics on the Web site (see Activity 5.3, Portfolio Assessments: A Student's Work with Problem Solving) to periodically rate themselves and their students on the necessary skills to become good problem solvers and teachers of good problem solvers.

Metacognition has been suggested as an aid for problem solving (Bransford et al., 1999). *Metacognition* is one's knowledge of how one's own cognitive processes work. Good problem solvers can learn from observing their own actions and mental processes as they work on problems. A checklist taken from Capper's work (1984) has been made into a rubric. It is included in the checklist assessment (Web site, Chapter 5, Extended Activities 5.1, "Checklist Assessment"). Capper cites research to show that elementary and middle school students can improve their problem-solving skills if a teacher makes them

LEARNING AREA	TYPES OF TASKS	POTENTIAL DIFFICULTIES	POSSIBLE STRATEGIES
Conceptual	Making generalizations Determining rules Identifying and extending patterns	Tends to think concretely Has difficulty generalizing	Provide manipulatives or models for patterning Provide an incorrect rule for the student to try out and correct Encourage students to consider several trials, and test the generalization after each trial
Language	Reading problems Listening[2] Writing explanations and justifying conclusions	Often misunderstands directions For SLL students, listening is their weakest academic language skill Describes the procedure (i.e., "I added the numbers together.") rather than the reasoning that led to using the procedure	Have students highlight essential parts of problems; restate directions Have someone read the problem and/or the directions aloud For SLL students, write words on the board or overhead as they are spoken or point to words; contextualize instruction by using models, drawings, and other visual aids; have students physically act out problems
Organization	Collecting and recording data Sequencing and carrying out procedures in a multi-step problem	Does not organize data; has information in many different places Loses track of next step in the problem	Use a notebook system, grid paper labeled for data being collected Check off each step as it is completed, and ask what the next step is
Attention	Sustaining the attention needed to carry out multi-step problems Attending to other students' explanations	Loses track of what needs to be completed Loses track of what is being said	Provide an organizer or be completed checklist of steps Schedule frequent check-in points
Psycho-Social	Working in pairs or small groups Giving an oral presentation	Distracts the group Causes tension because of weak social skills	Set clear expectations for student collaboration and individual accountability; continue to review and teach expectations throughout the year Use "think-alouds" to model appropriate expression and language Have students rehearse with a partner or small group

FIGURE 5.12 *Accessibility strategies for students with special needs[1].*

[1]Adapted from the Addressing Accessibility in Mathematics, Phase 2 Project.
[2]Adapted from Khisty (2002).

Group Members _____

A. _____ Understands the problem
   3 Group thoroughly understands the problem
   2 Group understands parts of the problem, some but not all of the constraints
   1 Group does not understand the problem
   0 Group does not attempt to understand the problem

B. _____ Selects a strategy
   3 Group selects a strategy that leads to an appropriate solution
   2 Group only partially selects a strategy that will work
   1 Group selects an inappropriate strategy
   0 Group does not select a strategy

C. _____ Determines a solution
   3 Group determines a correct/appropriate solution
   2 Group determines a solution that is partially correct
   1 Group determines an inappropriate or incorrect solution
   0 Group does not find any solution

D. _____ Verifies results
   3 Group logically verifies results
   2 Group verifies partial results
   1 Group does not know how the solution is workable
   0 Group cannot verify the results

FIGURE 5.13 *Analytic scoring rubric for cooperative group problem solving.*

Use the following scale to rate yourself in the problem-solving work that you are doing.

   1—Almost always
   2—Sometimes
   3—Never
   4—I need to try this

_____ While problem solving, I use the Polya 4 step plan.
   Do I understand the question?
   What strategy should I select?
   How did I work the problem out?
   Does my solution make sense?

_____ I use problem-solving strategies such as trial and error, make it simpler, make an organized list, and use or draw a picture.

_____ I like solving challenging problems.

_____ Problem solving is: (you fill in the blanks below)

_____

_____

FIGURE 5.14 *Self-reflection on my problem-solving work.*

routinely aware of their own thought processes in relation to the checklist assessment just described. There is ample research to suggest that people of all ages do a better job of problem solving if they are aware of how they structure and apply their own mental approaches to problem-solving tasks (Snowman and Biehler, 2006; Carey et al., 1995;). Therefore, it behooves all teachers who want to nurture good problem solvers to spend some time with metacognition in mathematics. Some questions that structure self-thought for children follow:

- "What did your brain tell you to do when you saw the _____?" (describe the task)
- "How does your brain help you remember what to tell a first grader about this problem?" (This is similar to the Labinowicz example seen earlier in the chapter.)
- "When does your mind tell you which steps you need to get the correct answer?"

Some children's answers are delightful and insightful at the same time. One very active first grader responded this way when asked:

Teacher: "What did your brain tell you to do when you saw the large and small shapes on the table to sort into sets by color?"
Child: "I said, 'Brain, I need help,' and my brain said, 'Sit down. You jump around too much. See the colors. Make color piles.' Then I said, 'Thanks,' and my brain said, 'You' e welcome. Come again.'"

An example of a form for written self-reflection is shown in Figure 5.14.

PUTTING IT ALL TOGETHER: A STUDENT'S WORK WITH PROBLEM SOLVING

We have covered a great amount of information on problem solving in a few short pages. Let's see how well you can reflect on what you have just studied. The guided reflection you will use in completing Activity 5.3 can be used in your professional portfolio to document your ability to evaluate student work and journal writing. This student's class had just begun journal writing. This was one of P.J.'s first attempts to show his work. The teacher had stressed that she wanted the students to explain how they arrived at their solutions. P.J. was happy with his work. He told the teacher that his work would show he really understood the problem. What do you think?

Supporting the NCTM *Principles and Standards* (2000):
- Mathematics as Problem Solving, Communication
- Worthwhile Mathematical Tasks for Teachers—The Teaching Principle
- The Assessment Principle

Activity 5.3

PORTFOLIO
PORTFOLIO SOLVING
ASSESSMENTS:
A STUDENT'S WORK
WITH PROBLEM
SOLVING

STUDENT PROBLEM SOLVER: P.J.

The following problem is a sample of the type found in some fifth grade textbooks:

> *This is the story of five friends in the fifth grade class, Mateo, Red Cloud, Maria, Shaloma, and Daniel. What is the order of the shortest to the tallest person in the group?*
>
> *Mateo is a super basketball player even though he is the next to shortest person in the class. Red Cloud is the tallest boy in the class but does not play basketball. He likes to play video games with the tallest person in the class who stands tall. Shaloma stands tall, a foot shorter than her best friend, Maria. Shaloma is taller than Mateo and shorter than Red Cloud.*

P.J. solved the problem this way:

DIRECTIONS

1. Which of the strategies does P.J. seem to use? How can you tell? Justify your answer.
2. Use one of the scoring rubrics presented in chapter 3 to score P.J.'s work.
3. Compare your score to the score given by the rubric.
4. What does that tell you about portfolio assessments with problems like these?

SUMMARY

- Problem solving is finding the answer to a problem that has no immediately obvious solution.
- An essential aspect of problem solving is basic logic and reasoning.
- In planning mathematics lessons, problem solving can be seen as a goal, as a process, or as a skill.
- Questions used in problem solving can be open-ended questions, discovery questions, or guided discovery questions.
- Process problems frequently call for logical reasoning and the use of a variety of strategies.
- Problems with too much, or not enough, information present difficulties for students who have reading problems or who have trouble focusing on the task at hand.
- There are a variety of processes that can be used to teach with or about problem solving including the Polya method, Cognitively Guided Instruction, and Share and Compare.
- Some researchers advocate that students learn many strategies to become effective problem solvers; others maintain that students should first develop their own natural problem-solving abilities and strategies.
- Strategies to be used in problem solving include acting out the problem; estimate and check; looking for patterns; drawing pictures, graphs, and tables; modeling; developing formulas and writing equations; working backward; flowcharting; and simplifying the problem.
- There are a variety of strategies that can be used to be a more effective teacher of problem solving.
- There are accessibility strategies that will increase the likelihood of success in problem solving for students with special needs.

relate to problem solving in life

PRAXIS II™-STYLE QUESTIONS

Answers to this chapter's Praxis II™-style questions are in the instructor's manual.

Multiple Choice Format

1. The discovery of the solution to a problem on one's own is called:

   a. heuristics

   b. metacognition

   c. NCTM's "no cheating" policy statement

   d. None of the above

2. Student D is asked to solve this problem:

   A person bought a television for 25 percent less than the original price of $375. How much was paid for the television (excluding tax)?

Student D's response:	18.75
.25 of 100 = 25	4)75.00
.25 of 100 = 25	4
.25 of 100 = 25	35
.25 of 75 = 18.75	32
	30
	28
	20

   ```
        75
     +18.75
      93.75
   ```

   ```
     375.00
     −93.75
     281.25      The answer is $281.25
   ```

   Student D is using which of the following problem-solving strategies?

   a. simplifying the problem

   b. working backward

   c. elimination of extraneous data

   d. Both a and c

3. If a student with special needs is having difficulties generalizing concepts when doing a problem-solving task, the text recommends that the teachers provide:

   a. manipulatives or models for seeing patterns

   b. an incorrect rule for the student to try out and correct

   c. use "think-alouds" to model appropriate expression and language

   d. Both a and b

4. Look at the problem below:

   Lydia, Hal, Maxie, and Henry play on a soccer team together. They each wear different numbers. The numbers are 4, 9, 18, and 36. From the clues listed below, tell what number each one wears.

   > Lydia's number is not divisible by 2 or 4.
   > Maxie wears a number that is divisible by 9.
   > Maxie's number is not the largest number.
   > Hal's number is smaller than Henry's number.

   This is an example of a _____ problem, using _____ questioning style.

   a. word; guided discovery

   b. process; open-ended

   c. process; guided discovery

   d. word; discovery

Constructed Response Format

5. Three students were asked to explain their reasoning after answering the problem posed in 4.

   Score each student on the 4+ scale originally presented in chapter 3 and explain your reasoning.

   Student A should receive a score of _____ because _____.

   Student B should receive a score of _____ because _____.

   Student C should receive a score of _____ because _____.

Student A	Student B	Student C
Lydia wears 4. Maxie wears 9. Hal wears 18. Henry wears 36 because the people and the numbers are in order for playing soccer.	Lydia wears 9 because it is the only one that fits. Maxie could wear 9 but it is already taken, so she wears 18. Hal could wear 4 or 36 because they are left, but Henry's number is bigger; so Hal is 4. So Henry is 36.	Lydia is wearing 9 because 9 is not an even number like the 2 and 4 and 4, 18, and 36 are even numbers. So the others wear those numbers.

6. Read the problem-solving task below and indicate which problem solving strategies could be used to solve the problem.

Mr. Gregor was delivering mail for his company. He got into the elevator on the fifth floor. He then made the following stops.

He went up nine floors to Mr. Fairbanks' office.

He went down six floors to Ms. Violette's office.

He went up three floors to Mr. Rodenbow's office.

He went down seven floors to Ms. Takagi's office.

On which floor is Ms. Takagi's office?

Which problem-solving strategies could be used to solve the problem?

_____**1.** Estimation and Check

_____**2.** Developing Formulas and Writing Equations

_____**3.** Drawing Pictures, Graphs, and Tables

_____**4.** Modeling

_____**5.** Acting out the Problem

_____**6.** Simplifying the Problem

_____**7.** Flowcharting

_____**8.** Working Backward

_____**9.** Looking for Patterns

Apply the strategies you chose to solve the problem. Explain **HOW** you solved the problem. Label each strategy.

7. Three questions are recommended in the chapter for teachers to use to stimulate student self-thought when problem solving. Write what they are.

8. The chapter listed numerous strategies for teachers to use for effective teaching of problem solving. One was to choose problems carefully paying special attention to interest and difficulty level. The three problems used in the Praxis II^{TM} questions were adapted from State and Regional Mathematics Contests for Grades 4 to 6. How might you change the problems to heighten interest or adjust the difficulty level?

Integrating Technology

Video Vignette

On the Web site, view the video vignette, "Doubling," found in chapter 5. Read the questions accompanying the vignette before viewing it. Be prepared to discuss your answers with your colleagues after you have watched the video vignette.

Doubling

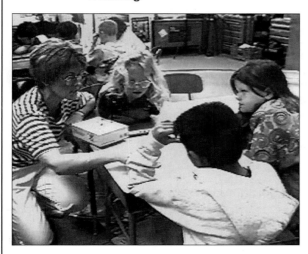

DIRECTIONS

1. When you first view the video segment, stop the tape once the children have made their choice of the first ($5 per day) option.
   a. Is this the choice you would make?

b. If it is, what would be your next step in this lesson?
   c. If not, how would you lead the class to explore the options further?

2. After you answer these questions, continue viewing the vignette.

3. Use the lesson plan for Video Vignettes (Table 3.0, page 00) to analyze Ms. Thomas's lesson in terms of tasks, discourse, and learning environment.

4. What evidence in the video vignette illustrates Ms. Thomas's attempt to monitor student learning?

Supporting the NCTM *Principles and Standards* **(2000):**

- Worthwhile Mathematical Tasks
- The Teacher's Role in Discourse
- The Student's Role in Discourse
- The Teaching Principle

Internet Activities

Scavenger hunt
"Road Trip" presents a problem solving situation in the context of an Internet-based scavenger hunt. It can be sound on the Web site for Chapter 5.

WebQuest

"Extrapolate and Interpolate: A Math WebQuest"
On the Web site for the text **www.wiley.com/hatfield**, open the WebQuest activity "Extrapolate and Interpolate: A Math WebQuest." Follow the directions there to complete this Web-based activity. Read the information on Fermi questions in "More Process Problems" found on the Web site (Extended Activities 5.1 in chapter 5) before beginning this WebQuest.

Web sites

For a series of problems based on stories, visit the Story Resource Center at the Mathematical Tale Winds Web site at **http://10.uwinnipeg.ca/jameis/**. Select the Land of Pome series for nonroutine problems set in the context of a fantasy story about the "pnomes" who live in the Land of Pome.
http://www.col-ed.org/cur/math/math45.txt has many lessons plans and units in mathematics developed by classroom teachers. A miniunit on "Estimating with Money" for chapter 1 students in grades 1 to 5 is an example of "real-world" mathematical problem solving.
Interactive: Home Page
http://www.shodor.org/interactivate
Developed for middle school mathematics explorations but several are adaptable to elementary mathematics.
NCTM: Elementary School Resources
http://www.nctm.org/resources/elementary.aspx
A wealth of teaching resources, recent research findings, and lesson plans for elementary teachers.
NCTM: Illuminations
http://illuminations.nctm.org/
Links to activities, lessons, the Standards, and other web resources.
NCTM: Middle School Resources
http://nctm.org/resources/middle.aspx?id=7860
A wealth of teaching resources, lesson plans, and tips for teachers of middle school mathematics.

CHILDREN'S LITERATURE

Clement, Rod. Co unting on Frank. Milwaukee, WI: Gareth Stevens Children's Books, 1991.

Cooney, Barbara. Miss Rumphius. New York: Viking Penguin, 1982.

Nolan, Helen. How Much, How Many, How Far, How Heavy, How Long, How Tall is 1000? Toronto: Kids Can Press, 1995.

Schwartz, David M. If You Made a Million. New York: Lothrop, Lee, & Shepard Books, 1989.

Schwartz, David M. If You Hopped Like a Frog. New York: Scholastic Press, 1999.

Scieszka, Jon and Lane Smith. Math Curse. New York: Penguin Books, 1995.

Tang, Gregory. The Grapes of Wrath: Mind-Stretching Math Riddles. Mexico: Scholastic Press, 2001.

Early Childhood Mathematics— Number Readiness

Chapter 6

A partial listing as it pertains to Number and Operations from NCTM *Curriculum Focal Points* (2006, pages11–12),

Although the majority of elementary school mathematics is focused on learning formal knowledge and skills, the preschool to early primary years (ages three to six) should focus on the intuitive, informal acquisition of mathematical concepts with many developmental activities to ensure a firm foundation in mathematics. All elementary teachers need to know how to analyze student understanding of beginning concepts if they are expected to build on what is known by the child. Children who have experienced some developmental delays will need a teacher who can restructure mathematical experiences that may have been missed along the way.

EARLY PRENUMBER UNDERSTANDINGS

This chapter is based on the growing volume of research on young children's early acquisition of mathematical concepts, especially those that lead to the basic understandings of number. Because the concept of number is foundational to building more complex mathematical understandings, this chapter focuses on the importance of understanding children's prenumber knowledge. It includes how to assess prenumber knowledge and how to develop quality teaching ideas to enhance prenumber concepts.

Emergent Mathematics
Geist (2004) has suggested the term "emergent mathematics" be used in much the same way as educators are now using the term, "emergent literacy" to talk about the early experiences necessary to develop good readers. In mathematics, it would mean immersing children in mathematics, giving them an opportunity to interact with mathematical ideas in a very "hands-on way," constructivist way. Geist points to the research that shows even very young children construct their math

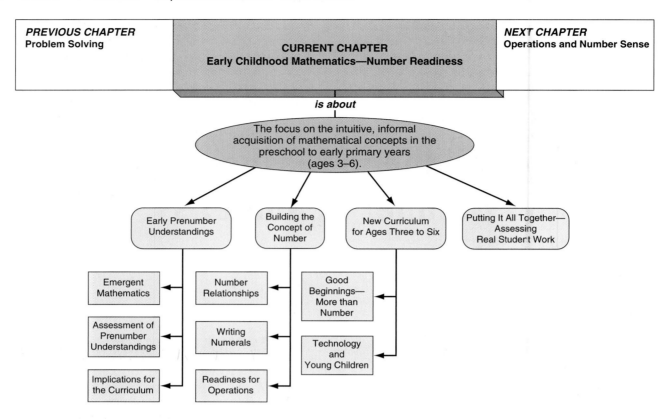

SELF-HELP QUESTIONS

1. How can I use the new research on emergent mathematics to be an effective teacher of children during their crucial early learning years?

2. How is technology used to foster quality mathematical understanding of young children?

3. How can I use assessment tasks in early mathematical understandings with young children in my classroom?

4. How can I use modeling, scaffolding, and learning styles to bring greater understanding of mathematics to young children in need of success?

5. How can I structure learning opportunities to help children experience quality number readiness activities?

knowledge, given some innate abilities to start the process. Through the new brain research, first mentioned in Chapter 3, we are learning that children are born with innate mechanisms that enable the construction of early intuitive learning about mathematics—the precursors of what will become more formal mathematical understanding with elementary school instruction. How the innate mechanisms affect later acquisition of mathematical understanding is speculative because we lack the research capability to give definitive answers.

As brain research advances, we look forward to more definitive answers in the future.

Patterns and Combinations—Precursors to Number Operations and Algebra Skills Patterns are inherent in mathematics and recognizing patterns are necessary if children are to acquire counting and number operations and early algebra skills. Pattern recognition means identifying the repetitive nature of something. Discovering a pattern requires detecting differences and similarities between the elements in the pattern. Monastersky (2004), citing a study by Gary F. Marcus, shows that infants as young as seven months recognize the difference in repeating patterns of syllables that modeled the patterns ABA and ABB. The syllables were nonsense syllables, such as wa ta wa and wa ta ta. Then new syllables in the same patterns were played, ga fe ga and ga fe fe. The infants reacted to the new patterns as if they were familiar even though they were completely new ones.

Patterns should be experienced visually, auditorially, and kinesthetically. The NCTM series, *Navigating through Algebra* (House, ed., 2001) asserts that children should be involved in recognizing, replicating, extending, completing, comparing, transferring, translating, predicting, and creating patterns, along with giving explanations for their work. To ensure success, patterns should begin simply—with an AB repetition. For example, red square, blue square, red square, blue square, or circle, square, circle, square, circle. When presenting patterns to children, it is important to include at least three repetitions. Once children have explored many varieties of this form, other simple patterns may be introduced: ABB, AAB, AABB, ABC, ABCD (Figure 6.1).

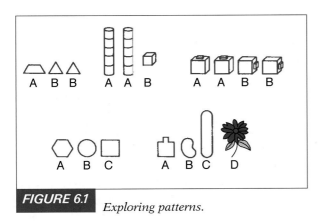

FIGURE 6.1 *Exploring patterns.*

Developing Patterning Skills Extended from the preschool to early primary years, children need to identify, analyze, copy, extend, and create many different patterns. Economopoulos (1998) suggests that comparing patterns helps children become careful observers of the structure of each pattern. Patterns should be presented to children in physical and concrete ways. They can participate in forming patterns with other classmates: boy, girl; sitting, standing; hands on head, hands on hips; short pants, long pants. Body movements can be used to make patterns: snap fingers, clap hands; touch your knees, touch your toes; step, hop. Patterns may be created by using some

manipulatives: pattern blocks, color tiles, peg boards, connecting cubes, dyed pasta, or whatever is available. The teacher creates a pattern such as "snap fingers, clap hands" and students can translate the pattern with the materials on hand (red circle, green circle; toothpick, macaroni). When they are comfortable with the concept of patterns, have them record their pattern by gluing construction paper shapes like the pattern blocks or connecting cubes, using stickers, or gluing the actual objects, if not intended for use again. Activities can connect to many concrete experience as in Activity 6.1

Activity 6.1

MATHEMATICAL CONNECTIONS **FINDING PATTERNS IN OUR LIVES**

PROCEDURE
1. Take a "pattern walk" to investigate where patterns occur in our everyday lives. (social studies)
2. Listen to songs or music that has a repeated pattern. (music)
3. Listen to stories that have a repeated pattern or a broken pattern. (reading)
4. Create a pattern that can be used in gym class with exercises such as hop, jump, hop, jump; touch toes, hands above head, touch toes, hands above head. (physical education)
5. Do an art project in which pattern is reflected: make strings of construction loops; string plastic or wooden beads on yarn; make a potato print pattern; paint a pattern. (art)

Constructions—Precursors to Geometry and Measurement From early infancy on, children construct with building blocks of all sizes. They stack boxes, pots, and pans—literally anything they can get their hands on. Hewitt (2004) says that the introduction of various building blocks from early wooden ones in the 1800s to the rods of George Cuisenaire in the 1930s to the plastic, sophisticated Lego™ blocks of today, has helped children gain an intuitive sense of geometric constructions with size, shape, color, and texture as attributes. They will be seen in Chapter 12. When children raise their two arms to play the game, "big" and place their arms further apart for "so big," they are experiencing the intuitive differences in number magnitude and in measurement. Children are using the intuitive sense of estimation and check (a problem-solving strategy discussed in Chapter 5) when they spread their hands apart to show which size block they want to use next. Daria-Wiener (2004) suggests that one way to judge a superior quality preschool is the presence of blocks for children to use in the development of crucial spatial and problem-solving skills.

Assessment of Prenumber Understandings

Young children develop a sense of number through kinesthetic experiences. Objects need to be matched, sorted, grouped, counted, and compared. Piaget's observations of young children offer great insight into their thinking and developmental stages (refer to Chapter 3). There are some prenumber concepts that children should acquire before formal work with numbers. Teachers should be able to assess a child's readiness for number by determining what abilities the child has acquired and what perceptions the child has about the world. The next section shows how the prenumber concepts of classifi-cation, class inclusion, number inclusion, seriation, number conservation, and set equivalence can be assessed through Piaget's classic tasks.

Early primary teachers must have background on how to conduct the interviews (refer to Chapter 3) with children on these Piagetian tasks and how to interpret the findings in terms of curriculum considerations. Piaget's findings provide several logical ideas that influence the child's understanding of number.

Classification   Classification experiences involve making decisions about certain attributes of objects and sorting them based on that classification. Attributes might include size, color, shape, thickness, texture, function, or any combinations of these.

Assessment Task   In Figure 6.2, a collection of three shapes in two sizes might be shown to a child. The child is asked to put the shapes into piles so that all of the objects in each pile are alike in some way. Classification is the earliest stage of logical thinking and is the foundation for graphing. The preoperational child does not determine a classification scheme but begins with one plan and changes as another feature of the material becomes obvious and important. There is no consistent thinking strategy for sorting the material.

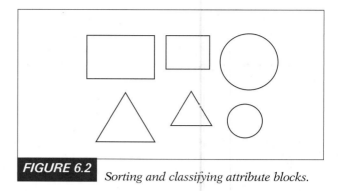

FIGURE 6.2   *Sorting and classifying attribute blocks.*

Most preschool and kindergarten children sort objects first by color because it is the most salient feature to them, but with maturity and experiences, sorting is done by shape and size.

Teaching Ideas   Because classifying is a fundamental task in life and appears across the curriculum, classification needs to be encouraged through many activities. Sorting can be done with shapes, dyed pasta, bottle caps, plastic animals, items from nature (shells, seeds, pine cones, leaves, and nuts), anything! The materials should be varied and interesting. Collections of fabric, pictures from magazines, junk such as old keys or nuts, bolts, screws, and buttons offer many varied opportunities for classification. Encourage children to describe and name their sets. Sorting should be done by using a sorting area with a defined boundary such as a chalked circle, yarn hoops, or a sorting mat. The teacher should circulate among the children asking key questions: How are these the same? How are these different? Why does this belong in your group? What is your sorting rule? It is important to sort materials many different ways (using different sorting rules). Children need to be encouraged to use different sorting criteria and be flexible. Sorting experiences offer means to assess the children's ability to think logically, to express ideas, to apply sorting rules, and to focus their observational skills. Blindfolds can be useful to involve using other senses and ways of describing their sorting rules. Other activities are seen in Activity.

The Sesame Street television program has a song, "One of These Things Is Not Like the Others." In this activity, children must form mental relationships between objects to determine which one does not belong. Children can compare seasonal pictures by attributes that they have in common (are alike) and not in common (are different). For example, in February compare pictures of Lincoln and Washington or in October compare two large poster pumpkins that are different in several ways.

These activities lead to more sophisticated mathematical logic in later grades such as Venn diagrams. Children need to explore relationships according to quantifiers such as "all," "some," and "none."

Associated with sorting is the idea of noting similarities and differences. This involves logical thinking. Children need a wide variety of experiences. See the Extended Activity, "Where Does It Go?", on the student companion Web site in Chapter 6 listed in Extended Activities 6.1. The teacher can group children from the class into two sets—long sleeves or short sleeves; with glasses or without glasses; wearing tennis shoes or other types, and so on. This can be an exciting way to explore materials in greater detail and to prepare children to think logically and draw conclusions. It also leads into graphing as a visual way to describe the results. Extend classification activities to involve two or more attributes (e.g., girls with pierced ears, wearing tennis shoes).

Activity 6.2

MATHEMATICAL CONNECTIONS **SORTING PROJECTS**

DIRECTIONS

1. Use the list of class members' names and have the children sort the names by a given letter.
2. Say a list of short words to the students and have them indicate all those that rhyme and those that do not rhyme.
3. In social studies, have children sort animals as farm or zoo.
4. In science, have children sort objects into those that sink and those that float or into those that a magnet attracts and those that are not attracted. Collect seeds or leaves and sort by type.

Class Inclusion A part of classification is the ability to see relationships between groups at different levels in the classification system. Grouping on the basis of class is one way to classify objects in the physical world. It is related to logical reasoning. To classify objects, their relation to other objects must be known. The idea is that all of one group can be

part of another group at the same time (e.g., the group of boys is part of the group of children). The Piagetian task to test class inclusion is discussed first, followed by some additional questions that prove insightful in a child's acquisition of this concept.

Assessment Task Show the child a box containing twenty yellow plastic beads and seven blue plastic beads. Discuss the properties of the beads with the child—plastic, a hole through it, uneven or bumpy surface, colored. Ask, "Are there more yellow beads or more plastic beads?" The characteristic response of younger children is to answer more yellow beads. Children have problems seeing the relationship of the two classes and end up basing their responses on appearances. This mistake indicates an inability to consider the quantity of plastic beads (the larger and general class) because the answer is based on appearances and the visible, bigger set is the yellow beads.

Teaching Ideas Additional experiences should include questions about children (are there more boys or more children), animals (are there more cows or more animals), fruit (are there more apples or more fruit). Suppose you give the child a collection of five plastic cows and three horses and ask, "Show me all the cows. Show me all the horses. Show me all the animals. Are there more cows or more animals?" The four-and five-year-old child answers, "More cows," because the whole group does not exist. Ask, "Than what," and the typical response is, "Than horses." The child cannot consider the whole because the two parts are horses and cows (what is seen). The child does not have the mental structures to form such classes. Most children younger than seven have difficulty seeing that all of one group can be some or part of another group. In terms of mathematical logic, a class may be considered in terms of its parts of partial classes. Thus, number can be related to logic. Piaget maintains that both class and number result from the same operational mechanism of grouping and both are needed to be understood. The young child is unable to think of one specific number in relation to other adjacent numbers; therefore, each number is approached in isolation. If the task asks the child to make a group of three blocks, followed by a task to make a group of four blocks, the young child is unable to place the two numbers and tasks into a mental relationship. This means the blocks used for the group of three will not be used to form the group of four.

Number Inclusion This mechanism is directly related to understanding the meaning of addition or number inclusion. Because addition is putting two sets together and naming it as a single number, the child who does not have the ability to place numbers into a mental relationship will have difficulty with the addition principle. The "counting on" strategy for addition (seen later in this chapter in "Building the Concept of Number") holds limited meaning for the preoperational child and probably should not be attempted. For the same reasons, using fact families or the inverse principle for addition and subtraction will be of limited value to the young child. Piaget (1965) contends that children at this stage of development are unable to have reversibility in thinking about whole to part and back to the whole again. Until these concepts are developed, which is around seven years of age (second grade), Piaget concludes: "In a word, it seems clear at this stage (stages 1 and 2) that the child is still incapable of additive composition of classes, i.e., of logical addition or subtraction" (p. 174). Therefore, although children can be taught to repeat answers to equations of basic facts, he warns that, "there is no true assimilation until the child is capable of seeing that six is a totality, containing two and four as parts, and of grouping the various combinations in additive compositions" (p. 190).

Assessment Task A quick assessment can be done by asking a child to count a collection of objects. Then add two more to the group and ask how many things there are now. Many first graders will count the entire group beginning at number 1 rather than arriving at the solution by thinking of the relation of five to adjacent numbers. The unnecessary counting is a result of being unable to count on from the first set and arrive at the solution sooner.

Teaching Ideas Children need many varied experiences of putting sets together to make the whole. They can make up number stories with counters, connecting cubes, or painted lima beans. Pattern block designs (Figure 6.3) offer opportunities to explore the class inclusion concept. Tasks, such as building a color square with Cuisenaire rods (Figure 6.4), then writing all the ways to show names for a given number, encourage children to mentally place numbers into an inclusive relationship. "Spill the Beans" Activity 6.3 and "the Number Four" Activity 6.4, as well as others described under number conservation in this chapter also foster class inclusion. Such experiences help children see that the total is constant regardless of how its parts are constructed.

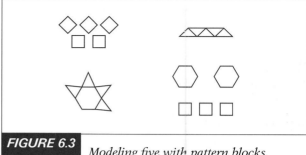

FIGURE 6.3 *Modeling five with pattern blocks.*

Seriation The ability to seriate involves the ordering of objects and events (e.g., the smallest blocks to the largest blocks). To seriate correctly, the child must make comparisons and make decisions about differences. The key to seriation is that the child understands how a single position in the series is related to both the position before and the position after it. This is similar to understanding that one object can belong to two classes at the same time, as in the class inclusion tasks. Ordering involves successive comparisons of objects so that each object or set has a unique place in the series: for example, to construct a series of ordered objects by locating the smallest object, then placing other objects in a series so that each is larger than the one before it and also smaller than the one after it. Objects may be ordered by various elements of dimension: capacity, mass, height, length, and quantity. Preoperational children have no overall plan for arranging things in a sequential order such as by length and cannot coordinate the relationships. According to Piaget, the ability to seriate is vital to the child's understanding of number. It also leads to the child's understanding of the relationship of cardinal and ordinal numbers. Children must mentally order numbers so that each one is one more than the previous number and also one less than the following number. The thinking processes necessary for seriation skills are important also in learning science, social studies, and language arts.

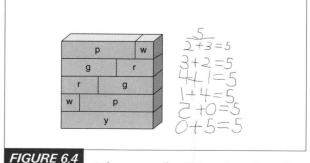

FIGURE 6.4 *Color square for Cuisenaire rods and child's number sentences.*

Activity 6.3

MANIPULATIVES   **SPILL THE BEANS**

MATERIALS
- Lima beans painted on one side *or*
- Colored counters
- Small cup

PROCEDURE
Put a given number of beans in the cup, which represents the total or sum. Shake and spill the beans. Group those beans with the painted side showing and count for the first addend. Group the beans with the white side showing and count for the second addend. Ask children to share their number stories (or equations) with each other, such as "4 red and 2 white makes 6; see Figure 6.5." When assessment indicates some children are ready to add written symbols, have them write the accompanying number sentence when the beans are spilled.

ASSESSMENT
Watch for children who continue to count the entire set and those children who use counting-on strategies. Notice if counting by twos occurs. Think about when each child is ready to move to the connecting level and attach numbers with the action.

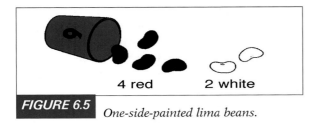

4 red   2 white

FIGURE 6.5   *One-side-painted lima beans.*

Supporting the NCTM *Principles and Standards* (2000):

- Concepts of Number and Operations—Flexibility
- Representation—The Teaching Principles

Activity 6.4

CULTURAL RELEVANCE   **THE NUMBER FOUR**

Four is an important number for many Native cultures. It symbolizes the four seasons, the four directions, Four Sacred Mountains in the Navajo Nation. Spiritual traditions often are performed in fours. The whole child is thought of in four aspects: Family, Spiritual (cultural), Education, and Self-Esteem. Indian education considers four circles of learning: Spiritual, Political, Social, and Intellectual. Find other examples in Native culture in which four plays a special number. Study other cultures to determine whether a special number is associated with any of them. Why do you think four might be chosen to be special? What about other special numbers?

Supporting the NCTM *Principles and Standards* (2000):

- Mathematics as Reasoning, Communication, Connections
- The Equity Principle

Assessment Task   To assess seriation, the child might be given a set of ten sticks or soda straws of graduated lengths and asked to arrange them from longest to shortest. The child could be given a set of pictures of graduated sizes. Because it is difficult for young children to establish a baseline for making comparisons, a ruler could be used as a straightedge or the pictures could be placed in a chalktray.

Teaching Ideas   Children could place rings on a spindle according to size relationships or they could arrange Cuisenaire rods into a staircase (Figure 6.6). Cuisenaire rods are different colored rods in graduated lengths from one centimeter to ten centimeters. Patterns for the rods are found in the appendix and on the student companion Web site.

Classmates can be placed in order of height. A set of shapes of a given region (e.g., rectangle), can be made in graduated sizes from heavy poster

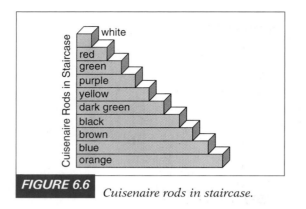

FIGURE 6.6 *Cuisenaire rods in staircase.*

board for the child to arrange in serial order. Ribbons or straws could be ordered from shortest to longest (or tallest). Have children think of other ways to order things such as coins by value, by size, by mass, and have them discuss their ideas. Children could order objects by a secret ordering rule and have others guess the rule.

Number Conservation   Conservation of number shows how the child perceives number invariance and the degree to which the child is tied to perceptual cues. Reversibility of thought is part of this task. Can the arrangement of a constant number of objects be changed without changing the number? The ability to maintain the equivalence of sets despite their arrange-ment is developmental and is acquired gradu-ally. Place a row of eight colored chips (blue for this example) before the child. Piaget recommends at least eight objects be used for the task. Otherwise, the child might know the number perceptually without the use of logic. Beside this row, have the child form an equivalent set with chips of a different color (e.g., yellow); see Figure 6.7. This task also tests the child's ability to establish one-to-one correspondence.

Assessment Task   Point to the first row. Ask, "Are there more chips in this row or in this row (point to the second row), or are there the same number of chips?" Child responds. Ask, "How do you know that?" Child responds. Now spread out the second row of yellow chips so that the length has been extended. Ask the same ques-tion about equiva-

lence. Ask, "Why do you think so?" Additional chips may be added to both rows, or the second row may be grouped in a stacked column or bunched together. Repeat the same questions with justification of the answers. The child who is a nonconserver cannot maintain the equivalence of number because of changes in length that are irrelevant to number. The real issue is that the child can-not reverse the line of reasoning back to where it started. Preoperational children are so focused on the perceptual aspects of the task that a lasting equivalence or number invariance is not possible. Conservers are not persuaded by changes in configurations or counter suggestions. They can justify their answers of "the same" by explaining that no chips were added or taken away, or that the chips could be arranged in the original position, or that the chips are spread out so the rows are longer but the number is the same. When we relate this discussion to mathematics instruction, Piaget claims that without reversibility of thought and number conservation, the additive property cannot be understood. The child cannot understand that five will remain five if grouped as four and one, one and four, three and two, or two and three. The number in the set is still five. "Fiveness" has no meaning for the child. Other educators or philosophers have studied Piaget's findings and have repeated his interviews and have confirmed his results. Direct instruction and schooling on conservation skills show that conservation cannot be taught with any lasting, permanent effects. Conservation abilities evolve from maturation due to experiences children have. Piagetian theory says that conservation abilities will not emerge until cognitive schemata, or the logico-mathematical structures, are in place. Number is something each human being constructs from within and not something that is socially transmitted (Kamii, 1985). Research (Kilpatrick, Swafford, and Findell, 2001) has shown that ability to do Piagetian tasks in conservation, class inclusion, and transitivity may not be needed to solve simple addition and subtraction problems. When the same arithmetic problems were compared with a task assessing a child's information-processing ability, a small but consistent correlation was seen. However, some students scoring low on the information-processing task could solve the arithmetic problems. The findings would seem to indicate that the information-processing task and the three Piagetian tasks may not be prerequisites for applying simple strategies to solve early number facts.

Teaching Ideas   Children need experiences exploring various numbers in different arrangements.

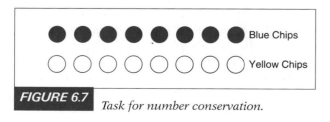

FIGURE 6.7 *Task for number conservation.*

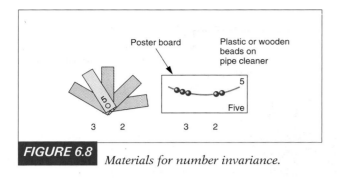

FIGURE 6.8 *Materials for number invariance.*

FIGURE 6.9 *Set equivalence task.*

Sets must be constructed and compared by children so that lasting equivalence can be achieved no matter what the configuration. Number fans and bead cards (Figure 6.8) are teaching devices that can be used to build understanding of relationships needed for conservation. A game with painted lima beans or two-sided colored counters develops number invariance (refer back to Figure 6.5 on page 129) and allows many repetitions without boredom. Connecting cubes can be joined together to represent the same sum with various configurations and color patterns.

Everyday Mathematics (University of Chicago School Mathematics Project, 2006) is one of the numerous early primary programs that promote the use of number stations and part-part-whole activities. Such activities encourage children to look for many number combinations and ways of grouping different materials for a specific number. In this way, children can see different configurations and combinations that lead to number sentences related to addition and subtraction.

Equivalence of Sets A task associated with understanding number is equivalence of sets. Here the child must form an equivalent set and be able to match sets for equivalence. Perceptual cues may interfere with the young child's understanding of this aspect of number. The tasks in the following paragraphs describe how to assess set equivalence.

Assessment Task Give the child a pile of lima beans. Make a set of five beans. Ask the child to make a set on a margarine lid (or any specific place to identify the set) that has the same number of beans. Ask, "Why do you think your set has the same number of beans as my set?" A child can have this understanding of one-to-one correspondence without being able to count. Another task is to make a line of counters. Below it, start a second line of counters but stop before the lines are equal in number. Have the child continue the second set until it equals the numbers in the first set. The next task tests set equivalence as well as the degree to

which the child is tied to perceptions. The teacher and child each have a paper cup or small container (Figure 6.9).

The child is given a group (around ten to twelve) of large lima beans or large counters. The teacher has an equivalent number of small lima beans (counters). The task is to simultaneously drop a bean into each of their cups. Because children love to race on this task, it might be advisable to say "drop" each time to keep the pace together. After all beans have been dropped into the cups ask, "Are there the same number of beans in each cup or do you have more or do I have more?" After the child responds, show the cups with the beans inside and repeat the question. The child may change the response because the size difference in the beans gives perceptual cues that may be interpreted as associated with the number. Ask for justification of each answer to gain valuable insight about how the child is thinking. The same thing holds true if the child is given two glasses of different sizes but the same size beads (Figure 6.10). Repeat the activity, but now the size of the container affects the child's perception of quantity even though a bead was placed simultaneously into each container.

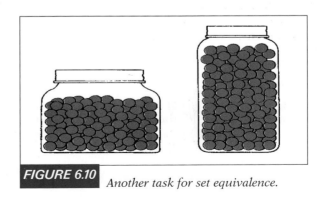

FIGURE 6.10 *Another task for set equivalence.*

FIGURE 6.11 *Developing set equivalence.*

Teaching Ideas Children need practice in naming the number when given a representative set and in constructing sets of a specific amount. Have children work in pairs with junk material. Each child, taking turns, makes a set, and the other child makes a set that is equal. Use yarn to establish one-to-one matching between sets and help the child see set equivalence. Relying on counting is sometimes insufficient for the young child. In the task with the beans, it is helpful for the developmentally young child who makes decisions about number from perception to take the beans from the cups, place them in matched pairs to see equivalency, and discuss differences. Set equivalence and one-to-one matching can be done with cups and saucers, juice cans or milk cartons and straws, toy babies and bottles, jars and lids, and plastic flowers and vases (Figure 6.11).

Implications for the Curriculum

If these Piagetian ideas are applied to the learning of mathematics, there are several implications for the curriculum. First, prenumber concepts should be developed prior to introducing the child to abstract symbols. Second, teachers must develop diagnostic skills described in this chapter to assess a child's logico-mathematical knowledge and developmental level. Third, children need a learning environment that permits free exploration with concrete materials. Because most of these concepts are attained around the age of six or seven, the kindergarten year and a good portion of the first grade year should be spent enjoying informal explorations with number. Some additional activities can be found in the Extended Activities for Chapter 6 on the Student Companion Web site.

BUILDING THE CONCEPT OF NUMBER

Number Relationships

Young children must experience seven essential relationships to build the mathematical understanding associated with number development. The remainder of the chapter presents activities to match the child's thinking to build a firm understanding of the concept of number.

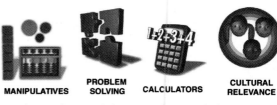

EXTENDED ACTIVITIES

MANIPULATIVES **PROBLEM SOLVING** **CALCULATORS** **CULTURAL RELEVANCE**

On the Web Site (Chapter 6, Extended Activities), read/do the following:

- Where Does It Go?
- Make Them the Same
- Part-Part-Whole
- Modeling Operations
- Use Calculators for Number Sense
- The Challenge of Diversity
- Family Math Packets
- Sample Lesson Plan for Number Readiness

One-to-One Correspondence Many of life's scenarios involve establishing a one-to-one correspondence between two sets of objects, such as giving a napkin to each family member. This task is easier than counting a set and saying only one number name as each item is counted. This counting process establishes a one-to-one correspondence between the set and the counting number. Preschool children can be asked to do many household tasks to build this foundation for number: setting the table, distributing cookies to a group, getting paired with a buddy to play a game, arranging chairs at the table, and so on. It is important that children realize that if a one-to-one correspondence exists, the items in the set can be rearranged and the matched relationship remains. This aspect of one-to-one correspondence is a necessary part of Piaget's number conservation task as viewed earlier in the chapter.

More, Less, and Same Another important consideration in early number development is the concept of comparing quantities as more, less, and same. As mentioned earlier, the young child who does not have class inclusion will not perform well on these tasks. This child does not understand relative relationships of number, namely that seven can be more (more than six) and also less (less than nine). The concept of number must be firmly established before the child is ready to make comparisons between numbers. One device that teachers have found helpful is a walk-on number line (the counting numbers beginning at zero). The child can step on each number as the numbers are counted; the relative position of numbers is sometimes easier to understand through this bodily kinesthetic positioning—one of Gardner's multiple intelligences. Other activities can be played as games (Activity 6.5), enabling children to work with the concepts frequently without tiring of the experiences. Only the concept of more, less, and the same should be the focus at first; then how many more or less can be addressed through counting activities as discussed in the next section.

Activity 6.5

MANIPULATIVES **DEVELOPING MORE AND LESS**

MATERIALS
- Connecting cubes
- Number cube with 0 to 6 on faces

PROCEDURE 1

First player rolls the cube. Get connecting cubes and make a train that long. Next player rolls and builds a train according to the number rolled. Compare trains and decide who has more (or who has less). A spinner divided into two equal regions with one-half labeled "more" and the other half labeled "less" can be used. After comparing the two trains, one child spins, and the pointer tells who is the winner (Figure 6.12).

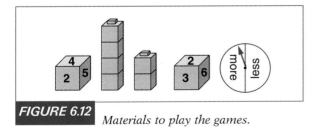

FIGURE 6.12 *Materials to play the games.*

- Connecting cubes
- More/less spinner

PROCEDURE 2

Each child makes a cube train out of the other's sight. They show their trains, compare them, and one child

spins. The winner is the child whose train matched the spinner. *Example*: One player made a train of six; other player made a train of three. Spinner points to "less." The child with three wins.

Rote Counting One of the first skills children learn in mathematics is rote counting. They count one, two, three . . . ten. Some children do this at an early age, and adults assume that the child will be a good math student. Rote counting is saying the number names in isolation without actually counting anything. It can be introduced from other children, parents, television, books, rhymes, games, and finger plays. References of picture books, finger plays, verses, and songs for counting experiences can be found in the Children's Literature section at the end of the chapter. Rote counting has no conceptual understanding of the numbers associated with it. It can be nothing more than nonsense names to some children said in a sing-song fashion. But when the rote counting skill is investigated for understanding, it is obvious that the child has little or no understanding of what the number name means or represents. Rote counting is similar to learning the alphabet but having no idea of the names of the individual letters. Early research by Fuson and Hall (1983) indicated that the three-and-a-half- to four-year-old group can count to thirteen on the average and the five-and-a-half- to six-year-old group can count to fifty-one on the average. Ordering the decades (counting by tens) presented the most difficulty to the counting sequence. They concluded that young children's counting is based more on language patterns than on the structure of our number system.

Rational Counting A more difficult counting stage is that of counting with meaning. At this point, a number meaning is assigned to the counting words. This stage develops slowly and is associated with developmental progress in the child as well as opportunities to explore the invariance or "manyness" of number. An important principle in counting is the cardinal-ity rule, which means after counting a set, the last number name said is the quantity of that set. Another aspect of cardinality is that the order of counting the set does not matter—the result is the same. Even though young children can extend their conventional string of count-ing words, the development of number mean-ing comes much later. A child may know "twenty-five" in the counting sequence but may not have a number-structure meaning of two tens and five ones. After children attach an association between counting and cardinality, they are more flexible in dealing with number as quantities that can be compared, broken into parts, and seen as groups (Payne and Huinker, 1993). Using children's literature from many cultures is one recommended way a teacher can construct connections across the curriculum and counting with meaning through careful questioning as the books are read. An example is shown in Activity 6.6.

Many adults fail to remember how difficult and abstract the idea of number is for children to grasp. Imagine a new counting system with nonsense number names that you have to remember in order and with meaning and you can identify better with the frustrations of the young child.

Activity 6.6

MATHEMATICAL CONNECTIONS   **CULTURAL RELEVANCE**

CULTURAL COUNTING BOOKS

MATERIALS
- Book, *Ten Little Rabbits* (Grossman and Long, 1991)
- Writing paper and crayons

DIRECTIONS
1. Read the book to the class. Stop and ask the class to predict the next counting number.
2. Have the class discuss the rabbits' clothing and activities. Use information from the back of the book to discuss which Native American tribe is associated with each number.
3. Ask students to discuss in pairs how many rabbits there were in all. Children can use drawings or tallies to show their thinking.
4. Have them use other animals or pieces of pottery from the Native American culture to create and draw their own counting books.
5. Use other counting books to explore specific cultures such as *Count Your Way Through Mexico* (Haskins, 1989) and *Bread, Bread, Bread* (Morris, 2000). The latter author uses different breads eaten throughout the world to explore cultural diversity. *Roman Numerals I to MM = Numberabilia Romana Uno ad Duo Mila* offers counters the way the Romans did it (Geisart, 1996).

Write the number.   Write the number.

FIGURE 6.13 *Writing numbers to match sets.*

Counting Sets One-to-one matching is necessary for the child to be able to accurately count the number of objects or people. Textbooks have pictures of sets and the child is to circle the number name for the number of objects in the set. Other pages may show the set of objects, and the child is to write the number for the set (Figure 6.13).

Children can rote count much farther than they are able to rationally count. It proves more difficult for a child to successfully count objects in a random array, whereas objects in a linear arrangement may pose no problem. Generally, the child physically touches the objects while counting and gradually will rely on visual counting. Counting does not become meaningful until about six years of age when the child has a mental structure of number. Involve the class in many counting activities to reinforce the one-to-one matching concept. Encourage children to keep records of objects by making tally marks. For example, have the children draw a tally mark for each boy that you ask to stand. Have them tally the number of children who are eating bag lunches. Children's first experiences with word-problem solving should involve counting and modeling. Such experiences should include a variety of problem structures (such as take-away, comparison, and missing addend) as suggested by the NCTM Principles and Standards (2000). Such problem structures are presented in Chapter 7 with a more detailed discussion of formal operations and number sense.

Counting On by Adding One More Cuisenaire rods are a good manipulative to show this strategy. Have children build a staircase with the ten different colored rods (see Figure 6.6 on page 134). Take a white rod and "walk" it up the staircase. With each step, the children see it is one more. Any material where one more can be added (connecting cubes, straws that show one more unit added, etc.) can be used.

Numeral-Set Association The relation of the number in a set, the number name, and the written

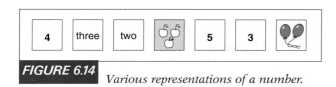

FIGURE 6.14 *Various representations of a number.*

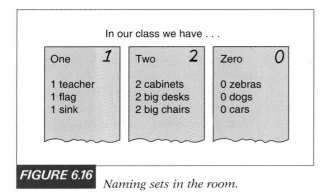

symbol must be well understood. An activity to develop this relationship for numbers through ten is illustrated in Figure 6.14. The child is given cards with the individual numerals 0 to 10 on them, pictures of sets from 0 to 10, and the number names. The child's task is to put appropriate cards together. The numeral-set associations should form a large part of an early primary mathematics program.

Various arrangements of patterns for a number provide flexibility and greater transfer later. Children need to be able to recognize any sets that represent a number, regardless of the direction or composition of the members of the set. For example, 8 may be associated with each of the sets in Figure 6.15.

In addition, students can name the words as they are counted for relating reading to a math lesson. When students have a clear understanding of the numerals and their matching sets, the numeral names can be introduced. This introduction should be made when the child has constructed a set in the classroom rather than according to the typical procedure followed in textbooks where it is a workbook page that may or may not mean anything to the child. When the situations come naturally out of real-life experiences, the numeral-set association has more meaning. Build number charts that list the items there are "one" of in the classroom. Post the number charts and add to the lists as children discover more items. Create number charts for other numbers (Figure 6.16). The video vignette shows a first grade class working with numeral-set activities.

In our class we have . . .

One *1*	Two *2*	Zero *0*
1 teacher	2 cabinets	0 zebras
1 flag	2 big desks	0 dogs
1 sink	2 big chairs	0 cars

FIGURE 6.16 *Naming sets in the room.*

FIGURE 6.15 *Number patterns for eight.*

Developing Meaning for Numbers As children become aware that the quantity in a set they counted is named by a specific name, they begin to associate meaning to numbers. A connection must be made between the number concepts and the symbols that represent the numbers. When symbols are introduced, they hold no meaning to the child. Directed activi-ties must be provided over a long period of time in the PreK–2 program. Numbers should be encountered through the stages of concrete experiences (physical materials and oral nam-ing as the counting is done), to the connecting stage (with physical objects associated with the written numeral), and finally to the sym-bolic stage (writing numerals with a meaningful visual image associated with the quantity). See Figure 6.17.

Everyday Mathematics (University of Chicago School Mathematics Project, 2001) and books from the NCTM Addenda series such as Number Sense and Operations (Burton et al., 1993) show detailed explanations and activities for setting up number stations with an abundance of activities similar to the ones described in this chapter. Children freely explore numbers through a variety of materials and activities that focus on the process rather than on the answer. They construct arrangements of objects (for numbers they can count) to develop numerosity, conservation, counting skills, number sequence, and number combinations. They allow for the gradual evolution of number from the intuitive concrete concept stage to the connecting pictorial/iconic mode and finally to the symbolic representation. The developmental sequence of activities takes into account the intellectual capacities and maturation of a child. The teacher's role is to provide ways to help children see the relationship between activities and the traditional mathematical symbols. The teacher must also be sensitive to know when to schedule activities at the next stage by assessing when each child has acquired real understanding of the quantity of a given number. The assessment strategy is described in Activity 6.7.

Writing Numerals

Recognizing numerals and writing numerals involve different skills. Children are asked to

Video Vignette

Numeral-Set Activities

In Mrs. Arroyo's first grade class, she orally gives a number and the children are to match the quantity with numerals. As you watch this video, consider these questions:

- What informal assessments can you make about these children's counting strategies?
- Are there any numbers that they can instantly recognize without counting? Children can look at a small group of objects and know the quantity without counting the discrete items. This skill is called *subitizing*. Is there any evidence of this skill?
- What different counting strategies did you notice?
- What mathematical experiences (in terms of instructional strategies) would you suggest for these children?

FIGURE 6.17 *Learning stages to build set-number meaning.*

match numerals to sets before writing them. The skill of associating a symbol with an amount is different from that of writing numerals. The physical skills of writing numerals include small muscle control as well as copying skills. Educators use various techniques to introduce the numerals 0 through 9. Associating a verbal sequential order with writing the numeral provides structure that helps recall. Some teachers use a color sequence for writing the numerals. The first segment is assigned a certain color, and the second segment is assigned a different color. The color sequence is the same for all the numerals. Baroody (1987) suggests having children reflect on the shapes of the numerals through verbal descriptions. He uses a "motor plan" that is practiced aloud as the children write the numerals. The motor plan describes where to begin and in which direction to proceed to form each numeral.

Teaching Ideas Children may experience reversed numerals. Many different problems exist. Some children have certain numerals they consistently reverse and others reverse numerals when they hurry. A great number of errors are made in writing the "teens." Many first graders write "71" for "seventeen." This error is made because children write the numbers according to how they hear the number spoken. This may also be a problem later in place value understanding and will be discussed further in Chapter 8. Because children often write numerals before they receive formal instruction at school, teachers see many strange procedures that are difficult to stop. For example, the numeral nine is formed starting at the baseline with a straight line and the top loop added last. To help establish the form of each numeral in the mind, teachers should provide tactile experiences accompanied with verbal structure of the sequential order of the writing. Make numerals from sandpaper or highly textured materials and have children trace the numerals. Fill a small cake pan with salt and have the child trace the numeral, shake the pan, and practice again. Care should be taken to have easy-to-see models available for copying. Tracing in the air, on each other's back, and on Magic Slates or individual chalkboards provides a variety of practice activities. Furnish opportunities for writing the numerals in association with a matching set rather than in isolation.

Activity 6.7

ASSESSMENT OF NUMBER ACQUISITION (BARATTA-LORTON, 1976, P. 287)

MANIPULATIVES

Situation 1

Teacher: Count five blocks into my hand. How many blocks do I have?

Child: Five (without counting). (Shows "fiveness" and understanding of number invariance.)

Teacher: (Divides set of blocks between hands. Opens one hand and shows the blocks. [3]) I have three blocks and how many blocks are hiding in my other hand?

Child: Two. (Answers immediately without counting or guessing.)

This procedure is repeated several times with different combinations for the number. After many successful times, the child is ready to move to number six.

Situation 2

Teacher: Count five blocks into my hand; see Figure 6.18. (Child performs task.)
How many blocks do I have in my hand?

Child: (Counts the blocks again.) Five.

The rest of the procedure is continued and the child needs to count on or randomly guess to give the answer. This result means the child has not mastered an under-

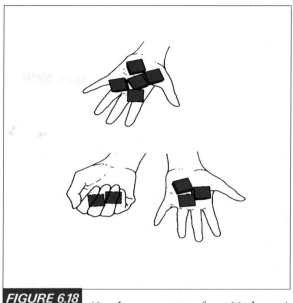

FIGURE 6.18 *Number assessment from Mathematics Their Way.*

standing of five and needs to have additional experiences with combinations for fives.

Readiness for Operations

Once children have well-developed concepts of numbers and understand the relationships among numbers, a broader concept of number can be undertaken to include readiness for working with operations. According to the NCTM *Principles and Standards* (NCTM, 2000), beginning in preschool, all children should understand meaningful situations that lead to the four operations addition, subtraction, multiplication, and division. Building on the informal mathematical knowledge children possess when they enter school, counting activities can be directed to include joining, separating, comparing, doubling, halving, breaking sets apart, and part-part-whole. The part-part-whole relationship is fundamental to developing the concept of the four basic operations. Many parents and teachers, as well as the traditional mathematics curriculum, move children too quickly into what might be considered as the "real mathematics." Textbook practice pages of basic facts in first grade are inappropriate for many children who are not developmentally ready for such abstractions. The child needs many experiences with number and symbols before being introduced to the signs for the operations. The child may be able to respond to questions about answers for basic facts, but often this ability is simply good recall or counting rather than solid understanding.

The importance of parental involvement during the early informative years of mathematics instruction is paramount to greater child success. The Family Math Packets on the Student Companion Web site in Chapter 6 show books and mathematics activities for developing a sense of number and readiness for operations. Web sites that support activities and knowledge for parents in mathematics are listed at the end of the chapter. The work is updated periodically, giving parents the benefit of the current research and approaches when working with their children. The sites can help back up the messages you want to send to parents on the ways they can be of most help to their children.

Developing Meaning for Operations   As children develop the mental structures to deal with numbers, they can explore the operations with concrete experiences. To gain understanding of the operations, children should manipulate materials and discuss and model the operations in problem-solving situations. They need to verbalize their actions and internalize the concepts before performing written work with the symbols. The same learning sequence should be followed for developing understanding about the symbols for operations that was used for developing number concepts discussed earlier in this chapter (refer back to Figure 6.16 on page 140). Activities are illustrated in Figure 6.19. After participating in and describing concrete experiences, the connecting mode with symbols is modeled. When a solid understanding of the language and action is shown, the formal symbolic notation is introduced.

Although the typical scope and sequence in textbooks present addition to six, subtraction to six, addition to ten, subtraction to ten, educators continue to debate whether addition and subtraction should be taught together or separately. A great deal of research has been conducted to investigate this question without any firm conclusions. Whichever approach is followed, children should be comfortable communicating about the operations orally and with objects to ensure understanding.

Building Part-Whole Understanding   Once children are able to see relationships between numbers and connect number and set, they should begin to think in groups. The skill to quickly recognize the amount in a group without counting, called subitizing, becomes an important aspect of thinking in groups. Seeing the part-whole approach to groups (seeing ten as two fives and seven as five and two) rather than single

Concrete Stages

Tree has 4 green apples and 2 red. Child models with felt apples on tree.

Connecting Stages

| 4 | 2 |

Same situation but child has number cards to show with apples.

Symbolic Stages

4 + 2 = 6

Same situation with equation cards to show symbolic level and child gives answer.

FIGURE 6.19   *Learning sequence for understanding number operations.*

counting by ones constitutes a valuable component for understanding addition and subtraction. Activities to build part-whole understanding include using ten-frames (Figure 6.20). Children can place counters on the ten-frame filling the top row to five and then continuing in the bottom row to ten. In Figure 6.20, some children may see seven as "5 and 2" but other children may subitize into "4 and 3"; still other children could see the number seven as "10–3".

Research (Fuson, 2003) suggests that ten-frames can be displayed to the children to help them recognize the number (whole) as well as visually recall the two parts that form the number. Children from European and Asian countries adapt to this approach more easily than do children in the United States and Canada. It would appear that the language for numbers in European and Asian cultures name the ten first (refer to Chapter 8 for a further discussion), so children think of a ten and some more. The video vignette shows two first grade classrooms using ten-frames in instructional settings. Kline (1998) offers many alternative ideas for using the "quick images" to

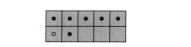

FIGURE 6.20 *Ten-frames.*

develop mental imagery of the numbers. She suggests using the ten-frames as five-to-ten-minute warm-up activities and to ask children to describe their mental images. Kline finds ten-frames used in a horizontal fashion help her kindergarten students become fluent with teen numbers. Additional explanations and suggestions for using ten trays are provided in Chapter 7.

NEW CURRICULUM FOR AGES THREE TO SIX

Although the NCTM *Principles and Standards* (2000) includes general guidelines for teaching the standards to PreK–2, there was no attempt to list specific knowledge and skills to be accomplished within the ages of three through six (see Figure 6.21). Many teachers felt the need for a curriculum to aid preschool and kindergarten teachers in the coordination of activities that could be developmentally appropriate for young children.

Good Beginnings—More than Number

The National Association for the Education of Young Children (NAEYC) and NCTM have cooperated in publishing a joint position paper, Early Childhood Mathematics: Promoting Good Beginnings (2003) that lists typical achievements and teaching strategies for working with children ages three to six. The materials show how a continuum of activities can help children develop quality knowledge and skills in early mathematics. Each of the content areas are represented—number and operations, geometry and spatial sense, measurement, pattern and algebraic thinking, and displaying and analyzing data. A sample learning path appears in Figure 6.22. The whole document may be found on the Web; the Web site address is listed at the back of this chapter.

Although this chapter has discussed early concepts of number and readiness for operations, other learning activities and assessments for young children (K–2) are included in each of the content chapters of this text: geometry and spatial sense (Chapter 12); measurement (Chapter 13); patterns and algebra (Chapter 14); and data analysis, graphing, probability, and statistics (Chapter 15). People who have not been in an elementary school for many years are amazed at the activities in algebraic thinking and data analysis that young children can do when presented

Video Vignette

Using Ten-Frames

Two first grade teachers are using ten-frames to help develop understanding of the power of ten.

- Watch the video of the two classrooms and compare the instructional uses of ten-frames. What do you think about the task in terms of "sound and significant mathematics?"

- Discuss your thoughts about the children's use of subitizing or counting. What can you conclude about the children's confidence with number?

- In the second sequence, what can you say about children's understandings of part-whole number relationships? Of number invariance? Of the operations being used?

with concrete experiences prepared by knowledgeable teachers.

Technology and Young Children

The International Society for Technology in Education (ISTE) and NCTM both espouse the use of technology with young children. It is the careful selection of developmentally appropriate Internet activities, computer software, and calculators that makes the difference in what young children can understand and accomplish. The activities on the NCTM Web site have passed the scrutiny of experts in the field of early childhood and can be trusted as quality activities for young children.

Calculators Calculators have a place in number explorations in early primary mathematics

Instructional programs from PreK through grade 2 should enable all students to

Problem Solving

Solve problems that arise in daily routines and mathematical situations arising from stories.

Solve problems related to classification, shape, and space.

Solve problems by comparing and completing collections.

Pose problems that generate new questions.

Create and modify multiple strategies for solving problems, deciding which ones are most useful.

Reasoning and Proof

Continue to develop logical reasoning skills begun before entrance into formal education.

Create justifications for mathematical results through perception; empirical evidence, and short chains of deductive reasoning.

Make conjectures and test their generalizations by examples and counter examples using pattern recognition and classification skills.

Use properties to reason about numbers.

Communication

Articulate, clarify, organize, and consolidate their thinking—orally, with gestures, pictures, objects, and symbols.

Reflect on their own knowledge and ways of solving problems.

Listen to others to learn alternative perspectives and to use more precise mathematical language through daily opportunities to write and talk about mathematics.

Explain their answers and describe their strategies by manipulating objects, drawing pictures, using diagrams and charts, writing explanations, and expressing ideas with mathematical symbols.

Connections

Connect intuitive, informal mathematics of their own experiences and the mathematics learned in school.

Eliminate the barriers that separate mathematics learned elsewhere and the mathematics learned in school.

See explicit connections between and among mathematical ideas such as subtraction with addition, measurement with number and geometry, and representations with algebra and problem solving.

Connect ideas with the use of concrete objects and in extended projects and investigations.

Representation

Use many varied representations to build new understandings and expressions of mathematical ideas.

Use the skills learned in the communication standard to link with representation.

Use calculators and computers as representations to enlarge one's thinking about mathematics along with concrete objects, use gestures, drawing pictures, diagrams and charts, writing explanations, and expressing ideas with mathematical symbols.

See the common mathematical nature of different situations.

Organize their thinking by translating between different representations of the same idea.

Understand that representations are tools to model and interpret phenomena of a mathematical nature found in different contexts.

Content Standards for PreK to grade 2 are shared in content chapters

Number and Operations	Chapters 7, 8, 9, 10, 11
Geometry	Chapter 12
Measurement	Chapter 13
Algebra	Chapter 14
Data Analysis and Probability	Chapter 15

FIGURE 6.21 *NCTM expectation for grades preK–2. A partial listing as it pertains to the Process Standards from NCTM Principles and Standards for School Mathematics (2000, pages 116–141).*

EXAMPLES OF TYPICAL KNOWLEDGE AND SKILLS FROM AGE 3————————————————→AGE 6		SAMPLE TEACHING STRATEGIES
Number and Counts a collection of 1 to 4 items and begins to understand that the last operations counting word tells "how many."	Counts and produces (counts, out) collections up to 100 using groups of 10.	Models counting of small collections and guides children's counting in everyday situations, emphasizing that we use one counting word for each object: ♥ ♥ ♥ "One . . . two . . . three . . . " Models counting by 10s while making groups of 10s (e.g., 10, 20, 30 . . . or 14, 24, 34 . . .).

FIGURE 6.22 *Sample element from* Learning Paths and Teaching Strategies *by NAEYC and NCTM. From* Young Children *(January, 2003), p. 41. Total Learning Paths may be viewed in the journal or online in NAEYC/NCTM joint position statement.*

programs. NCTM Principles and Standards (2000) call for appropriate and ongoing use of calculators beginning in kindergarten. Some calculators can be used for counting by having the child count and push the equal (=) key to see if the counting number matches the calculator display. Counting by multiples of a number follows naturally by having the first number in the series change to reflect the counting pattern. The calculator's constant feature causes the number automatically to keep increasing or decreasing by a given amount. Counting backward is another skill that can be done on the calculator. This skill is necessary when using the "counting back" strategy for subtraction. Calculators are valuable in counting, searching for counting patterns, and solving problems. Activity 6.8 shows an example of calculator use.

Computers Many computer programs are available for number recognition games, counting games, classification tasks, and exploring shapes and patterns. Clements (2002) has worked for almost two decades with young children using the computer programming language Logo. Children exposed to Logo did significantly better on tests of geometric skill than did their counterparts with no child computer programming. A new National Science Foundation project, Building Blocks, is developing modules for young children that integrate three modes together—learning computers, working with corresponding manipulatives, and doing the conventional print-pages. A Web site to preview the modules is online and the address is printed at the end of this chapter. The project is being field-tested across the United

States. Research (Clements and Samara, 2007) shows positive gains in essential multiple mathematical concepts beyond number concepts as measured in the Building Blocks project.

Activity 6.8

CALCULATORS   **ESTIMATION**   **NUMBER SEQUENCE ON A CALCULATOR**

MATERIALS
• Calculator

PROCEDURE
1. Count "one more" beginning at 0. Press "+" key, then "1," and "=" key. Display reads: 1. Press "=" key again (2), again (3), again (4), and continue. The calculator is counting by ones or showing "one more."
2. Count "one less" beginning at 20. Start with 20. Press "−" key, then "1" key, and "=" key. Display reads: 19.

Press "=" key again (18), again (17), and continue with each number showing "one less" or how to count backward.

3. Counting by other multiples is equally easy to show. Count by twos. Start with 0. Press "+," "2," and "=." Continue to press "=" to see multiples of two. Explore other operations using the same key sequence.

4. Add or subtract a constant to any number by this key sequence: To add 4, press "+," "4," "=" (display reads 4); "6," "=" (display reads 10); "2," "=" (display reads 6). To subtract a constant, begin with "−" as first input key. To incorporate *estimation*, have children make guesses about how many "=" keys it will take to reach a specific number. This relates to relative size of numbers for number sense. (Great practice for basic facts in Chapter 7.)

(*Note:* Some calculators work differently than the one described here.)

Supporting the ISTE Standards . . .

Use developmentally appropriate technology with support of classroom teachers, parents, and student partners.

PUTTING IT ALL TOGETHER—ASSESSING REAL STUDENT WORK

Here is a chance to organize one of your first student assessments from the concepts covered in this chapter. Reflection on what you learned as you prepare to work with real student work; it can be a valuable part of your professional portfolio.

Activity 6.9

PORTFOLIO MANIPULATIVES

PORTFOLIO ASSESSMENT

FOR TEACHER REFLECTION OF STUDENT'S WORK IN NUMBER READINESS

• Make a collection of materials to use for assessing young children's understandings of these mathema-

tical concepts: one-to-one correspondence, number conservation, seriation, set equivalency, class (number) inclusion, classification, patterning, and set-number association.

• Design an interview protocol based on the chapter's information to assess each of the concepts mentioned above.

• Design a rubric to help define levels of verbal responses and to take into account the variety of answers.

• Prepare activities (according to the curriculum implications) for the children who have not acquired these mathematical understandings.

• Find a child at the age level you targeted in the curriculum activities.

• Assess him/her by using your tasks and rubrics.

• Write about your assessment of the child's level of number acquisition. Collect readings about number readiness from mathematics journals to add to your portfolio.

SUMMARY

• The early primary curriculum for mathematics must take into account the aspects of active, direct participation by the child.

• Children in early primary years should have opportunities to make sense of mathematics, to engage in active mathematics learning, and to connect mathematical language to their informal knowledge.

• As we keep the child's needs in mind, the primary grade experiences must be structured to nurture young children and guide them toward logical, operational thinking about the world of mathematics.

• The environment must be child oriented with time provided for assessing the child's understanding of prenumber concepts with time to use the teaching ideas presented in the chapter if children need more background before moving to more formal symbolic arithmetic.

• A large part of PreK–grade 1 must be spent in building the conceptual understanding of number before moving on to basic fact, single-digit addition and subtraction.

• Calculators and computers may be used if careful selection of developmentally appropriate activities and software are chosen.

PRAXIS II™-STYLE QUESTIONS

Answers to this chapter's Praxis II(tm)-style questions are in the instructor's manual.

Multiple Choice Format

1. Which of these students understands **class inclusion** in Figure 6.23?

    a. Student A.

    b. Student B.

    c. Student C.

    d. Both a and c.

2. A first grader uses a calculator similar to the one in Figure 6.24.

    He starts with a "3" on the display and then presses "+1+1+1=" He looks at the display and writes down the numeral and then presses He

FIGURE 6.24

looks at the display again and writes down the numeral. Then he continues with "+1+1+1=" and so on. This child understands how to use the calculator to:

a. Find multiples of 3.

b. Count on to a beginning number by threes.

c. Fiddle around with no particular pattern in mind.

d. None of the above.

3. The kindergarteners are working on building the concept of number patterns as a readiness activity for number understanding. The task is shown below:

Directions to Students: Draw a rectangle or a sun to complete the pattern and tell what you were thinking (see Figure 6.25).

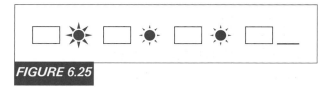

FIGURE 6.25

Give a rubric score of 1 to 4+ for each kindergarten explanation seen below and justify your answer (with 1 being low to 4+ being advanced).

FIGURE 6.23

Student A

"A rectangle because the first one is a rectangle and so the last one should be a rectangle."

Student B

"A sun because the first one and the last one are rectangles."

Student C

"A sun because the first one is a rectangle and then a sun, then another rectangle and a sun, and another rectangle and a sun, and then a rectangle. So next is a sun."

Student D

"A sun because there are four rectangles and three suns. So a sun makes four suns too."

a. Student A should score a ——.
b. Student B should score a ——.
c. Student C should score a ——.
d. Student D should score a ——.

Constructed Response Format

4. You have given a Piagetian assessment task for number conservation, and you see that the child needs more development of the concept. List two teaching ideas you could develop to help the child.

5. Adapt the assessment of number acquisition found in Activity 6.7 to test a child's knowledge of "seven-ness" and "eight-ness".

6. Write a scenario that shows what children might be doing if they understood only rote counting. Write another scenario that shows what children might be doing if they understood rationale counting.

Integrating Technology

Internet Activities

WebQuest

The Animal Habitat—A First Grade Mathematics WebQuest

| ESTIMATION | MATHEMATICAL CONNECTIONS | CULTURAL RELEVANCE | INTERNET SEARCHES |

1. On the text's Web site (**www.wiley.com/college/hatfield**), open the Web-Quest "The Animal Habitat".
2. You will see the work of a typical first grader using this WebQuest.
3. Follow the progression of directions in the WebQuest as you look at the student's work.

Web sites

- **http://gse.buffalo.edu/org/buildingblocks/writings/ECE_Comp_Math.pdf**
Computer modules may be viewed and findings from the current research with young children are shared by NSF Project Director, Douglas H. Clements.
- **http://www.lib.muohio.edu/pictbks/**
Lists over 5000 picture books to reinforce mathematics learning; abstracts for the books are given. The site is updated frequently.
- **http://www.nctm.org/profdev/default.espx?id=398**
This is NCTM's "Teachers Corner," which provides information about professional development opportunities, resources, and more.
- **http://www.naeyc.org/about/positions/psmath.asp**
Early Childhood Mathematics: Promoting Good Beginnings; A joint position statement of the National Association for the Education of Young Children (NAEYC) and the National Council for Teachers of Mathematics (NCTM), adopted April 2002.
- **http://www.mathperspectives.com**
Mathematical Perspectives Teacher Development Center provides PreK–grade 6 mathematics educators with tools, strategies, and assessments that will ensure that all students are successful in the study of mathematics and are able to use mathematics to solve problems and to think and reason mathematically.
- Sites to Help Parents:
  - **http://www.nctm.org/resources/families.aspx**
    NCTM's "Family Corner" provides information for parents and caregivers on helping children learn mathematics with links to educational video clips, tips for new teachers, information on special needs, and more. This link will also be further expanded in the near future.

- **http://www.ed.gov/pubs/EarlyMath**
  Early Childhood: Where Learning Begins—Mathematics. Mathematical activities for parents and their two- to five-year-old children. Online information for parents from the U.S. Department of Education.

CHILDREN'S LITERATURE

A number of books are available to develop concepts associated with early number readiness. Counting practice for both counting forward and counting backward are common such as

- Anno, Mitsumasa. *Anno's Counting Book*. New York: Harpercollins, 1977.

- Anno, Mitsumasa. *Anno's Counting House*. New York: Philomel Books, 1982.

- Carle, Eric. *The Very Hungry Caterpillar*. New York: Philomel Books, 1987.

- Tildes, Phyllis Limbacher. *Counting on Calico*. Watertown, MA: Charlesbridge, 1995.

- Crews, Donald. *Ten Black Dots*. New York: Greenwillow Books, 1986.

  Offers an interesting way to have children establish set-symbol relationships by incorporating a given number of dots into an illustration to make a counting book to ten.

- Geisert, Arthur. *Roman Numerals I to MM = Numberabilia Romana Uno ad Duo Mila*. Boston, MA: Houghton Mifflin, 1996.

- Grossman, Virginia and Sylvia Long. *Ten Little Rabbits*. San Francisco, CA: Chronicle Books, 1991.

- Haskins, Jim. *Count Your Way through Mexico*. Minneapolis, MN: Carolrhoda Books, 1989.

- McGrath, Barbara Barbieri. *The Cheerios Counting Book*. Watertown, MA: Charlesbridge, 1998.

Arranges cheerios into number patterns, shows groupings of ten and number relationships.

- McGrath, Barbara Barbieri. *M & M's Brand Counting Book*. Watertown, MA: Charlesbridge, 1994.

Shows numbers to twelve and some basic operations.

These books help children classify and sort objects. They show similarities and differences to promote logical reasoning:

- Hoban, Tana. *A Children's Zoo*. New York: Greenwillow Books, 1985.

- Hoban, Tana. *Is It Larger? Is It Smaller?* New York: Greenwillow Books, 1985.

- Giganti, Paul, Jr. *How Many Snails?* New York: Greenwillow Books, 1988.

To see classification of many attributes.

- Pluckrose, Henry, *Pattern*. Chicago: Children's Press, 1995.

Pluckrose (1995) has written a series of books to introduce sorting activities, pattern, shape, size, and number with colorful real-world photographs (for example, *Pattern*).

- Reid, Margarette S. *The Button Box*. New York: Dutton Children's Books, 1990.

It portrays many attributes of buttons that can extend to explorations with classification and patterns.

See Web site listings above for additional picture book references.

Operations and Number Sense

Chapter 7

At the Start ~~~~ *Know What Children Will Be Doing* . . .

NCTM Curriculum Focal Points—   See . . .

Grade 1 ~~ Developing understandings of addition and subtraction and strategies for basic addition facts and related subtraction facts	Activity 7.4
Grade 2 ~~ Developing quick recall of addition facts and related subtraction facts	Activity 7.9
Grade 3 ~~ Developing understandings of multiplication and division and strategies for basic multiplication facts and related division facts	Activity 7.6
Grade 4 ~~ Developing quick recall of multiplication facts and related division facts and fluency with whole number multiplication	Activity 7.7
Grade 5 ~~ Developing an understanding of and fluency with division of whole numbers	Web site . . . "Calculator Capers"

A partial listing as it pertains to Number and Operations and Algebra from NCTM *Curriculum Focal Points* (2006, pages 13–17).

WHERE'S THE MATHEMATICS? CONCEPTUAL UNDERSTANDING FOR OPERATIONS AND PROPERTIES WITH NUMBER SENSE

Few people today will deny that an elementary school teacher needs considerable mathematical knowledge and pedagogical skill. Teachers of young children must understand and be able to interpret models of operations with whole numbers. They must have a significant repertoire of models and teaching strategies, as well as applications of each of the operations and must understand the relationships among the operations.

This is especially true because a large percentage of a child's elementary school years is spent working with the whole number system. The operations, properties, and basic facts become an important part of daily mathematics instruction. In many, if not most, textbooks, children study the whole number operations in the following order: addition, subtraction, multiplication, and finally

division. The NCTM *Principles and Standards* (NCTM, 2000) state that all four operations should be developed throughout the elementary grades as young children have intuitions that can apply to operations. A preschooler knows that when mother says to share the candies fairly with little brother that means, "one for you and one for me," so why wait until third grade to explore division concepts? Young children can relate pattern skills to skip counting—a basis for multiplication.

A variety of problem situations, beginning in preschool and kindergarten, must be developed through modeling with physical materials. Activities to develop meaning for the mathematical language and symbols should link to the children's language and informal knowledge. The relationships between operations should be investigated, as well as the various problem structures such as the missing addend, comparison, and take-away approaches to subtraction. This chapter is designed to help teachers see how these relationships aid in the learning of number

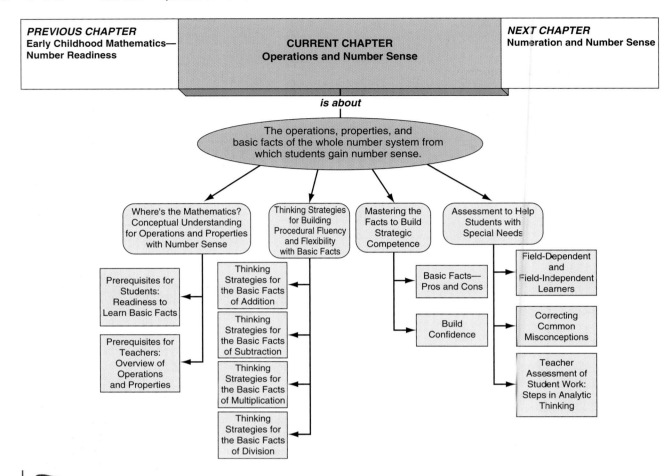

| PREVIOUS CHAPTER
Early Childhood Mathematics—
Number Readiness | CURRENT CHAPTER
Operations and Number Sense | NEXT CHAPTER
Numeration and Number Sense |

is about

The operations, properties, and basic facts of the whole number system from which students gain number sense.

- Where's the Mathematics? Conceptual Understanding for Operations and Properties with Number Sense
  - Prerequisites for Students: Readiness to Learn Basic Facts
  - Prerequisites for Teachers: Overview of Operations and Properties
- Thinking Strategies for Building Procedural Fluency and Flexibility with Basic Facts
  - Thinking Strategies for the Basic Facts of Addition
  - Thinking Strategies for the Basic Facts of Subtraction
  - Thinking Strategies for the Basic Facts of Multiplication
  - Thinking Strategies for the Basic Facts of Division
- Mastering the Facts to Build Strategic Competence
  - Basic Facts—Pros and Cons
  - Build Confidence
- Assessment to Help Students with Special Needs
  - Field-Dependent and Field-Independent Learners
  - Correcting Common Misconceptions
  - Teacher Assessment of Student Work: Steps in Analytic Thinking

SELF-HELP QUESTIONS

1. What does research say is the best way to teach the basic facts to early elementary children and students with special needs?

2. What are the prerequisites that children need before learning whole number operations, properties and basic facts?

3. Which assessment strategies will help my students who have difficulty learning the basic facts?

4. What do I need to remember about my own learning of number operations, prop-

erties, and basic facts to be an effective teacher?

5. What are some quality games and activities to help students learn number sense with whole numbers?

6. How should I use computer and calculator activities effectively for teaching whole number concepts?

sense in the elementary grades and on into middle school. Figure 7.1 show the concepts to be developed in operations and number sense in PreK–grade 8.

Prerequisites for Students: Readiness to Learn Basic Facts

What are basic facts? Where do they come from? How many facts are there? What does it mean to

master the basic facts? These are key questions approached in this chapter. Basic facts refer to the combinations of single-digit numbers (for addition and multiplication) and their corresponding inverse (for subtraction and division), such as $4 + 9 = 13$, $13 - 9 = 4$, and $4 \times 9 = 36$, $36 \div 9 = 4$. Although some textbooks and teachers continue basic facts through 12, in this

STANDARD

Instructional programs from prekindergarten through grade 12 should enable all students to:

Understand meanings of operations and how they relate to one another.

Compute fluently and make reasonable estimates.

GRADES PREK TO 2

In prekindergarten through grade 2 all students should:

Understand various meanings of addition and subtraction of whole numbers and the relationship between the two operations.

Understand the effects of adding and subtracting whole numbers.

Understand situations that entail multiplication and division, such as equal groupings of objects and sharing equally.

Develop and use strategies for whole-number computations, with a focus on addition and subtraction.

Develop fluency with basic number combinations for addition and subtraction.

Use a variety of methods and tools to compute, including objects, mental computation, estimation, paper and pencil, and calculators.

GRADES 3 TO 5

In grades 3 to 5 all students should:

Understand various meanings of multiplication and division.

Understand the effects of multiplying and dividing whole numbers.

Identify and use relationships between operations, such as division as the inverse of multiplication, to solve problems.

Understand and use properties of operations, such as the distributivity of multiplication over addition.

Develop fluency with basic number combinations for multiplication and division and use these combinations to mentally compute related problems, such as 30×50.

Develop fluency in adding, subtracting, multiplying, and dividing whole numbers.

Develop and use strategies to estimate the results of whole-number computations and to judge the reasonableness of such results.

GRADES 6 TO 8

In grades 6 to 8 all students should:

Use the associative and commutative properties of addition and multiplication and the distributive property of multiplication over addition to simplify computations with integers.

Understand and use the inverse relationships of addition and subtraction, multiplication and division, and squaring and finding square roots to simplify computations and solve problems.

FIGURE 7.1 NCTM expectation of number and operations. *Source: A partial listing as it pertains to Operations and Number Sense from NCTM Principles and Standards for School Mathematics (2000, pages 392–393).*

book basic facts will be only numbers less than 10. There are 390 basic facts: 100 facts for addition, subtraction, and multiplication, and 90 for division. Mastery of basic facts becomes a critical issue in elementary school starting in first grade. The term "mastery" refers to the automatic recall of a basic fact combination within a three-second time period.

In arithmetic, it is generally agreed that computational algorithms are more easily understood and learned if students have mastered the basic facts of addition, subtraction, multiplication, and division. More time can be spent in becoming successful problem solvers if students have memorized basic facts and are fluent in computation. However, as pointed out in Chapter 5, page 100, there is abundant evidence from research that memorization of basic facts and computational fluency are not prerequisites

for conceptual understanding and problem solving.

Meaning of Operations First, an understanding of the meanings of operations must be developed along with knowledge of basic number combinations. Children might use manipulatives to discover number patterns and relationships, to model particular word problems, and to explore the joining, separating, and partitioning of groups. Second, after extensive informal experiences in varied contexts, mathematical terms and symbols can be introduced. As children acquire operation sense, a solid conceptual framework will be established on which to build the basic facts and later, the algorithms (Chapter 9). As the *Principles and Standards* (NCTM, 2000) suggest, exploring numbers and operations helps children develop strategies to learn and recall basic facts. By linking the manipulation of materials to the steps of the procedures and developing thinking patterns, teachers can foster basic fact mastery.

It is important to consider a child's readiness to learn the basic facts. Understanding these prerequisites will ensure greater success in getting children to have quick recall of the facts. Many first graders are "taught" addition and subtraction facts before they can understand them. Parents are often misled into believing that early recall of facts implies an understanding of the operation. Two operations are essential as prerequisites to learning the basic facts: (1) number conservation and (2) class inclusion and reversibility.

Number Conservation Consider what Piaget tells us about children's learning and how this relates to readiness to learn basic facts. Number conservation (knowing that numbers remain the same despite various changes in configuration) is one important factor in evaluating readiness. If a child has five beans and forms them into a set of three and a set of two, there are still five beans. Until a child conserves number, counting is used to name the sum rather than the child knowing the sum remains unchanged. Refer to Chapter 6, page 130, of this text for additional details about this topic.

The ability to conserve number must precede the memorization of basic facts. Teachers should provide adequate time for children to internalize the invariance of number. For a child to verify the understanding of conservation, many experiences are needed with joining, separating, and comparing sets. The child who is a nonconserver will not see the relationships between families of number facts. Many of the strategies in this chapter hold little meaning for nonconservers.

Class Inclusion and Reversibility The principle of class inclusion (the ability to see that all of one group can be part of another group at the same time) also deserves careful study and evaluation before beginning a program of memorizing the basic facts. Review Chapter 6, page 131, for greater details on the bead experiments. Children younger than seven have difficulty seeing the whole as being larger than its parts. The logical relationship, the inclusion relation, might not be comprehended until a child is about seven years old.

The class inclusion problem can also be a class addition problem. To solve the problem, children must consider the whole set and its parts at the same time. Children need to add the parts to obtain the whole and to be able to reverse this

process (reversibility). Addition is an operation relating the parts to the whole.

$$6 + 1 = 7$$
$$2 + 5 = 7$$
$$3 + 4 = 7$$
$$5 + 2 = 7$$
$$1 + 6 = 7$$

The child who has not mastered the concept of class inclusion may not relate various number pairs with the same sum. To understand addition as an operation, the child must be able to look at various pairs of addends and realize that the number can be expressed as the same sum. The child must also be able to realize that the sum (7) can become all these combinations. Number combinations can be developed with concrete materials such as lima beans painted red on one side, of which the child counts a given number into a small cup. The beans are spilled from the cup, and the child reads the number of painted beans as the first addend and the number of white beans as the second addend. This activity is repeated many times to build the principle of invariance of number as well as to see the possible combinations for a given sum. Figure 7.2 illustrates this activity.

According to Piaget, until the child understands class inclusion and reversibility of thought, basic facts are learned at a meaningless level. Teaching facts using strategies described later in this chapter may be a questionable practice if children do not understand class inclusion. More activities to develop number meaning (described in the next section, "Number Meaning") should be included before children can apply thinking strategies to the operations of addition, subtraction, multiplication, and division.

Number Meaning Another prerequisite for working with number facts is to develop meaning

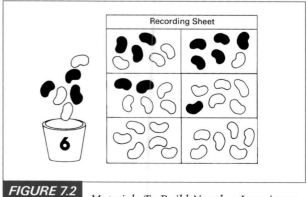

FIGURE 7.2 *Materials To Build Number Invariance.*

for the symbols ($+-\times\div$) that stand for the mental operations. An excellent idea is to use physical objects to model number combinations in many ways. When children can successfully create and label sets, they are ready to attach the symbols to the actions. Invite children to create number stories using concrete materials and storyboards (a picture of a forest, ocean, barn, store, airport, and so forth on which the children build their stories). An example is seen in Activity 7.1.

Activity 7.1

| MANIPULATIVES | PROBLEM SOLVING | MATHEMATICAL CONNECTIONS |

STORYBOARDS AND NUMBER MEANING

MATERIALS
- A picture or drawing of an airport landing strip.
- 10 small toy airplanes.

DIRECTIONS
1. Give the children the picture or drawing.
2. Place the 10 toy airplanes to the side.
3. Start with a problem situation to be modeled—for example:

   - *Problem Situation 1*
     "Lon Po has 3 airplanes on the landing strip and 5 airplanes in the hangar see Figure 7.3. How many airplanes are at the airport?"
     (Children can model the actions by placing the toy airplanes in the correct places on the picture before answering the question. Some children may answer first and then model the actions.)
   - *Problem Situation 2*
     "Terrill has 2 airplanes on the landing strip. Terrill needs 7 airplanes to fly people to Disney World. How many more planes does Terrill need to get for the trip?"

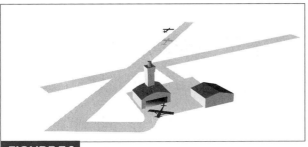

FIGURE 7.3 *Airport picture with runways and hangars.*

4. Children make up their own number stories using oral discourse to explain their actions and the resulting answers to the problem situations they create.
5. The teacher keeps assessment notes on the students' progress as they create their stories.

Supporting the NCTM *Principles and Standards* (2000):
- Mathematics as Problem Solving; Mathematics as Communication
- Worthwhile Mathematical Tasks; Mathematics as Oral and Written Discourse—The Teaching Principle
- Monitoring Students' Progress—The Equity Principle

According to the standards, mastery of basic facts should come after exploratory work with the operations in problem situations. Research shows that starting with problem situations yields greater competence in problem solving as well as equal or better computational competence (Fuson, 2003). However, understanding the concept or mental operation does not imply that facts will be mastered automatically. Also, learning facts by rote does not mean understanding the operation. Meaningful problem-solving situations should accompany each step in the learning sequence. Examples like Problem Situation 2 in Activity 7.1 can be solved in several ways. If we think about A as representing airplanes, most young children will model $2 + A = 7$. Few will think of $7 - 2 = A$. It will take the modeling of many situations before children are likely to see the situation as a subtraction example since the sentence order does not follow the actual action of the story. The important thing to remember is that children CAN solve the problem correctly in a valid way. Their way should be honored by the teacher, even if the elementary textbook wants children to see the subtraction possibility more quickly than children may be ready to do.

Teachers who provide a variety of contexts and tasks in which their students can encounter basic facts give them greater opportunities to develop and use thinking strategies and build number relationships that support and reinforce learning the basic facts. A solid mathematics program incorporates all of the components together.

Use the video vignette on the student companion Web site, Chapter 7, Video Vignettes, "Dinosaur Legs," to see a first grade teacher using a storybook to pose a problem situation; see Figure 7.4.

PROBLEM SOLVING   **MATHEMATICAL CONNECTIONS**   **PORTFOLIO**

Dinosaur Legs

FIGURE 7.4

On the Web site, view the video vignette "Dinosaur Legs" (Chapter 7, Video Vignettes). As you watch Mrs. Boch and her first graders, notice the number of different strategies the children used for solving this problem.

DIRECTIONS

- Before viewing this vignette, you might want to review what you read about problem solving strategies in Chapter 5.

- Compare the strategies the children used for solving this problem. Discuss the children's understanding of operations.

- How did Mrs. Boch encourage her children to develop flexible thinking?

- What techniques does the teacher use to build number sense?

Concrete to Symbolic   Operation concepts can be extended in the same manner as the number concepts are developed in Chapter 6 from the concrete experiences made to the connecting mode and finally to the symbolic mode. After children have used different materials and variations of the part-part-whole concepts, they can share their number "stories" with other classmates. They verbalize their actions and internalize the concepts before performing written work with the symbols. Children's informal experiences with operations can be linked to the mathematical language and symbols of operations as seen above in Activity 7.1.

After participating in and describing concrete experiences, the connecting mode with symbols is introduced. Activities to bridge these two modes help children relate the concrete with the symbolic. As children model with objects, the teacher writes the related number sentence on chart paper or the chalkboard. Another connecting activity is to pair children so that one child models with materials as the other child writes the number equation. Number equations written on sentence strips provide another variation. One child selects a number equation and makes up a word story while the other child constructs with models as shown in Figure 7.5.

When a solid understanding of the language and action is indicated, then and only then are children introduced to the symbolic mode. Operation meaning develops slowly through repeated exposure with numerous situational problems accompanied with modeling. The astute teacher assesses when each child is ready to make the transition from one mode to the next mode.

Curriculum units developed by Marilyn Burns, TERC, Encyclopedia Britannica, University of Chicago School Mathematics Project (Everyday Mathematics), and many others offer hands-on alternative mathematics programs. No Child Left Behind has caused programs to

FIGURE 7.5   *Working together in a connecting level activity.*

prove their quality by research studies in the schools (UCSMP, 2006). Teachers can now view a program's that record of student achievement before adopting a program to use in their classrooms.

PREREQUISITES FOR TEACHERS: OVERVIEW OF OPERATIONS AND PROPERTIES

This text assumes that the reader has completed at least one mathematics content course in a teacher education program. Only the parts of whole number operations and properties that affect a teacher's basic mathematical proficiency using conceptual understanding and strategic competence are discussed in this section. The topics are discussed in relation to how the teacher might extend the same learning to children in the elementary grades to develop their mathematical proficiency. Mathematics content review in greater depth is provided on the Web site Chapter 7, "Check Your Mathematics Knowledge."

Check

YOUR MATHEMATICS KNOWLEDGE

On Operations and Number Sense
- Properties and Principles
- Cartesian Products
- Why Not Division by Zero?
- More Word Problems
  . . . a refresher from mathematics content coursework . . . Lest you forget!

Addition and subtraction are inverse operations. That is, one "undoes" the other. If there are three cookies on a plate and Juan comes along and eats two, that can be described mathematically as $3 - 2 = 1$. If Marie brings two more cookies from the kitchen and puts them on the plate, there are once again three cookies on the plate. Mathematically, $1 + 2 = 3$. That all seems simple enough. Teacher candidates in an elementary math methods course were given linking cubes and asked to model the mathematical problem: After John gives his four tennis balls to Suzie who has three tennis balls already, how many tennis balls will Suzie have? Over half of the teacher candidates set out a stack of 4, a stack of 3, and a stack of 7 cubes. The rest of the candidates had a stack of 7 cubes sitting in front of them. Which group modeled the adding of a set of 4 and a set of 3? Which group demonstrated an understanding of addition as the process of joining sets together? If the teacher does not understand what happens in the process of addition, how is the student expected to understand addition?

This understanding is even more important when it comes to the operation of subtraction. Subtraction is a more complex operation and three interpretations of subtraction are covered in this book: take-away, comparison, and missing addend. Ma (1999) delineates a *Knowledge Package for Subtraction* that every teacher of elementary mathematics needs to have. Briefly, as you saw in Chapter 1, a knowledge package is a " . . . network of conceptual and procedural topics that support and are supported by its learning" (Ma and Kessel, 2001). In the diagram in Figure 7.6, repeated from Chapter 1, page 4, the symbols used represent different elements of the *Knowledge Package*. Ovals are the topics in the curriculum. Rectangles with rounded corners are the basic principles. Key pieces have thick borders. A rectangle represents the topic under discussion. Suppose that tomorrow's lesson involves subtraction with regrouping of numbers between 20 and 100. The *Knowledge Package* then would look like that in Figure 7.6.

Let's review what you learned in Chapter 1 about a knowledge packet for subtraction. What do you understand "composing and decomposing a higher value unit" to mean? What is "the rate of composing a higher value unit?" What importance does this have for children's knowing and doing mathematics? Consider the subtraction problem $15 - 8$. We know this as one of the "basic facts." But elementary students, before they are ready to memorize that fact, may already have discovered that they can decompose the 15 to $10 + 5$, then decompose the 10 to $7 + 3$, recompose the 15 as $7 + (3 + 5 [or 8])$, and finally subtract the 8 from the 8 and have a final answer of 7. As we noted earlier, many adults find this a confusing and tedious means of subtracting. But for children who are learning and doing mathematics, this is a meaningful approach to the original problem. How might a child who has not yet memorized all of the basic facts solve the problem $13 - 9$, using the method described here? The answer can be found in the instructor's manual. At the end of this chapter, you will have the opportunity to create a knowledge packet for one of the other operations.

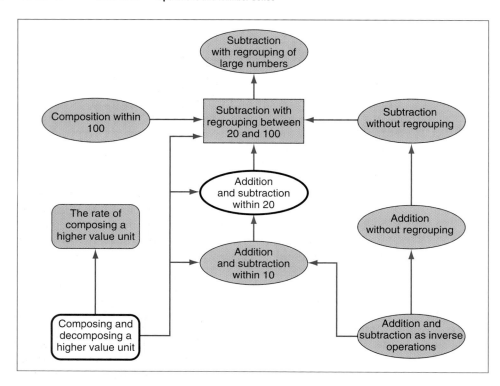

FIGURE 7.6 *Knowledge package for subtraction (Ma, 1999).*

Operation of Addition With addition, there are two types of problems that students need practice in modeling and creating. One is known as *combining* and the other is called *static*.

Combining A combining problem was illustrated above in the cookie problem on page 158 (Figure 7.5). The sets of cookies were physically joined. When the average adult is asked to define addition, he or she will most likely define the combining definition of addition.

Static Another type of addition problem, called "static," may involve the combining of two fixed sets (i.e., "Uriah's mom has one rose bush in the front yard and two rose bushes in the backyard. How many rose bushes does Uriah's mom have?"). The mathematical number sentence is the same (1 + 2 = 3), but in this example, the modeling would not have to involve the sets representing the bushes actually being moved together. It is not important that children distinguish between these two interpretations. It *is* important that they encounter a wide variety of problem structures and materials to model them.

All the materials that are used in modeling should represent two distinct parts (addends) that result in the whole (sum). The part-part-whole concept remains the same regardless of the material used—linking cubes of different colors, pattern blocks of two types, two-color tiles or lima beans, two types of keys or junk, or any other objects. See Figure 7.7 for examples of the part-part-whole concept modeled with a variety of manipulatives.

As students develop concepts and explore problem situations involving operations, the teacher should provide experiences to develop different meanings for operations. Mathematics learning in early grades should build an understanding of properties and relationships for each operation, develop relationships among operations, and acquire intuition about the effects of operating on a pair of numbers, such as increasing one addend and decreasing the other addend by one.

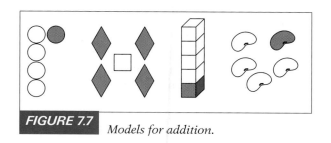

FIGURE 7.7 *Models for addition.*

Operation of Subtraction There are several types of problem situations that involve the operation of subtraction. Subtraction is more complex than addition. Subtraction can be defined as the inverse of addition and should be approached as a part-part-whole connection to addition. There are several types of problem situations that can be interpreted as subtraction when semantic differences in the word problem are evaluated. Fuson (2003, 1992) analyzed the problem subtypes for subtractive situations identified by research studies and found up to fifteen different structures. Research on Cognitively Guided Instruction (Carpenter, Fennema, and Franke, 1996), Conceptually Based Instruction (Hiebert and Wearne, 1993), and other such projects introducing children to a broad range of problem types improves children's problem-solving performance. Three interpretations for subtraction are covered in this book: take-away, comparison, and missing addend. All three concepts have the same subtraction equation but involve different problem situations.

Take-Away The "take away" idea means that a subset of the original set is actually removed. This is probably the most easily understood and the most often applied concept of subtraction. Concrete examples are found rather easily in real-life situations, such as eating cookies, spending money, or popping balloons. See Figure 7.8 for an example of this take-away word problem: "There were five cupcakes on the plate. Teri and Marcella each ate a cupcake. How many cupcakes were left?"

For many children, subtraction is a more difficult operation to understand, and the facts are memorized more slowly. The difficulty may be that there are various types of subtraction (take-away, missing addend, and comparison). The take-away concept is often overemphasized in the classroom to the detriment of the other two. Many teachers read the symbol for subtraction (−) as "take away" rather than minus. Minus is a word used for the sign " − ," not for the concept of "take away." However, owing to the overuse of this meaning for subtraction, many young children refer to this

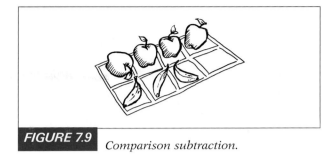

FIGURE 7.9 *Comparison subtraction.*

symbol as the "take away" sign and refer to subtraction as doing "the take-aways." You have the opportunity to evaluate yourself. If you are calling the minus sign, the "take-away" sign, it is now time to stop. Students deserve our best understandings!

Comparison The second meaning of subtraction is comparison. This concept is harder for children to understand and needs many modeling experiences to develop it. The comparison concept means that two sets are modeled and compared to one another and the difference, either more than or less than, is found as shown in Figure 7.9. The difference may be seen by a one-to-one matching as in this example: "In their lunches, four children had an apple and three children had a banana. How many more apples were there than bananas?"

Everyday examples of this may be experienced by children when comparing ages or height, comparing data on a bar graph, matching books to children in a reading group, setting the table, or getting chairs for members of a group. Comparison language of "how many more," "how many less," "how much younger," "how much heavier," accompany situational problems for this interpretation of subtraction.

Missing Addend The third concept of subtraction is missing addend or completion. This interpretation involves the relationship of subtraction to addition as a missing part. In addition, two parts are joined to make the whole. If a part is missing and the whole is known, then how much more must be added to the part to make the whole (the target number)? Often confusion comes by being misled by the word "more" and linking addition to the two numbers rather than adding on to the part to make the whole. Problem Situation 2 in Activity 7.1 was a comparison example. Another one is shown in Figure 7.10. For example, "Julio knows it costs 5 cents to buy the kite, but only has 2 cents. How much more does he need to buy the kite?"

This idea of finding "how many more are needed" is represented in real-world situations. Many experiences call for deciding the missing

5 cupcakes
- 2 were eaten
_____
3 cupcakes left

FIGURE 7.8 *Take-away subtraction.*

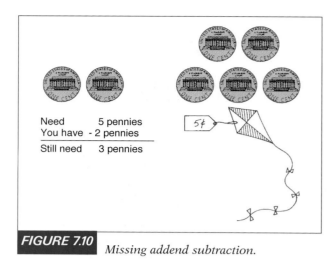

Need   5 pennies
You have - 2 pennies
Still need   3 pennies

FIGURE 7.10   *Missing addend subtraction.*

part and may be modeled as "counting on" to make the whole. The following examples ask the question of "how many more": Knowing the total cost and how much money you have, knowing the total mileage of a trip and how far you have traveled, determining the amount of change to be returned when a larger coin or bill has been given. Kamii, Lewis, and Booker (1998) suggest several games to help children focus on numerical reasoning for understanding missing-addend problems. A difficult aspect of missing addends is reversibility of the part-whole relationship, that is 3, + 2 = __, becomes 3 + __ = 5.

Now that you have studied the three types of subtraction problems, try Activity 7.2.

Activity 7.2

PROBLEM SOLVING

EXPLORING BASIC OPERATIONS OF SUBTRACTION

There are three ways to think about subtraction.

DIRECTIONS

1. Study the problems below and identify the type of subtraction problem each is.
2. Write the equation for each problem.

PROBLEM

1. Mateo's teacher gave him 8 pencils to sharpen and told him to make sure that each of his 17 classmates had a sharpened pencil. How many more pencils will Mateo need to sharpen for the class?
2. Sedona baked 15 cookies. If 9 cookies are eaten, how many cookies are left?

3. How many more cookies did Sedona bake than were eaten?
4. Jimmy has a collection of 12 matchbox cars. His friend has 15 matchbox cars. How many more cars does his friend have?
5. If Jimmy gets 5 more matchbox cars for his birthday, who has more cars? How many more?

Instruction in whole number operations should be embedded in modeling and real-world problem situations. It is important to build a context for the operation and to include various problem situations for the operation. For example, to construct meaning for the operation of subtraction, teachers must include situational problems that include comparison and missing addend rather than basing word problems only on the take-away situation. Children should be modeling the operation along with the word problem. The action of the operation (joining, adding on, separating, or partitioning) becomes a part of the activity. Use a story setting (the zoo, a picnic, a fish tank) to stimulate children's creation of their own word problems for understanding operations.

Properties of Addition and Subtraction   There are three properties that are helpful for children in understanding the operation of addition and in learning the basic facts. These properties are

- Identity property (zero property)—when 0 is added to any whole number the number remains the same; the identity stays the same. $7 + 0 = 7$
- Commutative property (order property)—the order of the addends (parts) does not change the whole (sum); the number equation can be "turned around" and the answer is the same. $3 + 4 = 7$ and $4 + 3 = 7$
- Associative property (grouping property)—the addends can be combined in any grouping and the sum does not change. $(2 + 3) + 6 = 11$ or $2 + (3 + 6) = 11$

It is important that the teacher understand that the properties of the number system are limited because the commutative property, the associative property, and the identity property result in inequalities when working with subtraction. Older students should examine these properties to explore such relationships for the operation. For example, $7 - 3 = 4$, but $3 - 7$ is not equal to 4.

Operation of Multiplication Multiplication and division are inverse operations, just as addition and subtraction are. Multiplication is also related to addition in that one explanation of the operation of multiplication is repeated addition. Likewise, division is sometimes described as repeated subtraction. Earlier in this chapter, you saw an example of a knowledge packet for subtraction. Team up with a classmate and one of you develop a knowledge packet for multiplication and the other, a knowledge packet for division. Compare your knowledge packets with others in your class.

The conceptualization of multiplication should involve investigations of various groups, arrangements, number lines, and arrays with many types of materials. As children experience the physical models and verbalize the action with problem situations, they will be ready for the written symbols.

Repeated Addition Although there are three different interpretations for multiplication, most textbooks devote primary time to combining sets of equal size, known as the concept of grouping or repeated addition. The aspect of multiplication that distinguishes it from addition is that for multiplication the sets must be the same size. Multiplication can be defined as repeated addition where the addends are of equal size or the addends must be the same number; for example, or 4 groups of 3 are 12. Multiplication should begin as ideas about repeated addition to connect children's prior understandings of addition. Children see multiplication as counting groups of objects rather than single objects. Figure 7.11 shows two examples.

Learning experiences should include children describing things in real life that naturally occur in groups (eyes, tricycle wheels, packs of soda, or days in a week). These groups can form problem situations when children are constructing their own word problems and modeling number sentences. Links between the language and modeling are valuable. Children need to move from a given number in a group to a given number per group. Another way to view multiplication word problems are rate situations such as, "Tenisha can earn $1.25 an hour babysitting her little sister. How much would she earn if she babysits for 4 hours?" Rate problems pose more difficulties because the language is not as clear as in the grouping situations (Kilpatrick, Swafford, Findell, [Eds.], 2001).

Language becomes important in expressing number equations for multiplication. Students must understand the exact wording of multiplication. For example, instead of saying "4 times 2," the teacher needs to say, "4 groups of 2." The use of the

"Pui Loo put 2 candles on each cupcake. She had 4 cupcakes. How many candles in all?"

$4 \times 2 = 8$
4 sets of 2 are 8

red	red	red	red
brown			

"Pui Loo had 2 cupcakes. There were 4 candles on each one. How many candles are there?"

$2 \times 4 = 8$
2 sets of 4 are 8

purple	purple
brown	

FIGURE 7.11 *Multiplication as repeated addition or grouping.*

word "of" is critical because it makes the nature of multiplication (equal sets) clearer than does the word "times." Activities using materials should begin in early grades to describe multiplication as repeated addition. In Figure 7.12, all these groups show three groups of two. In the resulting number sentence, 3×2, the first number (factor) defines the number of groups and the second number (factor) defines the size of each group.

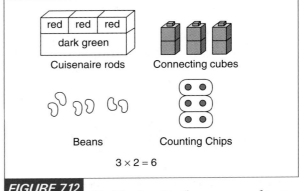

red	red	red
dark green		

Cuisenaire rods   Connecting cubes

Beans   Counting Chips

$3 \times 2 = 6$

FIGURE 7.12 *Models showing three groups of two.*

Involve children in physical groupings also: Give three books to each of two children; have four children each hold up five fingers; have five children stand and decide how many eyes or toes are there altogether. Using the wording "__groups of __" also helps children in later elementary grades when they study multiplication of decimal and rational numbers, covered in Chapter 10 of this text.

Combinations   Multiplication can also be defined in terms of combinations or possible pairings. Other names associated with this interpretation of multiplication are cross multiplication or Cartesian products. In this sense, all elements of one set can be matched one-to-one with all the elements of another set to find the number of total possible pairs. Real-life examples extend to selecting outfits for a trip (number of shirts matched to number of pants to produce different outfits), possible outcomes in probability experiments, or flavors of yogurt and different toppings.

Every college student on a budget uses the Cartesian product in wardrobe planning! See how the clothing combines to form different outfits in Figure 7.13: "Monique is packing for a trip. She has four tops to go with a skirt, a pair of shorts, and a pair of pants. How many different outfits can she make?"

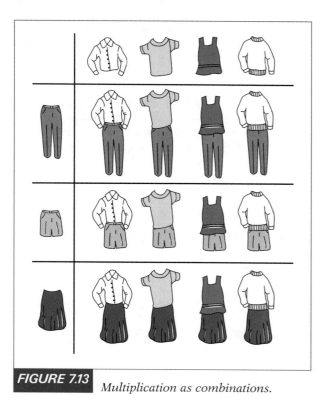

FIGURE 7.13   *Multiplication as combinations.*

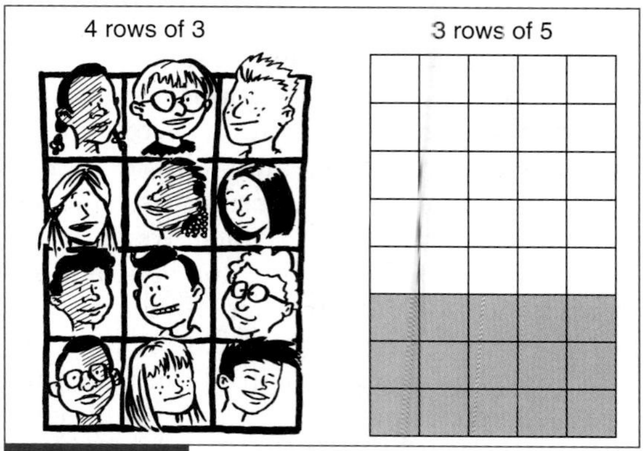

FIGURE 7.14   *Multiplication as an array.*

4 rows of 3   3 rows of 5

Arrays   The final interpretation of multiplication is that of an array model. This row-by-column problem compares to the width-times-length formula for areas of rectangular regions. The standards (NCTM, 2000) call for having students build arrays showing how a product is related to its factors and seeing relationships between factor pairs. Applications to real-world situations include rows in a theater and so many seats per row, or rows in a garden and a given number of plants per row to determine the total. Children can build various numbers with color tiles or cubes and make rectangles from graph paper as in Figure 7.14. Such activities offer readiness experiences for later work with factors, area, algebraic equations, and natural extensions to multidigit multiplication in Chapter 9. For example, "Mrs. Homeratha asked the children to sit in 4 rows with 3 in each row. How many children would this be?"

Perhaps it needs to be said again that all of the interpretations for an operation are written, recorded, and answered the same way. Only when situational word problems are attached to the number equation must appropriate modeling occur. Difficulty results when children translate word problems into number equations, and then flexible ways to model the problem are needed.

Operation of Division   Division is the mathematical operation used to separate a set into equal parts. Division is the inverse operation of multiplication—where multiplication is the operation used to combine sets of equal size into a new set. The operation of division has two other concepts that teachers need to understand if they are going to create viable opportunities for students to model and understand the action involved in division. The two concepts, partitive division and measurement division, can be easily modeled with

MEASUREMENT DIVISION	PARTITIVE DIVISION
You know:	*You know:*
1. Number of objects in the original set.	Number of objects in the original set.
2. Number of new sets to be in each new set.	Number of objects formed.
Need to find:	*Need to find:*
3. How many new sets can be made?	How many objects are in each new set?

FIGURE 7.15 *Comparison of two types of division.*

manipulatives. The difference between these two situations is noted in Figure 7.15.

Measurement Division (Repeated Subtraction) Measurement division involves the process of taking a group of objects and separating (measuring) them into equal size groups of a specific size until all are distributed. The number of groups made is the answer. Here is a real-world example: "Todd has 10 marbles and wants to give 2 to each friend. How many friends will get 2 marbles?" Figure 7.16 shows that if there are 10 marbles and 2 are taken away each time, this can happen 5 times. This process can also be thought of as repeated subtraction or, in equation form, as $10 \div 2 = 5$.

Partitive Division Partitive division involves the process of taking a group of objects and sharing (partitioning) them evenly into a specific number of groups until they are all gone, or none are left for another complete round. The number in each group is the answer. Dealing cards to people in a game is a common situation where partitive division is used. Here is another example of partitive

division: "Enrique has 4 friends and 8 pieces of candy. He wants to give his candy away to his friends so everyone has an equal amount. How many pieces will each friend get?" Figure 7.17 shows the thought process for partitive division.

A way to help you and the children remember the difference between the two types of division is by relating them in a meaningful fashion. The following is a common illustrative situation. There are 24 students in the class. You ask them to form groups by counting aloud 1–2–3–4 and then you have all the fours go into one group, the threes go to another group, and so on. This is partitive division.

Another example of partitive division is when you have four children chosen as team captains and they select people to be on their team. You know the number of groups, and you are finding the size of each group.

For measurement division, you would have children count aloud 1–2–3–4, and you would call

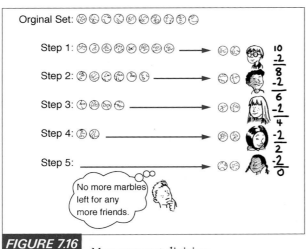

FIGURE 7.16 *Measurement division.*

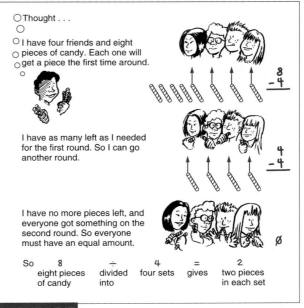

FIGURE 7.17 *Partitive division.*

that group 1. The next four children would form group 2, the next four are group 3, and continue in such a manner. Here you know the size of each group, and you are determining how many groups can be made. The same equation and recording fits both division situations, 24 ÷ 4 = 6, but the modeling with objects is different.

It is not important that children know the differences by name, but it is important that both types of exercises are included in building the division operation. Research (Kilpatrick, Jeremy and Jane Swafford, [Eds.], 2002) suggests that children use different strategies to represent measurement division problems than partitive division. These strategies should be observed, explained, and shared to help make sense of the operation. Remember that many students, even in upper elementary grades, commonly view multiplication as repeated addition and division as repeated subtraction as in Figure 7.18. They need to work with a variety of problem situations and expand their views of these operations (NCTM, 2000).

Properties of Multiplication and Division Several mathematical properties apply to multiplication. The mathematical principle called the commutative property (4 × 5 is the same as 5 × 4) relates to multiplication in the same way as it applies to addition. Although changing the order of the factors does not alter the product, when using grouping or rate problems, the roles being modeled by the factors must change. In other words, 4 groups of 5 cubes each (4 × 5) need to be rearranged to show the related commutative fact of 5 × 4, which is 5 groups with 4 cubes in each group. View the Video Vignette, "Cluster Problems," on the Web site, Chapter 7, Video Vignettes, to watch children in fourth grade exploring the commutative property and how repeated addition relates to multiplication see Figure 7.19. Review the questions provided at the beginning of the video before

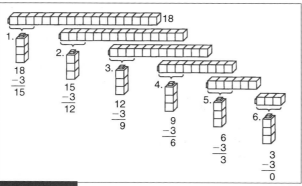

FIGURE 7.18   *Division as repeated subtraction.*

Video Vignette

PROBLEM SOLVING   MATHEMATICAL CONNECTIONS

Cluster Problems

FIGURE 7.19

On the Web site, view the video vignette "Cluster Problems" (Chapter 7, Video Vignettes). As you watch Mrs. Cordoba and her fourth graders, notice the number of different strategies the children used for solving this problem.

DIRECTIONS

- Why did Mrs. Cordoba select these four equations as a "Cluster Problems?" What do you think is the purpose of this activity?

- Compare the strategies the children used for solving this problem and discuss their effectiveness.

- What mathematical reasoning do you see the children using in this lesson?

- What meanings for multiplication do you notice?

- What would be another set of four equations that Mrs. Cordoba could use as a "Cluster Problem" if she were to continue this activity tomorrow?

watching the video. Be prepared to discuss your responses with your classmates. Practice with manipulatives helps develop understanding of the commutative property.

Four other properties relate to multiplication. These properties are the zero property, $0 \times 8 = 0$; the identity property, $6 \times 1 = 6$; the associative property, $(4 \times 2) \times 3 = 4 \times (2 \times 3)$, and the distributive property, $6 \times 5 = (3 \times 5) + (3 \times 5)$.

Like subtraction, the commutative and associative properties do not apply to division. The identity property for multiplication is one ($8 \times 1 = 8$) and this is true for division ($8/1 = 8$). The zero property in division is a special case and one that can be confusing to children. The property of division by zero says that dividing a number by zero does not compute or is undefined. Modeling and explaining this property to children is the challenge. It is not sufficient to say "dividing by zero is impossible." For example, what is the answer to $8 \div 0$? When expressed in inverse fashion (which works with other division facts such as $8 \div 4 = 2$ becomes $2 \times 4 = 8$), this would become $? \times 0 = 8$. Remember that any number multiplied by zero is zero, so any number used instead of the $?$ would produce a product of zero. Then 8×0 would equal 8, but that is not true. The only number that could replace 8, to make the inverse possible also, is zero. Because this does not permit computation to take place meaningfully, the situation inherently becomes "does not compute."

Children may still want to try to model examples that involve zero. As with other concepts, encourage students to make up word stories and try to model the action. Try problems with both partitive and measurement approaches to division. "How many groups of zero are in 8?" "Put 8 counters into zero groups."

Since division is the inverse of multiplication, write the related fact equations for the problem. Present the problem of $8 \div 0$ and write the corresponding multiplication sentence that checks that problem, $\_\_\_ \times 0 = 8$. Whatever number is placed as an answer, the product is still zero. This would indicate that 0 is not equal to 0; therefore, there is no answer to the problem and we say division by zero is undefined. If more explanation is preferred, use the extra examples on the Web site, Chapter 7, Check Your Mathematics Knowledge, "Why Not Division by Zero?"

Becoming comfortable with many different problem situations for the four operations takes time. Practice with recognizing problem structures may be needed before you ask children to analyze word problems. More opportunities and examples are found on the Web site, Chapter 7, Check Your

Mathematics Knowledge, "More Word Problems, Set 1" and "More Word Problems, Set 2."

Students need to know that all cultures have developed ways to handle different problem situations with arithmetic and that many of the numbers and numerals we use today originated in ancient times. Activity 7.3 connects students to many cultures and the geography of the world from which the ideas came.

Activity 7.3

CULTURAL RELEVANCE   MATHEMATICAL CONNECTIONS

ORIGINS OF MODERN ARITHMETIC

MATERIALS
- A globe
- Pictures of ancient and modern Egypt, Central America, India

DIRECTIONS
1. Tell the children that people in ancient days did the same things with numbers that they (the children) do in arithmetic.
2. Share the following information from the Chicago mathematics teachers (Strong, 1990):
   Students should know that many peoples contributed to the development of modern arithmetic and that the origins of arithmetic are international. For example, Africans were the first to use numerals. Ancient Egyptians in Africa invented a symbol for ten that represented 10 tally marks and a symbol for one hundred that replaced 100 tally marks. The Chinese were among the first to recognize and use number patterns. The Maya in Central America used a zero as a position holder hundreds of years before Europe imported modern numerals from Africa. Modern numerals were invented by the peoples of India. That is why modern numerals are known as Hindu-Arabic numerals. (p. 38)
3. Use the globe to show where the Maya lived in Central America, and where India and Egypt are located.
4. Show the pictures of the people going about their daily tasks. Talk of how they may be making up number stories about their work. Let the children pretend to live in each culture and tell a number story that could go with each picture.

Supporting the NCTM *Standards* (2000):
- Mathematics as Connections; Number Fluency
- The Learning Principle
- The Equity Principle

Exploring relationships and patterns between operations helps students acquire new understandings of operations. Conceptual understanding of the operations is an important aspect of knowing mathematics and must precede basic fact mastery and computation. Concept development activities are related to the symbolic mode of paper-and-pencil computation through careful bridging that connects and translates the two components of relationships and patterns. These bridging activities should encompass the oral (auditory) mode, the tactile (hands-on) mode, and the written (symbolic) mode. Extended Activities on the Web site in Chapter 7 are designed to give you some games and activities to help students with the bridging process.

THINKING STRATEGIES FOR BUILDING PROCEDURAL FLUENCY AND FLEXIBILITY WITH BASIC FACTS

The beginning step in developing basic facts is to build an understanding of the operation. Manipulatives are the important, beginning key. Children should have opportunities to represent the number equation with physical models. Teaching basic facts should center on the structure of mathematics. Simply going through the number combinations in numerical order is not enough. Numerous research studies over several decades have shown that certain thinking strategies help children learn the basic facts (Fuson, 2003; Siegler, 2003; Thornton, 1990; Steinberg, 1985; Rathmell,

1978). More research has been done with addition, less with subtraction, and much less with multiplication and division. Fuson (2003) reports that children worldwide follow much the same progression in working with single-digit addition and subtraction as seen in Figure 7.20.

It is in the thinking strategies where procedural fluency (the ability to find solutions efficiently, appropriately, and accurately) and computational flexibility (the ability to see more than one way to solve the problem) are nurtured and where the power of mathematics becomes visible to students. Therefore, a comprehensive analysis of the leading thinking strategies becomes important for teachers to know.

Thinking Strategies for the Basic Facts of Addition

The basic 100 addition facts, pictured in Figure 7.21, are those problems that are composed of two single-digit addends. Thus, the facts include $0 + 0 = 0$ through $9 + 9 = 18$. They serve as the basis for all further addition work and need to be developed from a concrete basis of understanding to an automatic response level if they are going to be useful in computation.

For many children the two basic forms—horizontal, $2 + 3 = 5$, and vertical,

$$\begin{array}{r} 2 \\ +3 \\ \hline 5 \end{array}$$

provide no real stumbling block to learning the addition facts. In teaching basic facts, both forms need to be used, and generally the horizontal form is introduced first. Children may be given help

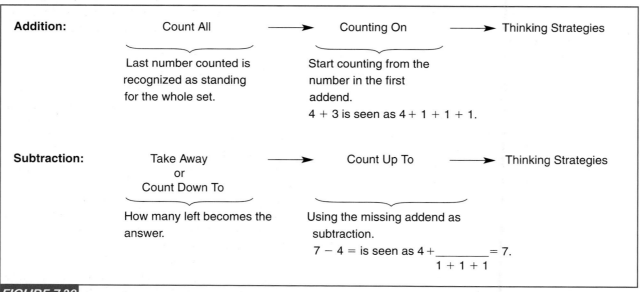

FIGURE 7.20   *Children's progression working with single-digit addition and subtraction.*

+	0	1	2	3	4	5	6	7	8	9
0	0	1	2	3	4	5	6	7	8	9
1	1	2	3	4	5	6	7	8	9	10
2	2	3	4	5	6	7	8	9	10	11
3	3	4	5	6	7	8	9	10	11	12
4	4	5	6	7	8	9	10	11	12	13
5	5	6	7	8	9	10	11	12	13	14
6	6	7	8	9	10	11	12	13	14	15
7	7	8	9	10	11	12	13	14	15	16
8	8	9	10	11	12	13	14	15	16	17
9	9	10	11	12	13	14	15	16	17	18

FIGURE 7.21 *100 Basic addition facts.*

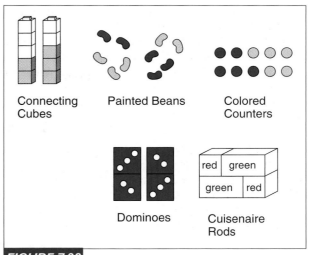

FIGURE 7.23 *Models to show commutative property—turnaround facts.*

recognizing that the combinations are the same by actually writing both forms of the same fact. This should be done at the same time children are performing actions with multiple's embodiments (various models).

Commutativity Understanding the mathematical properties associated with each operation is important to enhance learning. An important property of addition is the commutative principle. Figure 7.22 shows that 45 addition facts are learned readily if the principle of commutativity is applied. The facts that are related by the commutative property are shaded in the figure.

To internalize the property of commutativity, students need experiences with concrete materials. Figure 7.23 shows several effective manipulative devices to use. Students need to realize the power of this property in reducing the number of facts to learn.

Practice alone is not sufficient to facilitate memorizing the basic facts. Students need to increase their memorization abilities by using an organized list of the facts. This approach places

the facts into categories according to the structure of mathematics and their order of difficulty. It also capitalizes on the natural thinking strategies invented by children for learning the facts. Figure 7.24, the basic fact strategies for addition, assumes that the commutative property has been developed and continues to be emphasized. As you read each strategy, consider the definition and notice the systematic way the facts are related to each other. Also think about how organizing the facts in this manner reduces the number of facts to be learned and encourages retention.

The fact strategies should be shown and developed with concrete materials to ensure understanding. Many of these devices can be made inexpensively and quickly and are well worth the time. Activities with manipulatives are suggested for teaching the following fact strategies: adding one, counting on, near doubles, and bridging to ten.

Counting On by One, Two, and Three Although "counting on" was talked about in Chapter 6, it dealt with using concrete experiences and icon (pictorial) modes to achieve the understanding of number. The strategy now adds the counting on by two and three and focuses on the symbolic mode. Much time could be spent in quick practice sessions with counting one, two, or three more than a given number. Such sessions can be done easily when children are waiting in line to wash hands, to leave for another class, or when children are lining up for recess, music, or whatever. An effective aid that can be quickly made is shown in Figure 7.25. The first addend is written to the left with the second addend being plus two or plus three. Attached as flip cards are the counting numbers the child would say to reach the sum. If the child needs this prompt, the

+	0	1	2	3	4	5	6	7	8	9
0		1	2	3	4	5	6	7	8	9
1	1		3	4	5	6	7	8	9	10
2	2	3		5	6	7	8	9	10	11
3	3	4	5		7	8	9	10	11	12
4	4	5	6	7		9	10	11	12	13
5	5	6	7	8	9		11	12	13	14
6	6	7	8	9	10	11		13	14	15
7	7	8	9	10	11	12	13		15	16
8	8	9	10	11	12	13	14	15		17
9	9	10	11	12	13	14	15	16	17	

FIGURE 7.22 *Commutative property for addition.*

Definition

Identity Element

Adding 0 to any number does not change the number.
19 basic facts are learned.

+	0	1	2	3	4	5	6	7	8	9
0	0	1	2	3	4	5	6	7	8	9
1	1									
2	2									
3	3									
4	4									
5	5									
6	6									
7	7									
8	8									
9	9									

Adding One

Depends on understanding number seriation—adding one to any number is the same as naming the next counting number.
17 facts are learned.

+	0	1	2	3	4	5	6	7	8	9
0										
1		2	3	4	5	6	7	8	9	10
2		3								
3		4								
4		5								
5		6								
6		7								
7		8								
8		9								
9		10								

Counting One

Most effective when addend is 1, 2, or 3 more than any given number.
Involves two skills:
1. Knowing which number is greater and that counting begins here.
2. Knowing counting sequence beginning at any one-digit number.
28 additional facts are learned.

+	0	1	2	3	4	5	6	7	8	9
0										
1										
2			4	5	6	7	8	9	10	11
3			5	6	7	8	9	10	11	12
4			6	7						
5			7	8						
6			8	9						
7			9	10						
8			10	11						
9			11	12						

Definition

Doubles

Both addends are the same number.
6 facts are learned.

+	0	1	2	3	4	5	6	7	8	9
0										
1		2								
2			4							
3				6						
4					8					
5						10				
6							12			
7								14		
8									16	
9										18

Near Doubles

Use when addends are consecutive numbers.
If children know 8 + 8 = 16, then prompt them to reason that 8 + 9 is one more or 8 + 7 is one less.
10 additional facts are learned.

+	0	1	2	3	4	5	6	7	8	9
0										
1										
2				5						
3			5		7					
4				7		9				
5					9		11			
6						11		13		
7							13		15	
8								15		17
9									17	

Bridging to 10

Use when one addend is close to 10.
More difficult for children to understand because:
1. Mastery of sums to 10 must be developed first.
2. Ability to separate a number into two parts is required.
3. Must mentally keep track of changes in both addends.
16 additional facts are learned.

+	0	1	2	3	4	5	6	7	8	9
0										
1										
2										11
3									11	12
4								11	12	13
5									13	14
6										15
7						11				16
8				11	12	13				17
9			11	12	13	14	15	16	17	

Note: The blocks with numbers in the main body of the table denote new facts to be learned. The shaded part denotes facts already learned by a previous strategy. A shaded block with a number included indicates an overlap between a previously learned strategy and a new strategy.

FIGURE 7.24 *Thinking strategies for the basic facts of addition.*

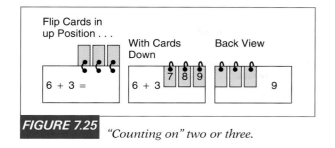

FIGURE 7.25 *"Counting on" two or three.*

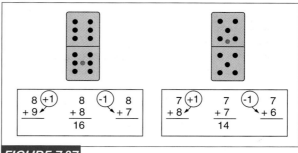

FIGURE 7.27 *Devices to learn near doubles.*

cards can be flipped over for help. If the child wants to check the answer, it appears on the back.

A simple game is to have a deck of cards of numbers that serves as the first addend. The child rolls a die that has two faces marked with 1, two faces marked with 2, and two faces marked with 3. The die indicates the number to be added to the card drawn from the deck. If the correct sum is given, the child can move on the number of spaces indicated on the die using the game board as shown in Figure 7.26.

Near Doubles The near-doubles strategy reinforces something a child already knows and feels comfortable with, the doubles. A teaching/practice device for near doubles is shown in Figure 7.27. We must always look for ways to build on prior knowledge to form new associations.

Bridging to 10 Many mathematics educators encourage the use of ten-frames to create mental imagery. The "Bridging to 10" activity below shows teaching techniques to develop this concept. These devices may be made from egg cartons. The sides of plastic fruit baskets, plastic canvas, or chicken wire may be used to project on the overhead for whole-class discussion. Ten-frames consist of a 2 × 5 array where one side must be filled to 5 before the other side is started. Counters are placed in the squares starting at the upper left and proceeding across until that row is filled. Review the video vignette, "Using Ten-Frames" from the Web site

for Chapter 6, if you need to refresh your memory. Number sense is developed as children predict how many more are needed to fill the row. Some children count backward from ten while others count on to ten. This reinforces relationships between the two operations as shown in Activity 7.4.

Another manipulative device to use for bridging to 10 that can be constructed easily and inexpensively is shown in Figure 7.28 and is composed of 18 plastic beads on a pipe cleaner. Ten beads are one color and eight beads are another color. When combinations are formed, the two colors indicate the two-digit number that results as the sum. The device allows for all facts through 9 + 9 (sum 18 or the total number of plastic beads) and visually indicates when a bridging to 10 occurs.

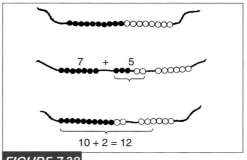

FIGURE 7.28 *Bead cards for "bridging to 10."*

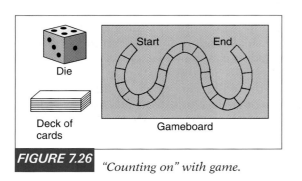

FIGURE 7.26 *"Counting on" with game.*

Activity 7.4

MANIPULATIVES   **ESTIMATION**   **MENTAL MATH**   **BRIDGING TO 10**

MATERIALS
- A set of dot cards for the ten-frames
- Counters and egg cartons

DIRECTIONS

1. Teacher flashes a card to child for a second. The child puts that number of counters in the egg carton trays and says the total amount. Teacher continues in similar fashion for other numbers.
2. Teacher can also flash a dot card to the child for a second and the child tells how many more dots are needed to form 10.

Variation

MATERIALS

- Counters and egg cartons to make two ten-frames

DIRECTIONS

Teacher (or child) shows addition fact with 7, 8, or 9 as one addend. The other addend is large enough to form a sum greater than 10. A 10 is made with the first addend by adding counters from the second ten-frame.

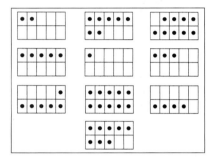

The answer appears as 10 + remaining number.

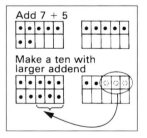

Children often regard learning the 100 addition facts as an insurmountable task. When the facts are broken into groups, the task becomes manageable and reasonable to attain. When thinking strategies and fact strategies are used rather than random memorization, the facts are learned faster and retained longer.

Thinking Strategies for the Basic Facts of Subtraction

There are 100 basic subtraction facts that are formed as the inverse of addition. There appear to be two different philosophies as to when subtraction facts should be introduced to children: at the same time as the related addition facts or after groups of addition facts (facts to 10 and facts to 18). Some teachers delay extensive work on subtraction facts until speed tests for addition have been mastered. Because many of the thinking strategies for subtraction are closely related to the addition facts, the authors support teaching the two operations together.

The fact strategies for subtraction are subtract zero; subtract the whole/almost the whole; counting back; counting on (counting up); and fact families. Keep in mind that it is critical to have children model these concepts with objects before the ideas are taught and before children are expected to use these strategies in meaningful ways. Practice with concrete manipulatives helps develop understanding and memory of these fact strategies. Fact strategies and the structure of the number system can be used to teach the facts shown in Figure 7.29.

Fact Families Analyzing the relationships between the facts of addition and subtraction helps the recall of fact families. Facts are organized into "families" to help children use a known fact to recall an unknown fact. Triominoes, pictured in Figure 7.30, are an effective device, made easily and inexpensively, to develop fact families. The triominoes can be color coded in clusters of facts such as facts to 6, facts to 10, facts to 14, or facts to 18. The teacher selects facts on which a child needs practice and gives that triomino to the child to write the four related equations.

When errors are noted, the teacher should ask the child to model the equation with concrete objects. This procedure will become self-correcting and a valuable learning experience. Triominoes can also be used as a practice device. If the top corner is covered, you are asking for a sum. If one of the side corners is covered, a missing addend is needed.

Using 10 The power of 10 cannot be overstated in developing thinking strategies for subtraction facts. When students master all the facts to 10 for subtraction using various strategies suggested, to subtract single-digit numbers from the teen numbers, students can think of a tens fact and then add on the rest. To use this strategy for this problem, 14 − 8, the child can think of the problem as 10 − 8, which is 2 and then add on the 4 from the ones place to get an answer of 6 as illustrated in Figure 7.31. In this manner, all subtraction facts greater than 10 can become two-step problems—subtract from 10 and then add the ones.

Definition

Subtract Zero
Easily learned—subtracting 0 from any number does not change the number.
10 facts learned.

+	0	1	2	3	4	5	6	7	8	9
0	0	1	2	3	4	5	6	7	8	9
1										
2										
3										
4										
5										
6										
7										
8										
9										

Definition

Counting Back
Most effective when the number subtracted is 1, 2, or 3. Related to "counting on."
24 facts learned.

+	0	1	2	3	4	5	6	7	8	9
0										
1		2	3	4	5	6	7	8	9	10
2		3	4	5	6	7	8	9	10	11
3		4	5	6	7	8	9	10	11	12
4										
5										
6										
7										
8										
9										

Subtracting the Whole/Almost the Whole
Subtracting the number from itself results in 0 left. Almost the whole means to subtract a number that is one less than the number: 8 – 7 = 1.
18 facts learned.

+	0	1	2	3	4	5	6	7	8	9
0	0	1								
1	1	2								
2	2	3								
3	3	4								
4	4	5								
5	5	6								
6	6	7								
7	7	8								
8	8	9								
9	9	10								

Counting On
Use when 3 or less is to be subtracted. Helpful to associate with "counting on" for addition.
Missing addend approach is emphasized: 5 + ? = 8.
12 additional facts learned.

+	0	1	2	3	4	5	6	7	8	9
0										
1										
2										
3										
4		5	6	7						
5		6	7	8						
6		7	8	9						
7		8	9	10						
8		9	10	11						
9		10	11	12						

Fact Families
Emphasizes inverse operation of addition/subtraction and interrelates them.
Last 36 facts learned.

+	0	1	2	3	4	5	6	7	8	9
0										
1										
2										
3										
4					8	9	10	11	12	13
5					9	10	11	12	13	14
6					10	11	12	13	14	15
7					11	12	13	14	15	16
8					12	13	14	15	16	17
9					13	14	15	16	17	18

Note: The blocks with numbers in the main body of the table denote new facts to be learned. The shaded part denotes facts already learned by a previous strategy. A shaded block with a number included indicates an overlap between a previously learned strategy and a new strategy.

FIGURE 7.29 *Thinking strategies for the basic facts of subtraction.*

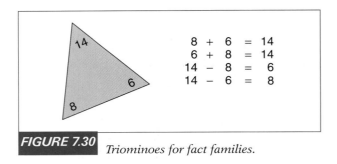

FIGURE 7.30 *Triominoes for fact families.*

$$8 + 6 = 14$$
$$6 + 8 = 14$$
$$14 - 8 = 6$$
$$14 - 6 = 8$$

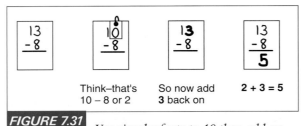

Think–that's   So now add $2 + 3 = 5$
10 – 8 or 2   3 back on

FIGURE 7.31 *Use simpler facts to 10 then add on the 1's.*

Part–Whole The important relationship between parts and wholes can be made as the four number sentences are generated with concrete modeling. If the facts related to 3, 6, and 9 are the goal, show three red counters as one set and six black counters as the second set and think of the corresponding two addition sentences for joining them and the two subtraction sentences for separating them. In the connecting mode, domino dot flip cards, shown in Figure 7.32, show the total as well as the two parts and can alternately cover the two parts or the whole. Children can write the appropriate number sentences.

Counting Back and Counting On Many teachers and parents consider only flash cards although some other devices are more effective. Because missing addends is a related concept for several strategies, several teaching aids can be made to reinforce this concept. Flip cards, illustrated in Figure 7.33, enhance learning the several strategies called subtract the whole/almost the whole, counting back, and counting on. Several studies (Fuson, 2003; Seigler, 2003; Kilpatrick, Swafford,

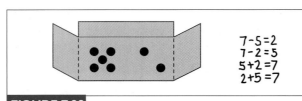

$$7 - 5 = 2$$
$$7 - 2 = 5$$
$$5 + 2 = 7$$
$$2 + 5 = 7$$

FIGURE 7.32 *Domino dot cards for fact families show a connecting level device.*

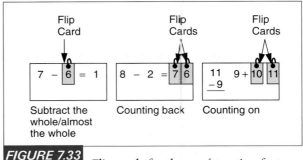

Subtract the   Counting back   Counting on
whole/almost
the whole

FIGURE 7.33 *Flip cards for three subtraction fact strategies.*

and Findell (Eds.), 2001) have shown that counting back (counting down) presents children with considerable difficulty, and research by Fuson (2003) indicates that counting up is an effective approach for first grade children.

Activity 7.5 describes a game that can be played to help students learn subtraction facts by using the "subtract almost the whole" strategy.

THINKING STRATEGIES FOR THE BASIC FACTS OF MULTIPLICATION

Readiness activities for multiplication should begin with talking about groups of the same size and exploring counting patterns. Activities that encourage children to visualize groups along with the related languages should precede any formal use of the multiplication table or the formal word "times." Children are eager to begin the multiplication chapter, usually included in the second grade text. Multiplication means the world of "big kids," and young children are eager to quote products of large numbers to teacher and others.

Activity 7.5

PROBLEM SOLVING

SUBTRACT THE WHOLE/ALMOST THE WHOLE

MATERIALS
- Four sets of 0–9 number cards (40 in all)

DIRECTIONS
1. Have the children work in cooperative groups of two or three.
2. Shuffle the cards.

3. Deal 4 cards to each player.

4. Put the remaining cards in a pile between two players.

5. On alternating turns, a player draws a card from the pile.

6. If the player can form an equation with two numbers that will give an answer with a difference of one, the player says, "UNO." The player says the number sentence (for instance, 4 minus 3 is 1) and lays down the two cards, 4 and 3.

7. Play continues until all cards have been drawn. The player with the most equations wins.

x	0	1	2	3	4	5	6	7	8	9
0		0	0	0	0	0	0	0	0	0
1	0		2	3	4	5	6	7	8	9
2	0	2		6	8	10	12	14	16	18
3	0	3	6		12	15	18	21	24	27
4	0	4	8	12		20	24	28	32	36
5	0	5	10	15	20		30	35	40	45
6	0	6	12	18	24	30		42	48	54
7	0	7	14	21	28	35	42		56	63
8	0	8	16	24	32	40	48	56		72
9	0	9	18	27	36	45	54	63	72	

FIGURE 7.35 *Commutative property of multiplication.*

When formal drill on the basic facts is needed, the following thinking strategies should be considered. There are 100 basic multiplication facts composed from all single-digit factors. Thus, the facts include $0 \times 0 = 0$ through $9 \times 9 = 81$. The resulting table is shown in Figure 7.34. As mentioned earlier, the commutative property reduces the number of facts to be learned by 45, as shown in Figure 7.35.

Most children develop strategies for recalling the multiplication facts. Many of these strategies involve the properties of the number system and counting patterns. The fact strategies are shown in Figure 7.36 with diagrams to identify which strategy is used. Remember that easier strategies should be taught first. The main fact strategies for multiplication are the identity element, zero property, skip counting, multiples of 9, and doubles.

Skip Counting Skip counting is another major strategy that shows patterns and the structure of

x	0	1	2	3	4	5	6	7	8	9
0	0	0	0	0	0	0	0	0	0	0
1	0	1	2	3	4	5	6	7	8	9
2	0	2	4	6	8	10	12	14	16	18
3	0	3	6	9	12	15	18	21	24	27
4	0	4	8	12	16	20	24	28	32	36
5	0	5	10	15	20	25	30	35	40	45
6	0	6	12	18	24	30	36	42	48	54
7	0	7	14	21	28	35	42	49	56	63
8	0	8	16	24	32	40	48	56	64	72
9	0	9	18	27	36	45	54	63	72	81

FIGURE 7.34 *100 basic multiplication facts.*

the number system. Calculators can provide an incentive to learn skip counting by pressing the keys, 2 + = . By continually pressing the = key, the view screen shows 2, 4, 6, 8, and so forth. Check to make sure that your calculator performs in the same way. The more expensive graphing calculators do not always work this way; the less expensive calculators are the ones to use with this activity. Skip counting by two begins in most first grade texts. Using examples in the child's world builds a visual frame of reference for these facts: two wheels on each bike, two socks in each pair, two rows in a six-pack of soda, two rows in an egg carton, two eyes on each child. Ask first graders what they would have to do to the calculator if they wanted to skip count by 3's and so forth, and they will know once they see the example with twos.

Skip counting with fives is familiar because of money (counting nickels) and time (counting five-minute intervals). If we look at the multiples of five on a hundreds chart, a pattern quickly emerges. These activities present some ways to develop an appreciation and curiosity in children about the interesting patterns of the multiples and counting numbers. Activities 7.6, 7.7 provide different ways to see number relationships by skip counting.

A further extension of the multiplication table is seen in the "Chinese Multiplication Table," Activity 7.8. Different techniques can be adopted to interpret the structure of this system and to examine the patterns. This activity reinforces culture awareness that multiplication is important to many cultures.

Finger Multiplication Finding multiples of 9 is another strategy that emphasizes number patterns and relationships. Finger multiplication is

Definition

Identity Element

Multiplying any number by 1 results in the same number.

17 basic facts are learned.

+	0	1	2	3	4	5	6	7	8	9
0										
1		1	2	3	4	5	6	7	8	9
2		2								
3		3								
4		4								
5		5								
6		6								
7		7								
8		8								
9		9								

Definition

Multiples of 9

Many interesting patterns and relationships can be used. Finger multiplication.

9 more facts are learned.

+	0	1	2	3	4	5	6	7	8	9
0										
1										9
2										18
3										27
4										36
5										45
6										54
7										63
8										72
9		9	18	27	36	45	54	63	72	81

Zero Property

Multiplying any number by 0 results in 0 for an answer.

19 basic facts are learned.

+	0	1	2	3	4	5	6	7	8	9
0	0	0	0	0	0	0	0	0	0	0
1	0									
2	0									
3	0									
4	0									
5	0									
6	0									
7	0									
8	0									
9	0									

Doubles

The number multiplied by itself—sometimes easier facts to remember.

4 more facts are learned.

+	0	1	2	3	4	5	6	7	8	9
0										
1										
2			4							
3				9						
4					16					
5						25				
6							36			
7								49		
8									64	
9										81

Skip Counting by 2, 5, 3

Relate "twos" to doubles in addition; "Fives" to counting nickels or telling time.

39 additional facts are learned.

+	0	1	2	3	4	5	6	7	8	9
0										
1			2			5				
2		2	4	6	8	10	12	14	16	18
3			6	9	12	15	18	21	24	27
4			8	12		20				
5		5	10	15	20	25	30	35	40	45
6			12	18		30				
7			14	21		35				
8			16	24		40				
9			18	27		45				

Note: The blocks with numbers in the main body of the table denote new facts to be learned. The shaded part denotes facts already learned by a previous strategy. A shaded block with a number included denotes an overlap between a previously learned strategy and a new strategy.

FIGURE 7.36 *Thinking strategies for the basic facts of multiplication.*

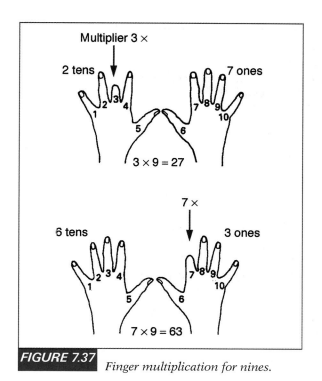

Multiplier 3 ×

2 tens | 7 ones

3 × 9 = 27

7 ×

6 tens | 3 ones

7 × 9 = 63

FIGURE 7.37 *Finger multiplication for nines.*

a fun way to determine facts of 9. Children enjoy the "magic" of this activity as they internalize some number combinations. Use both hands with fingers spread apart. Label the fingers consecutively from 1 to 10, as indicated in Figure 7.37. Bend the "multiplier finger," that is, 4 × 9, bend the fourth finger. To read the product, count the fingers to the left of the bent finger as the tens digit (3) and the fingers to the right of the bent finger as the ones digit (6), again as shown in Figure 7.38.

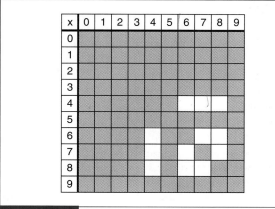

x	0	1	2	3	4	5	6	7	8	9
0										
1										
2										
3										
4										
5										
6										
7										
8										
9										

FIGURE 7.38 *Remaining 12 facts to learn.*

Activity 7.6

CALCULATORS

MULTIPLICATION AS REPEATED ADDITION

The first factor names the number of groups, and the second factor names the size of each group.
Check this on your calculator:

$$48 + 48 + 48 + 48 = ?$$

Now make this into a multiplication equation:

number of groups		size of each group	
4	×	48	= ?

Is the answer the same? Which way requires fewer steps?
Try some others: $5 + 5 + 5 + 5 + 5 = ?$
$$3 \times 9 = ?$$
Write the related multiplication equation and check on your calculator:

1. $3 + 3 + 3 + 3 = ?$
2. $8 + 8 + 8 + 8 + 8 = ?$
3. $1 + 1 + 1 = ?$
4. $7 + 7 + 7 = ?$

Try this on your calculator: $8 + = = =$.
What happens? Why?

Doubles The remaining 12 facts, in Figure 7.38, can be learned by using a variety of strategies. Because doubling is sometimes an easy mental computation task for children, it can be used to double multiples several times. The focus of this strategy is for multiples of 2, 4, 6, and 8 (to find 4 × 8, use 2 × 8 and 2 × 8 or think of doubling 8 twice). Figure 7.39 indicates the facts that can easily be solved by this doubling strategy. Think: I know 3 × 7 = 21; because 3 is half of 6, I need to double the answer. This will give me 6 groups of 7.

Friendly Facts The last three strategies entail using a known fact to derive an unknown fact. This approach asks students to find a friendly fact and mentally compute using addition to help. "Repeated Addition" might be a strategy to use when one factor is less than 5. The child simply changes the multiplication problem to an addition problem and solves 4 × 7 = 7 + 7 + 7 + 7. "Add Another Set" uses the distributive law of multiplication and helps a child use an easier known fact to find the answer to a more difficult fact.

x	0	1	2	3	4	5	6	7	8	9
0										
1										
2										
3					12		18		24	
4				12	16	20	24	28		
5					20				40	
6				18	24			42	48	
7					28		42			
8				24		40	48		64	
9										

FIGURE 7.39   *Facts covered by "doubling" strategy.*

Activity 7.7

PROBLEM SOLVING   ESTIMATION   CULTURAL RELEVANCE

FINDING MULTIPLES

Multiples of 5
MATERIALS
- Hundreds chart, paper

PROCEDURE
1. List the multiples of 5. What digits appear in the ones column? What kind of numbers are the fives facts?

1	2	3	4	5	6	7	8	9	10
11	12	13	14	15	16	17	18	19	20
21	22	23	24	25	26	27	28	29	30
31	32	33	34	35	36	37	38	39	40
41	42	43	44	45	46	47	48	49	50
51	52	53	54	55	56	57	58	59	60
61	62	63	64	65	66	67	68	69	70
71	72	73	74	75	76	77	78	79	80
81	82	83	84	85	86	87	88	89	90
91	92	93	94	95	96	97	98	99	100

Hundreds Chart

2. What pattern is found for the tens digits? Extend the chart and see if this pattern continues.
3. Add the digits together $(25 = 2 + 5 = 7)$, $(35 = 3 + 5 = 8)$, $(45 = 4 + 5 = 9)$, and so on.

Multiples of 9
PROCEDURE
Circle all the multiples of 9 and look for patterns such as

1. The tens digit in the product is 1 less than the number being multiplied by 9.

$$9 \times 4 = 36 \,(3 \text{ is less than } 4).$$

2. The sum of the digits in the products is equal to 9, for example, $3 \times 9 = 27$, $2 + 7 = 9$, and $7 \times 9 = 63$, $6 + 3 = 9$.
3. The digits in the ones column decrease by 1 beginning with 9 and the digits in the tens column increase by 1 beginning with 1.
4. The numbers that are one more and one less than a multiple of consecutive numbers can be added together and form another multiple of 9.

$$...17, 18, 19...$$
$$17 + 19 = 36$$

- Other interesting patterns of 9 are found in the culturally relevant teaching ideas in this chapter.

Multiples of 3
PROCEDURE
1. Circle the multiples of 3. What patterns do you notice?
2. Say the multiples of 3 to 30. How many multiples are in each row (decade) of the chart? List the multiples of 3. Add the digits of the two-digit numbers for each decade. What pattern do you see? ($12 \rightarrow 1 + 2 = 3, 24 \rightarrow 2 + 4 = 6$)
3. Starting with 3, tell whether the number is odd or even. What pattern is there? What other patterns exist?

Activity 7.8

CULTURAL RELEVANCE   MENTAL MATH

CHINESE MULTIPLICATION TABLE

The ancestors of Asians developed a unique "one digit" table from which many patterns can be seen. This makes an intriguing problem-solving puzzle for middle school.

DIRECTIONS
1. Start with a conventional multiplication table:
2. The objective is to have a table with only a one-digit number in each slot. Each digit of a two-digit answer is added. For example: $27 = 2 + 7 = 9$ where 27 was, it is now 9.
3. If adding the two digits gives another two-digit number like $48 = 4 + 8 = 12$, then the 12 is added to give $12 = 1 + 2 = 3$.

×	1	2	3	4	5	6	7	8	9
1	1	2	3	4	5	6	7	8	9
2	2	4	6	8	10	12	14	16	18
3	3	6	9	12	15	18	21	24	27
4	4	8	12	16	20	24	28	32	36
5	5	10	15	20	25	30	35	40	45
6	6	12	18	24	30	36	42	48	54
7	7	14	21	28	35	42	49	56	63
8	8	16	24	32	40	48	56	64	72
9	9	18	27	36	45	54	63	72	81

4. The following table results:

×	1	2	3	4	5	6	7	8	9
1	1	2	3	4	5	6	7	8	9
2	2	4	6	8	1	3	5	7	9
3	3	6	9	3	6	9	3	6	9
4	4	8	3	7	2	6	1	5	9
5	5	1	6	2	7	3	8	4	9
6	6	3	9	6	3	9	6	3	9
7	7	5	3	1	8	6	4	2	9
8	8	7	6	5	4	3	2	1	9
9	9	9	9	9	9	9	9	9	9

5. Many patterns can be seen. See how many you can find.

6. Here are thought clues to start:

Connect all the 8's to see a shape for 8.
Do the same for each number.
Many squares can be connected resulting in "reflecting" numbers, such as

9 3 6 9

3 7 2 6

6 2 7 3

9 6 3 9

For 6 × 8, *think:* I know 5 × 8 = 5 groups of 8
8 + 8 + 8 + 8 + 8 =; 40

So 6 × 8 = 6 groups of 8, so add 8 more to 40 to get 48

Split a Factor This strategy encourages students to split one of the factors into two or three friendly equations of known facts. Arrays and Cuisenaire rods work effectively to visually develop this concept. Cut graph paper into a specific array, apply the distributive law to fold it into two parts, as in Figure 7.40. Students can write the related number equations to be certain to see the total product. Group work promotes good discussions about various ways to split the factors. One student might select the first factor and split it into several parts

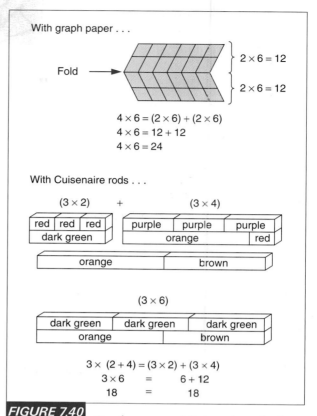

FIGURE 7.40 *Graph paper and Cuisenaire rods show "split a factor apart" strategy.*

(e.g., 7 × 9 = [3 × 9] + [3 × 9] + [1 × 9]), whereas another student may select the second factor and split it apart (e.g., 7 × 9 = [7 × 3] + [7 × 3] + [7 × 3]).

Such experiences build students' confidence that if a fact is not immediately known or remembered, some strategy can be used to find the product. Using a friendly fact, or a fact that is close to the target, unknown fact is an effective way to solve difficult facts. Group work with concrete materials, arrays, and sharing among students helps motivate children to remain on task. Remember there is not a "best" way to solve these facts. Individual students will find their own preferences and should be encouraged to share them with others. Assessment should reflect these preferred strategies so each child can relate to his or her own strengths.

Thinking Strategies for the Basic Facts of Division
The final operation is division and the question is how many basic facts are there for division? Most people answer "one hundred" because that was true for the last three operations, but division has a special property that must be considered. Because division by zero cannot be done or is

undefined, there are 90 basic division facts. Refer to the operation sense part of this chapter, page 166, to refresh your thinking about why division by zero is undefined.

Missing Factor The most useful strategy for learning division facts is to think of the problem as a missing factor and recall a related multiplication fact ($28 \div 4 = ?$; think $? \times 4 = 28$). This makes learning fact families for multiplication and division more important.

Triominoes are an effective device to help children practice fact families. Color coding keeps them in sets that allow for easier management. Facts can be clustered into categories, as described in the multiplication section, according to the strategies involved. When a corner of the card is covered, it means looking for the missing factor. Have children write, or say to a partner, the four related number sentences for a triomino.

$$6 \times 3 = 18$$
$$3 \times 6 = 18$$
$$18/3 = 6$$
$$18/6 = 3$$

The relatedness of the two operations must be emphasized and shown with concrete materials. Model the fact families with sets or arrays to establish the connection of the two operations. Figure 7.41 shows the relationship between the two operations using Cuisenaire rods as the manipulative.

When students learn the factors, there are many rich activities and strategy games that can be played. Factors and multiples of numbers can produce more intricate patterns and relationships

Rods to Manipulate	Words to Say	Symbols
red | red | red / dark green	3 sets of 2 are 6 / 6 is 3 sets of 2	Since $3 \times 2 = \boxed{6}$ / Then $6 = \boxed{3} \times 2$
dark green / red | red | red	6 divided into / 3 sets is 2 in each	And $6 \div 3 = \boxed{2}$

And it follows that . . .

green | green / dark green	2 sets of 3 are 6 / 6 is 2 sets of 3	Since $2 \times 3 = \boxed{6}$ / Then $6 = \boxed{2} \times 3$
dark green / green | green	6 divided into / 2 sets is 3 in each	And $6 \div 2 = \boxed{3}$

FIGURE 7.41 *Relatedness of multiplication and division.*

6	15
10	12

FIGURE 7.42 *Multiple answers depending on the factors chosen.*

than the basic facts of addition and subtraction. Buschman (2003) reports on such an exercise (Figure 7.42) that brought many answers. The task asked students, "Which one of the four numbers does not fit?" A series of student answers appears in the Buschman article. By reading the student explanations, you will be able to see the students who have a deep understanding of number operations and those who do not. Such activities can heighten your ability to assess student learning.

MASTERING THE FACTS TO BUILD STRATEGIC COMPETENCE

Mastering the basic facts means more than a student's ability to give the correct answer to all 390 facts. Mastery means that students show evidence of strategic competence (can use basic fact concepts and procedures appropriately) to arrive at accurate answers. If children are to be successful in mastering the basic facts, the operations must be developed through multiple embodiments. Children should have opportunities for informal activities with materials to model situations involving the different operations. When drill and practice are introduced, short, frequent sessions are recommended.

Basic Facts—Pros and Cons
Many teachers, administrators, parents, and the general public believe that learning basic facts should constitute a large part of the early grades mathematics instruction. Many of these people want today's children to learn mathematics in the same manners they learned mathematics. Children do need to be proficient in basic facts to solve problems and arrive at accurate calculations. However, arithmetic computation is only one part of mathematics, and attention given to basic facts can still be directed toward thinking, reasoning, and number relationships. As children work with problem-solving situations, they will find ways to solve a wide variety of problems and will build confidence in their own abilities to understanding the operations.

The NAEP results (NAEP, 2000) show that fourth and eighth graders can perform basic whole

number operations but only 37 percent of the fourth graders and 76 percent of the eighth graders can use them to solve multistep word problems that require reasoning and strategic planning. Activities like those listed in the technology section at the end of the chapter can reinforce basic skills while teaching multistep strategies. Students must have exposure to basic facts in a reasoning context if they are to be mathematically proficient in the upper grades and in the workforce.

The NCTM *Principles and Standards* (2000) acknowledge that a certain amount of practice is necessary to develop fluency with recalling basic facts. By fifth grade, students should have developed a number of thinking strategies to help them acquire fluency in computation. However, Burns (1996) warns against timed tests, worksheet drill, and flash cards. She contends these practices treat mathematics as isolated bits of information to memorize, do not support children's problem-solving abilities, and convey a message that rote memorization is more important than reasoning. There is evidence from research that facts and methods are connected when they are learned with understanding. If students know strategies that enable them to derive facts, it provides a critical and confidence-building fallback when memory fails them. "Learning with understanding is more powerful than simply memorizing because the act of organizing improves retention, promotes fluency, and facilitates learning related material" (Sutton and Krueger, 2002). The acquisition of single-digit basic facts is a recognized goal of the mathematics community so students in middle grades can approach mathematics full of competence and confidence.

Practice Devices   Remember that drill activities should be varied and interesting. Many simple, inexpensive devices can be made to practice the facts. Another effective way to provide drill is with teacher-made (or commercial) games such as board games, dice games, and card games. A number of teacher-controlled microcomputer software programs that provide instant reinforcement in a timed setting are available. Some of these are in the format of game challenges.

Audiocassette tapes with catchy songs about the facts serve as another way to help children recall the facts. Popular ones available are *I Can't Wait to Get to Math Class*, *Multiplication Motivation*, and *Mondo Math*. There are many activities from which a teacher may choose to help students learn the basic facts. The teacher who uses many forms of drill—calculators, games, computers, videotapes, and audiotapes—will find better atti-

tudes and performance by students. It is the teacher who must determine which activities and strategies are suited to the needs and interests of the students. Willis and Johnson (2001) describe a variety of activities using Gardner's theory of multiple intelligences to help students master basic multiplication facts.

Another procedure, which takes more time but seems to have more validity, is to show flash cards of facts to an individual child. In a timed sequence of no more than three seconds, show each fact to the child. The student must answer as quickly as possible. Correct cards are put in one pile and missed cards are put in another pile. This procedure can be repeated until you feel more assured that all the facts in the "correct pile" are known at an automatic level. Now drill and practice can begin on groups using strategies for these unknown facts as described earlier.

Calculators and computers serve as devices for learning too. Children should have many experiences with objects, calculators, computers, or arrays to help develop the concepts for multiplication and division and their related strategies. There are several simple computer programs that show the effect of multiplying by 1 (identity element) and multiplying by 0 (zero property). Some children like to run these programs to prove that any number when multiplied by 1 remains unchanged or when multiplied by 0 results in 0 for an answer. Multiplying by 0 confuses some children. They think that if you start with "something" and you multiply it by zero, you still have the "something" with which you began. In addition to serving as a way to practice, patterns and relationships of operations can be investigated.

Calculator activities using the constant function provide excellent experiences to help reinforce some of the strategies and relationships between the operations. One such calculator activity is described in "Using the Calculator with Basic Facts," Activity 7.9. Tests for commutativity, associativity, identity property, repeated addition, and repeated subtraction are only a few of the many relationships to be examined. A number of other calculator activities for learning basic facts are on the Web site, Chapter 7, Extended Activities, and others are listed by name from the NCTM Web site at the end of this chapter.

Build Confidence

Teachers should make a "big deal" out of passing each test and keep individual charts. These help students monitor their own progress and motivate children to continue mastering more facts. A student's progress should be measured by the

individual's progress in mastery—not by comparison to the rest of the class. Encourage parents to reinforce drill at home by keeping them informed of the facts on which their child is currently working. To tell parents to "work with your child on basic facts" is almost hopeless in terms of definite results. Typically, the parents will purchase a set of flash cards and drill will be intense for only a few weeks. This approach is inappropriate because the parents are trying to practice all the facts rather than taking them in small groups that relate to thinking strategies. Both parties (parent and child) become frustrated, and soon the practice ends. Praise and positive reinforcement should be given for learning each new group of facts rather than waiting until the entire set of facts has been mastered.

Activity 7.9

CALCULATORS

MENTAL MATH

USING THE CALCULATOR WITH BASIC FACTS

MATERIALS
- Calculator with a constant function

DIRECTIONS

1. To practice counting on 3: push 4, push + key, push 3, push = key, new number, push = key, new number, push = key, and so on.

2. Do you see how it is storing the number each time? Try it with other numbers. (If this activity does not work on your calculator, experiment with your calculator to determine how it handles the constant function.)

3. Mentally think of what the next answer will be *before* you press the = sign. See if you were correct each time.

4. This can be called mental skip counting!

Assess Mastery An often repeated phrase by teachers is, "Johnny doesn't know his basic facts." Presented in this negative fashion, the judgment sounds grim, but which facts and how many facts are not mastered remains unclear. It may become necessary to assess which facts are not mastered and then develop strategies to learn those facts. A procedure is suggested: Give a timed fact test for each operation with time guidelines of 3 seconds per problem (5 minutes for 100 facts and 4 1/2 minutes for 90 facts). Ask students to work the problems row by row, answering only those facts

EXTENDED ACTIVITIES

COMPUTERS   ESTIMATION   MANIPULATIVES   PROBLEM SOLVING

MATHEMATICAL CONNECTIONS   MENTAL MATH   CULTURAL RELEVANCE   PORTFOLIO

CHILDREN'S LITERATURE   WEBQUESTS

On the Web site (Chapter 7, Extended Activities), read/do the following:

- Calculator Capers
- Family Math Packets (with Children's Literature)
- Performance Assessment—Aunt Bee's Bakery

that they know automatically without any extra thought or counting. This test should be repeated on several occasions to ensure a higher validity. Isolate the "problem facts" into clusters and work on these with many different manipulatives and strategies.

Assess Strategy Preferences Children should be encouraged to develop other thinking strategies or associations that may hold particular meaning for them. The fact combinations suggested in this section do not mean that each basic fact has one and only one category into which it is placed and by which it should be learned. Children have preferred strategies based on their individual strengths that should be identified and encouraged. Strategies should be used to foster and promote analytic thinking as well as to form clusters of facts that reduce the number of isolated facts to learn. In this way, thinking strategies are useful for

students, especially students with special needs as it helps recall. When children resort to using their fingers to get answers, it simply tells us that they are not ready for the symbolic mode. More time should be spent at the concrete and connecting modes discussed in Chapter 6.

The standards (NCTM, 2000) state that encouraging children to develop their own strategies enables them to understand mathematical relationships and reasons. Teachers must help children build understanding by getting them to organize what they know and to disregard inefficient strategies.

ASSESSMENT TO HELP STUDENTS WITH SPECIAL NEEDS

Recent research now shows that students with special needs have the same type of problems learning whole number operations, properties, and basic facts as do other children (Fuson, 2003). Although they may learn at a different rate, the assessment techniques listed in this session apply to all learners.

Field-Dependent and Field-Independent Learners

Students preferring to use field-independent processing (the parts-to-whole strategy) may understand addition and multiplication (combining parts to make the whole) better than they understand subtraction and division (moving from the whole to the detailed parts). It is just the opposite for students preferring field-dependent processing. More research is needed before definitive statements can be made. However, teachers report definite preferences with some of their students. These observations suggest that some children adopt one processing style from which they find it difficult to decenter. Both groups can learn the basic facts more efficiently and more thoroughly by applying the following teaching techniques:

- *Subtraction and Division Basic Facts: Help for the Field-Independent Learner.* When a field-independent learner is faced with subtraction and division basic facts, it may be best to look on the combinations as "missing addends" for addition and "missing factors" for multiplication. The teacher should encourage the children to ask questions like those in Figure 7.43.

- *Addition and Multiplication Basic Facts: Help for the Field-Dependent Learner.* Field-dependent learners may be helped by using the idea of "subtracting as much as they can and adding

FIGURE 7.43 *Missing addends or missing factors help determine facts.*

as little as they can" when working with addition and multiplication. Subtracting from 10 or multiples of 10 will eliminate the largest amounts and students are left with as little as possible to add or multiply. Study the examples in Figure 7.44.

Both Learners Working Together with Basic Fact Tables Basic fact tables for each operation were illustrated in this chapter. Most elementary textbooks present the table in its incomplete form and ask the children to fill it in, a task that requires successive processing, which is used by field-independent learners. The table is completed square by square in a systematic way, so number relationships develop as each number combination is answered. The activity in the textbook may need

FIGURE 7.44 *Multiples of 10 to determine facts.*

to be modified for students preferring field-dependent approaches. They need to view the completed table before relationship patterns can be seen clearly. They become more confused by moving from row to row and column to column filling in blank squares.

It is effective to pair both learners together, allowing the field-independent learner to complete the table while the field-dependent learner watches for the overall patterns. Both learners can share what they discovered about the tables when the exercise is completed. Another cooperative learning venture is illustrated in Figure 7.45.

Correcting Common Misconceptions

Many misconceptions have been noticed through the years of working with children. Only the most common ones are noted here.

Failure to Perform the Operation A common error is to show sets for each number but fail to perform the operation. An excellent way to check understanding of the operations is to give a child physical objects and ask the child to model a number sentence, For example:

Teacher: Displays the equation 3 + 4 = 7. "Show me what this number sentence means using these counters."

Child: The child models a set of 3 counters under the numeral "3," a set of 4 counters under the numeral "4," and a set of 7 counters under the numeral "7."

Problem: The child is merely modeling sets for the numbers rather than showing addition as the union of two discrete sets.

FIGURE 7.45 *Paired learning to see patterns.*

Remediation: Give the child as many opportunities to represent the addition process in a problem-solving situation where the action of the operation is demonstrated.

Confusion with Multidigit Algorithms Children may experience difficulties with subtraction facts over ten once the regrouping algorithm for subtraction has been learned. They apply that procedure for the two-digit numbers of the subtraction facts. When children have this problem, the teacher must show them that the regrouping yields the same number as the original number (e.g., 13). Generally, this error will diminish with more time given to the subtraction algorithm:

$$\begin{array}{r} \overset{13}{\cancel{13}} \\ -\ 8 \\ \hline -\ 5 \end{array}$$

Anxiety Over Speed Testing Children with special needs should be given facts in small chunks and speed tests in a similar fashion. Too many facts are disturbing and overwhelming to the children who feel pressure when speed is an issue. One-minute quizzes over leveled facts work much better for children with special needs. It is suggested by Thornton and associates (1983) that a child who can write fifty digits per minute should be able to correctly write answers to thirty basic facts per minute. This five-to-three ratio may prove a useful guide in designing speed tests.

Failure to Handle Symbolic Notation

If students are having trouble going from the concrete mode to the symbolic mode, they may profit from the use of an individual number line placed at the top of their desks. Students can make their own from a sample. When such number lines are laminated, they have been known to last a whole school year under rugged use. If a student is growing overdependent on the number line as a crutch, it can be covered with a book and used only at the end of a session as a check. This makes an excellent connecting model to transition from concrete materials to the symbolic. Research (Damarin, 2000) reports that girls, even when they do abstract work well, still prefer to start problems using manipulatives and may need to use them longer than their male counterparts. In other studies, 75 percent of Latino students of both genders preferred to work with manipulatives longer than other groups (Garrison, 1999).

Failure to Understand Commutativity Failure to understand and apply the commutative law is another area of difficulty. Here the child can work $9 + 2$ by counting on, but does not readily change the order of the addends to help obtain the answer to $2 + 9$. The triominoes and fact families are techniques to emphasize this concept.

Children often use faulty reasoning when working with the basic facts. Some of the more common problems are described in the following paragraphs.

Faulty Reasoning 1: Position Counting

Can answer correctly   *Cannot answer correctly*
          or   or

$$
\begin{array}{cc}
9 & 7 \\
+3 & \times 4 \\
\hline
\end{array}
\qquad
\begin{array}{cc}
3 & 4 \\
+9 & \times 7 \\
\hline
\end{array}
$$

$$9 + 3 = \qquad 3 + 9 =$$
$$7 \times 4 = \qquad 4 \times 7 =$$

If this pattern is seen in a variety of basic facts, the children are likely to be "position counters"—they take whatever numeral appears in the top position or in the left position and add the numeral in the position next to it. Their count becomes confused when the larger numeral follows in the second position because there are more chances for mistakes in counting.

A teaching strategy to help remediate this problem is to develop a better understanding of the commutative property. Even if commutativity is too difficult for early primary children to understand, they can be taught the counting-on strategy as outlined earlier in this chapter. A modified approach can be seen with multiplication. The child sees 4×7 as 7 taken 4 times (or 4 groups of 7) and calculates the basic fact something like this:

$$
\begin{array}{l}
7 \\
+\,7 \\
\hline
14
\end{array}
\quad \text{and again} \quad
\begin{array}{l}
7 \\
+7 \\
\hline
14
\end{array}
\quad \text{and} \quad
\begin{array}{l}
14 \\
+14 \\
\hline
28
\end{array}
$$

Faulty Reasoning 2: Subtrahend/Divisor Substitution

Children answer problems in the following way:

In Subtraction   *In division*

$$
\begin{array}{cc}
4 & 9 \\
-1 & -4 \\
\hline
1 & 4
\end{array}
\qquad
\begin{array}{cc}
3 & 6 \\
3\overline{)} & 6\overline{)24}
\end{array}
$$

Children who answer basic facts in this manner often do not know the basic fact in question. To obtain a simple solution, they reason, "Sometimes the answer is the same number that is taken away [the subtrahend]. Since I cannot think of an answer, I'll use the one that is already there [in the subtrahend]."

A teaching strategy is to review the fact strategy for doubles in addition. They can learn to reason that if $1 + 1 = 2$ and $2 - 1 = 1$, then $1 + 1$ cannot equal 4 and $4 - 1$ cannot equal 1. The subtrahend and the difference can only be alike in doubles. What is commonly seen in subtraction and division can also happen with addition and multiplication, but it is usually less common. Examples would be:

$$
\begin{array}{cc}
2 & 7 \\
+8 & \times 5 \\
\hline
8 & 5
\end{array}
$$

When taught that the order of the numbers can be changed and the product is not affected, children can do the multiplication more quickly.

Faulty Reasoning 3: Missing the Answer by One

Children answer problems in the following way:

$$
\begin{array}{cc}
9 & 10 \\
-1 & -8 \\
\hline
7 & 1
\end{array}
$$

Children may miss the correct answer by one number. As stated in the teaching strategies section of this chapter, counting-back strategies are often found to be helpful in such a situation. Sometimes mistakes like these occur because some children count rapidly and lose track of the number being removed. Sometimes children have been taught the counting-back strategy, but when they try to apply it mentally, they reason that $9 - 1 = 7$ by saying, "When I count back it is 9, 8, 7. If I take one away it will look like this:

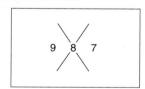

Since I have 9, the one to be taken away is the 8 and that means 7 is the next number that is left."

Another reasoning pattern is to think that $10 - 8 = 1$ by saying, "I'm at 10 and I need to know how many 8 is away from 10. It is 10, 9, 8. There is one number in the middle so 8 is one away from 10."

If students are struggling with keeping track of the counting when using some fact strategies, a number line can help only if the teacher emphasizes that the spaces between numerals are

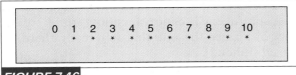

FIGURE 7.46 *Commercially prepared number line.*

important in the counting. Many commercially prepared number lines appear like the one shown in Figure 7.46. Without augmentation, many children will use this aid incorrectly, following the misguided reasoning outlined previously.

Figure 7.47 shows the same number line with the curved segment between numerals to emphasize the spaces in counting. Some elementary teachers refer to the spaces as "hops" up or down the number line. A teacher may say that $10 - 1 = 9$ because a person starts at the numeral 10 and hops back one space and lands on 9.

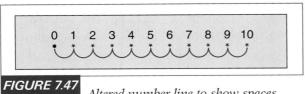

FIGURE 7.47 *Altered number line to show spaces in counting.*

Some students are just poor counters. Therefore, using any counting strategy for remediation will be unsuccessful. Such children should be encouraged to use derived fact strategies, known as DFS. The DFS have been explained earlier in this chapter. Research shows that the following ones are helpful to children needing help (Steinberg, 1985).

1. Doubles
2. Doubles $+ 1$ and $- 1$
3. Doubles $+ 2$ and $- 2$
4. Bridging to 10, such as

$6 + 8$ is $6 + 4 = 10$ with 4 more left to add to 10 so $10 + 4 = 14$

or

$12 - 7$ is $10 - 7$ which is 3 with 2 left so $3 + 2 = 5$.

Faulty Reasoning 4: Trying to Do Work without Manipulatives This faulty reasoning pattern belongs to the teacher rather than the children. Some teachers believe that students must move quickly from the use of concrete manipulatives

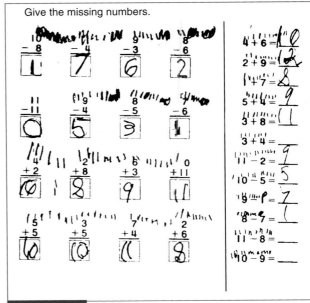

FIGURE 7.48 *Basic facts worksheet of primary child.*

to the symbolic stage where the children do worksheet after worksheet without the use of manipulatives or pictures. Children frequently give such teachers clues to their learning difficulties by their responses to basic fact problems on textbook pages or on worksheets. Figure 7.48 shows an actual worksheet of a primary child.

The child makes very few mistakes, but it is evident that the child needs some form of concrete or semiconcrete aid to arrive at the answers. The tally marks are needed in almost every problem. The child seems to understand the property of zero in addition with assurance; no tally marks are needed to check out the answers.

What should be done about this situation? More work with fact strategies and concrete materials is necessary. To demand that a child not use the tally marks would only force the child to use eye blinks, count fingers out of the teacher's view, or just guess the answer. Tally marks can help bridge the gap between concrete materials and symbolic numerals. This child needs to be encouraged to place the tally marks on a separate page where the marks can be separated for each problem and prevent the mislearning that occurs when the child thinks the answer counted was correct.

Some children will become overdependent on the tally marks. They will need to be "weaned" from them gradually, starting with the basic facts involving adding one or taking one away. These facts can be reasoned more easily. The next step is to adopt a systematized way to introduce the teaching strategies discussed earlier in the chapter.

Teacher Assessment of Student Work: Steps in Analytic Thinking

Some people might profit from writing down their thought processes in mathematics. It can bring clarity to processes that would otherwise be easily confused. An example of such a thought process is presented here as it relates to the assessment of a child's problems in learning basic addition and subtraction facts. Excellent teaching involves the analysis of what a child understands or does not understand and what misconceptions must be remediated.

A model outlining steps in analytic thinking is presented here so the teacher can see a way to approach the task of diagnosing a child's learning difficulties from answers a child has given to a textbook assignment. Exercises at the end of the chapter will ask the teacher to analyze the work of two other students. The analytic process applied here will be of help at the end of the chapter as well. Figure 7.49 shows the work of a first grade student who has several misconceptions about the basic facts of subtraction.

Steps in Analytic Thinking

1. Find the basic facts answered incorrectly.
2. Determine whether the same basic facts as those missed appear more than once on the

worksheet. If so, see if the student missed the problem or answered the problem in the same way as those marked incorrect.

   a. If the same mistake is made consistently, look for patterns like those mentioned in the learning styles section of the chapter and in the assessment section.
   b. If the student sometimes answers correctly, make a chart such as the one on page 188 to analyze the answers.

   Note: This student is correct more often than not. Now a teacher must decide whether the incorrect answers were the result of sloppy work habits or a real misconception.
   c. If sloppiness is the cause, answers tend to deteriorate the further down the worksheet the student goes. Is this the case here? No.
   d. If a real misconception is the cause, further scrutiny is needed. Often, all that the best teachers can do is to make an intelligent guess based on the pattern of answers. It appears that the student is doing each problem separately without seeing its connection with the other problems on the page. Hence, the student answers correctly sometimes but not other times.

3. Look for the pattern of reasoning used by the child. The most frequent pattern seen is faulty reasoning 2. The next most frequent pattern is faulty reasoning 3.
4. Refer back to the teaching strategies that help the child who makes the mistakes in faulty reasoning as listed in this section.

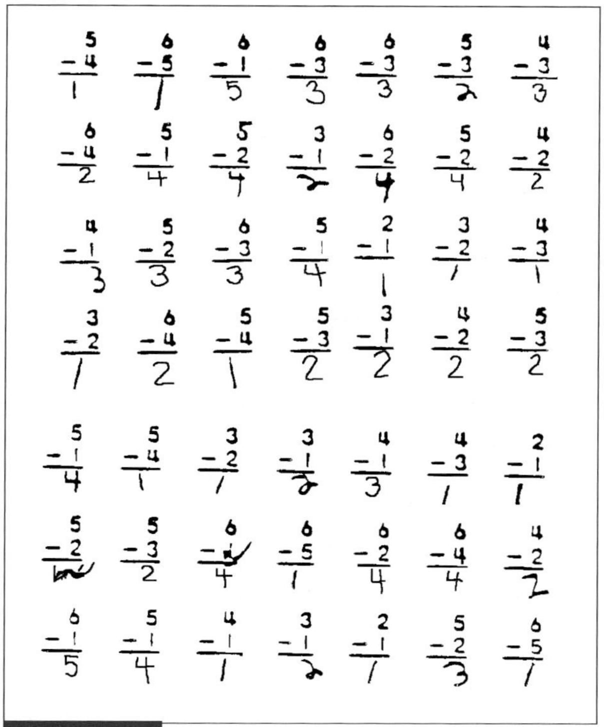

Teachers can make a table like the one in Figure 7.50 to keep record of their observations of the student's work.

When teachers have used this analysis process over time, their own mathematical proficiency improved with correlations to higher scores of national licensure tests as explained in Chapter 3.

FIGURE 7.49 *A first grader's misconceptions about subtraction.*

SUMMARY

- Three prerequisites for children to learn the basic facts are their ability to understand and perform tasks with (1) number conservation, (2) class inclusion and reversibility, and (3) number meaning for the operation symbols.
- Prerequisites for teaching operations and number sense include a teacher's conceptual understanding of the kinds of addition, subtraction,

BASIC FACT	ANSWERED	ANALYSIS
5 −2	5 −2 4	2 correct 2 incorrect — missed by one same answer
6 −1	6 −1 4	2 correct 1 incorrect — missed by one
6 −4	6 −4 4	2 correct 1 incorrect — missed by two
4 −1	4 −1 1	2 correct 1 incorrect — missed by two
4 −3	4 −3 3	2 correct 1 incorrect — missed by two

FIGURE 7.50

multiplication, and division, and the properties associated with the respective operations.

- Learning the thinking strategies for each operation builds students' procedural fluency and flexibility with the 390 basic facts.

- Ideas for teaching fourteen of the most frequently used thinking strategies were presented.

- Children worldwide follow much the same progression of development in working with single-digit addition and subtraction.

- Manipulatives are the important beginning key, followed by the connecting, transitional activities, and ending with the abstract, symbolic notation.

- Recent research indicates that children with special needs have the same common misconceptions and learning style challenges as do the typical students in the average classroom.

- Nine of the most common misconceptions were presented along with suggestions for remediation that have proven successful for teachers in current classrooms.

- The steps in analytic thinking required of teachers as they assess student work were demonstrated using actual student work as the example.

PRAXIS II™-STYLE QUESTIONS

Answers to this chapter's Praxis II™-style questions are in the instructor's manual.

Multiple Choice Format

1. The child who answers

   4
+9
15

   should be encouraged to use which of the following strategies to help remediate the problem
   a. bridging to ten
   b. counting on
   c. doubles
   d. None of the above

2. Analyze the movement of the Cuisenaire rods in the picture (Figure 7.51)

This is an example of
   a. the distributive property
   b. the commutativity property
   c. the associative property
   d. None of the above

3. A student comes to your class excited to show you the new way he has to remember answers

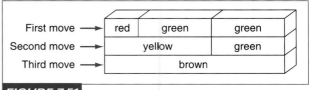

FIGURE 7.51

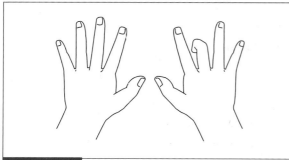

FIGURE 7.52

X	0	1	2	3	4	5	6	7	8	9
0	0	0	0	0	0	0	0	0	0	0
1	1	1	2	3	4	5	6	7	1	9
2	2	2	4	6	8	10	12	14	1	18
3	3	3	6	9	12	15	18	21	24	27
4	4	4	8	12	15	18	21	24	27	30
5	5	5	10	15	20	25	30	35	40	45
6	6	6	12	18	21	24	27	30	33	36
7	7	7	14	21	24	27	30	33	36	39
8	8	8	16	24	27	30	33	36	39	41
9	9	9	18	26	29	31	34	37	41	43

FIGURE 7.54 *Student's multiplication tables.*

to basic fact combinations. He shows you the hand math in Figure 7.52.
The student is modeling
a. 7 × 9
b. 8 × 9
c. 9 × 6
d. Not enough information to tell what the child is doing

4. Student A and Student B are using Cuisenaire rods to explore numbers. The teacher's only direction was to start their exploration with the orange and red rod in a train together. Each built the trains going down the page (Figure 7.53). Student A shows an early sense of_____ while Student B shows an early sense of_____.
a. class inclusion; seriation
b. commutativity; associativity
c. commutativity; seriation
d. one-to-one correspondence; commutativity

Constructed Response Format

5. The student's work (Figure 7.54) as a guide to help the teacher develop analytic thinking skills when doing assessment of student work. Score the student on the 4 + scale originally presented in Chapter 3. What should be the next teaching step in this student's development of multiplication understanding, keeping in mind all the material studied in Chapter 7?

This student has earned a score of_____

Which instructional approach is the **BEST** approach as **the immediate next step** for this child?
a. This child needs manipulatives for all the basic multiplication facts because .
b. This child needs to memorize the basic facts of 3 to 9 because .

Student A   Student B

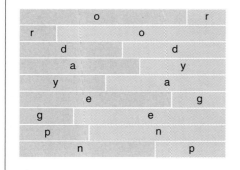
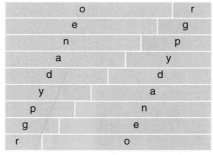

FIGURE 7.53

c. This child needs to do individual multiplication problems rather than filling in a chart because .

d. This child needs to practice $1 \times 0, 2 \times 0$, but not $0 \times 1, 0 \times 2$, and so on because .

6. A student in your class brings a bag of 36 butterscotch candies to class and asks if she can use them to help her do her work with multiplication and division concepts. Write a problem for each of the following ways to view multiplication and its inverse, division, using the butterscotch candies with each concept:

   a. as a combination or Cartesian product
   b. as repeated addition
   c. as partitive division
   d. as measurement division

7. Using the knowledge package of subtraction created by Liping Ma (1999) as an example, construct a knowledge package for addition, multiplication, and division. You may want to do this as a class project in small groups, with each group working on a different package. Cover up the title to your graphic organizer and give it to another group. See if they can identify which knowledge package you created. Talk as a class about what is similar and what is different from one group's work to another. In a test situation, you may be given one set and asked to describe which mathematics concept is being used. So this class activity is very much in line with national test examples.

Integrating Technology

Internet Activities

Web sites

Go to the NCTM website (**http://illuminations.nctm.org/ActivitySearch .aspx**) and do the interactive "Illuminations" activities. Try one from each of the grade levels: prek-2 3–5 6–8

Name of Programs

- National Library of Virtual Manipulatives
- **http://nlvm.usu.edu/en/nav/vlibrary.html**
- (also in Spanish)
- Virtual manipulatives, with suggestions for teachers and parents, useful for teaching the content standards in NCTM's Principles and Standards.

CHILDREN'S LITERATURE

Literature provides a wealth of creative activities to incorporate number operations in meaningful settings. No list of books for teaching whole number operations could ever be complete. A more extensive list with annotations, and ratings appears in *The Wonderful World of Mathematics* (Thiessen, Matthias, and Smith, 1998). Only children's books recommended by particular multicultural groups, classroom teacher workshop groups, or book reviews published after the 1998 Thiessen et al. book are printed here.

Video Vignette, "Dinosaur Legs," in this chapter showed a first grade teacher using a storybook to pose a problem situation. Other examples of the use of children's literature to teach mathematical concepts are found on the Web site and on the Web site, Chapter 7, Extended Activities, "Family Math Packets."

RECOMMENDED BOOKS

- Books promoting mathematical discourse with number sense (McDuffie and Young, 2003):

Coats, Lucy. *Neil's Numberless World.* Illus. by Neal Layton. New York: Dorling Kindersley Publishing, 2000.

Florian, Douglas. *A Pig Is Big.* New York: Harper Collins, 2000.

Thompson, Lauren. *One Riddle, One Answer.* Illus. by Linda Wingerter. New York: Scholastic Press, 2001. (Recommended for middle grades 5–8)

- Books supporting Native American cultural awareness; recommended by teachers (Secada, Hankes, and Fast [Eds.], 2002):

Blood, Charles L., and Martin Link. *The Goat in the Rug.* New York: Macmillan, 1990.

Caduto, Michael, and Joseph Bruhac. *Keepers of the Earth.* Golden, CO: Fulcrum, 1988.

Culin, Stewart. *Games of the North American Indians.* 1907. Reprint, New York: Dover Publications, 1975; reprint, with an introduction to the Bison book edition by Dennis Tedlock, Lincoln, NE: University of Nebraska Press, 1992. (After reading about the games, students play "Dish," a game that keeps score with number chart patterns like those developed in this chapter.)

Driving Hawk Sneve, Virginia. *The Navajos: A First Americans Book.* New York: Holiday House, 1993.
Duncan, Lois. *The Magic of Spider Woman.* New York: Scholastic, 1996.

Osofsky, Audrey. *Dreamcatcher.* New York: Orchard Books, 1992.

Roessel, Monty. *Songs from the Loom: A Navajo Girl Learns to Weave.* Minneapolis: Lerner Publications Co., 1995.

- Books supporting Asian cultural awareness; recommended by teachers (Whitman, 1999):

Au, Joy S. Illustrated by Jill Chen Loui. *Going to the Tide Pools in Hawaii Nei.* Honolulu: MnM Books, 1995.

Demi. *The Empty Pot.* New York: Henry Holt, 1990.

Flack, Majorie, and Kurt Wiese. *The Story about Ping.* New York: Penguin Group, 1966. (One-digit and two-digit addition and sequencing. Presented here for one-digit counting reinforcement.)

Friedman, Ina R. Illustrated by Allen Say. *Chopsticks in America.* New York: Houghton, Mifflin, 1984.

Ho, Minfong, and Saphan Ros. Illustrated by Jean and Mou-Sien Tseng. *The Two Brothers.* New York: Lothrop, Lee, & Shepard Books, 1995.

Louie, Ai-Ling. Illustrated by Ed Young. *Yeh Sheng: A Cinderella Story from China.* New York: Philomel Books, 1982.

Nunes, Susan. Illustrated by Cissy Gray. *To Find the Way.* Honolulu: University of Hawaii Press, 1992.

- Books supporting African cultural awareness; recommended by teachers (Chappell and Thompson, 2000):

The Story of Negro League Baseball
How Many Stars in the Sky?
Roots
Cookies
Roots: The Next Generation
Picking Peas for a Penny
The Boy and the Ghost
Zomani Goes to Market
The Chalk Doll
The Black Snowman
Wagon Train
Senefer
Shako: King of the Zulus

If You Traveled on the Underground Railroad

- Books recommended by classroom teacher workshop groups (Edwards and Morrow, 2003):

Anno, Masaichiro, and Mitsumasa Anno. *Anno's Mysterious Multiplying Jar.* New York: Philomel Books, 1983.

Birch, David. *The King's Chessboard.* New York: Dial Books for Young Readers, 1988.

Dee, Ruby. *Ten Ways to Count to Ten.* New York: Henry Holt, 1988.

De Regniers, Beatrice Schenk. *So Many Cats.* New York: Clarion Books, 1985.

Dunbar, Joyce. *Ten Little Mice.* New York: Harcourt Brace Jovanovich, 1990.

Hamm, Diane Johnston. *How Many Feet in the Bed?* New York: Simon & Schuster Books for Young Readers, 1994.

Hutchins, Pat. *The Doorbell Rang.* New York: Greenwillow Books, 1986.

Kellogg, Steven. *Much Bigger Than Martin.* New York: Dial, 1976.

Jackson, Ellen B. *Cinder Edna.* New York: Lothrop, Lee & Shepard, 1994.

Matthews, Louise. *The Great Take-Away.* New York: Dodd, Mead, 1980.

Mori, Tuyosi. *Socrates and the Three Little Pigs.* New York: Philornel Books, 1986.

Owen, Annie. *Annie's One to Ten.* New York: Alfred A. Knopf, 1988.

Pinczes, Elinor J. *A Remainder of One.* New York: Houghton Mifflin, 1995.

Stevens, Janet. *Tops and Bottoms.* New York: Harcourt Brace, 1995.

Walsh, Ellen Stoll. *Mouse Count.* San Diego, CA: Harcourt Brace, 1991.

Numeration and Number Sense

Chapter 8

At the Start ~~~~ Know What Children Will Be Doing . . .

NCTM Curriculum Focal Points—   See . . .

Grade 1 ~~ Developing understandings of whole number relationships, including grouping in tens and ones	Figure 8.9
Grade 2 ~~ Developing an understanding of the base-ten numeration system and place-value concepts	Activity 8.8 / Activity 8.9
Grade 4 ~~ Developing an understandings of decimals	Activity 8.15; 8.16
Grade 7 ~~ Developing an understanding of operations on all rational numbers, including positive and negative integers	Postman Stories

A partial listing as it pertains to Number and Operations and Algebra from NCTM *Curriculum Focal Points* (2006, pages 13–14; 16; 19).

In this chapter we prove that humans really ARE the most intelligent life form on the planet, and mathematics is the way to prove it! We see that mathematics is the intergalactic language by which intelligent "life forms" communicate with others from one galaxy to another by using the ideas of numeration and number sense. That communication has already begun with the space probe, Voyager, traveling into outer space. No student should leave middle school without a chance to appreciate mathematics as the universal language. The popularity of Star Trek, Star Wars, and other extraterrestrial venues over the years shows the interest level is ripe for the middle schooler to see how numeration and number sense fits in the universal setting. One of the most fascinating facts of civilization is that all highly developed cultures created some kind of numeration system at times when many cultures did not even know of each other's existence. This verifies the humans' innate intelligence for number sense. Whether using concrete objects or tally marks (strokes) to represent objects, the cultures came to the realization that an efficient way of counting beyond one-to-one correspondence was needed. The answer was to regroup, to arrange a certain set of symbols (digits) in varying positions or patterns to denote larger and larger numbers-a definition of a numeration system.

EARLY UNDERSTANDINGS OF NUMERATION

In a numeration system, the varying positions or places represent different values; so the same symbol has a different value depending on where it is placed (e.g., the digit 3 in 13, 37, 17389). This is

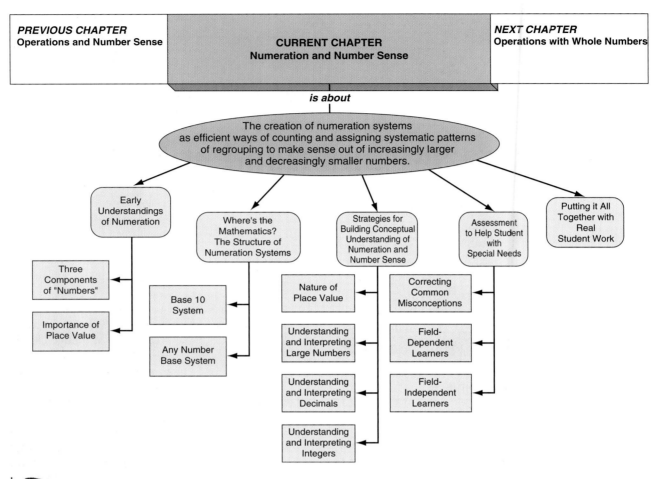

PREVIOUS CHAPTER
Operations and Number Sense

CURRENT CHAPTER
Numeration and Number Sense

NEXT CHAPTER
Operations with Whole Numbers

is about

The creation of numeration systems as efficient ways of counting and assigning systematic patterns of regrouping to make sense out of increasingly larger and decreasingly smaller numbers.

Early Understandings of Numeration
- Three Components of "Numbers"
- Importance of Place Value

Where's the Mathematics? The Structure of Numeration Systems
- Base 10 System
- Any Number Base System

Strategies for Building Conceptual Understanding of Numeration and Number Sense
- Nature of Place Value
- Understanding and Interpreting Large Numbers
- Understanding and Interpreting Decimals
- Understanding and Interpreting Integers

Assessment to Help Student with Special Needs
- Correcting Common Misconceptions
- Field-Dependent Learners
- Field-Independent Learners

Putting it All Together with Real Student Work

SELF-HELP QUESTIONS

1. In what ways do students learn how number names, symbolic numerals, and conceptual models with real-world situations?

2. How can I help students see the systematic organized patterning of our number system in such a way that they remember how to apply it when working with large and small numbers?

3. What can I do as a teacher to help students with special needs succeed in mathematics when working with the numeration system?

4. Which strategies are the most helpful to build conceptual understanding of number systems for young children and middle schoolers?

called the concept of place value. People can write and name any number to infinity without the need for too many digits. In our system, we have ten digits—0, 1, 2, 3, 4, 5, 6, 7, 8, and 9. So we must regroup to the next place value after 9. Ten (10) is our first regrouped numeral, so it is said that we have a base 10 system. Some cultures regrouped at different intervals, leading them to have different base systems. For example, the Mayans had a base twenty system, whereas the Babylonians had a

base sixty system with subbases to enable efficient counting. Computer scientists use the digits 0 and 1 for the off (0) and on (1) switches on computer boards—creating the base two or binary system used by diverse computer operating systems. Many of our students will work in the computer industry in which understanding the base two system is essential (Tepper, 2000). Most likely, you have studied some of these systems in other mathematics courses. They are excellent ways to

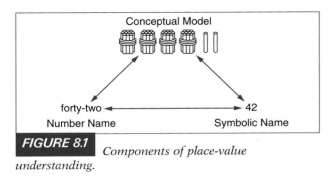

FIGURE 8.1 *Components of place-value understanding.*

connect mathematics with world history and multicultural appreciation. The Web site has some of the interesting ones used in school settings in Chapter 8 "Check Your Mathematics Knowledge."

Three Components of "Number"

Understanding place value involves three components of number: the number name (oral or written), the symbolic numeral, and the conceptual model represented with number base quantities. The coordination between these three components is the foundation for developing place-value concepts (Figure 8.1).

Starting in the early elementary grades, the part-whole understanding of number and the foundation work with addition and subtraction presented in Chapter 7 provide the conceptual base for later work with place value and larger numbers. The development of place-value understandings is an essential component of the elementary school mathematics curriculum. Children

Check

YOUR MATHEMATICS KNOWLEDGE

On Numeration and Number Sense
On the Web site (Chapter 8, check your math knowledge), read/do the following:

- Development of Numeration Systems
- Babylonian System
- Mayan System
- Roman System
- History of Hindu-Arabic System
  . . . a refresher from mathematics coursework . . . Lest you forget!

begin to develop number meaning by counting. Counting is related to counting groups to make ten. Counting groups is different from counting individual units in a one-to-one correspondence as featured in Chapter 6. Children need extended experiences to be able to integrate counting patterns and construct grouping relationships. Place-value understanding involves quantifying sets of objects by grouping by ten. Children's place-value ideas develop in a progression from seeing individual units of one and counting them by ones, to counting by groups (twos, fives, or tens), to developing notions about tens and ones that compose numbers.

Importance of Place Value

Miura (2001) presents compelling evidence from many studies that children speaking Asian languages have an advantage in the understanding of place value and its implications for an easy transition to addition and subtraction of multidigit numbers. For example, the name for twelve (12) in an Asian language would be "ten-two" and ninety (90) is "nine tens." Asian cultures spent less time on place-value teachings and use less pictorial representations in their work. Children come to school already understanding groups of ten and their representations; whereas non-Asian cultures spent many hours of extended experiences with manipulatives and pictorial representations for children to make the same connections. As number patterns are recognized and applied by the child, nonconventional number names often occur such as "twenty-ten" and "tenty-one." This shows that our English-speaking children are trying to make sense out of the patterns they see and supports the studies outlined by Miura. Throughout this chapter and the one to follow, you will see many pictorial representations of our numeration system in the suggested activities to build conceptual understanding because the children you teach will need this extended exposure to fully understand place value.

Data from the National Assessment of Educational Progress (NAEP) suggest that students at all grade levels (fourth, eighth, and twelfth) performed well on items requiring place value and rounding in familiar situations, but they had difficulty applying concepts and properties to unfamiliar situations (NAEP, 2006, 2000). Students could not justify their answers or explain their reasoning. Eighth grade students could not interpret the meaning of large numbers (only 22 percent answered correctly). The NCTM *Principles and Standards* (2000) call for students to develop well-understood meanings of our number system.

STANDARD

Instructional programs from PreK through grade 12 should enable all students to

Understand numbers, ways of representing numbers, relationships among numbers, and number systems.

PREK TO 2

In prekindergarten through grade 2 all students should

Use multiple models to develop initial understandings of place value and the base-ten number system.

Develop understanding of the relative position and magnitude of whole numbers and of ordinal and cardinal numbers and their connections.

Develop a sense of whole numbers and represent and use them in flexible ways, including relating, composing, and decomposing numbers.

Connect number words and numerals to the quantities they represent, using various physical models and representations.

GRADES 3 TO 5

In grades 3 to 5 all students should

Understand the place-value structure of the base-ten number system and be able to represent and compare whole numbers and decimals.

Recognize equivalent representations for the same number and generate them by decomposing and composing numbers.

Develop understanding of fractions as parts of unit wholes, as parts of a collection, as locations on number lines, and as divisions of whole numbers.

Recognize and generate equivalent forms of commonly used fractions, decimals, and percents.

Explore numbers less than 0 by extending the number line and through familiar applications.

Describe classes of numbers according to characteristics such as the nature of their factors.

GRADES 6 TO 8

In grades 6 to 8 all students should

Work flexibly with fractions, decimals, and percents to solve problems.

Compare and order fractions, decimals, and percents efficiently and find their approximate locations on a number line.

Develop an understanding of large numbers and recognize and appropriately use exponential, scientific, and calculator notation; use factors, multiples, prime factorization, and relatively prime numbers to solve problems.

Develop meaning for integers and represent and compare quantities with them.

FIGURE 8.2 *NCTM expectations of number systems.*[1]

[1] Partial listing as it applies to Numeration and Number Sense from NCTM *Principles and Standards for School Mathematics* (2000, pages 392–393).

Read through the components of the standards related to numeration in Figure 8.2 to see the concepts needed by our students.

Studying the numeration systems of other cultures provides some interesting comparisons to our number system. Researchers offer background understanding and activities for middle grade students to explore the rich history of number systems of the Chinese (Uy, 2003) and Native American tribes (Hughes and Anderson, 1996). The positional numerical system of the Mayans described in Wilson (2001) gives examples of representational materials and provides cultural links. Students need to explore other numeration systems for deeper understanding and appreciation of our own system. Students need to know that their ancestors and the ancestors of their fellow classmates were the intelligent people who invented number systems. The Chicago Public School District has developed a culturally relevant curriculum section around the origin of numerals coming from the major cultural groups. The Chicago

work is included here for you to use when planning mathematics lessons.

Cultural Contributions

CULTURAL RELEVANCE ORIGINS OF NUMERALS

Students need to know that their ancestors and the ancestors of their fellow classmates were the intelligent people who invented number systems.

Students should know that many peoples contributed to the development of modern arithmetic and that the origins of arithmetic are international. For example, Africans were the first to use numerals. Ancient Egyptians in Africa invented a symbol for ten that replaced 10 tally marks and a symbol for one hundred that replaced 100 tally marks. The Chinese were among the first to recognize and use number patterns. The Maya in Central America used a place-value system and they used zero as a position holder hundreds of years before Europe imported modern numerals from Africa. . . . Modern numerals were invented by the peoples of India. That is why modern numerals are known as Hindu-Arabic numerals. (Strong, 1990)

WHERE'S THE MATHEMATICS? THE STRUCTURE OF NUMERATION SYSTEMS

Exploring the structure of a numeration system generates an appreciation and understanding of how efficiently the system operates. It enables students to work within the system, building the conceptual knowledge that merely memorizing when to regroup numbers does not do. Numeration systems have a specific structure from which emerge place-value notations, powers, and exponents.

Base 10 System

The configuration of the base 10 system is shown in Figure 8.3. Notice that the system begins with a single basic building unit, often referred to as a *unit*. From there, each regrouping is done at ten. The models shown are known as the base 10 blocks (also referred to as place-value blocks, multibase blocks, Dienes blocks, and powers of 10 blocks).

All units are single ones until the first regrouping. The configuration of the first regrouping looks like a long set of units fused together, hence the name *long*. The 10 means one set of ten and no single units present except for those accounted for in the long.

The second type of regrouping occurs when there are ten longs (or ten groups of ten). The configuration looks like a flat with its ten longs fused together, hence the name *flat*. There are ten times ten sets of the basic building unit that can be seen in the flat, or one hundred pieces of the basic unit. The numeral 100 means one set in the second regrouping with no sets of ten and no single units present except for those already accounted for in the flat.

The third type of regrouping occurs when there are ten flats (or ten groups of hundreds). The configuration looks like a block with its ten flats fused together, hence the name *block*. There are ten times a hundred sets of the basic building unit that can be seen in the block, or one thousand pieces of the basic unit. Therefore, 1,000 means one set in the third regrouping with no sets of hundreds, no sets of tens, and no units except for those already accounted for in the block.

Exponents are known as powers of 10 when the base is 10. Exponents are introduced to students in the sixth or seventh grade in most textbooks. The exponent is just another way of indicating which type of regrouping is being considered. Notice that

$$10^2 \text{ is read as "ten squared."}$$

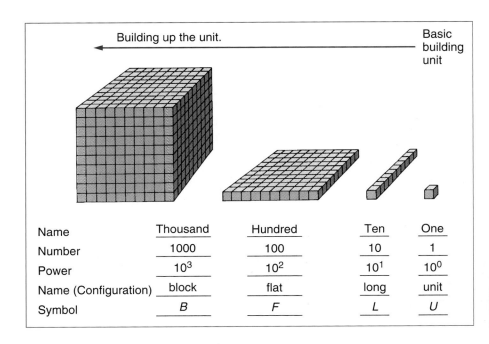

Name	Thousand	Hundred	Ten	One
Number	1000	100	10	1
Power	10^3	10^2	10^1	10^0
Name (Configuration)	block	flat	long	unit
Symbol	B	F	L	U

Building up the unit. ← Basic building unit

FIGURE 8.3 *Configuration of base 10 system.*

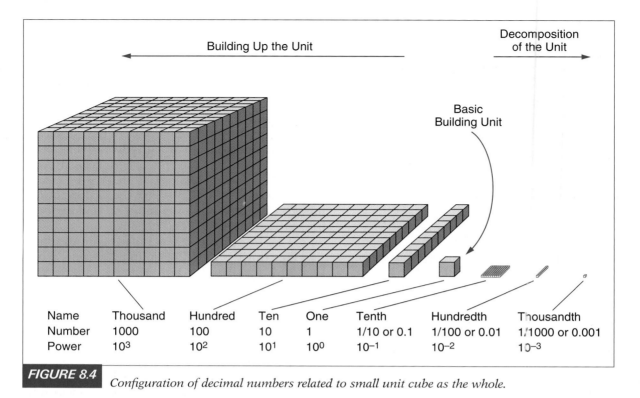

Name	Thousand	Hundred	Ten	One	Tenth	Hundredth	Thousandth
Number	1000	100	10	1	1/10 or 0.1	1/100 or 0.01	1/1000 or 0.001
Power	10^3	10^2	10^1	10^0	10^{-1}	10^{-2}	10^{-3}

FIGURE 8.4 *Configuration of decimal numbers related to small unit cube as the whole.*

It is not by chance that the configuration for "ten squared" is in the shape of a square (the flat), nor is it by chance that

$$10^3 \text{ is read as "ten cubed."}$$

As Figure 8.4 shows, the shape is a cube (the block). Many college students are unaware that any number squared or cubed becomes the shape of a square or cube, respectively, when using base models. When middle grade students are first introduced to exponents, the configuration and meaning of the base 10 system (as seen in Figure 8.4) should be shown to them.

Decimals The fractional parts of the base 10 system are known as the *decimal* part of the system. "Deci" is Latin for "part of ten" or "part of a whole broken down by tens." Elementary textbooks stress the point to students by writing a decimal part of a whole with a lead zero, like this:

$$0.625 \text{ instead of } .625$$

The zero in the above example reminds students that there is no whole number represented there. This text follows the same principle so that teachers can familiarize themselves with writing decimal representation in this way.

In Figure 8.4 a new part has been added to the right of the basic building unit. It illustrates the decomposition of the base 10 system. By extending the place-value system into smaller segments of the basic building unit and keeping the same configuration of units, we obtain the rational numbers or the fractional parts of the basic building unit.

Notice that throughout this section the discussion continues to focus on the basic building unit. It is the key from which all numbers are regrouped, larger to the left and smaller to the right. Just as the whole numbers are built up by groups of ten, so the fractional parts of the basic building unit can be partitioned (or decomposed) by groups of ten. Because the basic building unit is in the configuration of a cube, the configuration of the tenth is that of a flat or one-tenth of the basic building unit. The next regrouping is one-tenth of the small flat or one-hundredth of the basic building unit. It looks like a small long. The next regrouping is one-tenth of the small long or one-thousandth of the basic building unit. It looks like a little block. Notice that the three new categories of base 10 blocks fit into the same configuration as the whole number system, (i.e., block-long-flat, block-long-flat [reading from right to left]). The configuration shows the patterning and logic of the system.

Just as the powers of the whole numbers signify which regrouping is taking place in the

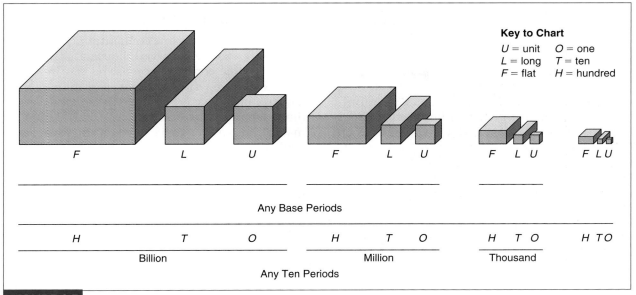

Key to Chart

U = unit O = one
L = long T = ten
F = flat H = hundred

Any Base Periods

| H | T | O | H | T | O | H | T | O | H | T O |
| Billion | | | | Million | | Thousand | | | | |

Any Ten Periods

FIGURE 8.5   *Family or period chart of the numeration system.*

buildup of the system by tens, so the negative (−) powers tell which regrouping is taking place in the decomposition of the base 10 system. So means we are talking about thousandths or the third regrouping decomposed from the basic building unit or 1.

Looking at 10^0 in Figure 8.5, it is clear that the value is 1 or the basic building unit. It is in middle school that students learn that any number to the zero power is one. For example, $395^\circ = 1$. Any number to the zero power means that no regrouping has taken place. The number is still being counted as a "one" as if there were 395 individual units or tally marks (strokes) with nothing regrouped. An informal proof would be

$$1 = \frac{395^1}{395^1} = 395^{1-1} = 395^0$$

Hisham E. Shaffey (2002, p. 133), a middle school student, developed still another proof by thinking of powers in a logical sequence:

$$2^3 = 2 \times 2 \times 2 = 8$$
$$2^2 = 2 \times 2 = 4$$
$$2^1 = 2$$
$$2^0 = 1$$

By reducing the power by 1, it divides the previous result by 2. It will work for any number; thereby, being able to state that if x equals any number, then x0 = 1. It is true for any numeration system. When students understand the logic and patterning of a system, they are able to explain many concepts in meaningful ways.

Relative Magnitude of Number Every time we move one place to the right anywhere along the continuum, the value of the digit is one-tenth as great (Figure 8.4). Thus, we can start from any position or place value and know that the number to the right will always be one-tenth of that number and the number to the left will always be ten times larger than the original number.

Place-value understanding in decimals requires a realization that the focal point of the place-value system is the number 1. As Sowder (1995) states, "So really 0.342 is 342 *thousandths of one*. Put another way, 0.3 is three-tenths of 1, while 3 is three ones, and 30 is three tens, or 30 ones. But by the same token that 0.3 is three-tenths of one, 3 is three-tenths of 10, 30 is three-tenths of 100, and so on up the line" (p. 21). Starting in any relative position enables us to tell the next magnitude of the number. Stated another way, if a student picks up any long as the starting point, he or she knows to pick up the unit that is one-tenth the size of the long to the right and to pick the flat that is ten times the size of the long to the left. Even if the long is shown to the student in isolation, the student can envision what would come to the right and left of any configuration. Students need to orally explain how they knew to pick the correct place value piece. Let's see how you would do. Without looking at Figure 8.5, think of the smallest flat in the figure; what would be to the right and left of its position? Can you explain in words how you knew what to pick? Now do the same thing with numerals:

50 is five-tenths of what number? Explain how you knew.

0.48 is forty-eight hundredths of what number? Explain how you knew.

You had to apply your knowledge of patterning and reason to get the answer. That is an example of conceptualizing the numeration system, seeing the embedded mathematics in the system. Before moving to operations with decimal numbers, Sowder recommends postponing work with operations on decimal numbers until these place-value concepts along the continuum are well developed. If students do not have a sound understanding of place value before they learn to add and subtract decimal numbers, many errors result from flawed computational procedures that are difficult to overcome. The NAEP results (2006; 2000) suggest that few connections exist between students' conceptual knowledge of decimals and the symbol manipulation of rules for computation. Hiebert (2003) provides a more indepth discussion of the research on decimal number understanding and its relationship to the relative magnitude of numbers.

Any Number Base System

Figure 8.5 depicts the regrouping configurations as they would appear for any number base. There are no individual unit markings on the place-value blocks because these "multibase blocks" apply to a multitude of bases.

Looking from right to left, from the basic building unit, the same three configurations keep reoccurring in any base. They are the block, the long, and the flat. Our system reads these sets of three as families or periods, and the names are consistent with the configurations. For example,

the **one** thousand place value is in the same configuration as the first **one** (block); the **ten** thousand place value is in the same configuration as the first ten (long); and the **hundred** thousand place value is in the same configuration as the first **hundred** (flat). When we write the place value numerals for large numbers, we group them in the same sets of three separated by commas: 974,023,922,071. It makes the number easier to read. Because some textbooks are taking a lesson from other countries and representing larger numbers with a space between periods or families instead of commas, the numeral would appear as

974 023 922 071

We discovered that the base 10 system progresses from one place value to the next by magnitudes of 10. If this were a base 4 system, the configurations would be the same, but each place value would progress by a magnitude of 4; a base 12 system would progress by a magnitude of 12, and so forth. Figure 8.6 shows what one flat, two longs, and three units would look like in base 4, base 10, and base 12. The numeral would be written the same way, but the magnitude of each place value would be by fours in base 4, by tens in base 10, and by twelves in base 12.

Activity 8.1 reconstructs numbers in different number bases by using pictures of the multibase blocks as the manipulatives. Activity 8.2 reconstructs numbers as they were used in different cultures. More activities are listed in the Extended Activities. They are on the Web site in Chapter 8. As you go through the activities, you will be challenged to think about the groupings and

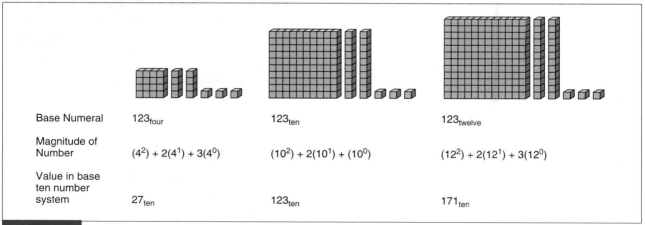

Base Numeral	123_{four}	123_{ten}	123_{twelve}
Magnitude of Number	$(4^2) + 2(4^1) + 3(4^0)$	$(10^2) + 2(10^1) + (10^0)$	$(12^2) + 2(12^1) + 3(12^0)$
Value in base ten number system	27_{ten}	123_{ten}	171_{ten}

FIGURE 8.6   *Representations in different number bases.*

Please Note: *When a numeral is written in a base other than base 10, students are taught to write out the number word as the subscript for that base so they can remember that there can be no individual numeral for the base number. In other words, there can be no numeral, 4, in base 4 because one always regroups to the next regrouping when a person has a group of four things. Mathematicians who understand base number systems use short notations like 1234, but beginning learners need ways to help them remember such details.*

relationships in much the same way that children must do as they learn the base 10 system. This is a good way for a teacher to simulate what it must be like to be a child and see our system for the first time.

Activity 8.1

PROBLEM SOLVING

MANIPULATIVES

BASE 4 NUMERATION SYSTEM

DIRECTIONS

1. Sketch the configuration of the base 4 numeration system to the third regrouping.

2. Now count by units in base 4 using the number line that appears below the multibase shapes. The first four have been done for you. Label each with the corresponding numbers.

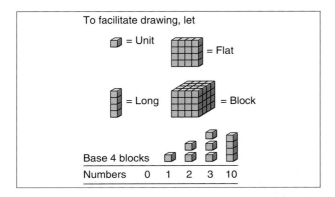

To facilitate drawing, let

$\quad$ = Unit $\quad$ = Flat

$\quad$ = Long $\quad$ = Block

Base 4 blocks				
Numbers	0	1	2	3	10

Activity 8.2

CULTURAL RELEVANCE

CHILDREN'S LITERATURE

NUMBERS ON THE WALL

The number system of early civilizations was primarily a notational system such as the Egyptians'. Investigate how we learned about other people's systems of numbers in the encyclopedia and other sources. What discovery converted the Hindu-Arabic notation into a place-value system? Explain the impact of this breakthrough finding.

Read *Talking Walls* by Margy Burns Knight (1992). How have walls been used by different cultures throughout thousands of years? Discuss how early people used

walls to record important events and what role number system played.

Generally, it is believed to be important to allow students opportunities to explore the structure of other number systems by performing activities in other number bases. This is usually done in upper elementary and middle school by using the type of activities seen on the web site (Extended Activities). Teisha's creation of her own numeration system in Chapter 2, page 22 is an example of the conceptual understandings that can emerge when given the opportunity to work in different base systems. Multibase activities were prevalent in the upper grade mathematics textbooks of the 1960s during the period in mathematics history known as the "New Math" era. Working with different number bases was considered quite new and revolutionary by many parents and teachers. "Scales of Notation," in Extended Activities, is from an upper elementary textbook published in 1892 (Milne, p. 398). If the word "scale" is replaced with the word "base," it becomes apparent that different number bases have been a part of the curriculum off and on for over one hundred years!

EXTENDED ACTIVITIES

CALCULATORS **MANIPULATIVES** **PROBLEM SOLVING** **MATHEMATICAL CONNECTIONS**

On the web site (Chapter 8, Extended Activities), read/do the following:

- Different Numeration Systems
- Quipu Knots
- Drawing Base Configurations
- Scales of Notation
- Review of Number Base Values
- Addition in Base 4
- Chinese Numeration System

The use of number bases keeps recurring in the curriculum because the creation of number bases is the mark of intelligent communication among people who may not have the same "word" language. When young people can place themselves in an unfamiliar setting using another base system, they are using logical reasoning patterns to arrive at the concept of the infinity of number-there is always a next number that can be created no matter how large or in what base people are working. They can continue to create the next number themselves, and once others discern the pattern, they also can communicate the next number in any base. They can take turns and continue to produce the next number together. That's what makes mathematics the intergalactic language.

The Voyager is on its way through outer space emitting sounds that increase in magnitudes, corresponding to the regroupings of several number systems. Each night in various observatories all over the world, astronomers turn on listening devices to see if there are any responses to the Voyager sounds. What are they waiting to hear? If the sounds come back mimicking the Voyager sounds, they will know there is life in other galaxies capable of mimicking what they hear. But what astronomers are **really** anxious to hear are sounds that show number systems other than the ones they have created on the Voyager. That would tell us that the "life forms" know what we are doing because they also have created mathematical systems that represent the infinity of number. The music from the film, *Close Encounters of the Third Kind*, gives you the idea of the sounds of number bases. In the film, the organist communicates with the space travelers until such a point that the aliens can regroup the sounds at larger magnitudes in quicker time than the organist can play. The movie, *Contact*, also uses number base patterning to show aliens' attempts to communicate with scientists on earth.

To date, we have heard no sounds from outer space that show such mathematical communication in the real universe. We have only the imagination of film writers to simulate what might happen. Now you can see why students should not leave middle school without a sense of the intergalactic power of mathematics through the creation of number bases. We owe it to our students to have them experience for themselves this power of mathematics.

STRATEGIES FOR BUILDING CONCEPTUAL UNDERSTANDING OF NUMERATION AND NUMBER SENSE

There is a growing body of evidence that without direct instruction, children will invent their own strategies for adding and subtracting multidigit numbers supported by what they know about base

10 number concepts (Fuson, 2003; Kilpatrick and Swafford, 2002; Miura, 2001). Children's invented strategies become important as they attempt to work with larger multidigit numbers in addition, subtraction, multiplication, and division as we will see in Chapter 9. There is an ongoing debate about the sequence for developing base 10 concepts and children's use of invented strategies. Which comes first—(1) a reasonably well-developed understanding of base 10 concepts or (2) learning set procedures for adding and subtracting multidigit numbers from which children develop their own strategies for quick analysis of answers (Carpenter et al., 1999)? The studies suggest that invented strategies develop as children reflect on their solutions with base 10 materials whether the set procedures are taught or base 10 concepts are well developed. The materials seem to be the key in our culture. Although initially children use various materials to represent tens and ones, as they become more comfortable with their invented procedures, their use of physical materials declines and mental calculations are done.

Whichever viewpoint you take, primary grade teachers recognize a wide range of misconceptions that students have when working with place value. An interesting research project (Nagel and Swingen, 1998) involving students from six to thirteen years of age noticed a close link between the language used by children and the depth of their understanding of place value. Opportunities for children to act out place-value exchanges, use physical materials, and use a shared language for these processes were critical components of solid place-value understandings.

Numeration often occurs in the first few chapters of the student's textbook. Unfortunately, inadequate coverage is frequently seen, and insufficient skill maintenance is offered. Our number system has certain properties that need to be fully developed in students' minds. The first property of the system is the nature of place value, followed by understanding and interpreting large numbers and decimals.

Nature of Place Value

Interaction with materials that can be formed into groups is the foundation for constructing understanding of place-value concepts. Young children need to physically join or group materials into sets of ten with discrete, "groupable" objects (e.g., toothpicks, straws, craft sticks, lima beans, or popcorn). In this manner, the child is responsible for forming the group rather than for trusting the trades of ten units for one ten. Some children need to continue to count and check to reassure themselves that the group represents ten. It is important to sequence the use of materials according to the developmental needs of each child. Ungrouped, discrete materials should be the beginning point of investigating grouping. Grouping with counting activities is presented first; next comes numeration models where the groupings have already been done. Then expanded notation with the use of numerals sets the stage for understanding large numbers.

Counting Activities   Counting can help construct base 10 concepts. Thompson (1990) identifies three ways to count a set (e.g., 42): Counting by ones (from one to forty-two), counting by groups of tens and singles (one, two, three, four groups of ten and one, two), and counting by tens and ones (ten, twenty, thirty, forty, forty-one, forty-two). He contends that counting by groups of tens and singles is a link between counting by ones and place-value concepts. The key is *many* activities should involve counting to accompany the action of the grouping. Four activities are presented here (Activities 8.3–8.6).

Learning about counting numbers through ten-frames, also discussed in Chapter 9, is an approach that develops benchmarks of fives and tens, which are helpful for numeration. The tens structure shows children how to develop numerosity rather than counting by ones (Figure 8.7). Each time the ten-frame is full, the beans are put in a portion cup to represent one ten and moved to the tens place on the place-value mat. Connecting the same activity to numerals is shown in Figure 8.8.

Activity 8.3

MANIPULATIVES   **HANDFULS**

MATERIALS
- Beans, popcorn, connecting cubes, buttons, pasta, and so on

PROCEDURE
Child takes a handful each of several different items. Count the total number of each item by putting it into groups of tens and singles. Compare the totals and write about why handfuls are different.

ASSESSMENT
Watch for counting procedures. What do you know about the child's understanding of place value?

Activity 8.4

MANIPULATIVES   **BEAT THE SAND!**

MATERIALS
- Egg timer with sand
- Stamps and stamp pad
- Paper and markers

PROCEDURE
The timer begins and the child stamps as many times as possible before the sand is gone. Then the child counts the stamps in several different ways and shows the grouping with different markers. Have the child write about how the grouping was done.

Activity 8.5

MANIPULATIVES   **HUNDREDS CHART FUN**

MATERIALS
- Hundreds chart—laminated or in protective plastic sheet
- Overhead pens or washable markers

1	2	3	4	5	6	7	8	9	10
11	12	13	14	15	16	17	18	19	20
21	22	23	24	25	26	27	28	29	30
31	32	33	34	35	36	37	38	39	40
41	42	43	44	45	46	47	48	49	50
51	52	53	54	55	56	57	58	59	60
61	62	63	64	65	66	67	68	69	70
71	72	73	74	75	76	77	78	79	80
81	82	83	84	85	86	87	88	89	90
91	92	93	94	95	96	97	98	99	100

Hundreds Chart

PROCEDURE
One child picks a beginning number and names it aloud as well as picking a "secret target number." Using arrow clues, the child tells his or her partner how to find the

secret number. Partner tries to name the ending target number. In order to get the point, partner must write the equation to describe the moves. Reverse roles.

For example: Begin at 47. (Target is 89.)

Arrow clues: → → ↓ ↓ ↓ ↓

$47 + 1 + 1 = 49 + 10 + 10 + 10 + 10 = 89$

VARIATION

Begin with an empty hundreds chart with only 10 to 15 numbers randomly filled in. Children can pick a number and tell directional moves they would make to land on positions for other numbers on the chart. For more teaching ideas see *Math By All Means* by Marilyn Burns (1994), a Place Value Replacement Unit, grade 2.

Activity 8.6

CULTURAL RELEVANCE

YUP'IK MATHEMATICS (ALASKAN ESKIMOS)

Yup'ik bilingual programs teach students to count to 10 using a "Western" base 10 system, but their cultural background uses a base 20 subbase 5. The basic Yup'ik number patterns use body parts to give literal meanings to the numbers. For example, the word for six is "arvin-legen," which means "cross over" because the finger counting changes from the left hand to the right hand. To count from 11 to 20, one starts over with the left end finger and repeats the process. The Mayan system of place value is similar to Yup'ik.

Investigate how this number system works.

1. What materials, patterns, and culturally based approach to mathematics would you suggest?
2. Write a reflective paper on what difficulties might be encountered for children when a concrete contextualized counting system is formalized in the classroom.

> **Supporting the NCTM *Principles and Standards* (2000):**
> * The Equity Principle
> * Number Systems; Number Representations and Relationships; Number Fluency and Flexibility
> * The Learning Principle

Counting by ones, tens, hundreds, starting at any number is an important activity to allow chil-

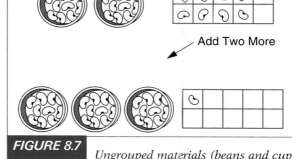

FIGURE 8.7 *Ungrouped materials (beans and cups) with ten-frames.*

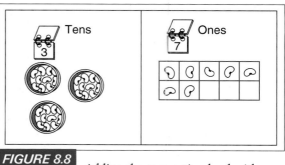

FIGURE 8.8 *Adding the connecting level with number flip cards.*

dren a sense of how and when numbers change. For example, when counting by ones even with six- or seven-digit numbers, only the digit in the ones column changes or increases. Some children who have not had opportunities to explore this concept will change several digits in a large number when asked to write the number that is one more or one less.

An excellent device to illustrate this concept is an odometer. If you can secure an old one from a junkyard or used car parts shop, it will demonstrate to children how the gears work together. For example, when the tenths dial is at 9, one rotation will cause the tenths dial to turn to 0, and the column on the left, the ones, will increase by one. Likewise, if the tenths and ones have a 9, the next rotation will cause both 9s to become 0 and the column on the left, the tens, to increase by one. Use odometers to show patterns for decimal numbers also.

A homemade odometer can be constructed to illustrate such counting patterns, and the student can control the moving of the places. Observing such counting patterns helps solidify how the number system is structured.

Students can profit from experiences with the calculator when dealing with large multidigit numbers. A quick counting activity is to use the constant feature of the calculator and input

$1 + = = =$. As the student continues pushing the equals key, the counting sequence of the numbers is displayed. Students can see the changing ones column and the 0 to 9 sequence recurring. As you assess children's understanding and confidence of counting in groups, watch for children who continue counting by ones to verify the number. For these children, more concrete exposure is necessary for longer periods of time.

Numeration Models   After initial grouping concepts are well established, proportional materials requiring trading can be introduced. Many texts call these numeration models. Base 10 blocks serve as excellent models for place-value concepts, especially in establishing an understanding of ones, tens, and hundreds. Keep in mind that numbers are abstractions and children need concrete materials to construct an understanding of number and place-value notation. When proportional models are used, the same configuration that indicates grouping occurs. Remember the repeating pattern of cube, long, and flat mentioned earlier in this chapter? This pattern continues as regroupings continue. The pictures and descriptions of place-value models in Figure 8.9 may help to demonstrate the differences between proportional and nonproportional models. Do you see which models provide a one-to-one correspondence with the number represented and which models do not? Some models attach irrelevant attributes to the place-value positions such as size or color. Which models would give less problems to children just learning about regrouping?

Activity 8.7

CULTURAL RELEVANCE   **ODOMETER MATHEMATICS**

MATERIALS
- Oak tag-cut in three equal strips to cover can
- Aluminum soft drink can
- Matte board or heavy cardboard
- X-acto knife

CONSTRUCTION

Cut three equal strips from oak tag to cover aluminum can. Tape strips individually to allow each to rotate independently around the can. Make an opening or "window" in the matte board that is large enough to expose one number from each strip. Cut with X-acto knife as shown and pull tabs to cover ends of can. Cut

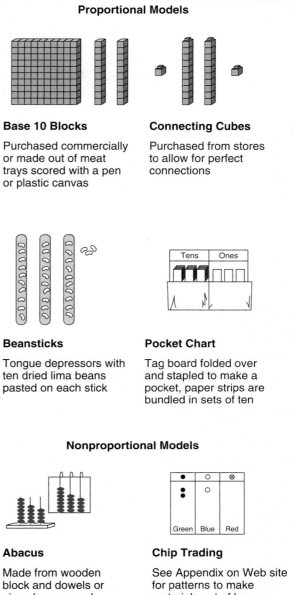

Proportional Models

Base 10 Blocks
Purchased commercially or made out of meat trays scored with a pen or plastic canvas

Connecting Cubes
Purchased from stores to allow for perfect connections

Beansticks
Tongue depressors with ten dried lima beans pasted on each stick

Pocket Chart
Tag board folded over and stapled to make a pocket, paper strips are bundled in sets of ten

Nonproportional Models

Abacus
Made from wooden block and dowels or pipe cleaners and heavy cardboard

Chip Trading
See Appendix on Web site for patterns to make materials out of heavy paper or plastic

FIGURE 8.9   *Models for numeration.*

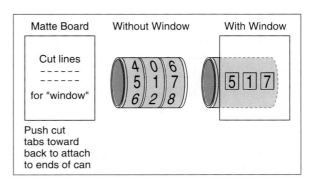

circles from oak tag to cover the ends of can and tape tabs and circles to can.

PROCEDURE

The three strips (or more if using the inner roll from paper towels) can be rotated to expose the digits on the face of the odometer through the "window." Rotate each strip to show children how the digits 0 to 9 form all the numbers through 999. Some activities to do with the odometer:

1. Teacher or partner dictates a three-digit number. The student forms that number on the odometer.

2. Teacher or partner announces which counting pattern is being used (e.g., adding 100 more or less). The student shows the next three numbers in that counting sequence.

> **Supporting the NCTM *Principles and Standards* (2000):**
> - Worthwhile Mathematical Tasks; Tools for Enhancing Discourse—The Teaching Principle
> - The Learning Principle

Any model that requires one chip or block to stand for 10, 100, or 1,000 things is problematic for children who are more literal thinkers. Nonproportional models should be used only after regrouping ideas are well established.

The game, Digit Hunt, can be played by using concrete models or child-drawn pictures of the concrete models if the child is not ready to work solely with the symbolic numerals as shown in Activity 8.8. For example, the child can choose 8

Activity 8.8

PROBLEM SOLVING   **DIGIT HUNT**

MATERIALS

- Game board with numbers in each "step" of the board
- Spinner with place-value names that agree with board numbers
- Spinner with numbers 0 to 9
- Game board markers

sets of 10 connecting cubes to represent 80 after the two spinners land on 8 and 10's, respectively. Then the child can search for the first number on the game board that shows an 8 in the 10's, position and place his or her marker on that number. Some children will see the pattern quickly and realize that they can get around the game board without the need to display the manipulatives first.

PROCEDURE

Determine who goes first by who spins the largest number. The first player spins the two spinners. The player's marker may be moved from start to the first space on the board that has that digit in the place noted on the place-value spinner. Players cannot occupy the same spot. In that case, the second player to land on that spot must return to start. Players must go to the *nearest* space that has the number in the place, even if it means a move backward. The first player to reach the end (finish) is the winner.

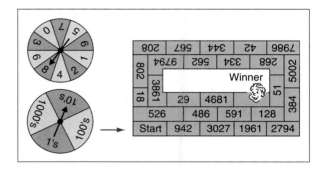

There are many mental math games that can build on the firm foundation shown here with numeration models. They are listed in the Extended Activities. See how the materials work in a college classroom as well as in the elementary school by viewing the Video Vignette on numeration games.

Many children's understanding of place value in second through fifth grades is delayed until grouping by ten is well established (Kamii, 2000). Repeated grouping experiences using multiple embodiments of materials help internalize number ideas. Labinowicz reports that interviews with children have indicated that many third grade children do not relate to the thousand block because they do not conserve volume until the approximate age of eleven. They focus on a surface area strategy and fail to consider the inside of the cube. Therefore, when asked how much the thousand block represents, a nonconserving child replies, "600," counting six sides of one hundred each. The assessment section of this chapter discusses how to deal with such learning problems.

EXTENDED ACTIVITIES

CALCULATORS

MANIPULATIVES

PROBLEM SOLVING

MATHEMATICAL CONNECTIONS

MENTAL MATH

CULTURAL RELEVANCE

On the Web site (Chapter 8, Extended Activities), read/do the following:

- Name the Operation
- Who Am I
- The Answer is 5. What's the Question?
- Number Tile Fun
- Number Tile Activities
- Remove that Digit
- Think about 32
- Make a Number
- High-Middle-Low
- 100 Chart Fun
- Count on Five-Game 1
- Count on Five-Game 2
- Chip Trading
- Place-Value Bingo
- Number Sense—From the Russian Perspective

Video Vignette

Numeration Games

Watch how the university professor's instruction becomes a reality in this fifth grade classroom.

- What significant mathematical ideas are included in the exchange games described by Dr. Hatfield?
- In what ways does Mrs. Torres encourage student discourse?
- How does she promote mental calculations? When she says the boys have "very good understandings," what do you think she is informally assessing?

To construct the ten-to-one relationship through counting and grouping materials takes more time than is typically allowed in schools. Teachers must be prepared with many materials like those shown here and on the Web site to supplement the limited exposure typically seen in most elementary textbooks.

Total Value and Expanded Notation Another aspect of our number system is the number's total value. *Total value* refers to the additive property of the system. This means that 358 represents the number 300 + 50 + 8 and 358 is the total value. *Expanded notation* refers to the actual value of each digit, such as 412 = 400 + 10 + 2, and *standard form* refers to writing the compact number, such as 412. During the modern math movement, heavy emphasis was placed on showing expanded forms of numbers using the distributive property $(4 \times 100) + (1 \times 10) + (2 \times 1)$, but much less time is currently devoted to this concept. Perhaps the reduced coverage on this topic in textbooks may prove to be a limitation on a child's understanding of the system. Uy (2003), the National Research Council Study (Kilpatrick, Swafford, and Findell, 2001), and Miura (2001) have shown the benefits of using the distributive property in Asian systems. The TIMSS test scores of Asian countries would suggest that there may be merit in spending more time with this approach. Activities 8.9, 8.10, and 8.11 focus on reinforcing expanded notation and developing more meaningful understanding of numeration. The mental math component of these activities helps children develop computational flexibility and strategic competence to see alternative ways to work with large numbers.

Understanding and Interpreting Large Numbers

Another aspect of number sense is the need to acquire a sense of the relative magnitude of numbers. Using proportional and nonproportional, manipulative models with smaller two-and three-digit numbers will hopefully create an understanding of the trading process and an understanding of how the powers of 10 function. Then, these concepts can be extended to larger numbers, working on a symbolic level.

Activity 8.9

MENTAL MATH

PLACE—VALUE STRIPS—AN AID TO MENTAL COMPUTATION

MATERIALS
- Felt-tip pens or any washable pens
- Laminated construction paper strips $1'' \times 9''$

PROCEDURE
The teacher says a three-digit number, and the students write the number on their strip in the rectangular region at the far left. After the equals sign, students place the single digit beside each appropriate place value name. In folded compact form, the strip should read $258 = 258$. In unfolded, expanded form, the strip should read $258 = 2$ hundreds $+ 5$ tens $+ 8$ ones. Various folds can be opened to expose different forms of the number, such as shown below. Such activities encourage students to be flexible in working with numbers and to see equivalent representations of numbers.

$$258 = 25 \text{ tens} + 8 \text{ ones}$$
$$258 = 258 \text{ ones}$$
$$258 = 2 \text{ hundreds} + 58 \text{ ones}$$

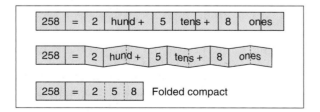

Activity 8.10

MENTAL MATH **EQUAL NAMES**

MATERIALS
- 48 cards—four forms for twelve numbers Samples:

$$600 = 60 \text{ tens} = 600 \text{ ones} = \text{six hundred}$$
$$8326 = 8000 + 300 + 20 + 6 = 83 \text{ hundreds}$$
twenty-six
$$= \text{eight thousand three hundred twenty-six}$$

PROCEDURE
Play in groups of four. Determine who goes first. Deal all cards to players. The object is to get books (total sets of four forms) of equivalent names for a number. When a book is formed, the player may lay down the cards as a set. When play begins, players may trade any cards to the player on the left. The game pauses for players to check on equivalent numbers and form books. Play continues until one player has succeeded in making all the cards into books.

Activity 8.11

CALCULATORS **MATHEMATICAL CONNECTIONS**

USING CALCULATORS WITH THE EXPANDED FORM

MATERIALS
- Set of number cards
- Calculator

PROCEDURE
Read the number on the card. Express the number in expanded form (such as $3000 + 40 + 6$). Enter the expanded form of the number into the calculator in any order. Did the same compact form of the number occur as the final number? This activity shows the additive property as well as the commutative property for addition.

Supporting the ISTE Standard of . . .
Using technology resources (calculators) for problem solving, self-directed learning, and extended learning activities.

Relative Magnitude of Numbers We live in a world that inundates us with large numbers. Any newspaper quickly illustrates this point: $41.2 million trade between two corporations, $3.23 million in shares traded, 2.4 billion cans of soda sold last year, $3.9 trillion national debt, to name just a few examples. Because these numbers are generally written in shortened form, a mystery is created about how much is represented by large numbers. People tend to ignore these large numbers and do not generally relate to them. Clearly, this situation is dangerous for society.

If we look to most middle school textbooks for instructional techniques to interpret these large numbers in standard form, we find limited coverage of this important skill. Findings from numerous interviews with adults and children indicate that few people know the difference between a million and a billion (in terms of their relationship to one another) and few understand how to translate the shortened form for large numbers into standard number form. Results from the NAEP assessment (NAEP, 2006; Kouba, Zawojewski, and Strutchens, 2000) imply that students in eighth grade have little sense of the relative magnitude of large numbers. More time needs to be spent on the concepts associated with large numbers-exponential, scientific, and calculator notation.

Exponential, Scientific, and Calculator Notation in the Middle School When numbers grow increasingly larger or decreasingly smaller, it is expedient to write the numbers in shortened form. For example, the number 1,000,000,000,000,000,000 may be written as 10^{18}, shown as exponents, called appropriately exponential notation. The number 0.000000000001 may be written as 10^{-12}. The addition property of exponents comes into play when we want to show products of large numbers such as: $1,000,000 \times 1,000$. By long multiplication, one could find the answer. It is 1,000,000,000, but exponential notation is more efficient to use, such that $10^6 \times 10^3 = 10^9$. Following the problem-solving strategies we learned in Chapter 5, it may be easier to see if we think of a simpler problem, $100 \times$

$10 = 1,000$. It may be written exponentially as $10^2 \times 10^1 = 10^3$. Exponents are added while the base number is multiplied. Think of $2,000 \times 300$ in exponential form: $(2 \times 10^3) \times (3 \times 10^2) = 6(10^5)$ We learned earlier in this chapter that 10^{-2} meant the decomposition of the basic building unit into its fractional parts (in this case to the hundredths). So $10-2 = 0.01$. So 2000×0.03 could be written as $(2 \times 10^3) \times (3 \times 10^{-2}) = 6(10^1)$ or 60.

When representing numbers with a few digits, this seems like more work to show numbers by exponential notation, but it becomes very efficient when working with extremely large numbers or extremely minute, decimal numbers. To allow for all cases, both whole numbers and decimals, a decimal notation is used. This can be done because we learned in the earlier section of this chapter that any regrouping can be seen as a fractional part of the grouping to its right (see Figure 8.5). Because the scientific community deals frequently with such numbers, the shortened form is called appropriately scientific notation. Scientific notation is defined as any number shown by its exponents using the addition property of exponents and its decimal representation. The idea is to find a decimal between 1 and 10 and multiply it by the exponential (power) of 10. Therefore

$$2,703 = \frac{2,703}{1,000} = 2,703 \times 10^3 \text{ to show its}$$
decimal form as a power (exponent) of base 10

$$0.0485 = 0.0485 \times 100 = 4.85 \times 10^{-2} \text{ is to}$$
show its decimal form s a power (exponent) of base 10
6.9 since 6.9 is already between 1 and 10, we need to only find its exponent $6.9 = 6.9 \times 10^0$
Therefore, a problem like this:

$$(3.5 \times 10^9) \times (4.2 \times 10^{-3}) = 14.7 \times 10^6 \text{ is}$$
much easier than doing the multiplication for $3,500,000,000 \times 0.0042 = 14,700,000$

A calculator can handle only so many digits in its display, depending on the type of calculator you have chosen to use. When the numbers become greater than the digit display, calculators represent numbers in scientific notation with some interesting symbols that may look like this on some calculators:

$$14.7 \times 10 \text{ E } 6 \quad \text{or}$$

14.7×10^6 or something similar that indicates the exponent is "to the 6th power."

These representations are called calculator notation. Calculators show different notations for handling large numbers and help students see patterning in the number system by efficient key strokes. St. John and Lapp (2000) show powers and regrouping with the previous entry feature (p. 163):

$10^\wedge 1 - 1 =$	$10^\wedge 5 - 1 =$	$10^\wedge 7 - 1 =$
9	99999	9999999

All are ways to show the relative magnitude of number using efficient notation systems. Once middle school students see the patterns, the seemingly strange notation systems are not as difficult to understand.

Activities 8.12, 8.13, and 8.14 and books for children by Schwartz called How *Much Is a Million?* (1985) and *If You Made a Million* (1989) provide some visualization of large numbers. Schwartz (1985) offers examples of million, billion, and trillion that children love to visualize. Other recommended books for numeration are given at the end of the chapter. The Video Vignette "Whale Math" shows a teacher's innovative lesson to develop the relative magnitude of number.

Activity 8.12

ESTIMATION

WHAT HAPPENS TO THE ANSWER IF . . . ? RELATIVE EFFECT OF OPERATING ON NUMBERS

$$26 + 38 = \underline{\hspace{1cm}}$$

What happens to the answer if . . .

- One is added to each addend?
- One is added to one addend?
- One is added to one addend and one is subtracted from the other addend?

$$4 \times 12 = \underline{\hspace{1cm}}$$

- What happens to the answer if . . .
- One is added to each factor?
- One is added to the first factor and one is subtracted from the other factor?
- One is added to each factor?
- One is subtracted from the first factor?

Activity 8.13

ESTIMATION **MATHEMATICAL CONNECTIONS**

WHAT'S A MILLION LIKE? RELATIVE MAGNITUDE OF NUMBERS

What's in your classroom that there could be a million of? In the school yard? What about a billion? Explain your reasoning. If you spend $10 every minute, how long would it take you to spend a thousand dollars? A million dollars? A billion dollars?

USA Today has lots of examples of statistics in the "USA Snapshots" section that uses large numbers. Find examples of large numbers in newspapers and magazines. Make a chart of the examples and write the standard number form (with all the place holders). Discuss the impact of large numbers on people and why the term "number numbness" is used regarding people's understanding of the relative magnitude of large numbers.

Design some activities that help others get an intuitive feel for these numbers. For example, a similar phrase to this one might be found, "The federal government ran a $88.9 billion deficit in October, up 60% from October a year ago. But so far this fiscal year, the budget deficit is down 5%." How much money is the difference? With some classmates, design ways to make large numbers meaningful to others and to visualize their numerical value.

> **Supporting the NCTM *Principles and Standards* (2000):**
> - Number Flexibility; Number Systems and Number Relationships; Reasoning; Communication; Problem Solving
> - Worthwhile Mathematical Tasks—The Teaching Principle
> - The Learning Principle

Reading Numbers There are several skills involved under the term "reading numbers." The skills involve numeral form, written form, and name form (orally reading the number from either its written form or numeral form). For example:

the numeral form is **3,425**

the written form is writing **three thousand four hundred twenty-five**

the name form is orally reading **"three thousand four hundred twenty-five"**

Activity 8.14

PROBLEM SOLVING

INTERPRETING LARGE NUMBERS

1. Ask children what is the largest number in the world and the smallest number in the world.
2. Explain the patterns in the names of the periods (families).
3. Is there such a number as a "zillion"? Why do you think this term was invented?
4. How long do you think it would take you to count to a million? A billion? A trillion?
5. What are some things in our environment of which we could quickly find a million? A billion?
6. Why do you think newspapers use the shortened form of large numbers?
7. Do you think you were living a million minutes ago? Figure this date to an approximate month and year. What about a million seconds ago?

Numbers literally need to be read aloud in the name form when seeing the numeral form. This is not given adequate time in most classrooms. The following activities need to be a part of the classroom throughout the year.

1. See and read the number in its written form and translate it into standard form. Example:
   two trillion, eig... hundred ninety-seven million, **three hundre**... ...illion, sixteen
   Translation i...
   2,897,345,00...
   (*Note:* You d... ...thousands... ...it you DO hav... ...ung to...
2. See the num... ...and or write the name form... ...reading from the above exam...
3. See the number in its exponential form and translate it into its standard military time written or (oral) name forms. Example:
   $$(293 \times 10^6) + (4 \times 10^3) + 58$$
   Translation into standard numeral form is **293,004,058**
   Translation into standard written or (oral) name form is **two hundred ninety-three million, four thousand, fifty-eight**
4. See the standard numeral or written form and write in exponential form—the opposite procedure from the above example.

Video Vignette

Whale Math

Mrs. Shanks' multiage classroom explores relative magnitude of number using a recent field trip to Sea World.

- What techniques does Mrs. Shanks use for clarifying number meanings for her students?
- How does this lesson develop ideas about the relative magnitude of number?
- What mathematical ideas are included?
- How does Mrs. Shanks show respect for students' thinking and promote discourse?

The teen numbers seem to present many problems for some children because they hear the ones digit first and then the tens ("teen"). Many number reversals occur in the teens because on hearing "seventeen," the child writes 7 and then 1. The child might read it back to you as 17, or, given some time away from that number, the name 71 might be given to the number. It is important to have many practice opportunities for modeling the teen numbers.

A word of caution: Never read whole numbers with the word "and" between the hundreds and tens. For example, 259 is read "two hundred fifty-nine" not "two hundred *and* fifty-nine." The word "and" indicates a decimal point in the number separating the whole number from its fractional (decimal) components. We also must be careful to read numbers in complete word form and not simply the single digits. Adults often read multidigit numbers such as 34,528 as "three four five two eight" to be efficient and faster. This method is a better way to read large numbers

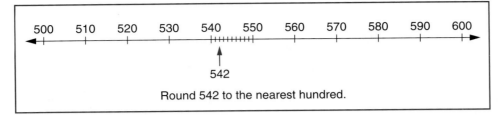

Round 542 to the nearest hundred.

FIGURE 8.10 *Rounding on number line.*

when comparing answers or reading answers from the calculator, but it can be destructive to children who need to read, hear, and interpret numbers with place-value labels. Writing checks is an application of this skill and one that students soon see a need to learn.

As seen in the examples above, when reading large, multidigit numbers, it is important for students to use commas to cluster the periods together. Then it becomes a matter of grouping the digits into groups of three and reading these numbers together followed by the period name (represented by the comma). As stated earlier in this chapter, some groups advocate using a space instead of a comma. However, most elementary textbooks still use the comma. Remember each period contains a group of hundreds, tens, and ones and the numeral form must show the place values for each period. Owens and Sanders (2000) show creative games and whole number naming machines that reinforce numbers through the trillions to be used with middle school students.

The period names also follow a pattern, which is fun to explore and about which students can speculate. Study the period names and see what patterns you notice, reading from left to right:

thousand, million, billion, trillion,

quadrillion, quintillion, sextillion, septillion,

octillion, nonillion, decillion, undecillion,

duodecillion, tredecillion, quattuordecillion.

Rounding   Numeration cannot be taught without considering the importance of rounding skills. Most textbooks begin simple rounding to tens around third grade and may include rounding to hundreds. Generally, rounding is introduced with number lines (Figure 8.10) so students can see the position of the number to be rounded in relation to other numbers (multiples of 10 or 100, and so forth) depending on the place to which the number is being rounded. This visual aid helps children see the relative position of the numbers to each other.

Another effective activity is to give students number lines with only some reference points labeled. The task is more challenging by adding fractions or decimals. This is an example of students using proportional thinking and reasoning to discover the relative position of numbers. Bay-Williams (2001) uses the life-sized number line whenever the goal of a lesson is to develop conceptual understanding. The next step is to do the same on paper as shown in Figure 8.11.

A similar activity is to have points of reference on the number line and have students place other given points on the number line (Figure 8.12). Such experiences encourage students to approach situations in a variety of ways rather than apply "rounding rules." Introducing such rules for rounding often inhibits developing a sense of number relationships.

Many times students do not see a purpose for rounding numbers because the final task is to work the problem using the actual numbers. Unfortunately, teachers often assign problems

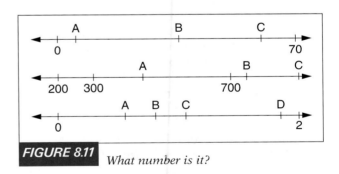

FIGURE 8.11 *What number is it?*

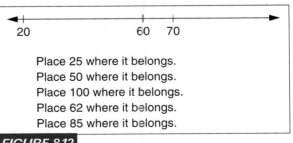

FIGURE 8.12 *Place the number where it belongs.*

to be worked both ways-estimated by rounding and with actual numbers-and this practice causes students to believe that rounding is extra work and does not matter. Estimation is a useful, important skill for determining the reasonableness of your answer, and estimation requires an understanding of rounding. Teachers should assign problems where rounding and estimating are the final answers and full credit is given as a bonafide exercise.

Understanding and Interpreting Decimals

As with whole numbers, reading, writing, and interpreting decimals are important skills. Opportunities should be provided for children to take oral dictation of decimals. It is important to note again that the word "and" is said for the decimal point. It separates the whole units and the parts of wholes. This is why students should read large whole numbers *without* the word "and." It can be emphasized by the following example:

Correct: 645.03—six hundred forty-five and three hundredths

Incorrect: 645.03—six hundred and forty-five and three hundredths

When learning about decimals, students should read the decimal point with the place-value terms (tenths, hundredths, thousandths) rather than as a "point" and the names of the digits. If this requirement is not stressed, students cannot acquire the place-value ideas as quickly, nor will the connection between fractions and decimals be seen as clearly. Modeling helps focus on the size of the number and provides the visual reference needed to correctly record numbers as fractions. After introducing hundredths, the difference between four-tenths and four-hundredths must be called to the students' attention. Confusion may occur when comparing and interpreting the numbers 0.20 and 0.02. Many opportunities with materials with concrete and pictorial materials are necessary for children to internalize the notation and values of decimals.

From students' earlier experiences with fractions, they should know that tenths represent a whole unit partitioned into ten equal parts. Likewise, they need to realize that 10 tenths equal the whole unit (10/10 = 1). In a similar fashion, they should know that if the whole unit is partitioned into one hundred equal parts, 100/100 = 1, each part is 1 out of the 100 or 1/100 (one hundredth).

Activity 8.15

MANIPULATIVES   **MENTAL MATH**

COVER UP GAME AND ADD SOME MORE

DIRECTIONS

Start with a mixed number:

1. Begin with

2. Cover up the decimal fraction

3. Read "and"

4. Read number following decimal point as if it were a whole number

5. Read place-value label of last digit

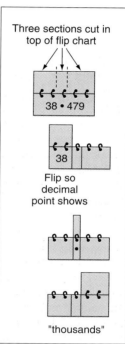

Three sections cut in top of flip chart

38 • 479

38

Flip so decimal point shows

"thousands"

Add the Skill of Mental Math

6. As students practice reading various numbers in the sequence suggested in steps 1 to 5, have them add one more tenth, hundredth, or thousandth to the number and read it again. The procedure could continue while students are waiting in line with a few minutes to spare. They get the needed practice breaking down the parts of the mixed fraction and have a chance to practice mental math at the same time.

Supporting the NCTM *Principles and Standards* (2000):

- Worthwhile Mathematical Tasks; Students' Role in Discourse—The Teaching Principle
- Mathematics as Problem Solving, Reasoning, Communication
- Number Systems and Number Relationships

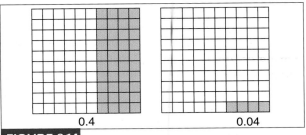

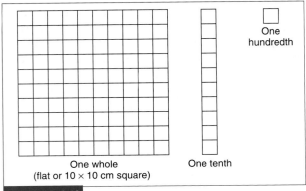
One whole
(flat or 10 × 10 cm square)
One tenth
One hundredth

FIGURE 8.13 *Models for decimals.*

FIGURE 8.14 *Base 10 models for decimal comparisons.*

0.4   0.04

Representing Decimals One of the most common and readily available models for decimals is place-value blocks (base 10 blocks). Another effective model is decimal squares made from chart or graph paper. Here, the unit square is divided into 10 equal parts (longs), and each one represents a tenth. If the unit square is divided into additional equal parts (each tenth is partitioned into 10 equal parts), the overall effect is to divide the unit square into 100 equal parts (Figure 8.13). Provide opportunities for students to practice reading, writing, and representing decimals (Figure 8.14).

An understanding of the place-value interpretation of decimals is a prerequisite to introducing computation with decimals. Students should identify the place-value positions of each digit as well as determine the relationships among the places, such as 10 hundredths equal 1 tenth (Activity 8.17).

Many of the games and activities mentioned earlier in this chapter for whole numbers could be easily adapted for decimal numbers. Materials for Digit Hunt (Activity 8.8) and Place-Value Bingo (on the Web site in Extended Activities) can be created with decimal numbers. Look at the other activities shown in this chapter and think about how these experiences can be modified to use with decimal numbers.

Activity 8.16

MANIPULATIVES **COMPARING DECIMAL NUMBERS**

MATERIALS

- Deck of cards with decimal numbers
- Base 10 blocks

PROCEDURE

1. Have students in groups of two or three members.
2. Each student draws a card, reads the decimal number, and models it with blocks.
3. All students in the group compare and order the numbers from least to greatest.
4. A new set of cards is drawn and these numbers are compared in a similar manner.

    Note: This activity can also be used with the big block representing the basic building unit (one whole) in order to include thousandths.

Activity 8.17

MANIPULATIVES **DIFFERENT WAYS TO REPRESENT DECIMALS**

DIRECTIONS

1. Read decimals like these: 0.4   0.7   0.45   0.758
2. Shade decimal squares to represent the decimals read. (See Figure 8.15.)
3. Model with flats, longs, and units as the decimals are read. (See introduction to the chapter.)
4. Connect with the pictorial level by drawing decimal squares and base 10 blocks for the above examples.
5. Use place-value grids and record each decimal.

Ones	Tenths	Hundredths	Thousands

6. Connect with the symbolic level by writing the two ways to represent decimals— $\frac{4}{10}$ and 0.4.

Comparing Decimals Before handling operations with decimals, students need to explore and understand relationships among decimals by comparing decimals. Again, it is important to provide experiences for modeling the numbers with place-value blocks or with graph paper (decimal squares) as concrete manipulatives.

Activities for comparing decimals should embed concrete proportional materials for modeling the numbers. The quick rule of "add a zero and make the numbers have the same number of digits" presents some confusing information. Such actions are inappropriate to build a sense of the relative size of decimals. Students need to represent numbers using manipulatives to interpret which is larger, such as 0.7 and 0.34. Many students see the two digits in 0.34 and think this represents a greater number than 0.7. However, placing 7 longs (tenths) on the flat (whole) shows 0.7 is closer to one whole than the 3 longs and 4 hundredths placed on the flat. Adapting activities like the one pictured in Figure 8.14 are appropriate for students to compare the meaning of decimals.

Estimation with Decimals Place-value understandings extend into estimation and building intuitions about the relative size of decimal numbers. Students need to explore estimation strategies rather than to be told rules and procedures. NAEP results (NAEP, 2006; 2000) indicate that routinely worded rounding tasks resulted in higher correct responses than nonroutine tasks in less traditional formats. For the nonroutine items fewer than one-fourth of the fourth-grade students and around half the eighth grade students answered correctly.

Extensions of comparing activities could include locating decimal numbers on number lines to see the relative position of the numbers to each other. Look again at Figures 8.11, 8.12, and 8.13 and substitute decimal numbers. Try some of these activities to help develop benchmarks for estimation. Other games listed in the Extended Activities are on the Web site in Chapter 8. The game, Decimal War, on the Web site may be modified by using base 10 blocks or pictorial representations of the decimal numbers.

Understanding and Interpreting Integers

Many textbooks introduce integers with a number line to help students see the relationship of positive and negative numbers to each other. Moving to the right of zero results in positive numbers, and moving to the left of zero results in negative numbers. Some children's card games have a situation in which the player might lose enough points to be "in the hole." This is an opportune time to discuss negative numbers. Another situation that involves the use and interpretation of negative numbers is below zero temperatures. It is important to encourage the correct way to read and write these numbers.

Activity 8.18

MENTAL MATH   **ESTIMATION**   **PLACE THAT DECIMAL!**

MATERIALS
- Deck of cards with decimal numbers
- Yarn, ribbon, or string with end points given such as 0 and 1 or 0.1 and 0.9

PROCEDURE
1. Determine the end points for the number line.
2. Students draw a number card and place the card on the number line where that number should be located.

Activity 8.19

ESTIMATION   **FIND A BENCHMARK**

MATERIALS
- Deck of cards with decimal numbers
- Yarn, ribbon, or string with benchmarks such as 0, 0.5, and 1

PROCEDURE
1. Each student draws a number card.
2. Place the card in relationship to being closer to 0, closer to 0.5, or closer to 1.
3. Use base 10 blocks if needed to see relationship to the whole.

Teaching students the four basic operations with integers is a difficult task. Many students

EXTENDED ACTIVITIES

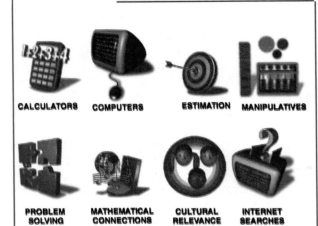

CALCULATORS   COMPUTERS   ESTIMATION   MANIPULATIVES

PROBLEM   MATHEMATICAL   CULTURAL   INTERNET
SOLVING   CONNECTIONS   RELEVANCE   SEARCHES

On the Web site (Chapter 8, Extended Activities), read/do the following:

- Form the Numbers with Expanded Notation Cards
- Decimal War
- Decimal Monopoly
- Links for Operations
- Abacus Action
- Rounding Large Numbers
- Reading Decimal Numbers
- Family Math Packets for Teaching Numeration
- Sample Lesson Plan for Mathematical Proficiency with Numeration
- Get a Charge out of Integers

learn to work problems with integers by memorizing rules such as "negative times a negative is a positive." The rule may not make sense, but it produces correct answers. Physical models are seldom used as teaching devices. A number line model has limitations and only partial explanations.

Postman Stories   When students are introduced to addition and subtraction of integers, one simple, effective approach is to use checks (money received) and bills (money spent). Davis (1967) introduced young children to integers through the "Postman Stories" from the Madison Project. In this setting, checks represent positive numbers and bills represent negative numbers. The action of "bringing" refers to addition and the action of "taking away" refers to subtraction. When the post-

man brings (+) a check, this indicates adding a positive number. When the postman takes away (−) a check, the action is subtracting a positive number. In the case of bringing (+) a bill, the action would be adding a negative number. If the postman takes away a bill, the effect would be to subtract a negative number. The concept emphasizes that when a check is received, we become richer, but when a bill is received, we become poorer. Likewise, if a check must be given up (subtracted), we become poorer. Read the examples in the next activity and try to visualize the possible events that could occur in the postman stories.

Students need to understand that the effect of the postman taking away a check is less money. Some teachers might want to relate this event to turning a paycheck over immediately to someone to whom you owe money so you are not richer as the end result. To help clarify this situation, Davis suggests including a time factor in the imaginary story about the postman. The use of time prevents misconceptions about the mathematical equation that is appropriate for each situation.

If the postman takes away (−) a check (+) for \$5 and takes away (−) another check (+) for \$2, the result would be $-^+5-^+2=^-7$. As a result of the postman's visit, we have less money because two checks were taken away from us.

If the postman takes away (−) a bill (−) for \$5 and takes away (−) a bill (−) for \$2, we would be richer in the end because bills were taken away. In symbols: $-^-5-^-2=^+7$. Again the time factor should be emphasized. We had to give the postman bills, an action that makes us richer in the long run because we had counted on paying those bills and now we do not have to pay them. One method to help children visualize these events is to use play money. When a bill comes for \$7, we set money aside to pay that amount and put the bill with it to remember it. If the postman makes an error (and errors could occur in the same amounts as bills) when we give the postman the bill, we can see the effect of making us richer.

The real challenge comes when trying to teach multiplication and division of integers with understanding. For multiplication, interpretation of the factors is a critical feature of the postman stories. The second factor is the money (bill or check), and the first factor tells how many times the postman brings the item or takes it away. Study these examples:

$^+2 \times ^+3 = ^+6$ The postman brings two checks of \$3 each.

$^+2 \times ^-5 = ^-10$ The postman brings two bills \$5 of each.

$^-3 \times {^+4} = {^-12}$ The postman takes away three checks of $4 each.
Remember—this means we are poorer when we have checks taken away.

$^-2 \times {^-6} = {^+12}$ The postman takes away two bills of $6 each. This is good. We are richer when bills are taken away.

The "Cartoon Corner" in the January 2002 issue of the NCTM Mathematics *Teaching in the Middle School* journal is entitled "Debit or Credit" and features Ziggy dealing with a bank teller. It is similar to the postman story approach.

Many educators suggest using physical models for teaching and representing integers. Dr. Henry Borenson's *Hands-On Equations*® is an example of a physical model for presenting essential algebraic concepts including positive and negative integers. The positive–negative charge model extends to the four operations illustrates how the model can show properties of the system of integers. Some of the more difficult concepts are covered in "Get a Charge out of Integers" (Extended Activities on the Web site). Other children's literature books are included in the end-of-chapter bibliography.

Bay-Williams (2002) present several models to teach addition and subtraction of integers: number line, play money (a technique that is similar to the postman stories), and color-block technique that uses negative and positive blocks. The articles outline the teaching strategies for all three approaches in a clear, concise manner.

Students in the middle grades need concrete materials and games to reinforce concepts as much as children in lower grades. The middle grade teacher may be more reluctant to use this technique, but it has been proven effective for all grades. Games with the football field or the thermometer provide scenarios to help visualize the computation with signed numbers. Teaching operations with integers is an opportune time to challenge students to apply their prior experiences in new situations.

ASSESSMENT TO HELP STUDENTS WITH SPECIAL NEEDS

Correcting Common Misconceptions

Many of the manipulative materials shown in the chapter can be used to help students when misconceptions occur. Several teaching ideas to avert misconceptions were discussed earlier in the chapter, especially those ideas dealing with interpreting larger numbers and decimals. Further ideas are developed for whole numbers and decimals in this section.

Whole Number Numeration One common error is that children write too many zeros in the number because they are relating to the number words. For example, two hundred forty-five is written as "20045." The first three digits are recorded for the 200 and then the 45. The remediation technique to use is to ask the child to model the number with base 10 blocks. Additional experiences with the place-value strips seen earlier in the chapter (Activity 8.9) also would be a valuable connecting level experience. Special-needs students need oral activities to build the language connection.

Another error is developmental in nature—when children do not conserve volume as mentioned previously. Because many children who do not conserve volume consider the thousand block as "600," it may be wise to construct 1,000 using 10 flats (hundreds blocks). Students with special needs can easily remove a layer at a time to recall there are more units inside that need to be counted. When they mistake 1,000 for 600, let them count by 100s to 1,000 to see that there are more blocks than 600.

Another common error in writing numerals is just the opposite problem—not using zeros as place holders in numerals where needed. In this case, because the child does not hear or read any numbers for that place value, it is simply ignored. For example, in the number "three thousand fourteen," the child would write "3,14." Again concrete models such as base 10 blocks with a place value mat or spiked abacus (Figure 8.15) help to visualize all place-value positions to know where zeros are needed as place holders.

Decimals *Nonalignment of the Decimal Points* Students are used to writing numerals from left to right, and some students proceed to write the decimals in the same manner as in the example on the left below. Students need practice transferring decimals written in the horizontal form to the

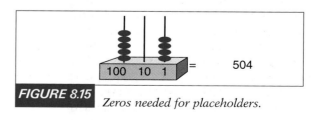

FIGURE 8.15 *Zeros needed for placeholders.*

vertical form. A teaching method to mark the decimal point is as follows:
Add: 235.06 + 41.25 + 9.345 = ?

$$
\begin{array}{c}
\downarrow \\
235.06 \quad \cdot \\
4.25 \quad \cdot \\
9.345 \quad \cdot
\end{array}
$$

| Ask students to place an arrow above the decimal points, marking the points before writing any numerals. |

Attention to Decimal Point as Place Holder   Some students, when faced with a number like .529, totally disregard the decimal point, treating .529 as if it were a whole number. We have already stressed the importance of writing such decimals as 0.529 to emphasize that 0.529 is a part of a whole. Calculators also reinforce this approach because every decimal without a whole number is automatically recorded with the zero as a place holder whether the child enters it that way or not. Perhaps students with special needs should be encouraged to use the calculator and then connect that number to place-value materials.

Annexing Zeroes   Some students see 0.500 as greater than 0.50 and 0.50 as greater than 0.5. They do not understand that annexing zeroes to the right of a decimal does *not* change the value of the decimal. Students must work with concrete manipulatives as shown in the teaching strategies section of fractions in Chapter 10. Some students with special needs will need many experiences representing decimals to see numerical relationships, although other students see the pattern after a few times. Let students use the concrete materials as long as needed, using a place-value chart for decimals.

Name Value Confused with Place Value   Just as young children become confused with the name forty-seven and write the numeral as 407, when students learning decimals hear such name values as "eight hundredths" or "fifty-two thousandths," they write:

0.800   or   0.80 (if they remember that hundredths has only two decimal places)
0.5200   or   0.520 (if they remember that thousandths has only three decimal places)

Writing the numeral on a place-value chart helps if students have a folder with the rule written out to the side, as in the following example rule:

1. Find the place that corresponds with the word you are saying.
2. Start writing the number there, moving from right to left.

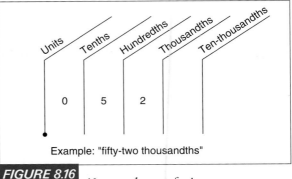

FIGURE 8.16 *Name value confusion.*

3. Fill in any 0s you need to get to the decimal point.

See example in Figure 8.16.

Field-Dependent Learners

Students who process information simultaneously (from the whole to the part) frequently do well with activities such as the computer spreadsheet model in which the table changes all at once when

---

Activity 8.20

PORTFOLIO   **PORTFOLIO ASSESSMENTS**

FOR TEACHER REFLECTION OF STUDENTS' WORK IN NUMERATION AND NUMBER SENSE

One important aspect of numeration and number sense is to understand the variety of equivalent forms of numbers and the multiple relationships among numbers. Look at these three examples of student's work on the next page and analyze what each child understands.

Develop a rubric that you could apply to assess this aspect of numeration.

What are the next steps you would do for continuing each student's progress? What else would you like to know about each child?

Child work on next page.

| **Supporting the NCTM *Principles and Standards* (2000):**
• Worthwhile Mathematical Tasks—The Teaching Principle
• The Assessment Principle |

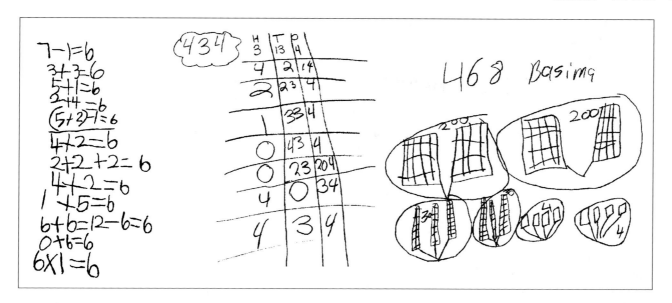

a number is generated. They can analyze patterns from the whole table seen simultaneously. They also perform well with materials like the place-value strips because everything is already there and just needs to be folded from the expanded notation to the compact form. The base 10 blocks can be used successfully in such activities as "trading down," where the base numbers are exchanged from a large set of base 10 blocks already assembled.

Field-Independent Learners

Students who process information successively (from the parts to the whole) frequently benefit from the use of the abacus and chip trading activities (on the Web site) because both materials require a detailed buildup of the place values from ones to tens to hundreds and so on. Such students may be more comfortable with computer software programs that allow students progress from one number to the next. The base 10 blocks can be used successfully, especially in activities like "trading up," where the student builds large numbers from exchanging smaller place-value units to make larger and larger numbers from the smaller blocks.

If materials like place-value strips are used, consider pairing a field-independent learner with a field-dependent learner. It is a cooperative learning effort in which both students can learn from watching the other if they talk about what they are doing as they work.

PUTTING IT ALL TOGETHER WITH REAL STUDENT WORK

Try applying what you have learned in this chapter to analyze the work of the three students in Activity 8.20. Pick one student and do a more detailed analysis and plan for relearning by following the assessment form seen in Chapter 3 (Figure 3.23). This can become an important part of a professional portfolio to show you can have a positive effect on student learning.

SUMMARY

- Early concepts of numeration and number sense develop gradually through understanding numbers in concrete, physical situations.

- Middle schoolers need to realize the power of numeration to be the intergalactic language by which all intelligent beings can communicate.

- Intuition about number relationships helps children decide about the reasonableness of computational answers in the early and intermediate elementary grades.

- Understanding place value is a crucial link to acquiring number sense.

- As number relationships are developed, students acquire an understanding of the relative magnitude of numbers.

- Number systems in any base have a definite structure that allows students to predict the next number.

- Decimal understandings need to be developed by many concrete and pictorial representations so students do not confuse decimal notation with whole number notation.

- Exponential, scientific, and calculator notations are used frequently in the twenty-first century and must be understood by students.

This requires more than the brief pages given to this knowledge in middle school textbooks.

- Common misconceptions when working with decimals include nonalignment of the decimal points, annexing zeroes, and attention to decimal points as place holders.

- There are specific ways to help children correct misconceptions of numeration and number sense.

PRAXIS II™-STYLE QUESTIONS

Answers to this chapter's Praxis II™-style questions are in the instructor's manual.

Multiple Choice Format

1. This number 471,000,000,495,000 is read as:

   a. four hundred seventy-one quadrillion four hundred ninety thousand

   b. four hundred seventy-one trillion four hundred ninety thousand

   c. four hundred seventy-one trillion and four hundred ninety-five thousand

   d. None of the above

2. The _____ were the first people to invent a symbol for ten and one hundred. They are the ancestors of the _____ children in our classrooms.

   a. Chinese; Asian American

   b. Mayans; Hispanic (Latino) American and Native American

   c. Egyptians; African American

   d. Greeks; European American

3. Analyze the materials seen in Figure 8.17. Place them in the correct order for teaching a new concept of numeration to children starting with the most proportional to the most nonproportional models.

   a. 1, 2, 3, 4, 5

   b. 2, 4, 3, 5, 1

   c. 4, 2, 3, 5, 1

   d. 4, 3, 2, 1, 5

4. The number 0.00075 is represented in scientific notation as:

   a. 7.5×10^{-3}

   b. 7.5×10^{-4}

   c. 75×100

   d. 0.75×10^{-3}

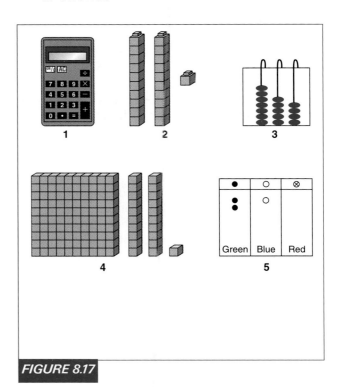

FIGURE 8.17

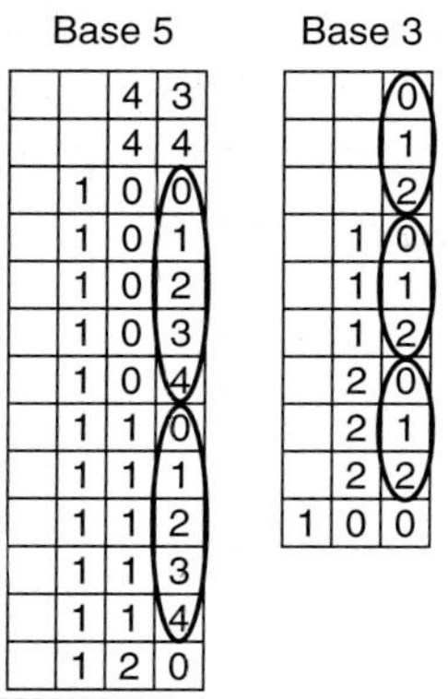

	Base 5			Base 3	
	4	3			0
	4	4			1
1	0	0			2
1	0	1		1	0
1	0	2		1	1
1	0	3		1	2
1	0	4		2	0
1	1	0		2	1
1	1	1		2	2
1	1	2	1	0	0
1	1	3			
1	1	4			
1	2	0			

FIGURE 8.18

Constructed Response Format

6. Give an assessment score, following the assessment score guide in Chapter 3, for each student's understanding of estimation. Justify your answers.

Student A	Student B	Student C
I could estimate 389 plus 432 to be 821.	This problem says 501 plus 213. Each is more than 500 + 200 so the answer is more than 700. So I will estimate 800.	16 + 24 + 32 can be estimated to about 24 because it is right in the middle.

7. Student B in the preceding example needs to be taught which concept is the next.

8. This activity is similar to the one in the chapter. A middle school student was learning about different number bases; the student drew the configurations in Figure 8.19 to represent whole numbers (no decimals) and wrote the numeral it represented correctly: Write the numeral as the student would have done. Also remember to indicate the base.

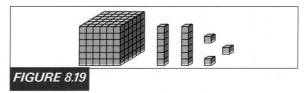

FIGURE 8.19

5. A student is doing the odometer activity adapted for middle school work with different bases. The student is creating her own base strip, working from an example like the one in Figure 8.18. The student picks any number to start with and builds on to the base counting by one unit at a time. If the student writes 666 and then immediately follows with 1,000, we can say that the student has created an odometer strip:

a. in the base six number system

b. that counts to the fourth kind of regrouping

c. in the base seven number system

d. Both a and b

Integrating Technology

Internet Activities

WebQuest

"A Creative Encounter of the Numerical Kind" is a WebQuest for middle school math students. It can be found at **http://studenthome.nku.edu/~webquest/gabbard**

Web sites

Go to the following Web sites and review the activities for the age level indicated.

http://www.edbydesign.com/kidsact.html—for young children to regroup ones to sets of tens and ones.

http://www.nctm.org/resources/elementary.aspx—for younger children. Look for the CFP (*Curriculum Focal Points*) related resources.

http://www.nctm.org/illresources/middle.aspx?id=7860—for middle schoolers. Look for illuminations activities that involve mathematical strategies based on the number system and magnitude of number.

http://nlvmousu.edu/eu/nav/index.html—for students to work with virtual manipulatives in different number bases of 10, 5, 4, 3, and 2.

NAEP site—to see sample test questions dealing with the topics in this chapter

http://www.nces.ed.gov/nationsreportcard/mathematics

Voyager site—to learn more about the space probe and the different base systems going out into space

http://voyager.jpl.nasa.gov

CHILDREN'S LITERATURE

Books for numeration are in two categories: counting books for numbers to ten and counting larger numbers or place value concepts. Counting books to ten are quite popular and plentiful. Check references in chapters 7 and 9 and on the CD for this type of book. Some appealing counting books exploring number patterns, decade numbers, and other number systems are:

Howard, Katherine. *I Can Count to One Hundred . . . Can You?* New York: Random Books, 1979.

St. John, Glory. *How to Count Like a Martian*. New York: Henry Z. Walck, 1975.

Sloat, Teri. *From One to One Hundred*. New York: Dutton Children's Books, 1991.

Pinczes, Elinor J. *One Hundred Hungry Ants*. Boston: Houghton Mifflin Co., 1993.

Geisert, Arthur. *Roman Numerals I to MM*. Boston: Houghton Mifflin Co., 1996.

Books with stories involving big numbers provide children with a sense of the relative magnitude of numbers. Besides the two books by David Schwartz discussed earlier, these stories fascinate children:

Lottridge, Celia Barber. *One Watermelon Seed*. New York: Oxford University Press, 1990.

Schwartz, David M. *How Much Is a Million?* New York: Lothrop Lee & Shepherd, 1985.

Schwartz, David M. *If You Made a Million?* New York: Zothrop Lee & Shepherd, 1989.

Friedman, Aileen, *The King's Commissioners*. New York: Scholastic, 1995.

Schwartz, David M. *G is for Googal: A Math Alphabet Book*. Berkeley, CA: Tricycle Press, 1998.

Birch, David. *The King's Chessboard*. New York: Dial Books, 1988.

Adler, Irving. *Integers:Positive and Negative: The Reason Why Books*. New York: John Day, 1972.

Barry, David. *The Rajah's Rice: A Mathematical Folktale from India*. New York: Scientific American Books for Young Readers, 1994.

Operations with Whole Numbers

At the Start ~~~~ Know What Children Will Be Doing . . .

NCTM Curriculum Focal Points—   See . . .

Grade 2 ~~ Developing quick recall of addition facts and related subtraction facts and fluency with multidigit addition and subtraction   Activity 9.15
Activity 9.16; 9.17

Grade 4 ~~ Developing quick recall of multiplication facts and related division facts and fluency with whole number multiplication and division   Activity 9.18

Grade 5 ~~ Developing an understanding of and fluency with division of whole numbers   Activity 9.20

A partial listing as it pertains to Number and Operations and Algebra from NCTM *Curriculum Focal Points* (2006, pages 14; 16–17).

WHERE'S THE MATHEMATICS? THE STRUCTURE OF ALGORITHMIC THINKING FOR COMPUTATIONAL FLUENCY AND FLEXIBILITY

How to Be An Algorithm

Be a big number with many digits,
Use with other multi-digit numbers,
Operate by adding, subtracting, multiplying and dividing,
Always regroup wherever you see ten sets of any number in any digit,
Always do the same thing—
Step by step . . . Every time the same way.

—Written by a Fourth Grader
Based on *Write-Traits* "How to" Poems in Writing

Development of Algorithms and Algorithmic Thinking

As the fourth grader's poem implies, an *algorithm* is a set of rules for solving a problem, a step-by-step sequence, a method that continually repeats some basic process. This chapter covers the algorithms for the addition, subtraction, multiplication, and division of multidigit numbers. These numbers, containing two or more place values, go beyond the basic facts, which are the combinations of single-digit numbers. Algorithms are efficient ways of incorporating the basic facts into larger, multidigit numbers.

Algorithmic thinking is the thought processing necessary to achieve solutions to problems in efficient ways that involve step-by-step sequences or repetitions of some basic processes. Algorithmic thinking requires application of what has been learned in number sense and number systems from the student's past experiences.

Student Readiness for Algorithmic Thinking The basic facts, number properties, and place-value concepts are applied in the computational skills required to work with algorithms. Therefore, young

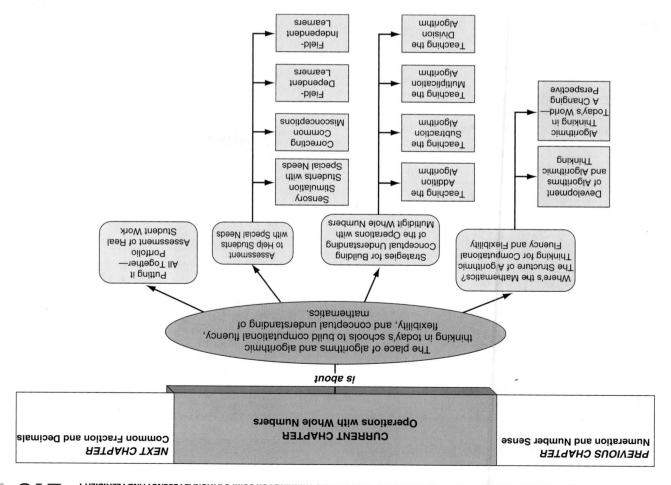

PREVIOUS CHAPTER
Numeration and Number Sense

CURRENT CHAPTER
Operations with Whole Numbers

NEXT CHAPTER
Common Fraction and Decimals

is about

The place of algorithms and algorithmic thinking in today's schools to build computational fluency, flexibility, and conceptual understanding of mathematics.

Where's the Mathematics? The Structure of Algorithmic Thinking for Computational Fluency and Flexibility
- Development of Algorithms and Algorithmic Thinking
- Algorithmic Thinking in Today's World—A Changing Perspective

Strategies for Building Conceptual Understanding of the Operations with Multidigit Whole Numbers
- Teaching the Addition Algorithm
- Teaching the Subtraction Algorithm
- Teaching the Multiplication Algorithm
- Teaching the Division Algorithm

Assessment to Help Students with Special Needs
- Sensory Stimulation Students with Special Needs
- Correcting Common Misconceptions
- Field-Dependent Learners
- Field-Independent Learners

Putting it All Together—Portfolio Assessment of Real Student Work

SELF-HELP QUESTIONS

1. What are the differences in terminology among student self-invented algorithms, alternative algorithms, and traditional algorithms?

2. What are the algorithms that make the most sense to children as they first learn to work with multidigit whole number operations?

3. How can I help my students bridge the gap between their own invented algorithms and the corresponding alternative algorithms?

4. How can I help my students learn the most appropriate times to use estimation, technology, and paper and pencil computation?

5. How can I assess my students' misconceptions in calculating and help them become computationally fluent and flexible?

students must have well-developed concepts of number (Chapter 6), know basic facts and number properties (Chapter 7), and have a solid understanding of place-value concepts (Chapter 8) *before* they are introduced to algorithms. Work with algorithms should proceed *only* when children have a firm foundation in these concepts.

Review Chapters 6, 7, and 8 for help remembering teaching aspects for these topics. Figure 9.1 shows the grade-level expectations recommended in the NCTM *Principle and Standards* (2000).

Exploratory experiences with the various interpretations of the operations (i.e., arrays, combinations, and repeated groups for multiplication)

develop meaning for discussing a variety of pro-blem situations when using the algorithm in every-day life. Place-value concepts incorporate trading and grouping with materials to understand the base 10 numeration system—a necessary prere-quisite to teach algorithms for the four operations. Students must have this basic foundation to build meaning for the algorithms.

Role of Algorithmic Thinking in Schools The NCTM 1998 yearbook, *The Teaching and Learning of Algorithms in School Mathematics* (Morrow and Kenney, 1998), presents many issues and ques-tions regarding the role of algorithms in today's mathematics curriculum. Topics include assess-ment of algorithms, the history of algorithms, alternative algorithms, and investigations of algo-rithms from addition to fractals. Carroll and Porter (1998) discuss the pros and cons of teaching specific algorithms. They list these points for teaching algorithms: written algorithms are needed for larger numbers; parents and adults see competence in computation as a measure of mathematical success; students benefit from hav-ing a range of computational options, including paper-and-pencil methods; and societal expecta-tions make written methods for computation necessary, including a computation section on standardized tests.

Elementary textbooks devote a great amount of time to the development of algorithms. Usually a textbook will present only one algorithm for each opera-tion. Teaching one algorithm for an opera-tion fails to consider the students' knowledge of

---

FIGURE 9.1 *NCTM expectation of operations with whole numbers. A partial listing as it pertains to Operations and Number Sense from NCTM* Principles and Standards for School Mathematics *(2000, pages 392-393).*

STANDARD

Instructional programs from prekindergarten through grade 12 should enable all students to

- Understand multidigit numbers, ways of represent-ing multidigit numbers, relationships among num-bers.
- Understand meanings of operations and how they relate to one another with multidigit numbers.
- Compute fluently and make reasonable estimates.

GRADES PREK TO 2

In prekindergarten through grade 2 all students should

- Develop a sense of whole numbers and represent and use them in flexible ways, including relating, com-posing, and decomposing numbers.
- Connect number words and numerals to the quanti-ties they represent, using various physical models and representations.
- Understand the effects of adding and subtracting whole numbers.
- Develop and use strategies for whole number compu-tations, with a focus on addition and subtraction.
- Use a variety of methods and tools to compute, including objects, mental computation, estima-tion, paper and pencil, and calculators.

GRADES 3 TO 5

In grades 3 to 5 all students should

- Recognize equivalent representations for the same number and generate them by decomposing and composing numbers.

- Understand the effects of multiplying and dividing whole numbers.
- Understand and use properties of operations, such as the distributivity of multiplication over addition.
- Develop fluency with basic number combinations for multiplication and division and use these combi-nations to mentally compute related problems, such as 30 × 50.
- Develop and use strategies to estimate the results of whole number computations and to judge the rea-sonableness of such results.
- Select appropriate methods and tools for computing with whole numbers from among mental compu-tation, estimation, calculators, and paper and pencil according to the context and nature of the computation and use the selected method or tool.

GRADES 6 TO 8

In grades 6 to 8 all students should

- Understand and use the inverse relationships of addi-tion and subtraction, multiplication and division.
- Develop meaning for integers and represent and com-pare quantities with them.
- Understand the meaning and effects of arithmetic operations with integers.
- Use the associative and commutative properties of addition and multiplication, and the distributive property of multiplication over addition to simplify computations with integers.
- Develop and analyze algorithms for computing with integers and develop fluency in their use.

place value, thinking strategies, and number relationships. As you read this chapter, you will encounter many of the issues facing teachers in the teaching and learning of mathematics. In the United States, we have maintained basically the same instructional approach to mathematics for over a hundred years. The traditional mathematics teaching emphasizes teaching procedures, especially computational procedures or algorithms. Current research is challenging the "one algorithm fits all" method of direct instruction. There are new ways to achieve algorithmic thinking that results in higher test scores and greater computational flexibility and fluency. These are presented in the teaching strategies section of this chapter.

Algorithmic Thinking in Today's World— A Changing Perspective

A large percentage of teaching time is spent on the algorithms for whole numbers. When we consider the impact and availability of calculators now, plus the increased use expected in the future, can we remain content to devote so much instructional time to the algorithms? Many of our present-day pencil-and-paper algorithms were developed over 500 years ago and yet remain a stable component of the mathematics curriculum. Perhaps we need to consider some arguments for teaching algorithms to students. Some people look to their own past experiences and say, "that's the way it's always been done." They were taught with rules and procedures and they are successful adults, so why change? Some parents, educators, and members of the general public think that learning the basic skills of arithmetic should be teacher-directive steps for the procedures. Students need a standard routine that works for numbers and when properly executed will produce accurate computations. Time is saved when students are "given" the direct, efficient method for written calculations. Yet, in everyday life, we *do* use alternative mental computations. Many adults think about the numbers and mentally compute in a variety of ways rather than use the standard algorithm. For example, double 38. Take a moment right now and mentally calculate this problem. Did you close your eyes and picture $38 + 38 = 8 + 8 = 16$, "carry the ten" then add $3 + 3 + 1$ to get 7, so 76? Or did you use some alternative strategy such as $40 + 40 = 80 - 4 = 76$? Or did you say $38 + 30 = 68$, then add 8 more and get 76? Many adults perform mental computations that are flexible and consider number and place-value relationships.

Some investigators contend that teaching algorithms conflicts with how children naturally approach computational situations. Kilpatrick, Swafford, and Findell (2001) report that on their own, children would universally begin adding from left to right. Carraher and associates (Carraher et al., 1985) studied the mathematics used by Brazilian children selling in the streets and found that children who used their own procedures made fewer errors than those using written algorithms. Researchers (Fuson, 2003; Pesek and Kirshner, 2000) conclude that once children are taught formal written algorithms, they lose conceptual knowledge and their development of numerical reasoning is hindered.

Promoting Student-Invented Strategies and Alternative Algorithms The NCTM *Principles and Standards* (2000) support the idea of allowing students to invent their own strategies for computing with large numbers. Many articles in the journals, *Teaching Children Mathematics* and *Mathematics Teaching in the Middle School*, show the rich conceptual understandings of students who invent their own strategies. Several projects designed to support children's mathematical thinking and the creation of alternative strategies for problem solving provide rich frameworks for thinking about mathematics instruction. Three such projects are Cognitively Guided Instruction (Fennema et al., 1996), Project IMPACT (Campbell, 1997), and Everyday Mathematics (UCSMP, 2001). For a more complete discussion, Fuson (2003) provides a comprehensive analysis of children's invented strategies for solving problems and describes several of the projects mentioned here. The projects advocate following student-invented strategies with compatible alternative algorithms that closely match their own invented strategies.

Alternative algorithms are defined as step-by-step sequences and procedures to solve problems different from the traditional algorithms taught in U.S. schools over the past hundred years. There is no end to the many alternative algorithms that can be used. There is no one right way to solve multi-digit problems. In fact, there are many algorithms that have been developed over time for each operation. Figure 9.2 shows addition examples from an 1892 and a 1909 textbook.

Examples for the other operations from textbooks ranging from 1848 to 1930 can be found in the Extended Activities, "Alternative Algorithms," on the Web site. As a teacher, you may need to show some of these algorithms to parents to convince them that alternative algorithms have been successful in the lives of others in the past. The idea of teaching their children a different way to do things is a scary proposition for some parents. They will want to know that there is sound

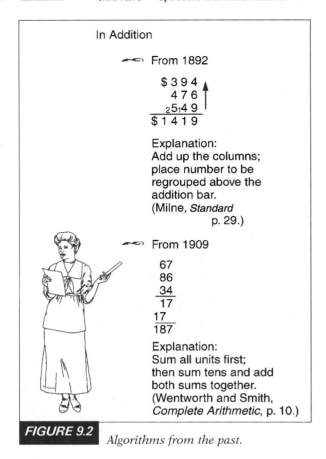

In Addition

⟜ From 1892

$$\begin{array}{r} \$394 \\ 476 \\ \underline{{}_25_14\ 9} \\ \$1419 \end{array}$$

Explanation:
Add up the columns;
place number to be
regrouped above the
addition bar.
(Milne, *Standard*
p. 29.)

⟜ From 1909

$$\begin{array}{r} 67 \\ 86 \\ \underline{34} \\ 17 \\ \underline{17} \\ 187 \end{array}$$

Explanation:
Sum all units first;
then sum tens and add
both sums together.
(Wentworth and Smith,
Complete Arithmetic, p. 10.)

FIGURE 9.2 *Algorithms from the past.*

reasoning behind your instructional program. A compilation of longitudinal and current research studies (Fuson, 2003) shows that students score higher on standardized achievement tests when allowed to use their own invented strategies first with follow-up using compatible alternative algorithms in formal instruction. These research findings are compelling and very important because they dispel the fear many people have had that students would not do well on the high-stakes testing if taught a new way.

Other mathematics educators (Burns, 2007, 1994; Kamii et al., 1993) suggest that teaching specific algorithms should be delayed in the early primary school curriculum so children can become more aware of what it means to think mathematically. The standard algorithms may be unclear to the students who learn them in meaningless ways. The notion of "ours is not to reason why, just invert and multiply" implies that these procedures will produce correct answers, so just do it! When there is a breakdown in the procedure, the child is left feeling helpless and insecure. Student-invented algorithms reflect their natural thinking and are based on their interpretations of the problem. When students develop their own

procedures for solving problems, they naturally incorporate more aspects of place value and less mindless procedures such as "carry the one." They show greater computational flexibility and the ability to solve a problem in a different way if the first way does not seem feasible, and make less errors (Randolph and Sherman, 2001). This may be one reason that test scores are on the rise. Students are not intimidated when they see problems that they have not directly experienced previously.

Importance of Appropriate Models A study of the research findings has led Fuson (2003), Thompson and Saldanha (2003), and Gravemeijer and Galen (2003) to conclude that when students are not successful in using algorithms, there is almost always a lack of concrete or pictorial modeling of the problem situation to some degree. Just using manipulative models does not guarantee a link to understanding, but careful selection of appropriate models to fit students' invented algorithms most assuredly helps in the beginning stages of learning new concepts.

The progression of concrete experiences to pictorial connecting modes to the symbolic (abstract) stage still holds as the teaching progression teachers need to follow as already discussed in Chapter 3 and subsequent content chapters in the text. When to use mental computation, estimation, and calculators as models in algorithmic thinking are also important decisions that teachers need to make. They are discussed in this section.

Concrete/Pictorial Models—Proportional versus Non-proportional Some algorithmic models are proportional in the sense that the concrete and pictorial models are based on the *structure* of the numeration system seen in Chapter 8. Every original unit in a problem is clearly seen as the unit is regrouped to a larger and larger place value. Some algorithmic models are nonproportional in the sense that the concrete and pictorial models do not account for every original unit as it is regrouped to larger place values. The inclusion of every original unit into the next larger place value is assumed but not clearly visible. Examples of proportional and nonproportional models are shown in Figures 9.3 and 9.4, respectively. They are presented throughout this chapter to show how such models work with the regrouping of multidigit numbers.

You will see many different algorithms as you proceed through the chapter—some representational and some nonrepresentational. *Representational models* show the regouping strategy that

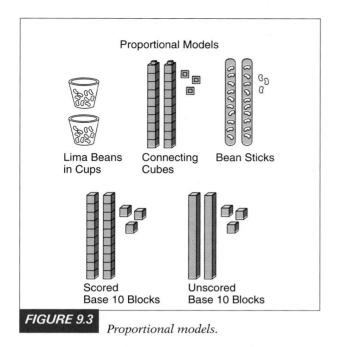

FIGURE 9.3 *Proportional models.*

Check

YOUR MATHEMATICS KNOWLEDGE

On Representational Models
On the Web site (Chapter 9 Check Your Mathematical Knowledge), read/do the following:

On Operations with Whole Numbers
- Distributive Property
- Associative Property and Expanded Notation
- Commutative Property
- Patterns with Multiples

   . . . a refresher from mathematics coursework . . . Lest you forget!

occurs between powers of 10 represented by the place value of numerals. The base 10 blocks are an example of a proportional, representational model, whereas the stylized number line seen in the subtraction section of the teaching strategies is nonproportional and nonrepresentational. If you need more examples of these models, go to the "Representational Models" in the Check Your Mathematics Knowledge in Chapter 9 on the Web site. Check Your Mathematics Knowledge

also contains a refresher on other concepts that will help your background understanding for the work in this chapter. These are concepts you have studied in mathematics content courses in the past.

Mental Computation Models Computation can also be considered as mental computation. Mental computation involves the use of number sense, alternative algorithms, and mentally regrouping numbers into "friendly numbers." It encourages students to look at different ways to solve a problem and should be developed and rewarded. Research (Kilpatrick and Swafford, 2002) indicates that students who use mental computation appear to have a better understanding of place value, number decomposition, order of operations, and number properties.

Children need encouragement to use flexible computing strategies rather than the typical step-by-step algorithm. Devise activities that promote mental computation such as those shown here. Remember there is *no* one way to mentally compute. Children need to share their strategies and compare approaches. When teachers stress the importance of using a variety of patterns for computation, children feel encouraged to seek inventive ways to compute. When numbers are put into context with real-world settings, applications can be seen. In Activity 9.1, "I Have" is an exciting circular game that involves children in mental computation and emphasizes listening skills.

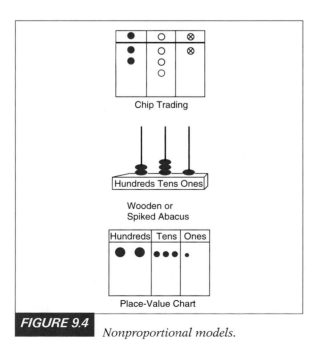

FIGURE 9.4 *Nonproportional models.*

Activity 9.1

MENTAL MATH "I HAVE . . . "

MATERIALS
- Prepared problem cards where one gives the answer to the next card

DIRECTIONS
Distribute the cards to the students. Have them listen carefully to each classmate read the problem card and respond if he or she has the answer card. Then read the problem on the card.

Sample Set
I have   5, who has 3 times as much?
I have   15, who has this much plus 3?
I have   18, who has this divided by 3?
I have   6, who has half of this?
I have   3, who has this times 7 plus 2?
I have   23, who has this plus the next even number?
I have   24, who has this minus 12?
I have   12, who has this minus −7?
I have   5—the beginning place

The game can be varied to accommodate grade and ability levels such as including fractions, decimals, percentages, and exponents. Teachers can substitute some interesting vocabulary terms in place of a number, such as, "Add the number of degrees in a right angle," or "Divide by the number of sides on a pentagon."

A variation of this game is to give children the number tiles 0 to 9 (or digit cards) and give a long string of mental computation, and at the end say, "Show me." Children take the number tiles to form the final answer. This individual response provides a quick assessment for the teacher and involves all children in showing the answer. If you see that several children are not following the sequence, throw in a multiplication by zero and "wipe out" or start over in a subtle way. Keep the pace going about the same and remember no pencils are allowed! Try one now. How much is 3 × 9, + 5, ÷ 4, − 2, square this number, + 4, × 8? Activity 9.2 shows how the Russian culture develops much of the same ideas using mental computation with number sense.

Notice that the "I Have" game begins with basic fact combinations and subtly moves to multidigit numbers. The same is true for Activities 9.3 and 9.4.

Activity 9.2

CULTURAL RELEVANCE **NUMBER SENSE—FROM THE RUSSIAN PERSPECTIVE**

These are number sense examples that appear in Russian textbooks. Make up some grade-appropriate problems based on them.

1. If you know that $126 + 35 = 161$, what is $161 − 26$? Explain your thinking.
2. A two-digit number minus 10 is a one-digit number. What could the two-digit number be?
3. Count from 6 to 27 and leave out the numbers that are divisible by 3.
4. Think up a number that 8 can be subtracted from 5 times.
5. Can 20 be expressed as the sum of two even numbers? Can 21 be expressed as the sum of two odd numbers? Explain your thinking and what other number can be substituted.

Activity 9.3

MENTAL MATH **USE THOSE FOURS!**

DIRECTIONS
You must use all four 4's to create number sentences to form the numbers from 0 to 10 as the answer. You may use all four operations and may use the same operation more than once. Even exponents and decimal numbers are allowed, but not necessary. For example (but you must make your own sentence for this number too!):

$0 = 4 \times 4 \div 4 − 4$
0 = _____   1 = _____
2 = _____   3 = _____
4 = _____   5 = _____
6 = _____   7 = _____
8 = _____   9 = _____
10 = _____   Make more!

As students use simple mental computations with growing ease, they can be led to more complex thinking as seen in Activity 9.5. There are a variety of mental computation strategies including breaking numbers into parts using the distributive property, compensation, dropping common zeroes, finding compatible numbers, and annexing zeroes. The strategies vary with the operation(s) involved. Notice in these activities how the principles of the operations are used.

Estimation Models   Mental computation is often used for determining estimated answers. Estimation provides a "ballpark guess" about a reasonable answer. Estimation provides a check to determine if the result is reasonable. Children should develop good estimation skills for their own sake, not to simply estimate and then compute a page of problems. The purpose for estimating should be rewarded rather than viewed as an extra step. The activity "Estimation Detectives" (Activity 9.6) provides a reward for being good estimators. Decisions can be made on the basis of the answers produced by estimation.

Activity 9.4

MENTAL MATH   **FILL IT UP**

Two to four players

MATERIALS

- Playing board per player
- Two regular number cubes (dice)
- Game markers (beans, clips, and so on)

DIRECTIONS

Players take turns and roll the cubes and may add, subtract, multiply, or divide the two numbers on top faces. If player gives correct answer, a marker may be placed on the number named as the answer. If player cannot make a number equation to cover a number, play goes to next player. Winner is the first player to cover all the numbers on his or her board.

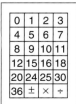

0	1	2	3
4	5	6	7
8	9	10	11
12	15	16	18
20	24	25	30
36	±	×	÷

Activity 9.5

MENTAL MATH   **USE YOUR HEAD AND LET'S COMPUTE!**

BREAK NUMBERS APART (DISTRIBUTIVE PROPERTY)

Hays traveled an average of 325 miles a day for 6 days. What is the total number of miles they traveled?

Think: 325×6 as $300 \times 6 + 25 \times 6$

COMPENSATION

What is the total of items priced $4.98 and $7.95?

Think: $\$4.98 + 2 = \$5.00$ and $\$7.95 + 5 = \$8.00$, so $\$5 + \$8 = \$13$, but count back $7 = \$12.93$.

COMPATIBLE NUMBERS

Jim has 25 cases of candy bars with 24 bars in each case. How many candy bars?

Think: $24 \times 25 = 6 \times 4 \times 25$, so

$4 \times 25 = 100 \times 6 = 600$

DROPPING ZEROES

Alisha needed to find the number of minutes there are in 5400 seconds.

Think: $5400 \div 60 =$ Cancel the common zeroes

(that's like dividing both by 10) so $540 \div 6 = 90$

ANNEXING ZEROES

Basima measured 34 meters on the playground. Her teacher asked her how many centimeters this would be.

Think: 34×100 means to annex or "stick on" two

more zeroes or 3400

Supporting the NCTM *Principles and Standards* (2000):

- Numbers and Estimation; Relationships; Reasoning
- The Learning Principle

Be sure you do not fall prey to the "best estimate" mentality. Often children get so locked into the "one right way" philosophy that they will ask "who had the best estimate?" Students cannot believe the teacher is really looking for a nonexact

Activity 9.6

ESTIMATION **ESTIMATION DETECTIVES**

DIRECTIONS

Look at this page of problems. Estimate the quotient for each problem. Use paper and pencil to compute the exact answer to all problems that have a two-digit quotient. Show your estimate for all the other problems.

$$6\overline{)125} \qquad 9\overline{)1869} \qquad 13\overline{)117}$$
$$29\overline{)221} \qquad 42\overline{)512} \qquad 53\overline{)312}$$
$$6\overline{)685} \qquad 8\overline{)665} \qquad 24\overline{)103}$$

answer. They believe the exact answer is the best estimate. A teacher needs to reward the students who truly estimate rather than doing quick mental computation to get the right answer if estimation is the goal of the activity. A Praxis II™ question at the end of the chapter may catch you in the same way if you are not careful!

A central idea in estimating is that there are many approaches that can be used. Children need to be exposed to a variety of estimation strategies and then encouraged to think about the situation, the numbers involved, and the type of precision needed. The strategies of front-end estimation, compatible numbers, clustering, and rounding are discussed here.

Front-End Estimation This strategy uses the leading digits in the number and considers the place value position of the digits. This approach incorporates number sense and provides a quick idea of the relative size of the answer as seen in Activity 9.7. After the initial estimate using the front-end numbers, children can consider the other numbers in the problem and adjust the estimate.

Compatible Numbers This strategy uses numbers that are easy to compute because they naturally go together or are "friendly numbers." Finding numbers that make 10 or 100 aids in quicker computation as seen in Activity 9.8.

Numbers are also rounded to numbers that are easier because they are "nice numbers." For division, one way to estimate is to find the closer number of tens, hundreds, or thousands in the quotient.

Activity 9.7

ESTIMATION **FRONT-END ESTIMATION**

For addition:
$$\begin{array}{r} 961 \\ 844 \\ +211 \\ \hline \end{array}$$

Think: 900 + 800 + 200 = 1900

Adjust: Since in the tens place we see 100 (6 + 4), we can adjust estimate to 2000.

For subtraction:
$$\begin{array}{r} 4189 \\ -2301 \\ \hline \end{array}$$

Think: 4000 − 2000 = 2000

Adjust: In tens place, we must regroup to subtract, so get closer and estimate 1800.

For multiplication:
$$\begin{array}{r} 8534 \\ \times\ 5 \\ \hline \end{array}$$

Think: 8000 × 5 = 40,000

Adjust: Multiply next digits, 500 × 5 = 2500 so estimate is around 42,500.

Activity 9.8

ESTIMATION **ARE WE COMPATIBLE?**

DIRECTIONS

Look for easy ways to group these numbers into Friendly Pairs to add more easily.

25	37	843
32	49	917
45	71	206
+74	56	684
	35	112
	−69	+388

Students may need to look for friendly multiples that make dividing easier. For example:

To divide 3417 by 4, *think:* 3200 ÷ 4 = 800

The same strategy is helpful to think of fractions. For example:

$$\frac{1}{5} \times 21, \text{use} \quad \frac{1}{5} \times 20$$

Compatible numbers can be mixed numbers with decimals. For example:

$$123.4 \div 3.45, \text{use} \quad 120 \div 3$$

More of these strategies are discussed in Chapter 10.

Clustering When numbers cluster around the same amount, you can use this number and multiply by the number of addends in the group. This approach is like finding an average value for the group of numbers and then making it into a simple multiplication or repeated addition problem. It reduces the numbers with which you are working, but it is more difficult to adjust the estimate.

Estimate the total cost of these items:

$$\$1.21 + \$1.29 + \$1.32 + \$1.25$$

Because all the numbers are around $1.25, *think:* $4 \times \$1.25 = \$5.00$

Rounding Rounding is deliberately discussed last because it is the most familiar estimation technique. The traditional rounding techniques ask students to round to a particular place-value position. When students are asked to estimate by rounding, they commonly ask "to which place?" Unfortunately, this situation occurs because rounding is often done in "rounding lessons" or to check computational problems, rather than taught in a contextual setting that provides clues to this question as demonstrated in Activity 9.9.

An effective technique is to search for compatible numbers and to consider flexible rounding adjustments. For addition and subtraction, both numbers may not need to be rounded to get a good estimate. The best approach is to round numbers to reasonable values to make the computation easier. Multiplication estimation often involves rounding numbers to multiples of 10. To reduce the rounding error when multiplying, students should try to adjust the estimate by rounding one factor up and the other factor down. Experiment with numbers where you use this approach and compare it to rounding both factors up and rounding both factors down. Just by doing this simple experiment, you will be ready to answer the question, "What do you think would be a reasonable range?"

Calculator Models Computation should be placed in a problem-solving environment in which stu-

Activity 9.9

ESTIMATION   **TARGETING PRODUCTS**

MATERIALS

- Digit cards or number tiles
- Calculators (optional)

DIRECTIONS

1. Place the digits 4 to 9 in the boxes to get a product as close to the target as possible.
2. Multiply and find out how far your answer is from the target. You get three tries for each one.

	Target
▢▢▢▢ × ▢ =	50,000
▢▢▢▢ × ▢ =	80,000
▢▢▢▢ × ▢ =	70,000
▢▢▢▢ × ▢ =	40,000
▢▢▢▢ × ▢▢ =	40,000
▢▢▢▢ × ▢▢ =	70,000

dents judge whether the answer can be determined by mental computation, estimation, using the calculator, or by paper-and-pencil computation. The NCTM *Principles and Standards* (2000) declare that children need to know when technology is an appropriate tool for learning mathematics. As we look at the skills and competencies needed in the workforce for the twenty-first century, the shopkeeper's computational skills play a diminished role. In the real world, computations of multidigit numbers or of several steps are handled by the calculator. The following chart in Figure 9.5 will help you devise a strategy for when to use calculators in your own classroom lessons. The chart can also help children decide when to use calculators themselves.

It is important to remember that access to calculators does not eliminate fluency with basic facts and mental calculations. In fact, calculators can enhance one's ability to think mathematically as the next four activities show (Activity 9.10, Activity 9.11, Activity 9.12, and Activity 9.13). Do the activities yourself. Although these activities are used in elementary and middle schools, we suspect that your mind was really thinking as much as the students you will teach!

Focus of the lesson is on . . .	Activity requires		
	laborious calculations to get an answer	one or two step calculations to get an answer	estimation to eliminate poor answers from feasible ones
how a concept, process, pattern, or system works	Use a calculator	Use mental math or pencil and paper	Use mental math or pencil and paper
finding a computational solution	Use a calculator	Use mental math or pencil and paper	Use mental math or pencil and paper

FIGURE 9.5 *Decision chart for when to use a calculator in classroom activities.*

Activity 9.10

MENTAL MATH **CALCULATORS** **MISSING NUMBERS**

MATERIALS
- Digit cards or number tiles
- Calculators (optional)

DIRECTIONS
Place the digits 5 to 9 to create the problems. Check your solutions with a calculator.

```
Create the LARGEST ANSWER

  □□□        □□□        □□□
 ×□□        +□□        −□□

  □□□□ ÷ □□ =

Create the SMALLEST ANSWER

  □□□        □□□        □□□
 ×□□        +□□        −□□

  □□□□ ÷ □□ =
```

Compare your answers with your classmates. Were you correct? Explain your thinking and what you found out about placement of the digits for each operation. Discuss with a partner the different strategies you used for the different operations. Make up new problems using five different digits and share with a classmate. More problems are on the Web site, "Find the Largest and Smallest Answers."

Activity 9.11

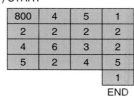

CALCULATORS **MENTAL MATH** **DIVISION PRACTICE WITH THE CALCULATOR**

Pathways—Find the path to the END answer by dividing. No diagonal lines allowed. Use your calculator as needed.

Example: START

1000	2	1	10
2	4	5	5
2	5	5	5
10	2	2	1
			1

END

1) START

800	4	5	1
2	2	2	2
4	6	3	2
5	2	4	5
			1

END

2) START

19683	6	9	27
5	4	3	3
18	3	5	6
6	5	3	0.9
			9

END

When parents, school boards, or administrators question the decreased attention given in your classrooms to tedious, complex computations,

Activity 9.12

ESTIMATION **CALCULATORS** **MULTIPLICATION**

The following activity can be used in a cooperative learning situation:

ESTIMATION—MULTIPLICATION
(a game for two or more players)

How to Play

1. Choose a number as your target. Circle it.

93	556	5444	57
212	491	649	303
1010		237	

2. Choose another number and enter it in your calculator, then enter the operation.

Example:

$23 \times \underline{\hspace{1cm}} = \boxed{93}$

$33 \times 3 = 99 \leftarrow$ almost!

$23 \times 4 = 92 \leftarrow$ closest

$32 \times 2 = 64$

3. Quick! In 5 seconds or less, enter a number that you think will produce the target number when you push the equal sign.

4. Each player tries reaching the same target number. The one who gets the closest wins one point. The first player to win 10 points wins the game.

Display:

Enter 23					2	3
Enter ×					2	3
Estimate						4
=					9	2

remind them of the instructional time you have saved to spend on developing computational strategies, reasoning, probability and statistics, proportional thinking, and other topics that might otherwise will not have time to be covered. Research (Bitter and Hatfield, 1992) also indicates that use of calculators with middle school students did not have adverse effects on their computational abilities but did enhance their problem-solving skills, and girls felt more mathematical empowerment using the calculator.

Activity 9.13

PROBLEM SOLVING **CALCULATORS** **SPEND EXACTLY $3.55**

How can you spend exactly $3.55? Can you find at least five different ways?

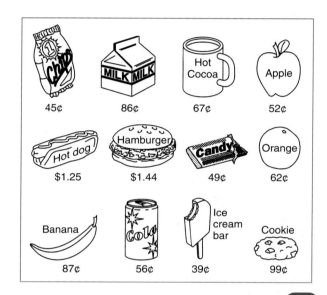

Additional activities to promote students' algorithmic thinking are in the Extended Activities on the Web site for Chapter 9.

With a growing consensus of mathematics educators emphasizing the discovery of procedures for computation rather than memorizing traditional algorithms, you are urged to watch some of the past video vignettes with this approach in mind, such as Mrs. Thomas in the "Doubling" problem on the Web site in Chapter 5. As you read more of this textbook, be aware of your own changing perceptions of the teaching and learning of mathematics.

STRATEGIES FOR BUILDING CONCEPTUAL UNDERSTANDING OF THE OPERATIONS WITH MULTIDIGIT WHOLE NUMBERS

In the first section of this chapter, a strong rationale was built in support of allowing students to

EXTENDED ACTIVITIES

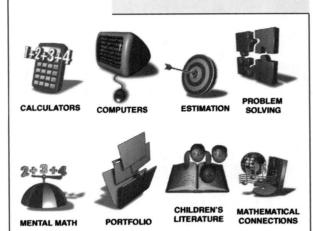

CALCULATORS COMPUTERS ESTIMATION PROBLEM SOLVING

MENTAL MATH PORTFOLIO CHILDREN'S LITERATURE MATHEMATICAL CONNECTIONS

On the Web site (Chapter 9, Extended Activities), read/do the following:

- Alternative Algorithms
- Number Sense and Mental Computations
- Eye Openers
- Find the Largest and Smallest Answers
- Addition Practice
- Estimating Quotients 1 Spreadsheet
- Estimating Quotients 2 Spreadsheet

invent their own strategies for solving multidigit problems based on many research studies. The recommended instructional sequence is

Start with Student-Invented Strategies

Continue with Corresponding Alternative Algorithms (each being shown with concrete/pictorial models based on real-world problem solving situations.

Higher test scores are associated with this approach. Therefore, each operation is shown with the most common student-invented strategies and the corresponding alternative algorithms that most closely match what students have done on their own. A concrete model with base 10 blocks accompanies each algorithm.

Analyze the algorithms with the knowledge that there is no one right algorithm. There are still more to be created. One of the higher thought activities at the end of this chapter asks you to design your own algorithm for operations on multidigit numbers. There is mathematical power in

Activity 9.14

CULTURAL RELEVANCE

ALGORITHMS FROM OTHER CULTURES

- Many cultures have developed different algorithms. Look in the library for mathematics books or texts from other countries to find different examples.
- Write a pen pal in another country and ask how the four operations are done. Share your findings with your classmates.
- Use a world map and plot your class findings about cultures and algorithms. What predictions can you make about why these differences have occurred?

the idea that any algorithm can be seen through progressively more abstract models, arriving at a correct answer no matter what model is used. Many cultures use different algorithms. Students may find Activity 9.14 an enjoyable way to learn about algorithms used in other countries.

A special attempt has been made to choose algorithms that are quite different from one another. Some elementary and middle school students may find one algorithmic model more understandable than another. It is hoped that you will see the variety of options as a way of meeting the diversified needs of students.

Teaching the Addition Algorithm
Children are introduced to addition with two-digit numbers without regrouping in most first grade textbooks. They are taught regrouping for addition and subtraction in second grade. The authors support teaching addition with regrouping and without regrouping together so that the mechanical aspect is replaced with thoughtful attention to the process. When word problems and situational problems accompany the presentation, children are less likely to ask, "Do I have to regroup on this one?" Manipulative materials are the key to understanding, and their use results in fewer remediation problems. Whatever the model, it should include some place-value boards (Hundreds—Tens—Ones labeled at the top) to help children focus on a logical organizational procedure.

Take time now to read through the activity, "Regrouping with Addition" (Activity 9.15). Can you follow the children's various thinking strategies?

Activity 9.15

MANIPULATIVES

PROBLEM SOLVING

REGROUPING WITH ADDITION

Situational Problem: Monday night 258 people watched the school play. Tuesday night 379 people watched the school play. How many people watched the play?

STUDENT-INVENTED ALGORITHM	ALTERNATIVE ALGORITHM FOR INSTRUCTION	MODEL OF THE REPRESENTATION (can be concrete or pictorial as needed)
$$258$$ $$+379$$ $$\overline{500}$$ $$120$$ $$+17$$ $$\overline{637}$$ This is one of the most common student-invented algorithms.	**PARTIAL SUMS** Advantage: Students never need to regroup. This is fairly straightforward with little adjustment needed if students keep columns straight so each place value is clearly seen.	Hundreds · Tens · Ones 500 · 120 · 17 NOTE: Since 120 is another name for 12 tens, students see no need to regroup. The same is true for 17 ones. $$500$$ $$120$$ $$17$$ $$\overline{637}$$
$$2\,|\,5\,|\,8$$ $$+\,3\,|\,7\,|\,9$$ $$\overline{5\,|\,12\,|\,17}$$ Some students may stop here thinking they have finished. If students see the adjustment on their own, they may say something like, "200 + 300 is 500 (Looking at next column) but I need to adjust because 50 and 70 is 120; so 5 is now 6. I need to do the same thing for the ones too." A notation like the one to the right helps students remember to regroup at the end.	**COLUMN ADDITION** Advantage: Students only need to regroup at the end. If students start left to right. $$2\,|\,5\,|\,8$$ $$+\,3\,|\,7\,|\,9$$ $$5\,|\,0^{1}2\,|\,0^{1}7$$ $$6\,|\,3\,|$$ $$\overline{6\quad 3\quad 7}$$ If students start right to left. $$2\,|\,5\,|\,8$$ $$+\,3\,|\,7\,|\,9$$ $$5\,|\,^{1}2\,|\,0^{1}7$$ $$6\,|\,0^{1}3\,|\,7$$ $$\overline{6\quad 3\quad 7}$$	Hundreds · Tens · Ones 6 ← 3 ←
$$260\;②$$ $$258↑$$ $$379$$ $$377↓②$$ $$300↑⑩$$ $$337↓⑩$$ Student says, "I go up 2 to get to a set of 10, but I go down 2 so all the numbers have the same value as before like they did when we started. I do the same with 40."	**RENAMING ADDENDS** $$258 \rightarrow 260 \rightarrow 300$$ $$379 \rightarrow 377 \rightarrow 337$$ $$\overline{637}$$ Adjust by 2, then adjust by 40 Students need only a way to record what they are doing that is more organized as they work, leaving less likelihood of simple errors.	Hundreds · Tens · Ones

Video Vignette

MANIPULATIVES

PROBLEM SOLVING

Regrouping with Addition and Base 10 Blocks

View the Video Vignette with Mrs. Arroyo (Chapter 9, Video Vignettes, "Regrouping with Addition and Base 10 Blocks"). Then

- Analyze the instructional style being used in the classroom.
- What are the advantages and disadvantages to the direct instructional model used by the teacher?
- How could the lesson be modified to allow for children's invented strategies?
- Analyze the instruction in terms of learning environment, focus on children's understanding, and building students' empowerment and confidence in mathematics.

Pose the situational problem to the children. Have materials available for those children who select to use them. Try doing other problems using the alternative algorithm strategies. Although the foundation for the algorithm begins with two-digit numbers, children need to continue to have concrete experiences with regrouping for hundreds and thousands.

That is why the situational problem in Activity 9.15 models place value in the hundreds.

When problems involve numbers in the hundreds and thousands, many teachers claim not to have sufficient time or materials to provide direct manipulation by children with place-value models. Time spent on these activities is well worth it in terms of long-range results. If a child is to truly internalize and "own" the concept, time and concrete experiences are required.

Use the Video Vignette in Chapter 9 on the Web site. Watch first graders learning regrouping with addition. Analyze the teacher's approach and the child's level of understanding.

Teaching the Subtraction Algorithm

Much has been written about the subtraction algorithm and alternative algorithms to use. The most common algorithm is the decomposition method, which is traditionally the one presented in student textbooks. It relates easily to place-value models and emphasizes the inverse relationship of addition and subtraction. Unfortunately, it is often the most difficult for young children to understand, producing frequent errors in regrouping. The alternative models shown in Activity 9.16 are the ones children find most compelling, even if they seem more difficult to adults seeing them for the first time.

Take-Away Subtraction The first kind of interpretation for subtraction is the take-away approach. It is the easiest for a child to understand and the most common one that a child encounters in real-life situations, and it is simple to represent physically. Modeling operations and algorithms with objects allow better understanding and prepare children to interpret the textbook pictures more clearly. Activity 9.16 is an example of the teaching strategies for the take-away interpretation of subtraction and alternative approaches students often take. Notice that children do not always explain what they are doing in eloquent terminology, but their actions, coupled with their explanations, can show the depth of their understanding that words alone could not do.

Comparison Subtraction The second interpretation of subtraction is the comparison idea. A comparison is made between the two sets of numbers. Usually, children do not encounter this interpretation in their textbooks until second grade. The questions for comparison involve ideas of how much more, how many more, how much less, how much older, and so on where the two sets must be compared. This is significantly more difficult for children to master. The algorithms in

Activity 9.16

MANIPULATIVES

PROBLEM SOLVING

TEACHING TAKE-AWAY SUBTRACTION WITH REGROUPING

Situational Problem: Grégor had 332 baseball cards. He gave 157 to his brother, Travis. How many baseball cards does he have left?

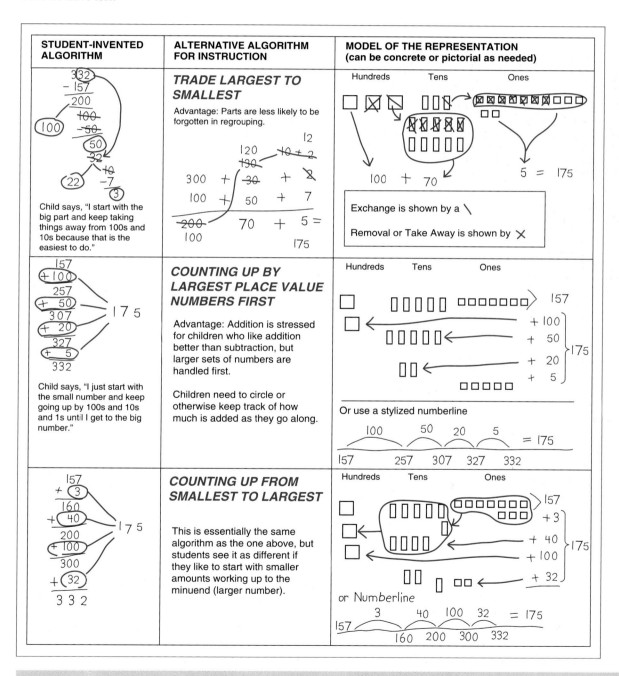

STUDENT-INVENTED ALGORITHM	ALTERNATIVE ALGORITHM FOR INSTRUCTION	MODEL OF THE REPRESENTATION (can be concrete or pictorial as needed)

Activity 9.17

MANIPULATIVES

PROBLEM SOLVING

CULTURAL RELEVANCE

TEACHING COMPARISON SUBTRACTION WITH REGROUPING

Situational Problem: Jana has 332 music Web sites? Her friend, Kara, has 157 music Web sites. How many more music Web sites does Jana have than Kara?

Alternative Question: How many more would Kara need so she could have as many as Jana?

STUDENT-INVENTED ALGORITHM	ALTERNATIVE ALGORITHM FOR INSTRUCTION	MODEL OF THE REPRESENTATION (can be concrete or pictorial as needed)
3 13 12 ~~332~~ − 2\6̸57 175 Child says, "I change things on top to a double-digit number. If the bottom number (subtrahend) is larger than the top number (minuend) at the beginning, then I rise the bottom number up by one. Then I just subtract everything at once."	**CANADIAN ALGORITHM** This is also known as the "European Algorithm" because it is used in so many European countries. The traditional algorithm would change minuend: 2̸ 2̸ 12 3̸ 3̸ 2 1̸ 5̸ 7 1 7 5	This is the most difficult to model with proportional models because it depends on the property of numbers, not on actual units counted. Decreasing the minuend has the same effect as Increasing the subtrahend while leaving the minuend unchanged 2 12 3 13 −1 −5 −2 −6 1 7 1 7
332 −157 −5 −20 200 ⟩ 180 −5 175 −7 (−5) −4 −3 −2 −1 0 1 2 −50 −30 (−20) −10 0 10 20 30	**ABSOLUTE DIFFERENCE** Disadvantage: This will always work, but students must remember to subtract what is a negative balance remaining in place values that would be regrouped in other algorithms. The number line is one way to keep students centered on the absolute difference.	Hundreds Tens Ones Step One Jana / Kara a difference of 5 or −5 for Kara a difference of 20 or −20 for Kara Step Two Jana Kara Step Three 1 7 5 Jana has more web sites

Activity 9.16 can be used here as well; it is a question of interpreting problem-solving situations and knowing that the subtraction operation is to be used. Many children confuse the word "more" with the idea of addition. Also in the comparison interpretation, the modeling involves making both sets and determining the difference by one-to-one matching. The two additional algorithms in Activity 9.17 can also be used in take-away subtraction.

Missing Addend Subtraction The third interpretation for subtraction is the missing addend concept. The problem involves knowing what you start with or have now and knowing how many you need in all. The idea is finding how many more are needed. Writing the problem as an addition problem with a missing addend may help visualize the procedure to use to solve the problem. The two "counting up" algorithms seen in Activity 9.16 match the action of missing addend subtraction although the other subtraction algorithms yield the correct answer if students realize that subtraction will give the needed solution.

An example of a situational problem would be

There are 332 miles from Phoenix to the trailhead. Consuelo drove 157 and bought a soda. How much further does she need to drive to reach the trailhead?

This part–whole concept, or adding to a part to make the whole, often appears in measurement situations such as making change, determining how many more days until a given date, figuring how many minutes left until the play is over, and so on. There are many other situational word problems for comparison subtraction in Extended Activities, "More Word Problems for Operations," on the Web site in Chapter 9.

Zeroes pose a problem in subtraction when students need to make trades, especially when two regroupings are needed. In numbers such as 500 – 256, a common misconception is to rename the number in the hundreds place and bring over ten to the tens place *and* to the ones place (because both need help!). The "Trade Largest to Smallest" algorithm does not present the zero regrouping problem that the traditional algorithm does (Figure 9.6). Estimation becomes a valuable way to focus attention on the reasonableness of the answers when working with subtraction examples.

Because students invent many different algorithms with varying sophistication in oral discourse, a teacher must become a good observer

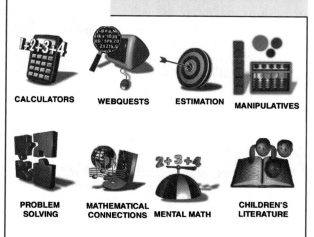

EXTENDED ACTIVITIES

CALCULATORS   WEBQUESTS   ESTIMATION   MANIPULATIVES

PROBLEM SOLVING   MATHEMATICAL CONNECTIONS   MENTAL MATH   CHILDREN'S LITERATURE

On the Web site (Chapter 9, Extended Activities), read/do the following:

- Napier's Bones
- Palindrome Pals
- Creating Your Own Problems
- More Word Problems for Operations
- Leftovers
- Problem Solving with a Spreadsheet
- Powers of 10 and Division Spreadsheet
- Family Math Packets
  - Ocean Math
  - As *the Crow Flies* Multiplication
- Lesson Plan for Mathematical Proficiency
  - Counting Numbers from 1 to 10

and evaluator. Praxis II™-style questions often show the work of real students for evaluation. Analyze the subtraction work of the student in the Praxis II™-style question #6 at the end of the chapter. This student has a unique way of dealing with zeros in subtraction problems. Ask yourself, "Will this algorithm work every time? If so, why? If not, why not?"

$$
\begin{array}{r}
500 \\
-256 \\
\hline
\end{array}
$$
300 → 100
200   −50
      50 → 10
      40   −6
           4 = 244

FIGURE 9.6 *Subtraction with zeros.*

Many of the difficulties that children have with word problems requiring addition or subtraction result from the various interpretations of the operations that are possible. Explanations of addition as "putting together" and subtraction as "taking away" place limits on the operations that are inaccurate when we consider the many other situations calling for these two operations. The opportunity to model many different situational problems relevant to children's experiences is the most helpful.

Teaching the Multiplication Algorithm

Before considering teaching strategies for the multiplication algorithm, a quick review of the language and mathematical concepts of multiplication is recommended. Multiplication also has several interpretations: repeated addition, a rectangular array or row-by-column, and a combination type. It is important not to limit the children's exposure to only one approach, or they will also be limited in their abilities to decide when a problem-solving situation calls for multiplication.

Repeated Groups Generally, explorations begin with repeated addition to extend the approach most likely used by children when developing competencies for basic facts of multiplication. The repeated addition meaning of multiplication seems the easiest for students to understand and apply. Research indicates that middle school students often have difficulty producing a pictorial representation or a word problem to accompany an equation. Instruction may be needed in the meaning of the mathematical expressions tied to drawings and manipulatives. The language of repeated addition focuses on the number of groups and the size of each group. Remember from Chapter 7 the importance of using the word *of* when describing groups for multiplying? For example,

Interpretation of multiplication: $4 \times 5 = 4$ groups of $5 = 5 + 5 + 5 + 5$
To change from equation to working form:

$$4 \text{ groups of } 5 = \begin{array}{r} 5 \\ \times\ 4 \\ \hline 20 \end{array}$$

Note: The vertical position places the 4 as the second number and still is read as 4 groups of 5.

Multiplication without regrouping usually appears in students' textbooks around the end of the third grade. This concept is easily taught and understood by children who have a reasonable proficiency with the basic facts and a firm understanding of place value. It can be modeled with base 10 blocks as shown in Figure 9.7. Expanded notation

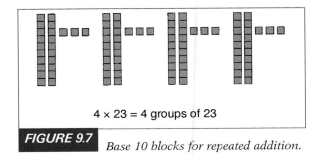

$4 \times 23 = 4$ groups of 23

FIGURE 9.7 *Base 10 blocks for repeated addition.*

and the distributive property help teach the multiplication algorithm with regrouping by showing how the partial products can be obtained and integrated into the shortened form of the algorithm.

The cognitive complexity of the traditional algorithm for multiplication causes difficulties for many students. Figure 9.8 shows the steps that the traditional algorithm requires. It is very easy for students to miss a step.

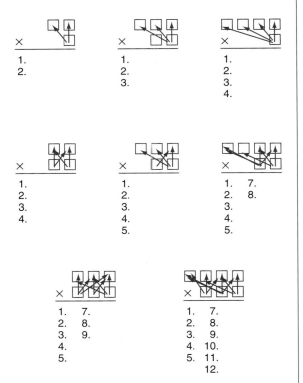

NOTE: In the student's folder each arrow is given a different color and each step is numbered in the same color to correspond with the appropriate arrow. This helps children remember the sequence with which to perform each procedure. The arrows and numbered steps appear in one color in this version of the form.

FIGURE 9.8 *Steps required in the traditional multiplication algorithm.*

Activity 9.18

MANIPULATIVES

PROBLEM SOLVING

CULTURAL RELEVANCE

TEACHING MULTIPLICATION WITH ALTERNATIVE ALGORITHMS

Situational Problem: Teshon wants to give 16 trading cards to each of the 24 people coming to his birthday party. How many cards will he need to buy?

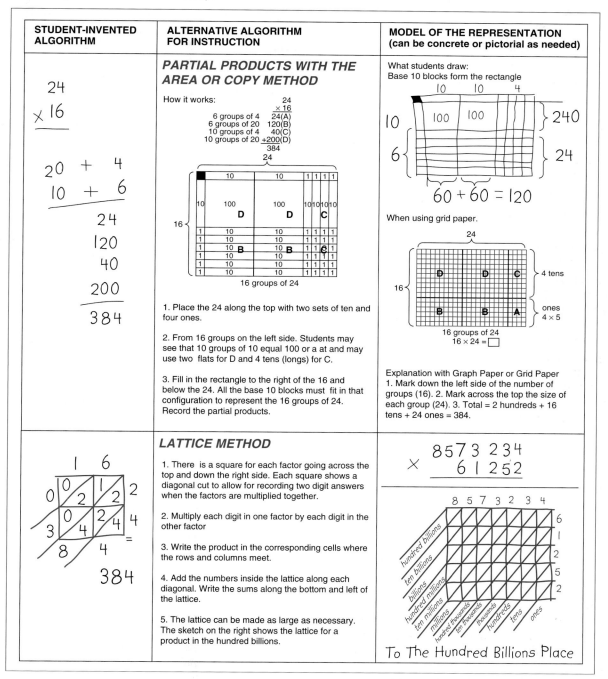

STUDENT-INVENTED ALGORITHM	ALTERNATIVE ALGORITHM FOR INSTRUCTION	MODEL OF THE REPRESENTATION (can be concrete or pictorial as needed)
24 × 16 20 + 4 10 + 6 24 120 40 200 ____ 384	**PARTIAL PRODUCTS WITH THE AREA OR COPY METHOD** How it works: 24 × 16 6 groups of 4 24(A) 6 groups of 20 120(B) 10 groups of 4 40(C) 10 groups of 20 +200(D) 384 24 16 groups of 24 1. Place the 24 along the top with two sets of ten and four ones. 2. From 16 groups on the left side. Students may see that 10 groups of 10 equal 100 or a at and may use two flats for D and 4 tens (longs) for C. 3. Fill in the rectangle to the right of the 16 and below the 24. All the base 10 blocks must fit in that configuration to represent the 16 groups of 24. Record the partial products.	What students draw: Base 10 blocks form the rectangle 60 + 60 = 120 When using grid paper. 16 groups of 24 16 × 24 = □ Explanation with Graph Paper or Grid Paper 1. Mark down the left side of the number of groups (16). 2. Mark across the top the size of each group (24). 3. Total = 2 hundreds + 16 tens + 24 ones = 384.
1 6 0	2	2 0	4	4 3 8 4 = 384	**LATTICE METHOD** 1. There is a square for each factor going across the top and down the right side. Each square shows a diagonal cut to allow for recording two digit answers when the factors are multiplied together. 2. Multiply each digit in one factor by each digit in the other factor 3. Write the product in the corresponding cells where the rows and columns meet. 4. Add the numbers inside the lattice along each diagonal. Write the sums along the bottom and left of the lattice. 5. The lattice can be made as large as necessary. The sketch on the right shows the lattice for a product in the hundred billions.	8573234 × 61252 8 5 7 3 2 3 4 hundred billions ten billions billions hundred millions ten millions millions hundred thousands ten thousands thousands hundreds tens ones 6 1 2 5 2 To The Hundred Billions Place

The researchers working with the Everyday Mathematics program (UCSMP, 2001) have turned to two other algorithms that more closely match the way students think about multiplication. They are shown in Activity 9.18. Another name for Lattice Multiplication is Napier's Bones. This algorithm is one of the oldest in mathematics history, tracing back to its Hindu origins before 1100 A.D. The authors of Everyday Mathematics discovered that children overwhelmingly favored this algorithm when given a choice between the traditional algorithm and the lattice approach.

Multiplication requires an understanding of place-value concepts along with some mathematical terminology and properties. For a quick review of these concepts and language, you may want to use the "Check Your Mathematical Knowledge" on the Web site for Chapter 9, shown on page 231 in this text.

Area Models The area or copy model for the standard multiplication algorithm has applications for showing multiplication across many dimensions of mathematics—fractions, decimals, and algebra. The NCTM *Principles and Standards* (2000) proclaim that area models are helpful in visualizing numerical ideas from a geometric point of view and provide a model to see relationships between factor pairs. Area models occur again in the study of algebra and probability. Activities such as renaming one factor in expanded notation as tens and ones and building the array formed help provide the mental visualization of what is happening with the multiplier ($4 \times 23 = 4 \times 20$ and 4×3. Take a look at some children using color tiles to build arrays in the Video Vignette "Operations with Whole Numbers Understanding Multiplication" in Mrs. Castenda's class on the Web site in Chapter 9. Notice how Mr. Dillon develops a framework for multiplication understanding in the same video.

When students are ready, transfer the modeling to centimeter graph paper or base 10 grid paper. If students record partial products, the steps can be more readily noticed. Base 10 grid paper serves as an alternative to base 10 blocks by allowing children to draw the outline of the problem. This is often called the "copy method" because a "copy" of the total problem is shown in a geometric area.

Remember to evaluate whether too much instructional time is being spent on becoming proficient in multiplying large numbers, when estimation and the calculator may be more appropriate. Activity 9.19, "Prove It," shows a quick way to

Video Vignette

Operations with Whole Numbers Understanding Multiplication

Listen to these two teachers building understanding of the operation of multiplication.

- What important mathematical ideas are being enhanced in Mrs. Castenda's lesson? Discuss how you see her classroom exemplifying suggestions from the *Standards*.
- What mathematical terms and language are developed?
- How is Mr. Dillon's lesson developing a framework for these students to understand multidigit multiplication? How are these children using partial products and seeing factor pair relationships?
- How do you see these lessons connecting conceptual knowledge to procedural knowledge?

check reasonableness of answers when multiplying large numbers.

Teaching the Division Algorithm

The standard division algorithm requires many prerequisite skills that create difficulties for children because of the numerous opportunities for error. The algorithm requires a knowledge of subtraction and multiplication algorithms, estimation skills, and an understanding of place value. Figure 9.9 shows the knowledge package required to do the standard algorithm for division. It is no wonder that many teachers regard division of multidigit

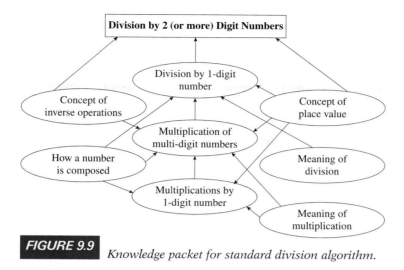

FIGURE 9.9 *Knowledge packet for standard division algorithm.*

numbers as the hardest concept to teach in elementary school mathematics.

A disproportionate amount of time is spent mastering this algorithm when we consider how often adults reach for a calculator to work long division problems. However, we do not recommend that teachers stop teaching multidigit division. Instead, the focus of instructional time should be on understanding division using one-digit divisors with three-digit or four-digit dividends. Students should use estimation or mental calculations and use calculators for dividing large numbers that involve tedious calculations. Even testing situations rarely go beyond problems with two-digit divisors. Some teachers create raps or chants for students to remember the various steps in division and encourage students to "sing" to themselves during testing. Consider this rap created by fourth graders:

First I divide

Then I multiply

Next I subtract

Last I bring down

Second verse, like the first

Don't shortcut or it'll be worse.

Partitive and Measurement Division Division problems result from two different situations—measurement division, which is related to successive subtraction, and partition division, which is related to fair sharing (see Chapter 7 for additional explanations about the differences). Remember that the actions using manipulative materials, the language used to describe the actions, and the corresponding steps of the algorithm must be in total agreement. This is especially important in division where the two different interpretations or approaches to the algorithm are possible. Word problems and manipulatives are easily shown in the partitive model. However, the measurement concept of

Activity 9.19

MENTAL MATH   **PROVE IT**

A quick way to check multiplication problems is to "add the digits." Add until only one number remains. Try this one!

$$673$$
$$\times\,236$$

$6 + 7 + 3 = 16, 1 + 6 = 7$
$2 + 3 + 6 = 11, 1 + 1 = 2$
The problem is $7 \times 2 = 14$

and

$1 + 4 = 5$

Now check all the partial products and the final product and see whether you get 5.

(Yes, $673 \times 6 = 4038 = 15 = 6$; $673 \times 30 = 20,190 = 12 = 3$; $673 \times 200 = 134,600 = 14 = 5$ and add these partial products together and get $14 = 5$. For the final product, $158,828 = 32 = 5$)

Try other examples and check this way.

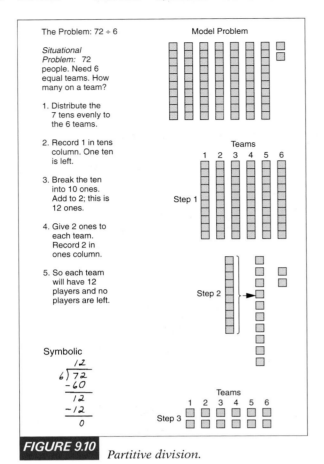

FIGURE 9.10 *Partitive division.*

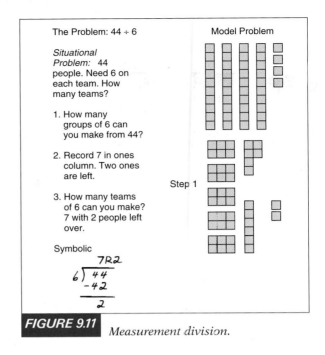

FIGURE 9.11 *Measurement division.*

division lends itself for division by a rational and decimal number and, therefore, must not be overlooked. The suggestion is to give children opportunities to create their own arguments and explanations about the division algorithm so that instruction can be matched to the way they think. Figures 9.10 and 9.11 show ways that it can be done.

Before the division algorithm requiring regrouping is introduced, students are exposed to division with remainders and to division of two-digit numbers where no regrouping is required. Dividing by tens and multiples or powers of 10 is a skill needed for estimation as well as a way to see the effect on the size of the quotient. It is advisable to relate multiplying and dividing by multiples or powers of 10 to note relationships and patterns.

$$4 \times 6 = 24 \qquad 4 \times 60 = 240$$
$$24 \div 6 = 4 \qquad 240 \div 60 = 4$$
$$4 \times 600 = 2400 \qquad 40 \times 60 = 2400$$
$$2400 \div 600 = 40 \qquad 2400 \div 60 = 40$$

Activity 9.20 shows the most commonly used student-invented algorithms for division. This is especially true if students have been exposed to the area or copy method of multiplication and multiples of powers of 10 in partial product multiplication as seen earlier in this section.

Remainders An area that causes difficulties for children is understanding how to interpret the remainders when word problems are involved. Part of the problem is that they need to reflect on the question in the word problem and label the quotient appropriately. This does not happen easily. Children work the problem and consider themselves finished with it. This is when cooperative learning experiences are valuable because students are given opportunities to verbalize the problems and to internalize meaning. Evidence of this difficulty is shown in the following situation with fourth graders and visualized in Figure 9.12. The problem was for them to decide how many six-packs of soda should be purchased for 45 people if each person was to have one can of soda. The division posed no difficulty with an answer of 7 remainder 3. The question (how many six-packs) was answered by the students: "We need 7 of them and will have 3 left over." Three what left over—cans? people? They claimed to have 3 cans of soda left over. They did not understand the need to increase the quotient.

Whatever the algorithm of choice, understanding how any algorithm works is pivotal to developing computational fluency. Bass (2003) points to the need for students and teachers alike

Activity 9.20

MANIPULATIVES **PROBLEM SOLVING** **CULTURAL RELEVANCE**

TEACHING ALTERNATIVE ALGORITHMS FOR DIVISION

Situational Problem: Davino has 32 people in his class and 997 trading cards to give away. He wants to know how many trading cards each person can have if each person gets an equal amount (a fair share).

STUDENT-INVENTED ALGORITHM	ALTERNATIVE ALGORITHM FOR INSTRUCTION	MODEL OF THE REPRESENTATION (can be concrete or pictorial as needed)
$$\begin{array}{c} \quad 10 \quad 10 \quad 10 \quad 1 = 31 \\ 10\,\overline{)100 \;\; 100 \;\; 100 \;\; 10} \\ 10\;\;\;100 \;\; 100 \;\; 100 \;\; 10 \\ 10\;\;\;100 \;\; 100 \;\; 100 \;\; 10 \\ 2\;\;\;\;\; 20 \;\; 20 \;\; 20 \;\; 2 \end{array}$$ $$\downarrow \quad \downarrow \quad \downarrow \quad \downarrow$$ $$\underbrace{320 \;\; 320 \;\; 320}_{960} \; 32$$ $$\begin{array}{r} 997 \\ 960 \\ \hline 37 \\ -\;32 \\ \hline 5 \end{array} \quad \begin{array}{l} R = 5 \\ \text{Answer} = \\ \quad 31R5 \end{array}$$ Student says, "I divide everything up by as many 100s, 10s and 1s as I can doing the bigger numbers first and fitting them side by side with the divisor. Then look above the division bar and see how many multiples I have. It always works because I use the place values of 1s, 10s, 100s, 1000s, and so on because that's our system."	### AREA OR COPY METHOD Explanation of How It Works with Base 10 Blocks: 1. The divisor, 32, is placed down the left side. 2. The dividend, 997, is represented by base 10 blocks going out to the right of the divisor to form a rectangle, showing how 997 is divided into 32 sets. 3. The quotient, 31, is represented on the top of the dark line (shown here by the dotted line above the base 10 blocks of 3 sets of ten and 2 ones). The quotient must fit exactly over the top line of the dividend. It shows how many things are in each group of the 32 groups. 4. The largest number of the base 10 blocks (in this case 9 sets of hundreds), represented rst as the dividend, is modeled from left to right at the right of the dark line, then come tens and ones. The representation is just like the written numeral representation: $\quad$ 997 = 900 (9 × 100) nine sets of 100 $\quad$ 90 (9 × 10) nine sets of 10 $\quad$ 2 (2 × 1) two sets of one with 5 remaining that $\quad$ will not make another set of 32 5. In some examples, the dividend may need to be regrouped to smaller powers of 10 so that its configuration will fit exactly to the right of the divisor with no parts "hanging down" past the end of the divisor (as shown by the arrow in the example to the right).	
$$32\,\overline{)997}$$ $$\begin{array}{r} 320 \\ \hline 677 \\ 320 \\ \hline 357 \\ 320 \\ \hline 37 \\ 32 \\ \hline 5 \end{array} \left.\begin{array}{l} 10 \\ 10 \\ 10 \\ 1 \end{array}\right\} 31R5$$ Student says, "It's easy to think of multiplying by 100s, 10s and 1s because you can do it in your head and just keep track of how many you've done on the side. When I cannot make any more sets, I stop. If I have some left over, it has to be less than the divisor or I could have made another set by multiplying the divisor by 1s."	### MULTIPLES OF THE BASE 10 SYSTEM Explanation of How It Works with Base 10 Blocks: 1. Looking at the dividend, the largest multiples of 1000, 100, 10, and 1 are subtracted from the dividend after being multiplied by the divisor. 2. In this case, the largest multiples are 10s. So $\quad$ 32 × 10 = 320 $\quad$ 32 × 10 = 320 $\quad$ 32 × 10 = 320 3. Each set of 10 is recorded on the side as it is pulled out or subtracted from the dividend. 4. When no more multiples of 10 can be subtracted, then 1s are used. $\quad$ 32 × 1 = 32 $\quad$ with a remainder of 5 of the next set of 32. 5. Since no more sets of 32 ones can be subtracted, the problem is finished and the remainder of 5 is shown as the only thing remaining in the dividend.	bring down what's left after doing multiples of 10 · not enough to make another set of 32 · = 31 R 5

What does the remainder mean?

to evaluate algorithms by four characteristics—reliability to produce accurate answers each time, efficiency or ease to work problems, less prone to errors, and mathematically transparent, meaning why an algorithm works mathematically is clearly visible to users. Analyze the work of the fourth grader in Praxis II™-style question #4 to see what level of computational fluency the student exhibits. Would you say he or she can compute fluently and flexibly? When students can explain why an algorithm works, they are becoming mathematical proficient, and this is the real goal of elementary and middle school mathematics.

ASSESSMENT TO HELP STUDENTS WITH SPECIAL NEEDS

Although some algorithms are less prone to errors than others, people still make errors when using algorithms. Sometimes errors become patterns that are hard to break without help. Although there are a variety of errors associated with whole number algorithms, a great many of them have to do with working with zeroes and applying place-value principles to the algorithm. Some errors are caused by difficulties with computation, such as not knowing the basic facts. Specific errors for each operation are discussed in this section, along with some remediation techniques when applicable. Generally, it can be said that most errors come when students mindlessly apply the step-by-step procedures for an algorithm, forgetting a

sequence, or misinterpreting what to do with the procedure. How does a teacher assess learning difficulties related to algorithm use? Oral interviews and teacher probing are valuable assessment techniques, as discussed in Chapter 3. Teachers should observe students working individually and collectively as they communicate about mathematics. In this way, the teacher can discover the strategies used by the child to arrive at answers along with any misconceptions the child has about the algorithm and the structure of the number system. We must ensure that assessment reflects significant mathematics.

Sensory Stimulation Students with Special Needs

The teacher should plan teaching strategies to use as many senses as possible in developing mathematical concepts, especially for special-needs students who may benefit more from one type of sensory stimulation than others. Manipulative materials may provide the visual mode, but if the child is allowed to work with them, tactile as well as visual skills can be used. Whenever possible, instruction should be based on concrete experiences that use as many sensory modes as possible. This should be the situation for initial instruction, but it is of paramount importance during remediation.

Another important aspect of assessment is selecting appropriate materials. There are many manipulative devices, including both proportional and nonproportional models, the teacher may select. Which device is most appropriate depends on several aspects of the learner: maturity level, previous experiences, materials used for initial instruction, visual or perceptual problems, fine motor skills, learner's intact skills, distractibility problems, and any other special needs of the child. Preparing an instructional hierarchy that takes these issues into account is a skill that takes much practice. Determining the proper instructional sequence is a most difficult task. For these reasons, the teacher must carefully read each section on assessment to become an effective teacher.

Correcting Common Misconceptions

Many errors with addition and subtraction result from difficulties with regrouping. Children may not know when to regroup and will regroup when it is not necessary or will fail to regroup. As mentioned earlier, the authors advise that problems with regrouping should be introduced at the same time as problems without regrouping. Beginners and children with special needs often benefit from using a learning mat (Figure 9.13) to center their attention on the materials.

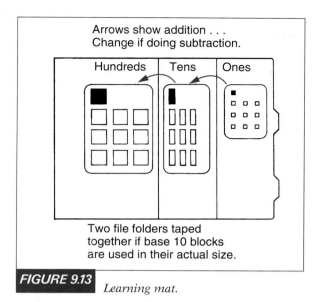

Arrows show addition . . .
Change if doing subtraction.

| Hundreds | Tens | Ones |

Two file folders taped
together if base 10 blocks
are used in their actual size.

FIGURE 9.13 *Learning mat.*

The mat can be a file folder, a shoebox, and so on. The important thing is that the child sees nine holes cut, so just nine ones can fit into the slots. The tenth one is covered in black to remind the students that when all the holes are filled and this is the only one left, it is a sign that it is time to regroup. The same thing is done for tens and hundreds. If the learning mat is plasticized, the arrows can be drawn in crayon so that they can be changed for addition or subtraction.

Corwin (2002) found that fourth and fifth graders worked better with money, naturally making piles of like coins. In essence, they organized their own learning mat with the piles of coins. For older students who may have been introduced to manipulatives without meaningful connections to mathematical concepts in the primary grades, money may be the best instructional tool. Each coin's value is clear to students, and the real-world importance of money is an obvious motivator. You will need to decide whether to use real money or play money, depending on the trustworthiness of the students involved. The general rule is never give students more real money than you are willing to lose.

Students with memory deficiencies will have problems learning algorithms. Steele's work (2002) shows excellent intervention strategies for middle school students. She emphasizes the use of mnemonic strategies similar to the chants and raps seen earlier in the chapter. She stresses gradual teaching from the concrete to the symbolic stage. Lerner (2000) stresses the use of lined paper to keep place values in the correct order. These

ideas are incorporated in the suggestions of materials and approaches to use with special-needs students detailed in the paragraphs that follow.

Common misconceptions for the traditional algorithms of the four basic operations are presented here because the traditional algorithms are still being used in many textbooks. Study the examples and decide what error the student is making. Then work the problems given by using the student's error pattern. Compare answers with those given below each example. Decide what remediation procedures you would use in each situation. In all cases, remediation involves additional experiences with place-value models so the algorithm is understood rather than just a series of memorized routines. Some additional teaching strategies are mentioned when appropriate.

Addition

Consider these problems: *Try these using the error:*

```
   37      297          48       306
 + 46    + 658        + 29     + 495
 ─────   ──────       ─────    ─────
  713    81415
                       (617)    (7911)
```

Error pattern: Adds by column without regrouping.

Remediation techniques: Estimate the answer and compare difference between the estimated and obtained sums. Use a closed abacus where regrouping is forced to occur because only nine chips or beads will fit in each column. Use graph paper with the rule that only one digit can be written in each section to focus attention on the need to regroup.

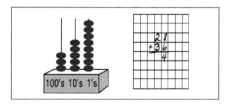

Consider these problems: *Try these using the error:*

```
   28      463          346      694
 + 37    + 358        + 39     + 137
 ─────   ──────       ─────    ─────
  515    7112
                      (3715)   (7212)
```

Error pattern: Adds from left to right.
Remediation techniques: Use a form that is placed over the problem to reveal only the ones column, then the tens, and continue in a right-to-left sequence. You could also write "A" over the ones column, "B" over the tens, column, and so

on to show the sequence. Color coding works well with some children who are visually challenged.

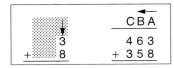

Consider these problems: *Try these using the error:*

$$\begin{array}{r} 27 \\ + 35 \\ \hline 52 \end{array} \qquad \begin{array}{r} 377 \\ + 94 \\ \hline 361 \end{array} \qquad\qquad \begin{array}{r} 85 \\ + 67 \\ \hline \end{array} \qquad \begin{array}{r} 219 \\ + 576 \\ \hline \end{array}$$

$$(142) \qquad (785)$$

Error pattern: Fails to add the regrouped digit.

Remediation techniques: Estimating the sum will work in some cases. May need to provide a "box" at the top of the columns to the left of the ones with a large plus sign to help remind the student of this step.

$$\boxplus\; \begin{array}{r} 27 \\ + 35 \\ \hline \end{array}$$

Subtraction

Consider these problems: *Try these using the error:*

$$\begin{array}{r} 300 \\ - 198 \\ \hline 298 \end{array} \qquad \begin{array}{r} 56 \\ - 29 \\ \hline 33 \end{array} \qquad\qquad \begin{array}{r} 512 \\ - 258 \\ \hline \end{array} \qquad \begin{array}{r} 309 \\ - 98 \\ \hline \end{array}$$

$$(346) \qquad (391)$$

Error pattern: Takes the smaller number from the larger without regard to position.

Remediation techniques: Estimate the answer. Have the student check using addition. In many cases, the answer is larger than the original number and makes no sense. Concrete materials can be used with a take-away model (rather than the comparison model) to show that the first number, or minuend, is modeled with the blocks or chips and the second number is removed from that set.

Consider these problems: *Try these using the error:*

$$\begin{array}{r} 315 \\ - 138 \\ \hline 172 \end{array} \qquad \begin{array}{r} 746 \\ - 159 \\ \hline 551 \end{array} \qquad\qquad \begin{array}{r} 452 \\ - 189 \\ \hline \end{array} \qquad \begin{array}{r} 315 \\ - 96 \\ \hline \end{array}$$

$$(221) \qquad (214)$$

Error pattern: Regroups all columns as ten and fails to add the previous digit.

Remediation techniques: Use concrete proportional models to review the subtraction algorithm.

Consider these problems: *Try these using the error:*

$$\begin{array}{r} ^{1\,1}206 \\ - 38 \\ \hline 78 \end{array} \qquad \begin{array}{r} ^{1\,1}715 \\ - 288 \\ \hline 437 \end{array} \qquad\qquad \begin{array}{r} 465 \\ - 97 \\ \hline \end{array} \qquad \begin{array}{r} 285 \\ - 189 \\ \hline \end{array}$$

$$(378) \qquad (96)$$

Error pattern: Regroups in the column farthest to the left and adds ten to each column rather than working column by column starting with the ones.

Remediation techniques: Concrete materials to reteach the steps of the algorithm. Could also use a form that allows only the column on the left to be seen at one time (as in an addition example mentioned earlier).

Consider these problems: *Try these using the error:*

$$\begin{array}{r} ^{2\;16}\cancel{36} \\ - 14 \\ \hline 112 \end{array} \qquad \begin{array}{r} ^{4\;12}\cancel{52} \\ - 36 \\ \hline 16 \end{array} \qquad\qquad \begin{array}{r} 27 \\ - 19 \\ \hline \end{array} \qquad \begin{array}{r} 98 \\ - 26 \\ \hline \end{array}$$

$$(8) \qquad (612)$$

Error pattern: Regroups all columns when regrouping is unnecessary.

Remediation techniques: This error occurs in second and third grades when the child is learning the algorithm and problems with mixed operations are included. The child continues to focus on the regrouping process and perseveres. Give mixed problems where the child is asked only if regrouping is needed. Also estimation will help alert the child to a problem in the answer.

Do you trade? Circle yes or no.

$$\begin{array}{r} 26 \;\; Yes \\ + 12 \;\; No \end{array} \qquad \begin{array}{r} 39 \;\; Yes \\ + 24 \;\; No \end{array} \qquad \begin{array}{r} 41 \;\; Yes \\ + 39 \;\; No \end{array}$$

$$\begin{array}{r} 52 \;\; Yes \\ + 27 \;\; No \end{array} \qquad \begin{array}{r} 90 \;\; Yes \\ + 26 \;\; No \end{array}$$

Multiplication

Consider these problems: Try these using the error:

$$\begin{array}{r} 37 \\ \times 5 \\ \hline 1535 \end{array} \qquad \begin{array}{r} 241 \\ \times 34 \\ \hline 8164 \\ 61230 \\ \hline 69{,}394 \end{array} \qquad\qquad \begin{array}{r} 23 \\ \times 47 \\ \hline \end{array} \qquad \begin{array}{r} 186 \\ \times 42 \\ \hline \end{array}$$

$$(9541) \quad (453{,}852)$$

Error pattern: Fails to regroup.

Remediation techniques: Estimation will help draw attention to the large difference in products. Use graph paper with the rule that only one digit per column can be recorded. Review the multiplication algorithm with concrete materials.

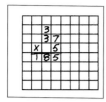

Consider these problems: Try these using the error:

68	68	29	52
× 5	× 26	× 3	× 87
500	608		
	1460	(127)	(5284)
	2068		

Error pattern: Adds carried digit before multiplying the next column.

Remediation techniques: This error could be a carryover of the drill with regrouping in the addition algorithm. Estimation may help clue the student about the difference in the two products—estimated and obtained. Review of the algorithm with concrete materials may reinforce sequence of steps.

Consider these problems: Try these using the error:

83	423	73	302
× 27	× 254	× 24	× 58
581	1692		
166	2115	(438)	(3926)
747	846		
	4653		

Error pattern: Fails to annex a zero as a place holder when multiplying tens and hundreds.

Remediation techniques: Worksheets with these zeroes already recorded may help. Another strategy is to use a form that exposes only the column multiplied and column labeled. Outlining the correct placement of steps with colored lines on graph paper helps draw attention to the sequence of the algorithm. Using concrete models is encouraged along with estimation.

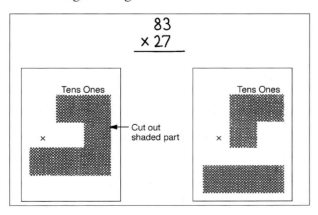

Consider these problems: Try these using the error:

56	584	75	185
× 38	× 73	× 29	× 37
198	4072		
		(185)	(575)

Error pattern: Multiplies column by column like the addition and subtraction algorithms.

Remediation techniques: Use a form to help show the sequence and use graph paper outlined with the steps. Graph paper can be color coded according to the multiplier to give visual clues. The distributive law will also indicate the partial products and help in understanding how to complete the steps. Estimation will clue the error.

Consider these problems: Try these using the error:

265	468	327	705
× 238	× 83	× 286	× 356
2120	1404		
7950	17440	(886,622)	(60,630)
5300	31,844		
63,170			

Error pattern: Does not keep columns straight and errors occur in the adding.

Remediation techniques: Use graph paper to help keep columns in proper alignment. Can also turn notebook paper sideways, which will cause the blue horizontal lines to become vertical lines to help with alignment.

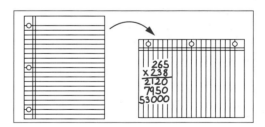

Division

Consider these problems: Try these using the error:

56 R 6	830		
9)4560	6)4818	8)5840	3)752
−45	−48	(73)	(25 R 2)
60	18		
−54	−18		
6	0		

Error pattern: Does not record zero as a place holder in the quotient when the division step cannot be done (the number is too small to be divided).

Remediation techniques: Estimation will offer the clue that there is an error. Estimating the size or range of the quotient, and then marking that in the quotient with lines (two for a two-digit quotient or three for a three-digit quotient) will help draw attention to the error when it occurs. However, some children will misuse this device and will simply record a zero in the ones place to satisfy the needs of the size of the quotient. Concrete models are the best device to use as the child will see from where the zero comes.

Consider these problems: Try these using the error:

$$4\overline{)352} \qquad \text{Think} \rightarrow 4\overline{)320} \quad \overset{80}{} \leftarrow \textit{2 digits} \qquad 4\overline{)352}$$

Consider these problems: Try these using the error:

$$
\begin{array}{c}
68 \\[-2pt]
6\overline{)516} \\
-48 \\ \hline
36 \\
-36 \\ \hline
0
\end{array}
\qquad
\begin{array}{c}
19 \\[-2pt]
3\overline{)273} \\
-27 \\ \hline
3 \\
-3 \\ \hline
0
\end{array}
\qquad
8\overline{)584} \atop (37)
\qquad
4\overline{)568} \atop (241)
$$

Error pattern: Records the problem (or perhaps even works the problem) from right to left as in the other three operations.

Remediation techniques: Use play money to model the division process and visualize the algorithm. Can also use a cover form to reveal numbers in the dividend beginning with the left. Stress where the quotient will go. Estimate the quotient to determine whether it is reasonable.

Consider these problems: Try these using the error:

$$
\begin{array}{c}
95\,R\,7 \\[-2pt]
4\overline{)387} \\
-36 \\ \hline
27 \\
-20 \\ \hline
7
\end{array}
\qquad
\begin{array}{c}
64\,R\,12 \\[-2pt]
9\overline{)588} \\
-54 \\ \hline
48 \\
-36 \\ \hline
12
\end{array}
\qquad
6\overline{)579} \atop (95\,R\,9)
\qquad
8\overline{)369} \atop (45\,R\,9)
$$

Error pattern: Remainder is greater than the divisor. The division was stopped too soon and is incomplete.

Remediation techniques: Stress estimation and use play money to focus on the size of the remainder.

Consider these problems: Try these using the error:

$$
\begin{array}{c}
15\,R\,3 \\[-2pt]
31\overline{)4696} \\
-31 \\ \hline
158 \\
-155 \\ \hline
3
\end{array}
\qquad
\begin{array}{c}
16\overline{)4650} \\
-32 \\ \hline
145 \\
-144 \\ \hline
1 \\
(29\,R\,1)
\end{array}
$$

Error pattern: Lost track of which numbers were left to "bring down."

Remediation techniques: This error happens because digits are not kept in proper alignment.

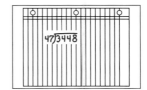

Graph paper or notebook paper turned sideways offers a help for alignment.

Consider these problems: Try these using the error:

$$
\begin{array}{c}
862 \\[-2pt]
47\overline{)3448} \\
-32 \\ \hline
24 \\
-24 \\ \hline
8 \\
-8 \\ \hline
0
\end{array}
\qquad
\begin{array}{c}
3236\,R\,1 \\[-2pt]
24\overline{)6473} \\
-6 \\ \hline
4 \\
-4 \\ \hline
7 \\
-6 \\ \hline
13 \\
-12 \\ \hline
1
\end{array}
\qquad
37\overline{)9846} \atop (3282)
\qquad
43\overline{)2867} \atop (716\,R\,3)
$$

Error pattern: Uses only the first digit of the divisor to divide.

Remediation techniques: Estimate the quotient. Use graph paper to record the answer with the size of the quotient indicated. Also, checking the answer may give a clue to the error.

Field-Dependent Learners

Students who process information from the whole to the parts often benefit from an organizing mat that forms an outline for placing base 10 blocks in the copy method (Figure 9.14). The copy (area) method of multiplication and division is also helpful because the *whole* rectangular area is easily seen. Students feel they have a compact area in which to work—the problem does not get away from them, so to speak. They also work better with the partial sums addition or renaming trades from largest to smallest parts.

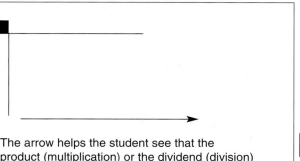

Place base 10 blocks touching the edge of the black square to the right and down the column. This helps the student see where to place base 10 blocks without the factors overlapping one another.

The arrow helps the student see that the product (multiplication) or the dividend (division) must be contained in the space above the line.

FIGURE 9.14 *Learning mat for area (copy) multiplication or division.*

Field-Independent Learners

Students who process information from details to the whole often benefit from the column addition algorithm and the counting up algorithm in subtraction because both of the algorithms take one column at a time, find the answer, and then move on to the next column. These students are often better at performing addition and multiplication algorithms than they are at subtraction or division. Perhaps it is because both addition and multiplication are joining activities ending in the whole at the culmination of the algorithm. The important thing is to use manipulatives where exploration is possible. The emphasis is on the meaning behind the algorithms. Remember to allow all learners to invent their own algorithms first and introduce algorithms that are compatible to the students' processing style.

PUTTING IT ALL TOGETHER—PORTFOLIO ASSESSMENT OF REAL STUDENT WORK

The work of students has been included here so that you can practice analyzing and planning instruction for typical solutions to students' difficulties. Figure 9.15 in Activity 9.21 shows the work of two students who are experiencing difficulty with the standard U.S. subtraction and multiplication algorithms. Follow the steps recommended in the teacher reflection.

SUMMARY

- This chapter targets a redefinition of teaching and learning of algorithms for multidigit whole number computation. The challenge is to develop computation through a rich conceptual development of the operations.

- Rather than emphasize the rules and procedures of teaching algorithms, the teaching focus is on children's understanding of the operations. This approach highlights the role of instructional activities that support children's thinking and numerical reasoning.

- Place value, number properties, and basic facts are also related to understanding the algorithms.

- If results obtained by paper-and-pencil computations are tested as reasonable, students need skills in estimation. Estimation and mental computation play a large part in obtaining a

---

Activity 9.21

PORTFOLIO   **PORTFOLIO ASSESSMENTS**

For Teacher Reflection of Student's Work with Operations on Whole Numbers
Review the student's work in Figure 9.15.

DIRECTIONS
1. Analyze the response made by this student. Create a reflective description of the error patterns you notice and the thought processing displayed by the student through the work shown.
2. Design a remediation plan to help the student overcome the misconceptions with the algorithms. Include the sequential development of concrete, pictorial, and symbolic models to reteach the concept.
3. Design a rubric that would take into account the diversity of answers while being open in your assessment.

Include the rubric in your Professional Portfolio for Job Interviews.

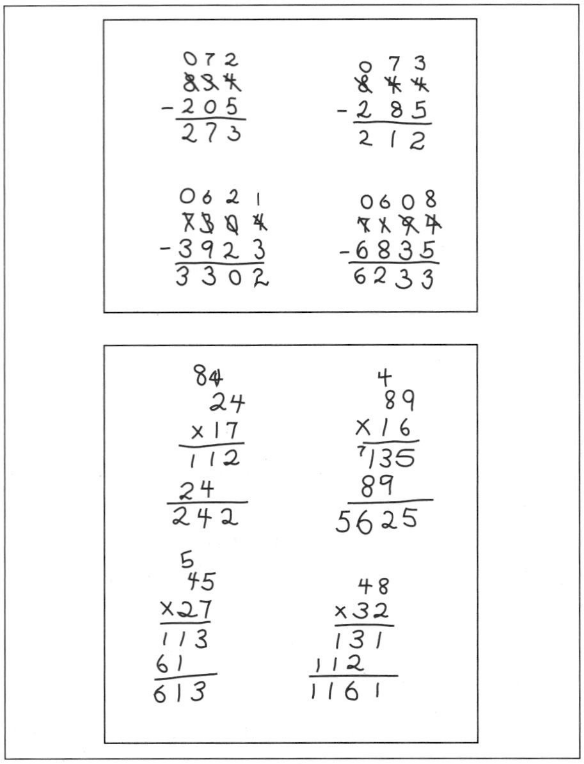

FIGURE 9.15 *Analyze the misconception patterns.*

"ballpark figure" or in simplifying the calculations.

- Calculators should be used when computation is laborious and may get in the way of understanding what the actual problem is asking students to solve.

- Research indicates that students given the chance to create their own invented algorithms first and shown alternative algorithms to match their invented ones will achieve higher test scores on standardized tests than their counterparts who were taught only one traditional algorithm per operation.

- If we want children to be empowered in mathematics, more time must be spent on developing flexible thinking and conceptual understanding about the algorithms in which the emphasis is on making sense of mathematics.

PRAXIS II™-STYLE QUESTIONS

Answers to this chapter's Praxis II™-style questions are in the instructor's manual.

Multiple Choice Format

1. A student answers number combinations this way:

   85
   +78
   153 "I know the answer is only in the hundreds"

   Which of the tools in Figure 9.16 would

   BEST handle the student's misconception?

2. Give a score on the five-point rubric scoring guide for each student's understanding of estimation.

Student A	Student B	Student C
I could estimate 389 plus 432 to be 821.	This problem says 501 plus 213. Each is more than 500 + 200 so the answer is more than 700. So I will estimate 800.	16 + 24 + 32 can be estimated to about 24 because it is right in the middle.

Student A's score_____
Student B's score_____
Student C's score_____

3. Student B in the preceding example needs to be taught which concept next.
   a. how to find the average number
   b. how to round numbers to the nearest place value by 10s
   c. how to add three-digit numbers
   d. None of the above

4. This student transfers into your room in the middle of the year. You give this problem to your class. When you ask the child to explain the work the child says, "I made up my own way to do these. I can work them fast. I always get done before the other kids." [NOTE: He did finish first.]

```
        363   R 26
   27)9827
       60
       38
       21
      172
      120
       52
       42
      107
       60
       47
       21
       26
```

Which of the following instructional approaches should come next for this child?

a. This child needs to go back to simpler problems with one-digit divisors and three-digit dividends because he cannot answer problems with larger numbers.

b. This child needs to memorize his basic facts better because he does not answer simple

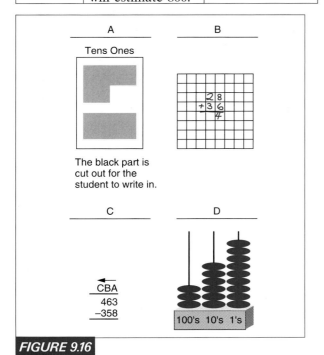

Tens Ones

The black part is cut out for the student to write in.

A   B

C   D

CBA
463
−358

100's 10's 1's

FIGURE 9.16

subtraction and multiplication facts correctly.

c. This child should be given a calculator to use because he is wasting valuable time doing such problems when he could work more efficiently.

d. This child should be encouraged to make up more algorithms on his own because he understands the mathematics involved and does it well.

Constructed Response Format

5. To analyze what the student in question #4 is doing, complete the following problem as the student would do it. Evaluate the level of computational fluency of this student. Justify your reasoning.

$$42\overline{)97801}$$

6. You are teaching multidigit subtraction and have given the students the following problem to do.

$$\text{The porblem:} \quad \begin{array}{r} 94257 \\ -\ 87969 \\ \hline \end{array}$$

Mateo says, "I found a way that is easier to do. All you have to do is subtract 1s and 0s to get the right answer at the end of each problem. It is much easier to do than changing everything on top." Mateo's work is in Figure 9.17.

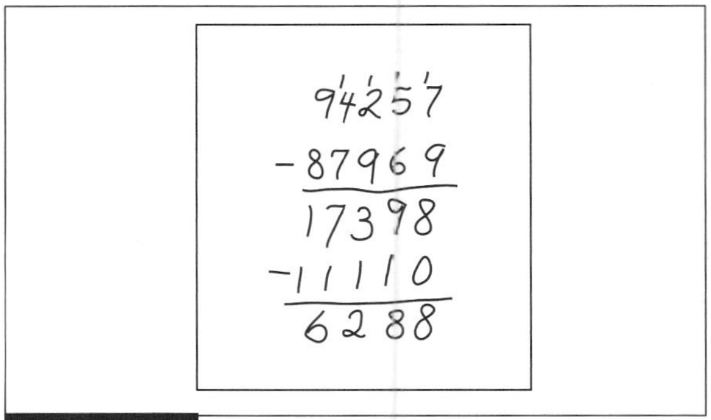

FIGURE 9.17 *Mateo's work.*

Analyze what Mateo is doing and tell what you, as a teacher, would have to find out next before responding to Mateo's idea.

7. Create a knowledge package for the multiplication of multidigit problems. (NOTE: You will not be asked to do this during the Praxis II™ test, but this activity will directly help answer the type of questions based on what you know about the algorithms for multiplication.)

8. Create a new algorithm for one of the four operations using multidigit numbers. Try several different numbers to see if your algorithm works in all cases. On what principles of mathematics is your algorithm based?

Integrating Technology

Internet Activities

WebQuest

Fall Leaves is a WebQuest integrating mathematics and science.

Web sites

Go to the NCTM Web site (**http://www.nctm.org**) and do both the CFP activities and the interactive "Illuminations" activities. Many of the activities start with numbers supporting the basic facts. Frequently, the later parts of the activities involve multidigit numbers and progressively more difficult mathematical reasoning is required. Examine activities for grades 3–5 and 6–8 that focus on computational algorithms.

CHILDREN'S LITERATURE

Most children's literature does not include multidigit computation, but these books provide some contextual setting for applying operations.

Trivett, John V. *Building Tables on Tables: A Book about Multiplication.* New York: Crowell, 1975, explores many grouping possibilities for the same number.

Pinczes, Elinor J. *One Hundred Hungry Ants.* Boston: Houghton Mifflin, 1993, provides different ways to group 100 ants involving division.

Griganti, Paul, Jr. *Each Orange Had 8 Slices.* New York: Greenwillow, 1992, lends itself to meaningful situa tions to introduce repeated addition, multiplication, and division.

Viorst, Judith. *Alexander, Who Used to Be Rich Last Saturday.* New York: Atheneum, 1978, offers a contextual setting to use subtraction with money problems and can serve as a stimulus for writing children's own stories using larger amounts of money and more difficult subtraction problems.

Anno, Mitsumasa. *Anno's Mysterious Multiplying Jar.* New York: Philomel Books, 1983, involves the concept of factorials, which could be used with calculators to explore large numbers.

Neuschwander, Cindy. *Amanda Bean's Amazing Dream: A Mathematical Story.* New York: Scholastic, 1998.

Common Fractions and Decimals

At the Start ~~~~ Know What Children Will Be Doing . . .

NCTM Curriculum Focal Points—	See . . .
Grade 3 ~~ Developing an understanding of fraction and fraction equivalence	Activity 10.5
Grade 4 ~~ Developing an understanding of decimals, including the connections between fractions and decimals	Figure 10.18
Grade 5 ~~ Developing an understanding of and fluency with addition and subtraction of fractions and decimals	Activity Concepts 1–6 Figure 10.20; 10.21
Grade 6 ~~ Developing an understanding of and fluency with multiplication and division of fractions and decimals	Activity 10.14; 10.15 Activity 10.22; 10.23

A partial listing as it pertains to Number and Operations from NCTM *Curriculum Focal Points* (2006, pages 15–18)

WHERE'S THE MATHEMATICS? CONCEPTUAL UNDERSTANDING FOR OPERATIONS AND PROPERTIES OF COMMON FRACTIONS AND DECIMALS

This chapter provides techniques and ideas for developing meaning for fractional and decimal numbers. The central theme is how we can teach fractions and decimals so that students develop a conceptual understanding for operations and properties of common fractions and decimals. Such conceptual understanding will include developing number sense and operation sense related to fractions and decimals and

applying them to problem situations. This is not an easy task because rules and tricks are associated with these topics. Think about how you were taught to multiply fractions—multiply the top numbers and multiply the bottom numbers. Did the answer make sense? Probably not! Take just a minute and create a realistic word problem for $\frac{1}{3} \times \frac{5}{6}$ and $1\frac{3}{4} \div \frac{1}{2}$ for.

Now think about how you were taught to multiply decimals—forget about the decimal points and just multiply like whole numbers, and then count up the number of decimal points in the two factors and move over that number of places in the answer. Do such rules build a sense for the operation to enable you to create realistic word

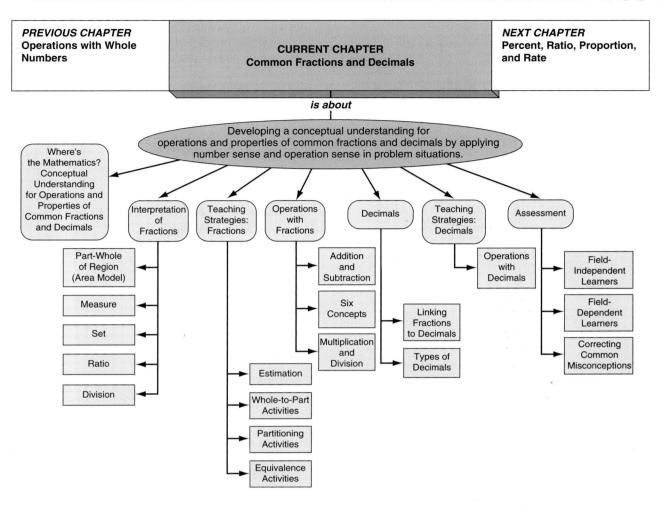

SELF-HELP QUESTIONS

1. Can I use different manipulatives and models to help students develop their conceptual understanding of fractions and decimals?

2. Do I know five different interpretations of fractions?

3. Can I use benchmarks in estimating the results of operations with fractions?

4. Do I understand the role of invented strategies when teaching the operations with fractions and decimals?

5. Can I use the common denominator approach when teaching division of fractions?

6. What do my students need to know about the reciprocal when studying fractions?

7. Do I understand the relationships among operations with whole numbers, fractions, and decimals?

problems? A major change must occur in how we view fractions and decimals. A careful study of this chapter will help you develop a better conceptual understanding of the operations and properties of fractions and decimals. The better your understanding of these topics in mathematics the more confident you can feel designing instruction for your students.

✓ *Check*

YOUR MATHEMATICS KNOWLEDGE

On Fractions

- Definitions of Rational Numbers
- Part of a Complete Set
- Ratio
- Division
- Properties of Rational Numbers
  Denseness
  Reciprocal
  Equivalency Rule
- More Word Problems

. . . a refresher from mathematics coursework . . . Lest you forget!

For more background on fractions, you may review the information found on the Web site, Check Your Knowledge, for properties, definitions, interpretations, and word problems to test your understanding of fractions and operations with fractions. Researchers recommend that more than one interpretation of fraction should be used and that initial instruction should begin from a part–whole perspective.

Figure 10.1 gives a partial listing for the NCTM Principles and Standards (2000). In this partial list, you can see the recommendation that students represent fractions in a variety of meaningful situations and that solutions should be based on students' sense of number. For the complete listing, visit the NCTM Web site at **http:// standards.nctm.org/index.htm**.

Experience with a variety of concrete models offers a foundation for building abstract ideas. Depending on the instructional approach, different types of concrete models are used—measurement models or unit set models. Examples of different models are shown in Figure 10.2. Both models, as well as others, are presented in the Teaching Strategies section.

We believe that multiple embodiments should always be used to help build concept development. However, in the interest of space, some of the teaching strategies described later in this chapter are covered by using only fraction kits made from circular or rectangular regions. Try using Cuisenaire rods, multiple bars, geo-

boards, and pattern blocks to teach the same strategies as modeled with fraction kits. It is important to use a variety of area models as well, such as rectangular and square regions. These models help children focus on the question of what is the basic unit. The widely recognizable shape of a half or fourth of a circle may give false impressions of understanding that can be detected more quickly by using other shapes. You may prefer certain materials to others. Generally, students learn best when teachers feel comfortable using the materials they have chosen. The patterns for making fraction kits are on the Web site, Appendix A, "Patterns." Making fraction kits for yourself now will enable you to do the activities in this chapter by using these manipulatives. In this way, you can build up your comfort level with what may be new manipulatives for you.

INTERPRETATION OF FRACTIONS

Fractions become more difficult to understand because they can be interpreted from several perspectives: part–whole region (area model), measure, set, ratio, and division. Streefland (1993) describes the many problems students have confusing the various meanings of fractions in different contexts (scale factor, unit of measure, part–whole, ratio, and so forth). Middleton, van den Heuvel-Panhuizen, and Shew (1998) suggest that some difficulties in teaching fractions can be attributed to the extent that the differences between rational and irrational numbers are emphasized and taught as isolated topics rather than the similarities emphasized and connections strengthened.

Part–Whole of Region (Area Model)

In this interpretation, a whole unit is subdivided into equal parts. The common circular and rectangular models play a key role. This fraction interpretation is often encountered in textbooks for elementary school. Teachers may use commercial materials such as fraction pizzas that have pre-marked pieces. These materials are important to explore; however, teachers should also provide opportunities for students to create their own fraction materials in which the activity requires the child to assign values to the regions. Such activities link the language labels to the materials and provide meaningful contexts. Paper folding, used in the activity "Cover Up" (later in the chapter) and illustrated in Figure 10.3, is a valuable experience. Children not only produce a fractional strip set to

STANDARD

Instructional programs from prekindergarten through grade 12 should enable all students to

Understand fractions and decimals, ways of representing them, and relationships among numbers.

Understand meanings of operations and how they relate to one another.

Compute fluently and make reasonable estimates.

GRADES PREK TO 2

In prekindergarten through grade 2 all students should

Understand and represent commonly used fractions, such as $\frac{1}{4}$, $\frac{1}{3}$, and $\frac{1}{2}$.

GRADES 3 TO 5

In grades 3 to 5 all students should

Develop understanding of fractions as parts of unit wholes, as parts of a collection, as locations on number lines, and as divisions of whole numbers.

Use models, benchmarks, and equivalent forms to judge the size of fractions.

Recognize and generate equivalent forms of commonly used fractions, and decimals.

Explore numbers less than 0 by extending the number line and through familiar applications.

Develop and use strategies to estimate computations involving fractions and decimals in situations relevant to students' experience.

Use visual models, benchmarks, and equivalent forms to add and subtract commonly used fractions and decimals.

GRADES 6 TO 8

In grades 6 to 8 all students should

Work flexibly with fractions and decimals to solve problems.

Compare and order fractions and decimals efficiently and find their approximate locations on a number line.

Understand the meaning and effects of arithmetic operations with fractions and decimals.

Use the associative and commutative properties of addition and multiplication and the distributive property of multiplication over addition to simplify computations with fractions and decimals.

Select appropriate methods and tools for computing with fractions and decimals from among mental computation, estimation, calculators or computers, and paper and pencil, depending on the situation, and apply the selected methods.

Develop and analyze algorithms for computing with fractions and decimals and develop fluency in their use.

Develop and use strategies to estimate the results of rational number computations and judge the reasonableness of the results.

FIGURE 10.1 *NCTM expectation of common fractions and decimals.[1]*

[1]*A partial listing as it pertains to Operations and Number Sense from* NCTM Principles and Standards for School Mathematics (2000, pages 392–393)

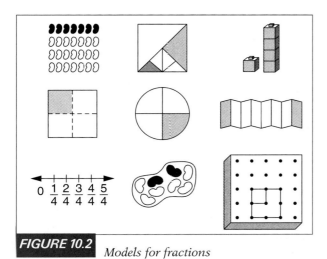

FIGURE 10.2 *Models for fractions*

use for developing operations, but they also see the result of folding congruent rectangular strips into smaller and smaller pieces.

Measure

Fractions as a linear measure can be viewed from an area perspective or a number line model. The fraction strips mentioned earlier can be used as a measure of a given length. Cuisenaire rods, shown in Figure 10.4, can serve as a measure of one specific rod to another. Activity 10.1 demonstrates one way to use Cuisenaire rods to develop the sense of fractions as measure. Or use a large piece of yarn to represent a given amount and have students subdivide it and label the points. Each of these activities represents a greater level of sophistication in the thinking required. Langford

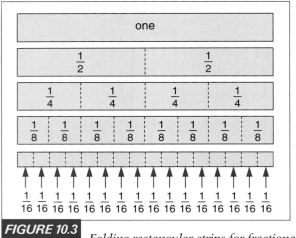

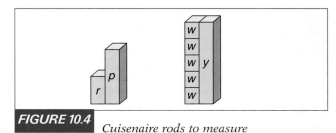

FIGURE 10.4   *Cuisenaire rods to measure fractional parts.*

Activity 10.1

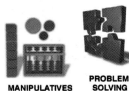

MANIPULATIVES   PROBLEM SOLVING

CUISENAIRE RODS AS FRACTIONAL PARTS OF A COMPLETE SET

Find as many Cuisenaire rods that represent $\frac{1}{3}$ as you can. How can you prove that each is exactly one-third of the basic unit of wholeness?

Now find Cuisenaire rods that represent $\frac{2}{3}$.

How can you prove that each is exactly two-thirds of the basic unit of wholeness? (*Hint:* if you proved one-third, proving two-thirds should follow easily.)

and Sarullo (1993) suggest connecting common fraction ideas to measurement ideas by using straws as a nonstandard unit of length to measure rectangular regions. Children can place segments of straws of a given unit along the edge of the region to determine fold lines.

Set

In fractional parts of a set, the whole becomes a given number of objects rather than a region. Figure 10.4 shows some examples of fractional parts of a set. Another example many students can relate to would involve situations using a dozen eggs. For instance, one-fourth of them are used to make a pie. In this example, the task becomes one of partitioning the set of twelve into four equal-size sets. The whole must be seen in a different way, which is harder for children and should be done in meaningful modeling situations. Hunting (in Bezuk and Bieck, 1993) found that students partition continuous quantities (such as a region) differently from sets (or discrete quantities). He concluded that students may need an understanding of fractions as continuous quantities before understanding problems involving sets.

Ratio

A fraction such as $\frac{2}{3}$ can also represent a ratio, which means that two elements of one set are present for every three elements of another set. Students may have more difficulty with this interpretation, illustrated in Figure 10.5.

Many middle school students who participate in sports activities often have experience with keeping team and individual stats. They know, for instance, that if Michele makes 3 out of 5 free throws ($\frac{3}{5}$) in Monday night's game and 3 out of 5 in Thursday night's game, she has made $\frac{3}{5} + \frac{3}{5}$ or $\frac{6}{10}$ (which equals $\frac{3}{5}$) of her free throws. In other words, when "adding" ratios, the rules are not the same as when adding fractions. If you find this confusing, think about your students and their confusion. But, as Smith (in Bright and Litwiller, 2002, p. 5) so aptly states, "(I)n your teaching, a simple principle follows: Work with your students to understand fractions and ratios in their own terms first. If they don't grasp those ideas, the formal concept of rational numbers will make little sense later on." More aspects of the concept of ratio are addressed in Chapter 11.

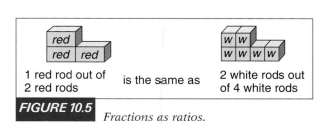

1 red rod out of 2 red rods   is the same as   2 white rods out of 4 white rods

FIGURE 10.5   *Fractions as ratios.*

Division

Fractions denote division of one set by the other. This concept is presented after much work with fractions has taken place in the elementary school. Many elementary texts introduce this concept after decimal representations are presented because the answers will be fractional parts. Here are the equivalent forms for 10/6:

$$\frac{10}{6} = 6\overline{)10}$$
$$= 10 \div 6$$

TEACHING STRATEGIES: FRACTIONS

Fractions are difficult to understand for several reasons. Frequently, models are not explored and used when concepts are developed. Many teachers demonstrate with pictorial models rather than with concrete aids. The study of fractional numbers should begin with a variety of models and shapes. Manipulative models should be used throughout the middle school years. Unless this practice is followed, fractions will continue to be difficult to learn and internalize. Too often the rule is presented before the underlying foundation has been laid. Many terms are unclear and ambiguous such as "reduce to lowest terms." Do we really mean to make the answer smaller? What about cancel and what does this term imply? Operations on whole numbers and on fractional numbers are not the same. For example, multiplying whole numbers yields a product larger than either factor, whereas multiplying two proper fractions results in a product smaller than either factor. Proper, concise language used when teaching operations with fractions plays an important role in the correct interpretation of the numbers.

The NCTM *Principles and Standards* (NCTM, 2000) specify a de-emphasis on paper-and-pencil computation with fractions. More time should be spent on creating a number sense for fractions through estimation with familiar fractions and mental computation. Oral language and concrete models are necessary components of building a conceptual understanding of fractions. In the *Standards,* it is recommended that operations with fractions and mixed numbers be limited to common fractions with simple denominators that can be visualized and correlated to simple real-world situations.

Estimation

Estimation is a skill that must be taught and used often with students. It is especially important in work with fractions and mixed numbers and should include some of the same estimation strategies used for whole numbers: nice numbers (or compatible numbers), front-end truncation, and rounding. These estimation strategies were described in Chapter 9, page 234, if you want to review them before proceeding with this chapter. One of the first teaching strategies in the area of fractions is to help students learn to establish **benchmarks** associated with recognizing numbers that are close to 1, $\frac{1}{2}$, or 0. This approach encourages them to consider the quantity represented by the fraction rather than get involved with the mechanics of changing to like denominators. Such activities help to emphasize that numbers in the numerator and denominator need to be compared to each other to determine their relative size. Number sense applies to fractions as much as it does to whole numbers.

Present situations in which students must estimate whether the fraction is closer to 0, to $\frac{1}{2}$, or to 1. Have students name some fractions near 0, $\frac{1}{2}$, and 1. Develop a sense of relative magnitude of a fraction, such as $\frac{3}{4}$ is large compared to $\frac{1}{3}$, about the same as $\frac{5}{8}$, and closer to 1 than to 0. It is important to establish the relationship of the numerator and the denominator (is the numerator about one-half of the denominator?) to help children become comfortable with this activity. They should also see that any fractional number close to 1 will have a numerator and a denominator that approach the same number. Develop activities where students must figure mentally fractional parts, such as 9 of the 20 people at the picnic were men. Was this about 0, about $\frac{1}{2}$, or about 1? If 12 of the 15 children in Mrs. Henry's class are girls, can we say over half the class is girls? Can you mentally picture a candy bar with $\frac{4}{10}$ of it cut off?

Whole-to-Part Activities

Early activities with fractions should begin with the whole–part meaning of fractions. Having children divide concrete objects such as a paper, egg cartons, or scored candy bars provides direct experiences to avoid such misconceptions as wanting the "biggest half." Young children do not understand the difference between the whole and parts of a whole. An orange broken into sections means more oranges to the young child. The emphasis is on developing the concept of a whole, parts, equal-size parts, and oral names (Smith, 2003; Empson, 2002; Steencken and Maher, 2002).

An important, and often disregarded, consideration is to discuss what is represented by a whole. The whole is whatever is designated as the unit. Take a sheet of $8\frac{1}{2} \times 11$ paper. Tear it in half. Each of the two congruent regions represents one-half. Show a notepad made of half sheets of paper. Tear off one sheet and ask if this sheet is a whole piece of paper. It is in relationship to the pad of paper, but it is one-half compared to the former whole sheet. Do the same for a pad consisting of paper the size of one-fourth the original sheet. Again ask the preceding questions and refer to the importance of knowing what is designated as the unit. This is important in terms of understanding operations with fractions discussed later in this chapter. Activity 10.2 demonstrates additional ways to help students build their understanding of fractions as a part–whole concept.

Fractions can be seen as parts of sets of objects when teaching for whole-to-part understanding. In this model, the unit represents the entire set.

Show a set of soft drinks.

How many cans are in the set? 6

Remove 2 cans. Suppose we drank 2 cans.

What part of the set did we drink?

What does the 6 represent?

What does the 2 represent?

Show an egg carton with 12 eggs.

How many eggs are in the set? 12

Suppose I use 5 eggs to make a cake. (Remove them.)

What part of the set did I use?

What does the 12 represent?

What does the 5 represent?

Repeat with connecting cubes, colored tiles, wooden cubes, and other concrete materials. Activity 10.3 can also be used for this purpose.

Partitioning Activities

Initial work with fractions should be based on the natural activities children experience with sharing. The sharing may be a region such as a candy bar or a set such as a bag of marbles. *Partitioning* relates to dividing parts into equal shares. In the concept development of fractions, the emphasis should be on unit fractions (where the numerator is one) and on common fractions.

The region model (a circle, square, or rectangle partitioned into parts) is usually the child's introduction to work with fractions and is found in most children's elementary school textbooks. It is important not to limit the shape to the "pie shape" or circle. Various regions should be used by exploring fractions with shapes on a geoboard, pattern blocks, Cuisenaire rods, and paper strips.

Activity 10.2

MATHEMATICAL CONNECTIONS

NAME THE FRACTION—FIND THE WHOLE

MATERIALS
- Pictures of real-world objects involving equal parts
- Shapes and parts of that shape

PROCEDURE
Hold up pictures or parts of a shape. Have students name the fraction. The purpose is to show that naming the fractional part cannot be done without seeing what represents the whole except in the case of some common fractions in circular form (one-half is always thought of as a half-circle regardless of the size of the circle). Include examples of egg cartons, ten-frames, all types of area models, and tires on cars or bicycles.

Activity 10.3

PROBLEM SOLVING   **WHAT'S THE PART?**

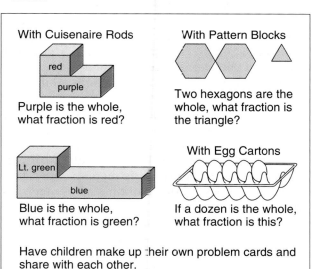

With Cuisenaire Rods

red
purple

Purple is the whole, what fraction is red?

Lt. green
blue

Blue is the whole, what fraction is green?

With Pattern Blocks

Two hexagons are the whole, what fraction is the triangle?

With Egg Cartons

If a dozen is the whole, what fraction is this?

Have children make up their own problem cards and share with each other.

Activity 10.6

MANIPULATIVES **ROLLING EQUIVALENTS**

MATERIALS
- Lima beans or counters
- Three dice
- Fraction strip chart (wholes, halves, thirds, fourths, fifths, sixths)

PROCEDURE
Players take turns rolling the three dice. When it is your turn, roll the dice and choose any two to make a fraction less than or equal to one using the fractions on the chart. (Roll a 2, 3, 3, and you make $\frac{2}{3}$ or $\frac{3}{3}$.) Put counters to correspond to the fraction you chose. If you chose $\frac{2}{3}$, you could put beans on 2 of the thirds or 4 beans on the sixths. The first person to fill the chart wins.

Activity 10.7

MANIPULATIVES **FRACTIONS ON THE GEOBOARD**

MATERIALS
- Geoboards and geobands
- Geoboard recording paper

PROCEDURE
Make equivalent fractions on the geoboard. Use different colored bands to partition the region. Draw on geoboard recording paper and write the equivalent fractions and why they represent the same amount. This approach helps students see the role of the whole and the parts. Encourage them to construct irregular regions and to name the fractional part represented.

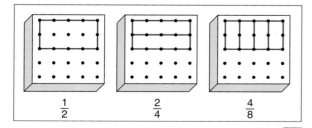

$\frac{1}{2}$ $\frac{2}{4}$ $\frac{4}{8}$

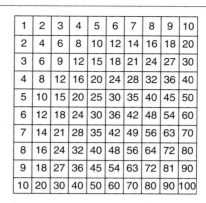

FIGURE 10.8 *Multiple bars.*

Activity 10.8

PROBLEM SOLVING **EQUIVALENT FRACTIONS: MULTIPLE BARS**

MATERIALS
- Multiple bars (Figure 10.8)

PROCEDURE
Place the 1 bar above the 8 bar to show a set of equivalent fractions for $\frac{1}{8}$. Read various equivalent names aloud. What name for 1 was used to multiply by $\frac{1}{8}$ to form $\frac{4}{32}$? ($\frac{4}{4}$). Write this number sentence:

$$\frac{1}{8} \times \frac{4}{4} = \frac{4}{32}$$

Repeat for other equivalent fractions. Place the 3 bar above the 4 bar. What fraction is formed? ($\frac{3}{4}$) Read other equivalent names for $\frac{3}{4}$. Tell what name for 1 was used to form each one.

1	2	3	4	5	6	7	8	9	10
8	16	24	32	40	48	56	64	72	80

or denominator. Some activities should include problems such as

$$\frac{2}{3} \times \frac{?}{?} = \frac{12}{18}$$

What name for 1 has been multiplied by $\frac{2}{3}$?

$$\frac{12}{20} \div \frac{?}{?} = \frac{3}{5}$$

What name for 1 has $\frac{12}{20}$ been divided by?

Additional equivalence activities and games are also on the Web site, Chapter 7, Extended Activities, as well as Video Vignette of fifth grade students exploring fractions.

Many experiences are necessary for children to feel totally comfortable with fractional equivalencies. Activities with a variety of materials as well as playing games in a comfortable, nonthreatening environment are helpful. The two games described in Activities 10.9 and 10.10 are from Marilyn Burns' *The Math Solution* (1984). They are to be played with the rectangular strip fraction kit described in Figure 10.2. These two games help children work on equivalent fractions, estimate fractions, compare fractions, and determine the relative size of fractions. After students have become familiar with these games and are ready to be introduced to the connecting level, have them record the steps on paper or small individual chalkboards as they do the action.

For example, in the game of "Uncover" (Activity 10.10), $\frac{1}{8}$ is rolled. On the strip, there is the $\frac{1}{4}$ piece.

We would most likely think to ourselves, "The problem then is $\frac{1}{4} - \frac{1}{8}$." The exchange is to trade $\frac{1}{4}$ for $\frac{2}{8}$ and in our adult understanding the exchange occurs like this:

$$\frac{1}{4} = \frac{2}{8}$$
$$-\frac{1}{8} = \frac{1}{8}$$
$$\frac{1}{8}$$

EXTENDED ACTIVITIES

PROBLEM SOLVING   **MENTAL MATH**   **ESTIMATION**

Name of Activity

- Build a Fraction
- Fracdecent
- Target One
- Edible Fractions
- Partitioning Regions
- Think About $\frac{1}{2}$
- Fraction War

Video Vignette

PROBLEM SOLVING   **MATHEMATICAL CONNECTIONS**

Rectangles and Fractions

In this video vignette, Mrs. Torres has posed a problem for her students. They are to use colored tiles to create a rectangle that meets the following specifications: $\frac{1}{2}$ of the rectangle is made of red tiles, $\frac{1}{4}$ yellow tiles, and $\frac{1}{4}$ green tiles. Before viewing the video, create this rectangle yourself. When you are finished, jot down the steps you went through to create the rectangle—including any wrong turns you took in the process. Now view the video.

Questions:

1. Mrs. Torres poses the task to create a rectangle that is composed of colored tiles such that $\frac{1}{2}$ of the tiles are red, $\frac{1}{4}$ are yellow, and $\frac{1}{4}$ are green. How many of each colored tile were used in Mrs. Torres' rectangle?

   a. Why does Mrs. Torres direct their thinking to the chart of factors?

   b. Is there another way to form this rectangle so that it meets the same requirements?

2. In the independent activity ($\frac{1}{3}$ red and $\frac{2}{3}$ green), what probing techniques does she use when talking with Carlos about his answer?

3. Be prepared to discuss your observations in class.

Supporting the NCTM *Principles and Standards* (2000):

- Mathematics as Problem Solving
- Tools to Promote Discourse; Student's Role in Discourse—The Teaching Principle

Activity 10.9

MANIPULATIVES COVER UP

MATERIALS

- Rectangular fraction kit (Figure 10.2)
- Number cube marked with these sides: $\frac{1}{2}, \frac{1}{4}, \frac{1}{8}, \frac{1}{8}, \frac{1}{16}, \frac{1}{16}$

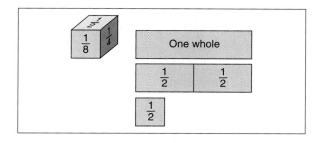

PROCEDURE

The object of the game is to be the first player to completely cover the whole strip with the other fractional pieces from the kit without overlapping.

Roll the number cube and the player rolling the least fractional number goes first. The first player rolls the number cube. This fraction tells the piece that the student puts on the whole strip. Each student builds the fractions on his or her own whole strip. If an overlap is the result, the player loses a turn and must wait until the fraction named on the number cube can be placed. For example, if the player needs only a small piece, such as an $\frac{1}{8}$ or $\frac{1}{16}$ to cover up and win, rolling a $\frac{1}{2}$ or $\frac{1}{4}$ cannot be used. The first person to cover up the entire strip wins.

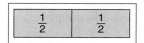

At this point in the students' understanding of fractions, writing the subtraction notation may be meaningless. Their notation may look more like this:

$\frac{1}{4}$ is the same as $\frac{2}{8}$. Trade $\frac{1}{4}$ for 2 of the $\frac{1}{8}$ pieces. Now I can take 1 of the $\frac{1}{8}$ pieces.

Activity 10.10

MANIPULATIVES UNCOVER

MATERIALS

- Rectangular fraction kit (Figure 10.2)
- Number cube marked with sides: $\frac{1}{2}, \frac{1}{4}, \frac{1}{8}, \frac{1}{8}, \frac{1}{16}, \frac{1}{16}$

PROCEDURE

The object of the game is to be the first player to uncover the whole strip completely. The player must roll exactly what is needed to uncover the strip in order to win. Each player has the whole strip covered with the two $\frac{1}{2}$ pieces.

Students roll the number cube, and the player rolling the least fractional number plays first. The first player rolls the number cube. The fraction on the cube tells how much the player can remove. An exchange or trade may be necessary before the fraction can be removed. This is the object behind the game as it focuses on equivalencies. For example, if a student rolls an $\frac{1}{8}$ on the first roll, one of the $\frac{1}{2}$ pieces needs to be exchanged in order to remove an $\frac{1}{8}$. Encourage students to verbalize the equivalencies exchanged.

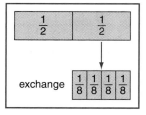

The important point in this connecting level activity is that a meaningful recording, created as the exchanges are made, ensures that the transfer from the concrete level to the symbolic level is much greater. These two games provide excellent readiness for addition and subtraction of unlike denominators. Check additional activities on the Web site, Chapter 10, Extended Activities, which develop multiple relationships of fractions.

Most calculator companies today market a fraction calculator that can simplify fractions automatically or by entering the greatest common

EXTENDED ACTIVITIES

MANIPULATIVES

MENTAL MATH

CULTURAL RELEVANCE

MATHEMATICAL CONNECTIONS

PROBLEM SOLVING

CHILDREN'S LITERATURE

On the Web site (Chapter 10, Extended Activities) read/do the following:

- Showing Geoboard Operations
- Fractions and the Eye of Horus
- Roll and Show
- Understanding Multiplication of Fractions
- Division of Fractional Numbers—Fraction by a Fraction
- Fraction Cube Toss
- Greatest Quotient
- Family Math Packets [using Children's Literature]
    Football Math
- Lesson Plans to Develop Mathematical Proficiency
    Simple Fractions
    Fractions with Food
    Introduction of Fractions and Fair Shares

multiple. Students can perform the four basic operations by using the built-in fraction algorithm. This calculator presents many possibilities for students to test their knowledge of fractions with the power of immediate feedback. Estimation should also be included with calculator activities.

OPERATIONS WITH FRACTIONS

Exploratory fraction work should introduce the use of physical materials to solve simple real-world problems involving fractions. Many students have learned computations with fractions as procedures without developing the underlying conceptual knowledge about fractions. Most instruction of operations with fractions occurs in the middle grades and instruction in computational procedures forms the major component of the textbook approach to fractions with limited coverage of quantitative reasoning about fractions.

Although an assortment of fraction models should be used, in the interest of space, the activities shown here focus primarily on the circular and rectangular fraction kits. Each activity, presented here with addition and subtraction, shows the sequence with which the operations should be taught. Notice that the activities grow gradually more complex.

Addition and Subtraction

Invented Strategies The same approach for developing alternative algorithms used in Chapter 9 for whole numbers applies as well to fractions. Students who have a rich background of solving problems through multiple means will likely not use the step-by-step process of the traditional algorithms. They will combine the wholes first and then approach the fractions. Subtraction will create a variety of alternative solutions. For example, students might find that the natural starting point for this problem would be to break down the wholes:

One characteristic of students' thinking about fractions is their successful use of solving problems in the context of real-life scenarios. Eating pizza or pie and sharing cookies or candy bars are situations that give meaning to fraction

procedures. More discussion of invented strategies is presented in the section in this chapter on multiplication and division.

Standard Algorithms As students' invented strategies become more sophisticated, they will be ready to learn the standard algorithms in meaningful ways because of the conceptual understanding of fractions and operation sense they have built through their work with models and invented strategies. Each step in the following procedures for the standard algorithms is outlined in detail. The actions should be replicated with many examples using different materials. Manipulatives model these concepts, but all action should be accompanied with verbal descriptions, followed by the written steps, to link the algorithm with the words. There must be a link and match between what is done, what is said, and what is written. As you read, you are encouraged to model each of the examples to solidify your understanding. Do the examples first with the fraction kits and then with another manipulative of your choice. Remember subtraction situations with fractions must include more than take away. All problem structures (missing addend, comparison, start unknown) that you encountered for whole numbers apply to fractions. In these examples, notice the modeling that accompanies the situation.

Six Concepts

Concept 1 *Adding Fractions with Like Denominators*

Situational Problem:
Alfinio ran $\frac{1}{4}$ mile to Jose's house, and then ran another $\frac{1}{4}$ mile to the country market. How far did he run in all?

Procedure:
  The problem: $\frac{1}{4} + \frac{1}{4}$

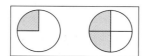

- Place a whole on the desk. Put a fourth on it.
- Add another fourth to it. How many in all?
- Record that one-fourth + one-fourth = two-fourths. Remember the numerators are added and the denominators are a label of the fractional pieces.
- Answer: $\frac{2}{4}$

Concept 2 *Adding Fractions with Mixed Numerals*

Situational Problem:
The recipe for cookies calls for $1\frac{1}{3}$ cups of white sugar and $1\frac{1}{3}$ cups of brown sugar. How much sugar is needed?

Procedure:
  The problem: $1\frac{1}{3} + 1\frac{1}{3}$
- Place two groups of one whole and one-third on the desk. Combine like units.
- Answer: $2\frac{2}{3}$

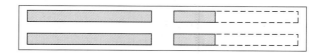

Concept 3 *Adding Fractions with Unlike Denominators*

Situational Problem:
Lucinda practiced her flute $\frac{1}{2}$ hour in the morning and $\frac{1}{4}$ hour in the evening. What fractional part of an hour did she practice that day?

Procedure:
  The problem: $\frac{1}{2} + \frac{1}{4}$

- Denominators are not the same, so the first step is to see whether one number is a multiple of the other.
- If it is, use the least common denominator. In other words, is one of the denominators a multiple of the other?
- Exchange $\frac{1}{2}$ for $\frac{2}{4}$. Record when ready for the connecting level.
- Proceed in the same manner as adding like denominators.
- Answer: $\frac{3}{4}$

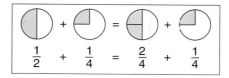

Concept 4 *Adding Mixed Numerals with Regrouping*

Situational Problem:
Mrs. Levison's pattern for a suit says yards are needed for the jacket and yards are needed for the skirt. How much material should she buy to make the suit?

Procedure:
     The problem: $2\frac{2}{3} + 1\frac{1}{2}$

- Form the two numbers with the fraction kit pieces.

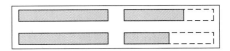

- Combine like units.

To combine the fractional units:

- Is one number a multiple of the other? (no)
- Exchange both pieces for the least common denominator (thirds and halves can become sixths). Exchange $\frac{2}{3}$ for $\frac{4}{6}$ and $\frac{1}{2}$ for $\frac{3}{6}$.
- Combine the sixths (7). Six-sixths can be regrouped as a whole with one-sixth left.
- Answer: $4\frac{1}{6}$

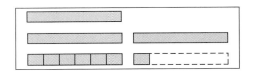

Concept 5 *Subtracting Fractions with Like Denominators*

Situational Problem:
Janet has $\frac{3}{4}$ cup of peanut butter. She uses $\frac{1}{4}$ cup for frosting. How much peanut butter does she have left?

Procedure:
     The problem: $\frac{3}{4} - \frac{1}{4}$

- Place three-fourths on a whole.
- To subtract one-fourth from three-fourths, simply take away the one-fourth piece.

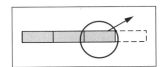

- Answer: $\frac{2}{4}$.

Concept 6 *Subtracting Fractions with Unlike Denominators (Take-Away Interpretation)*

Situational Problem:
Mr. Nyo has $\frac{2}{3}$ gallon $\frac{1}{4}$ of gasoline. He uses $\frac{1}{4}$ gallon for his chain saw. How much gasoline does he have left?

Procedure:
     The problem: $\frac{2}{3} - \frac{1}{4}$

- Place the whole piece with two-thirds on top.
- In order to subtract one-fourth, find the least common denominator. What piece can be exchanged for thirds and fourths?

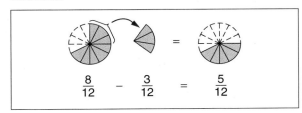

- Exchange $\frac{2}{3}$ for $\frac{8}{12}$ and $\frac{1}{4}$ for $\frac{3}{12}$.
- Now the denominators are the same, so subtract the numerators. Take away three-twelfths.

- Answer: $\frac{5}{12}$.

    With subtraction, the take-away method is most commonly used; however, modeling should be done for the missing addend and comparison interpretations. Be sure that appropriate word problems accompany the modeling.

For Missing Addend Interpretation

Situational Problem:
Marcus needs $\frac{2}{3}$ cup of solvent but discovers he only has $\frac{1}{4}$ cup. He calls a friend to get some more solvent. How much more does he need?

Procedure:
     The problem: $\frac{2}{3} - \frac{1}{4}$

- Begin with $\frac{1}{4}$ piece on the whole.
- How much must you add to $\frac{1}{4}$ to make $\frac{2}{3}$? (Optional—show $\frac{2}{3}$ as "target.")

- Exchange thirds and fourths for common equivalent pieces. Exchange $\frac{1}{4}$ for $\frac{3}{12}$ and $\frac{2}{3}$ for $\frac{8}{12}$.
- How much should you add to $\frac{3}{12}$ to get $\frac{8}{12}$?
- Add twelfths until you get $\frac{8}{12}$.
- Answer: $\frac{5}{12}$

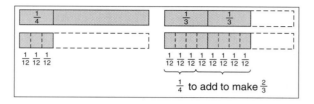

For Comparison Interpretation

Situational Problem:

The recipe for sugar cookies calls for $2\frac{1}{3}$ cups sugar. The recipe for oatmeal cookies calls for $1\frac{1}{3}$ cups sugar. How much more sugar is needed for sugar cookies?

Procedure:

The problem: $2\frac{1}{3} - 1\frac{1}{3}$

- Show the two whole pieces and the one-third piece.
- Show the one whole and one-half piece. (Remember, for comparison both numbers are modeled to be compared and the difference is found.)

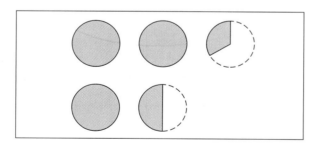

- Compare like pieces. The whole pieces "cancel" each other. Compare fractions.

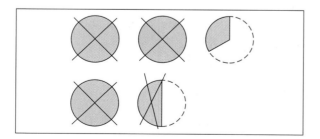

- The whole can become two halves and the halves "cancel" each other. How much is left? (one-half and one-third)
- Exchange for common denominators to give final answer. Exchange $\frac{1}{2}$ for $\frac{3}{6}$ and $\frac{1}{3}$ for $\frac{2}{6}$.
- Answer: $\frac{5}{6}$.

Activities 10.11 and 10.12 will also be helpful in estimating sums and differences of fractions and in giving children some checkpoint about the correctness of their answers in computational problems. You can write the problems on large cards to hold before the class in a whole class activity. Or you can write the problems on the overhead projector and control the time period they are shown by covering up the problem or turning off the overhead lamp. Or small groups of students can use the cards in a game situation during center time or during that part of the lesson often referred to as "independent practice." Children (and adults) have many insecurities about estimating with fractions because they have not had sufficient opportunities to practice this skill.

Activity 10.11

ESTIMATION ESTIMATE AND ORDER

MATERIALS

- Forty cards with a different addition or subtraction fraction problem on each one

PROCEDURE

Shuffle the cards and deal out five cards to each player facedown. When the dealer says go, the players arrange their cards by estimating the answers so that the answers are in order from least to greatest.

Winner: the first player to order the cards correctly wins the hand. That player is the new dealer.

Supporting the NCTM *Principles and Standards* (2000):
- Number and Operation; Mathematics as Reasoning, Problem Solving
- Worthwhile Mathematical Tasks—The Teaching Principle
- The Learning Principle

Activity 10.12

ESTIMATION WITH FRACTIONS

PROBLEM

Look quickly at the fractional number or numbers and decide whether they are about 1, about $\frac{1}{2}$, or about 0. Determine the sum or difference.

$$\frac{7}{12} + \frac{3}{6} = ? \qquad \frac{4}{10} + \frac{11}{10} = ?$$

$$\frac{2}{9} + \frac{7}{8} = ? \qquad \frac{9}{20} + \frac{4}{5} = ?$$

$$\frac{8}{9} - \frac{4}{5} = ? \qquad \frac{10}{9} - \frac{1}{12} = ?$$

Problems can also include mixed numbers. Ask students to round to the nearest whole number and add or subtract.

$$2\frac{4}{5} + 2\frac{9}{10} = ? \qquad 3\frac{1}{9} + 8\frac{8}{10} = ?$$

$$7 - 2\frac{6}{7} = ? \qquad 4\frac{8}{12} - \frac{7}{9} = ?$$

Remember the example from Chapter 4 about adding fractions incorrectly by adding the numerators and denominators as whole numbers? The problem posed was $\frac{7}{10} + \frac{3}{4}$. The student who answered it incorrectly gave $\frac{10}{14}$ as the solution. Another student in the class commented that that was wrong because then $3 + 5$ would equal 4 rather than 8. This student demonstrated a deep conceptual understanding of fractions, equivalence, and the operation of addition. Because any whole number can be written in fractional form by giving it a denominator of 1, $\frac{3}{1} + \frac{5}{1}$ would equal $\frac{8}{2}$ or 4 according to the reasoning of the first student. The second student understood that the operation of addition of whole numbers had to hold true even if the whole numbers were written in fractional form. Thus, adding the numerators together and the denominators together would not lead to a correct solution to the problem.

Mixed Numbers When adding and subtracting mixed numbers, students can benefit from knowing how to change a mixed number to an improper fraction. The terms *proper* and *improper fractions* are ones that may be difficult for students to remember. A *proper fraction* is one whose numerator is of a lower degree (less) than its denominator, and an *improper fraction* is one whose numerator is of a greater degree (more) or is equal to its denominator. Hence,

Proper	Improper
$\frac{7}{12}$	$\frac{12}{7} \quad \frac{8}{8}$

Elementary textbooks also show students how to change improper fractions to an equivalent proper fraction. This procedure necessitates changing the improper fraction to a *mixed number*, which is a whole number and a proper fraction. Check more activities with fractions and mixed numbers on the Web site, Chapter 10, Extended Activities.

Multiplication and Division

Multiplication and division of fractions are areas that pose many difficulties for children, primarily because the foundation for understanding the underlying concepts is not fully developed. The case too often is that the teacher uses the textbook examples and verbally explains them by using a chalkboard or the overhead. Students are moved too quickly to the symbolic level and are given the easy-to-remember but difficult-to-comprehend rules. Errors result when students move symbols around meaninglessly as they rotely learn rules for procedures like the following:

- When multiplying fractions, multiply the numerators and the denominators.

EXTENDED ACTIVITIES

MANIPULATIVES   **CALCULATORS**   **PORTFOLIO**

Name of Activity

- Changing Mixed Numbers to Fractional Numbers
- Changing Fractional Numbers to Mixed Numbers
- Freaky Fractions
- TIMSS Assessment: Chocolate Bar

- When dividing fractions, use the reciprocal. (Often rephrased as "Invert the second number and multiply the two numbers.")

Many teachers do not use manipulative materials in intermediate grades or in middle school. There may be a limited number of materials available to model various problems. One solution to the lack of materials is to use the patterns for manipulative pieces found in Appendix A on the Web site and have your students (or a parent volunteer or aide) make sets of manipulatives. Many examples and multiple embodiments are needed for adequate practice to solidify one's understanding of these operations with fractions.

An important aspect of multiplication is understanding the term "of" for multiplication and how it relates to whole number multiplication. It is important to build on the prior knowledge students have about whole numbers whenever possible when teaching fractions. Although there are several differences that occur with fractions and whole numbers, it is important to address them and to create bridges of understanding when desirable. The following teaching sequence is suggested:

Write this equation: $3 \times 4 = 12$

Ask students to give the mathematical language and draw the set pictures that model this equation. It says: 3 groups of 4. It means there are 4 in each group and there are 3 groups. This becomes a review of the meaning of multiplication seen in Chapter 7. If teachers use the word "of" from the beginning of teaching multiplication, the transfer of learning will help in problems like those that follow.

If children have only learned multiplication as repeated addition, they are going to have extraordinary difficulties when they study multiplication of fractions. In whole number multiplication you can say that 7×8 means $8 + 8 + 8 + 8 + 8 + 8 + 8$ (i.e., add 8 seven times). But what do you say that $7\frac{5}{6} \times 8$ means? Certainly adding 8 seven and five-sixths times makes no sense. That is one reason it is so important to teach multiplication in terms of "sets of" or "groups of" and not just in terms of repeated addition.

Invented Strategies Several studies (Thompson and Saldanha, 2003; Empson, 1995) indicate that students possess a great deal of intuitive knowledge about fractions. Children, even in first grade, can develop meaningful procedures for solving problems involving equal sharing without explicit instruction in the standard algorithm. Middle school teachers who continue the constructivist

teaching from elementary grades find that students are capable of inventing ways to add, subtract, multiply, and divide fractions without direct instruction on procedures or algorithms.

Presenting a context for understanding operations with fractions helps the students' development of understanding. Situations dealing with recipes naturally involve the concept of ratios and present opportunities for students to use familiar referents such as cups and teaspoons. Brinker (1998) presents the strategies her middle school students used to invent procedures for solving fractions and mixed-number multiplication problems. Samples of her students' thinking and their written explanations show a great deal of creative, powerful mathematical reasoning.

Many researchers are looking at the sophisticated mathematical thinking and powerful exchange of ideas that comes from children's invented solutions to fraction problems. Usiskin (2007b) points out that premature formalism leads to symbolic knowledge that children cannot connect to the real world and results in an inability to develop number sense and reasoning about fractions. You have heard those same warnings concerning whole number computation that is based on teaching the standard algorithm (Flores, 2002). The following two examples of children's thinking come from a first-grade classroom (Empson, 1995, p. 111). The problem was

Seven candy bars were equally shared among three children. How much candy would each child get?

Two students' drawings in Figure 10.9 show how the partitioning was done.

Another classroom example comes from fifth and sixth graders (Warrington, 1997) who had this problem presented to them:

I purchased 5 pounds of chocolate-covered peanuts. I want to store the candy in $\frac{1}{2}$-pound bags. How many $\frac{1}{2}$-pound bags can I make?

One student responded, "You get ten bags from the five pounds because five divided by one-half is ten, and then you get another bag from the three-fourths, which makes eleven bags, and there is one-fourth of a pound left over, which makes half of a half-pound bag" (Warrington, 1997, p. 393). Try this problem for yourself and think about the logical thought you might use. What aspects of equal sharing are included? How meaningful is the answer obtained in this manner rather than the "invert and multiply" approach?

The Standard Algorithms *Fraction* × *Whole Number* As noted earlier, as students' invented

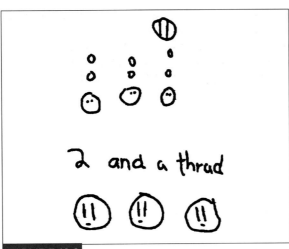

FIGURE 10.9 *Two examples of children's sharing seven candy bars among three children by partitioning the last candy bar into thirds.*

strategies become more sophisticated, they will be ready to learn the standard algorithms in meaningful ways because of the conceptual understanding of fractions and operation sense they have built through their work with models and invented strategies. In problems in which a fractional number is the first factor and a whole number is the second factor, encourage students to model the action. For example, $\frac{4}{3} \times 12$ means you start with 12 and want to find out how much is $\frac{4}{3}$ of that amount, as shown in Figure 10.10. The 12 must be divided into fourths, or four groups. Then the numerator tells how many groups to consider—three groups of 3, or 9.

Include examples and experiences that are not always the "friendly numbers" that are multiples of each other. For example, have students explore and model with materials or drawings how they would solve. Let them grapple with the notion of partitioning 14 into four groups. How would they subdivide the "leftovers"?

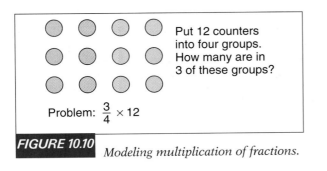

Put 12 counters into four groups. How many are in 3 of these groups?

Problem: $\frac{3}{4} \times 12$

FIGURE 10.10 *Modeling multiplication of fractions.*

Activity 10.13

MANIPULATIVES MATHEMATICAL CONNECTIONS

MULTIPLYING FRACTIONS—WHOLE NUMBER BY A FRACTIONAL NUMBER

MATERIALS
- Circular or rectangular fraction kits

PROCEDURE

Problem: $2 \times \frac{1}{2}$

Situational Problem: Lesley wants to double a recipe of cookies. The recipe calls for $\frac{1}{2}$ cup sugar. How much sugar will Lesley need to make 2 batches?

Take two groups of the one-half piece and place on a whole. These equal the whole.

In the problem of multiplying with a fraction, the language that accompanies the equation is that there are 2 groups of one-half.

Problem: $\frac{1}{2} \times 2$

Situational Problem: Andy's recipe calls for 2 cups flour. He wants to use only half of the recipe. How much flour will be needed?

Ask whether the commutative principle works for fractions. What is the mathematical language that accompanies this problem? It says: one-half a group of 2. What does it mean? It means there are two wholes and you take one-half of that amount. How do you model this problem? Was the answer the same? Why?

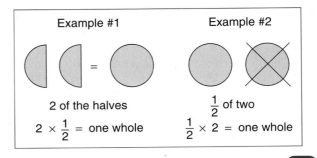

Activity 10.13 illustrates models of multiplying a whole number by a fraction using a fraction circle kit. What is at least one other manipulative you could use in modeling this activity?

Fraction × ***Fraction*** The next step is to multiply one fractional part by another, no longer relying on a whole number to make the concept easier to understand. Most textbooks represent this concept with an area model. Strips of paper, a modification of the area model, can substitute as a concrete model. One benefit of using an area model for multiplication is that the area model serves as a preview of models used in more advanced mathematics, including algebra and integral calculus.

Real-world situations should accompany the modeling. Practical problems should be used before the introduction of the algorithm. Remember that the easy path (and commonly used one) appears to just simply give the rule, "Multiply the numerators, multiply the denominators, and get the answer." However, such instruction limits children's intuitive feel for fractions. On the contrary, modeling develops quantitative reasoning so students can estimate the size of the product, observe relationships of the factors, create real-world applications, and judge the reasonableness of their answers.

For example, the problem $\frac{3}{4} \times \frac{1}{2}$ can be modeled with geoboards, counters, drawings, and rectangular or circular regions. Students should be able to explain how the physical materials are used and to interpret the entire operation. Generally, the situational problem the child creates to accompany the modeling matches the type of material used. Varying the materials becomes a powerful tool to break out of the typical mind-set of formulating problems using pizza or pies. Activity 10.14 demonstrates an approach to modeling the multiplication of a fraction by a fraction.

As teachers acquire more confidence in developing students' conceptual understanding of fractions, their observations can become more diagnostic in nature to determine a child's learning style as either part-to-whole or whole-to-part as shown in Figure 10.11.

It is important to provide many examples so that students become familiar with how multiplying two fractional numbers results in a smaller amount than either of the two proper factors. Give practice estimating with fractional numbers, adapting Activity 10.12, page 277. Test the students' understanding by asking them to evaluate answers to see if the answer is reasonable. This procedure helps when numbers become too cumbersome for manipulatives to work well, and students still need to check whether their answers are in the correct range of possibilities. Multiplying two mixed numbers is an example of a cumbersome set to manipulate. The fraction kits do not work well with such problems. If sufficient prior

work has been done with multiplying in ways mentioned previously, it is hoped that this process can be understood and estimations can be made to check for accuracy. Include predictions and estimations to develop quantitative understanding of fractions.

Activity 10.14

MANIPULATIVES   **MATHEMATICAL CONNECTIONS**

MULTIPLYING FRACTIONS—FRACTIONAL NUMBER BY A FRACTIONAL NUMBER

PROCEDURE

Problem: $\frac{1}{2} \times \frac{1}{4}$

Situational Problem: Lynn's lawn mower needs $\frac{1}{4}$ pint oil to be mixed with gasoline. If only half of the mixture is made, how much oil is needed?

Do we start with halves or fourths? Remember that the second factor tells the number in the group and the first factor tells how many groups.

To model this problem, it becomes critical to have the whole piece as the representative unit. *The one-fourth is one-fourth only in relationship to the whole circular region.* To take one-half of the one-fourth, the one-fourth piece needs to be partitioned into two equal parts. What fractional piece will do this? $\frac{1}{8}$.

Place the two one-eighth pieces on the $\frac{1}{4}$. How much is half of this group? $\frac{1}{8}$.

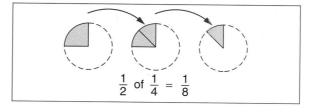

$$\frac{1}{2} \text{ of } \frac{1}{4} = \frac{1}{8}$$

Think about the answer. The one-eighth piece is one-half of the one-fourth, but it is one-eighth in relationship to the whole. Use the commutative property and have children see the other way to consider this problem and that the answer is still the same, but the modeling is different.

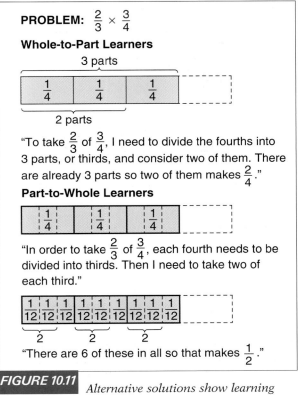

PROBLEM: $\frac{2}{3} \times \frac{3}{4}$

Whole-to-Part Learners

"To take $\frac{2}{3}$ of $\frac{3}{4}$, I need to divide the fourths into 3 parts, or thirds, and consider two of them. There are already 3 parts so two of them makes $\frac{2}{4}$."

Part-to-Whole Learners

"In order to take $\frac{2}{3}$ of $\frac{3}{4}$, each fourth needs to be divided into thirds. Then I need to take two of each third."

"There are 6 of these in all so that makes $\frac{1}{2}$."

FIGURE 10.11 *Alternative solutions show learning preference.*

Understanding Division Before beginning this section on division of fractions, study the knowledge packet for division of fractions based on Ma's work shown in Figure 10.12. Is there a key topic, basic concept, or principle that you would add to this knowledge packet? Why? Share your under-

standing of this knowledge packet with two or three of your classmates. Can you reach consensus on the changes to the knowledge packet you suggest?

Division with fractions is one of the most difficult concepts to understand. Again, it is important to relate the operation of division with whole numbers and discuss what mathematical language and models are appropriate. Consider the problem $\frac{12}{3} = 4$. What does it mean? There are 12 objects to be divided into groups of 3. The question is "How many groups of 3 are there in 12?" The answer tells you the number of groups of 3 you can get from 12. This is the measurement approach to division. You know the amount in each group and must determine the number of groups that can be made. This is the approach that will be used in division with fractional numbers. Although not every division situation (i.e., division by a whole number) can be interpreted as the measurement concept of division, it fits many problems as noted in this section. Read the situational problems for the activities and think about the mathematical language. Review the examples of word problems found on the Web site, Chapter 10, Extended Activities, "More Word Problems."

When students first work with division of fractions, we advocate using a common denominator approach. This keeps the operation as division rather than using the reciprocal, which converts the process into multiplication. Students are familiar with finding common denominators to add and subtract fractions, and the algorithm ties into that prior knowledge. The steps for division are the same as for addition and subtraction: find

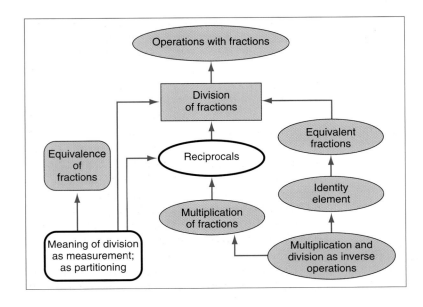

FIGURE 10.12 *Knowledge packet for division of fractions.*

common denominators and then perform the operation (division) on the numerators. This approach to the division of fractions is demonstrated in Activity 10.15.

Activity 10.15

MANIPULATIVES   **MATHEMATICAL CONNECTIONS**

DIVISION OF FRACTIONAL NUMBERS— WHOLE NUMBER BY A FRACTION

PROCEDURE

Problem: $2 \div \dfrac{2}{3}$

Situational Problem: Mrs. Morozzo needs 2 cups evaporated milk for her recipe. The milk comes in cans that contain $\frac{2}{3}$ cup. How many cans of evaporated milk must she buy? How many groups of two-thirds are in two wholes?

- Begin with 2 wholes.
- The first step is the 2 wholes must be renamed or exchanged for thirds. How many thirds are there in 2? There are 6.
- How many groups of two-thirds can be formed from six thirds?
- Answer = 3. Mrs. Morozzo needs 3 cans of evaporated milk.

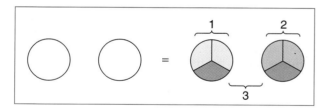

To show how the common denominator is used:

$$2 \div \frac{2}{3} = \frac{6}{3} \div \frac{2}{3}$$
$$= \frac{3}{1} = 3$$

Problem: $2 \div \frac{4}{12}$

Situational Problem: Maria has 2 yards of fabric that must be cut into sections of yard each to make costume pieces. How many costumes can be made?

How many groups of four-twelfths are there in 2?

- Rename two whole pieces as twelfths.

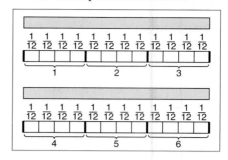

- There are 24 twelfths. Dividing them into groups of four means that 6 groups are made.
- Answer: 6.
  To show the common denominator:

$$2 \div \frac{4}{12} = \frac{24}{12} \div \frac{4}{12}$$
$$= \frac{24 \div 4}{12 \div 12}$$
$$= \frac{6}{1} = 6$$

How many groups of four-twelfths can be made from the 24 twelfths? Look at the numerators and perform the division of $\frac{24}{4} = 6$. The answer says that there are 6 groups of 4 twelfths in 24 twelfths.

Be sure students have many experiences with this kind of problem where the division results in an equal number of groups. Have them verbalize the steps and then record the symbolic numbers and model the procedures with the fraction kit. The important thing to remember is that using the common denominator method keeps the operation of division clearly in mind rather than the traditional "invert and multiply." For most children and many teachers, the latter approach can better be interpreted as "Ours is not to reason why, simply invert and multiply." The rule is easy to learn, but students have no idea about the reasonableness of answers when problem solving.

Activity 10.16 shows some more examples of the common denominator approach to division of fractions with mixed numbers as the final answer. See how the procedure works with them. Notice the relationship between the divisor and the remainder. The remainder needs to be expressed in terms of the size of the set. What part of a set or group is the remainder? Drawing on students' knowledge of whole number remainders may shed light on this new situation.

The common denominator method can also be used with fractional numbers divided by

fractional numbers. Activity 10.16 shows how it can be done with the circular fraction kit. The most difficult problems to show and correctly interpret are those in which the divisor is larger than the dividend. The fraction kit can be used to model this process, and some examples are given in this text. Curcio, Sicklick, and Turkel (1987) use rectangular fraction strips to illustrate the algorithm for the division of fractions. To solidify your understanding, you may want to read and compare both approaches.

Activity 10.16

MANIPULATIVES

USING THE COMMON DENOMINATOR METHOD

PROCEDURE

Problem: $2 \div \dfrac{3}{4}$

Situational Problem: Tenisha has 2 yards of cloth. She needs $\frac{3}{4}$ yard to cover a bar stool. How many stools can she cover? How many groups of three-fourths are there in 2?

- The first step is to rename the two wholes as fourths.
- How many are there? 8. Now the problem becomes:

$$2 \div \frac{3}{4} = \frac{8}{4} \div \frac{3}{4}$$

- How many groups of three-fourths are there in eight fourths?
- Take the eight fourths and place into groups of 3.
- There are two complete groups of 3 and a part of a group or a remainder.
- There are 2 pieces of fourths left. How many fourths make each group? 3. How many are left? 2. There are two-thirds of a complete group left. Answer is $2\frac{2}{3}$.

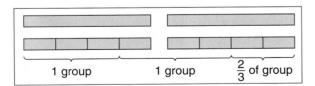

| 1 group | 1 group | $\frac{2}{3}$ of group |

To show the common denominator:

$$2 \div \frac{3}{4} = \frac{8}{4} \div \frac{3}{4} = \frac{8 \div 3}{4 \div 4} = \frac{8 \div 3}{1} = \frac{8}{3} = 2\frac{2}{3}$$

Problem: $2 \div \dfrac{5}{6}$

Situational Problem: The 2-foot board must be cut into segments that are $\frac{5}{6}$ foot long. How many segments can be made? What fractional part remains?

How many groups of five-sixths are there in two wholes?

- Rename the two wholes as sixths. How many groups of five-sixths are there in twelve sixths?
- Put the twelve sixths into groups of 5. There are 2 complete groups with 2 pieces left over. These are a part of the group—2 out of 5 that make a complete group.
- Answer: $2\frac{2}{5}$.

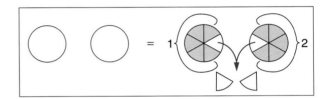

$$2 \div \frac{5}{6} = \frac{12}{6} = \frac{5}{6} \div 2\frac{2}{5}$$

How many $\frac{5}{6}$ are there in 2?

There are 2 sets of $\frac{5}{6}$ and $\frac{2}{5}$ of a set.

One important consideration—keep the numbers simple and within the realm of being conceptually understood. The NCTM *Standards* recommend that only common familiar fractions should be used. We must be reasonable about problem-solving situations that would require complicated fractional numbers. We cannot justify including difficult numbers that require a lot of valuable instructional time but have limited, or no, real-life application.

In dealing with common fractions, the easier approach to use is the measurement interpretation asking how many groups can be made. Partitive division is used in finding unit prices and averages. As you explore examples, think about how you can help students make sense of mathematics as the NCTM *Standards* recommend.

Reciprocal When middle school students are ready to work with the reciprocal, teachers must be ready to explain why the reciprocal works. This

is difficult for students to conceptualize. Consider the following:

> There are two groups of one-fourth: $2 \times \frac{1}{4}$
> There are one and one-half of the two-fourths: $1\frac{1}{2} \times \frac{2}{4}$

The multiplicative inverse is possible because answers to the division of fractions are inherently the inverse operation of multiplication. It was also shown that the reciprocal relationship is present, such as

$$2 \times \frac{1}{2} = 1 \qquad \frac{1}{2} \times 2 = 1$$

Notice that each example comes back to the same basic unit of wholeness or 1. When the numerator and the denominator can be inverted and multiplied by a corresponding number in such a way as to maintain the same basic unit of wholeness, it is said that one fractional representation is in a reciprocal relationship with the other. Putting two ideas together—(1) complete answers to division of fractions are really multiplication problems and (2) using a reciprocal of a fraction does not change the basic unit of wholeness—one has a justification for the rule "invert and multiply." In addition, the example has shown that another property of the multiplication of fractions,

$$2 \times \frac{1}{2} \text{ and } \frac{1}{2} \times 2$$

is referred to as the commutative property. You might enjoy the Math Playground blog about "Invert and multiply" found at **http://www.actionmath.com/blog/2006/03/invert-and-multiply.html**.

Estimation   As we suggested earlier, an important technique to help children get a sense about their answers is to encourage estimation. Experiences should be provided for students to estimate quotients. The procedure is to round each mixed number to the nearest whole number or to round fractions to more convenient numbers to allow for mental computation. Activities 10.17 and 10.18 demonstrate two estimation activities that can be used with the whole class, individuals, or small groups.

Using Other Manipulatives   A brief discussion of the teaching strategies using other manipulative materials shown in Figure 10.6, page 259, is presented in Figures 10.13 through 10.16 on pages

Activity 10.17

ESTIMATION   MENTAL MATH

ROUNDING MIXED NUMBERS IN DIVISION

$5\frac{3}{4} \div 2\frac{2}{3}$ Round to $6 \div 3$ so the answer is about 2.

$3\frac{1}{4} \div \frac{5}{6}$ Round to $3 \div 1$ so the answer is about 3.

$\frac{7}{8} \div \frac{1}{4}$ Round to $1 \div \frac{1}{4}$ so the answer is aout 4.

Activity 10.18

ESTIMATION   **ESTIMATE AND SORT**

MATERIALS
- Forty equation cards that each have a simple, common computational problem
- Playing mat or $4'' \times 6''$ note cards with the categories: *Closer to 1, Closer to $\frac{1}{2}$, Closer to 0*

PROCEDURE
Players take turns drawing a card from the deck and quickly mentally computing the answer and deciding into which category it should be placed. A time limit of 5 seconds should be allowed for each player. If the answer is correctly placed according to the other players, the card may be kept as a point card. If the answer is incorrect or not given within the time period, the card is replaced at the bottom of the deck.

Winner: The player with the most cards at the end of the playing time.

> **Supporting the NCTM *Principles and Standards* (2000):**
> - Mathematics as Reasoning; Number and Operation
> - Student's Role in Representation—The Teaching Principle
> - The Mathematics Principle

This method supports the way most textbooks teach the algorithm for addition and subtraction or fractions. It is the buildup of the basic unit of wholeness for one. The method finds the best common denominator without the need to find the lowest terms.

Add and Subtract: $\frac{1}{4}$ and $\frac{1}{6}$

Step 1. Represent each fraction in its original representation.

Step 2. Build up the denominator until both are the same length.

Step 3. The numerators are increased by the same respective magnitude as the denominators.

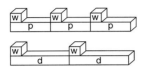

Step 4. Both numerators and denominators are represented in the equivalent rods, making an exchange for the least amount of rods to show any one number.

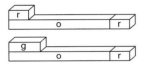

Step 5. For addition, add numerators, and represent the sum with the appropriate rod. Show the denominator as the part that stands for one. $\frac{5}{12}$.

Step 6. For subtraction, compare the green rod with the red rod and show the difference, one white rod. $\frac{1}{12}$. The answer in rods is shown as follows:

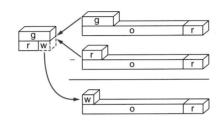

Note:
g = light green   w = white
r = red   p = purple
o = orange   d = dark green
y = yellow

FIGURE 10.13 *Cuisenaire rods—traditional algorithm.*

276–279 to show the power of using multiple embodiments. Always provide students with free exploration time using various materials to help them become familiar with the relationships between the components as well as to satisfy their innate need to explore new materials. This will ensure greater participation during the instructional time.

All four operations are presented together by using the same two fractions for each of the four operations. This approach has been taken so that you can see how the same rational numbers are affected when the operations change.

DECIMALS

Exploratory work with decimals should be included in primary grades. The study of fractions should encompass tenths to provide a natural link to decimals and money. In most textbooks, intensive work with decimals does not begin until students have acquired skill with the manipulation of common fractions. With the increased use of calculators by students, educators may need to reconsider when to start teaching decimals. Decimals

should be related to models, and the oral language should develop slowly. Early work with decimals in grades K to 4 should relate fractions to decimals. Building a number sense about decimals is an important goal. For example, students should recognize that 0.3 is less than $\frac{1}{2}$ because $\frac{1}{2}$ is the same amount as 0.5.

A summary of research findings (Usiskin, 2007b; Hiebert, 1992) indicates that many students, including high school students, do not realize that decimal fractions are just another way of writing common fractions and do not associate decimals as an extension of the base 10 place-value system. Researchers recommend that students have many introductory experiences with concrete materials before extensive rules are taught. The concrete materials discussed in this chapter provide a firm background with decimals.

There is a lack of conceptual understanding, perhaps because many students are being taught to compute with decimals before they fully grasp the basic decimal concepts. Owens and Super (1993) suggest that this situation is the result of basic decimal concepts being more difficult to teach and understand than the computational procedures along with the fact that computational

Pattern blocks may be made from various colors for various shapes. The shapes have an interrelationship with each other as the drawings show below. Find all the different ways to build the yellow hexagon with different combinations of other blocks—using all the same color.

Equivalent Fractions

- If yellow hexagon = 1, what are the fractional values for other combinations?
  1 green = ?   1 blue = ?   1 red = ?

- If red trapezoid = 1, find all the fractional values of the other blocks.
  1 green = ?   1 blue = ?   1 yellow = ?   1 red = ?

This activity can be repeated letting other blocks equal 1.

- To add or subtract with the blocks, you must decide which block to assign the value of one. It is good to estimate whether your answer will be greater than or less than 1, greater than or less than.

Add: $\frac{1}{2} + \frac{1}{3}$

If the yellow hexagon = 1, then the red trapezoid will be $\frac{1}{2}$, and the blue rhombus (parallelogram) will be $\frac{1}{3}$. When adding together, $\frac{5}{6}$ of the yellow hexagon is covered. Answer in symbols:

$$\frac{1}{2} + \frac{1}{3} = \frac{5}{6}$$

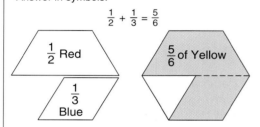

Subtract: $\frac{1}{2} - \frac{1}{3}$

If the hexagon = 1, then the blue rhombus = $\frac{1}{3}$ and the red trapezoid = $\frac{1}{2}$. The remaining part of the trapezoid is the green triangle, which is $\frac{1}{6}$ of the hexagon (the whole).

Answers in symbols:

$$\frac{1}{2} - \frac{1}{3} = \frac{1}{6}$$

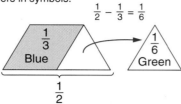

Multiply: $\frac{1}{2} \times \frac{1}{3}$

If yellow = 1, then $\frac{1}{3}$ is the blue rhombus and $\frac{1}{2}$ of $\frac{1}{3}$ is the green triangle. This is $\frac{1}{6}$ of the whole unit (yellow hexagon).

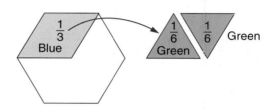

Divide: $\frac{1}{2} \div \frac{1}{3}$

If yellow = 1, then how many thirds (blue rhombus) are in the half (red trapezoid)?
Answer: There are 1 and $\frac{1}{2}$ more (green triangle) in the red trapezoid.

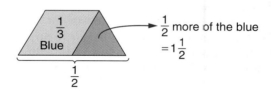

FIGURE 10.14 *Pattern blocks.*

algorithms are perceived by teachers to be more important or easier to teach.

Linking Fractions to Decimals

Many examples of common fractions becoming decimal fractions should be modeled by using base 10 blocks. Some problems to try might be $\frac{1}{2}, \frac{1}{4}, \frac{1}{5}$, and $\frac{1}{8}$. By problem solving, children can reason that if I find $\frac{1}{5}$ using the base 10 blocks as models, I can also find $\frac{3}{5}$. Children should predict the answer and then check with the blocks to make sure they were correct in their reasoning. Money provides another way to link fractions and decimals.

Types of Decimals

There are two kinds of decimal fractions: terminating and repeating decimals. Early and middle grades deal with terminating decimals, whereas repeating decimals are taught in the sixth, seventh, and eighth grades in most mathematics texts. Students should observe the patterns that emerge when exploring terminating and repeating decimals.

Terminating Decimals *Terminating decimals* are those that have a definite position or ending point in the base 10 number system. The point can be charted on a number line, or its position can be

Multiple bars were first introduced in the Teaching Strategies section. Review the use of multiple bars to show equivalencies. Then do the following activities:

Add: $\frac{2}{3} + \frac{1}{3}$

Place the 2 bar above the 3 bar to form the fraction $\frac{2}{5}$ at the left of the bars. All other fractions formed across the bars are equivalent fractions to this one.

2	4	6	8	10	12	14	16	18	20
5	10	15	20	25	30	35	40	45	50

Form the fraction with the one bar and the 3 bar.

1	2	3	4	5	6	7	8	9	10
3	6	9	12	15	18	21	24	27	30

Move one pair of the multiple bars until you have the same denominator lined up.
Once the denominators are alike, the operations can be performed with the numerators.

2	4	6	8	10	12	14	16	18	20
5	10	15	20	25	30	35	40	45	50

1	2	3	4	5	6	7	8	9	10
3	6	9	12	15	18	21	24	27	30

In this problem, the least common denominator is 15, and the two equivalent fractions are $\frac{2}{5} = \frac{6}{15}$ and $\frac{1}{3} = \frac{5}{15}$. The two numerators are 6 and 5 so, if these numbers are added, the result is 11 with the denominator or label of 15.

$$\frac{6}{15} + \frac{5}{15} = \frac{11}{15}$$

Subtract: $\frac{2}{5} - \frac{1}{3}$

The same procedure is used to subtract with the multiple bars, only once the numerators have been found, the operation of subtraction is performed on them. *Remember:* Move one pair of the multiple bars until you have the same denominator (the least common denominator) for both fractions. Line up the bars. Now you can subtract the numerators.

$$\begin{aligned} \frac{2}{5} &= \frac{6}{15} \\ -\frac{1}{3} &= \frac{5}{15} \\ \hline &\frac{1}{15} \end{aligned}$$

FIGURE 10.15 *Multiple bars.*

seen as a definite number of base 10 blocks. Common fractions can be seen as terminating decimals in the base 10 number system. An example would be $\frac{1}{2}$ as shown in Figure 10.17.

One-half $\left(\frac{1}{2}\right)$ can be seen as (0.5) or (0.50) or (0.500). It is the same position on the number line. The only thing that is different is whether the basic unit of measure (equaling 1) is subdivided into tenths, hundredths, or thousandths.

The same fraction, $\frac{1}{2}$, can be seen by using base 10 blocks as shown in Figure 10.18. Notice that $\frac{1}{2}$ can be seen in the first regrouping of the basic building unit as $\frac{1}{2}$ of the tenths or five-tenths of the basic unit (written as 0.5). The base 10 blocks also show the markings for the next regrouping (hundredths). If divided by hundredths, there are fifty-hundredths of the basic unit (written as 0.50). If divided by thousandths (the markings are not possible on the blocks), there are five hundred-thousandths in $\frac{1}{2}$ of the basic unit (written as 0.500). It represents the same amount whether one talks of tenths, hundredths, or thousandths. There is a definite amount of blocks that can be partitioned to show the termination of the fraction $\frac{1}{2}$; hence, it is a terminating decimal.

Activity 10.19 demonstrates the above reasoning using the fraction $\frac{1}{4}$. Try it now.

Repeating Decimals The existence of repeating decimals is proven in the seventh and eighth grades in most textbook series, although calculators may support an earlier introduction. A *repeating decimal* is a nonterminating decimal in which the same digit or block of digits repeats unendingly. As has been stressed numerous times previously, each new concept should be illustrated with manipulatives. The following exploration in Activity 10.20 can be used with students in middle school as well as adults learning the principle for the first time.

There are some decimal fractions for which we can find no definite point on a base 10 number line and no definite amount of base 10 blocks, but we know they are there just the same. Let's use the example of $\frac{1}{3}$. Using the same base 10 decimal number line, we can divide it so that there is exactly $\frac{1}{3}$ in each segment of the basic building unit as shown in Figure 10.19. Remember that the basic building unit equals one whole.

Notice that there is no position in tenths, hundredths, or thousandths when $\frac{1}{3}$ touches a definite point; hence, it does not terminate. If the number line were divided into ten-thousandths and beyond, $\frac{1}{3}$ would never meet at an exact point in the base 10 decimal system.

Each student is given a chart like the one pictured here. The strips have been already pasted on the chart. Each student also receives loose strips of paper measuring the same as the "whole unit" shown on the chart. The whole is clearly visible at all times; therefore, a student does not lose sight of the basic unit to which all fractions must be compared.

	unit
	halves
	fourths
	eighths
	thirds
	sixths
	twelfths
	fifths
	tenths

Multiply: $\frac{2}{3} \times \frac{1}{4}$

Read the problem as $\frac{2}{3}$ of $\frac{1}{4}$. Then the $\frac{1}{4}$ is found first and divided into thirds, and two of the thirds are found.

$\frac{1}{4}$

$\frac{1}{6}$

With the strip of paper at the top left edge, run the strip down until it matches an equivalent fraction, which is $\frac{1}{6}$. This way it is seen in its simplified form first.

Note one drawback: Because this method bypasses the $\frac{2}{12}$ that children would first find in the symbolic form, it makes the bridge from concrete to symbolic difficult to see.

Divide: $\frac{2}{3} \div \frac{1}{4}$

Read the problem as how many $\frac{1}{4}$'s in $\frac{2}{3}$. Find the $\frac{2}{3}$. Place a finger there and look at the $\frac{1}{4}$ strip. Compare the $\frac{2}{3}$ strip to the $\frac{1}{4}$ strip. It can be seen that there are 2 and $\frac{2}{3}$ of the $\frac{1}{4}$ strip in $\frac{2}{3}$.

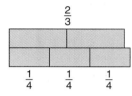

$\frac{2}{3}$

$\frac{1}{4}$ $\frac{1}{4}$ $\frac{1}{4}$

$1 + 1 + \frac{2}{3}$ of the next fourth $= 2\frac{2}{3}$

If the comparison is too difficult to do by just "eyeing" the strips, a $\frac{1}{4}$ strip may be marked from one of the loose strips and then moved down right on top of the $\frac{2}{3}$ strip for comparison.

Note: This procedure works well when the denominator of the second fraction is smaller than the denominator of the first fraction.

FIGURE 10.16 *Fraction strip chart.*

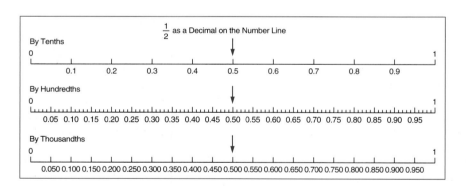

FIGURE 10.17 *Decimal values on a number line.*

TEACHING STRATEGIES: DECIMALS

Decimals are presented as an extension of the concepts of fractions in most elementary texts. An understanding of place value and common fractions helps students learn decimal notation. Therefore, a lot of work with fractions, such as $\frac{3}{10}$, proves valuable when connecting new symbolic notation (decimals) for fractions. Early exposure to decimal notation occurs in second or third grade when money concepts are developed. Pennies are related to hundredths and dimes are related to tenths. Children generally understand that pennies and dimes are parts of a dollar. Money notation found in textbooks provides experiences to count collections of dimes and pennies and to determine the total amount of money. This concrete, meaningful approach is an important bridge for learning ways to represent decimals. Although the cent sign is used with young children, decimal

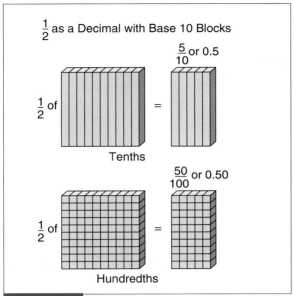

$\frac{1}{2}$ as a Decimal with Base 10 Blocks

$\frac{5}{10}$ or 0.5

$\frac{1}{2}$ of ___ = ___

Tenths

$\frac{50}{100}$ or 0.50

$\frac{1}{2}$ of ___ = ___

Hundredths

FIGURE 10.18   *Showing equivalency with base 10 blocks.*

notation is being used in earlier grades because calculators record money transactions easily and some primary economics units include collections of more than a dollar.

Activity 10.19

MANIPULATIVES   **PROBLEM SOLVING**

TERMINATING DECIMALS

What will happen if we try to find $\frac{1}{4}$ as a terminating decimal? Project what will happen before you test your assumptions with physical manipulatives.

1. Set up a base 10 decimal number line like the one in Figure 10.12.
2. Mark where $\frac{1}{4}$ of the basic building unit would be in tenths, hundredths, and thousandths. What did you discover?
3. Find $\frac{1}{4}$ using base 10 blocks in tenths, hundredths, and thousandths. What did you discover this time? Does it bear out what you discovered with the number line example? Is that to be expected? What will happen if we apply the same procedure to find $\frac{1}{8}$ as a terminating decimal?

Follow the same steps in reasoning as you did above. What did you discover?

Activity 10.20

CALCULATORS

NONTERMINATING, REPEATING DECIMALS

Enter $\frac{1}{3}$ into the calculator.* What is the result? It could be recorded as

$\frac{1}{3} = 0.\overline{333333333333}$ — The bar over the number means that it continues infinitely.

$\frac{1}{3} = 0.\overline{333333333333}$ — Now add two more thirds to the original one.

$+\frac{1}{3} = 0.\overline{333333333333}$

$\frac{3}{3} = 0.999999999999$

Mathematicians assert that $0.\overline{999999999999}$ is equal to one whole because of examples like the one above. When a whole unit is divided by thirds, nothing is taken away from or added to the basic unit; it remains intact. Therefore, $0.\overline{999999999999}$ is the nonterminating, repeating decimal for the whole number 1. It stands for one complete unit just as $\frac{3}{3}$ stands for one complete unit. This concept is a common question on college aptitude tests because it can be an easily forgotten mathematical principle.

*If the calculator has a M+ (memory plus) key, you can do the following explorations quickly by entering

$\frac{1}{3}$ M + M + M + [then press = or MT

(for memory total) or MR (for memory recall)]

Common fractions and decimal equivalence represent an important area to develop competence and understanding. Research (Thompson and Saldanha, 2003) suggests that students have minimal understanding of the relationship between fractions and decimals. Multiple representations for a number present conceptual difficulties for many students. Games can serve as an alternative form to practice skills and stimulate mental computations and comparisons. Extended Activities on the Web site shows ways to make and use games that focus on different names for the same number.

Operations with Decimals

In teaching the four basic operations with decimals, it is important to build on prior understanding of

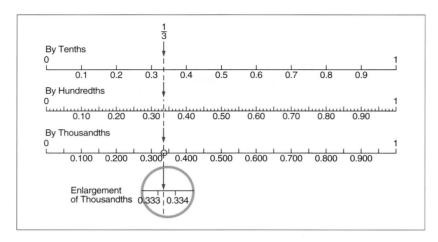

FIGURE 10.19 *Locating $\frac{1}{3}$ on a decimal number line.*

the place value of decimals and the algorithms used with whole numbers. Because the algorithms are the same, modeling them with a variety of materials is important for special-needs students and provides greater understanding and faster generalization for all students.

Addition Finding sums of decimal numbers should be an extension of whole number addition with the emphasis on lining up the place value associated with combining in each position or column. The following procedure should be followed when working with addition of decimals as modeled in Figure 10.20.

1. Represent the decimals with concrete materials.
2. Estimate whether the answer will be more than or less than 1. The same principle applies as discussed earlier with common fractions.
3. Combine like units making exchanges when necessary.
4. Record the actions and the answer in symbols.

An important task to master and remember when adding or subtracting decimal numbers is to align the decimal points so the place values are kept in mind. This is especially necessary when problems are presented in a horizontal form. Some textbooks stress the alignment of the decimal point while placing the zero in the appropriate decimal place values. The base 10 blocks seen in the introduction to decimals in this chapter show why 0.8 and 0.80 are the same amount. Working with the manipulatives makes this fact apparent to students. Pair students with special needs so one

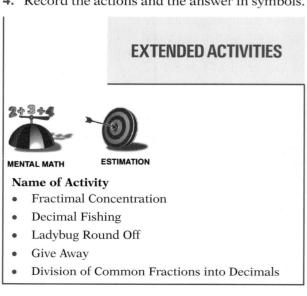

EXTENDED ACTIVITIES

MENTAL MATH   ESTIMATION

Name of Activity
- Fractimal Concentration
- Decimal Fishing
- Ladybug Round Off
- Give Away
- Division of Common Fractions into Decimals

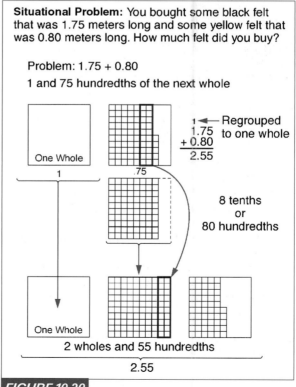

Situational Problem: You bought some black felt that was 1.75 meters long and some yellow felt that was 0.80 meters long. How much felt did you buy?

Problem: 1.75 + 0.80

1 and 75 hundredths of the next whole

One Whole

1   .75

$$\begin{array}{r} 1 \\ 1.75 \\ + 0.80 \\ \hline 2.55 \end{array}$$ ←Regrouped to one whole

8 tenths or 80 hundredths

One Whole

2 wholes and 55 hundredths

2.55

FIGURE 10.20 *Addition of decimals.*

Situational Problem: Rhea weighed a bag of nuts and found they were 2.32 kg. She took out 0.70 kg and weighed the nuts again. How much did she have then?

Problem: 2.32 − 0.70

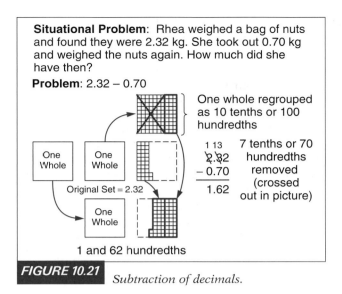

One whole regrouped as 10 tenths or 100 hundredths

7 tenths or 70 hundredths removed (crossed out in picture)

$$\begin{array}{r} {\scriptstyle 1\ 13} \\ 2.\cancel{3}\cancel{2} \\ -\ 0.70 \\ \hline 1.62 \end{array}$$

One Whole   One Whole

Original Set = 2.32

One Whole

1 and 62 hundredths

FIGURE 10.21   *Subtraction of decimals.*

ESTIMATION   MENTAL MATH

ROUNDING WITH DECIMALS

PROBLEM	MENTAL ROUNDING	ESTIMATED ANSWER
3.4 − 2.9	*Think:* 3 − 3	Less than 1
7.85 − 4.2	*Think:* 8 − 4	Around 4
11.34 − 0.895		
1.11 − 0.999		
345.25 − 245.5		
0.927 − 0.398		

DIRECTIONS

Look at the problems on the left and estimate how many whole numbers will be in the answer, if any. Fill in the rest of the chart. The first two are completed as a model. Check how close you came in this activity by computing the answer.

student works with the manipulative materials while the other student does the symbolic recording of the answer to incorporate a connecting level. Have them switch roles frequently so both have practice modeling and recording.

Subtraction

The same basic principles apply to subtraction as apply to addition because one is the inverse of the other. Figure 10.21 shows a subtraction of decimals with regrouping. It is important to include the three interpretations of subtraction when working with decimals: take-away, missing addend, and comparison. Review modeling with whole number subtraction, Chapter 9, pages 232–235, to refresh your memory. Children need to be allowed to investigate alternative solutions as they did for whole number computation.

Students need to experience many different situational and problem structures to gain confidence in computing with decimals. Estimation strategies can be used to make the problem more manageable. Using front-end estimation and rounding to whole numbers may be appropriate to check reasonableness of answers, as indicated in Activity 10.21.

Multiplication Multiplication of decimals follows the same rules as multiplication of whole numbers (Chapter 9). Therefore, multiplication of decimals can be modeled by using the same words and patterns using the base 10 blocks as the concrete manipulatives. In Figure 10.22, the flat is the basic building unit representing one

whole. The long represents tenths, and the small unit cube represents hundredths.

Products of two decimal numbers can be shown by using base 10 blocks or graph paper and the copy method. Students should build an array showing the two factors with number of groups on the left (or going "down") and number in a group going "across." Each of the partial products can be shown in the same manner as with whole numbers as already shown in Figure 10.22 and again shown in Figure 10.23.

The illustrations of a partial flat are enlarged in Figures 10.24 and 10.25 to make the demonstration of the commutative property easier to see. However, they may appear out of proportion to you as you study these pictures compared to the others you have just seen. They may be presented to students in the same manner as strips of paper that can be folded or measured into 100 parts.

Encourage students to find patterns and to generalize the rule for the multiplication of decimals as in Activity 10.22. It may seem easier and quicker to establish the rule of counting the number of decimal places for the product, but the rule is learned without meaning. Rather, teachers should ask students for place-value interpretations

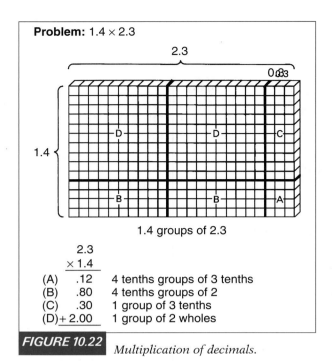

Problem: 1.4 × 2.3

1.4 groups of 2.3

          2.3
        × 1.4
(A)   .12   4 tenths groups of 3 tenths
(B)   .80   4 tenths groups of 2
(C)   .30   1 group of 3 tenths
(D)+ 2.00   1 group of 2 wholes

FIGURE 10.22 *Multiplication of decimals.*

and guide them in deciding on reasonable answers. Problems can be presented where the answer is given, but the students' task is to determine where the decimal point should be placed in the answer.

Provide experiences in which students decide where the decimal point should go in a given answer. Students can use estimation to justify their answers. There should be time spent on simple calculations without a calculator; however, valuable instructional time should not be spent on tedious paper-and-pencil calculations. These can be done more readily using a calculator.

Activity 10.23 provides students with an opportunity to practice a number of skills with operations of decimals. This activity will be extended to include proportions and percent in the next chapter.

Division Division of decimals follows the same rules as division of common fractions and whole numbers. Therefore, division of decimals may be

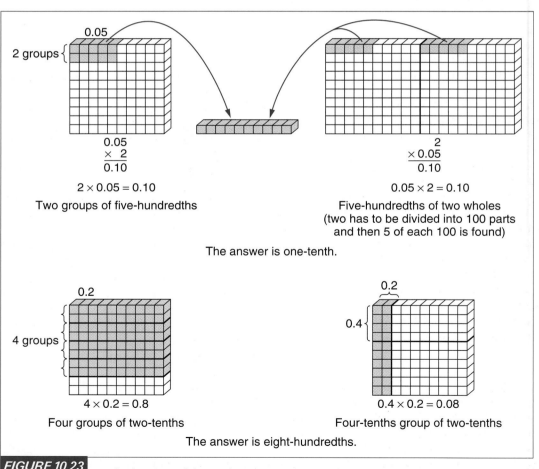

FIGURE 10.23 *Multiplication of decimals using base 10 blocks.*

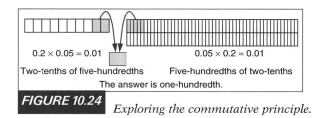

$0.2 \times 0.05 = 0.01$
Two-tenths of five-hundredths

$0.05 \times 0.2 = 0.01$
Five-hundredths of two-tenths

The answer is one-hundredth.

FIGURE 10.24 *Exploring the commutative principle.*

$0.02 \times 0.05 = 0.001$
Two-hundredths of five-hundredths

The answer is one-thousandth of the entire flat.

$0.05 \times 0.02 = 0.001$
Five-hundredths of two-hundredths

FIGURE 10.25 *Multiplying hundredths by hundredths.*

modeled with the same words and patterns as have been used before. For example, the base 10 blocks seen in the multiplication of decimals can be used if the question is changed to represent division. Figure 10.26 shows models in measurement division so you can become familiar with the language of dividing with decimals. (If needed, review Chapter 7 for discussion of the two kinds of division.)

As the decimal place values extend into the thousandths and ten thousandths, it becomes virtually impossible to do the entire problem with concrete manipulatives. The answers must be reasoned from past experiences. Estimation should be used in problem-solving situations with decimals. Students should learn to estimate answers and evaluate the reasonableness of answers. Calculators can be used to perform routine computations and should be the appropriate tool for solving division of multidigit numbers.

Suppose the problem is 1,000/0.001. Division asks the question, "How many sets of one-thousandths (0.001) are there in 1,000?" This is a measurement interpretation of division. Manipulatives can show the beginning of the thought process. If a cube represents one whole, then a tiny cube will be one-thousandth (0.001) of the whole as shown in Figure 10.27.

Activity 10.22

PROBLEM SOLVING

OBSERVATIONS OF MULTIPLICATION WITH BASE 10 BLOCKS

DIRECTIONS
1. Look at the pictorial and symbolic representations of multiplication shown in Figures 10.18, 10.19, and 10.20.
2. Fill in the chart. The first three are done as examples.

| | | NUMBER OF DECIMAL PLACES | |
| | | --- | --- |
PROBLEM	ANSWER	PROBLEM	ANSWER
2×0.05	0.10	2	2
0.05×2	0.10	2	2
4×0.2	0.8	1	1

3. Look for a pattern when working with decimals.
4. Generalize a rule for multiplying decimals using the pattern for clues.

Activity 10.23

CALCULATORS PROBLEM SOLVING **DIVISION OF DECIMALS**

This activity promotes problem solving as well as calculator use. Find the correct pathway by dividing the first number by the second one as you trace your way to the ending numeral.

Start			
1000	10	0.1	100
1000	1	0.001	0.01
0.001	1	0.01	10
100	100	10	100
			END 1

Figure	In Symbols	The Questions in Division
11.17	$0.05\overline{)0.10}$ with quotient 2	How many sets of five-hundredths are there in 0.10? *There are two sets of 0.05 in 0.10.*
	$2\overline{)0.10}$ with quotient 0.05	How many sets of two are there in 0.10? *There are five of the hundredths (0.05) in 0.10.*
11.18	$0.05\overline{)0.010}$ with quotient 0.2	How many sets of five-hundredths are there in 0.01? *There are five-hundredths of two-hundredths in 0.001.* (The 0.2 can be seen as $\frac{1}{4}$ of 0.05 with the base 10 blocks, but since $\frac{1}{5}$ is not a power of ten, 0.2 is the answer.)
	$0.2\overline{)0.010}$ with quotient 0.05	How many sets of two-tenths are there in 0.01? *There are five of the hundredths (0.05) in 0.01.*
11.19	$0.05\overline{)0.0010}$ with quotient 0.02	How many sets of five-hundredths are there in 0.001? *There are two-hundredths of 0.05 in 0.001.*
	$0.05\overline{)0.0010}$ with quotient 0.05	How many sets of two-hundredths are there in 0.001? *There are five-hundredths of two-hundredths in 0.001.*

FIGURE 10.26 *Measurement division.*

Now imagine that there are 1,000 cubes like the one in Figure 10.27 representing the whole number of 1,000. Then the same one-thousandth pictured here would make up a very, very tiny portion of the new number. So the question "How many sets of one-thousandth (0.001) are there in 1,000?" would result in a very large number.

By going over the division question, students become adept at predicting whether answers to such problems will be large or small numbers. Teachers can show problems, and students can state whether the answer will be a large or small amount. This is an excellent activity to use with the every pupil response cards (EPRs) (reviewed in Chapter 3). These activities help children visualize decimals to build number sense. Students with special needs need rich visualizations to make mental connections. Consider the situation of having eight-tenths and wanting to know how many groups of five-hundredths there are in eight-tenths as shown in Figure 10.28.

Money is a natural way to think about modeling division with decimals. When the divisor is a whole number, the partitive approach can be used. If $4.28 is to be shared among four people and the number of groups is known, what needs to be determined is how much will be distributed to each group as modeled in Figure 10.29.

Activity 10.24 promotes problem solving as well as calculator use. Find the correct pathway by dividing the first number by the second one as you trace your way to the ending numeral.

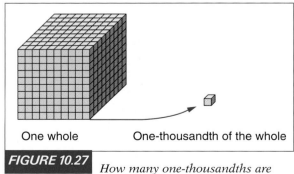

One whole   One-thousandth of the whole

FIGURE 10.27 *How many one-thousandths are in 1,000?*

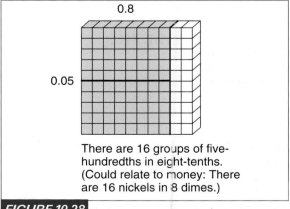

0.8

0.05

There are 16 groups of five-hundredths in eight-tenths. (Could relate to money: There are 16 nickels in 8 dimes.)

FIGURE 10.28 *How many nickels are in 8 dimes?*

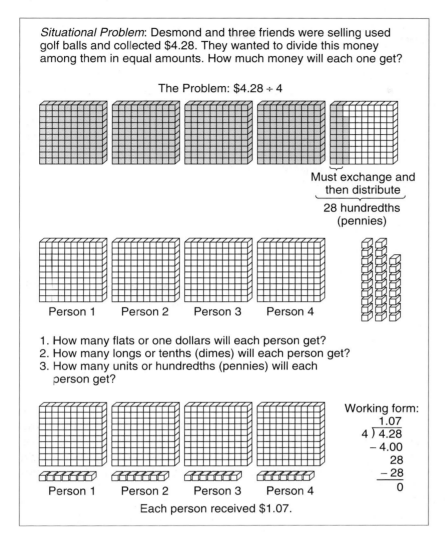

Situational Problem: Desmond and three friends were selling used golf balls and collected $4.28. They wanted to divide this money among them in equal amounts. How much money will each one get?

The Problem: $4.28 ÷ 4

Must exchange and then distribute

28 hundredths (pennies)

Person 1   Person 2   Person 3   Person 4

1. How many flats or one dollars will each person get?
2. How many longs or tenths (dimes) will each person get?
3. How many units or hundredths (pennies) will each person get?

Person 1   Person 2   Person 3   Person 4

Each person received $1.07.

Working form:
$$\begin{array}{r} 1.07 \\ 4\overline{)4.28} \\ -4.00 \\ \hline 28 \\ -28 \\ \hline 0 \end{array}$$

FIGURE 10.29 *Modeling division with money.*

Activity 10.24

PROBLEM SOLVING   **DIAGNOSTIC HELP**

The teacher asks: What did you do to $5\frac{1}{2}$ to get $\frac{11}{2}$?

Look at some more examples. Model the representation. Generalize a procedure to get these answers every time.

$$2\frac{3}{4} = \frac{11}{4}$$

$$3\frac{4}{10} = \frac{34}{10}$$

After working with division of decimals, it is easy to see why many mathematics educators believe that this concept must wait to be taught until the upper elementary grades when children can visualize intellectually what is happening with minute quantities. If upper grade students are at Piaget's concrete operational stage, there may be limited comprehension.

ASSESSMENT

Field-Independent Learners

Some students benefit from the gradual buildup of fractions from the parts to the corresponding whole. Materials, such as the fraction kits, the multiple bars, and the Cuisenaire rod algorithm for adding and subtracting fractions (explained in the earlier section on teaching strategies for

fractions), are all very helpful. These materials start with one fraction, find its equivalencies, and then compare them to the whole unit before performing the mathematical operation. If students do not respond well to one of these materials or seem to forget where they are in the sequence of building to the solution, materials supporting the simultaneous thought processing of field-dependent learners should be presented.

Field-Dependent Learners

Some students benefit from having a "whole" unit constantly within sight as they work on fraction relationships. The whole and its parts are more clearly seen in materials like the fraction strip chart. Such material allows for problems to be presented by partitioning from the whole to its parts. Students are not required to handle as many small pieces or make as many manipulations as they may be required to do in successive processing models.

Correcting Common Misconceptions

Adding or Subtracting Denominators as Whole Numbers

The denominator of a fraction serves as a label naming the number of parts into which the whole unit has been divided. Sometimes it is helpful for students with special needs to write the denominator in words to help focus on the numerator when teaching the symbolic level of adding and subtracting fractions. Because a common error is to add or subtract both the numerators and the denominators, this technique emphasizes that different parts or labels are involved, and until the parts or labels are the same, the numerators cannot be added or subtracted.

Common Errors: $\frac{2}{3}+\frac{1}{4}=\frac{3}{7}$

But: 2/thirds + 1/fourths = ?/?

Get labels or denominators the same and then perform the operation on the numerators:

8/twelfths + 3/twelfths = 11/twelfths

Changing Mixed Numbers to Improper Fractions

Students forget the sequence of steps and which part is added or multiplied. For the mixed number $5\frac{1}{2}$, the following answers may occur when it is changed to an improper fraction:

$$\frac{5}{2} \quad \frac{1}{10} \quad \frac{6}{2} \quad \frac{6}{10} \quad \frac{8}{2}$$

Analyze what happened to obtain each answer. There are other possible variations also.

One of the most efficient means of remediation is to model the action with manipulatives using concrete or pictorial materials. Often, many exploratory experiences are needed to build a conceptualization and visualization of the problem. In Activity 10.25, the circular fraction kit works well because the student can show five circles and one-half more of the next circle. Then the student can count the number of halves to find the eleven halves.

Inverting and Multiplying the Incorrect Factors

This problem occurs when the student "inverts and multiplies" the first factor instead of the second when attempting to divide one fraction by another. Some students may invert *both* fractions, thinking the rule applies to both factors.

Original Example	*Student's Work*
$\frac{1}{2} \div \frac{1}{4}$	$\frac{2}{1} \times \frac{1}{4} = \frac{1}{2}$

Switching to an entirely new algorithm is advisable. Just restating the rule may leave the student still confused. The teaching strategy for division using the circular or rectangular fraction kit would require a different setup and execution of the problem.

$$\frac{1}{2} \div \frac{1}{4} = \frac{2}{4} \div \frac{1}{4} = \frac{(2 \div 1)}{1} = \frac{2}{1} = 2$$

Activity 10.25

PORTFOLIO **PORTFOLIO ASSESSMENTS**

For Teacher Reflection of Students' Work with Operations on Fractions

Name *Nick*
Work this problem (showing all your work)

$$\frac{3}{4} \times \frac{1}{2} = \frac{3}{8}$$

Defend your answer—how do you know it is correct?

$$\frac{3}{4} \times \frac{1}{2}$$

Draw or visualize how to work the problem.

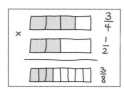

Write a word problem that will go with this problem to make sense of how to use this math in the real world.

Max has a pie; ¾ of it is left.

John has a pie; ½ of it is left.

Max and John put it together.

How much will they have?

$\frac{3}{8}$

DIRECTIONS

1. Analyze the response made by each student. Create a reflective description of what you think can be said about the student's degree of understanding of operations with fractions.

2. Describe how the drawings gave clarification of each student's level of understanding. What information was gained from their drawings? Compare the various levels of understanding between the students. What NCTM *Principles and Standards* (2000) are you including in your assessments? Explain your answer.

3. Design a rubric that would take into account the diversity of answers while being open in your assessment.

   Include the rubric in your Professional Portfolio for Job Interviews.

Name Dustin
Work this problem (showing all your work).

$$2 \div \frac{3}{4} = \frac{1}{4} \text{ R } \frac{1}{4}$$

Defend your answer—how do you know it is correct?

Because I drew below.

Draw or visualize how to work the problem.

Write a word problem that will go with this problem to make sense of how to use this math in the real world.

There were two people and I candy bar. The candy bar bar could break into 4 pieces 1 piece was missing so theres ¾ of the candy bar left. How much would each person get?

Focus the students' attention on the operation of dividing and the language of "how many groups can I get."

Multiplying and Dividing Mixed Numbers Students know they can add or subtract the whole numbers after they have found the equivalent fractional parts. They assume logically that they can do the same when multiplying or dividing mixed numbers, yielding answers like the following:

Original Example	*Student's Work*
$2\frac{1}{2} \times 4\frac{1}{4}$	$= 8\frac{1}{8}$

This type of problem is difficult to remediate. Some elementary textbooks insist on the change of mixed numbers to improper fractions as the first step in any addition or subtraction problem. Such texts hope that insistence on one procedure will eliminate problems with inappropriate transfer of learning later when multiplication and division of mixed numbers are taught. If students have learned different algorithms for addition and subtraction that are causing difficulties, it may be beneficial to go back to addition and subtraction, showing the improper fraction step first. After students have seen that it works with addition and subtraction, stress that the same procedure works for multiplication and division. For example,

With Addition

$$4\frac{1}{4} = \frac{17}{4} = \frac{17}{4}$$
$$+2\frac{1}{2} = \frac{5}{2} = \frac{10}{4}$$
$$\frac{27}{4} = 6\frac{3}{4}$$

With Multiplication

$$4\frac{1}{4} = \frac{17}{4} = \frac{17}{4}$$
$$\times 2\frac{1}{2} = \frac{5}{2} = \frac{10}{4}$$
$$\frac{170}{16} = 10\frac{10}{16} = 10\frac{5}{8}$$

Use the circular fraction kit to model the problem as shown in Figure 10.30. Students should build their understanding from the mathematical representation of $2\frac{1}{2} \times 4\frac{1}{4}$. When

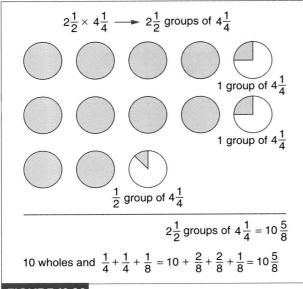

FIGURE 10.30 *Showing multiplication of mixed numbers.*

students are involved in problem-solving experiences, they can later generalize ideas gained through models. Figure 10.30 illustrates that the problem states that $2\frac{1}{2}$ groups of $4\frac{1}{4}$ yields $10\frac{5}{8}$.

Another way to help students with multiplication of mixed numbers is to have them estimate to see if their answers are reasonable. For example,

To estimate the largest value possible:

$2\frac{1}{2}$ becomes 3, $4\frac{1}{4}$ becomes 4, so

$3 \times 4 = 12 \neq 8\frac{1}{8}$

To estimate the smallest value possible:

$2\frac{1}{2} \times 4 = (2 \times 4) + \left(\frac{1}{2} \times 4\right).$

$= 8 + 2 = 10 \neq 8\frac{1}{8}$

The answer must be between 10 and 12. The student's answer of $8\frac{1}{8}$ does not fit reasonably in the problem, and this estimation technique alerts the student to check with a different algorithm like the one shown previously or to check with manipulative materials.

Regrouping Fractions as Whole Numbers Students frequently confuse the regrouping process of whole numbers with the regrouping process required in the subtraction of fractions.

Original Example   *Student's Work*

$5\frac{1}{4}$ =

$-3\frac{7}{8}$ $\cancel{5}4^{+1}\frac{2}{8} = 4\frac{12}{8}$

The student regroups the 5 as 4 and 1 but "carries" the 1 over to the renamed two-eighths as if the two were a whole number and not the numerator of a fraction. The student has forgotten that the whole number must be renamed as

$\frac{8}{8}$ and then added to $\frac{2}{8}$ to make $\frac{10}{8}$

The strategies section stressed the need to ask, "What name is being used for one?" *constantly* as a student performs the activities. Students who forget this important step should write the question down and save it in a folder where they can refer to it as they work. Perhaps going back to concrete materials may be the next step, particularly if initial instruction did not include them.

Activity 10.26 is designed to give you an opportunity to put your knowledge of fractions to work in assessing actual student work with fractions. Activity 10.26 refers to the work shown in Figure 10.31.

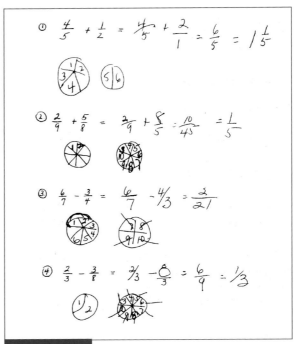

FIGURE 10.31 *Assessment of student's work.*

Activity 10.26

PORTFOLIO

ASSESSING UNDERSTANDING OF FRACTIONS

In the assessment example (Figure 10.31), to what extent do you feel this student has been exposed to concrete models? On what information do you base your decision? What conceptual understanding of operations with fractions does this student have? Think about a plan to develop meaning for operations and explain how you would instruct this child. What NCTM *Principles* (2000) will you include in your assessment?

Poor Estimation Skills in Multiplication and Division Some students have difficulty computing with decimals because they lack a sense of place value and estimation. Therefore, these error patterns occur:

$$0.3 \times 0.3 = 0.9 \quad 0.52\overline{)104}\,\overset{2}{}$$

They need to model such problems with manipulatives where possible, and at all times they should accompany the modeling with the oral language as shown in the Teaching Strategies part of this chapter. This procedure helps students determine whether their answers are reasonable or not. Activity 10.27 is an opportunity to apply your understanding of multiplication of decimals in assessing a student's work.

Activity 10.27

PORTFOLIO　**PORTFOLIO ASSESSMENTS**

For Teacher Reflection of Students' Work with Multiplication of Decimals

---

Name _Michelle_

Work this problem (show all your work).

1.5 X 3.2

$$\begin{array}{r} {\overset{1.5}{\times 3.2}} \\ \hline 3.0 \\ 4.50 \\ \hline 4.80 \end{array}$$

Defend your answer—how do you know it is correct?

It's correct because it's just like a multaction problum but with decimals it was like mutapiling

Draw or visualize how to work the problem.

$$\begin{array}{r} 1 \times \overset{1}{15} \\ 3.8 \\ \hline 3.0 \\ -4.50 \\ \hline 4.80 \end{array}$$
or
$$+\begin{array}{r}\overset{1}{32}\\32\\32\\32\\\hline 160\end{array}\,\begin{array}{r}\overset{1}{32}\\32\\32\\32\\\hline 60\end{array}\,\begin{array}{r}\overset{1}{32}\\32\\32\\32\\\hline 160\end{array}\,+\,\begin{array}{r}1.60\\1.60\\1.60\\\hline 4.80\end{array}$$

Write a word problem that will go with this problem to make sense of how to use this math in the real world.

The Worlds of fun roller coaster has 32 roller coaster cars each car carries 15 pepole in it. How many pepole can fit in all 32 cars?

Name _Danielle_

$2.88 X 0.4 pounds
$$\begin{array}{r}\overset{3}{2}\,\overset{3}{8}8\\ \times\ 0.4\\ \hline 1.152\end{array}$$

Work this problem (show all your work).

rounded from 2.88 x ⌐ to .4 X $3.00

Defend your answer—how do you know it is correct?

$$\begin{array}{r}2.88\\4\,\overline{)1.152}\\ -8\\ \hline 35\\ 32\\ \hline 032\end{array}$$

Draw or visualize how to work the problem.

$$\begin{array}{r}\overset{3}{0.08}\\ \times 0.4\\ \hline .032\end{array}\quad\begin{array}{r}\overset{3}{0.80}\\ \times 0.4\\ \hline .320\end{array}\quad\begin{array}{r}\overset{2}{}\\0.4\\ \times 0.4\\ \hline .8\end{array}\quad\begin{array}{r}.032\\ .320\\ +.8\\ \hline 1.152\end{array}$$

Write a word problem that will go with this problem to make sense of how to use this math in the real world.

She wants 0.4 pounds of candy each pound cost $2.88 How much does she spend?

DIRECTIONS

1. Analyze the response made by each student. Create a reflective description of what you think can be said about the student's degree of understanding of multiplication of decimals.

2. Describe how the drawings gave clarification of each student's level of understanding. What information was gained from their drawings? Compare the various levels of understanding between the students. What NCTM *Principles and Standards* (2000) are you including in your assessments? Explain your answer.

3. Design a rubric that would take into account the diversity of answers while being open in your assessment. Include the rubric in your professional portfolio for job interviews.

SUMMARY

- An overreliance on tricks and rules severely handicaps a student's ability to develop a conceptual understanding of fractions and decimals that will be the foundation for making sense of operations with fractions and decimals.

- Presenting new concepts with a variety of models and situational problems helps students develop stronger conceptual understanding.

- Fractions can be presented from many perspectives including part–whole of a region, measure, set, ratio, and division.

- Estimation skills should be developed and their use encouraged in the study of fractions and operations with fractions.

- Benchmarks, recognizing numbers as close to 0, $\frac{1}{2}$, and 1, should be taught as an estimation strategy early in the study of fractions.

- Whole–part activities that emphasize the role of the whole in understanding fractions should come at the beginning of fraction study.

- Partitioning, or equal shares, should be presented in many forms (i.e., not limited to pies, pizza, and other circular models).

- Equivalence (ways that show equal shares of the same portion) is a key concept to be developed before teaching operations with fractions.

- Standard algorithms for operations with fractions should follow students' development of invented strategies.

- A proper fraction is one whose numerator is of a lower degree than its denominator.

- An improper fraction is one whose numerator is of a greater, or equal, degree than its denominator.

- Present the operations within the context of a situational problem and use models in the performance of the operation.

- Introduce division of fractions with the common denominator approach.

- Work with fractions expressed in tenths provides a natural link to decimals and money.

- Terminating decimals have a definite position or ending point in the base 10 system.

- Repeating decimals are nonterminating decimals in which the same digit or block of digits repeats unendingly.

- Build on prior understanding of place value of decimals and whole number operations when teaching operations with decimals.

- When assessing student work with fractions and decimals, be alert for common misconceptions and strategies appropriate for reteaching.

PRAXIS II™-STYLE QUESTIONS

Answers to this chapter's Praxis II™-style questions are in the instructor's manual.

Mutiple Choice Format

1. Which child below would benefit MOST from fractional problems changed to this approach?

   The problem: Materials changed to

   $$\frac{3}{5} + \frac{1}{5}$$ $$\frac{3}{\text{fifths}} + \frac{1}{\text{fifths}}$$

   a. The child who answers problems like this:
   $$\frac{3}{5} + \frac{1}{5} = \frac{3}{25}$$

   b. The child who answers problems like this:
   $$\frac{3}{5} + \frac{1}{5} = \frac{2}{5}$$

   c. The child who answers problems like this:
   $$\frac{3}{5} + \frac{1}{5} = \frac{4}{10}$$

   d. The child who answers problems like this:
   $$\frac{3}{5} + \frac{1}{5} = \frac{4}{5}$$

2. Which of the following problems are modeled by the picture below?

   a. $\frac{3}{4} \times \frac{2}{3}$

   b. $\frac{2}{3} \div \frac{1}{4}$

   c. $\frac{2}{3} \times \frac{3}{4}$

   d. $\frac{2}{3} - \frac{3}{4}$

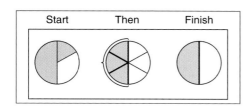

| Start | Then | Finish |

3. When the fraction $\frac{8}{12}$ becomes $\frac{2}{3}$, it is said that the fraction has been

a. reduced to lowest terms
b. simplified to its lowest term
c. expressed in its lowest reduced terms
d. Both b and c

4. Analyze Shenia's work below: It is the same as it appeared in Chapter 12 of your text.
   This is Shenia's worksheet:

   Work this problem (showing all your work).

   $$\frac{3}{8} \div \frac{1}{2} = \frac{3}{4}$$

   Defend your answer. How do you know it is correct?

   Because I need to no how many $\frac{1}{2}$ are in $\frac{3}{8}$

   Draw or visualize how to work the problem.

   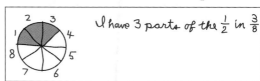
   I have 3 parts of the $\frac{1}{2}$ in $\frac{3}{8}$

   Write a word problem that will go with the division problem above.

   I have $\frac{1}{2}$ of a pizza and I want to eat $\frac{3}{4}$ of it how much do I eat? I get to eat $\frac{3}{4}$ of the pizza.

   On the five-point scoring guide (in Chapter 3), Shenia should receive a score of _____:

   a. "3" because she has answered the problem incorrectly, but her word problem is done well.

   b. "2" because her drawing is correct, but her word problem lacks understanding.

   c. "4" because her drawing and word problem show she understands the operation of division well.

d. "1" because both her drawing and her word problem lack understanding.

Constructed Response Format

5. What is the first phrase that a teacher must use when starting work with each common fraction activity?

6. This decimal activity was in the text to show what happens when decimals are divided in the base 10 system. What would the teacher expect students to understand after doing the activity?

Start			
1000	10	0.1	100
1000	1	0.001	0.01
0.001	1	0.01	10
100	100	10	100
			End
			1

7. In this performance-based task, children read from the *"Little House on the Prairie"* series in which Laura invited her family (six plus herself) to come to dinner. The task asked what Laura could do with the original corn bread recipe so everyone could be fed. The directions asked the children to tell in words and fractions what they did. The following was one student's work.

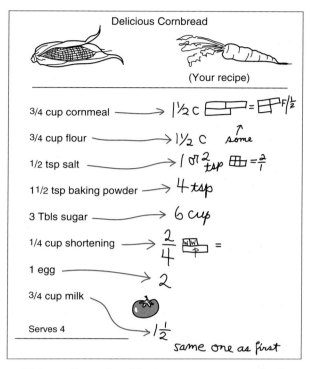

This student should score a _____ on the five-point scoring guide (in Chapter 3) because _____.

Integrating Technology

Video Vignettes

Rectangles and Fractions
Read the directions given for this vignette. Complete the tasks before viewing the video vignette.

Internet Activities

WebQuest

Volcano Encounter—Fractions in Action
Go to the Web site for the text for a WebQuest that integrates mathematics and science. Follow the directions given in the WebQuest.

Fraction Marathon
A review of fractions designed for grades 4–6.

Web site

Directions:
1. Go to each of the following Web sites. Select an activity or lesson plan that you could incorporate into a unit on fractions.

2. Write a two-to-three paragraph explanation of how you would incorporate the activity or lesson plan in your unit.

3. Describe any modifications you would incorporate either to bring the lesson plan or activity into greater alignment with the standards or to enable students with special needs to be successful in the performance of the activity or lesson plan.
   A brief description of what you will find at the Web site is provided here.
   A. *Casio, Inc.*
   http://casio.com/activities
   Lesson plans and activities developed by classroom teachers for a variety of grade levels can be found here. The materials are somewhat limited unless you are interested in purchasing activity books.
   B. *Texas Instruments, Inc.*
   http://education.ti.com/educationportal/sites/US/sectionHome/classroomactivities.html
   You need to become a subscriber (free) to see or download any of the free activities.
   C. *Teachers Helping Teachers*
   http://www.pacificnet.net/mandel/Math.html
   A variety of lesson plans, including mathematics lessons plans using manipulatives and calculators, are available here.
   D. *Columbia Education Center*

http://www.col-ed.org/cur/index.html Math
Mathematics lessons plans written by classroom teachers, categorized by grade level bands, are found here.

E. *NCTM Illuminations*
http://illuminations.org/LessonDetail.aspx?id=0113
"Fun with Fractions: A Unit on Developing the Region Model."

F. *Math Archives*
http://archives.math.utk.edu/k12.html
Here you will find a wide range of listings of Internet sites categorized as

- **Lesson Plans**
- **Software**
- **Topics in Mathematics**
- **Contests and Competitions**
- **Professional Societies**
- **Other**

National Library of Virtual Manipulatives
http://nlvm.usu.edu/en/nav/vlibrary.html
(also in Spanish)
Virtual manipulatives, with suggestions for teachers and parents, useful for teaching the content standards in NCTM's Principles and Standards.
Interactivate: Home Page
http://www.shodor.org/interactivate
Development for middle school mathematics explorations but several are adaptable to elementary mathematics.
Here are some additional Web sites for activities and lesson plans that you might like to visit:
www.hbschool.com/elab
members.learningplanet.com/directory/index.asp?sub=ma&lev=
www.visualfractions.com
www.gamequarium.com
www.coolmath4kids.com

CHILDREN'S LITERATURE

Adler, David A. *Fraction Fun.* New York: Holiday House, 1996.
Children see how fractions occur in real-life situations.

Dennis, Richard. *Fractions Are Parts of Things.* New York: Crowell, 1973.
The set model of fractions is demonstrated. Both partitive division and fractions can be used to describe the episodes.

Emberley, Ed. *Ed Emberley's Picture Pie: A CircleDrawing Book.* Boston: Little &Brown Publishers, 1984.
Equivalence is an important concept that is highlighted in this book.

Hutchins, Pat. *The Doorbell Rang.* New York: Greenwillow, 1986.
The set model of fractions is demonstrated. Both partitive division and fractions can be used to describe the episodes.

Leedy, Loreen. *Fraction Action.* New York: Holiday House, 1994.
Children see how fractions occur in real-life situations.

Mathews, Louise. *Gator Pie.* Denver, CO: Sundance, 1995.
The region or area model is portrayed. Some humorous complaints occur concerning equal parts, so the concept of equivalent fractions is demonstrated as well.

McMillan, Bruce. *Eating Fractions.* New York: Scholastic, 1991.
This book presents many examples of real-world pictures that show items being divided into parts. The text mentions the fraction in both written word and numbers.

40% % — part
─── = ────
100   100   whole

Percent, Ratio, Proportion, and Rate

Chapter 11

At the Start ~~~~ Know What Children Will Be Doing . . .

NCTM Curriculum Focal Points—   See . . .

Grade 6 ~~ Connecting ratio and rate to multiplication and division	Activity 11.5; 11.11
Grade 7 ~~ Developing an understanding and appling proportionality	Activity 11.6

A partial listing as it pertains to Number and Operations and Algebra from NCTM *Curriculum Focal Points* (2006, pages 18–19).

WHERE'S THE MATHEMATICS? THE MATHEMATICAL STRUCTURE OF PERCENT, RATIO, PROPORTION, AND RATE

The study of ratio, proportion, percent, and rate largely involves activities for grade 5 through grade 8. From decimals, students proceed to the study of ratio and percent, two other focal points in the study of rational numbers. Proportion is an extension of the comparisons developed when studying ratio. Rate is another way of comparing relationships. All four concepts have many real-world applications and frequently become topics of word problems in elementary and middle school problem solving. If you would like to review the definitions and some algebraic examples, go to "Check Your Knowledge" (Chapter 11, on the Web site).

Figure 11.1 gives a partial listing of the NCTM standards related to percent, ratio, proportion, and rate. For a more complete listing, check the NCTM Web site at **http://standards.nctm.org/index.htm.**

You may be asking, "Why are these four mathematical concepts placed together in a chapter?" It is of interest that they are related. Let's look at the following word problem as an example. *The pro*

blem: Mateo rewards himself with three bite-size candies every time he gets a hit in baseball.

Figure 11.2 shows how rewording can change the problem from one concept to another.

All these problems have a multiplicative relationship and a constant. In this example, the constant is the 3. The number of candies is three times the hits or $c = 3h$. We will see how that understanding is developed in each of the four concepts. In a school setting, each concept, although related, is initially presented separately, so we present them separately in this chapter as well.

Check

YOUR MATHEMATICS KNOWLEDGE

On Percent, Ratio, Proportion, and Rate

- Definitions and Algebraic Examples
- Mental Math and Its Relationship to Percentages
  . . . a refresher from mathematics content coursework . . . Lest you forget!

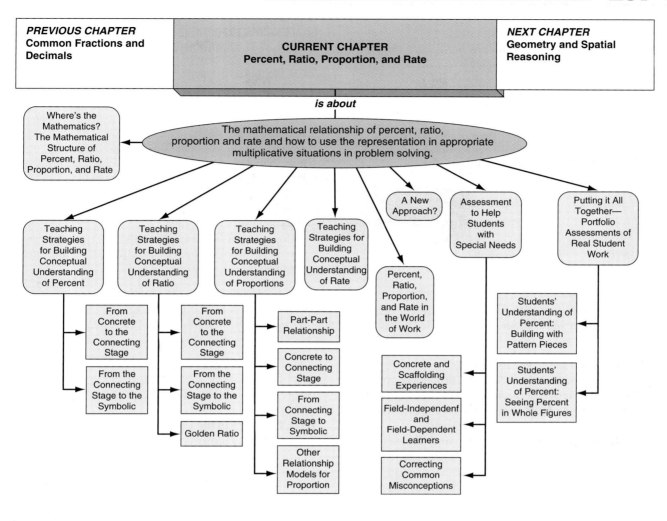

SELF-HELP QUESTIONS

1. Can I describe the relationships among percent, ratio, proportion, and rate?

2. How can I use manipulatives and children's literature to help students develop an understanding of percent?

3. What is meant by the part-part relationship in ratios?

4. What is meant by the part-part relationship in proportions?

5. What is the "rule of 3?"

6. How can coordinate graphs be used to help students develop an understanding of proportion?

7. Why do rates used in proportion problems create difficulties for students?

8. Do I know how to use calculators and computer spreadsheets in teaching percent, ratio, and proportion?

TEACHING STRATEGIES FOR BUILDING CONCEPTUAL UNDERSTANDING OF PERCENT

Percent means "by the hundred." Percent, when standing alone as in 32 percent, may be considered a ratio—32 parts out of 100. All percents are compared to a hundred parts or hundredths. Frequently, percent is the first ratio that students meet. Percent is usually taught right after fractions and decimals in fourth or fifth grade, but children

STANDARD

Instructional programs from prekindergarten through grade 12 should enable all students to

Understand numbers, ways of representing numbers, relationships among numbers, and number systems.

Understand meanings of operations and how they relate to one another.

Compute fluently and make reasonable estimates.

GRADES 3 TO 5 EXPECTATIONS

In grades 3 to 5 all students should

Understand various meanings of multiplication and division.

Recognize and generate equivalent forms of commonly used fractions, decimals, and percents.

GRADES 6 TO 8 EXPECTATIONS

In grades 6 to 8 all students should

Work flexibly with fractions, decimals, and percents to solve problems.

Compare and order fractions, decimals, and percents efficiently and find their approximate locations on a number line.

Develop meaning for percents greater than 100 and less than 1; understand and use ratios and proportions to represent quantitative relationships.

Develop and use strategies to estimate the results of rational number computations and judge the reasonableness of the results.

Develop, analyze, and explain methods for solving problems involving proportions, such as scaling and finding equivalent ratios.

FIGURE 11.1 *NCTM Expectations of Percent, Ratio, Proportion, and Rate. A Partial Listing as it Pertains to Operations and Number Sense from NCTM Principles and Standards for School Mathematics (2000, pages 392–393).*

have an intuitive sense of percent early in their school experience. This is seen in the assessment section of this chapter when the percent work of second and third graders is reviewed.

Moss (2002) and Lembke and Reys (1994) found that fourth and fifth graders, respectively, had a broad knowledge of percent in real-life situations. They found that fourth, fifth, and seventh graders used 25 percent, 50 percent, and 100 percent as reference points (called benchmarks by Lembke and Reys) more frequently when asked to solve problems than other approaches to find percent such as a fraction, ratio, equation, drawing pictures, or trial and error. By ninth grade, the reference points were not as prevalent a choice;

As a **rate** problem	Mateo eats at a rate of three candies per hit.
As a **ratio** problem	For every hit, Mateo eats three candies.
As a **proportion** problem	If Mateo eats three candies per hit, how many candies will he eat if he gets four hits?
As a **percent** problem	Of nine pieces of candy, what percent of the candy will Mateo have eaten after one hit?

FIGURE 11.2 *The questions coming from the situation.*

the idea of using an equation became the most frequent approach taken.

From Concrete to the Connecting Stage

Real-world situations occur in concrete activities in informal ways before the fifth grade. Early activities encourage teachers to model wording with percents and encourage children to speak of percents following the teacher's lead (i.e., oral discourse).

Money Using money is one of children's first experiences with an intuitive sense of percent. Money is a hands-on commodity that can buy other concrete things. Children learn that 50 cents is a half of a dollar and a dollar is equivalent to 100 pennies. It also helps that 50 cents and 50 percent sound much alike in oral speech. The same can also be said for 25 percent. A delightful children's book that helps with this idea is *If You Made a Million* by David M. Schwartz (1989). Children can be encouraged to see that they have 50 percent of a dollar when they have 50 cents and so on.

Shapes Early activities include subjects in which shapes and parts of shapes are used. Such activities include art where children are asked to cut a figure in half and in fourths so that they can use 50 percent of the circle and 25 percent of the circle. Notice in Activity 11.1 how a teacher can word examples so that percents can become a part of lessons in natural ways.

Activity 11.1

MATHEMATICAL CONNECTIONS **PROBLEM SOLVING**

CREATING ART PROJECTS WITH PERCENT OF SHAPES

MATERIALS

- Two circles, two rectangles, two triangles, scissors
- Crayons or paint (depending on the desire of teacher)
- Glue

DIRECTIONS

1. Have children cut out all the shapes.
2. Take one circle, one triangle, and one rectangle. Cut each in half and in half again. The teacher should ask, "Show me 50 percent of the circle, . . . ,25 percent of the circle." Do the same with the other shapes.
3. Have students create pictures (Figure 11.3) with the whole shapes and their 25 percent and 50 percent parts.
4. The children then tell each other what they have used to make each figure.
5. Teachers help children use the terminology of percent by asking such clarifying questions as

   "What percent of the circle made the hat?"
   "What percent of the triangle made each shoe?"

> **Supporting the NCTM *Principles and Standards (2000)***
>
> - Mathematics as Connections; Mathematics as Communication, Representations
> - Oral Discourse of Students—The Teaching Principle
> - Monitoring Students' Progress; Evaluating Students' Achievement—The Assessment Principle

Tangrams can also be used to connect percents with the fractional parts. Children who have physically manipulated the tangrams in activities like those presented in Chapter 12 know which pieces are congruent to each other and, therefore, equivalent in percent to each other. Figure 11.4 shows the connection to percent as a natural extension from the money concept.

FIGURE 11.3 *Percent pictures by children.*

Students can move from concrete figures to the connecting stage of pictorial images by using interactive computer programs that allow them to construct two-dimensional figures and shade in different percentages of the picture using the many colors available in computer programs.

From the Connecting Stage to the Symbolic

By the fifth grade, students have the opportunity to work with pictorial grids of a hundred parts. The

Name of Piece	Fraction of Cake	Cost	Percent of Cake	
Large triangle	$\frac{1}{4}$	$0.25	25%	× 2
Medium triangle	$\frac{1}{8}$	$0.12\frac{1}{2}$	$12\frac{1}{2}$%	
Small triangle	$\frac{1}{16}$	$0.06\frac{1}{4}$	$6\frac{1}{4}$%	× 2
Square	$\frac{1}{8}$	$0.12\frac{1}{2}$	$12\frac{1}{2}$%	
Parallelogram	$\frac{1}{8}$	$0.12\frac{1}{2}$	$12\frac{1}{2}$%	
	$\frac{16}{16}$		100%	

Tangram Cake Total Cost $1.00

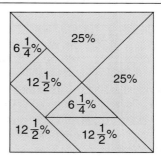

FIGURE 11.4 *Tangram cake: 100% sold for a dollar.*

grids gradually move from a literal representation of percent to symbolic representations of different amounts that stand for whole percentages and their parts. The grids help prevent some of the problems seen in the National Assessment of Educational Progress (NAEP) discussed next.

Data from the NAEP (NAEP, 2000; Kenney, Lindquist, and Hetternan, 2002) on items involving the understanding of percent, ratio, and rate were disappointing. There was improvement over the grades, but students at grade 4 and grade 8 tended to respond to multiple-step problems by reducing them to one-step operations. On the one multiple choice question that was the same over all three groups in the NAEP, 20 percent of the fourth graders, 36 percent of the eighth graders, and 50 percent of the twelfth graders answered it correctly. As noted throughout this chapter, it appears that more emphasis needs to be placed on understanding rather than routine procedures that do not seem to serve students well when multiple-step thinking is required.

Hundreds Grids   Hundreds grids are squares of 100 pieces. Students shade or color different parts to represent the percent of one hundred. Figure 11.5 shows an example as might appear in typical textbooks. Working with the grid, students do activities where the squares take on different symbolic representations of percent. An example based on the work of Bennett and Nelson (1994, p. 23) shows how middle school students can use the grid method as modeled in Figure 11.6 to solve word problems involving percentages. The Bennett–Nelson wording is used.

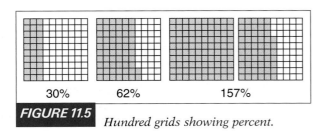

30%   62%   157%

FIGURE 11.5   *Hundred grids showing percent.*

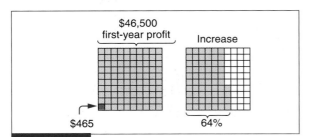

$46,500 first-year profit   Increase

$465   64%

FIGURE 11.6   *Grids showing problem solving with profit-increase problems.*

The Problem: The first-year profit from a small business was $46,500, and it increased 64 percent during the second year. What was the profit in the second year?

The hundreds grid represents the first-year profit of $46,500, and the 64 small squares in the second grid represent the percentage increase. So all 164 shaded squares represent the second-year profit. Because each small square has a value of $46,500 ÷ 100 = $465, the increase during the second year is 64 × $465 = $29,760. Thus, the second-year profit is $46,500 + $29,760 = 76,260.

A second way can also be seen with the grid. Once the $465 value of the small square is known, the total value of the 164 small squares, which is the second-year profit, is

$$164 \times \$465 = \$76,260$$

Therefore, students are given two ways to find the solution. One can be used as a check for the other. Bennett and Nelson (1994) show many more interesting ways to symbolically vary the representations in other difficult word problems with percent. Once children are familiar with the concept of increase over a two-year period, word problems can be extended to third-, fourth-, and fifth-year profits.

Unusual Shapes   Unusual shapes are used when divisions into parts is not so easily seen. The assessment section shows that elementary students are not the only ones who have a difficult time showing percentages with unusual shapes. Even preservice teachers have found the task more difficult than expected. Pattern blocks and grid paper are shown as the example in Activity 11.2. This activity shows the fractional equivalent way of finding percent, beginning with Step 4.

Although a circle is not an unusual shape, the diameter and radii dividing the circle into various sections, shown in Activity 11.3, present middle school students with an interesting challenge.

Percentages as Equations   Children do well with percent problems presented in an equation form if the numbers are kept simple so that students can visualize the answer. Figure 11.7 shows two ways the equations can be presented to children.

Real-World Mathematics   Spreadsheet programs, such as Microsoft Excel, are valuable tools in teaching percent. A real-world lesson involves having students keep track of the amount of time they spend in various activities such as eating, sleeping, playing, or being in school. Students can begin with keeping track of the hours for a

Activity 11.2

MANIPULATIVES   CALCULATORS

PERCENT WITH PATTERN BLOCKS OR GRAPH PAPER

DIRECTIONS

1. Using the actual pattern blocks as models, trace around them and shade the percent of the figure indicated below each one. Be ready to use graph paper also.

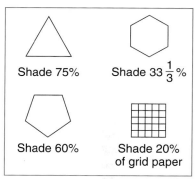

Shade 75%   Shade $33\frac{1}{3}$%

Shade 60%   Shade 20% of grid paper

2. Trace around other pattern blocks and shade a percent of the figure. Write the percent you chose to shade or color underneath each figure.
3. Do the same activity as in Step 2, using graph paper this time.
4. Check each figure to see whether it is the correct percentage by finding the common fractional equivalent. For example, in Step 1
   If 75 percent is shaded, then $\frac{3}{4}$ of the figure (or 3 out of 4 equal sections) should be shaded.
5. Write the fractional equivalent under each percentage to show you have checked each figure.
6. Check with a calculator to see whether the fractional equivalent is the same.

day and then using the spreadsheet with its formula capabilities to determine the percentage of each day spent in a given activity. That can be extended for a week or for a month. A sample spreadsheet, "Time Spent," for this activity can be found on the Web site in the Extended Activities.

The most common use of percent in the real world is with sale items. Students need to know how to figure percents when they are buying reduced items so they have a clear understanding of the discounted price. Often a store will have a sign over a counter announcing, "20 PERCENT

Activity 11.3

PROBLEM SOLVING

EXPLAIN YOUR THINKING WITH PERCENTS (A MIDDLE SCHOOL ACTIVITY)

Estimate the size (as a percent) of each section of the circle. Explain the mathematics used to arrive at the percent of each piece of the circle.

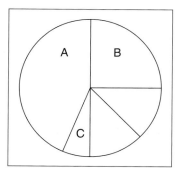

OFF THE TICKET PRICE." It is up to the consumer to figure out how much the item is reduced before deciding whether it is affordable at the sale price. Computer programs, such as the spreadsheet activity at the end of the chapter, can help students analyze what steps a person must take to find percentage reductions. Additional practice can also be done on the calculator.

FIGURE 11.7 *Percents represented as equations.*

EXTENDED ACTIVITIES

MATHEMATICAL CONNECTIONS   **CALCULATORS**

Name of Activity

• Consumer Math

• Percentages in Sports

• Time Spent

Children enjoy the idea of creating their own classroom stores. Many teachers integrate the study of percent with connections across the curriculum in economics. Students decide which items are to be sold at discounts by the percentage reduced on the sale price of items. Students can use (1) actual goods (penny toys, pencils, odds and ends collected by the teacher), (2) empty boxes and cans, or (3) pictures from catalogs or the newspaper. Figure 11.8 shows the work of one student.

This work can be adapted to computers. Students can use interactive computer programs such as Logo Turtle Math or a spreadsheet to write down the steps they need to remember when deciding on sale prices. By running the program and checking out some of their prices, the students discover if their mathematical reasoning led to the same answer as the computer program. If not, they should analyze what parts they need to redo by comparing their answers with the computer standard. This is a self-reliant way students can work with real-world situations without depending on a teacher. This takes computer use out of the drill and practice mode and into an aid to the children's own thinking.

More activities using consumer mathematics and percentages in the sports world can be found in the Extended Activities mentioned earlier. Students who are interested in sports may enjoy setting up their own sports charts with percentage of wins to losses for their favorite professional teams or use the Web site activity to keep track of their own school team's percentage of wins and losses.

Lembke and Reys (1994) report that the most popular to least popular ways to solve percent problems by fifth and seventh graders in their study were as follows: (1) using comparisons to benchmark reference points (i.e., 25 percent, 50 percent, and so forth); (2) setting up an equation (_____ is a_____ % of_____); (3) making a

---

Write what you will do step by step to find the sale price on items when you know the original price and what percent the item is to be reduced.

1. You put in the first price it cost.
2. Then you get the calculater to multiply the % off x .01 to get the real % and then on multipuly by the first price.
3. Then you take the first price and take away the answer in #2.
4. Then you have the sale price.

A Sample Problem: You are the sales manager and you must decide what percent to take off the orginal price of your items. What price will you charge customers at the checkout counter?

Paste items and original price tags here:

Take _20_% off the sticker price.

The sale price will be _$1.87_   The sale price will be _$14.38_

1. 2.34
2. 20 x .01 x 2.34 = 0.468
3. 2.34 - 0.468 = 1.872
   It's money so make it 1.87

1. $17.98
2. 20 x .01 x 17.98 = 3.596
3. 17.98 - 3.596 = 14.384
   It's money so make it $14.38

FIGURE 11.8   *Student's written journal worksheet of percent-off items.*

---

fractional equivalent; and (4) setting up a ratio. It is interesting to note that only the top quartile of students in both grades saw the ratio as a possibility to solve the problems.

TEACHING STRATEGIES FOR BUILDING CONCEPTUAL UNDERSTANDING OF RATIO

The concept of ratio is an extension from common fractions and may be written using the same symbolic notation:

$\frac{2}{5}$ The concrete manipulations are represented the same way as they were in common fractions.

Two ways to express the meaning of ratio *in words are*

2 : 5 Two to five, or For every two in one set, there are five in another set.

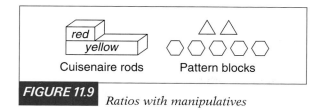

FIGURE 11.9 *Ratios with manipulatives*

From Concrete to the Connecting Stage

Pattern blocks and Cuisenaire rods are two of the materials children can use to express ratio as shown in Figure 11.9. Children can start doing teacher-made activities for ratio like Activity 11.4.

Activity 11.4

MANIPULATIVES   **EQUIVALENT RATIOS**

DIRECTIONS

1. Using attribute blocks and pattern blocks make equivalent ratios (ratios that have the same relationship). For children, one student can start and another student can make an equivalent ratio with different attribute and pattern blocks. Which of these represent the same ratio?

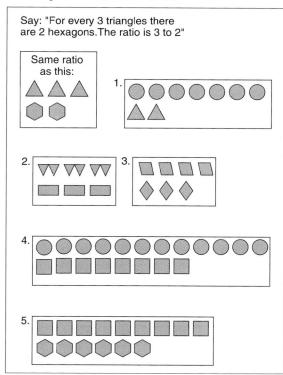

Say: "For every 3 triangles there are 2 hexagons. The ratio is 3 to 2"

Same ratio as this:

2. Continue the activity using Cuisenaire rods.
3. Think of other manipulatives that could show ratios.

4. Orally describe each ratio relationship.

> **Supporting the NCTM *Principles and Standards* (2000):**
> - Mathematics as Reasoning/Patterning; Mathematics as Communication, Representation
> - Oral Discourse of Teacher and Student; Tools That Enhance Discourse—The Teaching Principle
> - Mathematics Curriculum Principle . . . what all students need to know and do

Using it as an example, children can make their own activity cards. They write the answers in words (written discourse) on the back of the cards so other children can check their work after they explore the new activity cards. Two children can take turns seeing how many they can do correctly. These activities make good learning center or "extra time" activities when children find they have some free time on their hands.

Other activities celebrate children's literature and Native American culture. Activity 11.5 helps children see why it is important to have the right ratio of roaming area for the size of their pets. After completing this activity, children should be able to explain why a large dog needs more room to play than does a very small dog, or why a walk around a neighborhood of several blocks in area becomes important to a dog or a cat.

Activity 11.5

CULTURAL RELEVANCE   **MATHEMATICAL CONNECTIONS**   **PROBLEM SOLVING**   **CALCULATORS**

CREATING RATIOS WITH REPTILES IN NATIVE AMERICAN STORIES

MATERIALS
- "The Boy and the Rattlesnake" in *Keepers of the Animals* (Caduto and Bruchac, 1991, pp. 122–134), from the Apache Tribe in the Southwest
- Centimeter graph paper, meter sticks, newspapers, metric rulers
- Children to trace picture of lizards, snakes, turtles, salamanders, and so on, from animals, books, or encyclopedia

DIRECTIONS

1. Read the Native American story "The Boy and the Rattlesnake." Messages of story:
   - People need to use their common sense over persuasive talk.
   - Respect animals with the same respect we give humans.
   - Over 2 million reptiles are made into pets in a year's time and forced to live in a few square centimeters of cage space.

2. Reptiles need a roaming area of at least 25 square meters of space for each centimeter of their length. That's a square with the side of 5 meters for every 1 cm of reptile length.

3. How would this be expressed as a ratio? Take pictures of reptiles drawn by the students and have them measure the length in centimeters. Let them set up a ratio for how many square meters the reptile needs of living space.

4. With the centimeter graph paper, make a very tiny reptile and set up a ratio to its needed roaming area. There are several ways to do this—a factor-factor product model is shown here. Children can use a meter stick and newspapers taped together to measure their roaming area (Figure 11.10). Children are surprised at how large the area is for each reptile measured. One way is modeled in Figure 11.11.

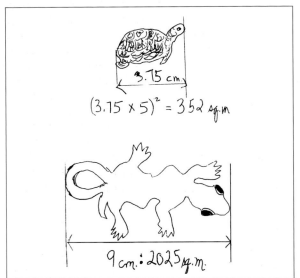

FIGURE 11.10   *Reptile drawn by child for ratio activity.*

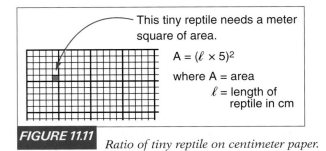

FIGURE 11.11   *Ratio of tiny reptile on centimeter paper.*

5. Share your thoughts with others. See what area other students came up with for their reptile pictures and centimeter reptiles. (These make great bulletin boards!)

Gomez (2002) and Brinker (1998) describe how ratio tables can help students plan strategies for proportions. The ideas can help students get ready for assessment tests that often expect the same mathematical modeling shown in Brinker's work, notably in recipes.

From the Connecting Stage to the Symbolic

Students can explore the several ways ratios are presented in mathematics as they become familiar with the symbolic forms of expression. The two most frequently used ways by students in problem solving were the part-part relationship and the factor-factor-product relationship (Barnett, Goldenstein, and Jackson, 1994). The part-part relationship was seen as the easiest method among middle schoolers as reported in research by Singer and Resnick (1992). Smith (2002) shows the seamless progression from reasoning with diagrams representing divided quantities to directly reasoning given numerators and denominators in the symbolic stage.

Part–Part Relationship   Computer programs help students move from the pictorial materials on the screen to the symbols that create the ratio. Commands like the ones in Logo Turtle Math such as **1part tri 4 2part pent 6** for the ratio 4:6 allow students to see that ratios are sometimes recorded symbolically as a first part to second part relationship.

Factor-Factor-Product Relationship   The previous Native American activity shows how ratio can be expressed by the part-to-part relationship and the factor-factor-product equation relationship.

The following are ratios students created by using the factor–factor product relationship after reading their favorite stories from children's literature.

For every inch that Pooh Bear was round, he dug a hole twice as wide to find honey.

p = inches of Pooh;
h = hole's width
$2 \times p = h$

developed using *Winnie the Pooh* (Milne, 1926)

For every Brachiosaurus's weight, there are 8 elephants to weigh the same amount.

w = B's weight;
e = elephant's weight
$8 \times e = w$

developed using *Creatures of Long Ago: Dinosaurs* (Buxton et al., 1988)

For every pup in a cup, there are three fish in a tree.

p = # of pups;
f = # of fish
$3 \times p = f$

developed using *Hop on Pop* (Seuss, 1963)

The children did not seem to have trouble writing the ratios in words because the form was fairly straightforward, "for every—— there are——." Lobato and Thanheiser (2002) show that the teachers need to help the students see how the same relationship could be shown mathematically as an equation. The students found it easier to make a table and then work out the equation from the table. Taking the pups in the cup is the example in Figure 11.12.

Students easily write _ p = _ f and then they figure by trial and error where the 3 goes so that the fish are equivalent to the correct amount in the equation. As we saw in Chapter 2, just recording the variables from the language frequently results in the "variable-reversal" error. The authors have found this to be a common difficulty among all groups of students with which they have worked.

Golden Ratio

Science, history, economics, art as well as mathematics are areas that share a commonality with regard to ratio. This commonality is referred to as the "Golden Ratio." The WebQuest, Golden Ratio (found on the Web site), provides the opportunity to explore the phenomenon of the Golden Ratio. The Golden Ratio has long been considered an eye-pleasing ratio. In this WebQuest, you will learn for yourself how the Golden Ratio was derived and explore some of its many applications. Then you

NO. OF PUPS	NO. OF FISH
1	3
2	6
3	9

FIGURE 11.12 *Ratio table.*

will modify this WebQuest so that it is appropriate for middle school students.

TEACHING STRATEGIES FOR BUILDING CONCEPTUAL UNDERSTANDING OF PROPORTIONS

Proportions are really equivalent ratios. The methods of finding ratios are also extended to proportions. You have already seen the start of proportional reasoning in the study of ratio as presented in the preceding section. When different values were introduced to make a new ratio, each relationship was in direct proportion to the original relationship given in the first ratio. It is a multiplicative relationship. This was seen in the Native American ratio activity when each new creature was compared with its roaming area. Each creature and its roaming area were in direct proportion to the first creature and its roaming area.

Proportional reasoning is important in the applications of mathematics. The NCTM *Principles and Standards* (NCTM, 2000) states that students need to have problem situations that can be solved through proportional reasoning. Scale drawings and similar figures involve proportional reasoning.

Making a picture or representation in direct proportion to another, either larger or smaller, is called scaling. This idea originated in the African continent. The Logo Turtle Math computer language allows children to do scaling quickly. Children have the chance to work with scaling in computer simulations that resemble the way the original work was done by early Africans. They have a first-hand "feel" for multiplicative relationships after using interactive computer programs.

Part–Part Relationship

A 12:8 ratio and a 3:2 ratio may be read as a proportion statement, "12 is to 8 as 3 is to 2." Proportions are checked the same way as equivalent fractions are:

$$\frac{a}{b} = \frac{c}{d} \; if \; ad = bc$$
$$\frac{12}{8} = \frac{3}{2} \; if \; 12 \times 2 = 8 \times 3$$
$$24 = 24$$

This is generally called the cross-product method. However, some mathematics educators have called the setup of $\frac{a}{b} = \frac{c}{d}$ by the term, the "rule of 3," meaning that it is easy to solve proportion problems if three of the four variables are known and only one variable is unknown. Charles and Lobato (1998) point out that expecting mastery of learning with the cross-multiplication method should be delayed from grade 6 to grade 7 to allow for more opportunities to solve proportions more informally by the "unit rate" or "factor of change" methods. *Unit rate* takes the original measure and enlarges it or decreases it by units until the desired proportion is reached. *Factor of change* focuses on the relationship to be maintained among factors even when a factor is changed; therefore, there needs to be a corresponding change to keep the relationship constant. Weinberg (2002) points to these methods as valid for students to study before the cross-product method. The unit rate and factor of change methods are presented in the next portion of this chapter.

Proportional reasoning is considered to be an important area for exploration in grades 5 to 8—so important, in fact, that we explore more than one approach in the remaining portion of the chapter. Activities 11.6, 11.7, and 11.8 present three different problems that involve proportional reasoning. Are there any of these for which you can show solutions found by the cross-product method in the part-part relationship model?

Activity 11.6

MATHEMATICAL CONNECTIONS   **CALCULATORS**   **ESTIMATION**

CREATING YOUR OWN WORLD 10 TIMES YOUR SIZE

MATERIALS
- Butcher paper, metric ruler, meter stick, pencil
- A set of student's choice—magic markers, crayons, paints, and so on
- Some favorite item to be measured
- Camera (optional)

DIRECTIONS
1. Estimate how large you think 10 times your item will look like. Get that much butcher paper to start the project.
2. Do the actual measurements of your item. Record them by length × width × height (for young children grades 2 and 3, measure only length × width).

3. Make each dimension 10 times as big and record the measures on paper. Use a calculator to check whether your measures are correct if you need to do so.
4. Draw the item's magnified measures on the butcher paper.
5. Color or paint the item so it looks like the real one.
6. Write a story about your adventures if you woke up one morning to find your favorite thing was 10 times its size but you were still the same size.
7. Some teachers have even taken pictures of the students sitting next to their favorite enlarged item (Figure 11.13).

FIGURE 11.13   *Student sitting next to his giant-sized roller blades.*

Concrete to Connecting Stage
Early experiences with proportion need to focus on things with which children are familiar and in which they have an interest. That's one reason why children enjoy activities like finding how much roaming area their own pets need as an extension of the Native American ratio activity. Children are fascinated with imagining a world in which everything they normally use could be 10 times or even a 100 times as big as they are. Integrated units can include children's literature that emphasizes the same theme.

Children can integrate art projects with proportion by measuring common things from their environment as demonstrated in Activity 11.6. Then they can enlarge the measurement dimensions by 10. These activities help children see proportion in concrete ways.

Kliman (1993) shares this story written by a student in the world of Brobdingnag. Notice how quickly it is apparent that the student understands size proportions in the story:

I was walking along one of Brod's huge sidewalks, which was like walking in a gigantic Logan Airport. Suddenly I bumped into something. It was a quarter-full Pepsi can 4 feet 2 inches, up to my chest. Then I figured out a way to get by it, somehow, and I found myself stuck on a piece of bubble gum bigger than my foot! I was about to step and I saw a 2-foot-6-inch, 5-inch-high log. What was it? A cigarette! My, does this place have litter! (p. 319)

Activity 11.7 begins to connect the pictorial models of graphing with the concrete models of collecting and measuring actual piles of newspapers.

Activity 11.7

CULTURAL RELEVANCE   **MATHEMATICAL CONNECTIONS**   **PROBLEM SOLVING**

CREATING PROPORTIONS WITH NATIVE AMERICAN STORIES

MATERIALS
- "Manabozho and the Maple Trees" in *Keepers of the Earth* (Caduto and Bruchac, 1989, pp. 144–145)
- Bring in some newspapers from home to get the stack of saved newspapers started
- Yardstick for measuring height of newspapers
- Poster board for making a graph

DIRECTIONS
1. Read the Native American story "Manabozho and the Maple Trees," an Anishinabe Tribe story from the Great Lakes Region. Messages of the story:
   - We must not let the trees do all our work for us. We must help save the earth and the trees too.
2. *Fact:* For every 3-foot stack of newspapers, one tree is saved.

3. Decide as a class how many trees the class would like to save. Decide how tall the stack of newspapers will need to be to save that amount of trees by recycling the paper. Set it up as a proportion:

   3 ft: 1 tree as_____ ft:_____ trees

4. Start making a graph of the proportion of trees saved to newspapers. You can use the newspapers you brought in to begin the measurement.
   - Another proportion: for every 1 foot of newspapers, you draw a third of a tree.
   - Ask the students, what could they do if there is only 1 foot of newspapers?

   $$1 \text{ ft}: \frac{1}{3} \text{ of a tree as 3 ft: 1 tree}$$

   - **Key to graph (Figure 11.14):**

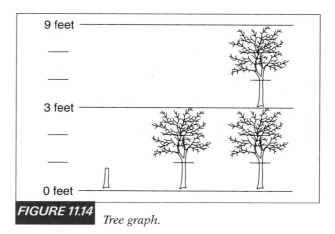

FIGURE 11.14   *Tree graph.*

5. Keep track by putting the graph up on a hall bulletin board. Ask students to talk about their project to other classes so that more newspapers can be collected.

> **Supporting the NCTM *Principles and Standards* (2000):**
> - Mathematics as Communication, Problem Solving, Connections, Representation
> - Worthwhile Mathematical Tasks; Oral Discourse for Students—The Teaching Principle
> - The Mathematics Curriculum Principle; Coherence

From Connecting Stage to Symbolic

Proportions are the essential elements of many problem-solving activities that appear as word problems in many elementary textbooks. Typically, one ratio is given, and the next ratio is only partially finished. The problem solver must "see" the two ratios as a proportion to figure out the missing segment. The typical analogy tests are an example of this type of proportion as seen in Activity 11.8.

Some of the most famous and infamous proportion problems from elementary and middle school texts have been the "travel" problems with the distance-to-time relationship implied. They are still seen with dread by many students and adults alike. However, one teacher found that students actually liked travel problems if they were presented in a new way. Notice the difference:

Textbook Type	**New Type**
If it takes 12 seconds to go 60 miles in a rocket ship, how many seconds will it take to go 55 miles?	If it takes 12 seconds for the villain to travel 60 miles to the finish line in your Nintendo game, how many seconds will it take you to win if you only need to go 55 miles to go to the finish line?

Solution:

$$\frac{12}{60} = \frac{?}{55}$$

Think: Expressing in Lowest Terms

$$\frac{12 \div 12}{60 \div 12} = \frac{1}{5}$$

SO

$$\frac{n \div 1}{55 \div 5}$$

SO

$$n = 11 \text{ seconds}$$

Think: Cross Multiplication

$$12 \times 55 = 60 \times n$$

$$\frac{660}{60} = \frac{60 \times n}{60}$$

$$11 = n$$
11 seconds

Labels for the proportions are important. In the preceding example, the following relationship patterns would produce valid proportions and arrive at the same answers.

Relationship (vertical)
$$\left[\frac{12 \text{ sec}}{60 \text{ min}} = \frac{N \text{ sec}}{55 \text{ min}} \right] \left[\frac{60 \text{ min}}{55 \text{ min}} = \frac{12 \text{ sec}}{N \text{ sec}} \right]$$
Relationship (horizontal)

Some of the new action-packed computer games lend themselves to new strategies for winning, many of which can be helped by the students' knowing how fast their action figure has to move to beat out the other action figures.

Activity 11.8

MATHEMATICAL CONNECTIONS   PROBLEM SOLVING

PROPORTIONS IN ENGLISH

DIRECTIONS

1. Proportions must maintain a definite relationship among four magnitudes such that the first is in relation to the second in the same way as the third is in relation to the fourth.

2. *Analogies* are really proportions with words as the magnitudes. For example:

   Oar is to rowboat as wheel is to car.

   Some standardized tests even use the mathematical symbols

   oar:rowboat = wheel:———.

3. Think of other word analogies and write them using the mathematical symbols.

4. These make great homework assignments.

Other Relationship Models for Proportion

Students need to realize that the "rule of 3" in proportion problems is not the only way to explore proportion. We have already seen the use of tables and of algebraic expressions when we discussed ratios in the preceding section. Remember the "pups in the cup" example, page 314?

Another model is the use of coordinate graphs to show proportions as shown in Figure 11.15. Middle school students should have exposure to this approach also. Taking the "pups in the cup" example, we can graph the proportion statement that "for every pup in a cup, there are three fish in the tree."

Activity 11.9 is another activity that provides additional practice in using coordinate graphs to solve proportion problems.

Proportional reasoning has so many applications in the real world that Thompson and Saldanha (2003) suggest that as much time as needed be spent with these concepts to ensure their careful development. Activity 11.10 provides a real-life example from farming. Hoyles, Noss, and Pozzi, (2001) show models from nursing. The 2002 NCTM yearbook supplement, *Classroom*

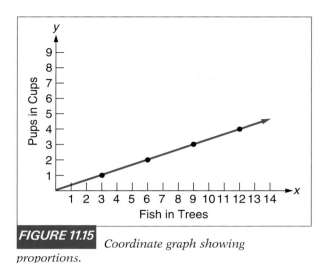

FIGURE 11.15 *Coordinate graph showing proportions.*

Activities for Making Sense of *Fractions, Ratios, and Proportions,* (Bright and Litwiller, 2002) shows many creative ideas to help students explore these concepts.

Activity 11.9

COMPUTERS

PROBLEM SOLVING

MATHEMATICAL CONNECTIONS

ESTIMATION

CALCULATORS

CREATING COORDINATE GRAPHS FROM OTHER PROPORTION EXAMPLES

MATERIALS
- Graph paper, pencils, or a computer coordinate graphing program or calculator

DIRECTIONS
1. Go back through this chapter and find ratio and proportion problems shown in other models.
2. Estimate what each proportion problem would look like on a coordinate graph before starting to graph each one.
3. Convert each example to the coordinate graph model.
4. Share orally with others how you set up your graphs and listen to their explanations. Compare and contrast any differences you find in your graphs.

Activity 11.10

PROBLEM SOLVING

CALCULATORS

MORE MIDDLE SCHOOL PROPORTIONS

1. Jo Farmer applied fertilizer to her cropland three times for the 1999 growing season. The first application, which occurred in November 1998, was anhydrous ammonia (82–0–0). She applied 150 pounds per acre of material at that time. A couple of weeks before planting, Jo applied diammonium phosphate (18–46–0) at a rate of 120 pounds per acre of material. At the time of planting, Jo applied a mixed fertilizer (9–23–30) at a rate of 100 pounds per acre. What were the total pounds of actual nutrients applied per acre to Jo's cropland? (Hint: The analysis (82–0–0) means that Jo applied 82% active nitrogen, 0% phosphorus, and 0% potash fertilizer. The remaining 18% is a carrier that helps hold the fertilizer to the soil particles.)

2. Joe Farmer is planning for this year's planting season by trying to figure out how much chemical he will have to purchase for weed control on 350 acres of corn. Joe has had trouble with cockleburs, so this year he will apply Atrazine and Buctril.

   The Atrazine will be applied at a rate of 2.5 pounds active ingredients (ai) per acre. The Atrazine Joe uses comes in a liquid form at a rate of 1.5 pounds ai per gallon. The Atrazine costs $8.00 per gallon and is applied two weeks before planting at the recommended rate; the final is applied two weeks after planting.

The Buctril is applied two weeks after planting at a rate of 0.25 pound ai per acre. Buctril also comes in a liquid form and the rate is 1 pound ai per gallon and costs $12.00 per gallon.

How many gallons of both Atrazine and Buctril will Joe need and what will the total cost be?

TEACHING STRATEGIES FOR BUILDING CONCEPTUAL UNDERSTANDING OF RATE

Rate is a term for a ratio when the ratio involves comparisons of two units uniquely different from one another. For example, 55 miles per hour is the ratio of miles to hour. Many textbooks include problems in which the ratios are expressed as rates. When the rate involves a proportion, the problem becomes more difficult. These are found frequently on standardized tests from the upper elementary grades through college entrance examinations. Activity 11.11 gives some examples of ratios expressed in rates and then asks you to add additional rates and their associated ratios to the list.

Technically, you have already seen rate examples in the previous section when the "travel"

Activity 11.11

MENTAL MATH **FINDING THE RATIO IN THE RATE**

DIRECTIONS

1. Think of the ratio that is implied in each of these rates:

Rate	Ratio
55 miles per hour	55 miles:1 hour
8 cans for a dollar	8:$1.00
12 eye blinks a minute	12 blinks:1 minute

2. Think of others you can add to the list.

EXTENDED ACTIVITIES

CALCULATORS

MATHEMATICAL CONNECTIONS

PROBLEM SOLVING

PORTFOLIO

CHILDREN'S LITERATURE

On the Web site (Chapter 11, Extended Activities) read/do the following:

- Proportions with Real-World Problems
- Proportions in Economics
- Finding the Height of the Flagpole
- Rates and Proportions
- Ratios with Robotics
- Emergency Medical Careers
- Response Time of Ambulances
- TIMSS Assessment: Can You Load an Airplane?
- Family Math Packet Proportions
- Lesson Plan to Develop Mathematical Proficiency Creating Your Own World 10 Times Your Size

problems were introduced. The Extended Activities provide further practice in working with proportions, including the cross-multiplication method.

Rates can be seen in the factor-factor-product relationship of algebraic expressions. For example, for problems involving distance, rate, and time:

Let d = distance r = rate t = time

There are three ways to set up the equation, depending on what needs to be found in the problem:

$$d = rt \quad r = \frac{d}{t} \quad t = \frac{d}{r}$$

CATEGORIES OF EMERGENCIES		MAXIMUM RESPONSE TIME ALLOWED
Priority 1	Life-threatening emergency	8 min 59 sec
Priority 2	Non-life-threatening emergency	12 min 59 sec
Priority 3	Urgent emergency	30 min 59 sec
Priority 4	Nonemergency	59 min 59 sec
Priority 5	Scheduled nonemergency	30 min 59 sec
Priority 6	Prescheduled nonemergency	15 min 59 sec

Response Time Performance

Response time penalties: for each priority 1, 2, or 3 call not handled in the agreed on response time, the contractor pays $15.00 per minute up to $250.00 per incident.

FIGURE 11.16 *Master contract for paramedic ambulance services.*

Return to the Extended Activities on the Web site, and using the activity "Rates and Proportions," analyze the rate examples to determine which equation should be used. You already know what the answers should be using other approaches. If you get the same answer using the formula approach as you did when you used another approach previously, you can be confident that you have a good grasp of proportional reasoning, ratios, and rates.

Middle school students have developed interesting ratio–rate problems using LEGO MINDSTORM Robotics (2003) and radio-controlled vehicles. The students working with the radio-controlled vehicles organized a race to measure rate to the finish line depending on the length of the track. They also discovered a way to use proportional reasoning when they noticed the shadow caused by their vehicles. One middle schooler said his truck, the Intruder, was made to a scale of 1:12. He said he could figure out how long the shadow would be on a life-sized Intruder by setting up a proportion using the shadow length of the radio-controlled Intruder.

PERCENT, RATIO, PROPORTION, AND RATE IN THE WORLD OF WORK

Middle school is the time when students think about themselves in many occupations. As seen in chapter 2, girls especially need a vision of the mathematics required for careers. In the Extended Activities activity on the Web site, "Emergency Medical Careers," middle school girls have the chance to see a female Emergency Medical Communications Officer using proportional reasoning and computers to save lives. Another series of rate and percent problems ("Response Time of Ambulances" in the same

Extended Activities) has been developed around the response time of ambulances. This problem's description comes from an ambulance company's contract with the city of Richmond, Virginia (Richmond Ambulance Authority, 2004). Use the information in Figure 11.16 for the extended activity "Response Time of Ambulances."

Many problems can be developed around the Richmond contract, or with information from a business in your local area, to help students realize that real people actually get paid to figure out percent, rate, and ratio in the real world.

The teaching strategies in this chapter require much practice to understand fully how they apply in a variety of real-world experiences. A teacher must avoid rushing from one principle to another without adequate exploration with manipulative models. Otherwise, students will have difficulties solving problems like the preceding examples, which require an integration of all the mathematical principles studied in this chapter. The NCTM *Principles and Standards* (NCTM, 2000) states that mathematics curriculum in grades 6 to 8 should investigate relationships between fractions, decimals, and percents. Students should understand the various representations of the same number, such as $\frac{15}{100}, \frac{3}{20}$, 0.15, 15%, and 15:100.

A NEW APPROACH?

We have presented the development of common fractions, decimals, percents, ratio, proportion, and rate in the usual order these topics are found in today's elementary textbooks. A recent research study (Moss, 2002), however, suggests that beginning with percents may be a better approach. Just as young students have intuitive understandings of fractions, so do students have substantial intuitive understandings of percent meanings and operations. Now that you have studied Chapters 10 and 11, and thinking back to your own elementary and middle school mathematics experiences, what do you think about changing the order of the curriculum and introducing percents and operations with percents prior to the formal study of fractions and decimals?

ASSESSMENT TO HELP STUDENTS WITH SPECIAL NEEDS

Concrete and Scaffolding Experiences

The bright young man who created the proportional reasoning problem with the Intruder has been diagnosed with Attention Deficit Disorder (ADD). This points out once again the danger of labels. Many times engaging, hands-on activities can bring out the best in all students if they are given time to think of new alternatives under stimulating conditions. Do not sell any student short. The work done with the radio-controlled vehicles and the animated robots can be seen in the Extended Activities with the activity "Ratios with Robotics." You can use the pictures and the activities to motivate your own students to do the same kind of activity at your school.

Stein and Bovalino (2001) remind us that students need concrete ways to compare and operate on quantities. This is as true with concepts such as fractions, percents, ratio, and proportion as it is for learning basic facts of addition. Another useful strategy, especially for students with special needs, is scaffolding. Scaffolding may take the form of offering a subtle hint, posing a similar problem, or asking for ideas (Kilpatrick, Swafford, and Findell, 2001). Scaffolding includes the introduction of a new concept in relation to a previously learned concept, gradually increasing the difficulty or complexity of concepts and applications, and providing frequent opportunities for review. Students with special needs, in particular, benefit from feedback that includes specific suggestions or a set of minimally different problems that addresses identified needs (Gersten et al., 2002).

Field-Independent and Field-Dependent Learners

Both thought-processing styles will be compared side by side to demonstrate how different students work together in cooperative learning situations.

Shaded Regions

Field-independent learners have more success finding their own fractional part from the percent given and then shading it. They should do the activity and then give it to a field-dependent learner to figure out the percent from a list of made-up answers with distractor items.

Field-dependent learners like to see the whole example and figure out the percent from there. They should explain how they get the answer for the field-independent learner because most standardized tests use this form.

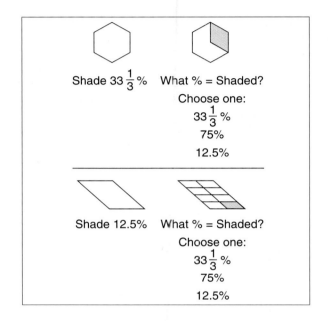

Spreadsheets

Observe the students as they work to see which of the actions described below are occurring and pair students with opposite processing styles together for computer work.

Field-independent learners enjoy building the table, working from cell to cell. Creating formulas such as +a2*bl for spreadsheet programs does not seem to be a problem. They often stop after each formula and study what has happened as the number appears in each cell. They may have trouble telling all the parts of the pattern if the table is shown to them fully constructed.

Field-dependent learners are bothered with what they perceive as long, tedious work building the formula. They can often "spot" patterns more quickly and in more depth than the field-independent learner once the table is constructed.

Correcting Common Misconceptions

Many of the common misconceptions presented here are the same ones seen in the work of students with special needs. These concepts may prove challenging for many students.

Writing the Decimal with the Percent It is common for children to hear 52 percent and write 0.52%, remembering that the number with two decimal places is "per hundredth." Reading the percent aloud with place-value labels is often all that is needed for the student to see the mistake. Fifty-two hundredths of a percent sounds much less than 52 percent.

If the problem persists, spreadsheet programs in which children can change the numbers quickly and see the results are often a good way for them to distinguish the difference because they can compare what 0.52% and 52% will give them. The use of a calculator to check percents is useful if the calculator has a % key.

Enter 0.52 and press the % key to see that the answer is 0.0052 instead of 0.52.

For some calculators that quick and simple check will not work. For those calculators, follow these steps:

1. Enter 1.00 × (the percent you wish to check) = ——

   (This fixes the number in the calculator as a variable.)
   Example: 100 × 0.52 = 0.52 (calculator answer)

2. Press the % key. Now the number on the calculator will be treated as a percent and the resulting number is the decimal equivalent.
   Example: [press % key] results in 0.0052

Percent of a Given Value There are three common mistakes when calculating percent of a given value.

Forgetting the Meaning of the Term "of" Students know that a percent of an original number means it will be less than the original quantity, so they divide rather than multiply to find the percent. They reason that multiplication yields a greater number rather than a lesser number. Again, the word "of" is crucial to the problem. If this point is stressed throughout the study of multiplication from basic facts to percents, students will recognize that "of" means multiplication and that the answer is smaller than the original number, which does make sense. For example:

29% of 52

Common Error   *With Multiplication*

52

179.31   ×0.29

0.29(52.00)   15.08

Stopping after Percent Is Found without Further Reduction In price-reduction problems students frequently find the percent correctly but forget that the problem is not finished because the original price must be reduced by that percent, meaning subtraction must be used. Role-playing many shopping examples with things they enjoy buying seems to help in two-step problem-solving situations.

Thinking of Percent as Money to Be Reduced When converting percents to decimals, the decimal reminds the student of the money that is involved in the answer. Therefore, in a price-reduction problem, 0.29 becomes $0.29 and it is reduced from the original price by subtraction. This is where estimation becomes valuable as a tool. If students have had much practice finding 10 percent of amounts, reasonable answers can be figured:

Faulty Reasoning

$52.00
− .29
$51.71

Reasoning by Estimation
10 percent of 52 = 5.20
30 percent of 52 = 5.20 × 3 = 15.60

29 percent is slightly less than 30 percent, so 29 percent, has to be a little less than 15.60 and 51.71 is nowhere close.

What will bring me closer to 15.60?

Answer: Multiplication *not* subtraction

Average and poor students will not be able to solve problems like this one unless they have had effective teachers who help them structure their thoughts.

PUTTING IT ALL TOGETHER—PORTFOLIO ASSESSMENTS OF REAL STUDENT WORK

Two concepts of percent are explored with students of different ages from kindergarten to adult. In Activity 11.12 students are asked to construct their own picture, building up to the whole. Then they are asked to find the percent. Activity 11.13 shows students' work based on a pictorial image provided on the assessment.

Students' Understanding of Percent: Building with Pattern Pieces

Four children worked on the task of building a picture with pattern pieces—Andrew, a

Activity 11.12

PORTFOLIO

CREATING YOUR OWN RUBRIC FOR PERCENTS WITH MANIPULATIVES

MATERIALS

• Work of the four children (see pages 314–315):
  Andrew, kindergarten
  Katelyn, third grade
  Mark, third grade
  Justin, sixth grade

BACKGROUND TO HELP IN YOUR ANALYSIS

None of the children have had formal instruction with percents. Justin's math series is just getting ready to introduce the concept.

DIRECTIONS

Use these questions to help you start thinking about a rubric:

1. What are the positive things that you see in all the answers to the percent questions?

2. What misconceptions about percents do the children seem to have?

3. Figure out what the percents actually were and see which student came the closest. Was the student's explanation one that showed a basic understanding of percent?

4. Is there a fair scale that could be used to give a numerical score to the creative work of all children?

   If yes—what is it?

   If no—what could you substitute instead of a numerical score?

5. Using some examples of rubrics presented in Chapter 4, how could you modify one or several to come up with a rubric that would assess this activity fairly?

6. What are the next steps you need to do to help all the children continue to grow?

7. Share your thoughts with others. See what your combined knowledge might be able to come up with.

kindergartner, Katelyn and Mark, both third graders, and Justin, a sixth grader. Both Mark and Justin had expressed an interest in building a rocket ship, so their paper directions were printed with their interest in mind. As you ana-

Because N is the smallest piece, all the pieces will be compared to it:

V = 8N	Z = 4N
U = 2N	Y = 4N

FIGURE 11.17 *Pattern pieces used in activity.*

lyze how much and what each student understands about percent, it may help to know the equivalencies of the pattern pieces, shown in Figure 11.17. The students' work follows the portfolio assessment activity.

Students' Understanding of Percent: Seeing Percent in Whole Figures

The next set of portfolio assessments is very interesting because it contains the work of both children and adults. Names have been omitted because some of the work of the adults shows major misconceptions that could prove embarrassing. It is not the intention of the authors to make fun of any learner, but rather to show the misconceptions that occur even among intelligent, successful adults.

It should be pointed out that this activity has been a part of one of the author's final exams for the past eight years. The work of Student C and

---

Andrew made a house.

Work with Pattern Pieces

Use the pattern pieces to make something of your choice. Trace what you did on this paper, so we can have a record to remember.

Answer these questions:
What percent of the picture is made out of "Y" pieces? __/__
What percent of the picture is made out of "Z" pieces? __4__
What percent of the picture is made out of "N" pieces? _____
Write how you figured out your answers:
_____
_____
_____
_____
_____

Mark

Rocket Ship with Pattern Pieces

Draw your rocket ship with the pattern pieces like you did in class. Trace it on to this paper, showing the pieces that make up the rocket ship.

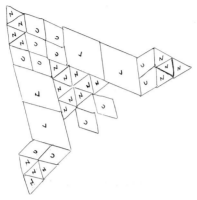

Answer these questions:

What percent of the rocket is made out of "U" pieces? _25 %_
What percent of the rocket is made out of "V" pieces? _22%_
What percent of the rocket is made out of "N" pieces? _16%_

Write how you figured out your answers:

```
        I counted the pieces
      37   37   37
     -12   -4  -21
     ----  ---  ----
      25    33   16
```

Justin

Rocket Ship with Pattern Pieces

Draw your rocket ship with the pattern pieces like you did in class. Trace it on to this paper, showing the pieces that make up the rocket ship.

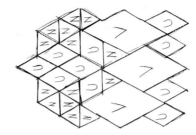

Answer these questions:

What percent of the rocket is made out of "U" pieces? _10/27_
What percent of the rocket is made out of "V" pieces? _14/27_
What percent of the rocket is made out of "N" pieces? _3/27_

Write how you figured out your answers:

I added all the pieces together and got a total of 27. Next I added all the U pieces together and got a total of 10 and came up with a percentage of 10/27. Then I performed the same procedure with V and N.

I made a chicken, Katelyn

Work with Pattern Pieces

Use the pattern pieces to make something of your choice. Trace what you did on this paper, so we can have a record to remember.

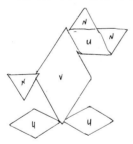

Answer these questions:

What percent of the picture is made out of "U" pieces? _40%_
What percent of the picture is made out of "V" pieces? _50%_
What percent of the picture is made out of "N" pieces? _10%_

Write how you figured out your answers:

There are very few Ns so I said 10% and Us looked like 40% because it wasn't 50% and wasn't 10% so it was 40% and V was a big part even if there was only 1 and I said 50% and all together it makes 100% of the chicken!

Student D represents answers seen about 25 percent of the time. All the adult students are juniors or seniors in an elementary education program. They have passed their college entrance exams with ACT scores of 21 or higher. Other pertinent information about all the students is given in the portfolio activity itself.

Activity 11.13

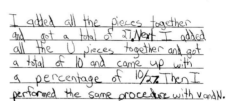

PORTFOLIO

ANALYZING CHILD AND ADULT KNOWLEDGE OF PERCENTS IN WHOLE FIGURES

MATERIALS
- Work of the five students (on page 316):

  Student A, age 8—Figure 11.18
  Student B, age 9—Figure 11.19
  Student C, adult—Figure 11.20
  Student D, adult—Figure 11.20
  Student E, adult—Figure 11.20

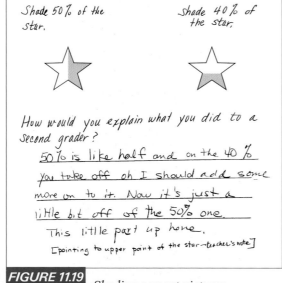

Shade 50% of the star.

Shade 40% of the star.

How would you explain what you did to a second grader?

Mainly I just thought That the whole star was a 100%. So I just shaded a haleof the star. I started at a point and end at a point, Then I did it all the way around. Then I times 4 and 10 together and got 40.

FIGURE 11.18 *Shading percent pictures by student A, age 8.*

DIRECTIONS

Use these questions to help you start thinking about the analysis:

1. How did each person attempt to break down the activity to find the percents?

2. Which shadings showed positive understanding of percent? Did it differ with age?

Shade 50% of the star.

Shade 40% of the star.

How would you explain what you did to a second grader?

50% is like half and on the 40% you take off oh I should add some more on to it. Now it's just a little bit off of the 50% one. This little part up here. [pointing to upper point of the star—teacher's note]

FIGURE 11.19 *Shading percent pictures by student B, age 9.*

Student C Student D Student E

FIGURE 11.20 *Shading percent pictures by adults.*

3. What misconceptions about percents do the students seem to have? Did it differ with age?

4. What is noticeably missing on the task as the adults were asked to do it and the task as the elementary students were asked to do it?

5. Do you think the adult answers would improve if the task was adjusted to match the task as asked of the children? Why or why not?

6. Using some examples of rubrics presented in Chapter 4, how could you modify one or several to come up with a rubric that would assess this activity fairly?

7. What are the next steps you need to do to help all the students continue to grow?

8. Share your thoughts with others. See what your combined knowledge might be able to create.

SUMMARY

- Percent, ratio, proportion, and rate involve a multiplicative relationship and a constant.

- Real-world contexts and the use of manipulatives are important in the development of conceptual understanding of percents.

- Computer spreadsheets and calculators are valuable tools in the teaching of percents.

- Ratios are an extension from common fractions and may use the same symbolic notation.

- Two of the most frequently used relationships of ratios in problem solving are the part-part and the factor-factor-product relationships.

- Proportions are equivalent ratios.

- Three common approaches to solving proportions are the rule of 3 or cross-product method, the unit rate method, and the factor of change method.

- The rule of 3 or cross-product method is the most common approach to solving proportions and is based on the fact that three of the four variables in a proportion are known.

- The unit rate method of solving proportions involves enlarging or decreasing the original measure until the desired proportion is reached.
- The factor of change method involves maintaining the relationship among factors even when a factor is changed.

- Rate refers to a ratio in which the comparisons involve two units uniquely different from one another.
- Students with special needs will benefit from a scaffolding approach and the use of real-world contexts.

PRAXIS II™-STYLE QUESTIONS

Answers to this chapter's Praxis II™-style questions are in the instructor's manual.

Multiple Choice Format

1. The method shown below is an example of an application of a mathematical concept,_____, used in ancient_____.
   a. ratio; Egypt
   b. percent; Babylonia
   c. scale drawing; France
   d. Both a and b

Total Shots Target	Shots Missing Target	% Hitting
1960	1375	?

The answer rounded to the nearest tenth is
   a. 99.3%
   b. 0.702%
   c. 29.9%
   d. 70.2%

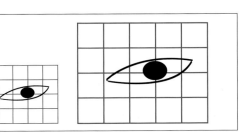

2. What is the ratio of the area of Tangram Shape A to the area of Tangram Shape B?

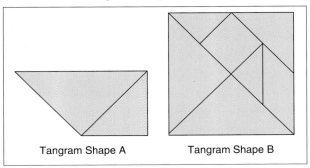

Tangram Shape A   Tangram Shape B

   a. 2:7
   b. 3:8
   c. 40:100
   d. $\frac{7}{2}$

3. Use a calculator to find the percent of arrows that missed the target in the archery example below.

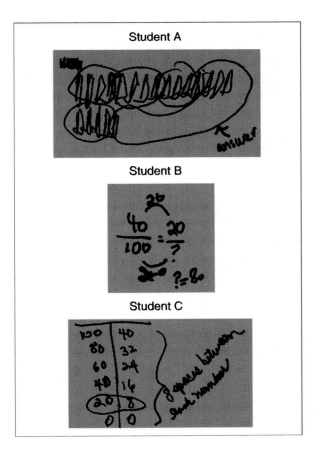

Student A

Student B

Student C

4. Students were asked to show how they would find 40% of 20. The solutions of three students appear below:

   Which student(s) understood how to find the accurate answer?

   a. Student A
   b. Student B
   c. Student C
   d. Both b and c

Constructed Response Format

5. In question #4, which students were using the rule of 3 method, the unit rate method, and the factor of change method? What misconceptions in the use of some of the methods lead to the inaccurate answers in question #4? Explain how you decided on your answers.

6. Restate the problem below in three ways—as a proportion, as a percent, and as a rate problem and solve each one.

   For every 2 completed homework papers, students will be rewarded with 5 additional minutes of free time in the classroom.

7. Shade 25% of the star below.

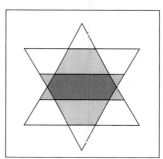

8. Both ratio and rate involve a comparison between two quantities. How would you answer the student in your class who asks, "How can I tell a ratio from a rate?"

Integrating Technology

Computer Spreadsheet

Time Spent

Internet Activities

Scavenger Hunt
Percents, Ratios, Rates, Proportions: Why Learn Them is an Internet-based scavenger hunt for grades 5–8.

WebQuest

WebQuest—Volcano Encounters—Using Percent, Ratio, and Rate

| **COMPUTERS** | **ESTIMATION** | **PROBLEM SOLVING** | **MATHEMATICAL CONNECTIONS** | **INTERNET SEARCHES** |

"Volcano Encounters—Using Percent, Ratio, and Rate" is on the Web site for the text. You will see how a teacher can adapt a WebQuest from one concept to another with relative ease. This is essentially the same WebQuest as the one in chapter 10. The common fraction materials have been changed to percent, ratio, and rate problems.

The Price is Right
A WebQuest integrating mathematics, language arts, and social students.

Web sites

National Library of Virtual Manipulatives
http://nlvm.usu.edu/en/nav/vlibrary.html
(also in Spanish)
Virtual manipulatives, with suggestions for teachers and parents, useful for teaching the content standards in NCTM's Principles and Standards.

Interactivate: Home page
http://www.shodor.org/interactivate
Developed for middle school mathematics explorations but several are adaptable to elementary mathematics.

CHILDREN'S LITERATURE

Briggs, Raymond. *Jim and the Beanstalk*. New York: Coward, McCann & Geoghegan, 1980.

Buxton, Jane H., ed. *Creatures of Long Ago: Dinosaurs*. Columbia, SC: National Geographic Society, 1988.

Caduto, Michael J., and Joseph Bruchac. *Keepers of the Earth: Native American Stories and Environmental Activities for Children*. Golden, CO: Fulcrum Publishing, 1989.

———. *Keepers of the Animals: Native American Stories and Wildlife Activities for Children*. Golden, CO: Fulcrum Publishing, 1991.

Carroll, Lewis. *Alice in Wonderland and Through the Looking Glass*. New York, NY: Putnam Publishing Group, 1981.

Cleary, Beverly, and S. Ralph. *Mouse*. New York: William Morrow, 1982.

Clement, Rod. *Counting on Frank*. Milwaukee: Gareth Stevens Publishing, 1991.

Dahl, Roald. *The BFG*. New York: Farrar, Straus and Giroux, 1982.

Milne, A. A. *Winnie-the-Pooh*. New York: E. P. Dutton, 1926.

Schwartz, David M. *If You Made a Million*. New York: Mulberry, 1989.

Schwartz, David M. *If You Hopped Like a Frog*. New York: Scholastic Press, 1999.

Seuss, Dr. *Hop on Pop*. New York: Random House, 1963.

Swift, Jonathan. *Gulliver's Travels*. New York: William Morrow, 1983.

White, E. B. *Stuart Little*. New York: Harper & Row, 1945.

Geometry and Spatial Reasoning

A partial listing as it pertains to Geometry from NCTM *Curriculum Focal Points* (2006, pages 11–13; 15; 17; 19–20).

WHERE IS THE MATHEMATICS? THE STRUCTURE OF GEOMETRIC THINKING AND SPATIAL REASONING

Wherever you are as you start to read this chapter—*STOP!* Lift your eyes from this page and look around. You are experiencing the spatial properties of the physical world. Our world consists of three-dimensional space and the objects found within it—both human-made and natural—a table, a chair, a tree, a mountain range, and so forth. You experience geometry and spatial reasoning every time you interact with the objects around you. Children also have an intuitive sense about spatial reasoning and geometry from interacting with everyday objects even before starting formal education in school. *Spatial reasoning* means a person can manipulate one-, two-, and three-dimensional objects in space and describe their orientations to other objects and form conclusions, judgments, and inferences about their properties and relationships. *Geometry* is defined as the study of spatial objects, their properties, and relationships in an organized, coherent system (UCSMP, 2001). Therefore, *geometric thinking* is the organization and application of spatial reasoning within a coherent system.

The earliest records of geometric thinking come from the ancient world of Egypt, Babylon, and China. Geometry and spatial reasoning were used to solve everyday problems—from finding area and volume for trading goods to constructing the

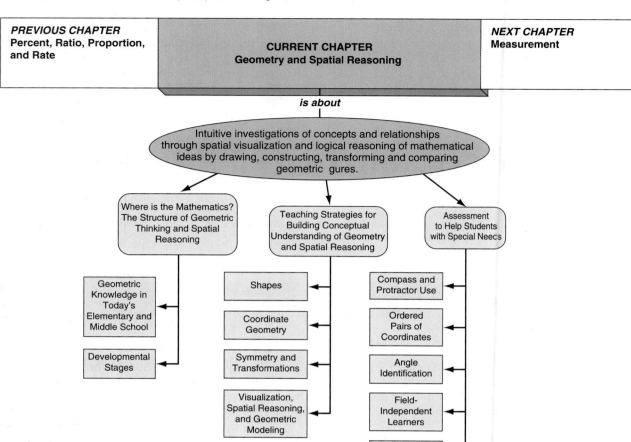

PREVIOUS CHAPTER	CURRENT CHAPTER	NEXT CHAPTER
Percent, Ratio, Proportion, and Rate	Geometry and Spatial Reasoning	Measurement

is about

Intuitive investigations of concepts and relationships through spatial visualization and logical reasoning of mathematical ideas by drawing, constructing, transforming and comparing geometric gures.

Where is the Mathematics? The Structure of Geometric Thinking and Spatial Reasoning

Teaching Strategies for Building Conceptual Understanding of Geometry and Spatial Reasoning

Assessment to Help Students with Special Neecs

Geometric Knowledge in Today's Elementary and Middle School

Developmental Stages

Shapes

Coordinate Geometry

Symmetry and Transformations

Visualization, Spatial Reasoning, and Geometric Modeling

Compass and Protractor Use

Ordered Pairs of Coordinates

Angle Identification

Field-Independent Learners

Field-Dependent Learners

SELF-HELP QUESTIONS _____

1. What is the current research on how students learn geometry?

2. How can I make sure that I am teaching to the appropriate developmental level of my students?

3. What is the best way to incorporate geometry into my mathematics curriculum?

4. Which materials appear to help children explore geometric concepts the best?

5. How can I celebrate the ingenuity of diverse cultures in the use of geometry?

ornate temples of Babylon and the magnificent pyramids of Egypt. Stemming from this early time, mathematicians have considered geometry and spatial reasoning central to all mathematics.

Many aspects of our world can be viewed from a geometric perspective. The study of geometry is important to develop adequate spatial skills. During childhood, children respond to the three-dimensional world of shapes as they play, build, and explore with toys and other materials. The development of spatial skills must be nurtured through geometric activities. Spatial skills include interpreting and making drawings, forming mental images, visualizing changes, and generalizing about perceptions in the environment. These abilities, in turn, will promote the ability to reason, to predict, and to represent knowledge in appropriate ways.

Another important benefit from geometry is that it provides opportunities to develop logical thinking and reasoning. Geometry provides an opportunity to use hands-on materials and to stimulate creative visualization of mathematical ideas. Activities involve drawing, constructing, measuring, transforming, and comparing geometric figures.

Geometric Knowledge in Today's Elementary and Middle School

Geometry has not always been part of the scope and sequence of an elementary mathematics program. Textbooks prior to the 1960s generally included only measures of area and volume. Geometry should be viewed as an opportunity to have lots of hands-on, interactive experiences with geometric concepts. Many people may think of geometry as a study of axioms, postulates, proofs of theorems, constructions, and so on. There are many kinds of geometry: motion geometry, solid geometry, plane geometry, Euclidean geometry, to name a few.

The important issue in the elementary and middle school years is not the name, but rather the type of experiences we intend students to have as part of the elementary school geometry curriculum. Experiences in geometry should allow for the intuitive investigation of concepts and relationships. Activities should provide a rich background and solid foundations for the generalizations about geometric relationships that come during the middle school grades. Geometry should encourage children to explore a variety of geometric concepts. This approach results in a study of what is called "informal geometry."

Research Research (Clements, 2003b) shows that geometry is the mathematics subject least taught in elementary school. Geometry remains the one area in mathematics where primary children can score better than their upper grade counterparts on standardized tests, the NAEP (2006) and TIMSS (1999), when asked to identify shapes and their properties. Clements cites many research studies that show instructors teaching the same low-level geometry skills regardless of grade level. The curriculum traditionally has not stressed on a progression of more complex skills as students advance from one grade level to the next. In fact, geometry may be overlooked entirely or mentioned much later than other mathematics areas. Some teachers reported skipping geometry instruction altogether.

Generally, the geometry curriculum in the United States has reflected a lack of focus and demanding content resulting in continued poor performance and lack of geometry knowledge of students. Suggestions for their resolution are presented in the NCTM *Principles and Standards* (2000) and the *Navigating through Geometry* Series (House, 2001, 2002). On the positive side, observations indicate that children may approach geometry as a challenging change from the more computational components of other mathematics topics. Special-needs students also frequently perform much better in geometry than in arithmetic if taught as outlined in the following section on recommendations.

Recommendations To teach informal geometry effectively, teachers must be familiar with the characteristics of geometric figures and the relationships between them. The NCTM *Principles and Standards* (2000) recommend four areas for geometric study with each area growing progressively more complex in the grade levels as seen in Figure 12.1. The teaching strategies in this chapter have been organized around the four major categories of study. Teachers are encouraged to teach geometry earlier in the school year with frequent revisits to topics during the year.

If elementary and middle school teachers do not feel competent to teach geometry, the low performance of students is likely to continue. A joint commission of the Conference Board of the Mathematical Sciences (2002) recommends at least one college course in geometry prior to licensure as an elementary or middle school teacher. The concepts are far more complex than can be covered in one chapter of a methods text. Ideally, you should have had the geometry course prior to reading this text. If such is not the case or if it has been a long time since taking the course, you are encouraged to read "Geometry Terminology Review" in Check Your Mathematics Knowledge in Chapter 12 on the Web site.

Another way to review is through the use of computer programs. One such program, Cabri™Jr. (2003), is available for download from Texas Instruments for use with the TI-83 Plus calculator or as software for the computer. Created for high school students, it will refresh your memory on building geometric constructions and on performing analytic, transformational, and Euclidean geometric functions. The address appears at the end of the chapter in the Web site section. It is good for teachers to have the knowledge of what

STANDARD: SHAPES

Instructional programs from prekindergarten through grade 12 should enable all students to

Analyze characteristics and properties of two- and three-dimensional geometric shapes and develop mathematical arguments about geometric relationships.

GRADES PREK TO 2

Recognize, name, build, draw, compare, and sort two- and three-dimensional shapes.

Describe attributes and parts of two- and three-dimensional shapes.

Investigate and predict the results of putting together and taking apart two- and three-dimensional shapes.

GRADES 3 TO 5

Identify, compare, and analyze attributes of two- and three-dimensional shapes and develop vocabulary to describe the attributes.

Classify two- and three-dimensional shapes according to their properties and develop definitions of classes of shapes such as triangles and pyramids.

Investigate, describe, and reason about the results of subdividing, combining, and transforming shapes.

Explore congruence and similarity.

Make and test conjectures about geometric properties and relationships and develop logical arguments to justify conclusions.

GRADES 6 TO 8

Precisely describe, classify, and understand relationships among types of two- and three-dimensional objects using their defining properties.

Understand relationships among the angles, side lengths, perimeters, areas, and volumes of similar objects.

Create and critique inductive and deductive arguments concerning geometric ideas and relationships, such as congruence, similarity, and the Pythagorean relationship.

STANDARD: COORDINATE GEOMETRY

Specify locations and describe spatial relationships using coordinate geometry and other representational systems.

GRADES PREK TO 2

Describe, name, and interpret relative positions in space and apply ideas about relative position.

Describe, name, and interpret direction and distance in navigating space and apply ideas about direction and distance.

Find and name locations with simple relationships such as "near to" and in coordinate systems such as maps.

GRADES 3 TO 5

Describe location and movement using common language and geometric vocabulary.

Make and use coordinate systems to specify locations and to describe paths.

Find the distance between points along horizontal and vertical lines of a coordinate system.

GRADES 6 TO 8

Use coordinate geometry to represent and to examine the properties of geometric shapes.

Use coordinate geometry to examine special geometric shapes, such as regular polygons or those with pairs of parallel or perpendicular sides.

STANDARD: SYMMETRY AND TRANSFORMATIONS

Apply transformations and use symmetry to analyze mathematical situations.

GRADES PREK TO 2

Recognize and apply slides, flips, and turns.

Recognize and create shapes that have symmetry.

GRADES 3 TO 5

Predict and describe the results of sliding, flipping, and turning two-dimensional shapes.

Describe a motion or a series of motions that will show that two shapes are congruent.

Identify and describe line and rotational symmetry in two- and three-dimensional shapes and designs.

GRADES 6 TO 8

Describe sizes, positions, and orientations of shapes under informal transformations such as flips, turns, slides, and scaling.

Examine the congruence, similarity, and line or rotational symmetry of objects using transformations.

STANDARD: VISUALIZATION, SPATIAL REASONING, AND GEOMETRIC MODELING

Use visualization, spatial reasoning, and geometric modeling to solve problems.

GRADES PREK TO 2

Create mental images of geometric shapes using spatial memory and spatial visualization.

FIGURE 12.1   *NCTM expectations for geometry. From* NCTM Principles and Standards for School Mathematics *(2000, pages 396–397).*

Recognize and represent shapes from different perspectives.

Relate ideas in geometry to ideas in number and measurement.

Recognize geometric shapes and structures in the environment and specify their location.

GRADES 3 TO 5

Build and draw geometric objects.

Create and describe mental images of objects, patterns, and paths.

Identify and build a three-dimensional object from two-dimensional representations of that object.

Identify and build a two-dimensional representation of a three-dimensional object.

Use geometric models to solve problems in other areas of mathematics, such as number and measurement.

Recognize geometric ideas and relationships and apply them to other disciplines and to problems that arise in the classroom or in everyday life.

GRADES 6 TO 8

Draw geometric objects with specified properties, such as side lengths or angle measures.

Use two-dimensional representations of three-dimensional objects to visualize and solve problems such as those involving surface area and volume.

Use visual tools such as networks to represent and solve problems.

Use geometric models to represent and explain numerical and algebraic relationships.

Recognize and apply geometric ideas and relationships in areas outside the mathematics classroom, such as art, science, and everyday life.

FIGURE 12.1 *NCTM expectations for geometry. From* NCTM Principles and Standards for School Mathematics *(2000, pages 396–397) (Continued).*

comes at the next level for students. Keep in mind that teachers are expected to know more than their students.

Recommendations for elementary and middle school students include the use of geometric models, designs, pictures, and shapes to help students analyze and make sense of geometric problems. They help students illustrate and describe their mathematical thinking and ideas. For example, area models can be used to approach multiplication, decimals, fractions, and percents. Students should be given the opportunity to explore mathematical concepts and relationships from a geometric or a spatial view. Many practical experiences involve problem-solving situations that require a knowledge of geometric concepts, such as making frames, determining the amount of wallpaper, paint, grass, or fertilizer to buy, and

other work situations. Geometry is an excellent way to involve relevant contributions from many cultures.

Geometry easily integrates with other disciplines. Many real-world performance assessment tasks designed for elementary and middle school have a geometric connection. Think of the Piagetian tasks in Chapter 3 and the problem solving tasks in Chapter 5, to name a few. By connecting geometry and spatial reasoning across mathematics topics, they are more likely to be given the instructional time they deserve in the curriculum.

Developmental Stages

There are two current theories assessing the developmental growth of students in geometry. One is called the van Hiele levels and the other is called the structured observation of learning outcomes (SOLO). Both stress going from simple to more complex understandings through certain levels or stages. A more advanced stage cannot be attained without the understanding of the previous stage. Both developmental theories are compatible, and the NCTM *Principles and Standards* (2000) for geometry and special reasoning are organized around the same developmental concepts. These findings hold many ideas that should be considered when reading this chapter.

The van Hiele Levels Two Dutch educators, Pierre van Hiele and Dina van Hiele-Geldof, studied

build blocks

Check

YOUR MATHEMATICS KNOWLEDGE

On Geometry
- Geometry Terminology Review
    . . . a refresher from mathematics coursework . . . Lest you forget!

Cultural Contributions

CULTURAL RELEVANCE

CULTURAL CONTRIBUTIONS TO GEOMETRY

The following material developed by the Chicago Public Schools should be shared with students at each of the appropriate grade levels.

K–3

Students should examine the contributions to geometry made by peoples all over the world. For example, the peoples of Egypt and Mesopotamia studied squares, rectangles, triangles, and circles. For greater strength, the Eskimos use geometric shapes to form their igloos. Mozambicans build rectangular houses by using equal-length ropes as diagonals.

4–8

Students should know that the first concepts of congruency were developed in Africa and Asia and that cotangents and similar triangle principles were used in the building of the African pyramids. The students should examine the contributions to geometry made by peoples all over the world. For example, Eskimos build strong dome-shaped igloos. Mozambicans build rectangular houses by using equal-length ropes as diagonals (Strong, 1990).

children's acquisition of geometric concepts and the development of geometric thought. van Hieles concluded that students pass through five levels of reasoning in geometry in much the same way that Piaget said children must proceed through the stages in cognitive development (Chapter 3). The five levels are described by Clements (2003b) and Fuys and Liebov (1993) as follows:

Level 0—Visualization   The student reasons about basic geometric concepts, such as simple shapes, by means of visual considerations. The student reacts to geometric figures as wholes. A square is a square because it *looks* like one.

Level 1—Analysis   The student reasons about geometric concepts by means of an informal analysis of the parts and attributes, and relationships among the parts of a figure. A square is a square because it has four equal sides and four right angles.

Level 2—Abstraction   The student logically orders the properties of concepts, forms abstract definitions, and can distinguish between the necessity and their sufficiency of a set of properties in determining a concept. A square's definition is dependent on some properties that are related to other shapes. The student sees that a square can be both a rectangle and a parallelogram.

Level 3—Deduction   The student reasons formally within the context of a mathematical system, complete with undefined terms, axioms, an underlying logical system, definitions, and theorems. This is the level needed to perform well in a high school geometry class as the student has developed the ability to prove theorems.

Level 4—Rigor   The student can compare systems based on different axioms and can study various geometries in the absence of concrete models. This is the level needed for success in college geometry courses because students have developed the ability to understand that many different geometries exist and can operate in any one when appropriate.

van Hieles proposed that progress through the five levels is more dependent on instruction than on age or maturation. They submitted five sequential phases of learning to be provided by the teacher. They coincide with the developmental levels. The learning phases carry teacher responsibilities to develop appropriate student thinking for each developmental level as Figure 12.2 indicates.

According to van Hieles, instruction developed according to this sequence promotes the acquisition of a level. The first three levels (0–2) should be the experiences in informal geometry during the elementary and middle school years. van Hieles asserted that children should have a wide variety of exploratory the experiences. Students should move through these levels with an understanding of geometry that will prepare them for the deductive study of geometry in high school and perhaps college where level 3 is required and level 4 is the aim at the finish of college.

Kilpatrick, Swafford, and Findell (2001) report that curriculum projects incorporating geometry as a regular strand since kindergarten with an emphasis on hands-on learning and problem-solving situations show higher gains in the van Hiele levels than comparison groups. This supports

DEVELOPMENTAL LEVEL	LEARNING PHASE	TEACHER RESPONSIBILITY TO DEVELOP STUDENT FOCUS
Level 0: Visualization	Information	Look holistically at one shape, concept at a time
Level 1: Analysis	Directed orientation	Tell properties of one shape, concept at a time
Level 2: Abstraction	Explication	Compare/contrast properties; tell commonalities of many shapes, concepts at a time
Level 3: Deduction	Free orientation	Tell logical relations, axioms, theorems for a system
Level 4: Rigor	Integration	Perform contrasts/connections between systems

FIGURE 12.2 *van Hiele learning phases and corresponding teacher responsibility.*

the assertion that the deductive study of geometry should be delayed until the student has developed the mental maturity required for advanced study as indicated in the van Hiele levels.

SOLO Levels The structured observation of learning outcomes (Hattie and Purdie, 1998) is a helpful way to see how students organize their thoughts as they learn new subject matter. Clements (2003b) and Pegg and Davey (1998) recommend SOLO as a way for teachers to understand the van Hiele levels more clearly. SOLO explains how students approach learning tasks. The SOLO thought process applies to any learning task, not just mathematics. SOLO is explained here by giving geometric examples. The van Hiele levels have been placed next to the corresponding SOLO levels:

Prestructural (Level 0—Visualization)
    There is preliminary preparation, but the task itself is not attacked in an appropriate way.

- Students ignore aspects of the concept . . . as if they were not there.
- Students just reiterate what has already been asked by the teacher.
    (Teacher: "What is a square?" Student: "It's a square because it looks like a square.")

Unistructural (Level 1—Analysis)
    One aspect of a task is picked up or understood serially; there is no relationship to other facts or ideas.

- Students talk about only one aspect of the concept or problem.
- Students can answer with only one thing at a time; they do not put multiple facts together.
    (Teacher: "What is a square?" Student: "A square has four sides." Teacher: "Are there other figures that have four sides?" Student: "Yes," and points to them.

Teacher: "So what do squares and other figures have in common?") Student just tells about each one separately once again. At this stage, children cannot see more than one thing at a time.

Multistructural (Level 2—Abstraction)
    Two or more aspects of a task are picked up or understood serially but are not interrelated.

- Students talk about two or more things but lack flow or connectedness.
    (Teacher: "So what do squares and other figures have in common?" Student: "They all have four sides—squares, rectangles, and parellograms.") But students would not see that they could all belong to the same larger category of quadrilaterals.

middle/high

Relational (Level 3—Deduction)
    Several aspects are integrated so that the whole has a coherent structure and meaning.

- Students directly attack the parts of the concept, looking for the connectedness.
- Students use quality discourse, emphasizing the elements of (1) depth (2) coherence (3) reasonableness.
    (Teacher: "What is a square?" Student: "I can prove what squares are by setting up a theorem and show logical steps to reach the conclusion that a square is a quadrilateral.")

high school

Extended Abstract (Level 4—Rigor)
    That coherent whole is generalized to a higher level of abstraction.

- Students see quality elements **quickly.**

- Students use connections with mathematically correct terms without prompts, give examples, organize categories, and so forth.
- Students deal with all the factors inherent within the system.
  (Teacher: "What is a square?" Student: "It depends on which axiomatic system I should discuss. I can prove what a square is by three systems of geometry.") The student goes on to set up the proofs in the correct systems and shows how the systems can be related in the study of geometry.

Several colleges of teacher education in the United States and Canada have adopted the SOLO model as a thought rubric for teacher candidates to monitor their own thought development as they go through their education courses because of its clarity in new circumstances. It is hoped that SOLO may add the precision needed to use the van Hiele levels more effectively in classroom situations. With a teacher's guidance, the student's thinking will gradually sharpen so that when a definition is needed, it will hold meaning for the student. As you read through the rest of this chapter, examine the activities and the van Hiele/SOLO thinking processes underlying them. Keep in mind that students need many experiences from a variety of materials to ensure the development of geometric concepts.

TEACHING STRATEGIES FOR BUILDING CONCEPTUAL UNDERSTANDING OF GEOMETRY AND SPATIAL REASONING

Activities for informal geometry are characterized by using manipulative materials, exploring concepts in both two- and three-dimensional space, discovering relationships through coordinate geometry, symmetry, and transformations, and using beginning techniques to develop visualization, spatial reasoning, and geometric modeling. Patterns are provided in the Appendix and on the Web site for the most used manipulatives—attribute blocks (pieces), geoboard, geometric recording paper, and tangrams. The focus is to provide experiences that will produce meaningful definitions and properties of geometric ideas across time.

Shapes

Shapes are said to have one-, two-, and three-dimensional space. *Dimension* as used here means "how much information is required to specify an exact location" (UCSMP, 2001). Students learn that a line segment is one-dimensional because it requires one piece of information to tell its dimension (i.e., the line segment is 4 centimeters long). The surface area of a room is two-dimensional because it requires two pieces of information to tell its dimension (i.e., measuring carpet requires length and width). The actual space taken up by an object is three-dimensional space because it requires three pieces of information to tell its dimension (i.e., a sofa has length, width, and depth [height]). Technically, even the two-dimensional carpet example has three-dimensions because the depth of the pile can also be measured.

Solid Geometry In reality, ours is a three-dimensional world. We walk through three-dimensional space, and the things around us have length, width, and depth. So it is easy to see why the teaching of young children starts with solid geometry. *Solid geometry* is defined as the study of three-dimensional shapes, their properties, and relationships. Children's early experiences with geometry are centered around objects with three dimensions—blocks, cans, cones, balls, and boxes. Many children had building blocks at home or at preschool with which they constructed structures and patterns. Collections of empty oatmeal containers, food cans, soda cracker boxes, paper towel rolls, and other various sized boxes provide representations of solids for children to explore, compare, and construct. Shape exploration of three-dimensional figures should begin informally with shape explorations and classifications (level 0 activities).

Greenes (2001) suggests activities to involve children in experiencing solids and their properties. In these teacher-directed activities, the children select a solid or pretend to be the solid. They describe the figure's properties in games like, "Guess What I Am?" in Chapter 12 in the Extended Activities on the Web site.

Children close their eyes, take a shape, and describe it to others who are trying to guess the shape selected. Using precise vocabulary becomes important in such activities and is the beginning experience where children learn that geometry has its own vocabulary. Activity 12.1 is an example of a level 0 activity for PreK to grade 2.

Younger children may call the shapes, "box, ball, can," but as they build greater understanding of the shapes, the proper names will become common, "prism, sphere, cylinder." As children learn to be more precise in describing and classifying solids, have them make a table of the properties (level 1 activity):

EXTENDED ACTIVITIES

| MANIPULATIVES | PROBLEM SOLVING | MATHEMATICAL CONNECTIONS | CHILDREN'S LITERATURE |

On the Web site (Chapter 12, Extended Activities), read/do the following:

- Guess What I Am?
- Can You Sort It?
- Change It and Describe It
- Working on Nets
- Geoboard Explorations
- Understanding Construction of a Pyramid
- Family Math Packets
  - Geometry—Basic Shape Recognition
  - Two- and Three-Dimensional Shapes

Students need to relate the study of geometry to their environment by finding examples in their homes of objects that look like the solids being studied. They can create wall charts with pictures of the shapes. In the classroom, com-

---

Activity 12.1

PROBLEM SOLVING   **CAN YOU BUILD IT?**

PARTNERS
MATERIALS
- Interlocking cubes or wooden cubes

PROCEDURE
Have children set a barrier such as a large notebook or an encyclopedia between them. One student makes a structure from the materials and then describes it to the other student who uses materials to try to duplicate the structure. Precise vocabulary and communication skills are developed along with spatial visualization skills.

Solid	Number of edges	Number of faces	Number of vertices

mercial materials should be available for play and exploration.

Level 2 activities become more abstract. Plastic models and wooden models are needed to provide different perspectives about the figures. The transparent plastic models help children realize that each figure has an inside and an outside. Ask children to describe and classify the shapes according these inside and outside properties in Activity 12.2.

Relating Three-Dimensional to Two-Dimensional Shapes   Once children begin to see how three-dimensional shapes are made up of various parts, they can design nets that make up the figures. A "net" is the pattern that can be made by covering ("wrapping") the figure in paper without any overlapping pieces. This activity allows children to identify the two-dimensional features of three-dimensional figures. Greenes (2001), Cuevas (2001), and Friel (2002) describe many activities using cubes and other three-dimensional shapes to improve spatial visualization skills using nets. They include activities where students find all the possible nets for a cube and record them on graph paper. Levels 0 and 1 can explore nets using familiar shapes from around home and school as seen in Activity 12.3.

Students can construct poster board or tagboard models from printed patterns. Cutting and assembling the figures help children learn about edges, corners, faces, and other parts of solid figures. With older children, these models can be used to develop understanding of the formulas in measurement, covered in Chapter 13. Level 2 activities involve middle grade students finding total surface area of the house, designing two-story houses, combining houses into apartments, and designing nets for the structures. Such activities use concrete representations to improve the perception of spatial relationships. Perhaps these experiences (Activity 12.4) will help students know how much wrapping paper is needed to cover the present they need to wrap—a real-world math performance! The African cultural activity (Activity 12.5) shows that traceable networks are in other cultures as well as in our own.

Activity 12.2

PROBLEM SOLVING **LET'S FACE IT**

MATERIALS
- Soma cubes or wooden cubes
- Isometric dot paper

PROCEDURE
Have students make a structure with the cubes (or select a soma cube). draw the structure from the various views—front, bottom, sides on isometric dot paper. See the example in Figure 12.3.

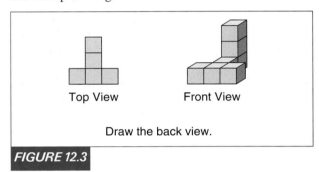

Top View   Front View

Draw the back view.

FIGURE 12.3

Activity 12.3

PROBLEM SOLVING **MANIPULATIVES** **MAKING NETS**

MATERIALS
- Different-sized containers (cereal boxes, oatmeal containers, and so on)
- Graph paper

PROCEDURE
Students will identify their solid by name and discuss the properties of it. draw a net to fold into the shape. explain how the drawing was done by describing the faces of the solid. verify that your net will fold into the shape. Estimate the area of each face, and then use the graph paper to determine the area. How much wrapping paper will be needed to cover your container without overlaps?

Sakshaug (2001) and Leu (2003) have developed excellent activities for levels 0, 1, and 2 relating two-dimensional objects to three-dimensional objects by using the problem-solving performance-based assessments and literature books, *Flat Stanley* and *Flatland*. The children's literature list is at the end of the chapter. A Web site where students can create and share their adventures with Flat Stanley is also included in the Web sites at the end of the chapter. You are encouraged to go to the Web sites to see what students can do when motivated to learn using technology.

Plane Geometry *Plane geometry* is the study, of two-dimensional figures, their properties, and relationships. An important aspect of teaching geometry is to have students become familiar with the properties of shapes. Early (level 0) activities include classifying or sorting cutout shapes or commercial materials such as pattern blocks or attribute blocks (also called attribute

Activity 12.4

PROBLEM SOLVING **MANIPULATIVES** **SOLIDS EXPLORATION**

1. Make nets of the containers (see Activity 12.3 on page 340). Which of the shapes can be folded into a topless box (without a lid)? Prove it using your nets.
2. The box problem
   Someone in a factory bought cardboard that was six squares by four squares. They figured that each sheet of cardboard could be cut into four pieces so each piece would fold into a topless box. How could the sheet be cut?
3. Have four to six empty containers. Label them with alphabet letters. Which one holds the most? Which one holds the least? Which ones hold about the same amount? Test your predictions with rice, milo, salt, or another granular substance.

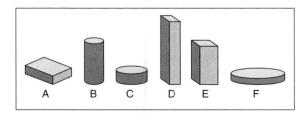

pieces). Children need concrete models of the shapes to feel the shape and relate the name to its properties—number of edges, corners, and other attributes. The common attributes used in early activities are

---

Activity 12.5

CULTURAL RELEVANCE

AFRICAN CULTURE AND MATHEMATICS

Claudia Zaslavsky has written a lot about mathematical projects that illustrate African societies. A unit on African network patterns illustrates how African children are able to carry out tasks to determine the conditions under which a network is traceable that adults find difficult to perform. Have students construct a house with the largest area for a given perimeter. Such experiences illustrate the wealth of mathematical ideas developed by African peoples and provide opportunities to appreciate other cultures. Check the chapter bibliography to obtain these journal references (Zaslåvsky 1989, 1990).

Supporting the NCTM *Principles and Standards* (2000)

- Mathematics as Reasoning; Communication; Representation, Connections; Geometry and Spatial Memory
- Worthwhile Mathematical Tasks—The Teaching Principle
- The Equity Principle

Attributes	Values
Size	Large, small
Shape	Circle, square, rectangle
Color	Red, yellow, green, blue
Thickness	Thin, thick

Children should find representatives of shapes in their environment. For example, the borders of the following could be selected: the file cabinet's sides are rectangles, the floor tiles are squares, the wastepaper basket rim is a circle, the flag is a rectangle, the traffic sign for yield is a triangle, the stop sign is an octagon, and so forth. "Can You Sort It?" and "Change It and Describe It" are

levels 0 and 1 activities, respectively, on the Web site in the Extended Activities in Chapter 12. All the plane geometry activities presented here and on the Web site offer strategies to reinforce properties of shapes as well as logical reasoning skills.

Level 1 activities help children see properties of one attribute and those that are not that attribute. For example, give children a set of shapes to sort into some classifying scheme—shapes with three sides and the others, shapes with four corners and the others, shapes with no corners and the others. Make cards with various cutout shapes pasted on them (one shape per card). Give children a sorting rule or have another stack of cards with sorting rules on them.

Activity 12.6 is an activity that can be adapted for level 0 to level 2. It is challenging for children because it requires logical reasoning and elimination of things that are different. A one-difference train is for young children (level 0), a two- to three-difference train is for grades 3 to 5 (level 1), and a four-difference train is for grades 6 to 8 (level 2). You will be asked to do a sample difference train activity as part of the Praxis II^{TM}-style questions at the end of the chapter.

Activity 12.6

PROBLEM SOLVING

ONE- AND TWO-DIFFERENCE TRAINS

MATERIALS
- Attribute blocks (or similar cutouts; see Appendix and Web sites)

PROCEDURE
Place the attribute blocks in a pile on the floor or table. Start with one block. Have students take turns adding one block to the train so that each block is placed next to one that is different from it in just *one* way. Have the student verbalize the difference as each block is added. For example, the starting block is a green, small triangle. The first player adds a green, *large* triangle. The next player adds a *yellow*, large triangle. The next player adds a yellow, large *square*. Play until all blocks are in the train. This goal may require some rearranging, which is allowed at the end of the round. Players can also see if they can get the end of the train to join to the beginning block. This objective may also require some rearranging.

VARIATION

Do the preceding activity and have each piece differ from the others by *two* attributes. For example, start with a thick, red, large square. The next player places a thick, *green, small* square in the train—two attributes are different (color, size). Thickness may be achieved by pasting attribute pieces on styrofoam, painted to match the color of each piece.

Variation—Three-Difference Train

Do the preceding activity and have each piece differ from the others by *three* attributes. For example, start with a *thin, small, blue triangle*. The next player places a *thick*, small, *green square* in the train—three attributes *are* different (thickness, color, shape).

Variation—Four-Difference Train

The same procedure is followed with all the pieces changing in all four attributes (thickness, color, size, and shape).

Variation—All Levels

A more difficult skill is to place several shapes in a train with one piece left out. The students have to choose a piece that fits the rule and place it in the missing spot. This requires logical thinking forward and backward in the student's mind—not an easy task by any means!

Properties and Attributes Using Geoboards Making shapes on a geoboard offers one of the best opportunities to explore the properties of shapes. A geoboard is usually a 6×6-inch board or plastic square with 25 nails or pegs placed into a 5×5 array. A geoboard pattern is provided in the Appendix and on the Web site. You may wish to print out and plasticize or laminate the pattern and use it as a model when making a wooden geoboard. (Other arrangements of nails or pegs are possible, such as circular, isometric, or

other dimensions of an array). The most common arrangement is shown in Figure 12.4.

Rubber bands can be stretched around the nails or plastic pegs to create shapes or designs. This is an invaluable teaching device for geometry because it allows children to create shapes, designs, and patterns to express ideas about geometry in a quick, accurate manner. Where it is impossible to ask a young child to make a square or octagon, the geoboard quickly provides such experiences.

Some teachers fear that rubber bands may become projectiles and have found that using the term "geobands" helps reduce the temptation. If a child *chooses* to use the rubber bands inappropriately, have plenty of geoboard papers on hand (patterns are on the Web site to appropriate scale). Children are then given paper to do what the rest of the class is doing with the real geoboard. The authors have found that telling students up front what the rules will be and following through with the geoboard paper if poor choices are made is a lesson learned quickly by the whole class. Children are encouraged to tell the teacher when they think they are ready to handle the real geoboard again. This is a way to teach students responsibility for their own actions. They know when they are ready to handle the activity better than the teacher knows.

Whatever procedure you use, provide adequate opportunities for free exploration with the geoboard. Young children almost always make designs or pictures with the geoboards. Have children copy their design or creation onto geometric dot paper (a replica of the 5×5 array using large dots for the nails), thereby keeping a record of their work. Both types of recording sheets are in the Appendix (reduced size) and on the Web site (full size). Activity 12.7 uses geoboards with children. More geoboard activities are discussed later in the chapter and on the Web site in Chapter 12 in "Geoboard Explorations" listed in the Extended Activities.

Properties and Attributes using Straws Another way to have children experience the properties and attributes of shapes is by making shapes with yarn and soda straws. The straws can be cut into various lengths to form other shapes such as scalene triangles parallelograms, and trapezoids. Cut straws in half if smaller shapes are easier for students to manage. Thread six or eight straws onto yarn. Have the children take the number of straws needed for the shape; for example, three straws will form a triangle and push the other straws apart from them on the yarn. See Figure 12.5 for additional sample shapes that can

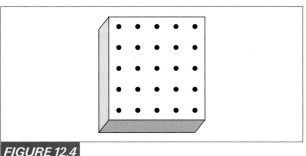

FIGURE 12.4 *Geoboard in 5×5 array.*

Activity 12.7

MANIPULATIVES   **MENTAL MATH**   **USING A GEOBOARD**

PROCEDURE

Copy This Shape (Level 0)

Hold up a large card with a shape on it. Have class copy the shape onto its geoboards. Discuss the name and properties of the shape. Have children copy other shapes and designs. Make a shape on an overhead geoboard and have the children copy it. Rotate the shape and see whether the children still call it by the same name. This is a good assessment technique.

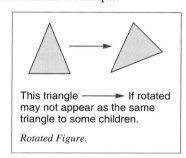

This triangle ⟶ If rotated may not appear as the same triangle to some children.

Rotated Figure.

Make This Shape (Level 1)

Ask students to make a shape with four sides. Have them compare their shapes and discuss the names and possibilities. Ask children to make a shape with four equal sides, a figure with six sides, or a figure that touches six nails. Depending on grade level you can vary the level of difficulty, for example, make a shape with one obtuse angle. Make the largest shape possible. Make the smallest shape possible. The possibilities are endless for this activity.

Dividing Our Shapes (Level 2)

Have students make a shape and subdivide it into other shapes. Make the activity more difficult by giving specific directions on the shapes that are to be formed. Incorporate vocabulary and terminology.

Have children make the largest square possible on their geoboards. Take another band and divide the shape into two congruent regions. What are the names of the regions formed? Divide one of the regions again. Now what shape is formed?

How Am I Classifying? (Level 1 or 2 . . . depending on depth of questioning)

Have students make a shape on their geoboards. Then decide a way to classify them into two groups. Ask them to put their geoboard figure into the appropriate set. Line the geoboards in the chalk tray. Do with many attributes.

be made. Figure 12.5 also shows how straws can be used to construct three-dimensional figures.

As relationships are explored, it might help to put the properties of the geometric figures into chart form. Write the name of the polygon, the number of sides, and the number of angles. Children in upper elementary grades classify triangles by sides (equilateral, isosceles, or scalene) or by angles (acute, right, or obtuse). When classifying shapes with four sides, children should realize there are many of these figures—rectangle, square, rhombus, trapezoid, or parallelogram. Additional information about their properties is needed to specifically identify the shape such as kind of angles, number of congruent sides, and number of parallel sides. Activity 12.8 shows a chart activity built from actions with triangles. This becomes a level 1 or 2 activity depending on the terminology used in the chart.

Coordinate Geometry

Coordinate Geometry may be defined as the study of spatial relationships by specifying location in position, distance, and space (House, 2001, 2002). The van Hiele/SOLO levels can be seen as children naturally develop their abilities to talk about relationships in position, distance, and space. For example, a person may ask, "Where is the math book?"

1. Young children (level 0) tell the location and position by references to other objects: "The book is near the chair."

2. In level 1: Analysis—Unistructural, children add distance, and direction to the location: "The book is a few feet to the right of the chair." They may also plan a route to get there (i.e.,

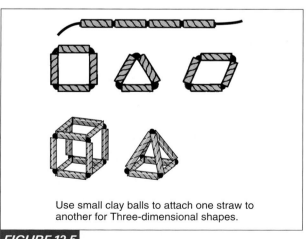

Use small clay balls to attach one straw to another for Three-dimensional shapes.

FIGURE 12.5   *Soda straw constructions.*

Activity 12.8

MANIPULATIVES   **ROLL A TRIANGLE**

MATERIALS

- Three dice
- Soda straws
- Yarn

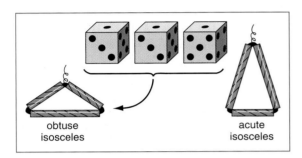

obtuse isosceles   acute isosceles

PROCEDURE

In groups have students try to build triangles. Roll three dice. Each face stands for the length of a side of the triangle to be cut from the straws. Using yarn to thread the pieces of straw make triangles. Record the lengths and whether a triangle was formed. Build ten triangles and study the data. Label the characteristics of the triangles and name them. Make a rule for deciding what conditions must be met with the length of the sides to make a triangle. What can be said about the angles needed?

ROLL	TRIANGLE	CHARACTERISTICS
3, 3, 5	Yes—isosceles	Two sides equal, Two angles equal

paths): "If I walk to the chair, then I can turn and walk a few feet to the right and get the book."

3. When students can see multiple paths to get to the same location and/or describe the path from another person's viewpoint, they are working on level 2: Abstraction—Multistructural. "The book is two feet to the right of the chair, which is four feet to your left." *Notice:* They are also more

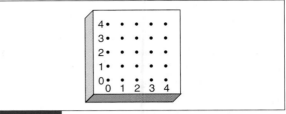

FIGURE 12.6   *Geoboard with coordinates.*

precise in their estimations of measure (a concept discussed in Chapter 13).

4. In middle school (level 2), coordinate geometry is linked to algebraic concepts with linear functions, slopes of line segments, midpoints of line segments, Pythagorean theorem, and so forth (concepts discussed in Chapter 14).

The computer language, Logo or "turtle geometry," has proved to be very successful in helping children see location, position, distance, and space. You can experience this for yourself in the activity, "Can You Get the Turtle to the Pond?" listed in the Web site activities at the end of the chapter.

Children can also learn to add simple coordinate systems to define a position more precisely. Geoboards can be used to practice coordinate geometry with ordered pairs. The arrangement of nails or pegs on the geoboard can provide a grid in which each place denotes a point and each point is labeled from 0 to 4 (Figure 12.6).

Activity 12.9

PROBLEM SOLVING   **MANIPULATIVES**   **WHAT IS THE FIGURE?**

MATERIALS

- Geoboards
- Rubber bands (geobands)
- Geoboard dot paper (Appendix and CD)

PROCEDURE

1. Connect these nails and record the figure formed: (1,1), (1,2), (1,3), (2,1), (2,4), (3,1), (3,2), (3,3)
2. Connect these nails and record the figure formed: (0,0), (1,0), (1,1), (2,1), (2,2), (3,2), (3,3), (4,3), (4,4)
3. Make a shape, record the coordinate pairs, and ask a friend to record the figure formed.

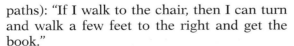

A strip of tape with the points labeled may help remind students of the numbers. The ordered pair notation of (1, 3) would refer to "over one peg and up three pegs" from the 0 point of orientation. Connecting cubes, household metal washers, plastic rings, and so forth can be placed over a chosen peg or nail. Working in pairs, students guess where the chosen piece or pieces are located on the unseen geoboard in the same way that the game Battleship is played. Activity 12.9 creates a shape or a design on the geoboard with a rubber band, and using ordered pair notation, children describe that shape to a partner who either makes the figure on a geoboard or on a geometric dot paper. This encourages precise language and accuracy of naming the coordinates. Activity 12.10 shows how children can use writing across the curriculum to make connections to coordinate geometry.

Activity 12.10

MANIPULATIVES   **PROBLEM SOLVING**   **MATHEMATICAL CONNECTIONS**

WRITING STORIES WITH GEOBOARD COORDINATES

MATERIALS
- Geoboards
- Rubber bands (geobands)
- Geoboard dot paper (Appendix and Web site)
- Scrap paper for making small pictures of one's house, ice cream store, pets, and so on.
- An option is to use pictures provided by the teacher of a generic boy, girl, house, pet, and so on.

PROCEDURE
1. Write a story using ordered pairs to show where to place the characters in the story.
2. Count how many spaces (units) from peg to peg it takes to get from one place to another. Allow no diagonals—Teachers of young children explain that one cannot cut across another person's yard.
   The reason in mathematical terms—The diagonal (hypotenuse) is longer than the two right legs of a triangle; therefore, it cannot be measured as the same length as the other units.
3. Then give the written story to someone else to reenact on the geoboard.

4. Then place the figures on the appropriate points and use the rubber band to show the path.

Here is a sample story based on similar work completed by second and third graders:

I am Juan. I live at (1, 3) and my friend, Temeka, lives at (4, 2). I want to walk to Temeka's house and go with her to the ice cream store at (1, 1). What is my path? How many spaces (units) did I walk to get to the ice cream store? If I go right home from the ice cream store, how many spaces will I walk? Could I have walked another path to Temeka's house? Would the path be the same length? What shape would I have walked from beginning to end if I went home from the ice cream store by the shortest way?

NOTE TO TEACHER: You may need to help children with the question part of the story at first because these questions extend the child's thinking beyond the lower level skills.

Symmetry and Transformations
Symmetry and transformations are the third area of geometry for study in elementary and middle schools in the NCTM *Principles and Standards* (2000). They are presented together because the transformation of figures is the most common way to prove that a figure has symmetry by sliding, flipping, or rotating one figure on top of the other.

Symmetry *Symmetry* is the correspondence in the size, shape, and arrangement of parts around a line or point. Symmetry around a line is called *line symmetry*. Symmetry around a point is called *rotational symmetry*. It is a way to describe geometric properties of shapes. Children have an almost intuitive sense of symmetry. Children may determine symmetry by visual inspection of a design. Paper folding and art designs offer opportunities to experience symmetry. Children might make a long line of paper dolls or cut out valentine hearts or Christmas trees and see the many lines of symmetry. "Symmetry in Art Activities" in Chapter 12 on the Web site, listed here in the Extended. Activities, is an example of connections to art across the curriculum.

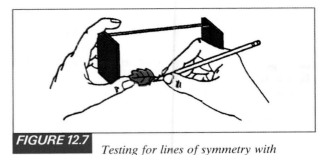

FIGURE 12.7   *Testing for lines of symmetry with a Mira.*

EXTENDED ACTIVITIES

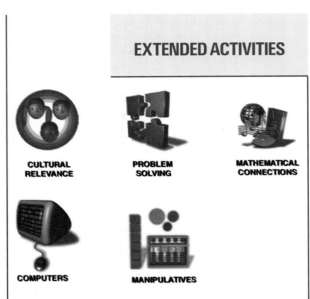

CULTURAL RELEVANCE   **PROBLEM SOLVING**   **MATHEMATICAL CONNECTIONS**

COMPUTERS   **MANIPULATIVES**

On the Web site (Chapter 12, Extended Activities), read/do the following:

- Symmetry in Art Activities
- Finding Native American Designs with Mirror Puzzles—*(see Chapter* 2 *on the* Web site)
- Mira, Mira, What do I see?
- Mira Transformations
- Tangram Quilts
- Can You Picture This?
- Geometry Surrounds Us
- Making Quilts Shows Our Culture
- Native American Beadwork with Logo
- Geometry Tell the Story
- Sample Lesson Plans for Mathematical Proficiency
  - A Tangram Folklore
  - Geometry Shapes and Symmetry
  - Finding Geometry Shapes

Line Symmetry   A figure with line symmetry has a line that can be determined, and the exact same image appears on both sides of the line. To test for lines of symmetry, use a mirror or a Mira (a

commercial device of red plexiglass), or have the figure traced and folded (Figure 12.7). To test for line(s) of symmetry using a mirror or Mira, place the mirror or Mira on the figure and move it until half the figure is reflected on the mirror or plexiglass. This portion should coincide with the portion of the figure behind the mirror. You have already used the "Finding Native American Designs with Mirror Puzzles" in Extended Activities of Chapter 2 on the Web site to do the Chapter 2 activity with the discovery and storytelling approaches on page 28. You are encouraged to review that activity. "Mira, Mira, What do I see?" and "Mira Transformations" are two more activities to test symmetry in the Extended Activities for this chapter.

Try folding a square to determine how many lines of symmetry you can create. A fold line is called an *axis of symmetry*. To test for symmetry using the folding method, have students fold the traced figure until the two halves match exactly. The tracing can also be flipped about the line of symmetry. Students can investigate familiar objects for symmetry (windows, wheels, human body) and will find that many objects have more than one line of symmetry.

Symmetry can also be explored by using geoboards and pattern blocks with older children. The figures or designs can be tested with mirrors, and the figures can be reproduced with geometric dot paper or pattern block paper and folded to show lines of symmetry. Letters of the alphabet can be used for younger children (Activity 12.11). Here are some additional suggestions to develop new connections for real-world experiences with symmetry. Because children (especially girls) love to cut out paper dolls by using folded paper, explore designing clothing by creating patterns. Have children bring other examples from home if possible. Other examples, such as leaves, snowflakes, hearts, and even humans, show that regularity of form abounds in our environment.

Activity 12.11

SYMMETRY IN LETTERS AND WORDS

MANIPULATIVES

DIRECTIONS

1. Symmetry can be found in letters of the alphabet or with some words (for example, "wow"). Use a small rectangular mirror and determine which students have names that begin with a capital letter with one line of symmetry or two lines of symmetry.

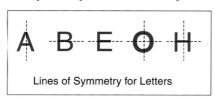

Lines of Symmetry for Letters

2. Ask the following questions:
   Whose initials are symmetrical? Which letters have rotational symmetry?
   Which shapes have an infinite number of lines of symmetry?
3. Use Venn diagrams to sort the letters by types of symmetry. Have children look at things that have line symmetry—buildings, people, pictures, leaves, plants, and cars.

Rotational Symmetry   A figure that has rotational symmetry can be rotated or turned (less than a full turn) around a point until a matched figure results. An example of a figure with rotational symmetry is a square (Figure 12.8). A quarter turn produces a square, a half turn produces a square, and a three-quarter turn produces another matched square figure. A square has four ways it can match the traced square, so it has rotational symmetry of order 4. The Chrysler Corporation trademark when tested for rotational symmetry has five turns that produce the matched figure (Figure 12.9).

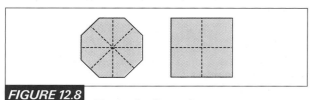

FIGURE 12.8   *Testing for lines of symmetry.*

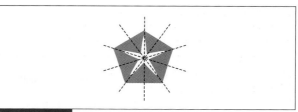

FIGURE 12.9   *Rotational symmetry in Chrysler symbol.*

Examine patterns, decorations, or designs to find examples of rotational symmetry.

Another interesting application of symmetry can be found in the arts of many cultures. Children can analyze the symmetrical patterns in quilts and rugs for line and rotational symmetry. Many connections with other subjects such as social studies, art, and history can be explored (Activity 12.12). Children can study the art of quilting through many children's books as well as design their own quilt patterns. Some books featuring African American and Native American activities with quilting appear in the children's literature section at the end of the chapter. Chappell and Thompson (2000) list 16 other books for geometry ideas in the African cultures. Numeral forms of the Iñupiaq culture (Bartley, 2002) and Navajo rugs are other rich settings for examining symmetry. Native Americans in Alaska are using the computer language, Logo, to create symmetrical patterns for their beadwork as seen in "Indian Beadwork with Logo" in the Extended Activities.

Transformations   Transformational geometry gives children some experience with changing their orientation and perspective about figures. This area of study deals with motion geometry and three basic motions: slides, flips, and turns. The motions follow certain rules, and the figure that results may produce a transformation that is a mirror image of the original figure. A *slide* motion is when the figure moves along a plane with no changes in the position of the points. A *flip* creates a reflected image of the original. A *turn* is a rotation around a point. Slides are generally easier for young children (level 0) to understand because the visual orientation of the figure does not change; it merely slides to a new position along the same plane (Figure 12.10).

The change in figure orientation created by flips and turns presents difficulties for young children's interpretation and perception of figures. For example, if an isosceles triangle is usually drawn with its base horizontal, a rotation of the triangle (Figure 12.11) may cause a change in perception about that figure, causing the child

Activity 12.12

CULTURAL RELEVANCE

CHILDREN'S LITERATURE

CULTURAL ILLUSTRATIONS

Read the book, *Less Than Half, More Than Whole* (Lacapa and Lacapa, 1994). Discuss the children's struggle with the questions raised in the book.

Why do you think the authors selected this title? What does this title mean to you? The book contains designs in the illustrations that represent many cultures. What patterns and symmetrical designs do you see? Explain your thinking. What examples of transformational geometry do you see?

Supporting the NCTM *Principles and Standards* (2000)

- Geometry and Spatial Reasoning; Mathematics as Reasoning, Communication, Connections, Representation
- Worthwhile Mathematical Tasks—The Teaching Principle
- The Equity Principle

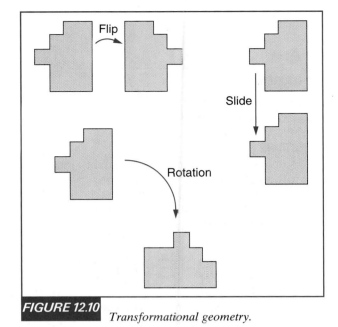

FIGURE 12.10 *Transformational geometry.*

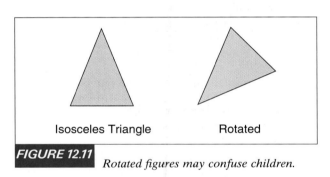

FIGURE 12.11 *Rotated figures may confuse children.*

not to recognize the isosceles triangle. Children may have such limited experiences with shapes that they may feel the triangle is not "right-side up." Children often think that the only figures that are triangles are those that are equilateral. They are unduly influenced by the orientation of figures even though they are familiar with the geometric vocabulary.

Children also think that right angles and right triangles are only those in the position shown in Figure 12.12. Applying "child logic," they term angles and triangles with the 90° angle in the flipped (reflected) position as "left" angles and "left" triangles, respectively.

The Video Vignette, "Shape Sort," shows college students learning about children's perceptions with figure orientation and a resulting activity with first graders sorting shapes. Notice that children within one class can be on different van Hiele/SOLO levels. This requires an alert teacher to adjust activities and vocabulary.

Congruent and Similar Figures *Congruent figures* are figures with the same size and shape so that one figure can be placed directly on top of the

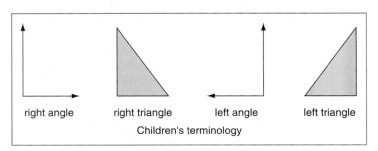

right angle   right triangle   left angle   left triangle

Children's terminology

FIGURE 12.12 *Children's perceptions of flipped or rotated right angles and right triangles.*

Shape Sort

View the Video Vignette (Chapter 12, Video Vignettes, "Shape Sort"). Then answer

- Where was the mathematics in this lesson?
- What did you learn about the first girl's understanding of triangles?
- What can be determined about the second girl's understanding of triangles? Compare to the boy's understanding of triangles.
- What follow-up assessment would you do?
- What instructional activities would you design?

Making Tangrams

View the Video Vignette (Chapter 12, Video Vignettes, "Making Tangrams"). Then answer

In this ELL classroom, Mr. Addcox's students create a set of tangrams.

- What techniques does Mr. Addcox use to have children analyze and describe the properties of shapes?
- Where was the mathematics in this lesson?
- What evidence do you see that he is incorporating components of the NCTM *Principles and Standards* (2000)?
- Use the video lesson plan in Chapter 3 to analyze the lesson.
- Listen to the number of precise geometric terms used in this lesson. How does Mr. Addcox support the mathematics learning of these ELL (English Language Learners) students?

are figures with the same shape and with all corresponding parts being proportional. Tangrams can provide many experiences for understanding congruent and similar figures. Students can use slides, flips, and turns to prove which tangram pieces are congruent and which are similar. The seven pieces of the tangram puzzle are illustrated in Figure 12.13.

The puzzle can be made by students through a series of folds and cuts to form the tans such as Mr. Addcox's lesson "Making Tangrams" in the Video Vignette. A discussion of how to discover the areas

of the square, parallelogram, triangle, and trapezoid can accompany a similar lesson for middle-level students (Duke, 1998).

Designs can be made by putting a square, parallelogram, and five triangles into silhouette patterns of people, animals, objects, or geometric figures. Many aspects of these shapes lend themselves to the discovery of concepts such as shape, congruence, similarity, properties of polygons, symmetry, area, and perimeter. Additional tangram activities can incorporate other mathematical topics including fractions, decimals, percents, proportions (see Chapters 10 and 11), and probability (Chapter 12). There are several stories about the tangram puzzle's origin and name. The

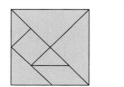

FIGURE 12.13 *Tangram puzzle.*

following myth offers an interesting introduction to the puzzle:

A very long time ago, in the land of China, there was a man named Mr. Tan. He had a beautiful porcelain tile of which he was extremely proud. He thought of it as a treasure. When he heard that the Emperor was coming to the village where he lived, Mr. Tan wanted to present the tile to the Emperor as a gift. As he began polishing his tile, he dropped it and it broke into the seven pieces of the tangram puzzle. Mr. Tan was very unhappy. Then he thought that if he could put the pieces back together, he would have the square tile again. Mr. Tan thought it would be easy to do, but it took him a very long time. While he was trying to form the square, he discovered lots of interesting shapes and designs—over 7000 in all. Let's see if we can make some of our own designs with the tangram puzzle pieces.

Activity 12.13

MANIPULATIVES | MATHEMATICAL CONNECTIONS | CULTURAL RELEVANCE

LITERATURE CONNECTION

PROCEDURE

1. Read the book, *Grandfather Tang's Stories: A Tale Told with Tangrams* (Tompert, 1990). Have the students make the figures from the story. Create tangram pictures to depict or "Illustrate" characters from other stories.

2. Students can create their own stories and use tangram designs to "illustrate" their stories. Have the students outline their puzzle picture and keep a copy of how to put the puzzle together again. The authors/creators could put their books at a center where other students can read the story and solve the puzzles.

Tangram dog.

Activity 12.14

MANIPULATIVES | PROBLEM SOLVING | **USING TANGRAMS**

MATERIALS
- Tangram sets (see Appendix and the Web site)

PROCEDURE

1. Sort the pieces into similar and congruent shapes. How many shapes are the same size (congruent)? How many shapes are the same shape but differ in size?

2. Take the two small congruent triangles and see what other shapes you can create with them. Are any of these new shapes congruent to other tangram pieces? Which ones?

3. It is possible to form many squares using different combinations of tangram pieces. How many squares can be formed?

4. With the two large congruent triangles, find what other shapes you can form with them. Name these shapes. Draw the tangrams used to form each shape—*if* you can make the shape.

SHAPE	NUMBER OF TANGRAMS USED					
	2	3	4	5	6	7
Triangle						
Rectangle						
Trapezoid						
Parallelogram						
Square						

5. What alphabet letters and which numbers can be made?

Many commercial books are available that contain activities with tangrams. The children's literature section at the end of the chapter lists some of them. The activities can provide experiences in spatial relationships as well as geometric concepts. Activity 12.13 can be used with level 0 children while Activity 12.14 is useful for level 1 and 2 activities. "Can You Picture This?" listed in the Extended Activities shows how precise language can be developed in level 2 activities. The

Video Vignette shows students working with tangrams in a classroom activity.

Tesselations Children can acquire an intuitive notion of slides (translation), flips (reflection), and bun (rotation) by working with pattern cards and tessellations. A *tessellation* is a design covering a flat surface without overlaps or gaps. Building a tessellation may involve motion geometry of slides, flips, and turns. Tessellations are also called tiling patterns. The study of tessellations has numerous application to other fields with a genuine, natural multicultural connection in the context of art. Children's storybooks such as *A Cloak for the Dreamer* (Friedman, 1994) present ways to investigate transformations. Geometric ideas and terms take on true meaning when students create and describe tiling pattern. These usually begin at level 1, grades 3–5, as in Activity 12.15 and become progressively more intricate in level 2, grades 6–8, as in Activity 12.16. Other tessellation activities are found in *Navigating through Geometry* in *Grades 1–5* (Cuevas, 2001) and in *Grades 6–8* (Friel, 2002).

Visualization, Spatial Reasoning, and Geometric Modeling

Spatial visualization an important aspect of geometric problem solving. The study of geometry should focus heavily on concrete and pictorial experiences. When students have opportunities to explore scale drawings, illustrate tessellations, work with coordinate geometry, and develop appropriate mathematical language, they are developing spatial reasoning as well as spatial visualization. Therefore, many of the activities explored in the preceding sections of this chapter have overlapping benefits for supporting visualization, spatial reasoning, and geometric modeling.

For example in tessellations, the preceding activities involved the ability to visualize images at both a perceptual and a representational level. Although the perceptual level is based on manipulation of objects and visual impressions, the representational level relies on mental manipulations, imagination, and thought (a spatial reasoning skill). Performing a mental operation (e.g., Euclidean transformation) is a more difficult task and may be limited by a child's developmental level in that it requires formal operational thought (in a Piagetian sense). So spatial reasoning must be viewed from a developmental point of view lest we ask students to do geometric activities that are not appropriate to their level.

The NCTM *Principles and Standards* (2000) call for the development of spatial sense that includes insights and intuitions about two- and three-dimensional shapes and their characteris-

---

Activity 12.15

CULTURAL RELEVANCE   MANIPULATIVES   **TESSELLATION TIME**

MATERIALS
- Pattern blocks
- Paper

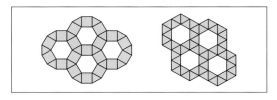

PROCEDURE

1. Have students predict which pattern blocks will tessellate and explain their thinking. Record on isometric dot paper the patterns that can be made (Appendix and Web site).
2. Combine pattern blocks into designs that will tessellate. These are called semiregular tessellations.
3. Find examples of tessellations in our world.
4. Explore why shapes or designs tessellate using angle measurements. Explore shapes other than regular polygons.
5. Investigate tessellations in Chinese lattice designs or Arabic patterns (Williams, 1993).

---

tics, the interrelationships of shapes, and the effects of changes made on shapes. Such experiences allow children to develop a more comprehensive understanding about shapes and their properties. Rich experiences with geometry will encourage children to see uses of geometry in their lives. To extend their knowledge of plane figures, children need to understand many properties of figures: the number of sides, the length of the sides, the size of the angles, parallel and perpendicular lines contained in the figure, and the number of angles.

As these concepts are encountered in the elementary mathematics program, it is important that experiences be provided to allow for guided discovery of what these concepts mean. Paper folding and origami are excellent ways to develop

Activity 12.16

PROBLEM SOLVING

ESCHER DESIGNS

MATERIALS

Study the work of M.C. Escher. Use the Internet to see whether there are clubs or forums that have Escher's work. Check the Internet for projects devoted to geometry. The Geometry Forum and the Geometry Center are two funded by the National Science Foundation.

Create your own interesting Escher-type design. Start with a square. Cut a section from one side and slide this cut-away part to the opposite side of the square and attach. Cut another section from one of the other two parallel sides and slide it to the opposite side and attach. You have made a shape that tessellates. Repeat four to six more times. Place the pieces together into a design. Use your imagination about what details you can add to show what your design could represent. Try to see many different interpretations (Kaiser, 1988, p. 24).

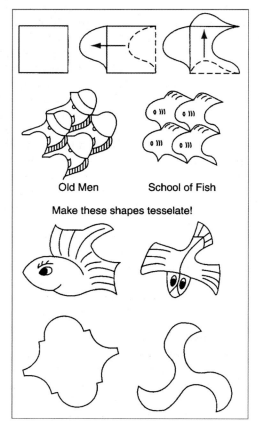

Old Men   School of Fish

Make these shapes tessellate!

the visualization, precise language, and careful thinking required to understand geometric principles. Inexpensive wax paper serves as an effective material for paper folding activities because it is clear and easy to see through, and when it is creased, leaves a visible line.

Visualization is helped when doing net activities. Students take a can or box and cut apart all the individual faces that compose that figure. Another activity is to have students build a solid from squares. These experiences help them visualize the individual components of the figure and how a vertex is formed. Students in middle grades often have not had such experiences with informal geometry and need to work with models just as younger children do. Participation in such activities helps build the visualization necessary in working with formulas for solids. Perimeter, area, and volume activities are presented as part of measurement concepts in Chapter 13, so preliminary work with geometry can be seen in the context of actual measurement systems.

Geometric Modeling with Constructions Students are encouraged to investigate geometric properties through constructions during grades 3 to 8. *Geometric constructions* are geometric drawings of angles and figures using a protractor, compass, and straightedge (a ruler without markings). Work with a straightedge is usually introduced early in the primary grades. The ruler with markings comes next and starts linear measurement concepts, a topic discussed in Chapter 13. Constructions with a protractor or a compass are generally delayed until middle school grades.

A *protractor* is a tool used to measure angles. To understand measuring angles, children should have experiences with Logo computer language where they move the turtle by degrees, use the hands of a clock, or even use their own arms to form angles. Students can see the effect of enlarging the size of the angle and compare how far they must move their arms or the hands of a clock to get certain angles. Without such preparation, they are unsure about what an angle is and are misled about the length of the sides. Often children say that angle *MNO* (Figure 12.14) is greater than

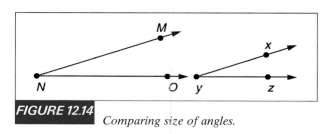

FIGURE 12.14
Comparing size of angles.

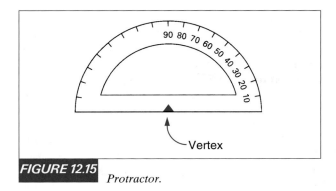

FIGURE 12.15 *Protractor.*

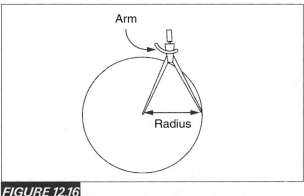

FIGURE 12.16 *Compass for constructing circles.*

angle *xyz* because they are comparing the length of the sides.

Students need to feel comfortable extending the length of the sides of an angle for a better measurement. Using a protractor (Figure 12.15) correctly means the child must know two things:

1. How to place the center of the protractor on the vertex of the angle.
2. How to read the degrees on the protractor by moving the eyes from the vertex of the angle to the degrees of the angle along the edge.

This is particularly important when using half-circle protractors with two sets of numbers in the half-circle formation. Children should be introduced to angle measurements with a circle protractor before using the half circle. They only need to focus on one set of numerals around the circumference. Include measuring angles shown in various positions, not just angles with one side on a horizontal line. Angles of shapes should be measured to learn that the sum of the measures of the angles of a triangle is 180 degrees and that the angles of a quadrilateral sum to 360 degrees. Also learned is that a 180 degree angle forms a straight line and a 90 degree angle forms a right corner. All of these concepts are much easier to visualize using a full-circle protractor. Patterns are available in the Appendix and on the Web site.

Billstein (1998) suggests making a real-world application by exploring angles used in designing airport runways. A device called a goniometer shows angles as an amount of rotation. Billstein also describes many extension activities using the next measurement tool, the compass.

A *compass* is a measurement tool that is used to make circles or portions of circles. One uses a compass by placing the spike of the compass at the center point of the circle. The measure from the spike to the pencil is the radius of the circle; it is that distance which is measured on the compass.

A compass may be difficult for students to manipulate because it takes a certain amount of coordination to swirl the compass around the radial point without slippage. For this reason, compass instruction is usually introduced later than protractors. A purchased compass (Figure 12.16) usually has two measurement systems, one on either side of the arm. The metric system (in centimeters) is on one side and the standard or customary measurement (in inches) is on the other side.

With many geometry topics being explored in the NCTM *Principle and Standards* (2000), the traditional focus on geometric constructions has decreased in favor of other modeling experiences seen earlier in the chapter. The construction tools are being reconsidered to be replaced by Mira, geometric dot paper, and Logo. Edwards, Bitter, and Hatfield (1990) provide ideas for using geometric constructions with Logo. If educational trends hold true, the construction tools will be used more prominently in the next few years. The pendulum will tend to swing back as people realize that students may be graduating without sufficient knowledge of these construction tools.

The Role of Technology One exciting potential for improving students' knowledge of geometric concepts lies in computer technology. The Web-Quest and Web site activities at the end of the chapter give you a chance to experiment with the power of computers in understanding geometry.

Logo Computer Language Logo, or "turtle geometry," presents many useful possibilities to foster children's spatial reasoning in a computer microworld. To create shapes, the child must analyze a shape into its parts. Research (Clements, 2003a) on the effectiveness of Logo indicates that such activities help children make a transition from a visual level to a descriptive–analytical level. Logo activities provide opportunities for students to study angle measurement of polygons in a problem-solving environment. Angles of rotation can also be discovered with older children using Logo.

Other Technologies Other valuable tools for technology use include the GPS, described in chapter 4 and software packages such as *The Geometric Supposer* (Sunburst Communications, 2003), Cabri, Jr. (Texas Instruments, 2003), and *The Geometer's Sketchpad* (Jackiw, 1995). Students using such software can construct a wide variety of figures using a toolbox including a compass, a straightedge, and a point tool. After the figures are a created, they can be explored and transformed into almost unlimited ways. Students can make conjectures about angles and triangles, examine transformations and symmetrical features, and make mathematical connections. The Web site activities will give you a "feel" for the power of these technologies to build geometric understandings.

ASSESSMENT TO HELP STUDENTS WITH SPECIAL NEEDS

Geometry is essentially a hands-on learning experience that tends to benefit the majority of students including those with special needs. A book for a children featuring an inquisitive boy and a girl, Collin and Catie (Robbins and Miller, 2006) travels through the sensory system learning the importance of understanding how our bodies use sensory-motor information to do the tasks of everyday life. The book was written to help children understand themselves and others who may find it challenging to do tasks that require sensory-motor manipulations. Informal geometry develops ideas requiring such manipulations (e.g., using transformations [slides, flips, rotations], repeated tessellations, and measurement tools, such as the compass and the protractor). The book can be used as a discussion starter for children to understand when there are those who cannot manipulate the geometric materials as well as others.

Compass and Protractor Use

Teachers of children with behavior challenges are cautious about the use of compasses in the classroom because the spike of the compass is very sharp and can do damage to property and people if students decide to inflict harm. The compass is also difficult to maneuver for those with orthopedic challenges. Teachers adapt lessons to have stu-

dents use plastic lids to draw circles when perfectly round figures are necessary. Plastic lids are easier to manipulate, harmless to use, and are readily available in a variety of sizes as any home kitchen can prove.

The educational advantages of the circle protractor have already been presented in this chapter. The added benefit is that it is less frustrating to use than the half-moon version for students who have little patience. Children who have trouble centering on two sets of numerals on the arc of a protractor will find the circle protractor much easier to use. Mathematics teachers of special-needs students will find it wise to have a set of circle protractors available for use even into the high school years.

Ordered Pairs as Coordinates

Children have trouble remembering in which direction to start counting when using coordinate pairs. Beginning activities should include the use of arrows over the pairs showing how to move from one pair location to another. The coordinated pair would look like this with the arrows applied:

$\overrightarrow{(3,}\overset{\uparrow}{5)}$ means 3 over to the right from 0 and 5 up from 0 as the location on the graph.

Angle Identification

Some students do not recognize an angle as the same if it is rotated. Students need many experiences making their own angles. Remember the Video Vignette called "Shape Sort" showing such situations? There are a sizable number of middle school and high school students who do not recognize a right triangle unless the 90 degree angle is in the lower left-hand corner of a triangle. Some children are successful if they fill in the angle they want to match in a bright color before they start to match it with other angles on a page. This way they do not lose sight of the angle match as the angle is rotated.

Field-Independent Learners

Field-independent learners enjoy constructing geoboard, working with individual attribute pieces, placing tangrams on top of each other to check for congruency or similarity, and finding locations by paired coordinates after they have had a change to move the figures one at a time themselves. They enjoy creating their own attribute trains by building up a piece of the train one at a time. If you notice that children are good at these kinds of task but have considerable trouble with the field-dependent approach, you should help the student redirect the learning tasks to the field-independent view.

Field-Dependent Learners

The field-dependent learners like tangram pieces especially if a figure is given and the student is asked to fill in the pieces while concentrating on the whole image. They also like the attribute trains when all the pieces are given but one. They enjoy moving the one piece around to complete the pattern. Angle identification is hard for them unless the angle is part of a whole figure that can be moved as one piece. If you notice children are successful at these kinds of tasks but have considerable trouble with the field-independent approach, you should help the student redirect the learning tasks to the field-dependent view.

SUMMARY

- The van Heile and SOLO developmental levels of thinking are being applied to the study of geometry.

- Children have an intuitive sense about spatial reasoning and geometry from interacting with everyday objects.
- The NCTM *Principles and Standards* (2000) stress four main areas for the study of geometry in today's elementary and middle schools.
- Shapes help students analyze and make sense of geometric problems.
- The computer language, Logo or "turtle geometry," has proved to be very successful in helping children see location, position, distance, and space in geometric concepts.
- Net activities allow children to identify the two-dimensional features of three-dimensional objects.
- Mira activities are replacing geometric constructions in the curriculum.
- Geoboards, tangrams, attribute pieces, mira cards, compasses, and protractors are materials used in elementary and middle school geometry.
- Teachers must take the commitment to feature geometry in classroom teaching more than research shows has happened in the past.

PRAXIS II™-STYLE QUESTIONS

 Answers to this chapter's Praxis II™-style questions are in the instructor's manual.

Multiple Choice Format

1. Look at the attribute train in Figure 12.17. It represents a _____-difference train. The next piece needed is a _____.

   a. two; large, thick, blue circle
   b. three; large, thin, yellow triangle
   c. three; large, thick, blue triangle
   d. four; small thin yellow rectangle

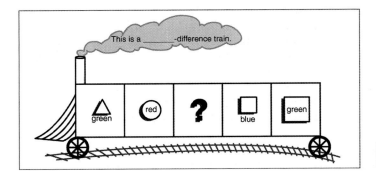

FIGURE 12.17

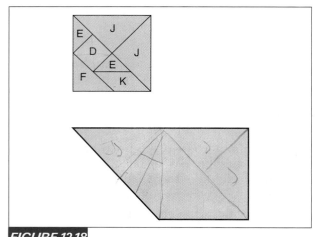

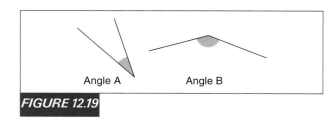

FIGURE 12.18 *Use the letters on the following tangram pieces to work with the polygon.*

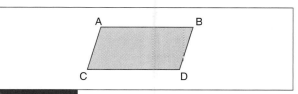

FIGURE 12.20

FIGURE 12.19

2. Which tangram pieces make a polygon similar to the one in Figure 12.18?

   a. {J, D, 2E, F, K}
   b. {K, 2E, 2J}
   c. {F, D. 2E}
   d. Both a and b

3. On a geoboard, Tye Rian lives at (2, 4) and she walked along the quickest way to Jamal's house at (0, 2).

   Please note that Tye Rian asked permission to walk across the neighbors' yards so she could take the shortest path to Jamal's house. Then both Tye Rian and Jamal walked to the ice-cream store at (2, 1). They decided to walk along the shortest route to see Pepé, the dog. His house is at (4, 3), and then they walked back to Tye Rian's house along the shortest route again. The path they walked was in the shape of a

   a. rhombus
   b. parallelogram

   c. scalene triangle
   d. trapezoid

4. When one figure can be placed directly on top of the other by a series of slides, flips, and/or rotations, then the figures are said to be:

   a. congruent
   b. equal
   c. similar
   d. Both a and b

Constructed Response Format

5. Measure the angles in Figure 12.19 using the circle protractor.

6. A student was asked to do the following activity:

   With your circle protractor, measure the angles of the parallelogram in Figure 12.20, naming the angles according to the illustration. Use the words "first," "then," and "finally" in your explanation so others can understand what you did.
   The student answers the task in the following way:
   "First, I only have to measure one angle. It is angle ABD for 130°. Then I subtract 130 from 180. Finally, I know the two small angles are 50° and the two big angles are 130° because to go around the shape is 360° like the circle protractor."
   This student should receive a score of _____ on the five-point scale seen in Chapter 3. On which level of van Hiele and SOLO is the student? Justify your reasons.

7. What is the next concept the student in question #6 needs to learn? Justify your reasons. How would you design an activity to help the student understand the concept you wish to teach?

Integrating Technology

Internet Activities

Scavenger Hunt Geometric Shapes
An Internet-based hunt for geometric shapes.

WebQuest

Shaping Up A mathematical WebQuest for primary grade students.

Web sites

ESTIMATION **MATHEMATICAL CONNECTIONS** **CULTURAL RELEVANCE** **INTERNET SEARCHES**

National Library of Virtual Manipulatives
http://nlvm.usn.edu/en/nav/vlibrary.html (also in Spanish)
Click on "Geometry" and try some of the Pre-K-2 Virtual Manipulative activities.

Go to Web site (**http://illuminations.nctm.org/ActivityDetail.aspx?ID=83**)
This program explores what Logo can do using commands to estimate length and angle measure to move the turtle to the pond in the activity, Can You Get the Turtle to the Pond?

Go to Web site (**http://standards.nctm.org/document/eexamples/chap4/4.2/index.htm**)
This is the teacher's Web site for the two activities using the interactive geoboard:
"Making Triangles" — The activity focuses attention on the concept of triangle, helping students understand the mathematical meaning of a triangle and the idea of congruence, or sameness, in geometry.
"Creating Polygons" — the activity allows students to make and compare a variety of polygons, describing the important properties of the shapes they create.
Go to Web site (**http://standards.nctm.org/document/eexamples/chap4/4.4/index.htm**)
The activity, "Tangram Challenges," develops geometry understandings and spatial skills through puzzle-like problems with tangrams by asking students to describe figures and visualize what they look like when they are transformed through rotations or flips.

Go to Web site (**http://education.ti.com/us/educationportal/activityexchange/ActivitySearch.do?lD=US**) to use interactive geometric concepts as a way to refresh your memory on basic geometric understandings.

The following two Web sites are for children in grades 3 to 5:

Go to Web site (**http://illuminations.nctm.org/ActivityDetail.aspx?ID=70**)

The activity, "Exploring Geometric Solids and their Properties," is a five-part activity that allows students to interact with geometric solids on the two-dimensional computer monitor, developing skills with two-dimensional representations of three-dimensional objects. Concepts include work with faces, edges, corners, constructing solids, and using jackets with solids (a net activity).

Go to Web site (**http://standards.nctm.org/document/eexamples/chap/5.3/index.htm**)

In the activity, "Exploring Properties of Rectangles and parallelograms Using Dynamic Software," students can explore geometric relationships and make and test conjectures. In this example, properties of rectangles and parallelograms are examined. The emphasis is on manipulating the dynamic rectangle and parallelogram by dragging the corners (vertices) and sides (edges), rotating or stretching the shapes, while they will retain particular features.

The following two Web sites are for students in grades 6 to 8:

Go to Web site (**http://illuminations.nctm.org/ActivityDetail.aspx?ID=125**)

In the activity, "Isometric Drawing Tool", students will explore polyhedra using different representations and perspectives for three-dimensional block figures. In addition, students will examine area and volume concepts for block figures within this context (area and volume are discussed in Chapter 13 of this text.)

Go to Web site (**http://standards.nctm.org/document/eexamples/chap6/6.4/index.htm**)

In the activity, "Understanding Congruence, Similarity, and Symmetry Using Transformations and Interactive Figures: Visualizing Transformations," students explore the concepts by moving shapes by slides, flips and turns to create shapes that are identical (congruent) and in another of the four-part activity, students are challenged to identify unknown transformations by seeing the original position and the ending position.

For all grade levels:

Go to Web site (**http://illuminations.nctm.org/**) and click on "Interactive Math Tools" to see other ways geometry can be reinforced by use of computer technology.

CHILDREN'S LITERATURE

The lists and categories were constructed from the recommendations of Moore and Bintz (2002); Strutchens (2002); Thiessen, Matthias and Smith (1998). Books marked with an * denote multicultural literature.

SHAPES

Bums, Marilyn. *The Greedy Triangle*. New York: Scholastic, 1994.

Coerr, Eleanor. *Sadako and the Thousand Paper Cranes*. New York: Dell Yearling, 1993.*

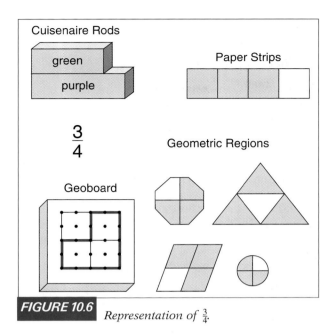

FIGURE 10.6 *Representation of $\frac{3}{4}$.*

Have children subdivide regions into equal-size sections. These multiple embodiments will help students develop their understanding of the meaning of the subdivisions (Figure 10.6).

An effective technique to develop the concept of comparing unit fractions is to take rectangular strips of construction paper, 4 × 18 inches, and fold each into various pieces. Activity 10.4 explains the procedure required to make the concrete material seen in Figure 10.2.

Use the rectangular fraction kit to compare unit fractions and to understand that the larger the denominator, the smaller the fractional size because the whole has been partitioned into more parts. A common misconception is that the larger number means more even when it appears as the denominator in a fractional number. The teacher can select three unit fractions and ask children to order them from least to greatest using the fraction kit as a concrete model.

The fraction strip chart in Figure 10.7 also serves as a powerful visual tool for comparing fractions. It is made essentially the same way as the rectangular fraction strips except somewhat smaller strips, 1 × 8, are folded, labeled, and pasted on a 9 × 12 piece of construction paper. Every strip can be compared with the whole unit 1, without the need to move many strips around.

Such activities develop flexible understandings of representing fractions. The tasks encompass a variety of concepts from equivalent fractions, use of the identity element for multiplication, multiplication as an area model, to the property of denseness.

Activity 10.4

MANIPULATIVES **MAKING A RECTANGULAR FRACTION KIT**

MATERIALS
- Five 4 × 18 inch strips of construction paper, each strip a different color
- Scissors
- Pen or pencil

PROCEDURE
1. Take one of the colored strips (indicate a specific color). Label it "one whole." Take another strip. Fold it in half lengthwise. How many equal pieces result? 2
2. Cut on the fold. What is each piece in terms of the whole (1 out of 2 or $\frac{1}{2}$). Label each piece "$\frac{1}{2}$."
3. Take a third strip. Fold in half and fold in half again. Open it out and count how many equal pieces. 4. With older children use the language that says "$\frac{1}{2}$ of $\frac{1}{2}$" to relate to multiplication later. What is each piece in terms of the whole? ($\frac{1}{4}$) Cut on the fold. Label each piece "$\frac{1}{2}$."
4. A fourth strip is folded into 8 equal pieces and labeled as "$\frac{1}{8}$," and the fifth strip is folded into 16 equal pieces and labeled as "$\frac{1}{16}$."
5. For connecting level activities, have students write about the equivalent names for one whole, one-half, and so on, and the patterns they notice (more folds make smaller pieces but larger denominator).

FIGURE 10.7 *The fraction strip chart.*

Equivalence Activities

Equivalence is another key concept associated with fractions. Equivalence relates to various ways that show equal shares of the same portion. Some educators believe that equivalence plays such a key role in the understanding of fractions that all work with the operations should be delayed until after the fourth grade. The NCTM *Principles and Standards* (NCTM, 2000) suggest that students should have efficient strategies to compute with fractions by the time they leave middle school. This practice would allow ample time to develop the concept of equivalence and would set the stage for later work with unlike denominators and mixed numbers. As part of equivalence, the identity element of multiplication, or property of one for multiplication, should be emphasized. The aforementioned fraction kit and fraction strip chart are ways to show how the one whole strip can be renamed, as is the problem-solving exploration in Activity 10.5 with the fraction strip chart (Figure 10.7).

Many experiences are needed to internalize the concept of equivalence of fractions before the symbolic level holds meaning. The identity element for multiplication should be related to whole numbers as well as to fractional numbers.

For example

What happens when you take any fraction and multiply it by 1?

$$\frac{1}{2} \times 1 = ? \qquad\qquad \frac{3}{4} \times 1 = ?$$

What happens if you substitute some equivalent name for 1 and multiply a fraction by it? Will it result in the same number?

$$\frac{1}{2} \times \frac{2}{2} = ? \qquad\qquad \frac{3}{4} \times \frac{4}{4} = ?$$

Is the outcome an equivalent name for that fraction? Why? Try several other fractions. What can you generalize from this experience?

Activity 10.6 is another problem-solving exploration of equivalent fractions that uses the fraction strip chart and a manipulative such as beans or counters. Activity 10.7 explores equivalent fractions using a geoboard. Activities 10.1 through 10.8 demonstrate some of the multiple embodiments that researchers describe as vital if students are to develop a conceptual understanding of fractions.

Activity 10.5

PROBLEM SOLVING

EQUIVALENT FRACTIONS: FRACTION STRIP CHART

MATERIALS
- Fraction strip chart (Figure 10.7)

PROCEDURE

For one whole—For each row, into how many pieces has the whole been partitioned? Write the name for one for each strip such as $\frac{2}{2}, \frac{3}{3}, \frac{4}{4}$. Discuss the pattern you see. What rule can you create? What other names for 1 can you name?

For one-half—Place a straightedge so that the edge is perpendicular to the mark showing $\frac{1}{2}$. Look down the rows of strips for pieces that also are equivalent to $\frac{1}{2}$ such as $\frac{2}{4}, \frac{3}{6}, \frac{5}{10}$. Make lists of all the equivalent names for $\frac{1}{2}$ and also a list of all the pieces that do not equal $\frac{1}{2}$. What patterns do you see? What kind of numbers will not be on the list of equivalent names? Repeat this procedure with all unit fractions on the chart.

> **Supporting the NCTM *Principles and Standards* (2000):**
> - Worthwhile Mathematical Tasks; Learning Environment—The Teaching Principle
> - Mathematics as Problem Solving; Mathematics as Representations, Patterns

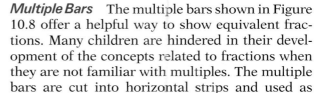

Multiple Bars The multiple bars shown in Figure 10.8 offer a helpful way to show equivalent fractions. Many children are hindered in their development of the concepts related to fractions when they are not familiar with multiples. The multiple bars are cut into horizontal strips and used as explained in Activity 10.8.

Multiple bars can be used to see how dividing a fraction by 1 or an equivalent name for 1 produces another equivalent name for that fraction. If the resulting fraction cannot be divided again, the fraction is said to be "expressed in lowest terms" or "expressed in simplest form." These terms are preferred by the authors because such terms are more meaningful to students than the phrase "reduced to lowest terms" and do not hold the misconception that reducing results in a reduction in the size of the region.

Practice activities should not always focus on finding an equivalent fraction given the numerator

Friedman, Aileen. *A Cloak for the Dreamer.* New York: Scholastic, 1994.

MacCarone, Grace. *The Silly Story of Goldie Locks and the Three Squares.* New York: Scholastic, 1995.

Pilegard, Virginia Walton. *The Warlord's Puzzle.* Gretna, La.: Pelican, 2000.*

Schwartz, David. "D is for Diamond." *G Is for Googol.* Berkeley, Calif.: Tricycle Press, 1998.

Tompert, Ann. *Grandfather Tang's Story.* New York: Crown Publishing Group, 1997.*

TWO-AND THREE-DIMENSIONAL REPRESENTATIONS

Abbott, Edwin A. *Flatland.* New York: Dover Publications, 1992.

Abbott, Edwin A., Dionys Burger, and Issac Asimov. *Sphereland: A Continuing Speculation on an Expanding Universe.* New York: HarperCollins, 1994.

Brown, Jeff. *Flat Stanley.* New York: Harper Trophy, 1992.

Grifalconi, Ann. *The Village of Round and Square Houses.* New York: Little, Brown & Co., 1986.*

Pappas, Theoni. "Penrose Discovers Pancake World." The Adventures of Penrose the Mathematical Cat. San Carlos, Calif.: Wide World Publishing/Tetra House, 1997.

Schwartz, David. "R is for Rhombicosido-decahedron." *G Is for Googol.* Berkeley, Calif.: Tricycle Press, 1998.

COORDINATE GEOMETRY

Glass, Julie. *The Fly on the Ceiling.* A Math Myth. New York: Random House, 1998.*

The following books featuring quilts represent a form of coordinate geometry as they are assembled on the concept of a grid pattern. Many of these books celebrate African-American Heritage:

Cobb, Mary. *The Quilt-Block History of Pioneer Women: With Projects Kids Can Make.* Illustrated by Jan Davey Ellis. Brookfield, Conn.: Millbrook Press, 1995.*

Hopkinson, Deborah. *Sweet Clara and the Freedom Quilt.* Paintings by James Ransome. New York: Alfred A. Knopt, 1993.*

Ringgold, Faith. *Aunt Harriet's Underground Railroad in the Sky.* New York: Crown Books for Young Readers, 1993.*

Smucker, Barbara. *Selina and the Bear Paw Quilt.* Illustrated by Janet Wilson. New York: Crown Publishers, 1995.*

TOPOLOGY

Pappas, Theoni. "Leonard the Magic Turtle," *The Adventures of Penrose the Mathematical Cat.* San Carlos, Calif.: Wide World Publishing/Tetra House, 1997.

Pappas, Theoni. "Penrose Discovers the Mobus Strip." *The Adventures of Penrose the Mathematical Cat.* San Carlos, Calif.: Wide World Publishing/Tetra House, 1997.

Schwartz, David. "M is for Mobus Strip," *G Is for Googol.* Berkeley, Calif.: Tricycle Press, 1998.

INDUCTIVE AND DEDUCTIVE REASONING

Anno, Mitsumasa, and Akihiro Nozaki. *Anno's Hat Tricks.* New York: Philomel Books, 1985.

Anno, Mitsumasa. *Socrates and the Three Little Pigs.* New York: Philomel Books, 1986.

Please Note: *47 additional books on shapes are listed in Thiessen, Matthias, and Smith (1998).

Measurement

Chapter 13

At the Start ~~~~ Know What Children Will Be Doing . . .

NCTM Curriculum Focal Points—   See . . .

PreK ~~ Identifying measurable attributes and comparing objects by using these attributes	Figure 13.2
Grade K ~~ Ordering objects by measurable attributes	Activity 13.3
Grade 2 ~~ Developing an understanding of linear measurement and facility in measuring lengths	Activity 13.4
Grade 4 ~~ Developing an understanding of area and determining the areas of two-dimensional shapes	Activity 13.7
Grade 5 ~~ Describing three-dimensional shapes and analyzing their properties, including volume and surface area	Figure 13.7
Grade 7 ~~ Developing an understanding of and using formulas to determine surface areas and volumes of three-dimensional shapes	Activity . . . 13.11
	Activity . . . 13.17
Grade 8 ~~ Analyzing two-and three-dimensional space and figures by using distance and angle	Activity 13.21

A partial listing as it pertains to Measurement from NCTM *Curriculum Focal Points* (2006, pages 11–12; 14; 16–17; 19–20).

WHERE IS THE MATHEMATICS? THE STRUCTURE OF MEASUREMENT SYSTEMS

Which weighs more—a pound of lead or a pound of feathers? Do you remember when you were first asked this question by classmates who thought it would be great fun to see if they could "trick" you? Many children knew the correct answer to the "riddle," but until they reached the age of nine or ten, they could not explain the answer. They memorized what others had told them. You may have fallen for the famed answer—"LEAD," but eventually you grew to know that a pound is a pound no matter how much or how little material it takes to reach that standard unit of weight. Throughout this chapter we will see how students' conceptual understandings grow as they experience the concepts of measuring space.

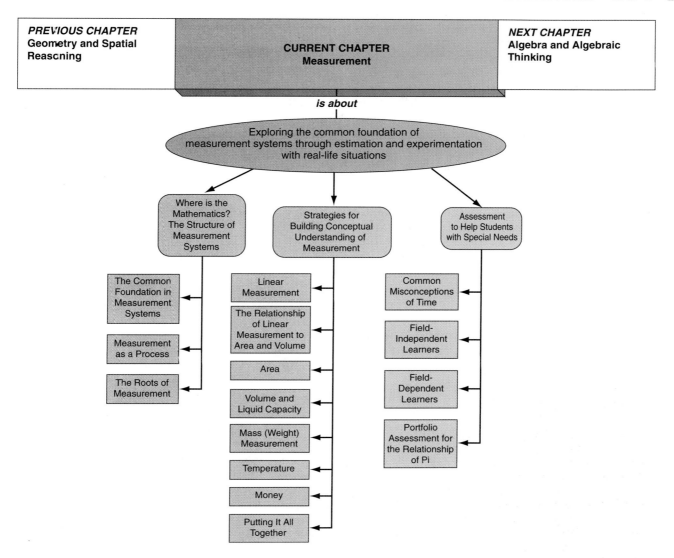

PREVIOUS CHAPTER
Geometry and Spatial Reasoning

CURRENT CHAPTER
Measurement

NEXT CHAPTER
Algebra and Algebraic Thinking

is about

Exploring the common foundation of measurement systems through estimation and experimentation with real-life situations

Where is the Mathematics? The Structure of Measurement Systems

Strategies for Building Conceptual Understanding of Measurement

Assessment to Help Students with Special Needs

The Common Foundation in Measurement Systems

Measurement as a Process

The Roots of Measurement

Linear Measurement

The Relationship of Linear Measurement to Area and Volume

Area

Volume and Liquid Capacity

Mass (Weight) Measurement

Temperature

Money

Putting It All Together

Common Misconceptions of Time

Field-Independent Learners

Field-Dependent Learners

Portfolio Assessment for the Relationship of Pi

SELF-HELP QUESTIONS

1. How can I use the mathematical ideas from other cultures to give my students a greater understanding of the accomplishments of others?

2. What can I do to help students from underrepresented populations realize how important their cultures have been to the development of mathematical ideas?

3. What can I do as a teacher to help bilingual students and those from underrepresented populations succeed in mathematics?

4. How can I use modeling, scaffolding, and learning styles to bring greater understanding of mathematics to students in need of success?

5. How can I use the power of storytelling to teach mathematics concepts?

Geometry and measurement are closely linked in the elementary and middle school curriculum. In the last chapter we developed an intuitive understanding of shapes, objects, their attributes, values, and relationships in geometry. Now we will assign a numerical value to the attributes of objects through the use of tools, techniques, and formulas—the definition of measurement in the NCTM *Principles and Standards* (2000). It involves the linear, area, and volume measures of one-, two-, and three-dimensional space, including liquid capacity, weight, and mass. Other measurement systems traditionally presented in the curriculum are temperature, time, and money. The NCTM *Standards* (2000) stress a progression of concepts and skills through the grade levels as seen in Figure 13.1. Angle measurement along with protractor and compass use are often covered as a part of geometric modeling in student textbooks, so these topics have been placed in the geometry chapter of this text. The development of formulas for working with circumference and area have been included here.

People have always measured things in the world around them. Cave dwellers judged distances by time or eye, and they compared sizes by paces or matched objects with trees, stones, or other objects common to their surroundings. There was no accuracy in that world.

As needs grew, greater accuracy was required. To measure clothing, weapons, and other items, rough methods of measurement were developed. Outstretched arms, heights, feet, and hands were all used for measuring. These measures differed between people and, therefore, were nonstandard. All persons had their own method of measuring. In 6,000 B.C., the first known standards of measurement, such as stones, feet, or hands, were established.

Today, measurement is used in many ways in our lives and is vital for communication. The sciences have always used measurement for communication. Most professions require measurement in some way or another. These uses vary in terms of scales, codes, numerals, and so on. For example, water hardness is measured in terms of mineral content, earthquake intensity is measured in terms of the Richter scale, and rock hardness is measured by Mohs' hardness scale. Oven and room temperatures are measured with a thermometer and may be controlled by a thermostat. Daily people weigh themselves, cut measured material to sew clothing, panel a room, figure the distance they have jogged, or mark off part of their yards for vegetable planting. So measurement can be different things to different people and professions.

Although the differences in measurement systems seem complex in the professional world, there are common elements and processes applied to all measurement systems. These common elements and processes present the structural basis for the experiences provided to students in the elementary and middle school.

The Common Foundation in Measurement Systems

There are eight elements that form the foundation or underpinnings of measurement systems (Stephan and Clements, 2003; Lehrer, 2003). Knowing these elements helps teachers see the cognitive demand that measurement places on the learner. Some authors have given slightly different names to the same elements. The most frequently used terms are represented here. The elements are partitioning, iteration, transitivity, conservation, zero-point orientation, continuous quantities, proportionality, and unit-attribute relationship. Each element, its definition, and an example (where appropriate) are presented in Figure 13.2.

Probably you have never thought of these elements as you have measured things in your daily life. We take the ability to measure things for granted, but the knowledge needed to successfully measure an object is quite complex. Study the knowledge package in Figure 13.3 to see what is required to measure even the simplest object. The knowledge package shows how the common elements are applied to a measurement task.

Carpet and tile installers acknowledge the difficulties adults have in measuring the floor area when ordering wall-to-wall carpeting or tile. The problem is so pervasive that the industry advises its installers to measure the areas themselves before placing an order at the factory. This phenomenon is more understandable after reviewing the knowledge package. When people lack experience with a particular measurement, the cognitive demand of the task may be too overwhelming, to guarantee success with out specific training. This applies to students too. Without attention to the eight common elements, students show difficulties with measurement concepts. The strategies section of this chapter will show ways teachers can give students experiences with the foundational elements of measurement.

Measurement as a Process

Measurement refers to a quality. In mathematics we attach qualities of measurement to describe

STANDARD

Instructional programs from prekindergarten through grade 12 should enable all students to

Understand measurable attributes of objects and the units, systems, and processes of measurement.

Apply appropriate techniques, tools, and formulas to determine measurements.

GRADES PREKINDERGARTEN TO 2

In prekindergarten through grade 2 all students should

Recognize the attributes of length, volume, weight, area, and time.

Compare and order objects according to these attributes.

Understand how to measure using nonstandard and standard units.

Select an appropriate unit and a tool for the attribute being measured.

Measure with multiple copies of units of the same size, such as paper clips laid end to end.

Use repetition of a single unit to measure something larger than the unit, for instance, measuring the length of a room with a single meterstick.

Use tools to measure.

Develop common referents for measures to make comparisons and estimates.

GRADES 3 TO 5

In grades 3 to 5 all students should

Understand such attributes as length, area, weight, volume, and size of angle and select the appropriate type of unit for measuring each attribute.

Understand the need for measuring with standard units and become familiar with standard units in the customary and metric systems.

Carry out simple unit conversions, such as from centimeters to meters, within a system of measurement.

Understand that measurements are approximations and understand how differences in units affect precision.

Explore what happens to measurements of a two-dimensional shape such as its perimeter and area when the shape is changed in some way.

Develop strategies for estimating the perimeters, areas, and volumes of irregular shapes.

Select and apply appropriate standard units and tools to measure length, area, volume, weight, time, temperature, and the size of angles.

Select and use benchmarks to estimate measurements.

Develop, understand, and use formulas to find the area of rectangles and related triangles and parallelograms.

Develop strategies to determine the surface areas and volumes of rectangular solids.

GRADES 6 TO 8

In grades 6 to 8 all students should

Understand both metric and customary systems of measurement.

Understand relationships among units and convert from one unit to another within the same system.

Understand, select, and use units of appropriate size and type to measure angles, perimeter, area, surface area, and volume.

Use common benchmarks to select appropriate methods for estimating measurements.

Select and apply techniques and tools to accurately find length, area, volume, and angle measures to appropriate levels of precision.

Develop and use formulas to determine the circumference of circles and the area of triangles, parallelograms, trapezoids, and circles and develop strategies to find the area of more complex shapes.

Develop strategies to determine the surface area and volume of selected prisms, pyramids, and cylinders.

Solve problems involving scale factors, using ratio and proportion.

Solve simple problems involving rates and derived measurements for such attributes as velocity and density.

FIGURE 13.1 *NCTM expectation of measurement. From NCTM Principles and Standards for School Mathematics (2000, pages 398—399).*

them in one way with some amount of precision and accuracy independent of the particular measurement unit used. Estimation and approximate measurements need to be emphasized. "About," "close to," "nearly," "almost," and "approximately" are common terms used by children when discuss-

ing their measurements. For example, "My finger is about ten centimeters long," or "It is nearly one kilometer to my home." All measurement is an approximation. Some measures are more precise than others, but there is never a time when the measurement tool is so exact as to be **the one**

Partitioning	Iteration	Transitivity	Conservation	Zero-Point Orientation	Continuous Quantities	Proportionality	Unit-Attribute Relationships
Separation into equalized units— Measure with the same size units Exception: Money	Can measure larger object by its smaller units by placing smaller units end to end in a continuous measurement	If a = b and b = c then a = c, making one element the referent to compare other things This shows why measurement devices can be used	If an object is moved, it does not change its measure	Accumulation of the measure from the starting point of zero on a measurement tool 1 2 3 4 5 0 2	Measurement is continuous counting of space between discrete points as opposed to discrete counting of the points themselves 2 continuous spaces not 3 discrete points	Different quantities can represent the same measure. 36 in. = 3 feet The smaller the unit, the more are needed in direct proportion to the larger unit. 36 in. = 1 yard 3 feet = 1 yard	Which unit is best to measure the attribute under consideration? A pencil should be measured in inches rather than in yards although an answer is possible using either measure.

FIGURE 13.2   *The common foundation of measurement systems.*

definitive measurement. Therefore, the processes of measurement rather than a definitive answer are developed and honed in the elementary and middle school grades.

Direct Comparison   When teaching measurement, we usually go through a procedure of comparison (indirect and direct), vocabulary building, instrument use, and reading the instruments. Therefore, no matter what the measurement, we usually begin with direct comparisons. With children we say, "Andrea is taller than Mario"; "Maggie's chalk is longer than Juan's"; "My glass holds more than your glass." These direct comparisons are common at all levels, but especially in the primary grades. Direct comparison is done by comparing like units to one another. This process leads to such nonstandard measures as calling this book ten paper clips long or three chalkboard erasers long.

Indirect Comparison   Soon a need for communication becomes apparent, and the nonstandard measures are compared to standard measures. A common vocabulary of measurement begins to develop. An example would be how many pencils long is a meter stick or how much clay weighs as much as one kilogram of butter. Measurement has now gone from general to specific units, and the general mechanics of measurement become apparent. This involves the element of transitivity, described in Figure 13.2; Transitivity explains why it is possible to use measurement tools.

Seriation   Reading rulers, balances, scales, and containers requires some proficiency on the part of the student. Not only are numbers used, but labels of specific measurement are also applied. For example, "The book is 15 cm wide," or "The coffee cup holds 250 mL." More generally, "I have a mass of 50 kg," or "I am 100 cm tall." These standard measures are now real to the student. The standard units require an awareness on the part of the student for the need to start the measurement process with estimation used for discussions or initial feelings. Proof and verification follow. For example, to prove that five cups of water is more than a liter of water, actual measurement can be done to prove the initial estimate. Experimentation and experience make these statements on estimation more accurate over time.

Frames of Reference   Students must have frames of reference for many of the standard units of measure. Specifically, the student must be able to discover that it is easier to measure a room in meters than in millimeters or kilometers. This involves the unit-attribute relationship seen in Figure 13.2. The tools for measuring should have the same quality as the object being measured. Obviously, liters are not an appropriate tool for measuring distance, and grams are not an appropriate tool for measuring area. Although these references seem apparent to us, many students confuse them without direct experiences with measurement. Measurement is a hands-on skill. Teachers who try to teach it without actual measurement activities find they have students who do not fare well on achievement tests.

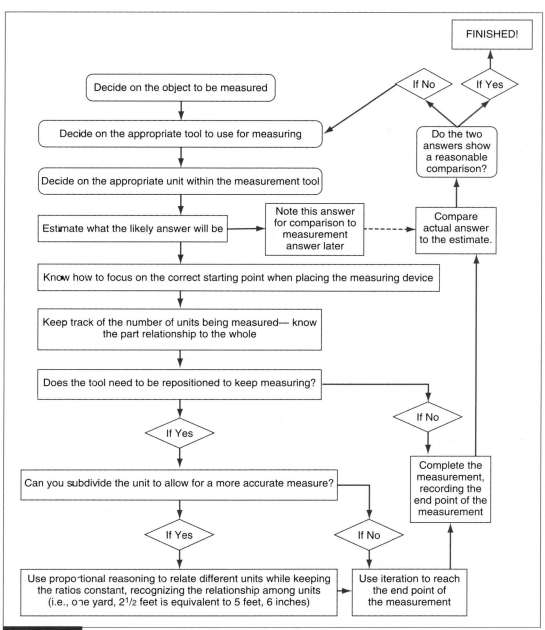

FIGURE 13.3 *The knowledge package for measurement, (Adapted from measurement actions set forth by Diana F. Steele (2002).*

The Roots of Measurement

The history of measurement tells a powerful story of who we are as human beings and what we have been able to accomplish since the days of the cave dwellers. Pictures on cave walls indicate that measurement may very well have been the first mathematical activity of human beings. This cultural connection is important to teach students along with the evolution of the two systems of standard measurement used in our world today.

The Cultural Roots of Measurement Before 6000 B.C., everybody had their own method of measurement. Many were quite different from each other. There was no known standard unit of measurement. People realized a standard was needed. The first known standards of measurement were stones, feet, and hands. The ancestors of the African Americans and the ancestors of the Native Americans were the first peoples to develop systems of standard measurement.

Activity 13.1 outlines what children can understand and should know at different grade levels in elementary and middle school. It is up to you, the teacher, to be cognizant of these knowledge levels and present the cultural awareness that is developmentally appropriate for each age group.

Activity 13.1

CULTURAL
RELEVANCE

MATHEMATICAL
CONNECTIONS

CULTURAL RELEVANCE FOR MEASUREMENT

The following material developed by the Chicago Public Schools should be shared with students at each of the appropriate grade levels.

K TO 3

Students should know that systems of measurement originated in ancient civilizations in response to real-life situations. For example, the annual flooding of the Nile River in Africa created a need to measure the area of triangles, rectangles, and circles. The unit of measure was the length of an early pharaoh's forearm. The 24-hour day—12 hours of day and 12 hours of night—originated in Egypt.

4 TO 5

Students should know that systems of measurement originated in ancient civilizations in response to real-life situations. For example, the annual flooding of the Nile River in Africa created a need to measure and resurvey field boundaries after the flood. The building of the pyramids created a need to develop formulas for the volume of pyramids. The unit of measure was the cubit, the length of an early pharaoh's forearm. The 24-hour day—12 hours of day and 12 hours of night—originated in Egypt.

6 TO 8

Students should be able to understand that systems of measurement were developed in response to the needs of real-life situations. For example, the building of the African pyramids required extremely accurate measurement to construct right angles in the base so that any error would be less than 1 part in 27,000 or 1/27,000. The unit of measure was the cubit, the length of an early pharaoh's forearm. The idea of a 24-hour day—12 hours of day and 12 hours of night—originated in Egypt. The Babylonians of Mesopotamia established the time measures of 60 seconds to 1 minute and 60 minutes to 1 hour. Native Americans, especially the Inca, Maya, and Aztec, developed a system of measures that was so accurate that they were able to lay out miles of direct highways

across high mountains and rugged terrain. The Ashanti of Ghana used standard gold weights to calibrate their scales with the accuracy required by their extensive commerce (Strong, 1990).

Supporting the NCTM *Principles and Standards* **(2000)**
- Mathematics as Connections, Communication
- Oral Discourse of Teacher and Student; Worthwhile Mathematical Tasks—The Teaching Principle.
- The Equity Principle

Piaget felt that tracing the order of development of mathematical concepts in history was a strong indicator of how the human brain develops its own cognitive structures. He pointed to the fact that different cultures, totally separated from one another, emerged with the remarkably similar developmental order of mathematical concepts and understandings (Piaget, 1989). This is most clearly seen in mathematics because language and customs do not get in the way of tracing a culture's ability to problem solve and reason.

Constructivists see wisdom in letting children explore mathematics like their foreparents did. They believe that if all cognitive structures develop in a similar order from stage to stage, students will move from one developmental stage to the next more effectively if asked to reconstruct the knowledge themselves (Brooks and Brooks, 1993). Therefore, activities like Activity 13.2 are encouraged.

The Two Standard Systems in Today's World

There are two common measurement systems in the world: the standard or customary system and

---

Activity 13.2

CULTURAL
RELEVANCE

MATHEMATICAL
CONNECTIONS

PROBLEM
SOLVING

ESTIMATION

CREATING YOUR OWN NEED FOR STANDARD MEASUREMENT TOOLS

MATERIALS
- Student's own body and any piece of furniture in the classroom.

DIRECTIONS

1. The following is a lesson plan dialogue created by one teacher. Plan your own dialogue lesson after reading the example.

> *"We are going to measure things today the way people did long ago before the ancestors of African Americans and Native Americans thought of a better way. Let's see if we can figure out why the ancient people of Egypt and the Mayans of Central America had to come up with a better way to measure things."*

Ask; "How many different ways can you measure the length and width of your desk using your body?" Have every student do this at least five different ways.

Compare and contrast the measurements after all students have had a chance to orally describe what they found with their measurements.

Then create a scenario like this one;

> *"Let's say I have to go to the furniture store to replace a certain desk in the classroom that just fits in a certain spot. It has to be the exact measurements, and I cannot take it with me. I tell the store owner that the desk is the same length as Tojan's foot '(take any one of the students' body measurements they have just used). Tojan cannot go with me and the store owner does not know Tojan. What could I do?"*

Let the students problem solve a variety of solutions. Eventually, someone will say you should take a paper copy of Tojan's foot so the store owner could see the correct measurement. Now it is time to do the drawing in Figure 13.4.

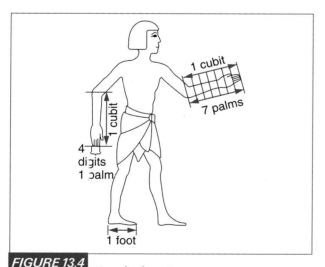

FIGURE 13.4 *Standard ancient measurements.*

Now you can explain that the students have shown that they are just as great as the ancient mathematicians were. Explain that the measurements first standardized were based on Pharaoh's body measurements because he was the famous king.

Now ask: "What happened when one Pharaoh died and some other king with different body measurements came to power?" Elicit from the students comments that the ancient people standardized even further to make a foot always the same measurement no matter what. Explain that that is how we have the name "foot" for 12 inches in our system.

Ask them what body parts they think an inch might have been in the old days. This is not a hard answer when the students are looking at a poster like the picture in Figure 13.4

the metric system. The United States uses the customary system and some metric, and most of the world uses the metric system exclusively. Most elementary textbooks include both systems, with each system taught separately and with no conversion of one system to the other. Only a few texts compare units between systems in the last part bf middle school. Consequently, the approach of this book is to treat each system independently of the other in the student activities.

Price (2001) points to the inherent qualities of the metric system. It is based on the decimal system of tens with the naming of prefixes in relation to their placement in the decimal system. Working solely with one system would give our students more time to concentrate on the metric system rather than spreading attention between two systems, and it would place our students on an equal footing with the other students around the world. International trade, Internet activities, and technology would no longer be a problem for our students who must now "translate" measurements, escalating the chance for errors. Despite opinions by the scientific community, change does not look likely for many years to come.

This book will not cover the systems in detail, assuming you have had exposure to the systems in a mathematics content course. If you are wondering what a decameter is after reading the cartoon, *Subscripts*, you need the refresher activity. Review the system of metric measurement on the Web site in Check Your Mathematics Knowledge.

You may have also forgotten the standard or the customary English measurement system. The customary system, often thought of as the English system until England adopted the metric system, has been the basic measurement system of the United States. People tend to forget such things as how many feet are in a mile and so forth. This is

Subscripts© . . . *little thoughts below the bottom line*

Check

YOUR MATHEMATICS KNOWLEDGE

- On Customary System of Measurement
- On Metric System of Measurement

    . . . a refresher from mathematics content course-work . . . Lest you forget!

of course, understandable, because most people do not have a real-world necessity to measure how many feet are in a mile. If you feel you need a refresher course on the customary system of measurement, it is also available on the Web site in Check Your Mathematics Knowledge.

STRATEGIES FOR BUILDING CONCEPTUAL UNDERSTANDING OF MEASUREMENT

Measurement concepts should build on the informal spatial understanding that students naturally have. A firm foundation in measurement concepts shows students the interconnectedness of measurement and geometry. The NCTM *Principles and Standards* (NCTM, 2000) emphasize that measurements should have real-world applications and be embedded in everyday situations.

The performance on national and international tests indicates a lack of concentration in the area of measurement and that all students suffer from a lack of an intensive, in-depth study of measurement (Lehrer, 2003). Some measurement items on the Seventh Assessment for NAEP (NCES, 2000) asked students to read measure-

ments from pictorial representations of instruments such as rulers, scales, thermometers, gauges, and protractors. In general, students in fourth grade had more difficulty reading instruments when the object to be measured was not aligned at the beginning of a ruler and when the scale on the instrument involved an increment other than one. Such findings are consistent with previous NAEP studies. Although scores improved greatly with ruler measurements (79 percent), by the time students were in eighth grade, only 35 percent of these students obtained the correct angle measurements using a protractor. When students were asked how often they used measuring devices such as protractors, 52 percent of the eighth graders reported they had never used them! This is a twofold indictment because protractor and compass use is a part of both geometry *and* measurement.

The test results show that children need as much help in building the language of measurement as they do in building the concept of counting. Once a general language of measurement has been accomplished, the language is refined to be more specific. The types of measurement include length, area, volume, liquid capacity, mass (weight), time, temperature, and money. General activities for introducing each of the concepts are essential, and numerous approaches are necessary for understanding. Therefore, building language, questioning techniques, and activities for each topic should be established, based on the growing research on children's measurement understandings. The most pertinent research will be mentioned throughout this section where appropriate. The strategies presented here are not meant to be exhaustive. You are encouraged to study the NCTM *2003 Yearbook* (Clements and Bright, 2003) and the *Navigation Series on Measurement* (House, 2003) for additional measurement ideas and research findings.

Linear Measurement

To teach linear measurements, activities should begin with concepts familiar to children. Research shows that students' understanding of linear measurement directly impacts their ability to understand area and volume later in the elementary and middle grades (Outhred et al., 2003).

NAEP results (Strutchens, Martin, and Kenney, 2003) show that fourth grade students have improved in their ability to recognize that a ruler is an appropriate measure for linear activities from the 1996 to the 2000 test, but students do not fare well when asked to do a problem like the one shown in Figure 13.2 in **zero-point orientation.**

Students center their attention on the end point of the line instead of moving the ruler to the starting point of the figure and measuring from that point as the zero.

A variation of this problem was given on the TIMMS test, requiring a higher level of cognitive knowledge about linear measurement. The students were asked to approximate the length of a pencil that lay next to a ruler. The end of the pencil was resting at 3 cm and it extended beyond the centimeter ruler about a centimeter and a half. This was a multiple choice item with a distracter item giving the common misconception as an answer choice. The item required students to perform a mental **iteration** (see Figure 13.2) in **continuous quantities of space counting** without the ruler extended to the end of the line. Internationally, about half of the students (49 percent of the seventh graders and 52 percent of the eighth graders) were able to answer the question correctly. For U.S. students, the percents answering correctly were 46 percent and 45 percent, respectively (Beaton et al., 1996).

The students also did poorly on constructed response items even though distracter items were not present to influence answers. Students were asked to draw a rectangle whose length was one and one-half times the length of a given rectangle and whose width was half the width of that rectangle. Only 24 percent of the seventh graders and 31 percent of the eighth graders answered correctly. It is obvious from these studies that students need far more work with the eight common foundational elements of measurement that extend beyond the quick page or two on measurement in most textbooks.

So time spent moving children from direct to indirect comparisons through seriation and frames of reference is important for success in later measurements. They are presented next to each other so you can easily see the progression needed to move from one skill set to another:

Direct Comparison	Indirect Comparison
Compare lengths, widths, heights— One part of body, pencil, etc. being longer, shorter, same as another.	Compare two sets of measurements by use of rulers, trundle wheels, etc., moving from small things to larger measurements.
Use nonstandard measures— Own footprints to others in class, etc.	Use both customary and metric measurements See Activity 13.3—

Measure the same item by two different people's footprints.	Guessing Metric Measurements
Students should see need for standard measures and request for using them.	Activity 13.4—Metric Olympics Activity 13.5—Estimation with Large Measures

Seriation	Frame of Reference
Students make their own nonstandard tools of measurement.	Use trundle wheels to measure long distances; meter sticks, and yard sticks for shorter ones, etc.
Partition tool into smaller, same-size units.	Measurement activities on the playground work with trundle wheels.
This helps the partitioning, iteration, transitivity, and continuous counting ideas of measurement when students see how their own measurement tool affects the answer to measuring common things around the room.	See Figure 13.6
Establish **benchmarks** for common measures– distance in miles; from school to home; a thumbnail is 1 cm wide, etc.	Produce riddles— "Why is this silly?" Ex.— 1. Measure the distance from Phoenix to Los Angeles in meters. 2. Measure the size of a book in kilometers. 3. Pictures like the cartoon can show the funny side of measuring inappropriately.

Activity 13.3

PROBLEM SOLVING **ESTIMATION** **MENTAL MATH**

GUESSING METRIC MEASUREMENTS

DIRECTIONS
How good are you at guessing your metric measurements? For this activity you will need a meterstick and a piece of string.

PROCEDURE

1. Using string, have a partner cut a piece as long as you are tall. How does that length compare to your arm span?

2. Count how many times the string can be wrapped around your head, waist, ankles, wrist, neck, and thigh.

3. Cut a piece of string that you guess would go around your waist. Don't measure until you have cut the string. Now try it around your waist.

   How many centimeters off were you? _____ cm
   Your waist is _____ cm.

4. Repeat this activity for other parts of your body.
   Your neck = ——— cm. Answers will vary.
   Your wrist = ——— cm.
   Your thumb = ——— cm.

5. Your waist measures about _____ times your neck. Your waist measures about _____ times your wrist.
   Your waist measures about _____ times your thumb.

6. Make a bar graph representing the different lengths of each body part.

---

people of Greek ancestry live in America today. We have their ancestors to thank for this fun activity.

3. Each student has a handout with the task cards to keep track of his or her score. An official scorecard is found at each of the four stations and each station has an official (student) as the recordkeeper. A child is assigned as the announcer who will do the commentary when a winner is determined. This supports speech across the curriculum. Each person keeps track of his or her own score and an awards ceremony can be planned for the winners in each category.

4. Addenda Series: *Measurement in the Middle Grades* (Geddes, 1994, p. 24) shows examples of other task cards that could be developed.

Supporting the NCTM *Principles and Standards* (2000)
- Mathematics as Connections; Communication; Measurement
- Worthwhile Mathematical Tasks; Mathematics as Oral Discourse; Representation—The Teaching and Learning Principles

---

Activity 13.4

MATHEMATICAL CONNECTIONS   **MANIPULATIVES**   **CULTURAL RELEVANCE**   **METRIC OLYMPICS**

MATERIALS

- Task cards like the one in Figure 13.5
- Cotton balls, straws, regular paper clips; plastic-coated paper clips, meterstick
- Clay and straight pins
- Pencil and paper

DIRECTIONS

1. Set up stations around the room for each Olympic activity: 1 —Straw and Paper Clip Pole Vault; 2 — Cotton Ball Shotput; 3 —Straw Javelin Throw; 4 — Standing Long Jump; 5 —Metric Sponge Squeeze.

2. Use these words to start the activity:

   "Since the Greeks in ancient Europe, people have enjoyed the competition of, the Olympics. Many

---

The metric pack in the Extended Activities on the Web site stores typical frames of reference found in classrooms. Each child has length, area, weight, and volume frames of reference in the pack to use in activities like the ones here and in Activity 13.15, Weight with Foil Boats, seen later in this chapter.

When students have gained facility with using standard units of measure, they will again begin finding discrepancies in measurements. They may even come to the conclusion that measurements can never be exact. Discussions and activities surrounding a theme of measurement accuracy are natural. The activities in the Extended Activities are examples of ways to blend several topics together in a busy classroom.

Highlights to Remember At first, children use units that are larger than the objects being compared or measured. Later, they move to smaller units counting how many smaller units are in the object being measured. Finally, children begin using various objects as the unit of measure from which comparisons are made. Working with parts of units is preliminary to working with standard units such as inches, feet, and yards. The more ways in which children learn to divide nonstandard unit measurements into parts, the better prepared

1. Stand at the throw line.
2. Attach a regular paper clip to the top of a straw.
3. Aim the straw, then tap the bottom to make the paper clip jump over the cross bar. Record your best measurement.

Your best score: _____cm (at height = _____)
Your best score: _____cm (at height = _____)
Your best score: _____cm (at height = _____)

4. Attach a plastic-coated paper clip to the top of a straw.
5. Tap the bottom of the straw aiming the paper clip over the cross bar. Did you notice a difference in the feel of the "pole?"

If yes, which one was easiest to do? _____

Your best score: _____cm (at height = _____)
Your best score: _____cm (at height = _____)
Your best score: _____cm (at height = _____)

6. The official will raise the crossbar to the next level after each person on the team has had a chance to compete.
7. Do the activity again at the new height. Try this activity at three different heights.

A straw is raised and attached with straight pins to the straw poles. The base is molding clay.

FIGURE 13.5 *Pole vault task card.*

they will be to understand how to use standard units of measure as they study the more complex ideas of area and volume.

Activity 13.5

ESTIMATION   MATHEMATICAL CONNECTIONS   CULTURAL RELEVANCE

ESTIMATION WITH LARGE MEASURES

DIRECTIONS

1. Have the class line up on a start line. At the signal to begin, all participants should go forward to their best estimate of a distance of 50 meters. Measure the results to determine the first three places based on those students nearest to 50 meters. Use the trundle wheel to measure.

2. Estimate other lengths using the same procedure as in number 1. Some meter lengths to use: 5 meters, 10 meters, 13 meters.

3. Metric Olympics could be planned for an entire class with activities such as a 25-meter measure, a 100-meter measure, or create a 1-kilogram clay ball.

4. Have teams of students each estimate 1 hectare. Verify the estimations by measuring each other's estimate. Rank order the groups by best estimate.

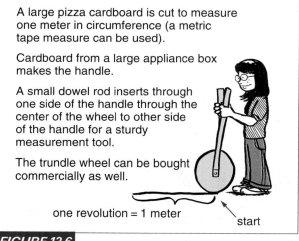

A large pizza cardboard is cut to measure one meter in circumference (a metric tape measure can be used).

Cardboard from a large appliance box makes the handle.

A small dowel rod inserts through one side of the handle through the center of the wheel to other side of the handle for a sturdy measurement tool.

The trundle wheel can be bought commercially as well.

one revolution = 1 meter   start

FIGURE 13.6 *Trundle wheel for large metric measurements.*

The Relationship of Linear Measurement to Area and Volume

Generally, it has been thought that area should be taught before volume, thinking that volume as a three-dimensional measurement of space is more complex than area. However, recent research (Outhred; et al., 2003) has shown that students can do either area or volume measurement following the use of linear measurement. Both area and volume involve "filling up" or "packing" units together until a whole object is covered. Success depends on how students view the basic building

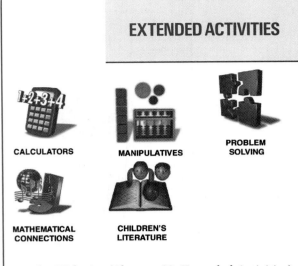

EXTENDED ACTIVITIES

CALCULATORS

MANIPULATIVES

PROBLEM SOLVING

MATHEMATICAL CONNECTIONS

CHILDREN'S LITERATURE

On the Web site (Chapter 13, Extended Activities), read/do the following:

- Map Scales in Social Studies
- Metric Measurements
- Making a Metric Pack
- Lesson Plans for Mathematical Proficiency
  - Discovering the Standard Measure of One Foot
  - Measurement Unit of Inches

Battista (2003) outlines four mental processes required before students can understand and work with area and volume measurement:

1. Forming and using mental model: This requires seeing mental images from past contexts and visualizing their placement in a new situation. This is analogous to thinking of directions to a new location without the presence of a map to guide you.

2. Spatial structuring: can see how the basic building unit can be structured to fill the object.

3. Units-locating: can see the dimensions required to locate any one unit of the composite units in the structure.

4. Organizing by composites: iterating from one basic scaled unit to others to form the entire array.

The three foundational elements of partitioning, iteration, and continuous quantities (Figure 13.2) seem most affected by the mental processes outlined by Battista. Figure 13.7 shows how a child might use the four mental processes in constructing either a square (area) or a cube (volume). Teachers must structure activities and ask questions to engender student answers like those in Figure 13.7. Think of these four thought processes as you explore the typical activities used to teach area and volume in the next two sections of the chapter.

unit as an array within the system. Apparently, it is the filling up of the space with the basic building unit, not the dimensionality of the task, that children see as important information.

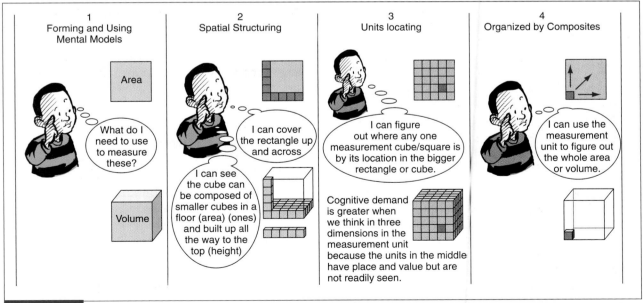

FIGURE 13.7 *Needed mental processes to move to area and volume.*

Area

Area is the number of square units required to cover a surface, and *perimeter* is the boundary or distance around an area. If the object being measured is a circle, the boundary is called *circumference*. These terms and the concepts behind them frequently confuse students. These concepts are frequently missed on slate assessment tests coming in second only to volume as the concept with the greatest difficulty for students in elementary through the middle grades. Many hands-on activities are required to set the concepts firmly in place. A quick review from year to year does not work when dealing with concepts of area and perimeter and circumference.

Area and Perimeter The Battista and Outhred research on area and volume seems in conflict to the Piagetian research on conservation. When one studies the eight foundational elements of measurement systems (Figure 13.2), one can see that conservation is a different concept from the four elements affected by the Battista and Outhred research. Plaget's tasks assessed conservation of length, area, and volume and were based on the child's ability to reason that the measure was unchanged by displacement. This is a different foundational element from the other four, and it may develop later. More research is needed before we can tell how significantly these subtle differences between elements may affect conceptual understandings in geometry and measurement.

Generally, conservation looks at the relationship of area to its perimeter requiring an understanding that area remains unchanged with different shape configurations even when the perimeter changes. From the assessment tests, it is apparent that many twelve- to fourteen-year-olds still had trouble being convinced that the area remains unchanged with different configurations such as in Figure 13.8. Children also had difficulty believing that perimeters could change but areas remain the same, as in Figure 13.9. The Video Vignette, "Pizza Perimeters," shows how fourth graders explore such concepts.

Pentominoes Pentominoes provide an exercise in perception and logical reasoning and help demonstrate some geometric principles of congruency as well as square unit measurement of area. Pentominoes are made of five (pent-) congruent squares that must have every square touching at least one side of another square (Figure 13.10). Have children cut squares out of graph paper or use plastic tiles to form the pentominoes.

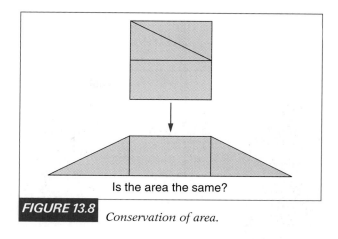

Is the area the same?

FIGURE 13.8 *Conservation of area.*

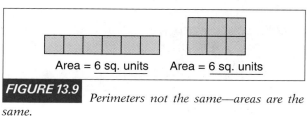

Area = 6 sq. units   Area = 6 sq. units

FIGURE 13.9 *Perimeters not the same—areas are the same.*

A common activity is to form the twelve different pentominoes that can be constructed. Individual squares such as mosaic tiles, which can be moved easily, work better with younger children. The shapes can then be cut from graph paper and kept as a record. Making the shapes out of paper allows children to test whether the newly formed shape is unique. The shape, when flipped or rotated, may produce a figure that has already been found. If the two shapes are congruent, they are the same shape and have the same square unit of area (Figure 13.11).

If this task is too hard for younger children, it can be made easier by starting with three squares,

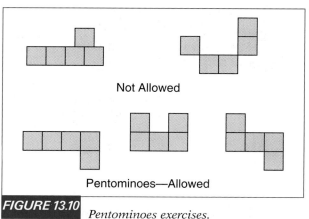

Not Allowed

Pentominoes—Allowed

FIGURE 13.10 *Pentominoes exercises.*

Video Vignette

Pizza Perimeters

View the Video Vignette with Mr. Dillion (Chapter 13, Video Vignettes, "Pizza Perimeters"). Then, Mr. Dillon's fourth graders are presented with a problem to solve involving area and perimeter. He uses a real-life scenario to give added meaning to the problem.

- Analyze this lesson in terms of the NCTM Teaching Principle, worthwhile mathematical tasks. Describe your reactions.

- What aspects of the NCTM *Principles* do you see exemplified in this lesson?

- What follow-up activities would you suggest should happen after this lesson?

for which there are only two different arrangements. Next try the different arrangements of four squares (Activity 13.6).

Tangrams and Geoboards Area and perimeter can also be explored with tangrams (Activity 13.7) and

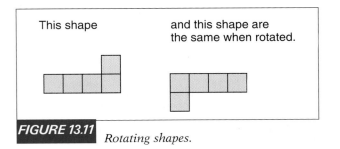

| This shape | and this shape are the same when rotated. |

FIGURE 13.11 *Rotating shapes.*

Activity 13.6

PROBLEM SOLVING **PENTOMINOES**

MATERIALS
- One cutout set of the 12 pentominoes (use graph paper—one inch or centimeter; see Appendix and Web site.

PROCEDURE
1. Find the area and perimeter of each pentominoe. Have you found all possible arrangements?
2. Which nets can be folded to make a cube without a lid? What do you notice about those that can be folded?
3. Use all 12 pentominoes and form a 6 × 10 rectangle (6 units wide and 10 units long). Form a 5 × 12 rectangle. What other rectangular arrangements can you make?
4. Use two pentominoes and make a 2 × 5 rectangle. Any others? Use three different pentominoes and make a 3 × 5 rectangle. Any others? Continue making rectangles with different numbers of pentominoes. Do you see a pattern? Write any predictions you can make.
5. Using two pentominoes, find all the tessellations that can be made. Color them using graph paper to show the tessellations.
6. Using a checkerboard, try to place all the pentominoes on the board without overlapping the places. As a partner game, each player draws six pieces and in turn places a pentomino on the board until no plays remain. The winner is the player with more places on the board.

> **Supporting the NCTM *Principles and Standards* (2000)**
> - Mathematics as Problem Solving; Representation; Reasoning
> - Representation—The Learning Principle, The Mathematics Principle
> - The Assessment Principle

geoboards (Activities 13.8 and 13.9). These teaching activities help develop an intuitive understanding about how area can remain the same regardless of various transformations. Students who rely heavily on perceptual cues gain understanding about

Activity 13.7

MANIPULATIVES MATHEMATICAL CONNECTIONS

DISCOVERING AREA WITH TANGRAMS

MATERIALS

• Tangram sets (see Appendix and Web site)

PROCEDURE

1. Use the two smallest triangles. Make a square. This square represents a square unit of measure. What is the area of the triangle?

2. Use the two smallest triangles. Make a parallelogram. What is the area of the shape?

3. Use the three smallest triangles. Make a square. What is the area? Use the same pieces and make a triangle, rectangle, trapezoid, and parallelogram. What is the area of each shape? If one edge of the square has a value of one unit, compare their perimeters. Write about your perceptions.

4. Using the five smallest pieces (all except the two large triangle) form the same five shapes. Compare the area and perimeter of each shape.

5. Which shape do you feel has the greatest area? Why? Greatest perimeter? Why?

6. If the total area for the square made from the seven tangrams is one, what fractions, decimal, percent relationships are there? What ratios are there for area and perimeter of the different places?

Activity 13.8

MANIPULATIVES

EXPLORING AREA AND PERIMETER WITH GEOBOARDS

MATERIALS

• Geoboards
• Rubber bands (geobands)
• Geoboard dot paper (Appendix and Web site)

PROCEDURE

1. The distance between two adjacent nails is considered a unit of length—(as it appears on the geoboard). What is the perimeter for the first row?

2. Make a figure with a perimeter of 6, 7, 10. Figures need right angles. How many different ways can you construct figures with a perimeter of 8?

3. Make the smallest square possible. This is called one square unit of area. Can you make squares with areas of 1 through 16?

4. Make these figures on a geoboard: perimeter 12, area 9; perimeter 8, area 4; perimeter 12, area 8.

5. Make the smallest right triangle possible. What is the area of the triangle? Construct a square on each side of the triangle. What is the area of each square? What is the relationship between these areas? Can you prove the Pythagorean theorem $a^2 + b^2 = c^2$? On a 10×10 geoboard investigate more right triangles.

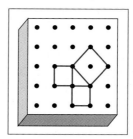

6. Consider line segment $\overline{MN}$. Can you predict the area of the square that has this line segment as one side? Can you predict the area of the right triangle that has this line segment as one side?

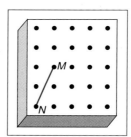

7. How many square units are in the figures below?

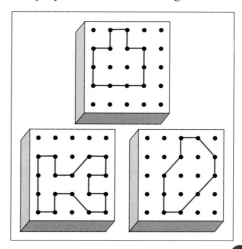

Activity 13.9

MANIPULATIVES

ADDITIONAL ACTIVITIES FOR AREA WITH GEOBOARDS

MATERIALS
- Geoboards
- Rubber bands (geobands)
- Geoboard dot paper (Appendix and Web site)

PROCEDURE

1. Make the smallest square. How many nails touch the rubber band? How many nails are inside?

2. Stretch the band around five nails. What is the area of this shape? How many nails are touching (T)? How many nails are inside (I)? Repeat questions with six nails. Continue in a similar manner. Develop these data into a table:

3. What patterns do you see? What can you predict?

Area (A)	Nails Touching (T)	Nails Inside (I)

4. Keep the number of nails inside as zero and increase the number of nails touching. What effect does this have on the area? Why? What patterns can be found?

5. Keep the number of nails touching as four and vary the number of nails inside. What effect does this have on the area? Why? What patterns can be seen?

6. If there is a relationship between these two variables, can a function be found to express that relationship?

7. Form a right triangle on the geoboard such as a base of 2 and a height of 3. Find the area by enclosing this figure with a rectangular region. Describe the area of the triangle.

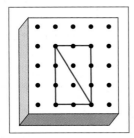

8. Form an acute triangle with a base of 3 and a height of 2. Find the area by enclosing this figure with two rectangles. Inside each rectangle is a right triangle. Since the area of a right triangle is half the area of the surrounding rectangle, add the two areas together to

find the total area of the acute triangle. Check using the formula for area of triangle: $A = \frac{1}{2} bh$.

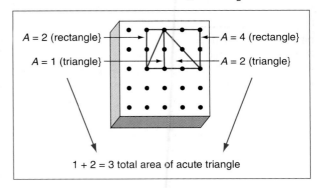

$A = 2$ (rectangle) $A = 4$ (rectangle)
$A = 1$ (triangle) $A = 2$ (triangle)

$1 + 2 = 3$ total area of acute triangle

9. Form a parallelogram. Form a rectangle around it and find the area of the rectangle. Children can see the relationship between the two figures and the computation of the area formula for a parallelogram, $A = h \times b$.

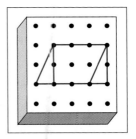

10. Write a formula to find the area of any region using the number of nails touching (T) and the number of nails inside (I). This formula is known as Pick's theorem. Check the area of the triangle in step 8. It is $T = 6, I = 1$, so
$$T/2 + I - 1 (\text{constant}) = \text{area, or } 6/2 + 1 - 1 = 3.$$

conservation of area. The geoboard is an effective device to show area formulas for parallelograms and triangles.

Rather than use the formula that requires the student to visualize a line segment as the height, the strategy with geoboards is to form a rectangle around the region, determine the area of the rectangle, and determine the area of the other figure. Notice in all of these activities the questions are framed by using the phrase, "square units of _____." This is essential if we are to help students understand that anytime one talks about area, one is measuring **square** units.

Measuring with Standard Units in Metric and Customary Measures   The unit of area measure is a square unit, which is a square with each side equal to one unit. Although the square inch, square foot, and square yard are the most common units of area measure in the United States, most of the world uses the metric system. Hence, children should experience activities with the square meter as well as the usual standard units. As the student constructs the square unit on each figure, there is the realization that a square unit takes up a certain amount of area regardless of the shape of the original figure. A vocabulary and a frame of reference still need to be established. Standard units can be reinforced by having children trace hands-on squared metric or customary paper and then count the number of squares covered. Estimation will be required to make whole squares.

The standard unit of area for small surfaces such as a book, notebook, or desk is the square centimeter. The square meter is appropriate for

Supporting the NCTM *Principles and Standards*(2000)
- Mathematics as Problem Solving, Connections, Reasoning/Patterns; Measurement
- Tools to Enhance Discourse—The Teaching Principle

determining the area of rooms in a home or school, or for finding how much carpeting is needed to cover a certain number of square meters or how much wallpaper is needed to cover a certain number of square meters. Frames of reference can be established for the square centimeter and square meter through experimentation. Hectare is the unit used for small land measure, and the square kilometer is used for measuring large areas of land and oceans. A region of land will be needed to establish a frame of reference for the square kilometer and hectare.

The activities should lead to discovery or reinforcement of the area formula of the square(s^2), rectangle ($l \times w$), and circle (πr^2). The NCTM *Principles and Standards* (2000) advocate less stress on memorizing formulas and measurement conversion equivalencies and more on estimation and setting benchmarks. Use lots of activities to "see" the formulas evolve through engaging mathematics activities. Students' exploration can help derive formulas. A typical example would be if students are asked to find the area of a parallelogram when they already know how to find the area of a rectangle. As Figure 13.12 shows, one can be deduced from the other without ever memorizing a formula. For more practice without formulas, see the area activities in the Extended Activities on the Web site.

Activity 13.10

PROBLEM SOLVING **ESTIMATION** **MENTAL MATH**

WITH CENTIMETER GRAPH PAPER

DIRECTIONS

1. Place your hand with the fingers closed on centimeter graph paper. Draw around your hand.

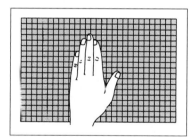

2. Guess the area of your hand in square centimeters, _____cm^2.
3. Count the square units to find the area of your hand. You should count a square if more than $\frac{1}{2}$ of it is inside the outline of your hand.
4. The area of my hand is about _____cm^2.
5. Now draw your foot on centimeter graph paper. Try to make a better guess.
6. Guess the area of your foot in square centimeters, _____cm^2.
7. Next count the square units to find the area of your foot.
8. The area of my foot is about _____cm^2.

I KNOW HOW TO FIGURE THE AREA OF A RECTANGLE SO I CAN FIGURE THIS PARALLELOGRAM OUT BY CUTTING THE RECTANGLE TO MATCH THE PARALLELOGRAM. IF THE ONE SIDE AND THE LINE PERPENDICULAR TO THAT SIDE ARE THE SAME AS THE TWO SIDES OF THE RECTANGLE, THE AREA MUST BE THE SAME. THERE, I GOT THE ANSWER!

FIGURE 13.12 *Deducing formulas from experience.*

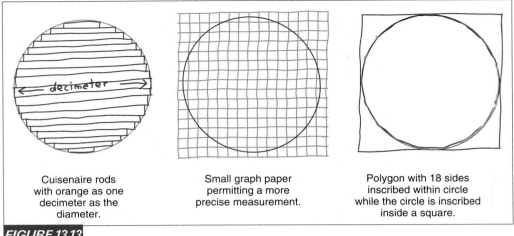

FIGURE 13.13 *Approximate measures of Pi.*

Cuisenaire rods with orange as one decimeter as the diameter.

Small graph paper permitting a more precise measurement.

Polygon with 18 sides inscribed within circle while the circle is inscribed inside a square.

Circle Area and Circumference The circumference is the distance or the perimeter of a circle. The diameter is the length of a straight line drawn from side to side through the center of the circle. The radius is the distance from the center to a side. Tent (2001) suggests a series of activities to help students see the constant relationship of pi to the area of circles. Figure 13.13 shows how students can explore using Cuisenaire rods, other graduated block measures, graph paper, and inscriptions of circles within squares to approximate more and more precise measurement of the area of the circle.

There are times when it is easier to learn a formula. Formulas involving circles seem to fall into this group. Even then exercises can be organized around the relationship between diameter and circumference rather than just memorizing a formula alone. The formula for circumference is

$$C = \pi d \quad \text{or} \quad C = 2\pi r$$

where d is the diameter and r is the radius. For further explorations, use the spreadsheet activities in the Integrating Technology section at the end of the chapter. Activity 13.11 shows how a performance activity may be explored so the proportional relationship of pi becomes clear. The portfolio assessment at the end of the chapter shows the work of a third grader doing the same task.

Volume and Liquid Capacity

Capacity and volume are referred to as synonymous terms in most elementary programs. These two terms have different dictionary meanings. Volume is defined as how much space a region

Activity 13.11

CALCULATORS   PROBLEM SOLVING

EXPLORING CIRCUMFERENCE AND DIAMETER

PROCEDURE

1. Use your calculator for the computations. Measure the following items and find the circumference and diameter in centimeters. What patterns or relationships do you notice?

Object	C	d	$C + d$	C/d	$C - d$	$C \times d$
Soda can						
Coffee can						
Plate						
Glass						
Waste basket						

Total = ____ ____ ____ ____

2. Which column shows a constant relationship between circumference and diameter?
3. What is the average value of circumference divided by diameter?
4. What can you say about the ratio between circumference and diameter?

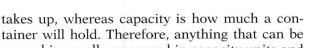

takes up, whereas capacity is how much a container will hold. Therefore, anything that can be poured is usually measured in capacity units and the space in a room is measured in volume units. Some elementary programs refer to it *as liquid capacity* so the students can remember the "pourable" aspect to the measurement. In working with young children, the terms can be used interchangeably, but upper elementary and middle grade students will need to distinguish between them. To begin working with these units, estimating how much a jar holds or which container holds more is necessary for a grasp of the concept.

The liter and milliliter are normally used for capacity unit measures, and the cubic centimeter and the cubic meter are common measurement units for volume. In the metric system, the volume, capacity, and mass measurements of water have a commonality: a cubic centimeter of pure water has a mass of one gram (weight) and a capacity of one milliliter.

Children should begin their work with volume and capacity by freely playing and experimenting with pouring sand and water into containers. In so doing, they are dealing with three-dimensional space and begin establishing basic notions about it. Although they may not wonder about how many cups of sand or how much water they have for some time, they will begin to wonder which of two containers holds more or how much water they need to fill an aquarium. This involves the common elements of transitivity, conservation, and continuous quantities (Figure 13.2).

Working with Volume   Remember, volume is the space that is occupied. The volume of the room is the number of cubic meters that will fit into the room. This includes length, width, and depth. For small measures such as the volume of a shoebox, use the cubic centimeter. Construct a cubic centimeter (or use the smallest unit from the base 10 blocks) and have the children estimate how many cubic meters would fit into the classroom.

Apparently, some people are beginning to think of these kinds of questions even when they are on vacation. The park service employees at Carlsbad Caverns National Park report that one of their most interesting (and entertaining) questions from a park visitor was, "How many Ping-Pong balls would it take to fill this up?" (Online Internet, 1995). Now there's a real activity that calls for estimation and mental math!

Computing Volume   Computing the volume of the shoebox in cubic centimeters and the classroom in cubic meters using length, width, and depth (height) measurements would help establish the formula for volume as length × width × height. The estimates could then be compared with the actual computed measurements for establishing

frames of reference for cubic meter and cubic centimeter. Which unit will be used for finding the volume of a basement or the volume of a dresser drawer? Activities 13.12 and 13.13 are two activities with which to start computing volume.

Working with Liquid Capacity   Containers of different sizes and shapes are needed for estimations practice. To make the distinction, several different size containers can be labeled, and sand or cereal can be available to fill them. Have the children estimate which container holds the most, the least, or about the same as an identified one. Next, have them verify their guesses. The children may also order the containers on the basis of how much

---

Activity 13.12

MANIPULATIVES   BUILDING CUBES

DIRECTIONS
1. Use a centimeter ruler to measure the length, width, and height of a block.
2. Build larger and larger cubes using blocks.
3. Record the number of blocks on any edge and the volume for each of these larger cubes.
4. What patterns do you observe?
5. Generalize to a formula for volume of a cube.

Activity 13.13

MANIPULATIVES   CUBIC CENTIMETERS

DIRECTIONS
1. Construct a cubic centimeter from heavy cardboard or with any other nonporous substance.
2. Fill with 1 milliliter of water.
3. Now set up an experiment to verify that it has a mass of 1 gram.
4. Experiments can also verify equivalencies for larger units.

they will hold, their heights, widths, or top circumference.

Teams could be selected to perform these activities while the rest of the class watches. This is less desirable than having each person doing the measuring of each activity, but this is more desirable than no measuring at all. Each child in the class should be on a team, and each team should have every member measuring at least one thing. The children must select a nonstandard unit to measure its capacity. They could give their answers in paper cups full, styrofoam cups full, or whatever units are selected. This method gives the children a feeling for capacity measurement depending on size and shape, not just size, as is often the case. The activity can be followed with the question, "How much does each container hold?"

Computing Liquid Capacity More specific activities would be to use standard units and guess which holds more than a liter, less than a liter, more than a milliliter, and so on. The answers should be proved by using the standard measures of milliliter or liter. Graduated cylinders and beakers are convenient to carry out the standard measure applications. Finally, a frame of reference can be established, (e.g., a can of soda holds _____mL). Familiarity with the unit has been established with the standard measure so the student would know when to use milliliters or liters. Discuss what units are used to measure milk, medicine, or soda pop.

It is hard to remember how the customary units of capacity fit together because the system has no predicable relationship among all its units as the metric system does. Therefore, teachers have found it helpful to create such things as the gallon coder in Figure 13.14. The activity, "Miniature Planet and Measurement" on the Web site in the Extended Activities uses the gallon coder. Children remember graphic organizers much better than memorizing how many quarts are in a gallon and so forth. Activity 13.14 is an activity enjoyed by upper-grade students. They can keep the results in their mathematics journal.

Comparing Liquid Capacity and Volume The strategy of comparing volumes and capacities by pouring water from one container to another is not easy for children to grasp. They find it difficult to believe that the quantity of the contents remains the same even though the shape of the container changes. Piaget claims that most children learn to conserve volume at about age eleven. Sometimes the water or sand that fills one container does not fill another. Is the first container bigger because it

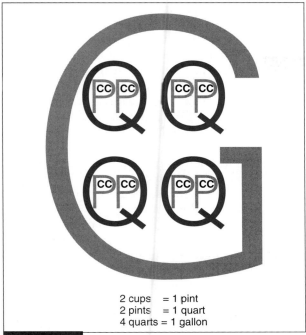

2 cups = 1 pint
2 pints = 1 quart
4 quarts = 1 gallon

FIGURE 13.14 *The gallon coder.*

is full, or is the second one bigger because more could be added to it? What if the water or sand overflows? Which container is larger then? Children must work through these puzzling questions in their own way and in their own time before they can be expected to make comparisons and measurements with any degree of understanding. Because there are so many factors to consider, volume and capacity concepts naturally evolve in the upper grades.

Once children have begun making volume comparison, they may begin considering how much one container holds. When sand or water is placed in many containers, it simply runs out. After some experimentation, children find that blocks or sugar cubes will better account for the space in such containers. Thus, they have begun to get the idea of the cubic unit of measure. As the need to interpret and communicate measurements arises, the need for standard units becomes apparent. Although the cubic inch, cubic foot, cubic yard, and gallon are the most common units of volume measure in the United States, as stated before, most of the world uses the metric system. Hence, children should experience activities with the cubic meter and cubic liter as well as the usual standard units.

Mass (Weight) Measurement

Mass and weight are often used interchangeably, but their meanings differ. Weight is related to the

Activity 13.14

PROBLEM SOLVING **ESTIMATION** **COMPARING CAPACITIES**

MATERIALS

* A piece of construction paper or clear acetate, scissors, tape, some beans or other dry material, and a pan

DIRECTIONS

1. Cut the construction paper or acetate in half.
2. Make a round tube by rolling one piece of the paper the long way ("hotdog" style). Put one edge of the paper over the other and tape them together.
3. Make another round tube, but roll the piece of paper the other way to make a shorter, fatter tube ("hamburger" style). Put one edge of the paper over the other and tape them together.
4. Place the shorter tube in the pan. Put the longer tube inside the shorter tube.
5. Use a measuring cup to fill the long tube with the dry material. Record how many cups it took to fill the long tube.
6. Mark where you think the dry material will come on the shorter tube if you pull the long tube out.
7. Now pull the long tube out. How close is your guess?
8. Because both tubes were made from the same size paper, did you expect the two tubes to hold the same amount?
9. Is the surface area the same for each tube?
10. Continue filling the shorter tube. How much more does it take to fill it?
11. In your journal, answer this question: How does this compare to the area and perimeter activity?

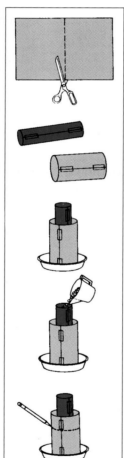

gravitational pull of the earth. It relates the action of a force (e.g., gravity) on a mass. Mass remains the same regardless of location. Children find measuring mass a more difficult concept to undertake. It is helpful for them to think of traveling through space on a spaceship. They have all seen the pictures of the astronauts beamed back to earth during space flights. They remember the floating bodies as the astronauts went through the spaceship. Their weight changed because they were no longer on earth to experience the gravitational pull of the earth. However, they still had mass because they did not turn into blobs. They looked like they did on earth before they got into the spaceship. Their form (mass) did not change.

The teaching of weight and mass can be seen through the four categories first introduced in the linear measurement section.

Direct Comparison	Indirect Comparison
Compare trucks, cars, dolls, blocks, and miscellaneous toys by hand comparison	Use a balance, where object A is compared to a known mass piece and then object B is compared to the known mass piece. The end result is a statement that object A is more or less massive than object B by transitivity.
See how much weight sinks a container in water. The book, *Who Sank the Boat?* (Allen, 1990) presents an excellent anticipatory set before children make their own foil boats (Activity 13.15) Simultaneous comparisons are seen in Activity 13.16.	Also that object A has a greater or smaller mass, than the mass piece. Some nonstandard units to use with a balance for units of mass (weight) are nails, pennies, interlocking cubes, and clay. See Activity 13.17.

Seriation	Frame of Reference
Use of rubber bands will probably be the child's first experience with spring scales. Light and heavy objects should be suspended by elastic bands and their length noted. Provide springs of all kinds—fragile and strong, long and short, extension and compression. Use a bathroom scale to measure things around the classroom as well as themselves. See Activity 13.18.	Standard weights are used on one side of a dual balance. Students begin to tell how much an object actually weighs in standard units—pounds or grams—depending on the system being studied at the time. See Activity 13.19.

Activity 13.15

| PROBLEM SOLVING | MANIPULATIVES | ESTIMATION | MATHEMATICAL CONNECTIONS |

WEIGHT WITH FOIL BOATS

MATERIALS

1. Children gather their own array of plastic toys, paper clips, and odds and ends found around the classroom.
2. Aluminum foil to make their own boats.
3. Charts and journals to record findings.
4. Metric packs—see Web site.

DIRECTIONS

1. Children form their own foil boats.
2. They predict which item will sink their boat if they put items in the boat in a particular order. They then change the order and predict again. Then they write journal entries to describe what happens.

Chart and journal sheet for foil boat activity

Round #1		Round #2	
Order into Boat	Mark When It Will Sink ✓ = Predict ☆ = Actual	Order into Boat	Mark When It Will Sink ✓ = Predict ☆ = Actual
1.		1.	
2.		2.	
3.		3.	
4.		4.	
5.		5.	
6.		6.	

Journal Entry: What did you discover? Was your prediction correct?_____

_____

Explain in your own words how the order and weight work together._____

_____

Activity 13.16

| ESTIMATION | PROBLEM SOLVING | **SIMULTANEOUS COMPARISONS** |

DIRECTIONS

1. Drop two different size balls (without a push) simultaneously from the same height.
2. Which one takes the least amount of time to reach the floor? How can you tell?

A word to the wise: If a teacher asks children to weigh in and keep a record of their weight, the teacher had better be prepared to do it too. It will be a sure request from the students. A teacher must be careful not to embarrass or cause humiliation to any student who may be overweight. Children in the United States are rapidly becoming overweight; so a health unit integrated with mathematics is quite possible, but dignity is the watchword of any such activity. If the scale has both English and metric measurements on its face, one set can be covered up with masking tape if the teacher feels that the students will be too confused with two sets of measurement tools. A teacher can convert a customary scale (usually cheaper to buy) into a metric scale by using the conversion chart in Activity 13.18. The scale is provided for the teacher to make the learning device. Children should *not* be asked to convert between scales in any activity until late in middle school if at all possible. Learning one system at a time is challenging enough! See the Extended Activities on the Web site for more practice.

Time Time is another aspect of measurement and is usually introduced with clocks and calen-

Activity 13.17

ESTIMATION   MATHEMATICAL CONNECTIONS

FINDING MASS WITH A BALANCE IN SCIENCE

DIRECTIONS

1. Build a balance to find the mass of objects using pennies, interlocking cubes, or clay, and make comparisons to determine objects with the greater mass see Figure 13.15.

   For example: five nails have a greater mass than two pennies; or three pennies have the same mass as ten interlocking cubes.

Start with a plastic ruler. The cutout parts are equidistant from each end and are measured more precisely than you can measure. This guarantees the balance will truly balance equivalent mass if cups are placed directly under the holes.

Glue wooden clothespins to plastic cups as shown. When dry, the cups will grasp the balance wherever you place them.

Drill a hole in the middle of a block of wood and screw in a wooden table leg.

Use a screw to tighten the ruler on to the table leg. Loosen the screw for easy storage. This set up costs a fraction of the price for commercial balances and will enable you to have more balances for your class.

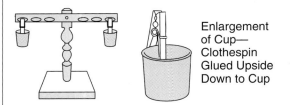

Enlargement of Cup— Clothespin Glued Upside Down to Cup

FIGURE 13.15 *Building your own balance.*

2. Estimate and record the answers before finding the actual mass.

3. Recordkeeping should indicate the status of the estimates. Hopefully, these estimates improve with experience.

---

dars. A clock measures the passage of time for each 24-hour period. Early experiences that are indirectly and unintentionally given to young children do not help them develop a clear feeling about the passage of time or the meaning of a minute or a

Activity 13.18

MATHEMATICAL CONNECTIONS   MENTAL MATH

MAKE IT LIGHT . . . REPORT THE MASS IN KILOS

WOW! LOOK HOW MUCH BETTER IT LOOKS IN KILOS.

Use the bathroom scale to do this activity. Make twenty labels for the numbers 5, 10, 15, 20 . . . 90, 95, 100. Peel back the material around the window of your scale so that the window may be removed. Then, using the table below, paste the labels over the appropriate numbers.

Weight Conversion—Bathroom Scale

kg	lb	kg	lb
5	11	65	143
10	22	70	154
15	33	75	165
20	44	80	176
25	55	85	187
30	66	90	198
35	77	95	209
40	88	100	220
45	99	105	231
50	110	110	243
55	121	115	254
60	132		

For example, the 5 would be pasted on the scale at 11, the 10 at 22, the 15 at 33, and so on.

---

second. For example, many adults and parents are guilty of saying phrases like "I'll be back in just a minute," or, "Just a second and I will help you." These inadvertent comments distort the child's understanding of how long a period of

Activity 13.19

CALCULATORS   **PROBLEM SOLVING**

MASS WITH SILVER DOLLARS

DIRECTIONS

1. If a silver dollar has a mass of 18 grams, use a calculator to determine how much money you would have if you had a kilogram of silver dollars.
2. What would be the mass of 1000 silver dollars?
3. Use a calculator to determine how many silver dollars you are worth based on your mass.
4. Do the above steps using a nickel as the unit of measure.

time is represented by the terms "minute" and "second."

Some of the children's first encounters with the concept of time measurement are general comparisons of which person or task took the least amount of time. Like other areas of measurement, since you cannot see time, you must infer it from observations of other things.

Activity 13.20

MATHEMATICAL CONNECTIONS

USE OF THE EGG TIMER IN SCIENCE

DIRECTIONS

1. Using an egg timer, record how many times you can do the following activities before the sand runs out: touch your toes, bounce a ball, play a chord on the piano, or hop in place.
2. Record how many seconds it takes for all the sand to run out.
3. Design a timer of your own, that is, water dripping from a can. Explain how the pioneers might have used your timer. Do this in your journal.
4. Explain to your class and your teacher how your timer works.

EXTENDED ACTIVITIES

CALCULATORS   **ESTIMATION**   **PROBLEM SOLVING**

MATHEMATICAL CONNECTIONS   **CHILDREN'S LITERATURE**

On the Web site (Chapter 13, Extended Activities), read/do the following:

- Using a Table and Square Centimeters
- Estimation with Graph Paper
- Metric Measurement with Area
- Using Volume
- Using Formulas
- Miniature Planet and Measurement—a Performance-Based Task
- Family Math Packets
  - Two- and Three-Dimensional Shapes
- Lesson Plan for Mathematical Proficiency
  - Learning About Capacity—Fill It Up!
- Area of 4
- Perimeter of 3
- Portfolio Assessment
  - Shiloh's Doghouse [area and perimeter]

Interpretation of Time Eventually, the need to communicate and interpret time leads to the desire for standard units of time: second, minute, hour. The teacher should give children opportunities to experience 1-minute intervals to help them gain a better perception of the passing of time. To help children develop a sense of time, have them do an activity, such as counting, bouncing a ball, listening to a story, or walking about the room, for a minute. Later, have children estimate 1-minute intervals. Have them close their eyes for about how long they feel a minute lasts and when they feel a minute has elapsed, indicate with a "thumbs-up" sign. Generally, there is a great variation among a group of children, which may be due to a lack of an intuitive feeling about the

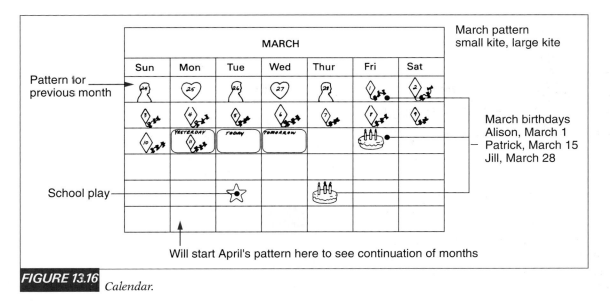

FIGURE 13.16 *Calendar.*

basic unit of time, a minute. Help children become more aware of time intervals such as 1 minute, 5 minutes, 10 minutes, and longer. This experience will clarify notions children have about the duration of time. The following activity stresses durations that go beyond 1 minute.

Understanding Passage of Time   To understand the concept of the passage of time, experiences should include activities to develop a sense of yesterday, today, and tomorrow along with the idea of the continuation of time through months. Daily calendar activities provide an excellent base. Children want to know how many more days until a special event such as a vacation, a holiday, or a school happening. With a calendar available as a reference point, the child builds some clear sense of the passage of time. The calendar shown in Figure 13.16 illustrates the many concepts included: yesterday, today, tomorrow, days of the week, days in a week, days in the current month, name of the current month, special days of that month. In the primary grades, including a pattern for the days adds interest, builds an awareness of the previous month and the coming month to see the continuation of time, and reinforces previous patterning skills. During the calendar time of each school day, the teacher can include discussion about the weather and temperature, which can be excellent graphing activities (covered in Chapter 15), as well as events that will occur that day and any sharing children might want to do.

Understanding Time Sequence   Understanding time sequence is another aspect of developing an awareness of time apart from the simple reading of

a clock. Have children arrange pictures of various events to indicate the order in which the events happen. For example, the pictures might include a child brushing his or her teeth, eating breakfast, just waking up, and leaving for school; another might be a child with a deflated balloon, with a large inflated balloon, the popped balloon, and the child just beginning to blow up the balloon. The task is to arrange these pictures in a logical time sequence. First experiences should involve comparing events during longer time periods such as events in their day: eat breakfast, go to school, play after school, go to bed. Many commercially made time sequence cards are available. In the classroom, many opportunities are present to discuss time sequence. For instance, the teacher might say, "First I want you to get your crayons, then color the worksheet, cut out the pictures, and put them in the collection tray."

Children also need to develop a sense of the duration of various events and decide which event takes longer. Have children think about how long it takes to do certain things. An activity might be to look at pictures of pairs of events and decide which takes longer: brushing your teeth or taking a bath; walking to school or time spent in school; giving a dog a bath or playing a soccer game. The problem of comparing events that cannot occur simultaneously or of indicating "how long" for a single event leads children to the use of various units of time measure.

Once the children are ready to begin telling time, clock-reading skills can be introduced. Children must learn to read a variety of clock faces with hands that have different sizes, colors, and lengths. Some clocks have a second hand, which may add confusion. Although digital clocks are popular and easier to read initially, they do not

Activity 13.21

ESTIMATION   PROBLEM SOLVING   MANIPULATIVES   **USING A PENDULUM**

DIRECTIONS

1. Set up a pendulum with a string and any object attached to the end of the string.
2. Can you change the beat of a pendulum? In what way(s) can you do this?
3. Make two pendulums that swing the same. Then alter one so that it swings twice as often as the other.
4. Use the pendulum to compute how long it takes to walk the length of the room.

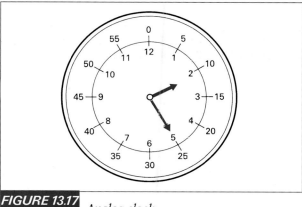

FIGURE 13.17 *Analog clock.*

allow children to see the relative position of the displayed time to the next hour or to the times that come before or after it.

To simplify the task of learning to tell time, one approach is to begin with only an hour-face clock. Using only an hour hand allows children to read the time as soon as the numerals 1 to 12 are recognized. The hour hand can be moved to a position a little past the hour and the child can learn to interpret this as "a little after," and when the hour hand is almost to a number the child can confidently call this "almost _____ o'clock."

When children have success with the hour hand and feel comfortable with it, the minute hand can be introduced. This process usually begins with the hour and half-hour times. The child should find the shorter hand first, read the hour, and then look at the longer hand. A large wooden clock with gears is helpful for children to see the hands moving together. Allow each child many opportunities to manipulate the clock to explore its features.

When children are ready to tell time to the nearest 5 minutes (usually in second grade), a prerequisite is being able to count by fives to 60. A paper plate clock may be made for the child to practice counting by fives as each numeral on the face is touched (Figure 13.17). The teacher should emphasize that these numbers indicate minutes after on-the-hour times. To simplify the task of understanding time, we suggest that children learn only to give the minutes after the hour. This is in agreement with reading time on digital clocks and

reduces teaching the concept of "minutes before the hour."

Children need practice on seeing how the time represented on a digital clock would look on an analog clock. They can begin with the digital time and use Logo to see the analog time. Another recommendation is to refrain from teaching the terms "quarter after," "quarter to," and "half past." These are outdated terms and add more confusion since the terms "quarter" and "half" are associated with 25 and 50 in money and now indicate 15 and 30 in time. It is better to reserve these terms for money.

Temperature

Label a thermometer with a common event for certain temperatures. This method helps the child build a frame of reference to relate the number to real events. Careful planning must be included in developing an ability for the child to read the thermometer. Introduce the concept of temperature into the curriculum with concrete experiences and establish frames of reference; for; example, 32°F is the freezing point of water and 212°F is the boiling point of water, whereas in the metric system, water freezes at 0°C and boils at 100°C.

Activity 13.22

PROBLEM SOLVING   MANIPULATIVES   **EXPERIMENTS WITH TEMPERATURE**

MATERIALS

- Thermometers with both Celsius and Fahrenheit measurements
- Ice cubes and a pan of boiling water (on a hot plate . . . teacher monitors this station carefully)

DIRECTIONS

Students work in pairs or small groups to do the following experiments, recording their findings in their math journals for later discussion in class:

MATH JOURNAL FOR TEMPERATURE EXPERIMENTS

	CUSTOMARY SYSTEM	METRIC SYSTEM
1. Place the thermometer under the arm for three minutes. Record temperatures.	____°F	____°C
2. Place the thermometer on an ice cube. Now in boiling water.	____°F	____°C
3. Place the thermometer on the asphalt part of the playground in the sun for four minutes.	____°F	____°C
4. Place the thermometer in the shade in the grass by the playground for four minutes.	____°F	____°C
5. Place the thermometer on your desk in the room for four minutes.	____°F	____°C

6. Think of other places to measure temperature. Check with your teacher before measuring.

Measured_____ ____°F ____°C
Conditions_____
Measured_____ ____°F ____°C
Conditions_____
Measured_____ ____°F ____°C
Conditions_____
Measured_____ ____°F ____°C
Conditions_____

Write what you learned from your observations. Be ready to share with others in class discussion.

Money

Of all the measurement systems, money is the one that finds its way into other topics most readily. Because money has a decimal component, it is a part of the study of the decimal system in many school textbooks. It also makes its way into many problem-solving tasks because it is a real-world reality. It helps make word problems authentic. So you have seen the application of money in various chapters throughout this text.

As a measurement system, it has every common foundational element as other measurement systems with the exception of partitioning (Figure 13.2). Because there is no separation into predictable, equalized units, money may be regarded as lacking full-fledged membership in the measurement system schema. It is possible to organize instruction into the four categories of measurement process.

Direct Comparison	Indirect Comparison
Children have sacks of pennies, nickels, etc. (the units must be the same denominations in all sacks) Pull money out of a sack and compare the amounts—for example: "Shalonda has more nickels than Topaz." "Benji has less pennies than Rachael."	From general units that are alike to comparison of different amounts to each other. For example—eight nickels is forty cents and four dimes is forty cents. Therefore, eight nickels is the same amount as four dimes. This is transitivity.

Seriation	Frames of Reference
The toy airplane cost $4.95. I have a five-dollar bill. I will have enough to pay for it. I will get $.05 back.	It is easier to count the amount of money to put into the bank if counting by tens to get to $100 than to count by pennies–
The concept of making change fits a seriation scale. For example—I gave the clerk a ten-dollar bill for something that costs $8.49. The clerk counted my change in continuous quantities (Figure I3.2) by giving me One penny, that's, $8.50 Fifty cents, that's, $9.00 One dollar, that's, $10.00	Similarly it is easier to count by nickels to get to $.10.
	Very young children have not conserved money nor do they have a realistic frame of reference when they ask their parents for a nickel because it is (physically) bigger than a dime; therefore they think it is worth more.

Generally, after children leave the very young years, they do not have trouble understanding how each denomination of coins and bills fits into the system. They learn to count money quite well. The built-in real reward of having money to buy the things they want helps this learning process.

Putting It All Together

The children's literature book, *Measuring Penny*, is a wonderful way to review all the measurement systems. The author, Loreen Leedy, shows how measurement systems are used in the real-world. She does this by using her dog, Penny, as the example. The book starts out with a school assignment on measurement. Many teachers use the

MANIPULATIVES MATHEMATICAL CONNECTIONS CULTURAL RELEVANCE

PORTFOLIO CHILDREN'S LITERATURE

EXTENDED ACTIVITIES

On the Web site (Chapter 13, Extended Activities), read/do the following:

- Social Studies and Science
- Cuisenaire Rod Clock
- Portfolio Assessment: The Bike Ramp
- Family Math Packets
  - Calendar Measurement
  - Time Measurement with Clocks
  - Money Game—Building and Buying
- Lesson Plans for Mathematical Proficiency
  - What Time Is It?

book to entice their own students to look for interesting things to measure from the perspective of all eight of the measurement systems. See the Extended Activities for more practice with time, temperature, and money.

ASSESSMENT TO HELP STUDENTS WITH SPECIAL NEEDS

As you can see by the six kinds of measurement we have covered in this chapter, measurement is a broad subject in elementary and middle school. Each kind of measurement could have its own rubric for assessment of what students know about the intricate workings within each measurement system. That could literally be a text in and of itself. We have chosen, instead, to concentrate on two areas where students have the most difficulty. For young elementary children, it is the concept of time. For older students, it is the concept of perimeter versus area.

Common Misconceptions of Time

Deficiencies in telling time may relate to insufficient real-life experiences reading time on a clock face. Today's child has quick access to a digital clock, which cannot give the needed exposure to telling time in a meaningful way. A child may be able to read "9:42" but will often not know that this time comes between 9:00 and 10:00. Time elapse becomes difficult to relate for the child. These children need experiences focused on constant reading of a clock face. They need to read the time every 5 minutes to actually witness the meaning of an hour and to see how the hour hand moves only a small distance during each 5-minute interval.

Because the minute hand is constantly changing position, some children have trouble seeing time elapse. When the previous minute hand remains in view as the count continues, children can see how many minutes have passed while doing an activity.

Correcting Misconceptions with the Concept of Time Two common errors in reading time are reversing the hour hand and the minute hand and reading the actual numbers indicated rather than assigning the minute hand appropriate time values.

Reversing the Hour and Minute Hands An example of the first error is the child reading 10:20 as 4:10, and an example of the second error is the child reading 10:20 as 10:04. See Figure 13.18.

To remedy these problems, children should be given a progression of clock faces; each one a little more detailed than the preceding one. This procedure allows children to focus on each part of the clock independently, first working with hour-face clocks then minute-face clocks.

Reading Actual Numbers Another aspect of understanding telling time is to relate the numbers 1 to 12 with counting by intervals of five. A flexible number line might help students to see this relationship. The

FIGURE 13.18 *Error patterns in telling time.*

Activity 13.23

MANIPULATIVES   MAKING CLOCKS

MATERIALS
- Paper plates
- Brad fastener
- Grosgrain ribbon or adding machine tape
- Permanent marking pen

PROCEDURE
Divide the paper plate into twelve congruent regions and label with the numbers 1 to 12 as on a clock face. Cut two clock hands from another piece of cardboard or poster board and attach in the center with a brad fastener. Take the grosgrain ribbon and stretch around the circumference of the plate. Cut the ribbon and tape it around the plate. Mark the ribbon at each place that matches with the clock numbers. Untape the ribbon and divide each segment into five equal regions. This will look like a flexible number line with the numbers marked in fives to 60 and with the increments by ones noted between the fives.

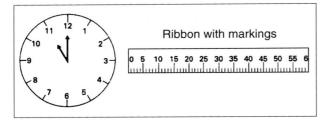

following activity is provided to show a teaching aid that can be made for the children's use.

Creating a Rubric for the Assessment of Time Concepts
The following child's work gives you an excellent opportunity to start developing rubrics you can use in your own classroom to assess children with difficulties. This activity is one that shows your ability to be a true professional in today's education community. Save it for your professional portfolio for job interviews.

Field-Independent Learners
Students who process information successively (from the parts to the whole) perform geoboard activities better if the area of the polygon to be measured is partitioned into segments within the polygon and then all the segments will be added up

Activity 13.24

PORTFOLIO   PORTFOLIO ASSESSMENTS

For Teacher Reflection of Students' Work in Measurement

DIRECTIONS
1. Look at this child's journal explanation in Figure 13.19. If you had to write your own rubric to score children on their understanding of time based on these problems, what would you consider prerequisite concepts?
   a. Decide what parts are crucial and what parts are just finishing touches to a true understanding of the concept.
   b. Give a numerical score to each part (more points for the important parts, less points for the less involved parts). Figure what would be the score for a person who had a perfect understanding of the concept of time as measured in the activities seen here.
   c. What would it look like as a score if the child totally misunderstood everything about the concepts of time as measured in these tasks?
2. How would this child's score measure based on your rubric? Perfect score = _____; lowest score = _____; percent this child understands_____?
3. Include the rubric in your Professional Portfolio for Job Interviews along with your analysis of each child's understanding in this activity. Other samples are on the Web site.

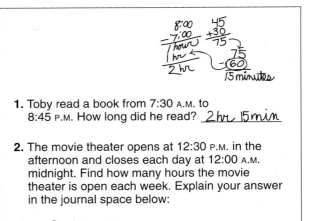

FIGURE 13.19   *Student's work with time concepts.*

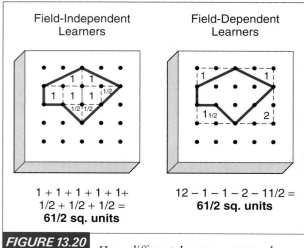

1 + 1 + 1 + 1 + 1+
1/2 + 1/2 + 1/2 =
61/2 sq. units

12 − 1 − 1 − 2 − 11/2 =
61/2 sq. units

FIGURE 13.20   *How different learners approach area with geoboards.*

to find the total area. The left geoboard in Figure 13.20 shows a sample activity as a field-independent learner would perform it. The solid black line identifies the original polygon. The student uses smaller geobands to divide the figure into unit segments.

Field-Dependent Learners

Students who process information simultaneously (from the whole to the individual parts) perform geoboard activities better if the polygon to be measured is included in a whole rectangular frame from which the outer segments can be subtracted. The remaining polygon inside the solid black line is the square area measurement. The geoboard on the right of Figure 13.20 shows the action movements as a field-dependent learner would perform them.

Students with special needs may have trouble obtaining correct answers to area geoboard problems when doing the calculations in one of the ways shown in Figure 13.20. Encourage them to try the other learning/processing style. Frequently, the change helps correct the misconceptions. This seems to hold true for all students—not just elementary ones. The authors have watched adult learners profit from a change in learning/processing style when errors occurred in geoboard activities. If the geoboard activities in this chapter seem difficult, try doing them again, using the opposite learning/processing style.

Portfolio Assessment for the Relationship of Pi

The third grader whose work appears in Figure 13.21 is a field-dependent learner who does very well in mathematics when given the chance to see

Object	C	d	C+d	C/d	C−d	C×d
Soda can	8.25	2.50	10.75	3.30	5.75	20.625
Coffee can	12.50	4	16.50	3.125	8.50	50
Plate	24	8	32	3	16	192
Glass	9	3	12	3	6	27
Wastebasket	25	8.50	33.50	3	16.50	212.50
	Total =		104.75	154.25	52.75	502.125

by Michael
Circumference and diameter project.

1. What patterns or relationships do you notice?

On 1st and total have all decimals.
On 3rd and 4th no decimals.
On 2nd row, − goes decimal no decimal decimal decimal decimal no decimal
On 5th row it goes no decimal decimal decimal no decimal decimal decimal

2. Which column show a constant relationship between circumference and diameter?

C/d

3. What is the average value of circumference divided by diameter? 3

4. What can you say about the ratio between circumference and diameter?

It would always come out to an answer of 3.

FIGURE 13.21   *Circumference and diameter project.*

the whole pattern of things. This task was given to him with the instructions that he was going to have the chance to measure three-dimensional objects and look for a pattern as he filled in the chart. As a part of the constructed response questions at the end of the chapter, you will be asked to give him a score on the five-point rubric scale. Are you surprised that a third grader could do this well? Learning style makes all the difference. Use the assessment scoring guide (Figure 3.23) to work out a more detailed evaluation of Michael's work and where you feel he should be directed in the study of measurement concepts.

SUMMARY

- More stress is being placed on the common foundational elements of measurement systems in the elementary and middle schools.

- Measurement studies are linking four specific mental processes with students' abilities to understand the concepts of measurement.

- Linear measurement is the key to understanding both area and volume.
- When studying area and volume, the order of study does not seem to matter as long as the understandings of linear measurement are firmly established.

- Time and money are frequently difficult concepts for young children.
- Measurement must be studied from a hands-on perspective if children are to grasp the subtleties of the seven measurement systems covered in elementary and middle school.

PRAXIS II™-STYLE QUESTIONS

Answers to this chapter's Praxis II™-style questions are in the instructor's manual.

Multiple Choice Format

1. A child -tells a playmate, "My doll is taller than your doll." The child is using
   a. transitivity
   b. iteration
   b. direct comparison
   b. indirect comparison

2. The _____ were the first people to use systems of standard measurement. They are the ancestors of the _____ children in our classroom
   a. Egyptians; African American
   b. Native Americans; Native American
   b. Chinese; Asian American
   b. Both a and b

3. The _____ of an object does not change location even when measuring its gravitational pull from the earth:
   a. mass
   b. weight
   b. capacity
   b. None of the above

4. After watching the Video Vignette, "Pizza Perimeters," a teacher had the elementary students make two figures with the same square units of area. Which student(s) below will more readily understand the next teaching concept that even when areas are the same, the perimeters may be different?

   Student A   Student B   Student C

   a. Student A
   b. Student B
   b. Student C
   b. Both a and c

Constructed Response Format

5. Name the eight common foundational elements of measurement and give an example of each one.

6. Choose the concept of area or volume measurement and create a chart showing the categories of direct comparison, indirect comparison, seriation, and frames of reference. Give an activity for each category that could be used when introducing students to area or volume.

7. Devise a graphic aid to help students remember a proportional relationship among units in one of the measurements systems studied in the chapter. The gallon coder is an example of one such devise.

8. Think of common things students know well from their environment. Create a benchmark or frame of reference for the following measures:

1 decimeter	1 inch
1 decagram	1 pound
l liter	1 quart

9. Think of Michael in the last portfolio assessment and score his conceptual understanding of *pi* using the five-point rubric scale. Justify your choice.

Integrating Technology

Internet Activities

Measurement Scavenger Hunts
Key one of these Internet-based scavenger hunts.

Web sites

Go to the *Figure This!* Web sites (**http://www.figurethis.org**) and follow their links to this NSF-funded program. Look for the area and volume measurement activities. They were written for parents and upper elementary and middle school students alike.

> A money challenge is called—"How can you use old Stamps?"
> Fitting popcorn into a cylinder (capacity) is called—"Which one would you buy?"

Go to the NCTM Illuminations Web site (**http://illuminations.nctm.org/**). The Web site is interactive and adapts measurement ideas to things young children can do. A good example is the measurement of the turtle paths in Logo or Turtle Geometry. One turtle step is a millimeter. Children are encouraged to have the turtle take 10 steps at a time . . . in effect moving the turtle 1 centimeter at a time.

Go to the megapennies Web site to practice counting huge sums of-pennies at (**http://www.kokogiak.com/megapenny/default.asp**)

National Library of Virtual Manipulatives
http://nlvm.usu.edu/en/nav/vlibrary.html
(also in Spanish)
Click on "Measurement" and try a variety of these activities with virtual manipulatives.

CHILDREN'S LITERATURE

Allen, Pamela. *Mr. Archimedes' Bath*. New York: Lothrop, Lee & Shepard Books, 1980.

Allen, Pamela. *Who Sunk the Boat?* Sandeastle Books, 1990.

Carle, Eric. *The Grouchy Ladybug*. New York: Crowell, 1977.

Clement, Rod. *Counting on Frank*. Milwaukee, WI: Gareth Stevens Publishing, 1991.

DiSpezio, Michael. *Visual Foolery*. Montreal: Tormont, 1995.

Hoff, Syd. *Lengthy*. New York: G. P. Putnam's Sons, 1964.

Lacapa, Michael, and Kathleen Lacapa. *Less Than Half, More Than Whole*. Flagstaff, AZ: Northland Publishing, 1994.

Lionni, Leo. *Inch by Inch*. New York: Astor-Honor, 1960.

Morris, Ann. *Houses and Homes*. New York: Lothrop, Lee &Shepard Books, 1992.

Myller, Rolf. *How Big Is a Foot?* New York: Dell Publishing, 1990.

Scieszka, Jon. *Math Curse*, New York: Viking, 1995.

Seuss, Dr. *Green Eggs and Ham*. New York: Random House, 1963.

Singer, Marilyn. *Nine O'Clock Lullaby*. New York: HarperCollins Children's Books, 1991.

Tompert, Ann. *Grandfather Tang's Story. A Tale Told with Tangrams*. New York: Crown Publishers, 1990.

Algebra and Algebraic Thinking

Chapter 14

At the Start ~~~~ Know What Children Will Be Doing . . .

NCTM Curriculum Focal Points—	See . . .
Grade 6 ~~ Writing, interpreting, and using mathematical expressions and equations	Figure 14.12
Grade 7 ~~ Developing an understanding of operations on all rational numbers and solving linear equations	Activity 14.20
Grade 8 ~~ Analyzing and representing linear functions and solving linear equations and systems of linear equations	Activity 14.11

A partial listing as it pertains to Algebra from NCTM *Curriculum Focal Points* (2006, pages 18–20).

WHERE'S THE MATHEMATICS? CONCEPTUAL UNDERSTANDING OF PATTERNS, FUNCTIONS, AND ALGEBRA

More than a few parents and teachers alike raised an eyebrow or two when NCTM included algebra in the curriculum standards for elementary school. If you think of algebra as that middle school or high I school course you took—learning how to solve equations for the "unknown *x*," finding the slope and intercepts of lines, for example—then you might have good reason to be nervous about introducing algebra in prekindergarten or any of the other primary and upper elementary grades. However, it is clear in the themes for the standard on algebra (see Figure 14.1 on p. 396), set forth in the *Principles and Standards* (NCTM,

2000), that the focus in the primary and upper elementary grades is on developing *algebraic thinking*.

What is algebraic thinking? Algebraic thinking has been described as "the kinds of generalizing that precede or accompany the use of algebra" (Smith, 2003). To think algebraically, you must.

1. Have a conceptual understanding of patterns, relations, and functions
2. Be able to represent and analyze mathematical situations and structures
3. Be able to use mathematical models in representing quantitative relationships
4. Be able to analyze change in a variety of contexts (Friel, 2001)

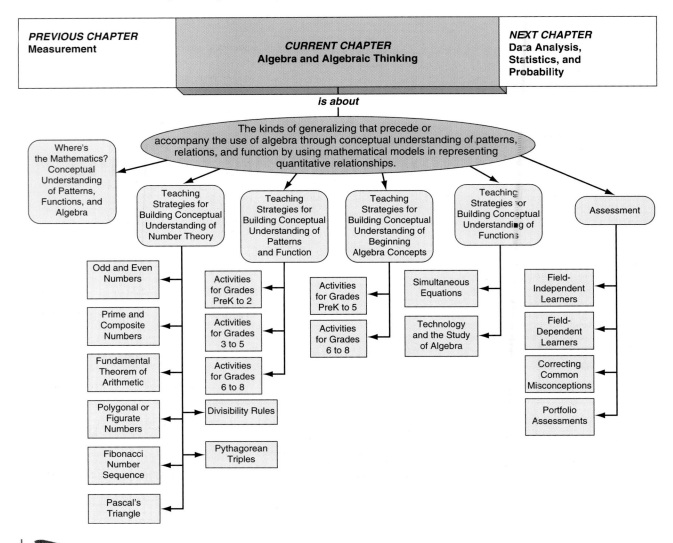

| PREVIOUS CHAPTER
Measurement | **CURRENT CHAPTER**
Algebra and Algebraic Thinking | NEXT CHAPTER
Data Analysis,
Statistics, and
Probability |

is about

The kinds of generalizing that precede or accompany the use of algebra through conceptual understanding of patterns, relations, and function by using mathematical models in representing quantitative relationships.

Where's the Mathematics? Conceptual Understanding of Patterns, Functions, and Algebra

Teaching Strategies for Building Conceptual Understanding of Number Theory

Teaching Strategies for Building Conceptual Understanding of Patterns and Function

Teaching Strategies for Building Conceptual Understanding of Beginning Algebra Concepts

Teaching Strategies for Building Conceptual Understanding of Functions

Assessment

Odd and Even Numbers

Prime and Composite Numbers

Fundamental Theorem of Arithmetic

Polygonal or Figurate Numbers

Fibonacci Number Sequence

Pascal's Triangle

Activities for Grades PreK to 2

Activities for Grades 3 to 5

Activities for Grades 6 to 8

Divisibility Rules

Pythagorean Triples

Activities for Grades PreK to 5

Activities for Grades 6 to 8

Simultaneous Equations

Technology and the Study of Algebra

Field-Independent Learners

Field-Dependent Learners

Correcting Common Misconceptions

Portfolio Assessments

SELF-HELP QUESTIONS

1. Do I understand the role of number theory in developing algebraic thinking skills?

2. Do I know the divisibility rules for 2, 3, 4, 5, 6, 7, 8, 9, 10, 11?

3. Do I know how to find the prime factors of a number?

4. Do I understand the difference between the least common multiple and greatest common factor?

5. Do I understand the importance of patterning in students' development of algebraic thinking skills?

6. What do my students need to know about algebra?

7. Do I understand how to use technology with my students as they develop algebraic thinking skills and study algebra?

Students' abilities to think algebraically evolve as they engage in learning activities that meet NCTM's expectations for algebra. For instance, in prekindergarten and kindergarten, students begin to develop their ability to recognize and extend patterns. By the end of the upper elementary, grades, students are generalizing patterns verbally and symbolically.

Standard

Instructional programs from prekindergarten through grade 12 should enable all students to

Understand patterns, relations, and functions.
Represent and analyze mathematical situations and structures using algebraic symbols.
Use mathematical models to represent and understand quantitative relationships.
Analyze change in various contexts.

Grades prekindergarten to 2	Grades 3 to 5
In prekindergarten through grade 2 all student	In grades 3 to 5 all students should
Sort, classify, and order objects by size, number, and other properties.	Describe, extend, and make generalizations about geometric and numeric patterns.
Recognize, describe, and extend patterns such as sequences of sounds and shapes or simple numeric patterns and translate from one representation to another.	Represent and analyze patterns and functions, using words, tables, and graphs.
Analyze how both repeating and growing patterns are generated.	Identify such properties as commutativity, associativity, and distributivity, and use them to compute the whole numbers.
Illustrate general principles and properties of operations, such as commutativity, using specific numbers.	Represent the idea of a variable as an unknown quantity using a letter or a symbol.
Use concrete, pictorial, and verbal representations to develop an understanding of invented and conventional symbolic notations.	Express mathematical relationships using equations.
Model situations that involve the addition and the subtraction of whole numbers, using objects, pictures, and symbols.	Model problem situations with objects and use representations such as graphs, tables, and equations to draw conclusions.
Describe qualitative change, such as a student's growing taller; describe quantitative change, such as a student's growing two inches in one year.	Investigate how a change in one variable relates to a change in a second variable.
	Identify and describe situations with constant or varying rates of change and compare them.

Grades 6 to 8

In grades 6 to 8 all students should
Represent, analyze, and generalize a variety of patterns with tables, graphs, words, and, when possible, symbolic rule.
Relate and compare different forms of representation for a relationship.
Identify functions as linear or nonlinear and contrast their properties from tables, graphs, or equations.
Develop an initial conceptual understanding of different uses of variables.
Explore relationships between symbolic expressions and graphs of lines, paying particular attention to the meaning of intercept and slope.
Use symbolic algebra to represent situations to solve problems, especially those that involve linear relationships.
Recognize and generate equivalent forms for simple algebraic expressions and solve linear equations.
Model and solve contextual problems using various representations, such as graphs, tables, and equations.
Use graphs to analyze the nature of changes in quantities in linear relationships.

FIGURE 14.1 *NCTM expecitation of algebra.* NCTM Principles and Standards for School Mathematics *(2000, pages 394–395).*

Mathematicians throughout the ages have been fascinated with patterns, and many interesting relationships have been developed during the evolution of mathematics knowledge. Children are usually exposed to these ideas first with manipulatives, then with numbers beginning in PreK to 2, extended in grades 3 to 5, and continuing through middle school. The units may be independent of the sequential skill development normally associated with the study of numeration; basic facts, and algorithms. Frequently, textbooks use a discovery approach to simulate activities similar to those experienced by early mathematicians. Some children enjoy this approach and are challenged to find new

patterns, but not all students will find patterns fascinating.

According to the NCTM *Principles and Standards* (NCTM, 2000), looking for patterns is the essence of inductive reasoning. As students explore problems with patterns, conjectures are made that must be Validated. This process encourages students to develop supporting logical arguments. Cooperative learning may help students maintain concentration during the study of number theory concepts.

Number theory explores the relationships (patterns) between and among counting numbers and their properties. Specific definitions and properties of each concept are introduced when appropriate in the following section on teaching strategies. Beginning concepts include odd and even numbers, prime and composite numbers, greatest common factor, and least common multiple.

Patterns, therefore, lead to relations and functions in the middle grades. When relations and functions are generalized to variables rather than specific numbers or values, the beginning understanding of algebra is developed. Algebra takes the relations in simple arithmetic and applies the pattern as a generalization statement. Hence, $3 + 2 = 5$ becomes any number x added to any other number y yields a different distinct number z such that $x + y = z$.

The term *relations* defines the relationships seen in sets of things and seen in patterns, either within the same set or among sets. A *relation* associates the elements or patterns seen in one set to the elements or patterns seen in another set. For example, 7 *is greater than* 5 tells a relationship between 7 and 5. A *function* is a specific relation in which every element in one set is associated with only one element in another set. Using the example of 7 and 5, there are many numbers that are greater than 5, but only one number, 7, is associated with 5 if the function $+2$ is applied to the number 5.

Chapter 6 presented many ideas and activities in working with patterns found in colors, shapes, and rhythms in the primary grades. The material related to patterns in this chapter will focus primarily on number patterns. There are activities in the primary grades that can be used to start children thinking about interesting patterns in numbers. A gradual progression is seen from primary grade number pattern relationships to functions to algebra by the end of middle school (Bay-Williams, 2001). The examples found in the Teaching Strategies section are meant to model this gradual transition from number patterns to algebra.

TEACHING STRATEGIES FOR BUILDING CONCEPTUAL UNDERSTANDING OF NUMBER THEORY

Children in PreK to 5 explore many number patterns. One of the first patterns is the concept of even and odd numbers. Beginning work with prime and composite numbers is also a part of the early grades. Some number sequences, like the Fibonacci sequence and Pascal's triangle, can be introduced near the end of the K to 5 period. The exponential ideas involved with Pascal's triangle will need to wait until the grades 6 to 8 middle school years.

Odd and Even Numbers

Children learn to tell the difference between odd and even numbers by pairing manipulative materials. A number is defined as *even* if it can be divided by 2 with no remainder. A number is defined as *odd* if it has a remainder of 1 when divided by 2. Activity 14.1 and Figure 14.2 show some of the materials children can use in the primary grades to discover odd and even numbers through pairing (which is dividing a counting number by 2).

Activity 14.1

MANIPULATIVES   PROBLEM SOLVING

MANIPULATIVES WITH ODD AND EVEN NUMBERS

MATERIALS
- See Figure 14.2.

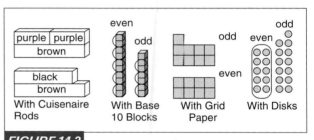

FIGURE 14.2 *Concrete manipulatives to explore odd and even numbers.*

DIRECTIONS
1. Look at the materials shown in Figure 14.2. These are just some of the many items that can be used to show the relationship of odd and even numbers.
2. Think of other manipulatives you could use to show the relationships. Draw them to share with others in a cooperative group setting.
3. Think of real-world mathematics where odd and even numbers occur.

    Example: Partitioned sections of candy boxes (even) after one person has chosen one candy (odd)

4. Prepare for oral discourse by thinking how children would be expected to explain odd and even numbers from the examples they bring to class. This could be a good homework assignment. Have them orally explain to others how the material shows odd or even concepts.

From the Concrete to the Connecting Stage

Children should be given the opportunity to draw the pictorial representations of many numbers while deciding whether the numbers are even or odd. Children will form an accurate definition of even and odd numbers if allowed to compare and contrast the paired and nonpaired sets as seen in Activity 14.1. The students can then apply their understanding of the definition of odd and even numbers to the number line as shown in Activity 14.2.

From the Connecting to the Symbolic Stage

Children can experiment with odd and even numbers to generalize a rule about the properties of such numbers in addition and multiplication. Activity 14.3 demonstrates one approach to such an experiment.

Students enjoy comparing charts of classmates to see whether the same rule will apply when other number combinations are used. Teachers should encourage students to see that the digit on the right (in the units' place) of any multidigit number is the one that determines whether a number is odd or even. Students can problem solve further possibilities.

Activity 14.2

PROBLEM SOLVING **MATHEMATICAL CONNECTIONS** NUMBER THEORY

MATERIALS

Number line

Manipulatives, such as those used in Activity 14.1

DIRECTIONS

1. Students model the counting numbers with manipulatives—pairing them to show odd and even numbers.
2. Then, the numeral for each even number, e, is designated on the number line. (The pattern will be clearer if the designation, e, is written above the even numbers and the designation, o, is written below the odd numbers.)
3. The same procedure is followed for each odd number, o.

Children will be able to predict what larger numerals will be even or odd once the pattern is established. Note that zero is considered an even number because it would fit the pattern shown on the number line.

Activity 14.3

CALCULATORS **PROBLEM SOLVING** ADDITION WITH ODD AND EVEN NUMBERS

DIRECTIONS

- Using a calculator, make a list of what happens when you add one even number to another even number. Do the same for odd numbers. Then combine both odd and even numbers and record the results.
- Set up a chart like the one below. Create more examples, following the pattern as established.
- Generalize a rule for each set.

Even + Even	**Odd + Odd**	**Even + Odd**
$2 + 4 =$	$7 + 3 =$	$2 + 11 =$
$106 + 38 =$	$201 + 55 =$	$348 + 29 =$
$1346 + 2794 =$	$2403 + 9825 =$	$7374 + 5689 =$

(Create some more examples of large and small numbers.)

Rule:	**Rule:**	**Rule:**
_____	_____	_____
_____	_____	_____

EXTENDED ACTIVITIES

PROBLEM SOLVING   **CALCULATORS**

Name of Activity
- Multiplication with Odd and Even Numbers
- Odd and Even Numbers

Students who enjoy problem-solving explorations like the preceding one can be challenged to find many more combinations on their own time and share them with the class. Two additional activities can be found on the Web site, Extended Activities in Chapter 14.

Prime and Composite Numbers

A *prime number* is an integer that is evenly divisible only by itself and 1; that is, only itself and 1 are factors of the number. Zero and 1 are not considered prime numbers. A *composite number* is a number that has more than itself and 1 as factors. Therefore, 7 is a prime number, whereas 8 is a composite number.

7	8
7 × 1	8 × 1
1 × 7	1 × 8
	2 × 4
	4 × 2
	2 × 2 × 2
	and so forth

There is only one even number that fits the definition for a prime number. Activity 14.4 invites you to consider this "mystery prime."

The Sieve of Eratosthenes   How can we know if a number is prime? The ancient Greeks had a method to find primes of a given number, and through the centuries it has become known as the Sieve of Eratosthenes. More than 2000 years ago the Greek mathematician Eratosthenes created a process to help sieve (filter out) the composite numbers, leaving only the prime numbers. There are many interesting patterns to be found by using the Sieve of Eraosthenes. Teachers can

Activity 14.4

MENTAL MATH   **THE MYSTERY EVEN NUMBER PRIME**

There is only one even number that fits the definition for a prime number. Think of many even numbers. Visualize their factors in your mind. Which factor, beside one and itself, does every even number have?

Did you think of two? The definition of an even number means that two will always be a factor of every even number. What about the two itself? Visualize the factors of two. What are they? The factors of two can only be one and itself (two). Therefore, two meets the criteria for a prime number, and it is the only even number that can be prime.

lead students to discover many of the patterns on their own by asking a few leading questions such as the ones found in the problem-solving exploration that follows in Activity 14.5

Activity 14.5

PROBLEM SOLVING   **CULTURAL RELEVANCE**   **NUMBER PATTERNS WITH THE SIEVE OF ERATOSTHENES**

DIRECTIONS

1. You are asked to use six colors on the Sieve of Eratosthenes (see chart at end of step 4) so that you can see the number patterns more easily. The colors of yellow, green, pink, light blue, red, and black are suggested, but any eye-catching colors will do.

2. On the chart in step 4, find the first prime number, which is 2, and circle it with a red marker. Now slash (/) all the multiples of 2 using the red marker. You have just eliminated all even numbers because they are composites. Note the color pattern you have just created.

3. Now find the next prime which is 3 and circle it with a green marker. Sieve (/) all the multiples of 3 using the green marker. Some numbers now have a red and a green slash. You can easily see the numbers that are multiples of both 2 and 3. Note the color pattern created by the green slashes.

4. Follow the same procedure using this color code:

Primes	Color
five	= yellow
seven	= black
eleven	= pink
all others	= light blue

1	2	3	4	5	6	7	8	9	10
11	12	13	14	15	16	17	18	19	20
21	22	23	24	25	26	27	28	29	30
31	32	33	34	35	36	37	38	39	40
41	42	43	44	45	46	47	48	49	50
51	52	53	54	55	56	57	58	59	60
61	62	63	64	65	66	67	68	69	70
71	72	73	74	75	76	77	78	79	80
81	82	83	84	85	86	87	88	89	90
91	92	93	94	95	96	97	98	99	100

Questions Based on the Sieve of Eratosthenes:

1. How many of the first 100 numbers are prime?

2. Of the first 25 numbers, what percent are multiples *of* three numbers? Of the second 25 numbers, what percent are multiples of three numbers?

3. Would you expect this number to Increase or decrease as we continue through the number system? Why?

4. The number of primes in the first 50 numbers is what fractional portion of the total primes in the first 100 numbers? What about the second 50 numbers?

5. Will the relationship found in question 4 hold for the second 100 numbers? What could be done to find out?

6. When is the first time that a multiple of 7 has not been crossed out by a multiple of a smaller prime?

7. What do you notice about multiples of 11? Predict at which number the multiple of 11 will be crossed out for the first time with no smaller primes as its multiple.

A person can figure out which multidigit numbers are prime by using the Sieve of Eratosthenes. The examples in the Extended Activities on the Web site are performed the way mathematicians and upper grade students figured the problem of primes for centuries. The same process can be placed in a computer program to show what Eratosthenes and others could have done with a computer if one had been available. Such a program is shown with middle

EXTENDED ACTIVITIES

COMPUTERS   CULTURAL RELEVANCE   CALCULATORS

Name of Activity

● Large Numbers with the Sieve of Eratosthenes

● Finding Prime Numbers Like the Ancient Ones Did

● Large Primes and the Computer with Middle School Students

school students using the computer language of Basic.

You can see that a calculator can be used with large primes such as 1033 or 1601. Early mathematicians used the long division algorithms to work such problems. In today's world, a computer can be programmed to check on large numbers without the need to use the Sieve of Eratosthenes in the detail we have just gone through.

A person exposed to long division algorithms, calculators, and computer methods can appreciate the power of computers. A student who has experimented with the Sieve of Eratosthenes can see the patterns and will not waste time checking numbers like 30, 125, 144, or 895. Those numbers can be noticed right away if students have been encouraged to look for easy patterns when working with the Sieve of Eratosthenes.

Mersenne Primes Middle school students can investigate *Mersenne primes*. Mersenne primes are named after the French monk Marin Mersenne and are those primes that can be expressed in the form $2^p - 1$, where p is a prime number. In 1999, the first known million-digit prime number, $2^{6972593} - 1$, was found. It contains 2,098,960 digits. To learn more about Mersenne primes and related classroom activities for middle school students, see Wanko and Venable (2002) or visit the Great Internet Mersenne Prime Search at **www.mersenne.org**.

Fundamental Theorem of Arithmetic

One interesting feature of our number system is known as the *Unique Factorization Theorem* or the *Fundamental Theorem of Arithmetic*. The Fundamental Theorem of Arithmetic states that every composite number can be expressed as a product of its primes. Applying this to what we learned about the number 201 on the Web site, it can be seen that 201 = 3 × 67. By checking the Sieve of Eratosthenes, we see that 67 is a prime, as is the familiar prime 3. Therefore, the number 201 can be expressed as 3 × 67 and will only have this one prime factorization.

Prime Factorization Another investigation of number theory is finding the prime factorization of a number. When a composite number is divided into its primes so that only primes are present as its factors, the process is known as *prime factorization*. The following illustration shows two methods for finding the prime factorization of the number 24:

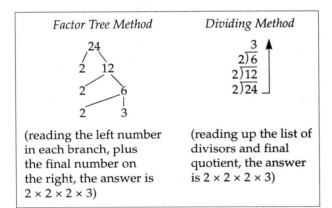

Factor Tree Method	Dividing Method
(reading the left number in each branch, plus the final number on the right, the answer is 2 × 2 × 2 × 3)	(reading up the list of divisors and final quotient, the answer is 2 × 2 × 2 × 3)

Both methods start with the smallest prime and continue its use until it is no longer a factor or a divisor of the number. Then the next appropriate prime is found and the process continues until all the factors are prime numbers (factor tree method) or until the final quotient is a prime number (dividing method). Both show 2 × 2 × 2 × 3 as the prime factors of the number 24. From the associative property, we know that any arrangement of the four prime numbers will yield the unique number 24 when multiplied as factors, but it is customary to write the prime factors from least to greatest.

Least Common Multiple and Greatest Common Factor The Least Common Multiple (LCM) and the Greatest Common Factor (GGF) can help students factor numbers efficiently. The GCF can also be called the Greatest Common Divisor, but most elementary textbooks choose the GCF terminology. The LCM and the GCF are useful when

relationships between and among patterns cannot be compared until common elements are found. For instance, $\frac{1}{3}$ and $\frac{1}{4}$ need a common denominator (the LCM) before one can use the two fractions together in the addition and subtraction operations of real-world mathematics from simple cooking and building to rocket fuel formulas. The LCM and GCF are stressed in schools because they help find comparison relationships more quickly, enabling the efficient use of mathematics in industry and business applications.

The *least common multiple* of two counting numbers is the smallest (least) nonzero number that is a multiple of both numbers. Because every number has an infinite number of multiples, every pair of numbers has an infinite number of common multiples. The smallest of the common multiples is known as the LCM. For example, although the numbers 4 and 5 have many multiples, the least (smallest) common one is 20.

4	8	12	16	**20**	24	28	32
5	10	15		**20**	25	30	35	40

The key word is *multiple*, which implies that the resulting number will be greater than either of the two numbers (or equal to the larger number as in the LCM of 3 and 6). When adding and subtracting fractions (e.g., $\frac{1}{3}$ and $\frac{1}{4}$), the common denominator is 12, which is the least common multiple of 3 and 4.

The *greatest common factor* (GCF) of two counting numbers is the greatest counting number, that is, a factor of each of the numbers. The key word is *factor*, which implies that the resulting number will be less than either of the two numbers (or equal to the smaller number as in the GCF of 5 and 10). The numbers 18 and 24 have several common factors (1, 2, 3, and 6) and the greatest common factor is 6.

A visual way to remember the idea is to think of the placement of each in relation to a diagram. Using the numbers 8 and 12

LCM (8, 12)	GCF (8, 12)
8)‾LCM 12)‾LCM	GCF)‾8 GCF)‾12

Both the LCM and GCF may be extended to more than two numbers, as seen in Activity 14.6 and Figure 14.3 where the LCM and GCF of three numbers are illustrated.

Activity 14.6

MANIPULATIVES

FINDING THE LCM AND GCF WITH CUISENAIRE RODS

MATERIALS
- Cuisenaire rods

DIRECTIONS

1. Study Figure 14.3 and see how the GCF and the LCM are figured.

2. Wording to use:
   - GCF = The color *every* tower has in common. (in this example, GCF = green or 3)
   - LCM = The most of any color in the towers when taken together (in this example, red × red × yellow × green × green or 180)

3. Prepare for oral and written discourse by thinking how children would be expected to explain LCM and GCF for the examples they bring to class.

4. Think of three more numbers for which you can build prime towers with Cuisenaire rods. Figure out the LCM and GCF for the prime towers.

5. Write how you would explain this to children.

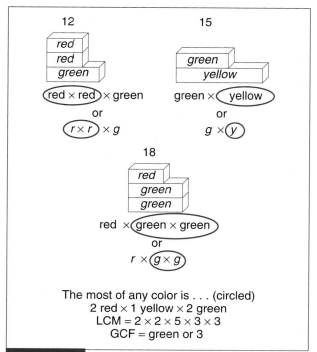

FIGURE 14.3 *Finding LCM and GCF with Cuisenaire rods.*

Supporting the NCTM *Principles and Standard* (2000)

- Mathematics as Reasoning/Patterning; Mathematics as Problem Solving; Connections; Representations
- Oral Discourse; Written Discourse—The Teaching Principle
- Active Engagement with Manipulatives—The Learning Principle
- The Mathematics Curriculum Principle . . .

Finding the LCM and GCF of Numbers Both the LCM and the GCF start by factoring each number to be compared into its primes (as shown in the following factor diagrams, known as factor trees, using the numbers 12, 15, and 18). The LCM is found by looking for the number of primes used most often in each composite number. Therefore, 2 × 2 is the most twos used (seen in the number 12), whereas 3 × 3 is the most threes used (seen in the number 18). Five is used only once but it still applies because it is the maximum times it is used in any number. The LCM is 2 × 2 × 3 × 3 × 5 or 180. The GCF is found by looking for the greatest divisor or factor that all numbers have in common. There is only one factor common to all the numbers and that is 3. Therefore, 3 is the GCF.

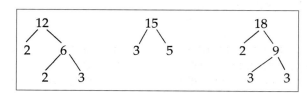

Figure 14.3 shows how the numbers 12, 15, and 18 can be factored by using Cuisenaire rods. Each set of primes is made into a "prime tower" with the prime rods stacked one on top of the other. The LCM is found by asking which is the color any prime tower uses the most. The answer is two reds, two greens, and one yellow, which equates with 2 × 2 × 3 × 3 × 5. The GCF is found by asking which is the largest color rod common in all three prime towers. The answer is the green rod or the numeral 3.

Venn diagrams, shown in Figure 14.4, are another useful tool for finding the LCM, and they may appeal to students who are comfortable with set diagrams. The LCM is 30. Although 60 and 90 are also common multiples, they are not the least common multiple.

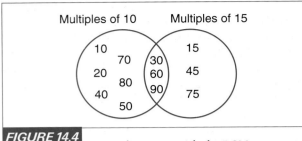

FIGURE 14.4 *Venn diagrams with the LCM.*

Number theory is an integral part of studying mathematics in the upper grades and middle school years. The following intermediate concepts are most often explored as sixth, seventh, and eighth grade material. Students are introduced to the concepts much as the topics are introduced here; however, time for individual exploration should be provided. These intermediate concepts are divisibility rules, polygonal or figurate numbers, Pythagorean triples, Fibonacci numbers, and Pascal's triangle.

Divisibility Rules

One number is said to be *divisible* by another number if and only if the first number divides evenly into the second, leaving no remainder. Sometimes a person needs to estimate quickly whether one number will divide evenly into a greater multidigit number. Knowing some simple divisibility rules can help a person conquer the time factor on standardized achievement and aptitude tests. Although other students are trying to perform laborious calculations taking up valuable time, the person who knows divisibility rules can answer more rapidly.

Divisibility rules also help economists and other professionals who have to deal with large population or demographic numbers too large to be recorded on a conventional calculator. A decision to divide the data by quarterly figures or by thirds can depend on which large number most easily divides into fourths or thirds. Divisibility rules also help children when selecting players for teams or dividing large amounts to be dispersed among many people. For example, students want eight school teams for a field day in a school with 1432 students. They know it will result in the same number of players on every team without the use of calculators or pencil-and-paper algorithms.

Divisibility rules can help find common denominators quickly. These rules were first introduced in Chapter 10. Middle school students who find number patterns interesting in arid of themselves will find the explanations for the divisibility rules of interest. Those students with a mathematical inclination will want to know why divisibility tests work. The following explanations may help the teacher who finds such a question hard to answer without some study.

Divisibility by 2, 5, and 10 From working with the Sieve of Eratosthenes, students can "see" patterns for the divisibility of numbers by 2, 5, and 10. They will be able to generalize that any number ending with an even number in the ones place will be divisible by 2. Any number ending with a 0 or 5 in the ones place will be divisible by 5, and any number ending with a 0 in the ones place will be divisible by 10. Other divisibility rules are not that easily seen and require more questions on the part of the teacher if rules are to be learned by students.

Divisibility by 4 and 8 Because our number system is based on regrouping at 10, the powers of 10 can help our understanding of divisibility rules. Look at the following divisibility pattern for 4:

Division by powers of 10	Does it divide evenly?
$10^1 + 4$	No
$10^2 + 4$	Yes . . . and all following powers of 10 will be divided evenly also.

Rationale for the rule: Some numbers in the tens and ones place (10 to the first power) are divisible by 4, such as $4 \times 4 = 16, 4 \times 5 = 20$. Therefore, if we look at the last two digits to the right in a multidigit number and find them divisible by 4, we know the entire number will be divisible by 4. The rule for divisibility by 4 is that *a number is divisible by 4* if and only if the last two digits of the number are divisible by 4.

Following the same reasoning, divisibility by 8 is examined on the Web site in the Extended Activities. Your instructor may wish to have you explain your reasoning for the rule of divisibility by 8. The rule for divisibility by 8 is that *a number is, divisible by 8* if and only if the last three digits of the number are divisible by 8.

Activity 14.7 gives students an opportunity to explore divisibility by 4 and 8 in more depth. Students will notice that any number divisible by 8 is also divisible by 4, but they should also notice that not every number that is divisible by 4 will be divisible by 8. Have students discuss in cooperative learning groups why this fact is true. How does this fact relate to divisibility by 2?

Bennett and Nelson (2002) use base 10 blocks to demonstrate another "rule" for divisibility by 8

EXTENDED ACTIVITIES

PROBLEM SOLVING **MATHEMATICAL CONNECTIONS** **CALCULATORS** **MENTAL MATH**

Name of Activity

- Divisibility by 3 and 9
- Divisibility by 8: Explaining the Rule
- Pythagoras and History

(which also holds for divisibility by 4). They go on to show how base 10 blocks and the powers of 10 can be used to demonstrated divisibility rules for 3, 6, 7, and 9.

Divisibility by 3 and 9   Look once again at the powers of 10 with the division by 9. Rationale for the rule: Any number divisible by 9 is also divisible by 3, and any number will always be divisible by 9 or 3 if and only if all the digits added together equal a number that is divisible by 9 or 3. See the Web site, Extended Activities for further explanation.

Quickly find which numbers would be divisible by 4, 8, 3, 9, or 5 . . .

$$?)\overline{2537887} \quad 7)\overline{7891302} \quad ?)\overline{1259945}$$

Change these numbers to make them divisible by the rest of the 4, 8, 3, 9, and 5 remaining. The NAEP results (2006, 2000), while gradually increasing in scores, show three-fourths of the fourth graders could answer yes/no responses to number theory questions but a little more then one-fourth of the students could give correct written explanation to the same questions. Most chose odd and even number explanations. Only a few fourth graders gave explanations involving higher

Activity 14.7

CALCULATORS **MATHEMATICAL CONNECTIONS** **MENTAL MATH**   **DIVISIBILITY BY 4 AND 8**

DIRECTIONS

Which numbers are divisible by 4 and 8? (Students should be encouraged to fill in the right side of the chart as they work with the problems. Some of the chart has been filled in for you.)

Numbers	Divisible by 4 and 8?	Divisible only by 4?	Divisible only by 8?	Explanation
197836	No	Yes		36 is divisible by 4 but 836 is not divisible by 8.
765872				
197836				

Check with a calculator to see whether you were correct. Make up others and check with your calculator. Write down what you would say to explain this to children.

Supporting the NCTM *Principles and Standards* (2000)
- Mathematics as Reasoning
- Using the Calculator—The Teaching Principle
- Using Inference—Assessment Principle

number theory concepts such as factors, multiplies, and divisibility. This further supports the need for written discourse early in the mathematical curriculum.

Polygonal or Figurate Numbers

Polygonal numbers (also known as figurate numbers) are numbers that take the shape of polygons or figures. We will explore several kinds in this section. There are polygonal or figurate numbers called triangular numbers, square numbers, pentagonal numbers, hexagonal numbers, octagonal numbers, and so on. The most common are known as square numbers and take the form of a square figure. These polygonal numbers will look like the drawings in Figure 14.5. Young children can create the polygonal numbers by using manipulatives or graph paper and can predict what will happen from an intuitive sense of beginning inductive reasoning. Middle schoolers can work with the embedded pattern.

There are many possibilities for figurate (polygonal) numbers. Pythagoras, a Greek mathematician and philosopher of 2500 years ago, started a society of persons interested in many issues of that day, including clever patterns dealing with numbers. Known as the Pythagorean Society, this secret society explored many possibilities with figurate numbers. Each figurate number is found by counting the number of units used to make the original figure (polygon) and the number of equivalent units needed to produce the polygon as it grows larger. Figure 14.5 shows the configurations for the triangular, square, and pentagonal numbers as the Pythagoreans discovered them.

Square Numbers Perfect squares are squares whose sides and areas are whole numbers. Figure 14.5 shows examples of perfect squares in the middle figurate numbers.

Squares can be drawn whose sides and areas are not Whole numbers. For instance, a square can be drawn whose sides are 2.1 × 2.1 which yields a square area of 4.41, and a square with an area of 3 will yield sides whose measure is an irrational number 1.7320508 (unending decimal). These are not considered perfect squares because the sides in both cases are not whole numbers. Therefore *a perfect square* is a square whose sides result in a whole number with no fractional parts. An *imperfect square* is a square whose sides result in a whole number plus some fractional part.

Pythagorean Triples

Pythagoras is thought by many to have created the Pythagorean theorem, which states that

$$a^2 + b^2 = c^2$$

where a and b are legs of a right triangle and c is the hypotenuse. The hypotenuse is the side opposite the right angle. The Extended Activities include an activity, "Pythagoras Theorem and History," that will describe the use of the Pythagorean Theorem long before Pythagoras was born. It is important that students have an appreciation of the role of all cultures in the development of mathematics.

A visual representation of the theorem is shown in Figure 14.6. Pythagoras found sets of three whole numbers, known as triples, that would fit this pattern. One triple given frequently as an

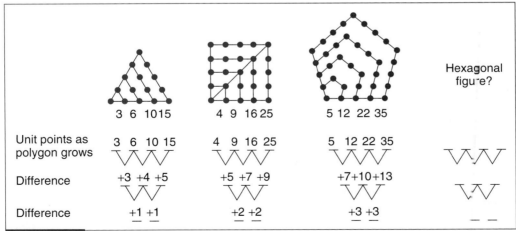

FIGURE 14.5 *Finding the embedded pattern to generate the next figurate numbers.*

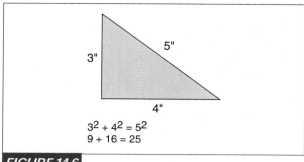

FIGURE 14.6 *One of the most frequently shown Pythagorean triples.*

example is the triple of 3, 4, and 5 as the sides of the right triangle. If asked to find other triples, middle school students are most likely to see multiples of the 3, 4, 5 triple as possibilities, as seen in Activity 14.8.

Activity 14.8

   TRIPLES

CALCULATORS   CULTURAL RELEVANCE   PROBLEM SOLVING

DIRECTIONS
1. Think of a pattern that might create triples from what you know about the triple 3, 4, 5.
2. Follow this theorem:

$$a^2 + b^2 = c^2$$

3. Use the calculator to see whether the triple fits the theorem.

Triples	Theorem
3 4 5	$9 + 16 = 25$
	$25 = 25$
6 8 10	$? + ? = ?$
	$? = ?$
? ? ?	$? + ? = ?$
	$? = ?$

4. Create four more triples, following the same pattern.
5. Generalize a rule for finding Pythagorean triples using the table you created in step 3.

There are other ways to create Pythagorean triples. Computer programs give students an excellent chance to analyze (problem solve) other techniques.

When middle schoolers analyze embedded formulas for finding patterns (as in Figure 14.5), they see one of the uses for beginning algebra concepts, where patterns can be generalized by using variables to stand for numbers.

Fibonacci Number Sequence

The Fibonacci number sequence is most often seen in the field of science, but it also occurs in other fields, including music, arts, and architecture. A *Fibonacci number sequence* is defined as a sequence of numbers where any number is generated by adding the two previous numbers together. Figure 14.7 shows a diagram of the number pattern as it might occur in growing things. The numbers to the right show the number pattern as it progresses through seven cycles.

Using the model of a tree branch, as in Figure 14.7, Fibonacci numbers must meet the following criteria:

1. An old branch can generate a new branch only once.
2. The old branch continues to generate itself at each new level.
3. A new branch can generate itself (becoming an old branch) and a new one (at the next level of procreation).

When the number pattern becomes apparent, one can predict the number of new and old branches for endless levels yet to come. It may be

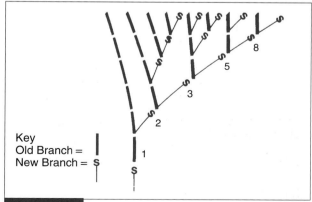

FIGURE 14.7 *Branching model of the Fibonacci number sequence.*

easier to see the number pattern if presented horizontally with numbers only:

$$1 \quad 1 \quad 2 \quad 3 \quad 5 \quad 8 \quad 13 \ldots$$

Notice that 13 is derived from adding the two numbers directly before it. Do you get 8 the same way? Do you get the other numbers the same way? Now you have established the number pattern of Fibonacci numbers.

Look at the three criteria needed in the preceding branch model. Substitute the word *Variable* for the word *branch* to generalize the Fibonacci sequence to all areas. The assessment section at the end of this chapter also shows how children from grade 2 to grade 6 handle the Fibonacci sequence and how they explain what they see in the number pattern. The children's literature book, *Math Curse* (Scieszka, 1995), features the Fibonacci sequence with its humorous commentary. Activity 14.9 demonstrates different fields where the Fibonacci sequence of numbers occurs.

Activity 14.9

MATHEMATICAL CONNECTIONS

MUSIC AND SCIENCE WITH FIBONACCI NUMBERS

DIRECTIONS

1. Because the Fibonacci sequence of numbers occurs in many fields, including music and science, students can be directed to choose a science or music topic and illustrate how the Fibonacci sequence is seen (Figure 14.7).

2. Find models in the science book and from nature. *A hint to start:* Rabbits help us see the sequence every few weeks. Think about roots and leaves of plants.

3. If students are creative, they may be able to compose their own examples of musical arrangements with the Fibonacci sequence.

Johnson (1999) shows how the Fibonacci sequence is used in basket weaving. Good middle school lessons are included too.

Pascal's Triangle

Pascal's triangle, shown in Figure 14.8, is a special arrangement of numbers thought to have been discovered by Blaise Pascal, a seventeenth-century

				1							start
			1		1						level 1
		1		2		1					level 2
	1		3		3		1				level 3
1		4		6		4		1			level 4
1		5	10		10		5		1		level 5
1	6		15	20		15		6		1	level 6
											etc.

FIGURE 14.8 *Pascal's triangle.*

mathematician. Pascal's triangle is in the configuration of a triangle with many number patterns visible as each row is added to the triangle. This arrangement of numbers relates to the number of possible outcomes in probability.

Pascal's triangle relates later to algebra and solving equations. A formal definition is left for the reader to discover during Activity 14.10. It is easy to see the symmetry of Pascal's triangle. It makes an excellent bulletin board, especially if a new row is added daily, starting after the initial pattern is established at level 6. Students find themselves anticipating what the next row will be. They should also be encouraged to look at emerging number patterns as the triangle develops. The following exploration in Activity 14.10 presents the kind of questioning that will help students begin to develop problem-solving strategies using the triangle.

Manouchehri and Enderson (1999) share ideas for promoting discourse using Pascal's triangle in an inquiry-oriented learning activity. They include answers by seventh graders as they worked in groups. The teachers are careful to use a form of the elaborating technique to keep the learning on task and bring out the mathematical potential of Pascal's triangle in the Extended Activity.

The patterns in number theory ban be very helpful to students as they work with the number system. The unique features can help students calculate more quickly, estimate-reasonable answers, perform mental computation *(mental math)*, and problem solve where expanded answers can lead to new discoveries. The latter supports Bruner's idea of discovery learning as a mark of a true education.

TEACHING STRATEGIES FOR BUILDING CONCEPTUAL UNDERSTANDING OF PATTERNS AND FUNCTIONS

"In preparing students for algebra, educators must consider the range of mathematics and the

Activity 14.10

PROBLEM SOLVING **CULTURAL RELEVANCE**

PASCAL'S TRIANGLE AND CULTURAL RELEVANCE

DIRECTIONS

Strong (1990) points out that the "modern method of using the so-called Pascal's triangle was actually invented in Asia by the Chinese and the Persians 500 years before Pascal was born" (p. 20). The curriculum of the Chicago Public Schools asks teachers to include this fact in the teaching of mathematics from grade 4 on.

1. This is the same as Pascal's triangle seen above. Some numbers have been removed to help you see some of the number patterns more clearly.

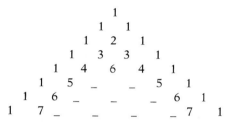

How many spaces will continue on the next two levels? Do you see a pattern developing?

2. The spaces give us an idea of the numbers required on each side to make the symmetry occur. By looking at the first diagram completed to level 6, we see that two tens come in the first two blank spaces after the numeral 5. Which numbers in the previous row help to produce the tens in level 5? In level 6, how were the numbers 15 and 20 chosen for that level? What numbers on the previous level helped? What will the numbers be on levels 7, 8, and 9?

3. Add the numbers horizontally on each level. What pattern do you notice? Turn the pattern into a definition of Pascal's triangle by explaining how the formula is derived.

Supporting the NCTM *Principles and Standards* (2000)

- Mathematics as Reasoning; Problem Solving, Connections, Representations
- Oral Discourse; Written Discourse — The Teaching Principle
- The Equity Principle

EXTENDED ACTIVITIES

CALCULATORS **CULTURAL RELEVANCE**

Name of Activity
- Pascal's Triangle

continued development of, mathematics as a science of pattern and order" (Fernandez and Anhalt, 2001). If students are to view algebra as more than the manipulation of symbols, then they must have opportunities to explore and reflect on problems that present algebra as the study of patterns and functions. These opportunities can be provided from the earliest grades.

There are two ways to look at functions. The first way is as a relationship between two sets (i.e., each element of the first set is related to a unique [one and only one] element of the second set). The second way to look at functions is as an input–output process. But, whichever way you look at functions you are stating a relationship between a number in one set with a number in another set. As you will see in the activities that follow, young children usually begin with the input–output or function machine.

Activities for Grades PreK to 2

Even very young children can achieve an understanding of functions by looking for the pattern rule that applies to every example within a set of objects. Students who have been exposed to work with attribute blocks, as seen in some of the activities found in Chapter 12 of this text, will find an easy transition to the use of functions to express relations and patterns between variables as shown in Figures 14.9 and 14.10.

From the Concrete to the Connecting Stage As always, the use of manipulatives is the first step in building an awareness of the functions. A box with a hole and funnel becomes the function input–output machine, as seen in Figure 14.9. The teacher puts one concrete object in the top of the function machine (in the input hole) and

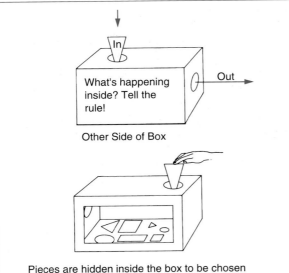

Function Table

In	Out
△ Red	△ Yellow
○ Red	○ Yellow
□ Red	□ Yellow
▭ Red	▭ Yellow

Same shape
small to large
red to yellow

What's happening? Tell the rule.

FIGURE 14.9 *From concrete to connecting stage.*

By third grade a stylized drawing is all that is needed before students generate a function table.

In	Out
3	8
7	12
6	11
The Rule:	
$x + 5$	

FIGURE 14.10 *From connecting stage to symbolic in 3 to 5 grades.*

pulls another object out the output slot. Children are asked to reason what is happening inside the machine and what rule is being applied that tells people what will come out of the machine. Children love the mystery idea of something "special" happening inside the machine and enjoy coming up with sounds for the machine to make as well as watching the teacher model the activity.

Children can make their own machines to use in cooperative grouping. As the link to the connecting stage, children are asked to make a table of input and output choices. They draw the pieces on paper as seen in the function table in Figure 14.9. First and second graders are given function relationships that differ by only one attribute. The portfolio assessment seen at the end of this chapter shows the typical response made by students at the end of second grade.

Functions that differ by two or more changes are difficult for young children and are introduced to students in the later grades after they have improved they can reason relationships involving one attribute change.

Activities for Grades 3 to 5
From the Connecting to the Symbolic Stage
Young children can switch from using objects to search for patterns by using facts they have learned about number combinations as seen in Figure 14.10.

Willoughby (1997) and Sulzer (1998) emphasize that fourth graders can use the "$x + 5$" notation instead of: saying "add 5." Sulzer also asserts that keeping the function box in the classroom all year enables fourth graders to grow in their mathematical thinking. Students create equations such as $\sqrt{x-1}$ and $\sqrt[3]{x-1}$ by the end of the year. A gradual progression of thought is included in Sulzer's article.

Activities for Grades 6 to 8
Middle schoolers can handle several attribute changes at one time, as in the function table shown in Figure 14.9, which changes size and color with only shape remaining the same.

From the Concrete to the Connecting Stage

Many attribute changes can be introduced in the middle grades. Attribute pieces that have varying values of shape, size, color, texture, and thickness may be used. The students still use manipulatives to start their activities with multiple variables. They record their actions by drawing function tables and writing the rule as the connecting stage activity.

From the Connecting to the Symbolic Stage

As they gradually handle more and more attributes at the same time, teachers introduce the change from drawings to working solely on the symbolic stage as in Figure 14.11.

Middle school students are encouraged to use a variety of variables with functions and relations. Students can use the ideas to develop their own functions and their relationships in cooperative group settings. Then they can switch with other cooperative groups in the class to see whether they can detect the rules that were used in formulating the other groups' functions.

These activities nicely lead into problem solving with algebraic, concepts in which equations represent many different kinds of function relationships between and among variables. The development of algebraic concepts is considered in the next section.

The NCTM *Navigating through Algebra* Series (House, 2001) for grades PreK to 2, 3 to 5, and 6 to 8 provide different lessons for introducing, developing, and extending some of the fundamental ideas of algebra: patterns; variable and equality, and relations and functions. The questioning skills are based on the NCTM *Principles and Standards for School Mathematics* (2000). The activities emphasize ways of communicating and questioning during problem solving, much like the questions found in the activities of this chapter.

TEACHING STRATEGIES FOR BUILDING CONCEPTUAL UNDERSTANDING OF BEGINNING ALGEBRA CONCEPTS

Algebra is the gateway to higher mathematics. Algebra must be accessible to all students if we are to reach the goal of equity in mathematics. The NCTM Navigation Series, *Navigating through Algebra*. (House, ed., 2001) points out that algebra is the entry-label skill in most sciences, business, industry, and technical jobs. What makes algebra seem difficult to some people is that algebra is really two things at once. First, it is a language that describes relationships and patterns between arid among elements; second, it is an abstract system of its own with its own rules and definitions.

Usiskin (1992) points to algebra as a language with symbols that stands for elements of sets and operations on those symbols. He stresses three facts (p. 27) about languages that should, therefore, apply to algebra:

- It is best learned in context.
- Almost any human being can learn it.
- It is more easily learned when one is younger.

Usiskin's thoughts are keeping with the ideas of brain research seen in Chapter 3, *use it or lose it* and *the sooner the better*. This means children must start early to see how different things from their world can be seen in a relationship with other elements using letters to emphasize the relationship patterns. This is the part of algebra started in elementary school. The abstract system of knowledge with its own rules and definitions is introduced in late middle school and high school in the traditional courses known as prealgebra, algebra I, and algebra II.

Students in the higher middle school grades can find more than one solution to the function table.

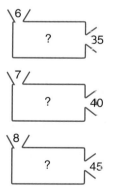

In	Out
6	35
7	40
8	45

The Rule:

Solution 1 = $(x + 1) \times 5$

Solution 2 = $(x \times 5) + 5$

The number in is called "*x*."

These problems can be made into beginning algebra equations, where *x* is the first number entered, which is 6 in the above:

$(x + 1) \times 5 = 35$ $(x \times 5) + 5 = 35$
$(x + 1 + 1) \times 5 = 40$ or $[(x + 1) \times 5] + 5 = 40$
$(x + 1 + 1 + 1) \times 5 = 45$ $[(x + 1 + 1) \times 5] + 5 = 45$

FIGURE 14.11   *From connecting stage to symbolic in middle school.*

Chappell and Strutchens (2001) would add that teachers must be aware of three aspects of algebraic thinking and algebra if their students are to see algebra as something more than "finding x." These three aspects are

- The study of patterns and relationships
- A tool for problem solving
- Generalized arithmetic

Look for these three aspects of algebraic thinking and algebra in the material that follows.

Activities for Grades PreK to 5

Children may be taken through the degrees of abstraction from manipulatives to symbols. Cuisenaire rods lend themselves nicely to go from a pure arithmetic level with concrete manipulatives to a more abstract knowledge in symbolic notation. Figure 14.12 shows how the transition works over the grades.

Children can start with one unknown variable where the relationship is the important emphasis. Connecting cubes may be used with a balance to show equations where an unknown is present. There are different bags marked x with various amounts of connecting cubes or rods that the children cannot see. They place each x bag on the balance until they get the bag that shows equivalence of sets by both sides balancing as seen in Figure 14.13. Students solve the equation first with

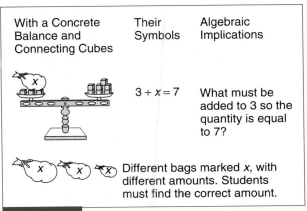

With a Concrete Balance and Connecting Cubes	Their Symbols	Algebraic Implications
	$3 + x = 7$	What must be added to 3 so the quantity is equal to 7?
		Different bags marked x, with different amounts. Students must find the correct amount.

FIGURE 14.13   *Equations with one unknown in the early grades.*

manipulatives and then proceed to the symbolic stage.

Note the questions asked in Figure 14.13: What must be added to 3 so the quantity ***is equal to*** 7? Howden (1990) stresses the importance of that wording for teachers of young children. Teachers must not ask: What is added to 3 to make 7? The word *make* gives the wrong interpretation to equations as children progress up the grades. It is better to start with the proper phrases in mathematics so "unlearning" does not need to occur later in the school years. For some children imprecise language is hard to abandon later in middle school.

Using what students already know is the best starting point for any concept. If students have been exposed to the use of Cuisenaire rods in the early elementary years, their use with beginning algebra concepts will be quite natural. Teachers report that even students who have never seen the rods before become quite adept at using them if given a day to explore their use on their own. The first example uses the letter variable y for the yellow rod. Early algebra concepts solve for one unknown, as shown in Figure 14.14.

Experienced rod users may translate "5" for the yellow rod too easily, and such easy solutions may inhibit the recognition of new ways of writing

---

With Concrete Rods

red | green
yellow

Their Symbols	Algebraic Implications
$2 + 3 = 5$	Actual whole numbers are shown.
$r + g = y$	Each letter stands for a definite rod; children see the relationship of one distinct rod to another without racing to a numerical answer.
$a + b = c$	The letters are now generalized to represent *any* number as it relates to any other unique number such that a third unique number is produced.

FIGURE 14.12   *A gradual transition to more abstraction in elementary grades.*

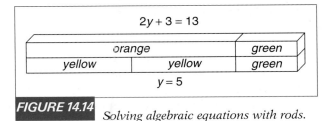

$$2y + 3 = 13$$

orange		green
yellow	yellow	green

$$y = 5$$

FIGURE 14.14   *Solving algebraic equations with rods.*

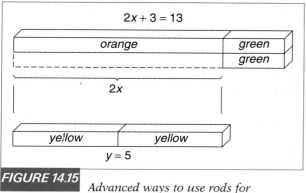

$$2x + 3 = 13$$

orange	green
	green

$$2x$$

yellow	yellow

$$y = 5$$

FIGURE 14.15 *Advanced ways to use rods for experienced users.*

equations. Teachers may place an x for the use of y and set up the equation as in Figure 14.15.

Activities for Grades 6 to 8

During the middle school years, students find themselves, their hormones, lifestyles, interests, everything in transition from child to teenager. It is an egocentric time when everything revolves around "what's in it for me and what will make me look good to the most peers?" an "I" of "me" view of life.

Into this world, the mathematics teacher brings abstract symbols and generalizations that seem a far cry from the more interesting topics of young adolescents—cars, the opposite sex, and wearing the "right" designer labels. But, even at this level, students must have an opportunity to use physical models to help them develop their understanding of the use of abstract symbols and generalizations (Hines, 2002; Fernandez and Anhalt, 2001; Chappell and Strutchens, 2001).

TEACHING STRATEGIES FOR BUILDING CONCEPTUAL UNDERSTANDING OF FUNCTIONS

To combat the egocentric nature of adolescence, teachers are choosing "real-life" mathematics, the kind that would be interesting to young people. "Math in Context" and "Algebra for All" (Driscoll, Moyer, and Zawojewski, 1998) are projects that teach algebra from real-world situations. The emphasis is on solving engaging problems rather than manipulating "x" and "y" variables in row after row of algebraic equations. A sample from the "Algebra for All" project is included (Driscoll, Moyer, and Zawo-jewski, 1998; p. 7)

Look at the following table. It is a table that describes tree growth in inches per month:

Months	0	1	2	3	4	5	6	—	10	n
Inches	?	1	4	7	10	13	—	—	28	—

1. *Write an equation that describes the growth of the tree from month to month.*
2. *Using the equation written for part 1, explain why in the first month the tree grows only one inch.*
3. *What is the value of the height in inches at Month Zero? What is this value's meaning?*

Half of grade 8 students are proficient at solving for the unknowns when the equation was presented to them, but only one-fourth can generate their own equation when shown a table like the one above with parts missing. If the questions asked students to give only the next value in the table, half of the grade 4 students and two-thirds of the grade 3 students responded correctly (NAEP, 2006; 2000). It is apparent that students continue to need more problem solving in the context of real-world examples. They need to generate the tables, graphs, and name the variables themselves. Such tasks were part of TIMSS (Mullis, 1997), another test in which U.S. students did poorly compared with other students around the world.

Functions that began as attribute relationships in the early grades are now extended to algebra and formula concepts. Glatzer and Lappan (1990, pp. 36–37) show how Cuisenaire rods can be used to see function relationships recorded in a table and generalized to any number rod. It is adapted here, in Activity 14.11 and Figure 14.16, as another example of a function table similar to that seen in the tree growth example.

Simultaneous Equations

Activity 14.12 is the same one found in Chapter 5, page 107. It, too, can be solved by tables (as in Chapter 5) or by simultaneous equations using the substitution method. One variable is defined in terms of the other (i.e., by substitution). Both variables have to be substituted for each other; therefore, it requires two equations: one to find n (number of nickels) and one to find d (number of dimes). Try Activity 14.12.

The answer is provided on the Web site. Extended Activities in "Jho-Ju's Problem." Also included in the same Extended Activities is a TIMSS assessment task involving the topics in this chapter—a good resource as you go into the classroom.

Activity 14.11

PROBLEM SOLVING

MANIPULATIVES

CUISENAIRE RODS AND FUNCTION TABLES

MATERIALS

With the Concrete Manipulatives

Table Showing Function with Different Rod Staircases

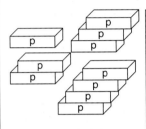

Purple Rods (4 units in length)

No. in Staircase	Volume	Surface Area
1	4	18
2	8	30
3	12	42
4	16	54
•	•	•
•	•	•
•	•	•
n	$4n$	$12n+6$

Yellow Rods (5 units in length)

No. in Staircase	Volume	Surface Area
1	5	22
2	10	36
3	15	50
4	20	64
•	•	•
•	•	•
•	•	•
n	$5n$	$14n+8$

Dark Green Rods (6 units in length)

No. in Staircase	Volume	Surface Area

You fill in the rest.

•	•	•
•	•	•
•	•	•

FIGURE 14.16 *Functions with any rod staircase generalizing a formula relationship*

DIRECTIONS

1. Work in cooperative groups to problem solve what should come next in the chart.
2. Fill in the chart found in Figure 14.16. Include a sketch of the dark green rods in staircases.

3. Generalize a formula for volume and a formula for surface area that will fit for any rod staircase. Listen to each other's ideas to see which formulas will work every time no matter which rod is chosen.

$$V = \underline{\qquad}$$
$$SA = \underline{\qquad}$$

Activity 14.12

PROBLEM SOLVING

SIMULTANEOUS EQUATIONS

Jho-Ju held a yard sale and charged a dime for everything, but would accept a nickel if the buyer was a good bargainer. At the end of the day, she realized that she had sold all 20 items and taken in the grand total of $1.90. She had only dimes and nickels at the end of the day. How many of each did she have?

A start to solving:

1. Using the facts of the word problem, the two simultaneous equations can be created:

$$0.05N + 0.10D = 1.90$$
$$N + D = 20$$

2. Now solve for N in terms of D in both equations.
3. Then solve for D in terms of N in both equations.

Simultaneous equations were a part of the culture of first century B.C. in China (Nelson, 1993). Some examples show three and four unknowns, not like the easy approach of two unknowns shown to middle schoolers today. Those who enjoy setting up simultaneous equations with unknowns may enjoy the activity from China. This activity is also found in the Extended Activities.

Binomial Expressions Manipulatives should still be used in beginning algebra so students can see how some of these strange-appearing notations are solved. Teaching-supply catalogs carry many manipulatives such as the *Algeblocks* to visualize equations.

EXTENDED ACTIVITIES

COMPUTERS

CULTURAL RELEVANCE

PROBLEM SOLVING

MANIPULATIVES

PORTFOLIO

MATHEMATICAL CONNECTIONS

Name of Activity

- Get a Charge out of Integers
- Jho-Ju's Problem
- Adolescent Literature with Equations in Spreadsheets
- Simultaneous Equations with Middle School Interests in Mind
- Math Dialogue with Middle School Students in Algebra for All
- Simultaneous Equations from China
- TIMSS Assessment: Earnings
- Origins of Algebraic Contributions

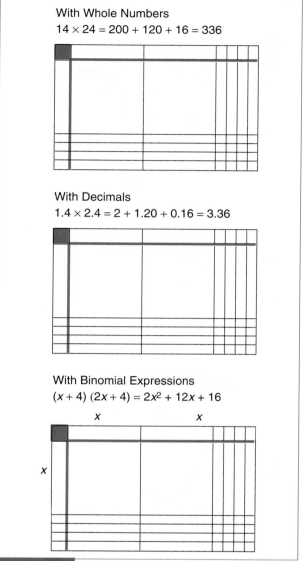

With Whole Numbers
$14 \times 24 = 200 + 120 + 16 = 336$

With Decimals
$1.4 \times 2.4 = 2 + 1.20 + 0.16 = 3.36$

With Binomial Expressions
$(x + 4)(2x + 4) = 2x^2 + 12x + 16$

FIGURE 14.17 *From whole number algorithms to binomial expressions.*

Many arrangements with manipulatives will look familiar to students who have worked with such items as base 10 blocks from the primary grades on, first with whole numbers, then with decimals, and now with x as the unknown. The configurations are essentially the same. This shows a connection to action movements with algebra notation that begins to make sense out of an equation pike this: $(2x + 4)(x + 4) = 2x^2 + 12x + 16$. Figure 14.17 shows how the ideas of arithmetic can blend with the concepts of algebra.

The examples given show subtle differences between functions and variables. Demana and Waits (1990) state that these subtle differences go unnoticed in most algebra curricula today and may be one of the reasons that so many students find algebra difficult. Variables have different meanings and different relationships depending on the particular situation in which they are used.

If a situation means we need to search for patterns, a table is a good way to focus on the functional relationship. We have just seen several examples of such functions in this chapter.

If the situation calls for a description on a certain aspect of the relationship, a graph is the best to use because students can see how the effects on one changes the other.

From One Unknown to Two Unknowns in Equations and Graphs The next step is to solve for two unknowns in the same equation. This step requires a cognitive awareness that there can be more than one pair of answers to the equation. This awareness can be proved by asking students to solve for at least three sets of the two unknown quantities, as seen in Figure 14.18.

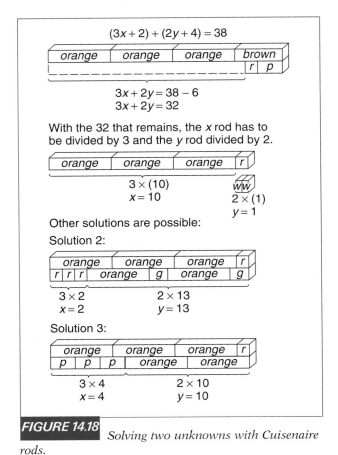

FIGURE 14.18 *Solving two unknowns with Cuisenaire rods.*

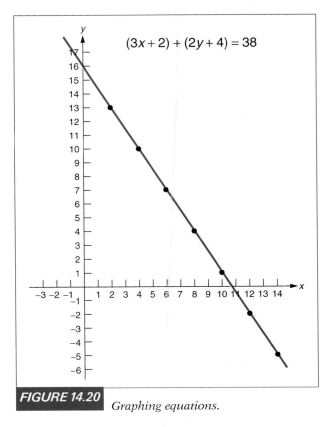

FIGURE 14.20 *Graphing equations.*

The next step is to set up a table in which the ordered pairs can be seen in a pattern of responses. If students have been working with tables from the early grades, the idea of a table to show the results will be easily grasped. Figure 14.19 organizes the information presented in Figure 14.18 and shows the variety of values assigned to x and y. Notice that negative integers are a natural part of algebra. The next step is to use the table to construct a graph showing the points and their relationship along the slope of a straight line (Figure 14.20).

x	y
2	13
4	10
6	7
8	4
10	1
12	−2
14	−5

FIGURE 14.19 *Variety of intercepts.*

To find where the y-axis is intercepted let $x = 0$:

$$(3x + 2) + 2y + 4 = 38$$
$$[3(0) + 2] + 2y + 4 = 38$$
$$(0 + 2) + 2y + 4 = 38$$
$$2 + 2y + 4 = 38$$
$$2y + 6 = 38$$
$$2y = 38 - 6$$
$$2y = 32$$
$$y = 16$$

When the line is extended to intercept the y-axis, one can see it crosses at the number 16. This point is called the y-intercept.

To find where the line intercepts the x-axis, the equation sets y at 0:

$$(3x + 2) + 2y + 4 = 38$$
$$(3x + 2) + [2(0) + 4] = 38$$
$$3x + 2 + (0 + 4) = 38$$
$$3x + 2 + 4 = 38$$
$$3x + 6 = 38$$
$$3x = 38 - 6$$
$$3x = 32$$
$$x = 10.66 \text{ or } 10\frac{2}{3}$$

EXTENDED ACTIVITIES

**MATHEMATICAL
CONNECTIONS**

Name of Activity
- Semantic Feature Analysis: Linear Equations
- Semantic Feature Analysis: Number Theory

Notice that the x-intercept has a fractional part. Intercepts do not have to be only whole numbers.

Gay and Keith (2002) describe the incorporation of a *semantic feature analysis*, a literacy strategy, in helping middle school students reason about linear equations. In a semantic feature analysis, students use their reasoning skills to analyze similarities and differences. Such an analysis requires that students use higher order thinking skills when completing the task. For examples of semantic feature analysis tasks, see the Extended Activities on the Website.

Technology and the Study of Algebra

The innovation of the graphing calculator allows students to go from the table of solutions to the graph without tediously drawing Coordinates themselves. This ability makes for more immediate feedback and helps students see the mathematical connections more quickly than was ever possible before this new technology was present. Try the problem in Figure 14.18, described in the preceding section, with the graphing calculator.

Demana and Waits (1990) advocate that students of prealgebra and beginning algebra I classes should draw some graphs by hand before moving to graphing calculators and computers. They believe that students will understand that there are many more points on the graph than a table can generate if they draw the lines on the graph themselves. It is not so apparent when a line is quickly drawn on a graphing calculator or computer.

The twenty-first century shows the promise of new ways to use algebra with new technologies yet unseen by all of us who have gone through the traditional algebra preparation. Nickerson,

Nydam, and Bowers (2000) describe using *SimCalc MathWorlds* in teaching graphing in the coordinate plane, writing and evaluating algebraic expressions, and understanding irate of change.

Technology, Algebra, and Students at Risk Research on the impact of the use of technology and constructivist learning environment for students at risk is just the beginning. A promising study is reported by Pugalee (2001). Although the students involved in the study were high school algebra I students, the methods and materials used in the study are readily adaptable to middle school mathematics classrooms. Questioning and discourse during the class encouraged students to become active participants in their own learning as they explored algebraic concepts and made connections essential to the development of algebraic thinking and understanding. Pugalee concluded that teachers of students who are at risk must incorporate "best practice" and increase student access to technology if algebra is to be the gateway to higher mathematics for all students.

ASSESSMENT

Field-Independent Learners

Throughout the examples in the teaching strategies section, material was presented in chart or table form so that one detail could build on another. Charts and tables, rather than diagrams, seem more helpful to students who find field-independent processing more to their liking. The step-by-step progression of the Sieve of Eratosthenes helps because primes are divided out one at a time and factors are combined in the end to see a pattern. The number pattern involved in the Fibonacci sequence may be seen more clearly if the numbers (minus the diagram) are presented in the following manner:

$$1 \quad 1 \quad 2 \quad 3 \quad 5 \quad 8 \quad 13 \quad 21 \quad 34 \quad 55$$

The diagram seems to "get in the way" of seeing the number sequence. If you found yourself confused rather than helped by the diagram, you may have been experiencing the same frustrations that successive thinkers feel at such times.

The dividing method for prime factorization is often more helpful than the stylized method of factor trees. Computer programs that develop any number pattern one step at a time may be more easily understood.

Field-Dependent Learners

Throughout the teaching strategies section, material was also presented in a diagram or stylized picture form. It is thought that such an approach may be more beneficial field-dependent thinker who can see patterns more easily if expressed in relationship to a whole picture or idea from the beginning. Factor trees, figurate (polygonal) numbers, Venn diagrams, graphs, and the branch drawing of the Fibonacci sequence are some of the teaching materials that can help students develop specific patterns in number theory. Logo computer programs that show the whole pattern in a drawing may prove more helpful to field-dependent learners.

Correcting Common Misconceptions

Jumping to Premature Conclusions Frequently students will decide on an answer before the real pattern can be discerned. In their desire to find a pattern, they have been too hasty in their conclusions. A good example is the false pattern emerging from this attempt to find the solution for Pascal's triangle.

```
          1               start
        1   1             level 1
       1  2  1            level 2
      1  3  3  1          level 3
     1  4  5  4  1        level 4
    1  5  6  6  5  1      level 5
```

Students who are asked to find the number pattern of Pascal's triangle after seeing only the first three levels may quite naturally jump to the wrong conclusion about the pattern. The best remediation technique is a preventive one—a teacher must anticipate the points at which a misinterpretation could easily occur and make sure that enough examples of the pattern have been given to ensure a correct analysis of the pattern. As was mentioned earlier, it is good to present at least six levels of Pascal's triangle before asking children to find the pattern involved.

Correcting Unknown Errors . . . the Reason for Oral Discourse Some students discover the correct pattern, but a teacher may not know it because the students make careless errors that do not show what they know. In the following Fibonacci example, the student understands the pattern but might be overlooked by a teacher who was checking only the answers in the blanks. Examples like this continue to emphasize the need for the teacher and student to engage in dialogue about the pattern. The teacher must analyze the step-by-step work of

each student when answers appear to be incorrect. This is where the new ideas on assessment become very important.

$$1 \quad 1 \quad 2 \quad 3 \quad 5 \quad \underline{8} \quad \underline{14} \quad \underline{25} \quad \underline{39} \quad \underline{64}$$

Not Seeing the Pattern There are some special needs students who cannot see a pattern or will not search for one it is not seen easily. Teachers must ask more probing questions in such cases. It is tempting to tell the answer rather than construct more and more decisive questions. If problem solving and self-discovery of patterns are the important components of the lesson, then probing questions and clues are the best helps a teacher can give. Notice that clues appear throughout this chapter, especially when you were asked to problem solve a pattern in number theory that could be quite difficult for the nonmathematics major. Such clues did not provide the answer but should have helped you discover a way to the solution.

Portfolio Assessments

Fibonacci Number Sequence In Activity 14.13, there are five students' work evaluated in this set of portfolio assessments. Four of the activities come from first, second, and third graders. A final journal entry was made by an eighth grader and shows the differences that occur as students mature at the end of their middle school experience.

Activity 14.13

PORTFOLIO **PORTFOLIO ASSESSMENTS**

For Teacher Reflection of Student's Work in Number Patterns
DIRECTIONS

1. Analyze the responses made by the students. Consider the age and the grade level of the work.

2. What likenesses do you see? What differences in reasoning do you see
   - between students of the same age and grade level?
   - between students of different ages and grade levels?

3. Two of the children chose to use Cuisenaire rods to help them figure out a pattern. Do you see a difference in their answers? Look at their sense of symmetry in the answers compared to the students who did not use rods. What is your impression of their

answers? Notice that Mark drew the rods while Matthew just talked about using them.

4. Design a rubric that would take into account the diversity of answers while being fair in your assessment strategy.

- Include the rubric in your Professional Portfolio for Job Interviews along with your analysis of each child's understanding in this activity.
- Enjoy the student work on Fibonacci numbers seen in Figures 14.21 through 14.25.

Name **Shawn – age 6 – first grade**

The Mystery Numbers

Look at the five numbers in a row. Can you think of the three mystery numbers that would come next? Place them in the blank spaces.

1   1   2   3   5   **5**   **6**   **7**

Write how you figured out the answer.

because there's two ones. Then
6 becames next in the numbers.
7 comes next in numbers.

FIGURE 14.21

Name **Mark –age 8 –grade 3**

The Mystery Numbers

Look at the five numbers in a row. Can you think of the three mystery numbers that would come next? Place them in the blank spaces.

1   1   2   3   5   **6**   **6**   **7**   **8**   **10**   **11**

Write how you figured out the answer.

I used Cuisenaire rods.
Made stair steps and
double six.

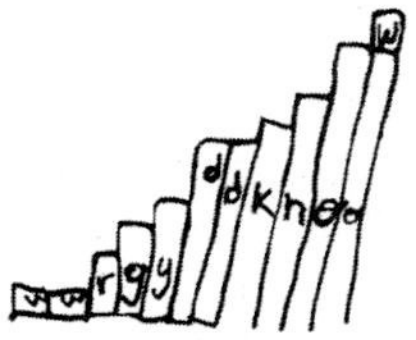

FIGURE 14.23

Name **Matthew** –age 8–grade 2

The Mystery Numbers

Look at the five numbers in a row. Can you think of the three mystery numbers that would come next? Place them in the blank spaces.

1   1   2   3   5   **5**   **3**   **2**

Write how you figured out the answer.

I Poot The Rods The
tox ~~Gither~~ and
macht The coLers

FIGURE 14.22

Name **Kate –age 9– grade 3**

The Mystery Numbers

Look at the five numbers in a row. Can you think of the three mystery numbers that would come next? Place them in the blank spaces.

1   1   2   3   5   **7**   **8**   **8**

Write how you figured out the answer.

The skiped 4 so I skiped 6 and dubbled 8.
They dubbled the first 2 numbers so I
thougt I should dubble the end 2 numbers.

FIGURE 14.24

Name _Tyler_ -age 14 -grade 8

The Mystery Numbers

Look at the five numbers in a row. Can you think of the three mystery numbers that would come next? Place them in the blank spaces.

1 1 2 3 5 _8_ _13_ _21_

Write how you figured out the answer.

Just add the last two numbers each time.

FIGURE 14.25

It's interesting to note that all of the younger children had excellent patterns with reasonable logic to the sequences they chose. They just did not see the Fibonacci sequence. By the eighth grade, it is the first one seen and no other sequence was attempted. This particular eighthgrade class had not had a formal introduction to Fibonacci numbers, nor had Tyler heard of the sequence from any other source.

Functions—Input–Output Tables   Two students responded in Activity 14.14.

Activity 14.14

PORTFOLIO   **PORTFOLIO ASSESSMENTS**

For Teacher Reflection of Students' Work on Attribute Functions

DIRECTIONS

1. Analyze the responses made by the students. Consider the age and the grade level of the work.

2. What likenesses do you see? What differences in reasoning do you see? Notice there is one year and one grade level apart.

   Notice how many attribute changes Kate is able to handle compared to the one Greg is able to handle with only a year's developmental level apart.

Note: Piaget says that there is quite a developmental leap that occurs around the eighth to ninth year.

3. Design a rubric that would take into account the diversity of answers while being fair in your assessment strategy.

   • Include the rubric in your Professional Portfolio for Job Interviews along with your analysis of each child's understanding in this activity.

   • Enjoy the student work on attribute function tables (See Figures 14.26 and 14.27) seen in Activity 14.15.

Algebra   The last portfolio assessment (Activity 14.15) shows the work of an eighth grader at the end of the prealgebra course. The problem is the same linear equation example shown in the algebra section of this chapter. This student did not use a graphing calculator. Rote symbol manipulation was the technique used for almost all of the prealgebra instruction. There were real-math applications shown in each section of the textbook, and students were encouraged to read them on their own as they went through the chapters. One of the most interesting comments comes when the student is asked how problems like these could be used in the real world of work. Notice the answer given by Travis. Why do you suppose he got an answer like this one?

Activity 14.15

PORTFOLIO   **PORTFOLIO ASSESSMENTS**

For Teacher Reflection of Students Work on Attribute Functions

DIRECTIONS

1. Analyze the responses made by the student in Figure 14.28. Consider the age and the grade level of the work.

2. Consider the student's answers in light of the background information given to you about the algebra course. What can you infer about the student's experiences with algebra after reading these answers?

   • What kind of answers would you expect if Travis had had experiences with manipulatives as well as the graph paper as shown in Activity 14.1?

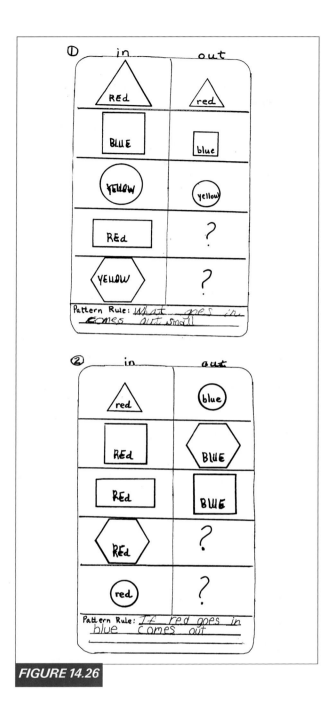

FIGURE 14.26

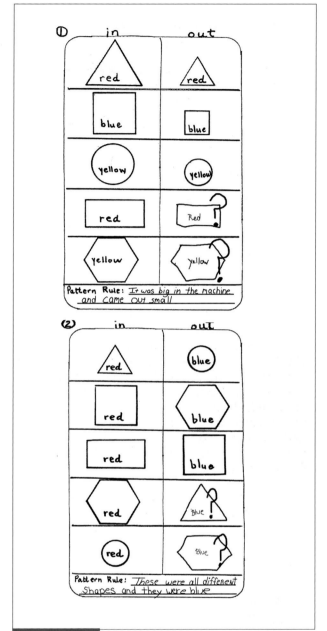

FIGURE 14.27

- What does Travis know and not know about linear equations from his answers on this paper?

3. It may be interesting to note that this student is considered gifted by the schools testing results and was placed in an accelerated prealgebra program for the eighth grade.

4. Design a rubric that would take into account the diversity of answers while being fair in your assessment strategy.

- Include the rubric in your Professional Portfolio for Job Interviews along with your analysis of the student's understanding in this activity.

- Enjoy the student work on algebra seen in Figure 14.28.

Name _Travis_

Complete this equation. Show how you solved it.

(3x + 2) + (2y + 4) = 38

$3x + 2y + 6 = 38$

$3x + 2y = 32$

$3x = 32 - 2y$

$x = 10.6 \cdot \frac{2}{3}$

$y = 1 \quad x = 10$

$32 + 2 + 2y + 4 = 38$

$38 + 2y = 38$

$y = 0$

$x = 10\frac{2}{3}$

Can you think of another way you can validate if you have solved the problem correctly? Please explain what you could do.

NO

How are the problems like these used in the real world of work?

If you have two types of one froit and you want to find out what kind, or how many of the froit in all.

What do you remember most about algebra after finishing your first year of study in algebra?

It wasn't easy remembering all the steps.

FIGURE 14.28

SUMMARY

- Algebraic thinking embodies a conceptual understanding of patterns, relations, and functions, the ability to represent and analyze mathematical situations and structures, the ability to use mathematical models to represent quantitative relationships, and the ability to analyze change in a variety of contexts.

- Number theory explores the relationships between and among the counting numbers and their properties.

- The term *relation* refers to the relationships seen in sets of things and in patterns, either within the same set or among sets. A relation associates the elements or patterns seen in one set to the elements or patterns seen in another set.

- A function is a specific relation in which every element in one set is associated with one and only one element in another set.

- Learning activities in number theory and algebra should begin at the concrete stage and proceed to the connecting stage and finally to the symbolic stage.

- A prime number has only two factors—itself and 1.

- The Video Vignette, "Connections to Algebra" found on the web site is an opportunity for you to apply what you have learned in this chapter.

PRAXIS II™-STYLE QUESTIONS

Answers to this chapter's Praxis II™-style questions are in the instructor's manual.

Multiple Choice Format

1. Babylonians used the right triangle theorem 1500 years before the time of Pythagoras, and the same understandings were used to build the pyramids generations before Pythagoras. Therefore the ancestors of _____ and _____ should be acknowledged for these findings.

   a. Asian-Americans and African-Americans

   b. Native-Americans and Hispanic-Americans

   c. Hispanic-Americans and Asian-Americans

   d. African-Americans and Native-Americans

2. What score on the five-point scale (Chapter 3) should be given to Mark as a result of his work in Figure 14.29?

   a. 2; because he does not understand the Fibonacci pattern although he attempted to answer.

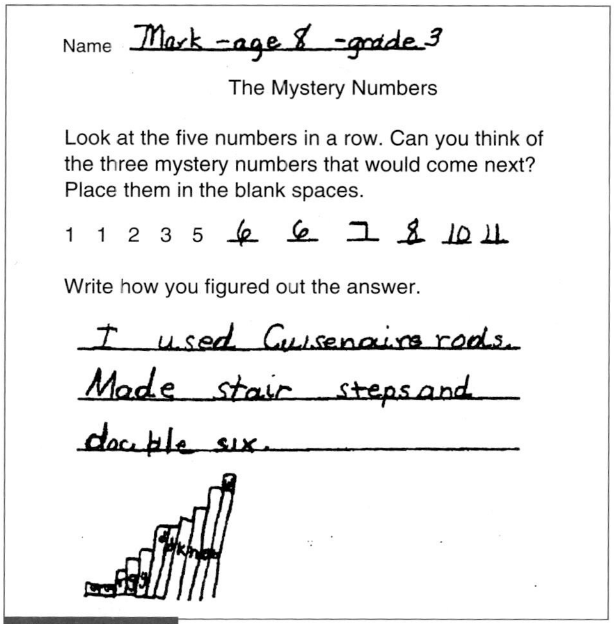

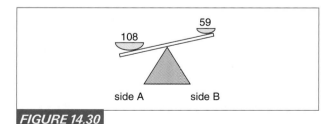

Name _Mark -age 8 -grade 3_

The Mystery Numbers

Look at the five numbers in a row. Can you think of the three mystery numbers that would come next? Place them in the blank spaces.

1 1 2 3 5 _6_ _6_ _7_ _8_ _10_ _11_

Write how you figured out the answer.

I used Cuisenaire rods.
Made stair steps and
double six.

FIGURE 14.29   *Name Mark-age 8-grade 3*

b. 3; because he is progressing in his understanding of number patterns although his explanation was not well formed or supporting of the pattern he showed.

c. 4; because he understands the concept of patterning and can write his justification.

d. 4+; because he understands the Fibonacci number sequence and goes beyond what is expected in the assignment.

3. The beginning algebra concept of the missing variable in an equation is seen in balance in Figure 14.30. The student who says that $n = 51$ has most likely:

FIGURE 14.30

a. added 51 objects to side B to balance the equation physically.

b. found the equation by subtracting quickly using mental math.

c. added both side A and side B together.

b. added 51 objects to side A to balance the equation by mental math.

4. The following problem involves the divisibility rules presented in this chapter. The following number is NOT divisible by

$$?\sqrt{2270382093432}$$

a. 3 and 9

b. 4 and 8

c. Both a and b

d. None of the above

Constructed Response Format

5. Using the information in question #4, create a new number that CAN be divided by the answer in question #4.

6. When the line is extented to intercept the y-axis, one can see it crosses at the number 16. This point is called the y-intercept.

7. This equation below is used to find where the line intercepts the x-axis. A student asks you why you changed the y to 0. What would be your explanation to the student?

$$(3x + 2) + 2y + 4 = 38$$
$$(3x + 2 + [2(0) + 4] = 38$$
$$3x + 2 + (0 + 4) = 38$$
$$3x + 2 + 4 = 38$$
$$3x + 6 = 38$$
$$3x = 38 - 6$$
$$3x = 32$$
$$x = 10.66 \text{ or } 10\frac{2}{3}$$

8. Create an engaging problem (one that young adolescents would enjoy) that involves the concept of the Fundamental Theorem of Arithmetic. How would you structure a classroom activity, using your problem, that could help students develop an understanding of the Fundamental Theorem of Arithmetic for themselves?

Integrating Technology

Computer Spreadsheet

Time Spent

Internet Activities

WebQuests

**CULTURAL
RELEVANCE**

PORTFOLIO

**MATHEMATICAL
CONNECTIONS**

The Pythagoream Theorem Revisited
Choosing a Cell Phone Plan: An Algebra WebQuest
http://home.austin.rr.com/esbhani/webquest.htm

National Library of Virtual Manipulatives
http://nlvm.usu.edu/en/nav/vlibrary.html
(also in Spanish)
Virtual manipulatives, with suggestions for teachers and parents, useful for teaching the content standards in NCTM's Principles and Standards.

Interactivate: Home Page
http://www.shodor.org/interactivate
Developed for middle school mathematics explorations but several are adaptable to elementary mathematics.

Video Vignette

Connections to Algebra

Choose one of the following three videos that you have seen previously. Watch the video of your choice this time, looking at the lesson for its connections to algebra and algebraic thinking.

Chapter 3, Video Vignette "Candy Sales"
Chapter 8, Video Vignette "Whale Math"
Chapter 7, Video Vignette "Dinosaur Legs"

Questions
1. What aspects of algebraic thinking did you see? Are there ways in the course of the lesson that these aspects could be emphasized?
2. Did the lesson involve number theory or patterning? What ways might that be extended in future lessons?
3. Be prepared to discuss your observations in class.

Supporting the NCTM *Principles and Standards* (2000)
- Mathematics Curriculum Principle
- Oral Discourse—The Teaching Principle

CHILDREN'S LITERATURE

Adler, David A. *A Picture Book of Frederick Douglass.* New York: Holiday House, 1993.

Blume, Judy. *Superfudge.* New York: E. P. Dutton, 1980.

_____. Blubber. New York: E.P. Dutton, 1974.

_____. *Otherwise Known as Sheila the Great,* New York: E. P. Dutton, 1972.

Forbes, Esther. *Johnny Tremain.* New York: Houghton, 1943.

Kelsey, Kenneth, and David King. *The Ultimate Book of Number Puzzles.* New York: Barnes and Noble, 1992.

Scieszka, Jon, and Lane Smith. *Math Curse.* New York: Viking Press, 1995.

Snape, Charles, and Heather Scott. *Puzzles, Mazes, and Numbers.* London, England: Cambridge University Press, 1995.

Solyom, Catherine, ed. *Big Block World Atlas.* Montreal: Tormont, 1997.

Data Analysis, Statistics, and Probability

Chapter 15

At the Start ~~~~ Know What Children Will Be Doing . . .

NCTM Curriculum Focal Points—

See . . .

| Grade 8 ~~ Analyzing and summarizing data sets | Figure 15.3
Activity 15.5
Activity 15.7 |

A partial listing as it pertains to Data Analysis from NCTM *Curriculum Focal Points* (2006, page 20)

WHERE'S THE MATHEMATICS? CONCEPTUAL UNDERSTANDING OF DATA ANALYSIS, STATISTICS, AND PROBABILITY

Nowhere does the concept of "real-world mathematics" show up more predominantly than it does in the concepts of graphing, statistics, and probability. Our information society revolves around the analysis of categorized information. Information is summarized and tested for its dependability and significance in nonbiased ways that call for numerical collection of data and tests for statistical significance. Data analysis, statistics, and probability have become increasingly more important topics in the elementary and middle school curriculum.

The NCTM *Principles and Standards* (NCTM, 2000) list data analysis, statistics, and probability as a part of the curriculum beginning in preschool. Students must work with data—collect it, organize and display it, analyze and interpret it—and understand how decisions are made on the basis of collected evidence. The *Standards* also call for

studying probability in real-world settings as shown in Figure 15.1 on page 427. Students need to investigate the notion of fairness (a natural PreK disposition) and chances of winning, a human interest of all ages. Because many predictions are based on probabilities, time should be allowed to make predictions based on experimental results or mathematical probability. Some items on the National Assessment of Educational Progress (2006, 2000) assessed organization and interpretation of data presented in graphs and tables. The NAEP also included items about finding and using measures of central tendency. As expected, students did better at making direct readings from graphs and tables than at deciding relationships among data.

An analysis of NAEP data shows gains on data analysis items. Students performed less well on the constructed response questions than they did on the multiple choice questions. Bar graphs were easier for fourth graders to understand than pictographs. Half of the fourth grade students and almost all of the eighth graders could interpret data from a graph. When asked to construct a

Kids see lists always (handwritten marginal note)

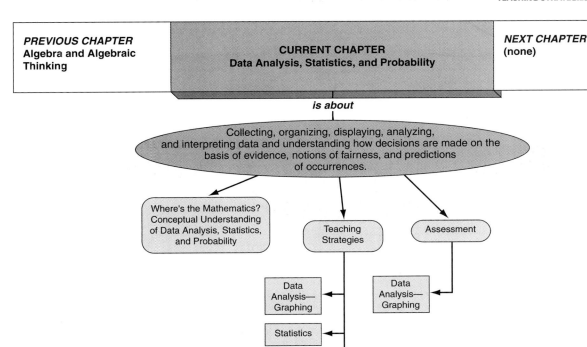

PREVIOUS CHAPTER	CURRENT CHAPTER	NEXT CHAPTER
Algebra and Algebraic Thinking	Data Analysis, Statistics, and Probability	(none)

is about

Collecting, organizing, displaying, analyzing, and interpreting data and understanding how decisions are made on the basis of evidence, notions of fairness, and predictions of occurrences.

Where's the Mathematics? Conceptual Understanding of Data Analysis, Statistics, and Probability

Teaching Strategies

Assessment

Data Analysis— Graphing

Data Analysis— Graphing

Statistics

Probability

SELF-HELP QUESTIONS

1. Do I know the four stages of the data analysis process?

2. Do I know how to create pictographs, bar, line, circle, scatterplot, stem and leaf, box and whisker and other types of graphs?

3. Do I know appropriate ways of using each of the various kinds of graphs?

4. Do I understand the difference among mean, median, and mode and the appropriate time to use each of those measures of central tendency?

5. Do I know the difference between combinations and permutations?

6. What do my students need to know about statistics and probability?

7. Do I understand how to use technology with my students as they study data analysis?

graph from data provided, one-third of the fourth graders and 80 percent of the eighth graders could construct the graphs. This suggests that proportional reasoning may be well defined by the eighth grade, accounting for the high scores. When asked to explain their reasoning in data analysis items, bale majority of the eighth graders received a score of satisfactory or higher. Once again, there is evidence that written discourse is a needed part of the mathematics curriculum (NAEP 2006; 2000).

This chapter emphasizes the different methods of representing information as well as producing the results. *Graphing* is a common method of displaying data pictorially. *Statistics* are used to discuss data numerically. *Probability* is the mathematics used to predict outcomes.

TEACHING STRATEGIES

If students are to develop mathematical proficiency in statistics and probability, then it is essential that a coherent curriculum, not just a collection of fun activities, is used. This means that you, the teacher, must understand the core ideas of data analysis. Data analysis is a process that involves four stages: (1) formulating the question

Standard

Instructional programs from prekindergarten through grade 12 should enable all students to

- Formulate questions that can be addressed with data and collect, organize, and display relevant data to answer them.
- Select and use appropriate statistical methods to analyze data.
- Develop and evaluate inferences and predictions that are based on data.
- Understand and apply basic concepts of probability.

Grades PreK to 2

In prekindergarten through grade 2 all students should

- Pose questions and gather data about themselves and their surroundings.
- Sort and classify objects according to their attributes and organize data about the objects.
- Represent data using concrete objects, pictures, and graphs.
- Describe parts of the data and the set of the data as a whole to determine what the data shows.
- Discuss events related to students' experiences as likely or unlikely.

Grades 3 to 5

In grades 3 to 5 all students should

- Design investigations to address a question and consider how data collection methods affect the nature of the data set.
- Collect data using observations, surveys, and experiments.
- Represent data using tables and graphs such as line plots, bar graphs, and line graphs.
- Recognize the differences in representing categorical and numerical data.
- Describe the shape and important features of a set of data and compare related data sets, with an emphasis on how the data are distributed.
- Use measures of center, focusing on the median, and understand what each does and does not indicate about the data set.
- Compare different representations of the same data and evaluate how well each representation shows important aspects of the data.
- Propose and justify conclusions and predictions that are based on data and design studies to further investigate the conclusions or predictions.
- Describe events as likely or unlikely and discuss the degree of likelihood using such words as certain, equally likely, and impossible.
- Predict the probability of outcomes of simple experiments and test the predictions.
- Understand that the measure of the likelihood of an event can be represented by a number from 0 to 1.

Grades 6 to 8

In grades 6 to 8 all students should

- Formulate questions, design studies, and collect data about a characteristic shared by two populations or different characteristics within the population.
- Select, create, and use appropriate graphical representations of data, including histograms, box plots, and scatterplots.
- Find, use, and interpret measures of center and spread, including mean and interquartile range.
- Discuss and understand the correspondence between data sets and their graphical representations, especially histograms, stem and leaf plots, box plots, and scatterplots.
- Use observations about differences between two or more samples to make conjectures about the populations from which the samples were taken.
- Make conjectures about possible relationships between two characteristics of samples on the basis of scatterplots of the data and approximate lines of fit.
- Use conjectures to formulate new questions and plan new studies to answer them.
- Understand and use appropriate terminology to describe complimentary and mutually exclusive events.
- Use proportionality and a basic understanding of probability to make and test conjectures about the results of experiments and simulations.
- Compute probabilities for simple compound events, using such methods as organized lists, tree diagrams, and area models.

FIGURE 15.1 *NCTM expectation of data analysis and probability.* Source: NCTM Principles and Standards for School Mathematics *(2000, pages 400–401).*

that will elicit the data desired; (2) gathering the data; (3) analyzing the data; and (4) forming and communicating conclusions based on the data analysis (Friel and Bright, 1998).

Formulating a question to elicit the desired data is a fine art. The question must be specific enough that relevant data are collected without being so specific that it is a trivial question. Sometimes that's a fairly easy task, as in testing the claim of Steak 'n Shake that "You could order a platter every night for a year and never have the same meal" (Hardy, 2001). Investigations about the number of languages spoken by classmates or

the number of states visited (Russell, Schifler, Bastable, 2000) call for more work in formulating the appropriate question.

Once the question is formulated, data can be collected. In the primary grades, students are most interested in themselves and their immediate surroundings. Often a show of hands or a collection of things (shoes, stuffed animals) is the preferred method of data collection. As children's interests expand, their questions become more complex and the amount of data available grows. Only through repeated experiences, frequent discussion, and the guidance of skilled teachers will children learn to refine their questions, collect data, and organize and display their data in ways that will help them to answer the question they posed (Friel, 2003).

By the time students reach middle school, their questions will expand from seeking information about a single population to asking about relationships among several populations or relationships between two variables in a given population. Their data collection methods expand to include experiments that require controlling variables or choosing samples. Their methods for representing data will also increase to include stem and leaf graphs, box and whisker plots, and relative frequency bar graphs (Friel, 2003).

Let's take time now to look at ways to represent data.

Data Analysis—Graphing

Graphing presents data in a concise and visual way that allows relationships in the data to be seen more easily. Students need to learn how to tally information, arrange data in a table, and display the information visually using a graph. Students can be introduced to graphing as a means of representing or organizing data early in the elementary years. Young children can make their own graphs and will benefit from collecting and organizing the information. A suggested developmental sequence for presenting graphs is generally followed in textbooks for young children.

1. Real graphs: actual objects to compare two or three groups.
2. Picture graphs: pictures or models to represent real things to compare two or three groups.
3. Real graphs: actual objects to compare up to four groups.
4. Picture graphs: pictures or models to compare up to four groups.
5. Symbolic graphs: most abstract using only symbols.

There are eight kinds of graphs frequently used in the elementary and middle grades, gradually proceeding from one to the other in level of difficulty—real, picture, bar, line, circle, scatter graphs. Stem and leaf and box and whisker graphs, introduced in the middle school years, will be discussed as a part of the statistics section of this chapter. As presented throughout this book, the introduction of each new concept (graph) should be from concrete to the connecting stage (pictorial) to the symbolic. Figure 15.2 shows the progression of learning experiences from real graphs to picture graphs to graphs with symbolic representation of data. Please pay special note to the written descriptions under each kind of graph. It will help you plan activities for your own classroom.

When working with any graph, ask students questions about it to help focus the discussion on information available for the graph. Questions should include comparisons such as which has the most or the least, how many more or how many less, and how many in all. Students enjoy taking a survey, collecting information, and constructing opinion graphs about their classmates or school. These graphs can be displayed in the hallway and create student interest and attention. Graphing should be at least a weekly activity because it is a part of daily exposure in newspapers, magazines, and other forms of media.

Creating Real Graphs   The possibilities for topics to graph are endless and should be determined by the interests of the class. Many articles have appeared in teacher journals and books showing clever ideas for real graphs with children. House([Ed.], 2002; 2003) as well as others, has reviewed ideas that can be used with group graphing as well as individual graphing projects. Some projects move naturally from the concrete stage of real graphs to the pictorial or connecting stage of picture graphs. Some of the more clever ideas suggest the use of finger puppets as a transition because they fit the description of real objects on the graph, yet they have the "look" of a picture graph.

Creating Picture Graphs   A *picture graph* represents data in the form of pictures, objects, or parts of objects as seen earlier in Figure 15.2. Be sure not to extend the categories to four until many experiences have been provided for comparing two and three groups.

There are many examples in the professional literature of innovative activities using picture graphs. Axelson (1992) shows how picture graphs can naturally lead into the symbolic stage using the real-world mathematics idea of the supermarket. She shows how journal writing can be blended into the activities after the children show the same information with a variety of graphs. Sgroi and coworkers (1995) show how children's literature, such as Dr. Seuss's *Green Eggs and Ham*, can be used effectively with picture graphs.

Another connecting stage idea is to use the actual pictures of the children in the classroom. Class pictures are usually taken at the beginning of the school year with each child receiving a sheet of small pictures. Many photographers also send a roll of small proofs to the teacher. These small

	Concrete	Pictorial (Connecting Stage)	Symbolic
Real Graphs Form actual graphs of themselves using hair color, sex, short pants/long pants, shoes with laces or without, who eats hot lunch or bag lunch, etc. Plastic or oil cloth can make the graph magic markers or masking type.			
Transition from Real Graphs to Picture Graphs Use actual pictures of children from their small class pictures. See two ways of using the bar graphs.		Individual Clothespin with Child's Picture Clothespins with the Bar Graph Hot Lunch Cold Lunch Bag Lunch No Choices Made ??? Clothespins with the Bar Graph Bag Lunch / Hot Lunch / Cold Lunch No Choices Made ??? *Actual pictures of children used in two graphs.*	
Picture Graphs Cut pictures of real things to paste. Draw pictures to represent real things or use models to stand for objects. Make the situations natural ones like the topic of how many girls are in each row in the class.		Children in Class Represent each girl with the symbol Row 1. Row 2. Row 3. Row 4. Row 5. *Picture symbols of children in class.*	
Transition from Picture Graph to Symbolic Representation A symbol represents multiple units. Use when multiplication is being studied in grades 3–4. Use fractional parts only after students have shown they understand multiple units without fractional parts represented.			Children in Class Let = 2 students Row 1. Row 2. Row 3. Row 4. *Children in class with multiple representations.*

FIGURE 15.2 *Developmental sequence for bar and line graphs.*

pictures are just the size to fit on the end of a clothespin. Two ways of using the graphs are shown in Figure 15.2. If the child's picture is not on the graph in the morning, the teacher knows who is absent very quickly. Children can ask comparison questions as a part of the morning mathematics activities known as "calendar math" in many schools. For example, "How many students brought their lunch today? How many are going to buy the cold lunch choice today? . . . hot lunch choice today? . . . How many more boys than girls brought their lunch?" This last type of comparison question is frequently difficult for children in the primary grades and should be asked on a regular basis so children can see how the idea is used in a real setting that has meaning for them. Lunch choice is one of those areas where children see real meaning in mathematics!

Native Americans used the picture graph, or pictograph, in sandpaintings as ways to communicate with each other. Children in PreK to grade 6 can have fun creating their own pictographs. Activity 15.1 is an extension of ideas that originally appeared in lesson material written by Native American teachers at their annual institute at Haskell Indian University in Lawrence, Kansas (Haines, 1992). A similar activity is found on the Web site in the Extended Activities. At the same time that students work with Native American pictographs, they can also learn about the contributions that other cultures have made to the development of data analysis, statistics, and probability as shown in the cultural contributions box.

Activity 15.1

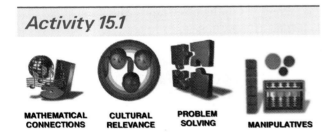

| MATHEMATICAL CONNECTIONS | CULTURAL RELEVANCE | PROBLEM SOLVING | MANIPULATIVES |

NATIVE AMERICAN PICTOGRAPHS

What Teachers Need to Tell Children
"Picture graphs originated in the pictographs used by early American Indians to communicate with each other. These pictographs were of two kinds: those that represented objects and those that represented ideas." (Riley and Stonehouse, 1992, p. 70)

MATERIALS
- *From nature*—leaves, bark, stones, soil samples, and so forth, gathered from a nature walk around the

school environment or brought from home as a homework assignment. Any object from their environment or picture of it can also be brought in.

DIRECTIONS
1. Students will learn the environment around them by comparing local plants, rocks, stones, other soil samples, animals, and objects from their environment.
2. Students organize their materials by categories on a picture graph. They decide how they will place the categories on the graph.
3. This can be done individually or in cooperative groups.
4. The gathering of things from nature gives the assignment a connection with science.

> **Supporting the NCTM *Principles and Standards* (2000)**
> - Mathematics as Connections; Problem Solving
> - Worthwhile Mathematical Tasks—The Teaching Principle
> - The Mathematics Curriculum Principle

EXTENDED ACTIVITIES

Name of Activity
- Pictographs with Sandpaintings
- Picture Graph with School-Community Activities
- One Picture = Many Students: Making a New Picture Graph
- Native American Pictographs
- Family Math Packet
  - Seas and Oceans (Graphing)
- Lesson Plans for Mathematical Proficiency
  - Graphs
  - Learning How to Read and Use Graphs Effectively

Teachers can see why multiple units represented with one symbol seem incomprehensible to PreK to grade 2 children as shown in Figure 15.2. Not only does it require allowing one symbol to stand for multiple representations but it also shows fractional parts of the symbol, implying that they stand for fractional parts of the multiple representations. PreK to grade 2 children are literal in their interpretations of concepts and half a person does not equate well to literally minded young children!

Students in grades 3 to 5 can use the other two activities found on the Web site in the Extended Activities to start real-world mathematics projects. Oral and written discourse can be integrated with graphing activities if you ask students what they can determine about the data from the graph. Their responses can become writings in their student journals.

Creating Bar Graphs A *bar graph* uses discrete (separate, distinct) data on each axis. Bars represent the information by the *x*- and *y*-axes. Figure 15.3 shows the development progression of bar graphs as students proceed through the grades.

Students need experiences constructing graphs in both vertical and horizontal formats. They also need activities in which they decide the labels for the two axes. Increments should be in consecutive whole numbers; in later grades, bar graphs can have other increments such as counting by twos, fives, or tens. Be sure to limit the list of choices to no more than six, such as the transition graph activities seen with the students' favorite academic subjects in Figure 15.3; otherwise, the comparisons become too difficult. Please note the written explanations in Figure 15.3. There are also additional bar graph activities in the Extended Activities.

Creating Line Graphs Our experiences indicate that upper elementary students have more problems interpreting information on a line graph than on a bar graph. It may be related to the visual interference from all lines seen simultaneously— horizontal, vertical, and broken diagonal lines. Perhaps the child does not know where to center attention. When given identical information in a bar graph and a line graph, children make fewer errors in interpreting the data than when interpreting the same data on a line graph. One way to help students see the relationship in bar and line graphs of the same data is to create the line graph by connecting the midpoint of the top of the bars in the bar graph, as seen in the explanation in Figure 15.3.

Line Graphs with Stationary Point Values Start with the simple line graph in the symbolic stage in Figure 15.3. What information can be obtained from this line graph? The graph expresses the relationship between Greg's and Travis's height and weight. Students can write a message under the graph to explain what is happening. One message could be "Travis is taller, but Greg is heavier." This connects written discourse with data analysis.

For additional practice the Extended Activities contains more examples of line graphs for various grade levels.

Continuous Line Graphs Line graphs are often used to illustrate a continuous activity, as seen in Figure 15.3. This requires higher level problem solving on the part of students. Young children can envision continuous graphs by working with toy cars on various kinds of inclined planes or straight raceways. The Extended Activities on show how to set up such graphs for PreK to grade 2 children. Upper grade students who own radio-controlled cars can come and demonstrate their moves while children graph what they see as the "motion line" on the graph.

EXTENDED ACTIVITIES

PROBLEM SOLVING   MANIPULATIVES

Name of Activity

- Bar Graphs with Favorite Sports
- Line Graphs
- More Practice with Messages in Line Graphs
- Pre-K–2 Continuous Graphs with Cars
- Line Graphs in Science
- More Practice with Plotting Continuous Graphs in Science
- Line Graphs with Speed and Time

Activity 15.2 demonstrates the use of continuous line graphs. When a continuous line graph is created, the data points are plotted and lines are drawn connecting the data points. The scale of a graph is very important. The scale used should be uniform and appropriate for the quantities to be displayed. The scale should be large enough to adequately represent the quantity being plotted. It is often necessary to use multiple units to keep the graph in reasonable proportions. Line graphs are often used because they provide a continuous representation of data. Therefore, the scale is important to adequately reflect the data. More

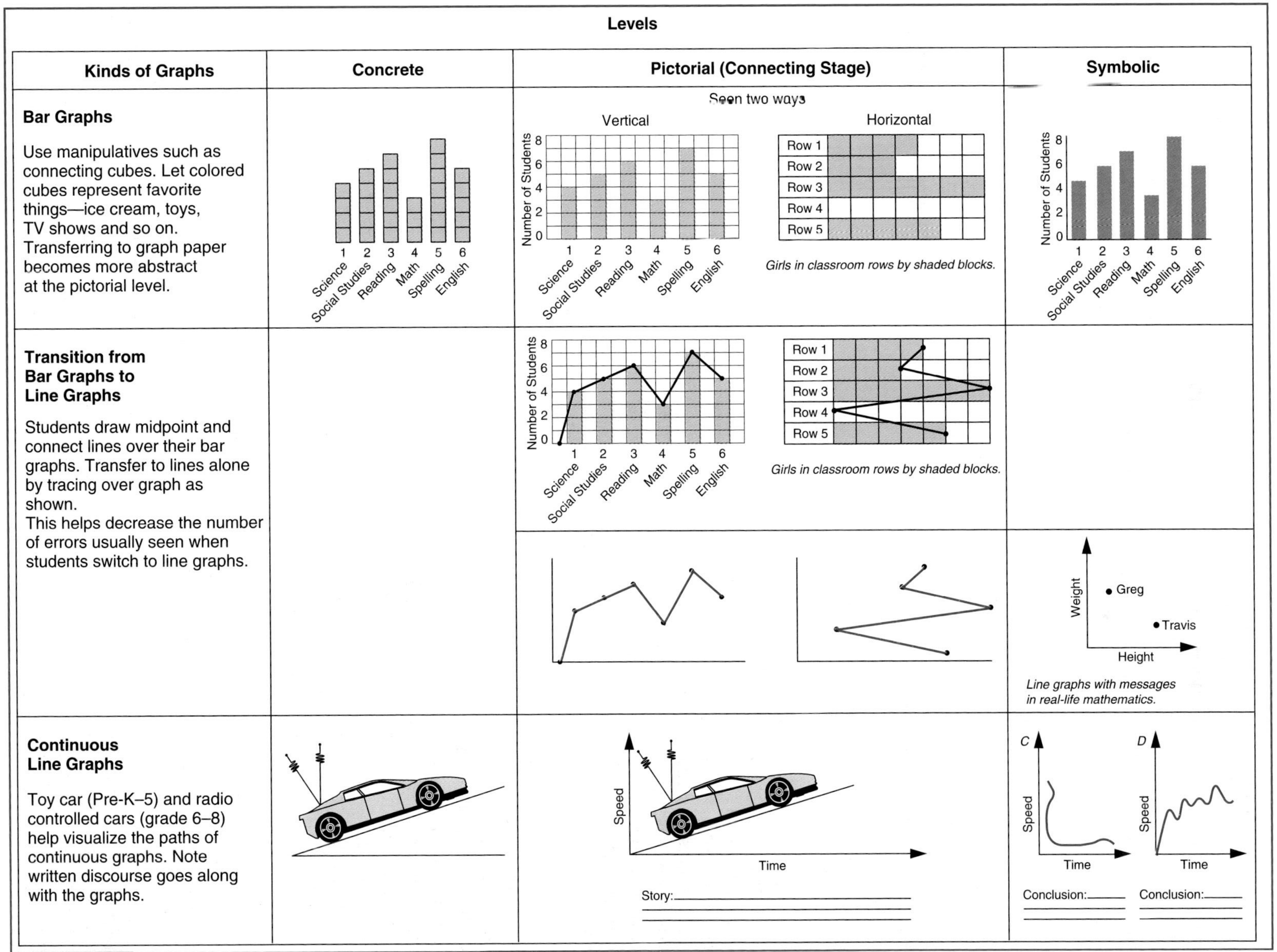

Levels
Kinds of Graphs
Concrete
Pictorial (Connecting Stage)
Symbolic
Bar Graphs
Use manipulatives such as connecting cubes. Let colored cubes represent favorite things—ice cream, toys, TV shows and so on. Transferring to graph paper becomes more abstract at the pictorial level.
Science
Social Studies
Reading
Math
Spelling
English
Seen two ways
Vertical
Horizontal
Number of Students
Row 1
Row 2
Row 3
Row 4
Row 5
Girls in classroom rows by shaded blocks.
Transition from Bar Graphs to Line Graphs
Students draw midpoint and connect lines over their bar graphs. Transfer to lines alone by tracing over graph as shown.
This helps decrease the number of errors usually seen when students switch to line graphs.
Girls in classroom rows by shaded blocks.
Weight
Greg
Travis
Height
Line graphs with messages in real-life mathematics.
Continuous Line Graphs
Toy car (Pre-K–5) and radio controlled cars (grade 6–8) help visualize the paths of continuous graphs. Note written discourse goes along with the graphs.
Speed
Time
Story:
C
D
Conclusion:
Conclusion:

FIGURE 15.3 *Developmental sequence for bar and line graphs.*

continuous line graphs can be found in the Extended Activities.

Graphs in the Middle School Years   By grades 5 to 8, middle school students can combine their knowledge of simple continuous graphs to plot more complex problems. In addition, the Extended Activities shows how middle school students can use radio-controlled cars to plot speed under different conditions, including racing times with and without various inclined planes. The Extended Activities show a number of excellent math problems that were generated by students when asked to make up problems involving the radio-controlled cars and the use of graphs to analyze the data collected. The pictures shown on the Web site can be a motivational start for your students to create problems with radio-controlled cars as well.

Activity 15.2

MATHEMATICAL CONNECTIONS   **PROBLEM SOLVING**

PLOTTING CONTINUOUS LINE GRAPHS IN SCIENCE

DIRECTIONS

These graphs show a *continuous* activity. The first set shows the graph and asks for an interpretation. The second is open-ended for the student to create. What is the message in each graph?

1. How could you label and plot these graphs? Be sure they give the message intended. An example is presented first.

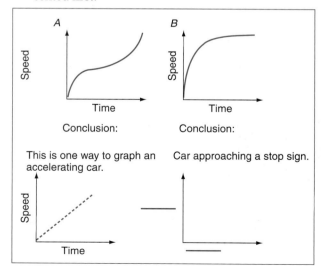

A

Conclusion:

This is one way to graph an accelerating car.

B

Conclusion:

Car approaching a stop sign.

EXTENDED ACTIVITIES

PROBLEM SOLVING   **MATHEMATICAL CONNECTIONS**

Name of Activity
- Middle School Data with Radio-Controlled Cars
- Graphs and Answers to Three Cars and a Race
- Buying at Super Target

Students' love of cars in the middle school years makes data collection and graphing activities more motivational even when the actual concrete items are not present as they were in the aforementioned example with the radio-controlled cars. The solution steps and the answers to Activity 15.3 appear on the Web site.

Creating Circle Graphs   The circle or "pie" graph is used to show the relationship between a whole and its parts as shown in Figure 15.4. Note the explanations under each part of the figure.

Circle graphs define the whole and it is easy to see how each part compares to the whole. Axelson (1992) cautions that many kinds of graphs are appropriate for comparing different kinds of information. Students gain the most from graphing activities when they can decide which graph best displays the needed information. Graphing calculators can compare different graph displays quickly, enabling students to analyze differences among graphs without losing concentration in the process. Such analysis promotes higher ordered mathematical thinking.

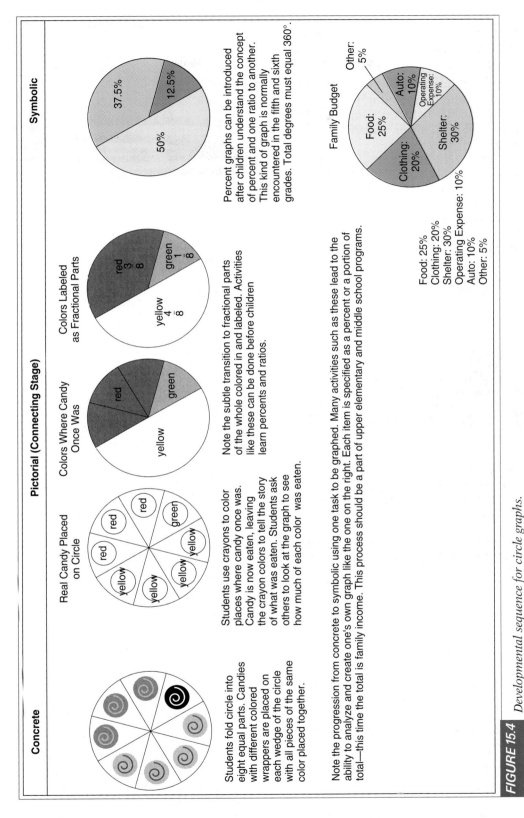

Concrete	Pictorial (Connecting Stage)			Symbolic

Real Candy Placed on Circle

Colors Where Candy Once Was

Colors Labeled as Fractional Parts

Students fold circle into eight equal parts. Candies with different colored wrappers are placed on each wedge of the circle with all pieces of the same color placed together.

Students use crayons to color places where candy once was. Candy is now eaten, leaving the crayon colors to tell the story of what was eaten. Students ask others to look at the graph to see how much of each color was eaten.

Note the subtle transition to fractional parts of the whole colored in and labeled. Activities like these can be done before children learn percents and ratios.

Percent graphs can be introduced after children understand the concept of percent and one ratio to another. This kind of graph is normally encountered in the fifth and sixth grades. Total degrees must equal 360°.

Note the progression from concrete to symbolic using one task to be graphed. Many activities such as these lead to the ability to analyze and create one's own graph like the one on the right. Each item is specified as a percent or a portion of total—this time the total is family income. This process should be a part of upper elementary and middle school programs.

Food: 25%
Clothing: 20%
Shelter: 30%
Operating Expense: 10%
Auto: 10%
Other: 5%

FIGURE 15.4 *Developmental sequence for circle graphs.*

Creating Scatter Graphs   A *scatter graph* is the plotting of pairs of values and observing the "scatter" form they take on. Often, real-world data are not "very uniform," and it is difficult to construct an accurate picture, line, bar, or circle graph. Students can plot the pairs of points and attempt to find some trend or tendency from the scatter pattern. For example, the scatter graphs in Activity 15.4 can be used to help students increase their problem-solving skills. This is usually a middle school activity.

Activity 15.3

MATHEMATICAL CONNECTIONS   **PROBLEM SOLVING**

THREE CARS AND A RACE

A Hyundai, a Ford, and a Mazda enter a 10-mile race. Because the Hyundai can average only 60 miles per hour, the Ford can average 90 miles per hour, and the Mazda can average 120 miles per hour, the Hyundai is given a 2-minute head start over the Ford and a 4-minute head start over the Mazda to make it a fairer race. In what order do the cars finish the race?

Data Collection

Create a table showing how far each car had traveled at the end of each minute. Why are there zeros under 1 and 2 minutes for the Hyundai and under the 1, 2, 3, and 4 minutes for the Mazda?

Graphing

The distance each car travels versus the time can be plotted on a coordinate graph. Graph the distance for each car (make sure you are able to distinguish the graph of each car). The first point for the Hyundai is (0, 0), for the Ford (2, 0), and for the Mazda (4, 0).

Related Equations

The distance each car travels can be represented by an equation. To write the equation representing the distance each car travels, you may use two points from your table or graph, or one point and the slope from your graph. To compare the equations, you will need to see them in slope-intercept form, $y = mx + b$. List the equations for each of the cars.

Use the data you have generated to answer the following questions. Explain how you arrived at the solution.

1. What is the order of finish?
2. If the race had been a 15-mile race, which car would have won?

3. How far will the Hyundai and the Ford have gone when the Ford catches up with the Hyundai?
4. How far will the Hyundai and the Mazda have gone when the Mazda catches up with the Hyundai?

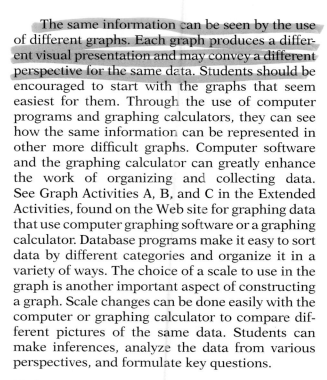

The same information can be seen by the use of different graphs. Each graph produces a different visual presentation and may convey a different perspective for the same data. Students should be encouraged to start with the graphs that seem easiest for them. Through the use of computer programs and graphing calculators, they can see how the same information can be represented in other more difficult graphs. Computer software and the graphing calculator can greatly enhance the work of organizing and collecting data. See Graph Activities A, B, and C in the Extended Activities, found on the Web site for graphing data that use computer graphing software or a graphing calculator. Database programs make it easy to sort data by different categories and organize it in a variety of ways. The choice of a scale to use in the graph is another important aspect of constructing a graph. Scale changes can be done easily with the computer or graphing calculator to compare different pictures of the same data. Students can make inferences, analyze the data from various perspectives, and formulate key questions.

Technology: Creating All the Graphs Together

Biehler (1994) points to the availability of technology programs as one of the reasons that innovations in presenting more intricate graphing techniques are possible at earlier and earlier grade levels.

Graphing Computer Models   It is now possible for a child to enter material to be graphed into a computer program and touch a key for each kind of graph. The graphs instantly appear, allowing the child to see how differently the material looks with each kind of graph presentation. Five of the seven graphs explored in this section are shown in the the Extended Activities called "Kinds of Graphs Compared." The graphs represent the fifth grade scores of children on a posttest compared with the amount of math anxiety each had before they studied a new mathematical concept with personalized mathematical problems. The scores showed that the students scored higher than would be expected for the amount of math anxiety originally experienced by the children (Habrock and Edwards, 1995). Which kinds of the graphs

Activity 15.4

PROBLEM SOLVING **MATHEMATICAL CONNECTIONS**

STORY WRITING WITH SCATTER GRAPHS

DIRECTIONS

1. Graphs I, II, and III all use the same data.
2. Label the *x* values and *y* values with identifiers.
3. Write a brief newspaper story using the data.
4. What has changed in Graph II? Does your newspaper story change from Graph I?
5. What has changed in Graph III? Does your newspaper story change from Graph I or II?

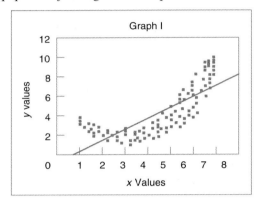

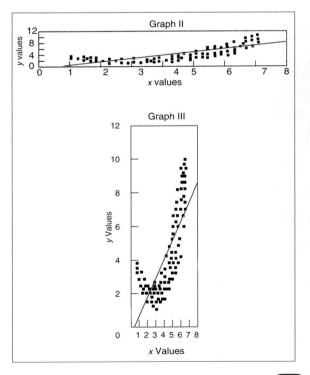

EXTENDED ACTIVITIES

MATHEMATICAL CONNECTIONS **PROBLEM SOLVING**

Name of Activity

- Kinds of Graphs Compared

presented in the Web site activity told the story of math anxiety best?

Graphing Calculator Models Graphing calculators are being used more frequently in the upper elementary and middle school settings at present. The graphing calculator can plot the same five graphs seen in the preceding activity. Perhaps the availability of many computers in the elementary and middle school laboratories makes the running of data seem more accessible on a computer as opposed to the graphing calculator. If you have a graphing calculator, use the information from the scatterplot activity and the Web site activity to plot the graphs. Many good analysis questions can come from the work with new technologies.

As you can see, graphs can tell many stories, and the same data can be represented in different ways. Newspaper reporters using microcomputers and graphing programs can present data in many views. Pick up any newspaper presenting statistical data and you can use a computer graphing program to display the information in another way. It is important that students understand how the presentation of data can take on different forms. Each gives a unique visual presentation and yields a different impact. Check out the NCTM *Navigating through Data Analysis and Probability* Series (House, 2002). To be an intelligent consumer, we must be aware of how different forms of data presentation can convey different perspectives.

Statistics

The study of statistics is important in the elementary grades because society frequently organizes and expresses data numerically (statistically). Since early childhood, we have been exposed to statistics in weather predictions, newspaper ads, and test grades, and with advances in technology, additional statistical data are available. Daily living requires decisions to be made on the basis of the processing of statistical information continuously.

Students need to be aware of how statistics can be manipulated to say whatever one desires. Media experts can use statistics to mislead consumers. Reports of medical information or opinion surveys must be examined carefully before drawing conclusions. Students should be aware of how statistics shape our lives and influence our decisions. There are many misconceptions about data because key questions have not been asked: How many people were in the sample? How was the population sampled? Who conducted the survey? How were the data summarized? We are inundated with statistical information and we must learn how to process this information accurately and effectively to function as knowledgeable citizens in society.

One of the first concepts of statistics encountered in daily life is that of average. The doctor tells a child "your height is about average for a six-year-old girl" or "your shoe size is a little over the average for an eight-year-old boy." The teacher says, "The class average on the last test was 68," or, "You scored above the average of the class on the last exam." The *average* is a measure of central tendency of data, or an attempt to describe what is "typical" in a set of data. There are three measures that are commonly used to describe ways of viewing what is typical in a data set. They are mean, mode, and median.

Mean The first measure of central tendency is the mean. The *mean*, or *arithmetic mean*, is most commonly used to describe the "average" of a set of data. The mean is computed by dividing the sum of the numbers by the number of members in the set. For example, if we want to know the average weight of four boys who weigh 105, 99, 110, and 90 pounds, we add $105 + 99 + 110 + 90 = 404$ and divide by 4. Thus, the average weight of the four boys is 101 pounds.

From the Concrete to Connecting Stage Students should be encouraged to perform simple activities to develop an understanding of the arithmetic mean. Have students work with objects until they understand the algorithm for determining the average (arithmetic mean) of a set of data. Two examples are shown in Activity 15.5. A stylized drawing of Cuisenaire rods can be sketched much like the second example in the activity when students are ready to move to the connecting (pictorial) stage.

Activity 15.5

MANIPULATIVES **MEAN**

DIRECTIONS

1. The weight of the bags of apples can be represented by objects, such as Cuisenaire rods. If the purple rod is 1 pound and the red rod is $\frac{1}{2}$ pound, the six bags of apples could be represented as follows:

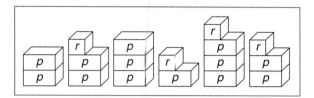

2. Rearrange the rods so there are six stacks of equal heights:

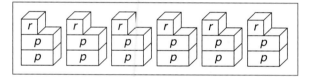

3. This is a method to discover that the arithmetic mean or average of six bags of apples weighing 2 pounds, $2\frac{1}{2}$ pounds, 3 pounds, $1\frac{1}{2}$ pounds, $3\frac{1}{2}$ pounds, and $2\frac{1}{2}$ pounds is $2\frac{1}{2}$ pounds.

4. Another approach using Cuisenaire rods is to have the students find the average height of four boys in a class. Their heights are 63 inches, 65 inches, 64 inches, and 68 inches. Use Cuisenaire rods to represent the heights:

10	10	10	10	10	10	111
10	10	10	10	10	10	5
10	10	10	10	10	10	1111
10	10	10	10	10	10	5 111

5. Rearrange the rods to make each one the same length:

10	10	10	10	10	10	5
10	10	10	10	10	10	5
10	10	10	10	10	10	5
10	10	10	10	10	10	5

The average height of these four boys is 65 inches.

From the Connecting to Symbolic Stage An additional example of using pictures in the connecting stage is shown in the Extended Activities found on the Web site. Calculators enable students to work with many numbers to find the mean on the symbolic level. An example with magic squares is also found in the Extended Activities.

Provide experiences in calculating means in practical problems using a calculator. A good source of practical problems is the daily newspaper. Class discussions could include "average rainfall," "batting average," "average speed," "stock market average," and "average points per game."

Mode The second measure of central tendency is the mode. Because an extremely high number or an extremely low number can distort the picture of the tendency shown by the arithmetic mean, the mode is frequently used. The *mode* of a set of numbers is the number that occurs most frequently in the set. For example, the following shoe sizes were recorded for 10 pupils: 8, 7, 6, 8, 9, 6, 8, 5, 7, 8. If we put these data into a frequency table, the mode becomes more readily apparent.

Shoe Size	Number of Pupils
9	/
8	/ / / /
7	/ /
6	/ /
5	/

We can see that the most frequent score was 8, hence the mode of this set of numbers is 8.

Median A third measure of central tendency is the median. The ***median*** of a set of numbers is the middle number of the set. For example, take a group of shoe sizes such as 7, 9, 3, 1, 6, 4, 10, and arrange them in order from greatest to least: 10, 9, 7, 6, 4, 3, 1. There are seven sizes. Now determine the position of the middle score. It must be the fourth score from either end; therefore, 6 is the median of this set of shoe sizes.

Here is another example, showing how to find the median of the following ages of a class:

$$12, 6, 7, 8, 7, 9, 10, 6, 7, 11, 12, 11$$

First, arrange the ages in order:

$$6, 6, 7, 7, 7, 8, 9, 10, 11, 11, 12, 12$$

How many ages are there? Twelve. Now determine the position of the middle age. It must be between the age of 8 and the age of 9. The median age is $8\frac{1}{2}$ because half of the ages are below 8 and half of the ages are above 8. Because there is an even number of ages, the median age lies halfway between the sixth and the seventh age, 8.

Range Another common statistical measure is the range. The range of a set of numbers is the difference between the highest and lowest numbers in a set. The range tells us the spread of a set of data.

Looking at one of our earlier examples of students' shoe sizes:

Shoe Size	Number of Pupils
9	/
8	/ / / /
7	/ /
6	/ /
5	/

The range here (or spread of shoe sizes) is 9–5 or 4. Here is another example with ages:

$$6, 6, 7, 7, 7, 8, 9, 10, 11, 11, 12, 12$$

The range of ages here is 12–6 or 6.

Range, like the mean, is sometimes not a good measure of a distribution because it includes the extremes and often gives a distorted picture of the data. For example, look at these two sets of numbers:

$$1, 1, 7, 7 \quad \text{mean 4; range 6}$$
$$1, 4, 4, 7 \quad \text{mean 4; range 6}$$

These two sets of numbers have the same mean and range, but they have a very different "scatter." The mean and range in the example do not give us an accurate picture of what is happening. We do not know that the points in the second set are grouped near the mean and those in the first set are located in the extremes of the range.

Stem and Leaf Plots In recent years, a new way of showing the median and the mode of a distribution has gained popularity in the middle school curriculum. The chart at the left shows the number of things to be "plotted" from a list of data gathered. The stem and leaf plot for the same data is shown to the right:

Ages of Female Students in Math Methods Class

23	18	38	49
17	39	48	52
19	31	42	33
23	20	37	23
19			

Stem and Leaf Plot

1	8	7	9	9	
2	3	3	0	3	
3	8	9	1	3	7
4	9	8	2		
5	2				

↑ ↑

ten ones

digits digits

(stem) (leaf)

Reordered to see mode and median more easily:

Stem and Leaf Plot

1	7	8	9	9	
2	0	3	3	3	
3	1	3	7	8	9
4	2	8	9		
5	2				

The stem and leaf plot looks like a horizontal graph of sorts, and the plot is easy to see because of its visual capabilities to explain data quickly. What can you tell from these data about the math methods class? What is the mode and the median?

See what else the stem and leaf plot can do for a visual analysis when men in the math methods class are added to the stem and leaf plot.

Ages of Male Students in Math Methods Class

17	18	19	43
27	19	18	22
19			

Stem and Leaf Plot

Male						Female					
9	9	9	8	7	1	7	8	9	9		
				7	2	0	3	3	3		
					3	1	3	7	8	9	
					3	4	2	8	9		
					5	2					

What can be told from the data now? What is the advantage of seeing data presented like this rather than in a normal chart formation? As you do the next activity, think about how the stem and leaf plot might have gotten its name.

The following approach is an example of the Learning Principle of the NCTM *Principles and Standards for School Mathematics* (2000). The activity emphasizes the purpose behind the stem and leaf plots used in middle school rather than calculations done without understanding what real-world examples apply.

Here is an example of another stem and leaf plot. It is similar to those found on some state assessment tests:

Stem			Leaf					
6	1	1	3	4	5			
7	0	2	2	5	6	7	9	9
8	4	6	7	8	8			
9	3	5	6	7	8	8	8	

What is the median?
What is the mode?

Here is an example of the kind of problem that could be solved by the stem and leaf plot above:

In a local mall arcade, the owners and the part-time workers want to report different salary options. The owners want to report the average salaries by the mean, but the part-time workers want to report the average salaries by the median.

The stem and leaf plot represents the amount of part-time salaries report in thousands of dollars (that is, $\frac{6}{1} = \$6100$). Now the question for students becomes "What does a stem and leaf plot do for data like that shown in the example? Why would a normal coordinate graph not work with these data? How do you suppose the stem and leaf plot got its name?" Look for the answers on the CD-ROM under " Stem and Leaf Dilemma."

Box and Whisker Plots Like the stem and leaf plots, the box and whisker plots have gained popularity in the middle school curriculum because of their ability to show how the different ranges of data affect the distribution. Different distributions may have the same mean and mode yet represent a very different median. Think about the following report of salaries for workers in town A and town B:

Town A : 2000, 5000, 5000, 8000, 15000, 25000, 25000, 25000, 35000, 100,000
Town B : 5000, 12000, 15000, 15000, 20000, 20000, 25000, 25000, 25000, 30000

What is the mode, median, and mean of each distribution? Which "average" or measure of central tendency misrepresents the financial well-being of each town? If one takes the mean for each town, town A would appear very well off, but is it? If one compares the mode and the median of both towns, they appear to be very similar towns. Comparing the two sets of information by range and differences from the median of each distribution tells the true story. That's what box and whisker plots do. See the plots for town A and town B in Figure 15.5.

A more appropriate picture of the towns can be seen. In the real world, this comparison of data matters when considering which town should receive federal funding for its less fortunate people and which may not qualify for aid. It may be easy to "eyeball" the disparity of salaries in this example, but the real-world model would have many more data points. The ability to see the disparity can get lost in the sheer volume of data.

Box and whisker plots are used when two or more sets of data need to be compared. First find the median and the quartiles (the lowest 25 percent and the highest 25 percent of the data). That makes the box and the vertical line within the box show the median. Now the highest and lowest data points are marked and a line, or whisker, is drawn from the box to the highest and lowest data points. The visual image of the box and whisker can show differences in the range (whisker) and cluster of scores in the second and the third quartile (the box). A graphing calculator can plot the box and the whiskers configuration once you know how and why the calculations are needed.

Another middle school activity for box and whisker plots shows more data that involve variation. An example from the NCTM **Standards** shows an application with an actual plot (Figure 15.6)

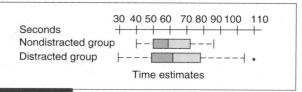

FIGURE 15.6 *Box and whisker plot.*

A class is divided into two large groups and then subdivided into pairs. One student in each pair estimates when one minute has passed, and the other watches the clock and records the actual time. All the students in one group concentrate on the timing task, while half the students in the second group exert constant efforts to distract their partners. The box plots show that the median times for the two groups are about the same but the times for the distracted group have greater variation. Note that in the distracted group, one data point is far enough removed from the others to be outlier. (NCTM, 1989, p. 107)

Putting It All Together: Statistical Information about Real-World Mathematics In the Extended Activities on the Web site, the activity called "Native American Lesson on Natural Resources with Statistics" shows how middle school students can learn of other cultures at the same time they are learning how to take care of the environment in real-world problems. The Native American Medicine wheel is used to show that the individual at the center of life is firmly connected to Mother Earth. Responsibility for the Earth and its resources is the theme of the sample statistical activity

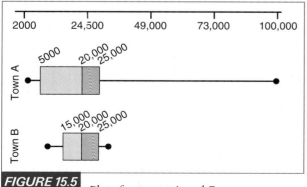

FIGURE 15.5 *Plots for towns A and B.*

EXTENDED ACTIVITIES

MATHEMATICAL CONNECTIONS   **CALCULATORS**   **CULTURAL RELEVANCE**

Name of Activity

- Finding the Mode
- Finding the Average in Sports
- More Box and Whiskers
- Stem and Leaf Dilemma
- Native American Lesson on Natural Resources with Statistics
- Poetry and mathematics

as adapted from the 1993 Summer Institute of Native American lessons on National Resources in Mathematics and Science conducted at Haskell Indian University in Lawrence, Kansas. All the lessons from K to12 are available through the U.S. Bureau of Indian Affairs (Darden et al., 1993).

Scavo and Petraroja (1998) describe creative activities in which teachers produce real-world statistics problems of interest to students. One activity asked students to find out whether the average areas of sixth grade rooms were larger than fifth grade rooms. Competition among middle schoolers being what it is, sixth graders eagerly took on the project. No sixth graders want to be in smaller rooms than fifth graders.

Other teachers use children's literature to spur interest in data collections and graphing representations. One such lesson used the book, **Visual Foolery** (DiSpezio, 1995), to learn what the average number of people would see in a variety of perceptual tasks designed to trick the eye. There are many child and adolescent books that can relate to statistics and data analysis (Thiessen [Ed.], 2004). Some of the best are listed in the bibliography at the end of the chapter.

Probability

Probability is the branch of mathematics concerned with analyzing the chance that a particular event will occur. The basic purpose of probability theory is to attempt to predict the likelihood that something will or will not happen. Probability is computed on the basis of observing the number of actual outcomes and the number of possible outcomes.

$$\text{Probability of an event} = \frac{\text{Number of actual outcomes}}{\text{Total number of possible outcomes}}$$

Studying probability will help children to develop critical thinking skills and to interpret the probability that surrounds us daily. The study of chance needs to begin in an informal way in the early grades. Many students and teachers have misconceptions about the outcome of real events in life. For example, if the Watson family has three girls and is expecting a fourth child, is there an equally likely chance of having a boy or girl? Many people feel the next child "is bound to be a boy" because there are already three girls in the family. They base their predictions on their opinions about what they feel should happen (a baised reaction) rather than on factual data. Statements involving probability abound in everyday situations, and it is important to make students aware of them. Students should be introduced to probabil-

ity through activities with measuring uncertainty. Choice devices can be used to provide initial experiences for the study of chance—tossing a coin, rolling a die, drawing a card from a deck or a colored cube from a bag.

Students should begin by doing experiments, predicting the outcome, and recording the results. In most cases, a sample must be selected. A *sample* is a small number that represents a large group called a *population*. In most cases, it is impossible to test the total population, so a sample or samples are chosen.

A simple rubric can be selected that helps structure students' thoughts. Probability is one of those areas that appears to be less defined to a lot of students and teachers since the answers are always framed as "probables" with no exact endings ever finalized.

Early Experiences: The PreK to 5 Grades Simple activities like the coin and dice toss give students in the early grades a limited number of choices from which to make predictions. Even young children can write a fraction to show how many heads they recorded out of how many total coins tossed. Charts or other recording devices need to be provided for young children. Free computer programs are available on the Internet for all grades. See Integrating Technology at the end of the chapter.

Rubric for Probability Problems		
Begins by doing experiment	0:	Does not organize a start to the experiment
	1:	Starts experiment, but does not record results after each trial
	2:	Starts experiment, records results, but stops before enough trials are completed
	3:	Finishes experiment with results recorded with all trials completed
Predicting the outcome	0:	Does not predict an outcome
	1:	Predicts outcome only after 75 percent finish of trials
	2:	Predicts outcome after 50 percent finish of trials
	3:	Predicts outcome *before* trials begin
Checking the probability	0:	Does not compare prediction to outcomes of trials
	1:	Tells whether prediction was close, same, or far from actual outcomes of trails
	2:	Compares prediction to outcomes and explains *why* prediction was same, close, different, and so on
	3:	Explains why and projects what a general rule would be if applied to the next set of trials

Tallies		Heads	Tails
Heads Count	=		
Out of Total	=		
Tails Count	=		
Out of Total	=		

As children come closer to the middle school grades, they can be encouraged to make up their own recording forms as a means of problem solving all the categories and the options that need to be considered. This situation is like the real world where the boss expects the worker to come up with some form to handle the business at hand after being given a problem to solve.

Dice and Coin Tosses, Two Color Counters From experiences like the coin toss (Activity 15.6), students can begin to predict the probability of certain events occurring. If a coin is tossed, there are two probable outcomes: heads or tails. There is an equally likely chance of it landing as a head or as a tail. If a coin is tossed 12 times, the theoretical probability is that it will land heads 6 times and tails 6 times. If one were actually to do this act, the experimental probability (actual outcome) may be quite different. Children need experiences with experimental probability.

Another study of chance is tossing a die. Toss a die 100 times and record how many times each number appears. The results will indicate on the average that each number occurs about $\frac{1}{6}$ of the time. The theoretical probability of the number 4

Activity 15.6

MANIPULATIVES **COIN TOSS**

DIRECTIONS

1. A good experiment is to toss a coin 30 times and record how many heads and how many tails you get from a set number of tosses.

2. Represent the occurences as a fraction. For example, if the outcome was 16 heads, the fraction $\frac{16}{30}$ would be the ratio of heads to the numbers of tosses, and $\frac{14}{30}$ would be the ratio of tails to the number of tosses.

   Heads $\frac{16}{30}$ Tails $\frac{14}{30}$

3. Record your results as a ratio.

appearing on the toss of a die is $\frac{1}{6}$. Likewise, the probability of the number 2 is $\frac{1}{6}$.

Activity 15.7 will let students experiment themselves.

Students should engage in many experiments to explore probability problems such as tossing a coin, tossing a die, or flipping two-colored counters until they become skillful in assigning probabilities.

Activity 15.7

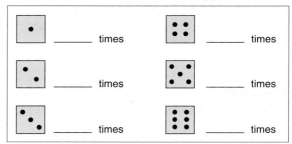

ESTIMATION **PROBLEM SOLVING** **MANIPULATIVES** **DIE TOSS**

DIRECTIONS

1. Take one die and roll it 100 times. Keep a record of the number of times each number appears.

_____ times	_____ times
_____ times	_____ times
_____ times	_____ times

2. Divide the number of times you threw the die into the number of times your number appeared. This ratio tells you the chances of your number appearing in a certain number of trials.

3. Compare your results in the die activity to the theoretical probabilities.

4. From your record, what was the probability of a number less than 3 showing? What is the theoretical probability of this event occuring?

5. What is the theoretical probability of an odd number (1, 3, 5) showing?

6. What is the theoretical probability of a prime number (2, 3, 5) showing? A multiple of 3 (3, 6) showing? A multiple of 2 (2, 4, 6) showing?

Supporting the NCTM *Principles and Standards* (2000)

- Mathematics as Problem Solving; Estimation; Probability and Data Analysis

- Tools for Enhancing Discourse—The Teaching Principle

- The Learning Principle

From experiments of this type with one coin or one die, the teacher should progress to experiments with two coins, Activity 15.7 colored balls and checkers. Discussions should include notions of fairness. Have students work through these activities as they continually ask, "Is this a fair situation?"

Video Vignette

Graphing Probability

Before viewing the Video Vignette "Graphing Probability" found on the Web site, Chapter 15, Video Vignettes, do the task assigned to the children described below. Then read over the following questions. After viewing the vignette, answer the questions independently. Then discuss your answers with a small group. Be prepared to defend your answers to the task and your responses to Questions 1 and 2.

Task

1. On a sheet of paper, draw a 3 × 4 grid.
2. List the possible outcomes from rolling two die (the sum of the upper faces), one per box in the grid that you drew.
3. Take 11 counters (beans or other small objects) and place them in the numbered boxes. You can put all 11 counters in one box, put 1 counter in each numbered box, or put more than 1 in some boxes and none in other boxes.
4. You will be rolling two dice. Each time the sum of the two upper faces matches a box with a counter in it, you may remove 1 counter from that box. You may remove only 1 counter at each roll.
5. On a separate piece of paper, numbered 2 through 12, keep a tally with each roll of the dice of the sum you rolled—regardless of whether you had, or still have, a bean on that box. You are

keeping track of the number of times you rolled each sum and, at the end, you will add that up to see how many rolls of the dice it took to remove all 11 counters.
6. After completing this task, read the following questions before watching the video vignette, "Graphing Probability." After viewing the video vignette, discuss what you learned from doing the task and your responses to the questions about the video vignette.

Questions

1. At the beginning of the lesson from the children's predictions, what can be determined about Ms. Bennett's students' understanding of probability?
2. Why does Ms. Bennett have the paired learning situation as the next part of her lesson? What do you think about the appropriateness of this task?
3. The students combine their data into the class chart. What do you think Ms. Bennett hoped would occur from this experience? What are their explanations about the likelihood of probability?
4. At the end of the lesson, what variables do her students suggest to explain the differences in the data? What follow-up activities would you suggest for students at this level of understanding?

The Extended Activities, found on the Web site, require students to set up charts and tables to record tosses with more than one coin and to record tosses of two dice at once. The tables may be printed from the Web site. See *Mathematics Teaching in the Middle School* (NCTM, 1999) for a focus issue on probability. The Video Vignette "Graphing Probability" found on the Web site illustrates an activity that can be used in grades 5–8.

EXTENDED ACTIVITIES

MANIPULATIVES   **PROBLEM SOLVING**   **ESTIMATION**

Name of Activity
- Money Toss
- Creating Tables with Dice Tosses
- Probability Games on the Internet

An interactive WebQuest, "Is This Your Lucky Day?" is explained in *Mathematics Teaching in the Middle School*, (Arbaugh, Scholten, and Essex, 2001). Unfortunately, the Web site is no longer available. However, you may want to use the ideas given in the article to develop your own WebQuest on probability. The URL for a WebQuest using statistics can be found at the end of this chapter.

Common Usage of Probability   Activity 15.8 provides a setting for students to work together in cooperative groups with common materials. The students use oral discourse as they make their predictions and naturally explain to each other what is happening as they participate in the actual trials. Each student should have a copy of the rubric shown earlier to remember all the parts of the activity.

Activity 15.8

MANIPULATIVES   **PROBABILITIES WITH CARDS**

DIRECTIONS

1. Place five cards with the numbers 0 through 4 on them in a cardboard box.
2. What is the probability of drawing a card with a number less than 5 on it? There are five possible outcomes, and they are all favorable; therefore, the probability of drawing a card with a number less than 5 on it is $\frac{5}{5} = 1$.
3. What is the probability of drawing a card with a number greater than 4 on it? There are five possible outcomes and none of them are favorable—the probability of this occurring is $\frac{0}{5}$ or 0.
4. If an event is sure to happen, the probability is 1. If there is no favorable outcome and an event is sure not to happen, the probability is 0.

In most experiments, we have more than one set of outcomes associated with the experiment. For example, in our previous example of tossing two coins, our probable outcomes were H–H, H–T, T–H, T–T. A pictorial way of illustrating all possibilities is with a *tree diagram*. To illustrate, use a bag containing five red and three black marbles. Draw twice with replacement (return the marble to the bag before making the second draw). What are the possible outcomes of this experiment?

You could draw a red marble first then a black marble, a red marble first and then another red marble, a black and then a red, or a black and a black. We can abbreviate this as: rb, rr, br, bb.

We can represent this visually as follows (Figure 15.7, p. 446). On the first draw, we can obtain either a red marble or a black marble.

Assigning Probabilities: The 6 to 8 Middle School Grades   Middle school children need to approach problems in which they represent the probability of the outcome of a certain experiment in a mathematical way. For example, use a bag with twelve red marbles and four black marbles, and represent the probability that a red marble is drawn or that a black marble is drawn. Because the red marbles make up $\frac{12}{16} = \frac{3}{4}$ of the total number of marbles, $\frac{3}{4}$ can be used to represent the probability of drawing a red marble. The black marbles represent $\frac{4}{16} = \frac{1}{4}$ of the total number of marbles. Therefore, $\frac{1}{4}$ can be used to represent the probability of drawing a black marble.

In another situation, if the same bag contained four black, three green, and three red marbles, the probability of drawing a black marble would be $\frac{4}{10}$ (0.4) a green $\frac{3}{10}$ (0.3), and a red $\frac{3}{10}$ (0.3).

Probability of red or black on first draw.

Regardless of what occurred on the first draw, there are still two possibilities for the second draw as seen below. The tree diagram is very useful in determining possible outcomes of an experiment. The possible outcomes of the second draw are shown below.

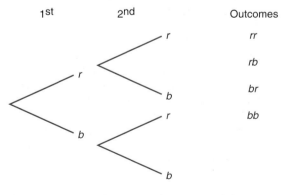

Probability of red or black extended to second draw.

FIGURE 13.7   *Probability of drawing red or black on successive draws.*

The probability of each outcome will be a number between 0 and 1, and the sum of all the probabilities in the experiment must equal 1. What is the probability that in the toss of a coin, "tails" will appear? $\frac{1}{2}$. What is the probability of rolling a 3 when tossing a die? $\frac{1}{6}$. Students should be allowed to perform experiments and record the results while learning to assign probabilities. Toss a die and ask how often does a 3 occur? About $\frac{1}{6}$ of the time. How often does a 2 occur? About $\frac{1}{6}$ of the time.

Activity 15.9 demonstrates another example of the use of tree diagrams.

Activity 15.9

PROBLEM SOLVING   **TREE DIAGRAMS**

DIRECTIONS
1. Draw a tree diagram illustrating the outcomes of draws from a bag containing twelve red marbles and four black marbles.
2. Marbles are drawn from the bag with replacement. Three draws are made. What are the possible outcomes?

   The solution is in the *Instructor's Manual.*

Experiments can be developed using dice, coins spinners, cards, or whatever to give students experience assigning probabilities. Assigning probabilities (making selections) without bias is essential for computing the probability of events occurring. Activities using probability paths, such as Activity 15.10, help give a sense of concreteness to a probable happening.

Identifying Different Types of Events After working with different arrangements of probability paths, the next step is to identify different types of events. Developmentally appropriate activities for middle schoolers include the recognition that there are different types of events that can occur in the real world of mathematics. These are called events that are independent of any other event that is occurring and events that are dependent on other events that are occurring. As you can see from the explanations, the Web site; but topic an understanding

Activity 15.10

PROBLEM SOLVING   **MANIPULATIVES**   **PROBABILITY PATH**

DIRECTIONS
Follow the probability path. Tossing a die five times will get you from the start position to one of the lettered boxes.

1. Toss the die. If the number on the die is odd, follow the odd path. If the number is even, follow the even path.
2. Follow the path twenty-five times. Keep a tally mark record of the box in which you finish each time. Which boxes do you end in most often? Least often?
3. What percent of the twenty-five tosses lands in each box?

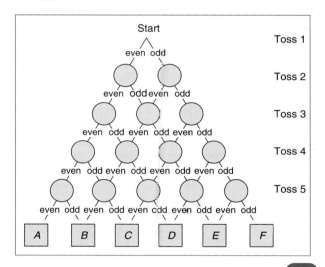

of set theory is helpful. This can be explained to middle school students without the set theory symbols for intersection and union. In these cases oral discourse of the teacher and written words on the board or overhead projector are needed at the start of developing an understanding with the manipulatives.

- **Mutually Exclusive Events (Independent Events)** Two events are said to be *mutually exclusive* if they have no outcomes in common. For example, if x and y are mutually exclusive events with a finite (z) set of outcomes, we could represent these sets as

The addition property of two mutually exclusive events is the sum of their probabilities. For example, if a marble is drawn at random from a bag containing four red, five black, and six green marbles, what is the probability of drawing

1. A green marble?

$$P(G) = \frac{6}{15}$$

2. A green or red marble?

$$P(G) = \frac{6}{15}$$

$$P(R) = \frac{4}{15}$$

The probability of drawing a red or a green marble is mutually exclusive, and so the combined probability is

$$P(G \text{ or } R) = \frac{6}{15} + \frac{4}{15} = \frac{10}{15} = \frac{2}{5}$$

To check our answer, compare this answer with the probability of drawing some color other than black.

$$P = 1 - \frac{5}{15} = \frac{10}{15} = \frac{2}{5}$$

Two dice are thrown. What is the probability that the sum is 5 or the sum is 7?

The possible outcomes $5 = (1, 4)(2, 3)(3, 2)(4, 1)$

The possible outcomes $7 = (1, 6)(6, 1)(2, 5)(5, 2)$
$$2(3, 4)(4, 3)$$

The probability of either event happening:

$$P(5 \text{ or } 7) = \frac{4}{36} + \frac{6}{36} = \frac{10}{36} = \frac{5}{18}$$

Practice is recommended to understand the concept of mutually exclusive events. However, if students are continually reminded that mutually exclusive events are two events that have no common outcomes, they will have less difficulty with the topic.

Using the phrase "either–or" is a helpful oral discourse technique for students to reason if occurrences are mutually exclusive. Activity 15.11 shows if the pencil is *either* on the line *or* off the line. Other examples would be tossing a die that yields one choice of six numerals. You *either* get that numeral *or* don't.

- **Known Conditions Imposed on Events: Conditional Probability (Dependent Events)** In probability experiments we are often restricted by certain conditions imposed on the outcomes. How does the outcome change when a "known" is imposed on the experiment?

Activity 15.11

MATHEMATICAL CONNECTIONS   **PROBLEM SOLVING**   **MANIPULATIVES**   **SCIENCE**

DIRECTIONS

1. Get a pencil and measure its length.
2. Draw parallel lines on the paper that are 1.5 times as far apart as the length of the pencil

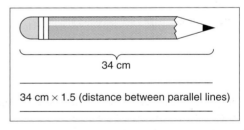

34 cm

34 cm × 1.5 (distance between parallel lines)

3. Drop the pencil onto the paper from a height of about 1 meter.
4. Record on a chart, such as the one shown here, how many times the pencil touches a line or does not touch a line. Don't count it if the pencil doesn't land on the paper.

	Tally	Total
Touches a line		
Doesn't touch		

5. After a certain number of trails, such as 50, figure the probability that the pencil will touch a line when dropped. Does it make a difference whether your pencil is longer or shorter?

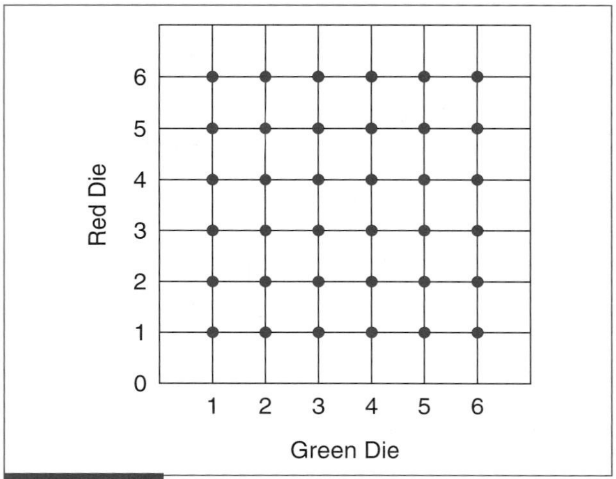

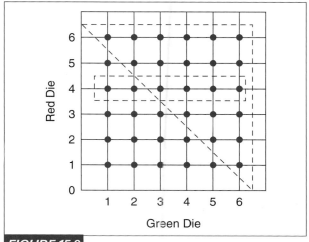

FIGURE 15.8   *Red and green dice with all possibilities shown.*

FIGURE 15.9   *Red and green dice with conditions applied.*

Suppose we throw two dice, one red and one green. If the red die shows a number that is divisible by 4, what is the probability that the total of the two dice is equal to or greater than 7? This condition that has been imposed on the experiment (the red die has a number divisible by 4) cuts down the sample or outcome.

The original sample of 36 possibilities is shown in Figure 15.8.

When the condition that the number on the red die has a number divisible by 4 is imposed, the sample reduces to 6 possibilities, and the probability of having a total greater than or equal to 7 is $\frac{4}{6} = \frac{2}{3}$ (Figure 15.9).

Probability that is *dependent* on an outcome is referred to as *conditional probability* and is represented as $P(A|B)$. This means the probability of A happening once B has occurred.

In the previous example, A equals the set of points representing a total dice sum of 7 or over; B equals the set of points for which the number on the red die is divisible by 4.

The 4 points common to A and B ones (7, 8, 9, 10), and the probability of B, $P(B) = \frac{6}{36} = \frac{1}{6}$. So, the probability of A occuring after B has occured is the intersection of A and B divided by the probability of B.

For example:

$$P(\text{sum} > 7 \mid \text{red die divisible by } 4) = \frac{\frac{4}{36}}{\frac{6}{36}} = \frac{4}{6} = \frac{2}{3}$$

- **Independent and Dependent Events Compared** There are certain events that are not dependent on what occurred prior to their occurrence. These events are called *independent events*. For example, if a coin is tossed, the probability of it being a tail on the second toss is not dependent on what it was on the first toss. The probability of it being a tail on the second toss is $\frac{1}{2}$ regardless of whether it was a head or a tail on the first toss.

The definition for the *multiplicative property for independent events* is that the probability of independent events X and Y to occur is the product of their probability.

Previous bag problems, where marbles were being drawn from a bag with replacement after each draw, were examples of an independent event. Our original problem had a bag containing five red and three black marbles. Two marbles were drawn one after another, with replacement after each draw.

The probability of red on the first draw is $\frac{5}{8}$. Because the bag is restored to its original state after the drawing, the probability of drawing a red marble on the second drawing is $\frac{5}{8}$ also. A tree diagram of this experiment would look like Figure 15.10.

Repeat the same experiment without replacing the marbles. Again, make two draws, but this time do not replace the first marble drawn. The probability of a black marble being drawn on the first draw is $\frac{3}{8}$. If the marble is drawn and not replaced, there are now seven marbles in the bag. The probability of a black marble being drawn on the second draw is $\frac{2}{7}$. A tree diagram of this experiment looks like Figure 15.11.

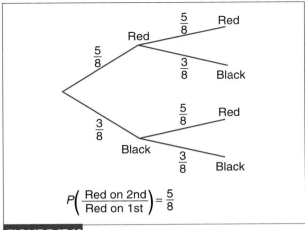

$$P\left(\frac{\text{Red on 2nd}}{\text{Red on 1st}}\right) = \frac{5}{8}$$

FIGURE 15.10 *Probability of marbles with replacement after each draw.*

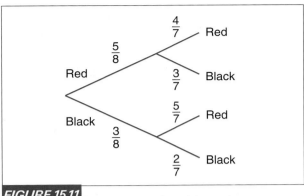

FIGURE 15.11 *Probability of marbles without replacement after each draw.*

The probability for the second draw changes because the marbles are not replaced and the content of the bag changes.

Cards, colored dice, and coins are good manipulative aids for probability experiments. Drawing diagrams and recording data can be used to develop skills in determining whether events are independent or dependent. Probability is rich with interesting problems to experiment and stimulate. It provides a setting to engage middle school students in making hypotheses, testing conjectures, and justifying their conclusions. Once students have experimented, a computer can generate hundreds of simulated results.

Permutations and Combinations Probability includes the study of permutations and combinations. These probability applications have to do with mathematically predicting the results of games and real-life situations. Before discussing permutations and combinations, the term *factorial* needs to be defined. *Factorial* is a series of multiplications of consecutive integers. For example, 6! means $6 \times 5 \times 4 \times 3 \times 2 \times 1 = 720$ and is read "six factorial."

Factorial is used in evaluating combinations and permutations.

Zero factorial is defined to be equal to one; that is, $0! = 1$.

Calculator keys with the factorial key [!] make it easy for middle schoolers to figure problems with permutations and combinations. Simple factorial problems like 6! shown above can be done with any calculator without the student losing track of how many times the factors are to be multiplied. No special keys are really needed when the factors are held to ten or less.

Permutations There are many problems involving permutations. Here is one example: Suppose we wish to seat four students (Al, Beth, Cathy, and Diego) in four seats in the front of the room. How many different ways are there to seat these students?

The problem can be solved by experimenting with the actual arrangements and constructing a tree diagram following this explanation.

How many different ways are there to fill seat 1?
It can be filled with

1. Al
2. Beth
3. Cathy
4. Diego

Seat 1 can be filled in four ways. When seat 1 is filled, how many ways are there to fill seat 2? If Al is in seat 1, seat 2 can be filled with

1. Beth
2. Cathy
3. Diego

There are 3 ways of filling seat 2. Suppose Beth is in the first seat, how many ways are there of filling seat 2?

1. Al
2. Cathy
3. Diego

There are three ways of filling seat 2 with seat 1 being occupied by Beth. The same is true when the first seat is filled by Cathy and when it is filled by Diego.

So there are $3 + 3 + 3 + 3 = 12$ different ways of filling seats 1 and 2. They are as follows:

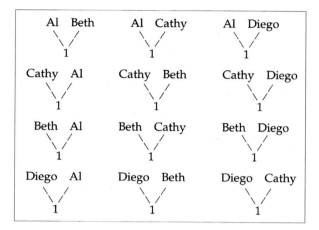

There are twelve ways of filling the first two seats. There now remain two different ways of filling the remaining two seats. For each way of filling the first two seats, there are a total of twenty-four ways to seat the four children in four seats. The tree diagram of this seating would look like Figure 15.12.

This experiment and others like it should actually be done cooperatively with students so they can visualize the concept of ordered arrangements. Placing n objects in a particular order gives the following result:

$n = 4 : n(n - 1)(n - 2)(n - 3)$ ways
or $4 \times 3 \times 2 \times 1 = 24$
$n = n :$ or $n! = n(n - 1)(n - 2)(n - 3) \ldots 3, 2, 1$

The generalization of an ordered selection of x of the n objects can be done in $n(n - 1)(n - 2) \ldots (n - x)$ ways, which is equal to $n!/(n - x)!$. The generalized formula can be applied to the previous example as follows:

Example : 4 students
4 chairs

$$\frac{4!}{(4 - 4)!} = \frac{4 \times 3 \times 2 \times 1}{0!} = \frac{24}{1} = 24$$

A *permutation* of a number of objects is an ordered arrangement of those objects—that is,

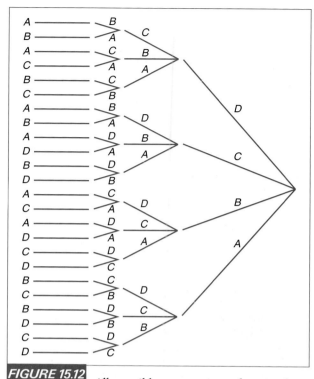

FIGURE 15.12 *All possible ways to seat four students in four chairs.*

placing the objects in a definite order. The formula for the number of permutations is

$$_nP_x = n!/(n - x)!$$

where

$x = $ the number of objects to be ordered
$n = $ the original set of n objects from which x was taken

Let's do another experiment in Activity 15.12 to determine the number of ways a set of letters can be ordered and then check the answer with the permutation formula.

Some middle school students may not be developmentally ready to handle the step-by-step logic of the formula developed above. The answer can be obtained if the students have a calculator with a permutation button. It would look like this on most calculators: $\boxed{_nP_x}$. The guidebook provided with the calculator will explain how the key can be used.

For those who want to practice with more activities, they are available in the Extended Activities on the Web site.

Combinations As can be seen, permutation situations require a specific arrangement and order. Events that ignore order are called *combinations*. A solution is shown by exhausting all possibilities.

Activity 15.12

MATHEMATICAL CONNECTIONS · **CALCULATORS** · **PROBLEM SOLVING**

PERMUTATIONS WITH LETTERS

DIRECTIONS

1. How many three-letter arrangements can be made from the letters in the word *favorite?*

    Here the original set n contains 8 letters, and we want to order 3 of the letters, so $x = 3$.

$$_8P_3 = \frac{8!}{(8-3)!} = \frac{8!}{5!} = 8 \times 7 \times 6 = 336$$

    So there are 336 ways of combining 3 letters out of the original set, *favorite*.

2. We are having a school competition this Friday. There are 9 students entering in the broad jump. If we are going to give medals to the first 4 students, how many ways can the medals by awarded?

    For example: one way—first place to Billy, second to Jane, third to Sam, and fourth place to Lin.

$$_9P_4 = \frac{9!}{(9-4!)}$$
$$= \frac{9!}{5!}$$
$$= 3024 \text{ ways}$$

3. How many different 7-digit phone numbers can the telephone company make from the digits 0 through 9 without repeating a digit?

$$_{10}P_7 = \frac{10!}{(10-7)!} = \frac{10!}{3!} = 10 \times 9 \times 8 \times 7 \times 6 \times 5 \times 4$$
$$= 604,800 \text{ phone numbers}$$

4. List other situations that use the concept of permutations.

Supporting the NCTM *Principles and Standards* (2000)

- Mathematics as Problem Solving; Connections; Representations, Probability
- Tools that Enhance Discourse—The Teaching Principle
- The Learning Principle—Power to Solve New Problems

Three People	The Possibilities
Larry	Larry, Julie
Julie	Julie, Jeff
Jeff	Jeff, Larry

Notice: Order is not important.
The total is 3.

Three people form a line at the post office counter. How many different combinations are possible to be the first two in line?

When we want to take x number of objects from a set of n objects *without regard to order*, we are dealing with combinations instead of permutations.

The formula for combinations is as follows:

$$_nC_x = \frac{_nP_x}{x!} = \frac{n!}{x!(n-x)!}$$

Applying the formula for three objects taken two at a time gives the following results:

$$_3C_2 = \frac{3!}{2!} = \frac{3!}{2!(3-2)!}$$
$$= \frac{3 \times 2 \times 1}{2 \times 1 \times 1} = 3$$

Some calculators also have a key for combinations. It would look like this on most calculators: $\boxed{nCx}$. Following is Activity 15.13 using manipulatives. Some children actually need to move the

Activity 15.13

MANIPULATIVES · **CALCULATORS** · **EXPLORING COMBINATIONS**

DIRECTIONS

1. Place eight different books on a table in the classroom. How many pairs of books may be selected? (Order doesn't matter.)

2. Keep a tally of the different pairs of books that are selected. Then use the formula

$$_nC_x = \frac{n!}{x!(n-x)!}$$

    to see if you get the same answer as the experiment gave.

$$_8C_2 = \frac{8!}{2!6!} = \frac{8 \times 7}{2} = \frac{56}{2} = 28 \text{ pairs}$$

books around before using the calculator to see another way of solving the problem.

For those who want to practice with more activities, they are available on Web site.

Homework Possibilities   There are many ways to extend activities when students need some thought time to work out solutions. Such activities make excellent homework assignments because they do not involve the normal thought of drudgery in boring, repetitive work. The following ideas are taken from Project AIM, developed at the Teachers College of Emporia State University (Morrow and Mehring, 1993). They are meant for grades 3 to 8. More homework examples are found in the Extended Activities on the Web site.

---

1. Draw a spinner with at least three sections so that half the time the spinner should stop on red.

2. You have a bag with ten colored tiles. There are six blue, three red, and one yellow. If you draw from the bag one time, predict the color you would get and why you think this would happen.

    Extension: Keep the same bag as above. Explain how you could change the bag to improve the probability of drawing a yellow.

3. You have a regular deck of playing cards containing fifty-two cards. Shuffle this deck of cards. Place facedown. Draw one card at a time. Player A keeps only numbered cards that he or she draws. Player B keeps only face cards when he or she draws them. Other cards are discarded. Which player would you rather be? Explain why.

Source: Morrow and Mehring, 1993, pp. 14–15.

EXTENDED ACTIVITIES

Name of Activity
- Set Theory Notation for Probability Formulas
- Permutations with Selecting People and Other Interesting Things
- Boxes of Candy
- Combinations with Cards
- Homework Examples

ASSESSMENT

Data Analysis—Graphing

The following student work demonstrates how students can interpret graphs made by others as well as those made by themselves. It is very revealing to students when they give their graphs to others who try to interpret what is happening. Rubrics that can be used by students to evaluate their own work are included.

Bar Graph Stories

The bar graph activity seen in Figure 15.13 has been used in classrooms in several different ways. Students were asked to create their own bar graphs about something they liked.

Some teachers chose to extend the activity by asking other students to use the rubric to evaluate the work of their fellow students. The rubric critique was originally created for the Project AIM grant (Morrow and Mehring, 1993) mentioned earlier in the chapter. The rubric can be used by the student creator of the graph without the critique by another student. The different critiques and stories that accompanied this graph are seen on the Web site as listed in the Extended Activities.

Notice that Lauren takes issue with Michael's critique of her graph. Some teachers find that there can be deep hurt on the part of sensitive children when their work is critiqued by other students in a formal rubric sheet like those on the Web site. Some teachers argue that students

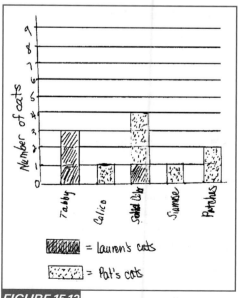

FIGURE 15.13   *Lauren's bar graph.*

EXTENDED ACTIVITIES

Name of Activity

- Lauren's Story . . . about her own graph
- Michael's Story . . . about Lauren's graph
- Michael's Critique . . . of Lauren's graph
- Lauren's Critique . . . of her own graph
- Bar Graph Rubric and Critique Form (Blank Rubric to Copy for Your Own Portfolio)
- TIMSS Assessment: Pasta Graphing
- TIMSS Assessment: Who's Going to Win the World Series?

like Lauren, even though they may be sensitive, will not forget the titles on graphs after such an evaluation by a peer. To use or not to use the critique sheet—it is a professional decision that each teacher must make for himself or herself with each new class in mind.

Continuous Graph Stories Figures 15.14 and 15.15 in Activity 15.14 show two third graders,

FIGURE 15.14 *Continuous graph interpretation by Mark.*

FIGURE 15.15 *Continuous graph interpretation by Kate.*

Kate and Mark, working on the same task. This is the first activity either one has ever worked with continuous graphs. Both have a sense of what the graph is about but each has approached the task differently. How could you make up a rubric that

Activity 15.14

CREATING YOUR OWN RUBRIC FOR CONTINUOUS GRAPHS

MATERIALS
- Two continuous graphs by third grade children

DIRECTIONS
- Use these questions to help you start thinking about a rubric:
1. What are the positive things that you see in both answers to the graph questions?
2. What misconceptions about the graphs do the children seem to have?
3. Is there a fair scale to use to give a numerical score to the children's creative work? If yes, what is it? If no, what could you substitute instead of a numerical score?
4. What are the next steps you need to do to help both children continue to grow?
5. Share your thoughts with others. See what your combined knowledge may be able to come up with.

Characteristics of the Five Predominant Approaches to Solving the Problems

---

Average as mode. Students with this predominant approach:
Consistently use mode to construct a distribution or interpret an existing one.

Lack flexibility in choosing strategies.

Are unable to build a distribution when not allowed to use the given average as a data point.

Use the algorithm for finding the mean infrequently or incorrectly.

View the mode only as "the most," not as representative of the data set as a whole.

Frequently use egocentric reasoning in their solutions.

Average as algorithm. Students with this predominant approach

View finding an average as carrying out the school-learned procedure for finding the arithmetic mean.

Often exhibit a variety of useless and circular strategies that confuse total, average, and data.

Have limited strategies for determining the reasonableness of their solutions.

Average as reasonable. Students with this predominant approach

View an average that is representative of the data, both from a mathematical perspective and from a common-sense perspective.

Use their real-life experiences to judge if an average is reasonable.

May use the algorithm for finding the mean; if so, the result of the calculation is scrutinized for reasonableness.

Believe that the mean of a particular data set is not one precise mathematical value, but an approximation that can have one of several values.

Average as midpoint. Students with this predominant approach

View an average as a tool for making sense of the data.

Choose an average that is representative of the data, both from a mathematical perspective and from a common-sense perspective.

Look for a "middle" to represent a set of data; this middle is alternately defined as the median, the middle of the x axis, or the middle of the range.

Use symmetry when constructing a data distribution around the average. They show great fluency in constructing a data set when symmetry is allowed, but have significant trouble constructing or interpreting nonsymmetrical distributions.

Use the mean fluently as a way to "check" answers. They seem to believe that the mean and middle are basically equivalent measures.

Average a mathematical point of balance. Students with this predominant approach:

View an average as a tool for making sense of the data.

Take into account the values of all the data points.

Use the mean for the beginning understanding of the quantitative relationships among data, total, and average; they are able to work from a given average to data, from a given average to total and from a given total to data

Break problems into smaller parts and find "submeans" as a way to solve more difficult averaging problems.

FIGURE 15.16   *Mokros and Russell Study. Source: Mokros and Russell, 1995, p. 26.*

---

would give each one of them credit for what they were able to do?

Averages   The concept of average is one of the most commonly used mathematics concepts in

Activity 15.15

PORTFOLIO

CREATING YOUR OWN RUBRIC FOR AVERAGES

MATERIALS
- Two journal entries of students working with the concept of averages

DIRECTIONS
Use these questions to help you start thinking about a rubric:

1. What are the positive things that you see in both answers to the averages questions?

2. What are the misconceptions about averages that the children seem to have?

3. Is there a fair scale that could be used to give a numerical score to the creative work of both children?

> If yes, what is it?
> If no, what could you substitute instead of a numerical score?

4. What are the next steps you need to do to help both children continue to grow?

5. Share your thoughts with others. See what your combined knowledge may be able to produce.

Supporting the NCTM *Principles and Standards* (2000)

- Mathematics as Reasoning/Patterning; Problem Solving; Communication
- Worthwhile Mathematical Tasks—The Teaching Principle
- Monitoring Students' Progress; Evaluating Students' Achievement—The Assessment Principle

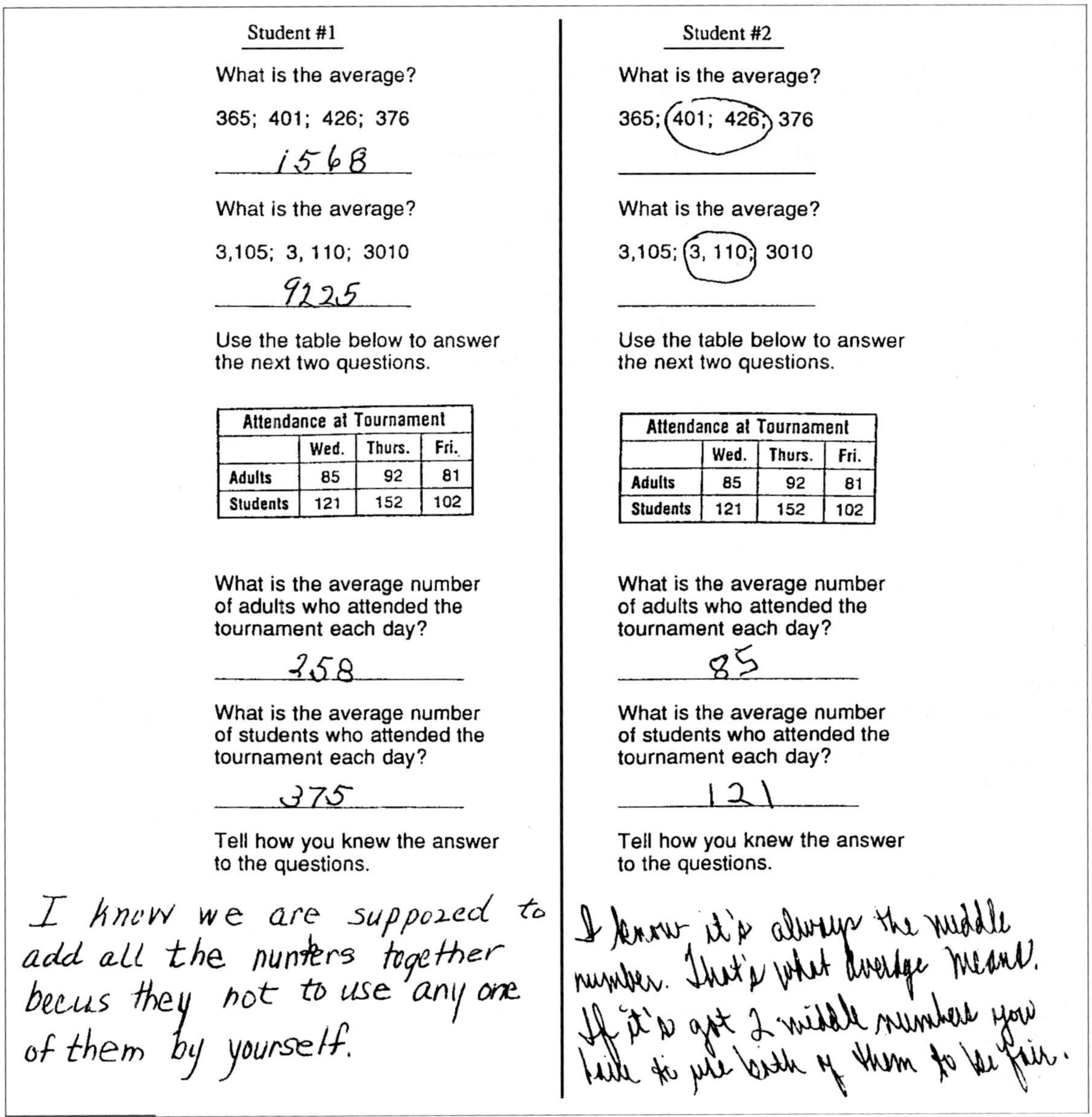

Student #1

What is the average?

365; 401; 426; 376

1568

What is the average?

3,105; 3, 110; 3010

9225

Use the table below to answer the next two questions.

Attendance at Tournament

	Wed.	Thurs.	Fri.
Adults	85	92	81
Students	121	152	102

What is the average number of adults who attended the tournament each day?

258

What is the average number of students who attended the tournament each day?

375

Tell how you knew the answer to the questions.

I know we are supposed to add all the numbers together becus they not to use any one of them by yourself.

Student #2

What is the average?

365; (401; 426;) 376

_____

What is the average?

3,105; (3, 110;) 3010

_____

Use the table below to answer the next two questions.

Attendance at Tournament

	Wed.	Thurs.	Fri.
Adults	85	92	81
Students	121	152	102

What is the average number of adults who attended the tournament each day?

85

What is the average number of students who attended the tournament each day?

121

Tell how you knew the answer to the questions.

I know it's always the middle number. That's what average means. If it's got 2 middle numbers you have to use both of them to be fair.

FIGURE 15.17 *Two students' interpretation of the average.*

everyday circumstances. Mokros and Russell (1995) tested children and mathematics education students to see what their understanding of averages is and how they go about finding an average. In a study with fourth graders, sixth graders, and eighth graders, they found the students see average as one of the five interpretations described in Figure 15.16.

Analyze the work of the following two students in Figure 15.17. Their teacher modified the worksheet of a leading math series (HBJ) to include a question at the end that became an entry in their math journals. Use Figure 15.16 as a starting point to discover the understanding of averages by each of the two students. Activity

15.15 asks you to develop a rubric for evaluating the work of these students.

Students with Special Needs Creating one's own rubric and judging others by their own rubric may give some children with special needs a difficult time. They do better if they can start with only three data points to place on the graph with category labels that make sense easily. It should be noted however, that the activities with radio-controlled cars for the middle school found on the Web site were all ideas generated and solved by students with Attention Deficit Disorder (ADD). Their ideas flowed throughout the assignment; they were highly motivated during the lessons. It may be that students with ADD need more interesting stimuli to pay attention. Certainly the chance to "drive" a radio-controlled car is highly motivational in middle school.

SUMMARY

- Data analysis is a process that involves the four stages of formulating the question, gathering the data, analyzing the data, and forming and communicating conclusions based on the data analysis.

- Graphing is a common method of displaying data pictorially.

- The introduction of each new graph should be from concrete to the connecting stage (pictorial) to the symbolic.

- One way to help students see the relationship in bar and line graphs of the same data is to create the line graph by connecting the midpoint of the top of the bars in the bar graph.

- Graphing calculators, spreadsheets, and other graphing software programs are valuable tools for students as they study data analysis.

- Statistics are used to discuss data numerically.

- Key questions to ask when looking at statistical information are: How many people were in the sample? How was the population sampled?

Who conducted the survey? How were the data summarized?

- The *average* is a measure of the central tendency of data, or an attempt to describe what is "typical" in a set of data. There are three measures that are commonly used to describe a typical data set: mean, mode, and median.

- The mean, or arithmetic mean, is most commonly used to describe the "average" of a set of data.

- The mode of a set of numbers is that number that occurs most frequently in the set.

- The median of a set of numbers is the middle number of the set.

- The range of a set of numbers is the difference between the highest and lowest numbers in a set.

- Probability is the mathematics used to predict outcomes.

- Mutually exclusive or independent events have no outcomes in common.

- Probability that is dependent on an outcome is referred to as conditional probability.

- A permutation of a number of objects is an ordered arrangement of those objects; in other words, order matters!

- A combination of a number of objects ignores order; it is an arrangement—an exhaustive list—in which order does not matter.

PRAXIS II™-STYLE QUESTIONS

Answers to this chapter's Praxis II™-style questions are in the instructor's manual.

Multiple Choice Format

1. Six friends eat dinner together once a week. If each person sits in a different position at the table each week, how many weeks will it take before the six friends have used every possible arrangement?

   a. 30
   b. 36
   c. 120
   d. 720

2. The problem in question #1 is an example of a _____ in the content area of_____
   a. permutation; probability
   b. combination; probability
   c. stem and leaf plot; statistics
   d. Both a and c

3. The continuous graph in Figure 15.18 represents students' quickness to do homework assignments before their favorite TV shows start. The *x*-axis stands for_____while the *y*-axis stands for_____.

FIGURE 15.18

    a. amount of homework completed; time before their favorite TV shows start
    b. time before the TV shows start; amount of homework examples completed
    c. the amount of homework that will be completed; the time after the TV shows end.
    d. None of the above.

4. Which graph(s) in Figure 15.19 give(s) the accurate representation of the following information? There are 24 students in the class who like ice cream best. Twelve students like cake best. Eighteen students like spaghetti best. Six students like apple best. Eighteen students like pizza best.

    a. Graph A
    b. Graph B
    c. Graph C
    d. both b and c

Constructed Response Format

5. Take the data from the problem in question #4 and organize it into a bar graph, a line graph, and finally into a picture graph.

6. Create two probability problems using dice whose answer would be $\frac{1}{36}$ and $\frac{1}{216}$, respectively.

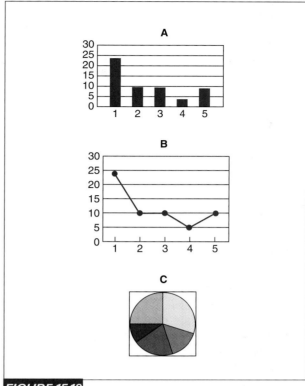

FIGURE 15.19

7. Data analysis is a process that involves four stages in which a teacher must become proficient when structuring activities for students. Create an activity for students and label the four stages as they apply to the problem.

8. Would a typical fourth grade student be able to read the data from all of the graphs in question #3 easily and accurately? Justify your answer.

Integrating Technology

Video Vignettes

Graphing Probability
Read the directions given for this vignette. Complete the task before viewing the video vignette.

Internet Activities

Scavenger Hunt: Probability

WebQuest

"Major League"
To find this WebQuest that uses statistics, go to the following Web site:
http://www.socs. k12.in.us/
Click on "Links," then click on "WebQuests," and finally, "Major Educational League."

http://www.macomb.k12.mi.us/wq/sw2cl.htm

"Math Lesson 1 on Olympics" is the name of a WebQuest found on this site. It is designed to use the 1996 Olympics and consequently, the NBC link is no longer active. We offer this WebQuest for you to study and see if you would like to adapt it for the 2004 Olympics.

Web sites

http://www.cut-the-knot.org/probability.shtml

Cut-the-knot is a Web site with many games and activities suitable for a variety of mathematical lessons. The information on probability given on the opening page is at a reading and "explanation" level suitable for high school students and above. It does offer a variety of activities with explanations for the teacher.

http://www.edhelper.com/Probability.htm

edhelper.com has a multitude of ideas, lesson plans, and activities.

National Library of virtual Manipulatives

http://nlvm.usu.edu/nav/vlibrary.html
(also in Spanish)

Virtual manipulatives, with suggestions for teachers and parents, useful for teaching the content standards in NCTM's Principles and Standards.

Interactive: Home Page

http://www.shodor.org/interactivate

Developed for middle school mathematics explorations but several are adaptable to elementary mathematics.

NCTM: Elementary School Resources

http://www.nctm.org/resources/elementary.aspx

A wealth of teaching resources, recent research findings, and lesson plans for elementary teachers.

NCTM: Illuminations

http://illuminations.nctm.org/

Links to activities, lessons, the Standards, and other web resources.

NCTM: Middle School Resources

http://nctm.org/resources/middle.aspx?id=7860

A wealth of teaching resources, lesson plans, and tips for teachers of middle school mathematics.

A

Paper Models and Patterns

(Reduced size — full size in color on Web site)

PAPER PATTERN BLOCKS

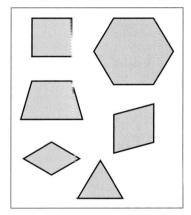

TANGRAM

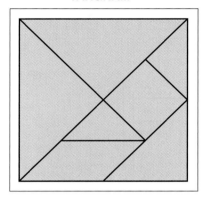

CIRCULAR FRACTION KIT

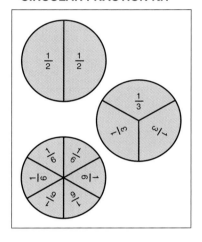

GEOBOARD RECORDING PAPER

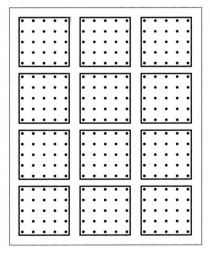

ISOMETRIC DOT PAPER

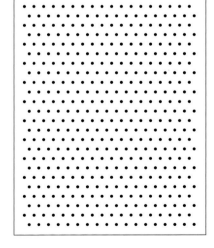

CENTIMETER GRID PAPER

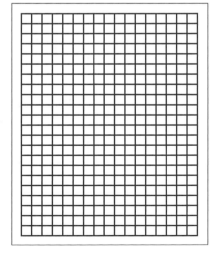

FRACTION BARS

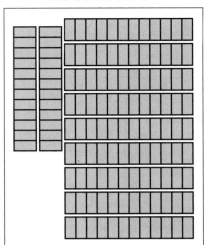

BASE 10 BLOCKS

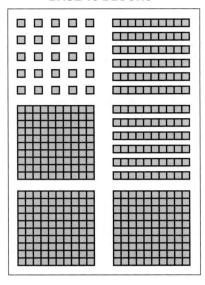

PENTOMINOES

CHIP TRADING MAT

Red	Green	Blue	Yellow

CHIP TRADING CHIPS

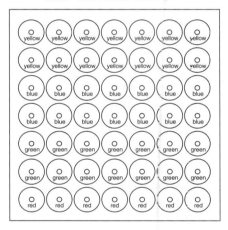

RECTANGULAR GEOBOARD TEMPLATE

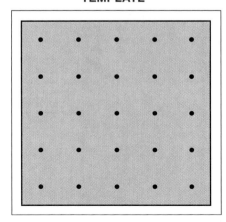

REGULAR POLYHEDRA

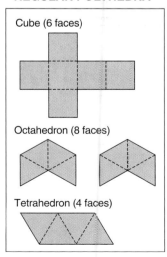

Cube (6 faces)

Octahedron (8 faces)

Tetrahedron (4 faces)

PRISM, PYRAMID, AND CYLINDER

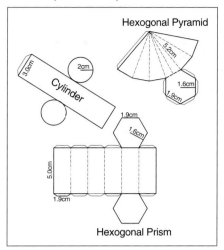

PROTRACTOR

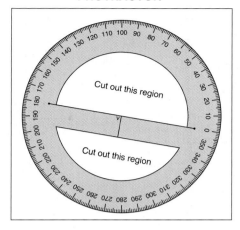

CUISENAIRE RODS

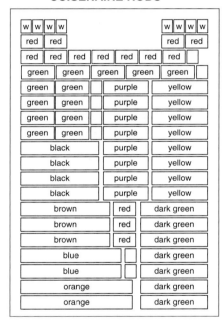

ATTRIBUTE PIECES

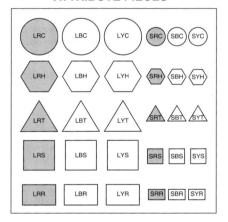

Bibliography

For an extended bibliography, see the Web site.

Abrams, Judy, Julia Ferguson, and Leslie Laud. "Assessing ESOL Students." *Educational Leadership* 59 (November 2001): 62–65.

Akoto, Agyei, ed. *Positive Afrikan Images for Children.* Trenton, NJ: The Red Sea Press, 1990.

American Federation of Teachers and National Center for Improving Science Education, ed. *What Students Abroad Are Expected to Know about Mathematics: Defining World Class Standards.* Vol. 4. Reston, VA: National Council of Teachers of Mathematics, 1997.

Arbaugh, Fran, Carolyn M. Scholten, and N. Kathryn Essex. "Data in the Middle Grades: A Probability WebQuest." *Mathematics Teaching in the Middle School* 7 (October 2001): 90–95.

Armstrong, Thomas. *The Best Schools: How Human Development Research Should Inform Educational Practice.* Alexandria, VA: Association for Supervision and Curriculum Development, 2006.

Axelson, Sharon L. "Supermarket Challenge." *Arithmetic Teacher* 40 (October 1992): 84–88.

Ball, Deborah L. "Magical Hopes: Manipulatives and the Reform of Math Education." *American Educator.* 14 (1992): 46–47.

———. "Setting the Stage." In *Studying Classroom Teaching as a Medium for Professional Development. Proceedings of a U.S.-Japan Workshop,* edited by Hyman Bass, Zalman P. Usiskin, and Gail Burrill, 49–52. Mathematical Sciences Education Board, Division of Behavioral and Social Sciences and Education, and U.S. National Commission on Mathematics Instruction, International Organizations Board. Washington, DC: National Academy Press, 2002.

Baratta-Lorton, Mary. *Mathematics Their Way.* Menlo Park, CA: Addison-Wesley, 1976.

———. *Workjobs II.* Menlo Park, CA: Addison-Wesley, 1978.

———. *Childrens Mathematical Thinking: A Developmental Framework for Preschool, Primary and Special Education Teachers.* New York, NY: Teachers College Press, Columbia University, 1987.

Baroody, Arthur J. and Dorothy J. Standifer. "Addition and Subtraction in the Primary Grades." In *Research Ideas for the Classroom: Early Childhood Mathematics,* edited by Robert J. Jensen, 72–102. Reston, VA: National Council of Teachers of Mathematics, 1993.

Barnett, Carne, Donna Goldenstein, and Babette Jackson. *Research and Development of Fractions, Decimals, Ratio and Percent: Hard to Teach or Hard to Learn.* Portsmouth, NH: Heinemann, 1994.

Bartley, William Clark. "Counting on Tradition: Inupiaq Numbers in the School Setting." In *Changing the Faces of Mathematics: Perspectives on Indigenous People of North America,* edited by Judith Elaine Hankes and Gerald R. Fast, 225–235. Reston, VA: National Council of Teachers of Mathematics, 2002.

Bass, Hyman. "Computational Fluency, Algorithms, and Mathematical Proficiency: One Mathematician's Perspective." *Teaching Children Mathematics* 9 (February 2003): 322–327.

Battista, Michael T. "A Complete Model for Operations on Integers." *Arithmetic Teacher* 30 (May 1983): 26–31.

Battista, Michael T. "Understanding Students' Thinking about Area and Volume Measurement." In *Learning and Teaching Measurement 2003 Yearbook,* edited by Douglas H. Clements and George Bright, 122–142. Reston, VA: National Council of Teachers of Mathematics, 2003.

Bay-Williams, Jennifer M. "What is Algebra in Elementary School?" *Teaching Children Mathematics* 8 (December 2001): 196–200.

———. and Sherri L. Martinie. "Thinking Rationally about Number and Operations in the Middle School." *Teaching Middle School Mathematics,* 8 (February 2003): 282–287.

Beaton, Albert, E., Ina V. S. Smith, Michael O. Martin, Eugenio J. Gonzalez, Dana L. Kelly, and Teresa A. Smith. *Mathematics Achievement in the Middle School Years: IEA's Third International Mathematics and Science Study (TIMSS)*. Chestnut Hill, MA: TIMSS International Study Center, Boston College, 1996.

Bennett, Albert B., Jr. and L. Ted Nelson. "A Conceptual Model for Solving Percent Problems." *Mathematics Teaching in the Middle School 1* (April 1994): 20–25.

———. "Divisibility Tests: So Right for Discoveries." *Mathematics Teaching in the Middle School 7* (April 2002): 460–464.

Bezuk, Nadine S. and Marilyn Bieck. "Current Research on Rational Numbers and Common Fractions: Summary and Implications for Teachers." In *Research Ideas for the Classroom: Middle Grades Mathematics*, edited by Douglas T. Owens, 118–136. Reston, VA: National Council of Teachers of Mathematics, 1993.

Biehler, Rolf. "Functional Thinking with Graphs." *Journal for Research in Mathematics Education 25* (November 1994): 526–533.

Billstein, Rick. "You Are Cleared to Land." *Mathematics Teaching in the Middle School 3* (May 1998): 452–456.

Bitter, Gary G. and Mary M. Hatfield. "Implementing Calculators in a Middle School: A Comprehensive Approach." In *Calculators in Mathematics Education, 1992 Yearbook*, edited by James T. Fey and Christian R. Hirsch. Reston, VA: National Council of Teachers of Mathematics, 1992.

Blume, Glendon, W. and David S. Heckman. "What Do Students Know about Algebra and Functions?" *Results from the Sixth Mathematics Assessment of the National Assessment of Education Progress*. Reston, VA: National Council of Teachers of Mathematics, 1997.

Bohan, Harry and Susan Bohan. "Extending the Regular Curriculum through Creative Problem Solving." *Arithmetic Teacher 41* (October 1993): 83–87.

Bohan, Harry, Beverly Irby, and Dolly Vogel. "Problem Solving: Dealing with Data in the Elementary School." *Teaching Children Mathematics 1* (January 1995): 256–260.

Bradley, Claudette. "Teaching Mathematics with Technology: The Four Directions Indian Beadwork Design with Logo." *Arithmetic Teacher 39* (May 1992): 46–49.

———. "Teaching Mathematics with Technology: Making a Navajo Blanket Design with Logo." *Arithmetic Teacher 40* (May 1993): 520–523.

Bransford John D., Ann L. Brown, and Rodney R. Cocking, *How People Learn: Brain, Mind, Experience, and School*. Washington, DC: National Academy Press, Committee on Developments in the Science of Learning, Commission on Behavioral and Social Sciences and Education, 1999.

Brewster, Cori and Jennifer Fager. *Increasing Student Engagement an Motivation: From Time-on-Task to Homework*. Portland, OR: Northwest Regional Educational Laboratory, 2000.

Bright, George W. and Bonnie Litwiller, eds. *Classroom Activities for Making Sense of Fractions, Ratios, and Proportions 2002 Yearbook of the National Council of Teachers of Mathematics*. Reston, VA: National Council of Teachers of Mathematics, 2002.

Brinker, Laura. "Using Recipes and Ratio Tables to Build on Students' Understanding of Fractions." *Teaching Children Mathematics 5* (December 1998): 218–224.

Brooks, Jacqueline Grennon and Martin G. Brooks. *The Case for Constructivist Classrooms*. Alexandria, VA: Association for Supervision and Curriculum Development, 1993.

Browder, Atlantis Tye, with Anthony T. Browder. *My First Trip to Africa*. Washington, DC: The Institute of Karmic Guidance, 1991.

Bruer, John T. "In Search of . . . Brain-Based Education." In *Annual Editions: Educational Psychology 2001/2002*, edited by Kathleen M. Cauley, Fredric Linder, and James H. McMillan, 84–90. Guilford, CT: McGraw-Hill/Dushkin, 2001.

Bucko, Richard L. "Brain Basics: Cognitive Psychology and Its Implications for Education." In *Annual Editions: Educational Psychology 2001/2002*, edited by Kathleen M. Cauley, Fredric Linder, and James H. McMillan, 78–83. Guilford, CT: McGraw-Hill/Dushkin, 2001.

Burk, Donna, Allyn Snider, and Paula Symonds. *Box It or Bag It Mathematics: Teachers Resource Guide*. Salem, OR: Math Learning Center, 1988.

———. *Math Excursions:* Project-Based Mathematics for First Graders, Portsmouth, NH: Heinemann, 1992.

Burns, Marilyn. *The Math Solution: Teaching for Mastery through Problem Solving*. Sausalito, CA: Marilyn Burns Education Associates, 1984.

———. "Arithmetic: The Last Holdout." *Phi Delta Kappan 75* (1994): 471–476.

Burrill, Gail. "The President's Report: Changes in Your Classroom: From the Past to the Present to the Future." *Journal for Research in Mathematics Education 29* (November 1998): 583–593.

Buschman, Larry. "Children Who Enjoy Problem Solving." *Teaching Children Mathematics 9* (May 2003): 222–227.

Bustamante, Maria L. and Betty Travis, "Teachers' and Students' Attitudes toward the Use of Manipulatives in Two Predominately Latino School Districts." In *Changing the Faces of Mathematics: Perspectives on Latinos*, edited by Luis Ortiz-Franco, Norma G. Hernandez, and Yolanda De La Cruz. Reston, VA: National Council of Teachers of Mathematics, 1999.

Caduto, Michael J. and Joseph Bruchac. *Teacher's Guide to Keepers of the Earth: Native American Stories and Environmental Activities for Children*. Golden, CO: Fulcrum Publishing, 1988.

———. *Keepers of the Earth: Native American Stories and Environmental Activities for Children*. Golden, CO: Fulcrum Publishing, 1989.

———. *Keepers of the Animals: Native American Stories and Wildlife Activities for Children.* Golden, CO: Fulcrum Publishing, 1991.

———. *Keepers of Life*, 1994.

Campbell, Patricia F. "Connecting Instructional Practice to Student Thinking." *Teaching Children Mathematics* 4 (October 1997): 106–110.

Campbell, Patricia F. and Thomas E. Rowan. "Teacher Questions + Student Language + Diversity = Mathematical Power." In *Multicultural and Gender Equity in the Mathematics Classroom: The Gift of Diversity*, edited by Janet Trentacosta and Margaret J. Kenney. 1997 Yearbook. Reston, VA: National Council of Teachers of Mathematics, 1997.

Capper, Joanne. *Research into Practice Digest, Vol. I, No. 1a, and Vol. II, No. 1b.* Thinking Skills Series: Mathematical Problem Solving: Research Review and Instructional Implications. Washington, DC: Center for Research into Practice, 1984.

Carey, Deborah, A., Elizabeth Fennema, Thomas P. Carpenter, and Megan L. Franke. "Equity and Mathematics Education." In *New Directions for Equity in Mathematics Education*, edited by Walter G. Secada, Elizabeth Fennema, and Lisa Byrd Adajian. Cambridge, England: Cambridge University Press, 1995.

Carpenter, Thomas P., Elizabeth Fennema, Megan L. Franke, Linda Levi, and Susan B. Empson. *Children's Mathematics: Cognitively Guided Instruction.* Portsmouth, N.H.: Heinemann, 1999.

Carroll, William M. and Denise Porter. "Alternative Algorithms for Whole-Number Operations." In *The Teaching and Learning of Algorithms in School Mathematics 1998 Yearbook*, edited by Lorna J. Morrow and Margaret J. Kenney, 106–114. Reston, VA: National Council of Teachers of Mathematics, 1998.

Center for the Study of Poverty, *Statistical Report.* New York, NY: Columbia University, 2002.

Chappell, Michaele F. and Marilyn E. Strutchens. "Creating Connections: Promoting Algebraic Thinking with Concrete Models." *Mathematics Teaching in the Middle School* 7 (September 2001): 20–25.

Chappell, Michaele F. and Denisse R. Thompson. "Fostering Multicultural Connections in Mathematics through Media". In *Changing Faces of Mathematics: Perspectives on African Americans*, edited by Marilyn E. Strutchens, Martin L. Johnson, and William F. Tate, 135–150. Reston VA: National Council of Teachers of Mathematics, 2000.

Charles, Randall and Joanne Lobato. "Ratio, Proportion & Percent." *Future Basics: Developing Numerical Power.* Monograph of the National Council of Supervisors of Mathematics (April 1998): 26–27.

Cheek, Helen Neely. "Increasing the Participation of Native Americans in Mathematics." *Journal for Research in Mathematics Education* 15 (March 1984): 107–113.

Choate, Joyces S., ed. *Successful Inclusive Teaching: Proves Ways to Detect and Correct Special Needs*, ed. Boston, MA: Allyn and Bacon, 2003.

Chocolate, Deborah M. Newton. *My First Kwanzaa Book.* New York: Scholastic, 1992.

———. *Contemporary Issues in Early Childhood.* Vol. 3 No. 2 (2002) Paper also on Web site **http://gse.buffalo.edu/org/buildingblocks/writings/ECE_Comp_Math.pdf**

———. (2003a) Web site for NSF grant materials development for computer use by young children, **http://www.gse.buffalo.edu/org/buildingblocks/index_2.htm**

———. (2003b) Web site for early childhood links from NSF grant materials for computer use by young children, **http://www.gse.buffalo.edu/org/buildingblocks/**

Clements, Douglas H. and Michael T. Battista. *Logo and Geometry. Journal for Research in Mathematics Education*, Monograph Series, Reston, VA: National Council of Teachers of Mathematics, 2001.

Clements, Douglas H. and George Bright, eds. *Learning and Teaching Measurement.* Reston, VA: National Council of Teachers of Mathematics, 2003.

Clements, Douglas H. and Julie Sarama. "Effects of a Preschool Mathematics Curriculum: Summative Research on the *Building Blocks* Project." *Journal for Research in Mathematics Education* 38 (March 2007): 136–163.

Clements, D.H., Julie Sarama, and A. M. DiBlase, eds. *Engaging Young Children in Mathematics: Findings of the 2000 National Conference on Standards for Preschool and Kindergarten Mathematics Education.* Mahwah, NJ: Lawrence Erlbaum Associates, 2004.

Closs, Michael P., ed. *Native American Mathematics.* Austin: TX: University of Texas Press, 1986.

Cohen, Ira S. and Joan V. Fowler. "Create Assessments That Do It All." *Mathematics Teaching in the Middle School* 4 (September 1998): 44–47.

Conference Board of the Mathematical Sciences. *The Mathematical Education of Teachers: Part I.* Mathematical Association of America in cooperation with American Mathematical Society. Washington, DC: Mathematical Association of America, 2002.

Cooney, Miriam P., ed. *Celebrating Women in Mathematics and Science.* Reston, VA: National Council of Teachers of Mathematics, 1996.

Cooper, Harris. "Homework for All—in Moderation." *Educational Leadership* 59 (April 2001): 34–38.

Corwin, Rebecca. "Assessing Children's Understanding: Doing Mathematics to Assess Mathematics." *Teaching Children Mathematics* 9 (December 2002): 229–233.

Cuevas, Gilbert J., ed. *Navigating through Geometry in Grades 3–5.* Reston, VA: National Council of Teachers of Mathematics, 2001.

Damarin, Suzanne K. "Equity, Experience, and Abstraction: Old Issues, New Considerations." In *Changing Faces of Mathematics: Perspectives on Multiculturalism and Gender Equity*, edited by Walter G. Secada, 75–83. Reston, VA: National Council of Teachers of Mathematics, 2000.

D'Arcangelo, Marcia. "Wired for Mathematics: A Conversation with Brian Butterworth." *Educational Leadership 59* (November 2001): 14–19.

Darden, Phyllis, Ivadene Dhority, Grover Parsons, Steve Poppe, Reggie Rowland, and Rae F. Thompson. "Science/Math—Seventh & Eighth Grade." *Natural Resources in Mathematics and Science: Summer 1993*. Washington, DC: U.S. Bureau of Indian Affairs, 1993.

Daria-Wiener, Irene. "10 Signs of a Great Preschool." In *Annual Editions: Early Childhood Education, 2003/2004*, edited by Karen Menke Paciorek and Joyce Huth, 79–80. Guilford, CT: McGraw-Hill/Dushkin, 2004.

Davidson, Ellen and Leslie Kramer. "Integrating with Integrity: Curriculum, Instruction, and Culture in the Mathematics Classroom." In *Multicultural and Gender Equity in the Mathematics Classroom: The Gift of Diversity*, edited by Janet Trentacosta and Margaret J. Kenney. 1997 Yearbook. Reston, VA: National Council of Teachers of Mathematics, 1997.

Davis, Robert B. *Explorations in Mathematics: A Text for Teachers*. Palo Alto, CA: Addison-Wesley, 1967.

De La Cruz, Yolanda. "A Model of Tutoring That Helps Students Gain Access to Mathematical Competence." In *Changing the Faces of Mathematics: Perspectives on Latinos*, edited by Luis Ortiz-Franco, Norma G. Hernandez, and Yolanda De La Cruz, 147–158. Reston, VA: National Council of Teachers of Mathematics, 1999.

DeLoria, Vine Jr. and Daniel R. Wildcat. *Power and Place: Indian Education in America*. Golden, CO: Fulcrum Resources, 2001.

Demana, Franklin D. and Bert K. Waits. "Instructional Strategies and Delivery Systems." In *Algebra for Everyone*, edited by Edgar L. Edwards, 53–61. Reston, VA: National Council of Teachers of Mathematics, 1990.

Driscoll, Mark, John Moyer, and Judith S. Zawojewski. "Helping Teacher Implement Algebra for All in Milwaukee Public Schools." *Mathematics Education Leadership NCSM Journal 2* (April 1998): 3–12.

Dunn, Rita. "The Goals and Track Record of Multicultural Education." In *Annual Editions: Educational Psychology 2001/2002*, edited by Kathleen M. Cauley, Fredric Linder, and James H. McMillan, 61–64. Guilford, CT: McGraw-Hill/Dushkin, 2001.

Economopoulos, Karen. "What Comes Next? The Mathematics of Pattern in Kindergarten." *Teaching Children Mathematics 5* (December 1998): 230–233.

Edwards, Carol A., ed. *Changing the Faces of Mathematics: Perspectives on Asian Americans and Pacific Islanders*. Reston, VA: National Council of Teachers of Mathematics, 1999.

Edwards, Nancy Tanner, Gary G. Bitter, and Mary M. Hatfield. "Measurement in Geometry with Computers." *Arithmetic Teacher 37* (February 1990): 64–67.

Edwards, Nancy Tanner and Peter A. Judd. *Stewardship: The Response of My People*. Independence, MO: Herald Publishing House, 1976.

Einhorn, Kama. "Welcoming Second-Language Learners." *Instructor* (September 2002): 54–56.

Empson, Susan B. "Using Sharing Situations to Help Children Learn Fractions." *Teaching Children Mathematics 2* (October 1995): 110–114.

Empson, Susan B. "Equal Sharing and the Roots of Fraction Equivalence." *Teaching Children Mathematics 7* (March 2001): 421–425.

Erlauer, Laura. *The Brain-Compatible Classroom: Using What We Know About Learning to Improve Teaching*. Alexandria, VA: Association for Supervision and Curriculum Development, 2003.

Fantauzzo, Michael. *The Mind of the Middle School Student. The Complexities of the Middle School Student*. On-line portfolio. **http://www.frontiernet.net/~mikef/portfolio/adol.htm**. (2002).

Fennell, Francis (Skip). "Go Ahead, Teach to the Test!" *News Bulletin 43* (December 2006): 3.

Fennema, Elizabeth, Thomas P. Carpenter, Megan L. Franke, Linda Levi, Victoria R. Jacobs, and Susan B. Empson. "A Longitudinal Study of Learning to Use Children's Thinking in Mathematics Instruction." *Journal for Research in Mathematics Education 27* (1996): 403–434.

Fernandez, Maria L. and Cynthia O. Anhalt. "Transition toward Algebra." *Mathematics Teaching in the Middle School 7* (December 2001): 236–241.

Flores, Alfinio. "Si Se Puede, 'It Can Be Done': Quality Mathematics in More than One Language." In *Multicultural and Gender Equity in the Mathematics Classroom: The Gift of Diversity*, edited by Janet Trentacosta and Margaret J. Kenney. 1997 Yearbook. Reston, VA: National Council of Teachers of Mathematics, 1997.

Flores, Alfinio. "Profound Understanding of the Division of Fractions." In *Making Sense of Fractions, Ratios, and Proportions: 2002 Yearbook*, edited by Bonnie Litwiller and George Bright, 237–246. Reston, VA: National Council of Teacher of Mathematics, 2002.

Forgione, Pascal D., Jr., ed. *Introduction to TIMSS: The Third International Mathematics and Science Study*. Washington, DC: U.S. Department of Education, 1997.

Freiberg, H. Jerome. "Essential Skills for New Teachers." *Educational Leadership 59* (March 2002): 56–60.

Friel, Susan N., ed. *Navigating through Algebra in Grades 6–8*. Reston, VA: National Council of Teachers of Mathematics, 2001.

———. *Navigating through Geometry in Grades 6–8*. Reston, VA: National Council of Teachers of Mathematics, 2002.

Friel, Susan N. "Setting the Stage for Data Analysis." In *Navigating through Data Analysis in Grades 6–8*, edited by Peggy A. House, 11–19. Reston, VA: National Council of Teachers of Mathematics, 2003.

Friel, Susan N. and George W. Bright. "Teach Stat: A Model for Professional Development in Data Analysis and Statistics for Teachers K–6." In *Reflections on Statistics: Learning, Teaching, and Assessment in Grades K–12*, edited by S. P. Lajoie, 89–117. Mahwah, NJ: Erlbaum, 1998.

———. "Developing Mathematical Power in Whole Number Operations." In *A Research Companion to Principles and Standards for School Mathematics*, edited by Jeremy Kilpatrick, W. Gary Martin, Deborah Schifter, 68–94. Reston, VA: National Council of Teachers of Mathematics, 2003.

Fuson, Karen and James W. Hall. "The Acquisition of Early Number Word Meanings: A Conceptual Analysis and Review." In *The Development of Mathematical Thinking*, edited by H. P. Ginsburg. New York: Academic Press, 1983.

Fuys, David J. and Amy K. Liebov. "Geometry and Spatial Sense." In *Research and Classroom Early Childhood Mathematics*, edited by Robert J. Jensen, 199–222. Reston, VA: National Council of Teachers of Mathematics, 1993.

Gallagher, Ann M. and James C. Kaufman, eds. *Gender Differences in Mathematics: An Integrative Psychological Approach*. Cambridge, England: Cambridge University Press, 2005.

Gardner, Howard. *Multiple Intelligences: The Theory in Practice*. New York: Basic Books, 1993.

Garrison, Leslie. "Portafolio de Matemática: Using Mathematics Portfolios with Latino Students." In *Changing the Faces of Mathematics: Perspectives on Latinos*, edited by Luis Ortiz-Franco, Norma G. Hernandez, and Yolanda De La Cruz, 85–97. Reston, VA: National Council of Teachers of Mathematics, 1999.

Garrison, Leslie and Jill Kerper Mora. "Adapting Mathematics Instruction for English-Language Learners: The Language-Concept Connection." In *Changing the Faces of Mathematics: Perspectives on Latinos*, edited by Luis Ortiz-Franco, Norma G. Hernandez, and Yolanda De La Cruz, 35–47. Reston, VA: National Council of Teachers of Mathematics, 1999.

Gay, A. Susan and Charlotte J. Keith. "Reasoning about Linear Equations." *Mathematics Teaching in the Middle School* 8 (November 2002): 146–148.

Gazin, Ann. "Focus on Autobiography." *Instructor*. (January/February 2000): 49–52.

Geist, Eugene. "Lessons from the TIMSS Videotape Study." *Teaching Children Mathematics* 7 (November 2000): 180–185.

———. "Children are Born Mathematicians: Promoting the Construction of Early Mathematical Concepts in Children under Five." In *Annual Editions: Early Childhood Education, 2003/2004*, edited by Karen Menke Paciorek and Joyce Huth Munro, 178–183. Guilford, CT: McGraw-Hill/Dushkin, 2004.

Gersten, Russell, David Chard, and Scott Baker. *A Meta-Analysis of Research on Mathematics Istruction for Students with Learning Disabilities*. Eugene, OR: Eugene Research Institute, 2002.

Given, Barbara K. *Teaching to the Brain's Natural Learning Systems*. Alexandria, VA: Association for Supervision and Curriculum Development, 2002.

Glatzer, David J. and Glenda Lappan. "Enhancing the Maintenance of Skills." In *Algebra for Everyone*, edited by Edgar L. Edwards, 34–44. Reston, VA: National Council of Teachers of Mathematics, 1990.

Glickman, Carl D. *Leadership for Learning: How to Help Teachers Succeed*. Alexandria, VA: Association for Supervision and Curriculum Development, 2002.

Gomez, Cristina. "Multiplicative Reasoning: Developing Student's (sic) Shared Meanings." In *Making Sense of Fractions, Ratios, and Proportions: 2002 Yearbook of the National Council of Teachers of Mathematics*, edited by George W. Bright. Reston, VA: National Council of Teachers of Mathematics, 2002.

Gravemeijer, Koemo and Frans van Galen. "Facts and Algorithms as Products of Students; Own Mathematical Activity." In *A Research Companion to Principles and Standards for School Mathematics*, edited by Jeremy Kilpatrick, W. Gary Martin, Deborah Schifter, 114–122. Reston, VA: National Council of Teachers of Mathematics, 2003.

Greene, Rebecca. *The Teenagers Guide to School Outside the Box*. Minneapolis, MN: Free Spirit Publishing Inc., 2001.

Greenes, Carol E., ed. *Navigating through Geometry in Prekindergarten–Grade 2*. Reston, VA: National Council of Teachers of Mathematics, 2001.

———. *Navigating through Algebra in Prekindergarten–Grade 2*. Reston, VA: National Council of Teachers of Mathematics, 2001.

———. *Navigating through Data Analysis in Prekindergarten–Grade 2*. Reston, VA: National Council of Teachers of Mathematics, 2002.

Grouws, Douglas and Smith. "Findings from NAEP on the Preparation and Practice of Mathematics Teachers." In *Results of the Seventh Mathematics Assessment of the National Assessment of Educational Progress*, edited by Edward A. Silver and Patricia Ann Kenney. Reston, VA: National Council of Teachers of Mathematics, 2000.

Habrock, Tanya and Nancy Tanner Edwards. "Manipulatives or Personalized Math Problems: Which Is Better for Students-at-Risk?" Address. Central Regional Conference of the National Council of Teachers of Mathematics, Springfield, MO, 13 October 1995.

Haines, Joyce E., ed. *Culturally-Based Mathematics and Science Curriculum 1992*. Washington, DC: U.S. Bureau of Indian Affairs, 1992.

Hale-Benson, Janice E. *Black Children: Their Roots, Culture, and Learning Styles.* Baltimore: John Hopkins University Press, 1986.

Hall, Charlotte. "Virtual Africa." *Instructor* (January/February 2000): 74–75.

Hankes, Judith Elaine and Gerald R. Fast, eds. *Changing the Faces of Mathematics: Perspectives on Indigenous People of North America.* Reston, VA: National Council of Teachers of Mathematics, 2002.

Hardy, Michael. "Burgers, Graphs, and Combinations." *Mathematics Teaching in the Middle School 7* (October 2001): 72–76.

Hattie, John A. and Purdie, N. "The SOLO Method and Item Construction". *Learning in Higher Education,* edited by G. Boulton-Lewis and B. Darts. Hawthorn, Australia: ACER, 1998.

Haynes, Judie. *Getting Started with English Language Learners: How Educators Can Meet the Challenges.* Alexandria, VA: Association for Supervision and Curriculum Development, 2007.

Heddens, James W. "Bridging the Gap between the Concrete and the Abstract." *Arithmetic Teacher 33* (February 1986): 14–17.

Heid, M. Kathleen, Charlene Sheets, Mary Ann Matras, and James Menasian. "Classroom and Computer Lab Interaction in a Computer-Intensive Algebra Curriculum." Paper presented at the annual meeting of the American Educational Research Association, San Diego. April 1998.

Henley, Cynthia. "Math—Grade 2 'Wild Animal Math.'" In *Culturally-Based Mathematics and Science Curriculum 1992,* edited by Joyce E. Haines. Washington, DC: U.S. Bureau of Indian Affairs, 1992.

Hernandez, Norma G. "The Mathematics—Bilingual-Education Connection: Two Lessons." In *Changing the Faces of Mathematics: Perspectives on Latinos,* edited by Luis Ortiz-Franco, Norma G. Hernandez, and Yolanda De La Cruz, 49–57. Reston, VA: National Council of Teachers of Mathematics, 1999.

Heuser, Daniel. "Mathematics Workshop: Mathematics Class Becomes Learner Centered." *Teaching Children Mathematics 6* (January 2000): 288–295.

Hewitt, Karen. "Blocks as a Tool for Learning: Historical and Contemporary Perspectives." In *Annual Editions: Early Childhood Education, 2003/2004,* edited by Karen Menke Paciorek and Joyce Huth Munro, 148–154. Guilford, CT: McGraw-Hill/Dushkin, 2004.

Hiebert, James. "Mathematical, Cognitive, and Instructional Analyses of Decimal Fractions." In *Analysis of Arithmetic for Mathematics Teaching,* edited by Gaea Leinhardt, Ralph Putnam, and Rosemary A. Hattrup, 283–322. Hillsdale, NY: Lawrence Erlbaum Associates, 1992.

Hill, Jane D. and Kathleen M. Flynn. *Classroom Instruction that Works with English Language Learners.* Alexandria, VA: Association for Supervision and Curriculum Development, 2006.

Hines, Ellen. "Exploring Functions with Dynamic Physical Models." *Mathematics Teaching in the Middle School 7* (January 2002): 274–278.

Honey, I Blew Up the Kids. Dir. Joe Johnston. Perf. Rick Moranis. Burbank, CA: Walt Disney and Amblin Entertainment, 1992.

Honey, I Shrunk the Kids. Dir. Joe Johnston. Perf. Rick Moranis. Burbank, CA: Walt Disney and Amblin Entertainment, 1989.

House, Peggy, ed. *Navigating through Geometry* [Book 1 and 2 of 3 in series]. Reston, VA: National Council of Teachers of Mathematics, 2001.

———. *Navigating through Algebra* [Book 1, 2, 3 in series]. Reston, VA: National Council of Teachers of Mathematics, 2001.

———. *Navigating through Geometry* [Book 3 of 3 in series]. Reston, VA: National Council of Teachers of Mathematics, 2002.

———. *Navigating through Data Analysis* [Book 1 and 2 of 3 in series]. Reston, VA: National Council of Teachers of Mathematics, 2002.

———. *Navigating through Data Analysis* [Book 3 of 3 in series]. Reston, VA: National Council of Teachers of Mathematics, 2003.

———. *Navigating through Measurement* [Book 1, 2, 3 in series]. Reston, VA: National Council of Teachers of Mathematics, 2003, Book 1 (2003); Books 2 and 3, 2004.

House, Peggy A. Carol E. Greenes, ed. *Navigating through Problem Solving* [Book 1, 2, 3, 4 in series]. Reston, VA: National Council of Teachers of Mathematics, 2004.

Howden, Hilde. "Prior Experiences." In *Algebra for Everyone,* edited by Edgar L. Edwards, 7–23. Reston, VA: National Council of Teachers of Mathematics, 1990.

Hoyles, Celia, Richard Noss, and Stefano Pozzi. "Proportional Reasoning in Nursing Practice." *Journal for Research in Mathematics Education 32* (January 2001): 14–27.

International Society for Technology in Education. *National Educational Technology Standards for Teachers: Preparing Teachers to Use Technology,* Eugene, OR: International Society for Technology in Education, 2002.

Ivory, Gary, Dolores R. Chaparro, and Stanley Ball. "Staff Development to Forster Latino Students' Success in Mathematics: Insights from Constructivism." In *Changing the Faces of Mathematics: Perspectives on Latinos,* edited by Luis Ortiz-Franco, Norma G. Hernandez, and Yolanda De La Cruz, 113–122. Reston, VA: National Council of Teachers of Mathematics, 1999.

Jackiw, Nickolas. *The Geometer's Sketchpad.* software. Berkeley, CA: Key Curriculum Press, 1995.

Jacobs, Judith E. and Joanne Rossi Becker. "Creating a Gender-Equitable Multicultural Classroom Using

Feminist Pedagogy." In *Multicultural and Gender Equity in the Mathematics Classroom: The Gift of Diversity*, edited by Janet Trentacosta and Margaret J. Kenney. 1997 Yearbook. Reston, VA: National Council of Teachers of Mathematics, 1997.

Jensen, Eric. *Teaching with the Brain in Mind*. Alexandria, 2nd ed. VA: Association for Supervision and Curriculum Development, 1998–2005.

———. "Fragile Brains." *Educational Leadership*. 59 (November 2001): 32–36.

Judd, Wallace. "Instructional Games with Calculators." *Mathematics Teaching in the Middle School 12* (February 2007): 312–314.

Johnson, Art. "Now & Then: Fiber Meets Fibonacci: The Shape of Things to Come." *Mathematics Teaching in the Middle School 4* (January 1999): 256–262.

Kamii, Constance K. *Young Children Reinvent Arithmetic: Implications of Piaget's Theory*. New York: Teacher's College Press, 1985.

Kamii, Constance and Ann Dominick. "The Harmful Effects of Algorithms in Grades 1–4." In *The Teaching and Learning of Algorithms in School Mathematics 1998 Yearbook*, edited by Lorna J. Morrow and Margaret J. Kenney, 130–140. Reston, VA: National Council of Teachers of Mathematics, 1998.

Kamii, Constance, Lynn Kirkland, and Barbara A. Lewis. "Representation and Abstraction in Young Children's Numerical Reasoning." In *The Roles of Representation in School Mathematics 2001 Yearbook*, edited by Albert A. Cuoco and Frances R. Curcio. Reston, VA: National Council of Teachers of Mathematics, 2001.

Kansas State Board of Education. *Kansas Mathematics Curriculum Standards: Mathematical Power for All Kansans*. Topeka: Kansas State Printing Office, 1993.

Kappan (Phi Delta Kappa, October 2002): 97–177.

Karp, Karen S. and Rhonda C. Niemi. "The Math Club for Girls." *Mathematics Teaching in the Middle School 5* (March 2000): 425–432.

Kenney, Patricia A., Mary M. Lindquist, and Cristina L. Herrernan. "Butterflies and Caterpillars: Multiplicative and Proportional Reasoning in the Early Grades." In *Making Sense of Fractions, Ratios, and Proportions: 2002 Yearbook of the National Council of Teachers of Mathematics*, edited by George W. Bright. Reston, VA: National Council of Teachers of Mathematics, 2002.

Kersaint, Gladis and Michaele Chappell. "Capturing Students' Interests: A Quest to Discover Mathematics Potential." *Teaching Children Mathematics*. 7 (May 2001): 512–517.

Khisty, Lena Licón. "Making Inequality: Issues of Language and Meanings in Mathematics Teaching with Hispanic Students." In *New Directions for Equity in Mathematics Education*, edited by Walter G. Secada, Elizabeth Fennema, and Lisa Byrd Adajian, 279–297. Cambridge, England: Cambridge University Press, 1995.

———. "Making Mathematics Accessible to Latino Students: Rethinking Instructional Practice." In *Multicultural and Gender Equity in the Mathematics Classroom: The Gift of Diversity*, edited by Janet Trentacosta and Margaret J. Kenney, 1997 Yearbook. Reston, VA: National Council of Teachers of Mathematics, 1997.

Khisty, Lena Licón and Gerald Viego. "Challenging Conventional Wisdom: A Case Study." *Changing the Faces of Mathematics: Perspectives on Latinos*, edited by Luis Ortiz-Franco, Norma G. Hernandez, and Yolanda De La Cruz. Reston, VA: National Council of Teachers of Mathematics, 1999.

Kilpatrick, Jeremy, Jane Swafford, and Bradford Findell. eds. *Adding It Up: Helping Children Learn Mathematics*. Washington, DC: National Academy Press, 2001.

Kilpatrick, Jeremy and Jane Swafford eds. *Helping Children Learn Mathematics*. Washington, DC: National Academy Press, 2002.

Kliman, Marlene. "Integrating Mathematics and Literature in the Elementary Classroom." *Arithmetic Teacher 40* (February 1993): 318–321.

———. "What Do Students Know about Numbers and Operations?" In *Results from the Seventh Mathematics Assessment of the National Assessment of Educational Progress*, edited by Patricia Ann Kenney and Edward A. Silver. Reston, VA: National Council of Teachers of Mathematics, 2000.

Krause, Marina. *Multicultural Mathematics Materials*. Reston, VA: National Council of Teachers of Mathematics, 1993.

Krulik, Stephen and Jesse A. Rudnick. *Roads to Reasoning: Developing Thinking Skills Through Problem Solving*. New York, NY: Wright Group/McGraw-Hill, 2001.

Krutetskii, Vadim A. *Psychology of Mathematical Abilities in Schoolchildren*. Chicago: The University of Chicago Press, 1976.

Kunjufu, Jawanza. *Lessons from History: A Celebration in Blackness*. Elementary Ed. Chicago: African American Images, 1987a.

———. *Lessons from History: A Celebration in Blackness*. Jr.-Sr. High Ed. Chicago: African American Images, 1987b.

———. *Lessons from History: A Celebration in Blackness*. Elementary Ed. Chicago: African American Images, 1987c.

Ladson-Billings, Gloria. "Making Mathematics Meaningful in Multicultural Contexts." In *New Directions for Equity in Mathematics Education*, edited by Walter G. Secada, Elizabeth Fennema, and Lisa Byrd Adajian, 126–145. Cambridge, England: Cambridge University Press, 1995.

Lampert, Magdalei, and Paul Cobb. "Communication and Language." In *A Research Companion to Principles and Standards for School Mathematics*, edited by Jeremy Kilpatrick, W. Gary Martin, and Deborah

Schifter, 237–249. Reston, VA: National Council of Teachers of Mathematics, 2003.

Langford, Karen and Angela Sarullo. "Introductory Common and Decimal Fraction Concepts." In *Research Ideas for the Classroom: Early Childhood Mathematics,* edited by Robert J. Jensen, 223–247. Reston, VA: National Council of Teachers of Mathematics, 1993.

Lara-Alecio, Rafael, Beverly J. Irby, and Leonel Morales-Aldana. "A Mathematics Lesson from the Mayan Civilization." *Teaching Children Mathematics 5* (3) (November 1998): 154–159.

Leder, Gilah C. "Equity Inside the Mathematics Classroom: Fact or Artifact?" In *New Directions for Equity in Mathematics Education,* edited by Walter G. Secada, Elizabeth Fennema, and Lisa Byrd Adajian. Cambridge, England: Cambridge University Press, 1995.

LEGO Group. *MINDSTORMS Robotics Invention System.* Billund, Denmark Europress, Interactive Factory, and SRI International, 2002.

Lehrer, Richard. "Developing Understanding of Measurement." In *A Research Companion to Principles and Standards for School Mathematics,* edited by Jeremy Kilpatrick, W. Gary Martin, Deborah Schifter, 179–192. Reston, VA: National Council of Teachers of Mathematics, 2003.

Lembke, Linda O. and Barbara J. Reys. "The Development of, and Interaction Between, Intuitive and School-Taught Ideas about Percent." *Journal for Research in Mathematics Education 25* (May 1994): 237–259.

Lemme, Barbara. "Integrating Measurement Projects: Sand Timers." *Teaching Children Mathematics 7* (November 2000): 132–135.

Lerner, Janet. *Learning Disabilities.* Boston, MA: Houghton Mifflin, 2000.

Leu, Donald Jr. "Flat Stanley Goes Cyber." *Instructor* (January/February 2003): 28–29.

Levi, Linda. "Gender Equity in Mathematics Education." *Teaching Children Mathematics 7* (October 2000): 101–105.

Lindeman, Betsy. "Speaking Their Language." *Instructor.* (September 2002): 34–36.

Litwiller, Bonnie, ed. *Making Sense of Fractions, Ratios, and Proportions: 2002 Yearbook.* Reston, VA: National Council of Teachers of Mathematics, 2002.

Lobato, Joanne E. and Eva Thanheiser. "Developing Understanding of Ratio as Measure as a Foundation for Slope." In *Making Sense of Fractions, Ratios, and Proportions: 2002 Yearbook,* edited by Bonnie Litwiller, 162–175. Reston, VA: National Council of Teachers of Mathematics, 2002.

Lo Cicero, Ana Maria, Karen C. Fuson, and Martha Allexsaht-Snider. "Mathematizing Children's Stories, Helping Children Solve Word Problems, and Supporting Parental Involvement." In *Changing the Faces of Mathematics: Perspectives on Latinos,* edited by Luis

Ortiz-Franco, Norma G. Hernandez, and Yolanda De La Cruz, 59–70. Reston, VA: National Council of Teachers of Mathematics, 1999.

Lott, Johnny W. and Terry A. Souhrada. "As the Century Unfolds: A Perspective on Secondary School Mathematics Content." In *Learning Mathematics for a New Century,* edited by Maurice J. Burke and Frances R. Curcio, 96–111. 2000 Yearbook. Reston, VA: National Council of Teachers of Mathematics, 2000.

Ma, Liping. *Knowing and Teaching Elementary Mathematics: Teachers' Understanding of Fundamental Mathematics in China and the United States.* Mahwah, NJ: Lawrence Erlbaum, 1999.

Ma, Liping and Cathy Kessel. "Knowledge of Fundamental Mathematics for Teaching." In *Knowing and Learning Mathematics for Teaching: Proceedings of a Workshop.* Mathematics Teacher Preparation Content Workshop Program Steering Committee, Center for Education, Mathematical Sciences Education Board and National Research Council. Washington, DC: National Academy Press, 2001: 12–16.

Malloy, Carol E. "Including African American Students in the Mathematics Community." In *Multicultural and Gender Equity in the Mathematics Classroom: The Gift of Diversity,* edited by Janet Trentacosta and Margaret J. Kenney. 1997 Yearbook. Reston, VA: National Council of Teachers of Mathematics, 1997.

Manouchehri, Azita. "A four-point instructional model." *Teaching Children Mathematics, 8* (November 2001), 180–186.

Manouchehri, Azita, and Mary C. Enderson. "Promoting Mathematical Discourse: Learning from Classroom Examples." *Mathematics Teaching in the Middle School 4* (January 1999): 216–222.

Mark, June, ed. *Selected Bibliography for Gender Equity in Mathematics and Technology Resources Published in 1990–1997.* South Hadley, MA: Women and Mathematics Education (WME), 1998.

Martin, Carol L., Becky Young Bear, Georgie Riley, John Wray, Vera M. Freeman, and Mary Stonehouse. "Math—Kindergarten Bar and Picture Graphs." *Culturally-Based Mathematics and Science Curriculum 1992,* edited by Joyce E. Haines. Washington, DC: U.S. Bureau of Indian Affairs, 1992.

McCoy, Leah P., Stefanic Buckner, and Jessica Munley. "Probability Games from Diverse Culture." *Mathematics Teaching in the Middle School 12* (March 2007): 394–402.

McDonald, Joseph P. "Teachers Studying Student Work: Why and How?" *Phi Delta Kappan* (October 2002): 120–127.

Merz, Alice and Patricia Moyer. "Investigations: Hurry Up and Weight," *Teaching Children Mathematics 10* (September 2003): 8–14.

Mestre, Jose P. and William J. Gerace. "A Study of the Algebra Acquisition of Hispanic and Anglo Ninth Graders: Research Findings Relevant to Teacher Training and Classroom Practice." *NABE Journal* (Winter 1986): 137–165.

Meyer, Margaret R. with Georgianna Diopoulous. "Anchored Learning in Context." *Mathematics Teaching in the Middle School 8* (September 2002): 16–21.

Michael-Bandele, Mwangaza. "The African Advantage: Using African Culture to Enhance Culturally Responsive Comprehensive Teacher Education." *Being Responsive to Cultural Differences: How Teachers Learn,* edited by Mary E. Dilworth. Thousand Oaks, CA: Corwin Press, 1998.

Milne, William J. *Standard Arithmetic.* New York: American Book Co., 1892.

Mingo, Clo. "Grounded Practice: Lessons in Anasazi Mathematics Emerging from the Multicultural Classroom." In *Multicultural and Gender Equity in the Mathematics Classroom: The Gift of Diversity,* edited by Janet Trentacosta and Margaret J. Kenney. 1997 Yearbook. Reston, VA: National Council of Teachers of Mathematics, 1997.

Miura, Irene T. "The Influence of Language on Mathematical Representations." In *The Roles of Representation in School Mathematics 2001 Yearbook,* edited by Albert A. Cuoco and Frances R. Curcio. Reston, VA: National Council of Teachers of Mathematics, 2001.

Mokros, Jan and Susan Jo Russell. "Children's Concepts of Average and Representativeness." *Journal for Research in Mathematics Education 26* (January 1995): 20–39.

Monastersky, Richard. "Look Who's Listening" In *Annual Editions: Early Childhood Education, 2003/2004,* edited by Karen Menke Paciorek and Joyce Huth, 31–33, 2004.

Moore, Sara Delano, and William P. Bintz "Teaching Geometry and Measurement through Literature." *Mathematics Teaching in the Middle School. 8*(2) (October 2002) 78–84.

Morales-Jones, Carmen A. "Understanding Hispanic Culture: From Tolerance to Acceptance." *The Delta Kappa Gamma Bulletin* (Summer 1998): 13–17.

Morgan, Candia and Anne Watson. "The Interpretative Nature of Teachers 'Assessment of Students' Mathematics: Issues for Equity." *Journal for Research in Mathematics Education 33* (March 2002): 78–107.

Morris, Helen. "Universal Games from A to Z," *Mathematics Teaching in the Middle School 5* (January 2000): 300–305.

Morrow, Charlene. "Women and Mathematics: Avenues of Connection." In *Learning Problems in Mathematics,* edited by Lyn Taylor, 4–18. 18 (1, 2, 3) 1996.

Morrow, Charlene and Teri Perl, eds. *Notable Women in Mathematics: A Biographic Dictionary.* Westport, CT: Greenwood Press, 1997.

Morrow, Jean and Tes Mehring, eds. *Project A.I.M.: Assessment Activities and Rubrics for Mathematics.* Emporia, KS: The Teachers College, Emporia State University, 1993.

Morrow, Jean and Ruth Harbin-Miles. *Walkway to the Future: Implementing the NCTM Standards in K-4 Grades.* Dedham, MA: Janson Publications, 1996.

Morrow, Lorna J. and Margaret J. Kenney, eds. *The Teaching and Learning of Algorithms in School Mathematics, 1998 Yearbook.* Reston, VA: National Council of Teachers of Mathematics, 1998.

Moschkovich, Judit N. "Understanding the Needs of Latino Students in Reform-Oriented Mathematics Classrooms." In *Changing the Faces of Mathematics: Perspectives on Latinos,* edited by Luis Ortiz-Franco, Norma G. Hernandez, and Yolanda De La Cruz, 5–12. Reston, VA: National Council of Teachers of Mathematics, 1999.

Moskal, Barbara M. "Understanding Student Responses to Open-Ended Tasks." *Mathematics Teaching in the Middle School 5* (April 2000): 500–505.

Moss, Joan. "Percents and Proportion at the Center: Altering the Teaching Sequence for Rational Number." In *Making Sense of Fractions, Ratios, and Proportions: 2002 Yearbook of the National Council of Teachers of Mathematics,* edited by George W. Bright. Reston, VA: National Council of Teachers of Mathematics, 2002.

Mullis, Ina V. S. *Benchmarking to International Achievement: TIMSS as a Starting Point to Examine Student Achievement.* Washington, DC: U.S. Department of Education, 1997.

Myles, Brenda Smith, Katherine Tapscott Cook, Nancy E. Miller, Louann Rinner, and Lisa A. Robbins. *Asperger Syndrome and Sensory Issues: Practical Solutions for Making Sense of the World.* Shawnee Mission, KS: Autism Asperger Publishing Co., 2000.

Nagel, Nancy G. and Cynthia Carol Swingen. "Students' Explanations of Place Value in Addition and Subtraction." *Teaching Children Mathematics 5* (November 1998): 164–170.

National Assessment of Educational Progress. *The Nation's Report Card™ Mathematics 2005.* Washington, DC: National Center for Educational Statistics, U.S. Department of Education, 2006.

National Association for the Education of Young Children (NAEYC) and National Council of Teachers of Mathematics (NCTM). *Early Childhood Mathematics: Promoting Good Beginnings.* Reston, VA: NAEYC/NCTM, 2003.

National Centers for Implementation of Standards-Based Mathematics Curricula. *Services of the Centers and Satellites.* Under Grant ESI-9729328, ESI-9714999, and ESI-961968. Washington, DC: National Science Foundation; 1999.

National Center for Educational Statistics [NCES]. *Pursuing Excellence: Comparison of 8th Grade Mathematics and Science Achievement from a U.S. Perspective, 1985 and 1999.* Washington, DC: U.S. Department of Education, 2000.

———. *The Nation's Report Card: Mathematics 2000.* Washington, DC: U.S. Department of Education, 2001.

National Commission on Mathematics and Science Teaching for the 21st Century. *Before It's Too Late: A Report to the Nation from the National Commission on Mathematics and Science Teaching for the 21st Century,* 2000.

National Council for the Accreditation of Colleges of Teacher Education. *Elementary Education Program Review Standards.* Washington, DC: NCATE, 2007.

———. *Mathematics Program Review Standards.* Washington, DC: NCATE, 2005.

National Council of Teachers of Mathematics. *Assessment Standards for School Mathematics.* Reston, VA: NCTM, 1995.

———. *Curriculum and Evaluation Standards for School Mathematics.* Reston, VA: NCTM, 1989.

———. *Mathematics Teaching in the Middle School 4* (January 1999): 213–276.

———. *Mathematics Teaching in the Middle School.* Focus issue on Probability. *4* (May 1999): 493–557.

———. *Principles and Standards for School Mathematics.* Reston, VA: NCTM, 2000.

———. *Professional Standards for Teaching Mathematics.* Reston, VA: NCTM, 1991.

———. *Algebra for the Twenty-first Century: Proceedings of the August 1992 Conference.* Reston, VA: NCTM, 1992.

National Council of Teachers of Mathematics and National Action Council for Minorities in Engineering. *Figure This!: Math Challenges for Families.* software. No. ESI-9813062. National Science Foundation. Reston, VA: KnowNet Construction, 2002.

National Council of Teachers of Mathematics. "Interdisciplinary Connections in the Middle School." *Mathematics Teaching in the Middle School 11* (January 2006) [Focus Issue]

National Research Council. *Everybody Counts: A Report to the Nation on the Future of Mathematics Education.* Washington, DC: National Academy Press, 1989.

———. *Global Perspectives for Local Action: Using TIMSS to Improve U.S. Mathematics and Science Education.* Washington, DC: National Academy Press, 1999.

———. Studying classroom teaching as a medium for professional development. Proceedings of a U.S.–Japan workshop. Hyman Bass, Zalman P. Usiskin, and Gail Burrill, eds. Mathematical Sciences Education Board, Division of Behavioral and Social Sciences and Education, and U.S. National Commission on Mathematics Instruction, International Organizations Board. Washington, DC: National Academy Press, 2002.

Nelson, David. "Simultaneous Equations: A Numerical Approach from China." In *Multicultural Mathematics: Teaching Mathematics from a Global Perspective,* 126–141. New York: Oxford University Press, 1993.

Nelson, David, George Gheverghese Joseph, and Julian Williams. *Multicultural Mathematics: Teaching Mathematics from a Global Perspective.* New York: Oxford University Press, 1993.

Nichols, Beverly W. "Calculating Women: 1600 Years of Beating the Odds, Classroom Activities and Interdisciplinary Ideas." National Council of Teachers of Mathematics Annual Meeting. San Diego, CA: April 1996.

Nickerson, Susan D., Cherie Nydam, and Janet S. Bowers. "Linking Algebraic Concepts and Contexts: Every Picture Tells a Story." *Mathematics Teaching in the Middle School 6* (October 2000): 92–98.

Ormrod, Jeanne Ellis. *Educational Psychology: Developing Learners.* 4th ed. New York, NY: Pearson Education, 2002.

Ortiz-Franco, Luis. "Latinos, Income, and Mathematics Achievement: Beating the Odds." *Changing the Faces of Mathematics: Perspectives on Latinos,* edited by Luis Ortiz-Franco, Norma G. Hernandez, and Yolanda De La Cruz. Reston, VA: National Council of Teachers of Mathematics, 1999.

Ortiz-Franco, Luis, Norma G. Hernandez, and Yolanda De La Cruz, eds. *Faces of Mathematics: Perspectives on Latinos.* Reston, VA: National Council of Teachers of Mathematics, 1999.

Outhred, Lynne, Michael Mitchelmore, Diane McPhail, and Peter Gould. "Count Me into Measurement. A Program for the Early Elementary School." In *Learning and Teaching Measurement 2003 Yearbook,* edited by Douglas H. Clements and George Bright, 81–99. Reston, VA: National Council of Teachers of Mathematics, 2003.

Overbay, Shannon R. and Mary Jean Brod. "Magic with Mayan Math." *Mathematics Teaching in the Middle School 12* (February 2007): 340–347.

Owens, Katherine D. and Richard L. Sanders. "Travel the World—An Addition Game." *Mathematics Teaching in the Middle School 5* (February 2000): 392–396.

Owens, Douglas T. and Douglas B. Super. "Teaching and Learning Decimal Fractions." In *Research Ideas for the Classroom: Middle Grades Mathematics,* edited by Douglas T. Owens, 137–158. Reston, VA: National Council of Teachers of Mathematics, 1993.

Pallascio, Richard, Richard Allaire, Lousie Lafortune, and Pierre Mongeau. "The Learning of Geometry by the Inuit: A Problem of Mathematical Acculturation." In *Changing the Faces of Mathematics: Perspectives on Indigenous People of North America,* edited by Judith Elaine Hankes and Gerald R. Fast. Reston, VA: National Council of Teachers of Mathematics, 2002.

Payne, Ruby K. *A Framework for Understanding Poverty,* 4th ed. Baytown, TX: RFT Publishing, 2005.

Pegg J. and Davey, G. "Interpreting Study Understanding in Geometry: A Synthesis of Two Models." In *Designing Learning Environments for Developing Understanding of Geometry and Space,* edited by R. Lehrer and D. Chazan, 109–135. Mahwah, NJ: Eribaum, 1998.

Perl, Teri. Math Equals: *Biographies of Women Mathematicians + Related Activities*. Menlo Park, CA: Addison-Wesley, 1978.

Perl, Teri Hock, and Joan M. Manning. *Women, Numbers and Dreams*. Santa Rosa, CA: National Women's History Project, 1982.

Perlin, Michael H. "Rewrite to Improve." *Mathematics Teaching in the Middle School 8* (November 2002): 134–137.

Pesek, Dolores, and David Kirshner. "Inferences of Instrumental Instruction in Subsequent Relational Learning." *Journal for Research in Mathematics Education 31* (November 2000): 524–540.

Phi Delta Kappa. *Phi Delta Kappan.* (April 2002) [entire issue].

Piaget, Jean. *The Child's Conception of Number*. New York: Humanities Press, 1965.

———. perf. *Piaget on Piaget*. film. 1989.

Polya, George. *How to Solve It: A New Aspect of Mathematical Method*. 2nd ed. Princeton, NJ: Princeton University Press, 1957.

Prescott, Jennifer O. "We Love Math." *Instructor.* (April 2001): 24–27.

Price, Tom J. "On My Mind—Which One, America?" *Mathematics Teaching in the Middle School 7* (September 2001): 4–5.

Pugalee, David K. "Using Communication to Develop Students' Mathematical Literacy." *Mathematics Teaching in the Middle School 6* (January 2001): 296–299.

———. "Algebra for All: The Role of Technology and Constructivism in an Algebra Course for At-Risk Students." *Preventing School Failure 45* (Summer 2001): 171–176

Ramirez, Olga M. and John E. Bernard. "The Minority Mathematics and Science Education Cooperative (MMSEC) Success Story." In *Changing the Faces of Mathematics: Perspectives on Latinos*, edited by Luis Ortiz-Franco, Norma G. Hernandez, and Yolanda De La Cruz. Reston, VA: National Council of Teachers of Mathematics, 1999.

Randolph, Tamela D., and Helene J. Sherman. "Alternative Algorithms: Increasing Options, Reducing Errors." *Teaching Children Mathematics 7* (April 2001): 480–484.

Rathmell, Edward C. "Using Thinking Strategies to Learn Basic Facts." In *Developing Computational Skills, 1978 Yearbook of the National Council of Teachers of Mathematics*, 13–38. Reston, VA: National Council of Teachers of Mathematics, 1978.

Ray, Joseph. *Intellectual Arithmetic*. New York: Van Antwerp, Bragg, 1850.

Richmond Ambulance Authority. *Master Contract for Paramedic Ambulance Services*. July 1, 2000–2004. City of Richmond, VA, 2000.

Riley, Georgie and Mary Stonehouse. "Math—Kindergarten Bar and Picture Graphs." In *Culturally-Based Mathematics and Science Curriculum 1992*,

edited by Joyce E. Haines. Washington, DC: U.S. Bureau of Indian Affairs, 1992.

Riley, Jocelyn, Producer. *Math at Work: Women in Nontraditional Careers*. Madison, WI: Videotaped by Her Own Words, 1999.

Robbins, Lisa A. and Nancy E. Miller. *Sensation Station*. Shawnee Mission, KS: Autism Asperger Publishing Co., 2004.

Robert, Margot F. "Problem solving and at-risk students: Making 'mathematics for all' a classroom reality." *Teaching Children Mathematics 8* (January 2002), 290–295.

Robbins, Lisa A. and Nancy E. Miller. *Autism Resources: A Different Kind of Boy and Girl*. Shawnee Mission, KS: Autism Asperger Publishing, 2006.

Russell, Susan, Deborah Schifter, and V. Bastable. *Developing Mathematical Ideas: Working with Data*. Parsippany, NJ: Dale Seymour Publications, 2002.

Sakshaug, Lynae. "Responses to the Nets and Polyhedra Problem." *Teaching Children Mathematics. 8*(1) (September 2001): 44–48.

Scavo, Thomas R. and Bryon Petraroja. "Adventures in Statistics." *Teaching Children Mathematics 4* (March 1998): 394–400.

Schucker, Mike. Results Now: *How We Can Achieve Unprecedented Improvements in Teaching and Learning*. Alexandria, VA: Association for Supervision and Curriculum Development, 2006.

Secada, Walter G., ed. *Changing the Faces of Mathematics: Perspectives on Multiculturalism and Gender Equity*. Reston, VA: National Council of Teachers of Mathematics, 2000.

Secada, Walter G., Elizabeth Fennema, and Lisa Byrd Adajian eds. *New Directions for Equity in Mathematics Education*. Cambridge, England: Cambridge University Press, 1995.

Seda, Milagros M. and Carmen M. Seda. "There's More to Mathematics than Choosing the Letter C: The Limitations of Test-Driven Intervention." In *Changing the Faces of Mathematics: Perspectives on Latinos*, edited by Luis Ortiz-Franco, Norma G. Hernandez, and Yolanda De La Cruz. Reston, VA: National Council of Teachers of Mathematics, 1999.

Shaffey, Hisham E. "Zero Power." *Mathematics Teaching in the Middle School 8* (November 2002): 133; 173.

Shannon, George. *More Stories to Solve: Fifteen Folktales from Around the World*. New York: Beech Tree Paperback Books, 1994.

Sharp, Earl and Rosemary Ingram. "Workshop on Problem Solving Using TIMSS Approach in Performance Assessment." Lake Contrary Accelerated School, St. Joseph, MO, October 30, 1998.

Siegler, Robert S. "Implications of Cognitive Science Research for Mathematics Education." In *A Research Companion to Principles and Standards for School Mathematics*, edited by Jeremy Kilpatrick, W. Gary

Martin, and Deborah Schifter. Reston, VA: National Council of Teachers of Mathematics, 2003. 289–303.

Silver, Edward A., Margaret Schwan Smith, and Barbara Scott Nelson. "The QUASAR Project: Equity Concerns Meet Mathematics Education Reform in the Middle School." In *New Directions for Equity in Mathematics Education*, edited by Walter G. Secada, Elizabeth Fennema, and Lisa Byrd Adajian, 9–56. Cambridge, England: Cambridge University Press, 1995.

Singer, Janice-Ann, and Lauren B. Resnick. "Representations of Proportional Relationships: Are Children Part-Part or Part-Whole Reasoners?" *Educational Studies in Mathematics 23* (June 1992): 231–246.

Slavin, Robert E. "Mounting Evidence Supports the Achievement Effects of Success for All." *Phi Delta Kappan 83* (February 2002): 469–480.

Smith, Erick. "Stasis and Change: Integrating Patterns, Functions, and Algebra Throughout the K-12 Curriculum." In *A Research Companion to Principles and Standards for School Mathematics*, edited by Jeremy Kilpatrick, W. Gary Martin, and Deborah Schifter, 136–150. Reston, VA: National Council of Teachers of Mathematics, 2003.

Smith, John P. III. "The Development of Students' Knowledge of Fractions and Ratios." In *Making Sense of Fractions, Ratios, and Proportions: 2002 Yearbook of the National Council of Teachers of Mathematics*, edited by George W. Bright. Reston, VA: National Council of Teachers of Mathematics, 2002.

Smith, John P. III. "The Development of Students' Knowledge of Fractions and Ratios." In *Making Sense of Fractions, Ratios, and Proportions: 2002 Yearbook*, edited by Bonnie Litwiller and George Bright, 3–17. Reston, VA: National Council of Teachers of Mathematics, 2002.

Snowman, Jack and Robert Biehler. *Psychology Applied to Teaching.* 11th ed. New York, NY: Houghton Mifflin, 2006.

Sofaer, Anna. *The Sun Dagger.* Bethesda, MD: Atlas Video, Videotaped by Bullfrog Films, 1993.

Solmon, Lewis C. and Kalyani R. Chirra. *The Last Silver Bullet? Technology for America's Schools.* Charlotte, NC: Information Age Publishing, 2006.

Sowder, Judith T. and Judith Klein. "Number Sense and Related Topics." In *Research Ideas for the Classroom: Middle Grades Mathematics*, edited by Douglas T. Owens, 41–57. New York: Macmillan, 1993.

St. John, Denny and Douglas Lapp. "Tech Time: Developing Numbers and Operations with Affordable Handheld Technology." *Teaching Children Mathematics 7* (November 2000): 162–168.

Steele, Marcee M. "Strategies for Helping Students Who Have Learning Disabilities in Mathematics." *Mathematics Teaching in the Middle School 8* (November 2002): 140–143.

Steele, Diana F. "Assessment in Action: Mrs. Grant's Measurement Unit." *Mathematics Teaching in the Middle School 7* (January 2002): 266–272.

Steencken, Elena and Carolyn A. Maher. "Young Children's Growing Understanding of Fraction Ideas." In *Making Sense of Fractions, Ratios, and Proportions: 2002 Yearbook of the National Council of Teachers of Mathematics*, edited by George W. Bright. Reston, VA: National Council of Teachers of Mathematics, 2002.

Stein, Mary Kay and Jane W. Bovalino. "Manipulatives: One Piece of the Puzzle." *Mathematics Teaching in the Middle School, 6* (February 2001): 356–359.

Steinberg, Ruth M. "Instruction on Derived Facts Strategies in Addition and Subtraction." *Journal for Research in Mathematics Education 16* (November 1985): 337–355.

Stephan, Michelle and Douglas H. Clements. "Linear, Area, and Time Measurement in Prekindergarten to Grade 2." In *Learning and Teaching Measurement, 2003 Yearbook*, edited by Douglas H. Clements and George Bright, 3–16. Reston, VA: National Council of Teachers of Mathematics, 2003.

Stiff, Lee. "Beliefs and Expectations," *NCTM News Bulletin 38* (January/February 2002): 3–4.

Strong, Dorothy S. (Mathematics Ed.). *Systemwide Objectives and Standards.* Vols. 1–3. Chicago: Board of Education of the City of Chicago, 1990.

———. *Mathematics Instruction Planning Manual I.* Chicago: Board of Education of the City of Chicago, 1991a.

———. *Mathematics Tutor Training Manual I.* Chicago: Board of Education of the City of Chicago, 1991b.

———. *Mathematics Tutor Training Manual II.* Chicago: Board of Education of the City of Chicago, 1991c.

Strong, Richard, Harvey F. Silver, and Amy Robinson. "What Do Students Want (And What Really Motivates Them)? *Educational Leadership 53* (September 1995).

Strutchens, Marilyn E. "Multicultural Literature as a Context for Problem Solving: Children and Parents Learning Together." *Teaching Children Mathematics. 8*(8) (April 2002): 448–454.

Strutchens, Marilyn E., Martin L. Johnson, and William F. Tate, eds. *Changing the Faces of Mathematics: Perspectives on African Americans.* Reston, VA: National Council of Teachers of Mathematics, 2000.

Strutchens, Marilyn E., W. Gary Martin, and Patricia Ann Kenney. "What Students Know about Measurement: Perspectives from the National Assessment of Educational Progress." *Learning and Teaching Measurement 2003 Yearbook*, edited by Douglas H. Clements and George Bright, 195–207. Reston, VA: National Council of Teachers of Mathematics, 2003.

Stylianou, Despina A., Patricia Ann Kenney, Edward A. Silver, and Cengiz Alacaci. "Gaining Insight into Students' Thinking Through Assessment Tasks." *Mathematics Teaching in the Middle School 6* (October 2000): 136–144.

Sunburst Communications. *Geometric Supposer.* software. Pleasantville, NY: Sunburst Communications, 2003.

Sullo, Bob. *Activating the Desire to Learn*. Alexandria, VA: Association for Supervision and Curriculum Development, 2007.

Sulzer, James S. "The Function Box and Fourth Graders: Squares, Cubes, and Circles." *Teaching Children Mathematics 4* (April 1998): 442–447.

Sutton, John and Alice Krueger, eds. *EDThoughts: What We Know About Mathematics Teaching and Learning*. Aurora, CO: Mid-continent Research for Education and Learning, 2002.

Sylwester, Robert. *A Biological Brain in a Cultural Classroom*. Thousand Oaks, CA: Corwin Press, 2000.

Taylor, Lyn. "Integrating Mathematics and American Indian Cultures." In *Multicultural and Gender Equity in the Mathematics Classroom: The Gift of Diversity*, edited by Janet Trentacosta and Margaret J. Kenney. 1997 Yearbook. Reston, VA: National Council of Teachers of Mathematics, 1997.

Tent, Margaret W. "Circles and the Number π." *Mathematics Teaching in the Middle School 6* (April 2001): 452–457.

Tepper, Jonathan R. "Basing a Career on Base Two." *Mathematics Teaching in the Middle School 6* (October 2000): 116–199.

Texas Instruments. *Cabri^{TM} Jr.: Geometric Software Applications*. Houston, TX: Texas Instruments, 2003.

Thiessen, Diane. ed. *Exploring Mathematics through Literature: Articles and Lessons for Prekindergarten through Grade 8*. Reston, VA: National Council of Teachers of Mathematics, 2004.

Third International Science and Mathematics Study [TIMSS]. Washington, DC: U.S. Department of Education, 1999.

Thomas, Jan. "Teaching Mathematics in a Multicultural Classroom: Lessons from Australia." In *Multicultural and Gender Equity in the Mathematics Classroom: The Gift of Diversity*, edited by Janet Trentacosta and Margaret J. Kenney. 1997 Yearbook. Reston, VA: National Council of Teachers of Mathematics, 1997.

Thompson, Patrick W. and Luis A. Saldanha. "Fractions and Multiplicative Reasoning." In *A Research Companion to Principles and Standards for School Mathematics*, edited by Jeremy Kilpatrick, W. Gary Martin, and Deborah Schifter, 95–113. Reston, VA: National Council of Teachers of Mathematics, 2003.

———. "Strategies for Learning the Basic Facts." *Teaching and Learning Mathematics for the Young Child*, edited by Joseph N. Payne, 133–151. Reston, VA: National Council of Teachers of Mathematics, 1990.

Thornton, Carol A., Benny F. Tucker, John A. Dossey, and Edna F. Basik. *Teaching Mathematics to Children with Special Needs*. Menlo Park, CA: Addison-Wesley, 1983.

United States Bureau of Indian Affairs. *National Resources in Mathematics and Science: Summer 1993*. Washington, DC: Bureau of Indian Affairs, 1993.

University of Chicago School Mathematics Project. "CMSI Evaluation Report." *UCSMP Newsletter 34* (Wiater 2006): 3–7.

University of Chicago School Mathematics Project [UCSMP]. *The University of Chicago School Mathematics Project 2002–2003*. [Quarterly Brochure] Chicago, IL: UCSMP, 2003.

University of Chicago School Mathematics Project. *Everyday Mathematics: Teacher's Reference Manual*. Chicago, IL: Everyday Learning Corporation, 2001.

Usiskin, Zalman. "Where Does Algebra Begin? Where Does Algebra End?" *Algebra for the Twenty-first Century: Proceedings of the August 1992 Conference*, 27–28. Reston, VA: National Council of Teachers of Mathematics, 1992.

Usiskin, Zalman P. "The Future of Fractions." *Mathematics Teaching in the Middle School 12* (March 2007a): 366–369.

Usiskin, Zalman P. "Some Thought about Fractions." *Mathematics Teaching in the Middle School 12* (March 2007b): 370–373.

Uy, Frederick. "The Chinese Numeration System and Place Value." *Teaching Children Mathematics 9* (January 2003): 243–247.

Van Hiele, Pierre M. "The Child's Thought in Geometry." In English Translation of *Selected Writings of Dina van Hiele-Geldof and Pierre M. van Hiele*, edited by David Fuys, Dorothy Geddes, and Rosamond Tischler, 243–252. EDRS No. ED287 697. Brooklyn, NY: Brooklyn College, School of Education, 1984.

Vogt, Sharon. *Multicultural Math*. Greensboro, NC: Carson-Dellosa, 1994.

Voolich, Erica Dakin. "Using Biographies to 'Humanize' the Mathematics Class." *Arithmetic Teacher 41* (September 1993): 16–19.

Vygotsky, Lev Semenovich. *Thought and Language*. Trans. E. Haufmann and G. Vakar. Cambridge, MA: MIT Press, 1962.

Vygotsky, Lev Semenovich. *Mind in Society*. Cambridge, MA: Harvard University Press, 1978.

Wanko, Jeffrey J. and Christine Hartley Venable. "Investigating Prime Numbers and the Great Internet Mersenne Prime Search." *Mathematics Teaching in the Middle School 8* (October 2002): 70–76.

Warren, Beth and Ann S. Rosebery. "Equity in the Future Tense: Redefining Relationships Among Teachers, Students, and Science in Linguistic Minority Classrooms." In *New Directions for Equity in Mathematics Education*, edited by Walter G. Secada, Elizabeth Fennema, and Lisa Byrd Adajian, 298–328. Cambridge, England: Cambridge University Press, 1995.

Warrington, Mary Ann. "How Children Think about Division with Fractions." *Mathematics Teaching in the Middle School 2* (May 1997): 390–394.

Waters, Kenneth L. Sr. *Afrocentric Sermons: The Beauty of Blackness in the Bible*. Valley Forge, PA: Judson Press, 1993.

rs, Kenneth L, Sr. "Made in God's Image." In *Discovering Your Personal Spirituality*. Independence, MO: Community of Christ, 2001.

Weinberg, Suzanne Levin. "Proportional Reasoning: One Problem, Many Solutions!" In *Making Sense of Fractions, Ratios, and Proportions: 2002 Yearbook of the National Council of Teachers of Mathematics*, edited by George W. Bright. Reston, VA: National Council of Teachers of Mathematics, 2002.

Weiss, Iris. Report of the 2000 National Survey of Science and Mathematics Education. Chapel Hill, NC: Horizon Research, Inc, 2001.

Wentworth, George and David E. Smith. *Complete Arithmetic*. New York, NY: Ginn, 1909.

White, Judith A., ed. "Cartoon Corner." *Mathematics Teaching in the Middle School 7* (January 2002): 293.

Whitin, David J. and Phyllis Whitin. "Building a Community of Mathematicians." *Teaching Children Mathematics 9* (April 2003): 464–469.

Whitin, David J. and Phyllis Whitin. *New Visions for Linking Literature and Mathematics*. Reston, VA: NCTE/NCTM, 2004.

Wiest, Lynda R. "Multicultural Mathematics Instruction: Approaches and Resources." *Teaching Children Mathematics 9* (September 2002): 49–55.

Williams, Julian. "Geometry and Art." Ed. David Nelson, George Gheverghese Joseph, and Julian Williams. *Multicultural Mathematics: Teaching Mathematics from a Global Perspective*. Oxford, Eng.: Oxford University Press, 1993.

Willis, Jody K. and Aostre N. Johnson. "Multiply with MI: Using Multiple Intelligences to Master Multiplication," *Teaching Children Mathematics 7* (January 2001): 260–269.

Willoughby, Stephen S. "Functions from Kindergarten through Sixth Grade." *Teaching Children Mathematics 3* (February 1997): 314–318.

Wilson, Amos N. *Awakening the Natural Genius of Black Children*. New York: Afrikan World InfoSystems, 1992.

Wolfe, Pat. *Brain Matters: Translating Research into Classroom Practice*. Alexandria, VA: Association for Supervision and Curriculum Development, 2001.

Womble, Myra N., Helen C. Hall, and Jeff P. Turner. "Middle School Vocational Teachers' Knowledge of the Characteristics of At-Risk Learners." *Journal of Vocational and Technical Education 14* (Fall, 1997).

Yoshida, Makoto. "Framing Lesson Study for U.S. Participants." In *Studying Classroom Teaching as a Medium for Professional Development: Proceedings of a U.S. Japan Workshop*, edited by Bass, Hyman, Zalman P. Usiskin, and Gail Burrill, National Research Council, 58–64, Washington, DC: National Academy Press, 2002.

Young, Sharon L. and Robbin O'Leary. "Creating Numerical Scales for Measuring Tools." *Teaching Children Mathematics 8* (March 2002): 400–405.

Zaslovsky, Claudia. "People Who Live in Round Houses." *Arithmetic Teacher 37* (September 1989): 18–24.

———. "Symmetry in American Folk Art." *Arithmetic Teacher 38* (September 1990): 6–12.

———. *The Multicultural Mathematics Classroom: Bringing in the World*. Portsmouth, N.H.: Heinemann, 1996.

———. Counting on Your Fingers African Style. New York: Black Butterfly Children's Books, 2000.

———. "The Inka Quipu: Positional Notation on a Knotted Cord." *Mathematics Teaching in the Middle School 6* (November 2000): 164–166, 180–184.

———. "Exploring World Cultures in Math Class." *Educational Leadership 60* (October 2002): 66–69.

Zaslavsky, Claudia. *Multicultural Mathematics*. New York: J. Weston Walch, 1993.

Credits

PRAXIS II™ is a trademark of Educational Testing Service (ETS). This publication is not endorsed or approved by ETS.

Excerpts reprinted with permission from *Curriculum and Evaluation Standards for School Mathematics,* copyright 1989 by the National Council of Teachers of Mathematics. All rights reserved.

Excerpts reprinted with permission from *Professional Standards for Teaching Mathematics,* copyright 1991 by the National Council of Teachers of Mathematics. All rights reserved.

Excerpts reprinted with permission from *Assessment Standards for School Mathematics,* copyright 1995 by the National Council of Teachers of Mathematics. All rights reserved.

Excerpts reprinted with permission from *Principles and Standards for School Mathematics,* copyright 2000 by the National Council of Teachers of Mathematics. All rights reserved.

Excerpts reprinted with permission from *Curriculum Focal Points,* copyright 2006 by the National Council of Teachers of Mathematics. All rights reserved.

Taxman game reprinted with permission from *Measuring Up: Prototypes for Mathematics Assessment,* copyright 1993 by the National Academy of Sciences. Courtesy of the National Academy Press, Washington, DC.

Figures 4.3 and 4.4 reprinted with permission from Key Curriculum Press, 1150 65th Street, Emeryville, CA 94608, 1-800-995-MATH, www.keypress.com.

Figure 10.9 adapted with permission from *Teaching Children Mathematics,* copyright 1995 by the National Council of Teachers of Mathematics. All rights reserved.

Emergency Medical Careers Activity on CD (Chapter 11), photos and excerpts reprinted courtesy of David P. Edwards, Clinical & Research Director, Richmond Ambulance Authority.

Figure 15.7 reprinted with permission from *Mathematics Teaching in the Middle School,* copyright 1998 by the National Council of Teachers of Mathematics. All rights reserved.

Index